"The complex structure of the Epistle to the Hebrews has long intrigued readers. Michael Clark offers a novel analysis of that structure using contemporary discourse theory, showing how repetitive patterns and well-defined chiastic structures contribute to the homily's rhetorical effect. His approach will no doubt stimulate further reflection on the dynamics of this early Christian literary masterpiece."

—**Harold Attridge**, professor of divinity, Yale Divinity School

"The structure of the Letter to the Hebrews has been so examined by so many previous scholars that one wonders initially if there is anything fresh to be said about it. Michael Clark amply dispels this anticipation by his consistent inductive approach to the text by his discriminating use of insights from general linguistics and by showing the implications for exegesis of his structural analysis. I find this an extremely thorough and systematic treatment of which future scholars will need to take account."

—**Paul Ellingsworth**, author of *The Epistle to the Hebrews: A Commentary on the Greek Text*

"Michael Clark has made a substantial contribution to scholarship.... I think he has done outstanding work and has made a significant contribution to the ongoing study of the structure of Hebrews, further developing and enhancing the works of Guthrie and Westfall, for instance. To be sure, given his subject matter, his thesis will be met with critique, criticism, as well as praise. To that end he has significantly succeeded."

—**Barry C. Joslin**, associate professor of Christian theology, Southern Baptist Theological Seminary

"Michael Clark surveys and critiques landmark studies on the structure of Hebrews and builds on them to develop his approach. Following the wider linguistic discipline of Cohesion Analysis, he notes 'link clusters' of repetition and considers how they function individually, in relation to one another, and to the wider discourse as a whole. With helpful summaries at the end of each section, this complex study provides fresh and significant exegetical and structural insights for the interpreter of Hebrews."

—**David Peterson**, emeritus faculty member, Moore Theological College

"Following Vanhoye, scholars have sought to use literary devices to unlock the difficult sections of Hebrews. Michael Clark's study of repetition follows suit, providing stimulating alternatives in the quest to understand this central New Testament text."

—**Matthew Jensen**, research associate, Department of Hebrew, Biblical, and Jewish Studies, Sydney University

"Michael Clark's investigation of repetition in Hebrews examines, in addition to recognized clusters of repeated words, countless more that have gone unnoticed. Attending to repetition generates fresh insights into both the implications of words and the structure of the treatise. *Patterns* is especially effective in showing *how* Hebrews generates meaning and therefore how it elevates Christ."

—**Philip H. Kern**, head of New Testament, Moore Theological College

"The Letter to the Hebrews is rightly esteemed for the depth of its theological understanding on the one hand and the complexity of argument on the other. In this study of the 'mystery' of Hebrews, Michael Clark has appreciatively analyzed the major efforts of scholars before him, before advancing his own thesis. This is a work of outstanding scholarship that will chart new directions in the understanding of the Letter to the Hebrews."

—**Paul Barnett**, lecturer emeritus, Moore Theological College

Patterns of Repetition, Structure, and Meaning in the Book of Hebrews

Patterns of Repetition, Structure, and Meaning in the Book of Hebrews

Michael C. Clark

☙PICKWICK *Publications* • Eugene, Oregon

PATTERNS OF REPETITION, STRUCTURE, AND MEANING IN THE BOOK OF HEBREWS

Copyright © 2024 Michael C. Clark. All rights reserved. Except for brief quotations in critical publications or reviews, no part of this book may be reproduced in any manner without prior written permission from the publisher. Write: Permissions, Wipf and Stock Publishers, 199 W. 8th Ave., Suite 3, Eugene, OR 97401.

Pickwick Publications
An Imprint of Wipf and Stock Publishers
199 W. 8th Ave., Suite 3
Eugene, OR 97401

www.wipfandstock.com

PAPERBACK ISBN: 978-1-6667-8337-7
HARDCOVER ISBN: 978-1-6667-8338-4
EBOOK ISBN: 978-1-6667-8339-1

Cataloguing-in-Publication data:

Names: Clark, Michael C., author.

Title: Patterns of repetition, structure, and meaning in the book of Hebrews / Michael C. Clark.

Description: Eugene, OR: Pickwick Publications, 2024. | Includes bibliographical references.

Identifiers: ISBN 978-1-6667-8337-7 (paperback). | ISBN 978-1-6667-8338-4 (hardcover). | ISBN 978-1-6667-8339-1 (ebook).

Subjects: LSCH: Bible. Hebrews—Criticism, interpretation, etc.

Classification: BS2775.52 C57 2024 (print). | BS2775.52 (epub).

VERSION NUMBER 03/22/24

Unless otherwise noted, all biblical translations are the author's.

to Caroline and the kids (Tom, Ben, Joel, and Abigail),
with joy, love, and gratitude

Contents

Acknowledgments | ix

1. Introduction | 1
2. Literature Review | 8
3. Questions of Methodology | 48
4. Micro Link Clusters in Hebrews 1:1—3:8 | 80
5. The Combined Function of Micro and Macro Link Clusters in Hebrews 1–4 | 203
6. Macro Link Clusters in Hebrews 4:14—13:22 and the Epilogue of 13:22–25 | 243
7. Conclusion | 307

Appendix: Micro Link Clusters in Hebrews 3:5—13:25 | 317
Bibliography | 367

Acknowledgments

THIS STUDY REPRESENTS A modified version of a thesis which was awarded the degree of Doctor of Philosophy in 2011 by the University of Sydney in association with Moore Theological College. It owes much to many.

I am grateful to my supervisory team as a whole: Prof. Iain Gardner and Drs. Peter O'Brien and Peter Bolt, for their wise input, suggestions, and support, and to Dr. Bolt in particular for his wholehearted, tireless efforts and advocacy on my behalf—I could not imagine a better supervisor. Thanks also to the staff and faculty at Moore Theological College for their encouragement and financial assistance; to Vanda Gould for his warm and generous support; and to my church family, friends, and parents for their love and constant encouragement throughout this period.

Though too many to mention by name, special thanks is also due two (or three) further groups. First, I owe a deep debt of gratitude to those who committed to praying *and then prayed* for this project and its successful outcome. Regardless of its merits or otherwise, it is these prayers which have brought this study to completion. Second, I am so thankful to my students at the Martin Bucer Seminar in Munich and the saints at St Thomas', North Sydney, for the opportunity to take this study for a "test drive" in the form of a series of lectures and sermons on the Book of Hebrews delivered in German and English on opposite sides of the world (though not at the same time). What a joy and privilege to be able to share some of the riches of Hebrews with others! What a relief to discover that it "preaches"! Your enthusiasm for this mighty "Word of Encouragement" and the fruit of my labors buoyed me onwards.

ACKNOWLEDGMENTS

Final thanks to Ruben, my true brother in the Lord, for his inspirational example of radical, costly discipleship; to Caroline, my lily among thorns, without whose beauty, grace, gentleness, and loving support this book could not have been written; and above all to the God and Father of the Lord Jesus Christ for all his undeserved goodness and mercy to me.

> All I have needed thy hand has provided.
> Great is your faithfulness, Lord, unto me.

1

Introduction

1.1 Introduction

THIS THESIS SEEKS TO investigate the combined effect of repetition in Hebrews so as to shed light on important and as-yet-unresolved questions relating to Hebrews' choice and use of language, structure, genre, relationship to the LXX, authorship and meaning. As Marohl observes, "it has become almost commonplace to refer to the 'mystery' of Hebrews, to speak of Hebrews as an 'enigma.'"[1] Despite centuries of research and a wide variety of methodological approaches, many questions remain unanswered, relating not only to the details of Hebrews' historical background (the identity of the author and original recipients, date, purpose and social context of its composition) but also to the text itself. While Hebrews' "literary virtuosity" is widely acknowledged,[2] there is still considerable uncertainty regarding *how* this text works,[3] *why* its author has communicated in the way he has, and even *what* he is attempting to

---

1. Marohl, *Faithfulness*, xiii.
2. Vanhoye, *Structure*, v, 19, describes the author as "a master of writing," possessed of "a talent without equal." Cf. Thompson, *Beginnings*, 158; Stanley, "The Structure of Hebrews," 254; Attridge, *Hebrews*, 20; and Lindars, "Rhetorical Structure," 382, who claims that "Hebrews is the most accomplished writing in the New Testament."
3. Cf. O'Brien, *Hebrews*, 1, who notes that "it is difficult to see how the author moves from one argument or stage to the next."

say at times.⁴ Indeed, though frequently contrasted with "Paul,"⁵ many of the most distinctive elements of Hebrews' "style"—its striking use of repetition, parallelism, polyvalent and at times ambiguous language, and a certain circularity in argumentation—remain largely unexplored. Similar uncertainty also prevails concerning the structural arrangement of this text which is "still very much an unsolved problem," despite decades of research.⁶ As Westfall notes:

> While on the one hand many have declared it [Hebrews] to be the only literary masterpiece in the NT, on the other hand there is little consensus on the nature of its design. There is no agreement on the major and minor divisions of the book or the development of its argument. This is a paradox, because by definition, a literary masterpiece would require an identifiable argument or a clear train of thought—it should be relatively cohesive and coherent.⁷

The recent demonstration of an oral dimension to the work has also raised questions about its genre.⁸ Traditionally understood as "an epistle" and analyzed purely as written text, the fact that Hebrews has been crafted for the ear as well as the eye has led to a growing consensus which views it as something *more*.⁹ How then should we think of this "word of exhortation" (τοῦ λόγου τῆς παρακλήσεως, 13:22)? Finally, although Hebrews'

---

4. For the purposes of this thesis, Hebrews' author will be assumed to be male in light of the masculine form of the participle (διηγούμενον) he uses with respect to himself in 11:32: καὶ τί ἔτι λέγω; ἐπιλείψει με γὰρ διηγούμενον ὁ χρόνος περὶ Γεδεών, Βαράκ, Σαμψών, Ἰεφθάε, Δαυίδ τε καὶ Σαμουὴλ, καὶ τῶν προφητῶν.

5. Calvin, *Hebrews*, 1, claims "the manner of teaching and style sufficiently show that Paul was not the author."

6. Aune, *New Testament*, 213. Cf. Gelardini, "Linguistic Turn," 38–66; Martin and Whitlark, *Inventing Hebrews*, 1; Joslin, "Can Hebrews be Structured?," 99, 122; and MacLeod, "Literary Structure," 197.

7. Westfall, *A Discourse Analysis*, xi, 21.

8. Guthrie, "New Testament Exegesis," 597, notes that "the book is replete with qualities pointing to the orality of this text; for example, alliteration, rhyme, short sentence structure, and forms of direct address."

9. See Martin and Whitlark, *Inventing Hebrews*, 258–61, who read Hebrews as "our earliest self-identifying Christian speech (or sermon) . . . [which] conforms to expectations and instructions outlined in rhetorical education of the ancient Mediterranean world, and prevalent in the early Roman imperial context of Christian origins"; and Gelardini, " Rhetorical Criticism," 135, who describes Hebrews as an "epistle, homily, and oration" or "mixed type of these forms." Cf. Gelardini, "Hebrews, Homiletics, and Liturgical Scripture Interpretation," 88, and "Rhetorical Criticism," 117-19, 122; and Trotter, *Interpreting the Epistle*, 64.

dependence on the LXX is universally recognized,[10] there is ongoing uncertainty regarding the precise identity of its source material in places, the function of this material in its new context and the reasons behind many of the seemingly deliberate alterations to the original text.

While not offering a full-scale structural or topical investigation, the fresh approach of this thesis yields a new understanding of the structure of Hebrews as well as a number of important insights into these literary questions.

1.2 Statement of Thesis

In the past, many have observed that the book of Hebrews abounds with unusual and striking patterns of repetition,[11] and that these patterns seem to play a role in structuring the discourse as a whole and clarifying its meaning. However, while particular instances of repetition have been individually considered by various scholars at various times, their significance within the text, viewed as one piece, has not been fully appreciated. Given the length of the text of Hebrews and the variety, scope and frequency of its connections, it will not be possible to address every pattern of repetition within the discourse. However, in light of Michael Hoey's suggestion that "we are more likely to arrive at a satisfactory account of how cohesion works if we concentrate on the way repetition clusters in pairs of sentences,"[12] this thesis will focus primarily on clusters of repetitive ties, or link clusters, within Hebrews, seeking to understand both their present *location* and distinctive *function* in the discourse. For as James Barr rightly notes, it is not words or "morphological and

---

10. Gheorghita, *The Role of the Septuagint in Hebrews*, 3, acknowledges the contributions made by "several monumental studies in the field" including K. J. Thomas, F. Schröger, J. J. McCullough, and P. Ellingworth. Cf. also Harris, "Use of the Old Testament"; Kistemaker, *Psalm Citations*; and Docherty, *Use of the Old Testament*.

11. While there exists a multiplicity of ways by which an author might establish a connection between particular words, for the purposes of this study, repetition refers to repetitive ties within a discourse which may be grouped under five broad categories (each of which will be further developed in chapter three): (a) lexical, (b) referential, (c) grammatical; (d) phonological, and (e) intertextual relations. Understood in this way, repetition may be deemed to occur when a textual item, whether a word, phrase, clause, sentence or even sentence cluster refers back to another.

12. Hoey, *Patterns of Lexis*, 20, follows Winter, "Replacement," 95–133, at this point.

syntactical mechanisms" that bear theological meaning, but their function within the sentence and literary discourse as a whole.[13]

For present purposes, a "link cluster" may be defined as two sentences or larger semantic units which demonstrate a higher degree of linkage than would be expected from common lexical repetition and thereby show convincing evidence of textual organization.[14] "Intratextual link clusters" are link clusters which exist between texts *within* Hebrews and which may be further categorized as "micro link clusters," which operate at the paragraph level of the discourse, or "macro link clusters," which join together texts separated on occasion by considerable distance. "Intertextual link clusters," meanwhile, represent link clusters which exist between texts in Hebrews and other external texts, most commonly (though not exclusively) taken from the LXX.

The study proposes, *first*, that the author of Hebrews chooses and uses particular words and phrases to establish connections with other words and phrases both within and without the discourse; that these connections are marked as significant by their co-location within contexts containing several other similarly-connected words and phrases (i.e. link clusters); and that such clusters of links occur frequently and consistently throughout Hebrews, spanning both small and large portions of the text.

Second, it claims that link clusters perform a range of important formal functions within the text. Perhaps most importantly, intratextual link clusters serve to indicate Hebrews' structure. Micro link clusters group the text into a series of overlapping, concentric and coherent textual units or paragraphs which combine together in linear fashion to form logical steps in the argument. Macro clusters, meanwhile, serve a similar function within the wider discourse by marking out the beginning and end of each of the thirteen overlapping subsections, and four sections, which may be found within this text.

Third, it argues that link clusters also play two key topical roles in Hebrews. In the first place, link clusters (both micro and macro) function to clarify and/or amplify the intended meaning of particular words, phrases, sentences and even whole sections of the discourse. Hebrews' delight in "the polyvalence of language,"[15] seen in its frequent use of ambiguous words and phrases, and tendency to bring out more than one

---

13. Barr, *Semantics*, 263.

14. See 3.3.2 for discussion on the meaning of common lexical repetition and the criteria by which a "higher degree of linkage" might be observed.

15. Attridge, *Hebrews*, 118.

meaning from the same word in different contexts,[16] has led some commentators to question whether its author provides sufficient guidance to its correct interpretation at times.[17] In response, this thesis claims that by carefully arranging his discourse into a series of balanced parallel phrases through repetition, the author clearly indicates his understanding of a coherent relationship between any given text and at least one other text, thereby providing his readers with additional contexts (both within and without the discourse) by which to understand its meaning.[18] In this way, it is possible *both* for readers to come to a precise understanding of the meaning of any word in any context *and* for a single word to have more than one meaning simultaneously, corresponding to its participation in more than one parallel context. This hermeneutical discovery yields many new exegetical insights which will be introduced as our method is applied to different parts of the text.

Macro link clusters also serve as parallel topic sentences which together summarize the content of the material they surround. Since, by their very nature, summary statements unite together the information they summarize,[19] a summary of the discourse as a whole may be obtained by compiling these sentences in one summary.[20]

1.3 Chapter Overview

In what follows, chapter 2 offers a survey of scholarship in the field, summarizing and assessing the six most significant structural approaches (Nauck, Vanhoye, Guthrie, Rhee, Westfall and Heil).

Chapter 3 locates this analysis within the wider linguistic discipline of "cohesion analysis" as practiced by Halliday, Hasan, and especially Michael Hoey, so as to establish parameters for responsible Biblical semantic analysis.[21] A methodology is outlined by which link clusters may be identified and their function analyzed.

---

16. Ellingworth, *Hebrews*, 419.

17. By way of example, Ellingworth, *Hebrews*, 198, claims with regard to Hebrews 3:1 that "it is difficult to decide whether the κλῆσις ἐπουρανίου is a call from heaven (e.g., Peshitta, Bleek) or to heaven (e.g., Windisch, Monetefiore), or both (e.g., Bengel, Spicq, Braun, Attridge, Grässer) . . . The immediate context in Hebrews gives little guidance."

18. See chapter three for more discussion on this.

19. Levinsohn, *Discourse Features*, 198.

20. Westfall, *A Discourse Analysis*, 73.

21. "Cohesion Analysis" represents a branch of modern linguistics which seeks to

Chapter 4, which constitutes the bulk of the research, presents a detailed analysis of the first seven micro link clusters in Hebrews (1:1–4; 1:3–6; 1:7–14; 2:1–4; 2:5–9; 2:8c–18; 3:1–8) according to the method outlined in chapter 3. Having first identified their location, it seeks to understand the particular function of each of these clusters in the text with fresh exegetical insights to be presented as they are discovered along the way. While it is claimed that similar clusters may be found consistently throughout Hebrews,[22] these seven have been chosen not only as typical examples of their kind but also as part of a linear sequence of link clusters, thereby allowing for further research into the relationships between them and with other macro clusters in the discourse (see chapter 5). The chapter demonstrates that intratextual and intertextual link clusters represent a commonly occurring and significant feature of Hebrews 1:1–3:8 which unite this text into a series of overlapping concentric units, thereby forming parallel contexts both within and without Hebrews which in combination clarify its meaning and emphasis.

Following this, chapter 5 investigates the relationships *between* the units/micro clusters identified in chapter 4; and between these units, taken together, and other macro link clusters within the same part of the text in light of further evidence provided by topic markers.[23] It seeks to uncover *why* the author has structured Hebrews 1–4 in the way he has and *how* each of these macro and micro units combines together within it to create meaning. The chapter demonstrates, first, that macro link clusters (between 1:1–5 and 1:13–2:4, 2:1–5 and 2:16–3:2, 3:1–2 and 4:14, and 1:1–4 and 4:12–14) function as matched pairs of topic sentences

---

uncover the properties of language which contribute to the production and interpretation of "cohesion" within texts by investigating what Halliday and Hasan, *Cohesion in English*, 329, describe as *cohesive ties*. The key notion is that, in all texts, connections exist between an item at one point and an item at another point which make at least one of the items dependent on the other for its interpretation. Consequently, by enquiring into the nature and location of such connections, it is possible to gain a better understanding of the discourse as a whole since such connections "signal the author's intentions of how the discourse is grouped." Westfall, *A Discourse Analysis*, 55.

22. Our findings suggest that link clusters function at the micro-level of the text to structure the discourse into a series of thirty-nine overlapping concentric textual units as follows: Heb 1:1–4; 1:3–6; 1:7–14; 2:1–4; 2:5–9; 2:8c–18; 3:1–8; 3:5–19; 4:1–12; 4:12–13; 4:14–5:10; 5:11–6:12; 6:9–18; 6:19–7:3; 7:4–10; 7:11–17; 7:15–26; 7:26–8:1; 8:1–5; 8:6–13; 9:1–8; 9:6–12; 9:11–28; 10:1–4; 10:5–22; 10:19–38; 10:39–11:4; 11:3–7; 11:8–16; 11:17–22; 11:23–28; 11:29–40; 12:1–13; 12:14–25; 12:25–29; 12:28–13:10; 13:10–14; 13:15–21; and 13:22–25.

23. For present purposes, a "topic marker" is a formal device used by the author to alert his readers/hearers to the beginning of a new topic in the discourse.

which mark out the beginning and end of three overlapping subsections (1:1—2:4; 2:1—3:2 and 3:1—4:14) and one major section (1:1—4:14) with a summary of its content. Second, that within this overall arrangement, micro units function as steps in an argument which proceeds in linear fashion from beginning to end. Third, that Hebrews also employs a further type of patterning, involving repetition (and frequently contrast) within the introduction to each of these units to draw the attention of readers/hearers to the start of each new topical point in the discourse. Fourth, that overlap represents a common feature of this text which allows the author both to effect smooth transitions between sections without wasting words and to express more than one meaning or emphasis simultaneously through particular words and phrases.

In light of these insights, chapter 6 identifies and investigates each of the remaining macro link clusters in Hebrews so as to better understand the text's overall structure and meaning. Based on the location of these clusters, it argues that Hebrews consists of four overlapping sections (1:1—4:14; 4:14—8:3; 8:1—10:22; and 10:19—13:22) and thirteen overlapping subsections (1:1—2:4; 2:1—3:2; 3:1—4:16; 4:14—5:10; 5:11—6:12; 6:9-20; 6:17—8:2; 8:1—9:12; 9:11—10:24; 10:19-38; 10:35—12:2; 12:1-13; 12:12—13:21) which are surrounded in each case by matched pairs of sentences (i.e. macro link clusters). The chapter also offers a topical analysis into the relationship between each of these sentences and their corresponding sections and subsections. It finds that a coherent summary of the discourse in either thirteen or four parts may be attained by reading each of the introductory topic sentences identified (at either the subsection or section level of discourse) in a linear fashion. Chapter 6 concludes with a brief analysis of the final micro link cluster in Hebrews (13:22-25), demonstrating the parallelism within it (consistent with the form of the units identified in chapter 4), and offering a new reading of these verses which yields two important clues regarding the authorship of Hebrews.

A number of conclusions relating to Hebrews' structure, genre, choice, and use of language and the LXX, authorship and meaning, which arise from this analysis, will then follow together with a number of suggestions for further research.

2

Literature Review

2.1 Introduction

FOLLOWING ON FROM THE seminal work of Wolfgang Nauck, Leon Vaganay, and Albert Vanhoye, most modern scholars recognize the presence of distinctive patterns of repetition within Hebrews which form connections between different parts of the text, and the fact that at least on occasion these patterns seem to serve an important function or functions within the discourse.[1] Despite this, however, though particular instances of repetition have been individually considered, the phenomenon of repetition in general remains largely unexamined: To date, no comprehensive study of repetition within Hebrews has been undertaken. Consequently, while many links have been observed, the sheer volume and extent of this text's connectedness has not been fully appreciated, nor has a coherent and comprehensive understanding of the function of repetition within it been properly established.

This chapter seeks, first, to provide a brief survey of those patterns of repetition in Hebrews deemed significant by modern scholarship, and, second, to investigate how their *function* has been understood by summarizing and critiquing the work of six scholars who have made the greatest and most distinctive contributions to this point: Wolfgang Nauck, Albert Vanhoye, George H. Guthrie, Victor (Sung-Yul) Rhee, Cynthia Long Westfall, and John Paul Heil.

---

1. Westfall, *Discourse Analysis*, 9, notes that "Vanhoye's observation of repetition throughout the discourse . . . has convinced many people concerning the unity of the discourse."

2.2 General Observations of Repetition within Hebrews

Over the past fifty years or so, many scholars have found significance in a large number of lexical and other kinds of repetitive ties within the text of Hebrews. While different scholars have deemed different connections significant for different reasons, links between non-adjacent texts that have been viewed as significant in some way include: 1:1–4 and 4:12–13;[2] 1:1–4 and 2:1–4;[3] 1:5 and 1:13 (τίνι . . . εἶπέν ποτε τῶν ἀγγέλων / πρὸς τίνα δὲ τῶν ἀγγέλων εἴρηκέν ποτε);[4] 1:5 and 5:5 (the quotation from Ps 2:7);[5] 2:5 and 2:16 (οὐ γὰρ ἀγγέλοις / οὐ γὰρ δήπου ἀγγέλων);[6] 2:10 and 2:17–18 (ἔπρεπεν / ὤφειλεν and παθημάτων / πέπονθεν);[7] 2:17–18 and 4:14–5:3 (which share "no fewer than eight words or phrases");[8] 3:1–4:14 (ἐποθανίου /οὐρανούς, Ἰησοῦν / Ἰησοῦν, ἀρχιερέα, and τῆς ὁμολογίας);[9] 3:12 and 3:19 (βλέπω and ἀπιστία);[10] 4:1 and 4:5 (εἰσερχομαι and κατάπαυσις);[11] 4:14–16 and 10:19–23;[12] 5:1–3 and 7:27–28 (καθίστημι; θυσία; ἀσθένειαν / ἔχοντας ἀσθένειαν and τοῦ λαοῦ);[13] 5:1 and 8:3;[14] 5:1–10 (ἀρχιερεύς, θεός, καθίστημι / προαγορεύω);[15] 5:11 and 6:12 (νωθροὶ γεγόνατε / νωθροὶ γένησθε);[16] 5:11 and 6:20 (Μελχισέδεκ); 6:17–20

---

2. Nauck, "Zum Aufbau des Hebräerbriefes," 204–05, sees connections between the "logos-hymn" of 1:2b–3 and the "sophia-hymn" of 4:12–13. Cf. Joslin, "Can Hebrews be Structured?," 108.

3. Ellingworth, *Hebrews*, 134; Westfall, *Discourse Analysis*, 93, 96–99.

4. Vanhoye, *Structure*, 80–81; Lane, *Hebrews 1–8*, n.p.

5. Guthrie, *Structure*, 104–5.

6. Vanhoye, *Structure*, 82–83; Lane, *Hebrews 1–8*, n.p.

7. Guthrie, *Structure*, 78–79; Westfall, *Discourse Analysis*, 100.

8. I.e. "high priest," "sin," "merciful/mercy," "tempted," "help," "in service (of matters related) to God," "the people," and the obligation to do something. Guthrie, *Hebrews*, 111, and *Structure*, 96–100; Cf. Vanhoye, *Structure*, 83, 86; and Ellingworth, *Hebrews*, 179–80.

9. Ellingworth, *Hebrews*, 213.

10. Guthrie, *Structure*, 78–79; Macleod, "Literary Structure," 187.

11. Macleod, "Literary Structure," 187.

12. Nauck, "Zum Aufbau," 204–05. Cf. Joslin, "Can Hebrews be Structured?," 108; and Guthrie, *Structure*, 80–81. Guthrie claims that Nauck's extension of the second passage to verse 31 "seems M

13. Guthrie, *Structure*, 82–83.

14. Guthrie, *Structure*, 85, 104–05.

15. Neeley, "Discourse Analysis," 15; Guthrie, *Structure*, 82–83.

16. Vanhoye, *La Structure*, 115; Lane, *Hebrews 1–8*, n.p.; Guthrie, *Structure*, 83–84; and Ellingworth, *Hebrews*, 54, who sees the second reference as the "structural counterpart" to the first.

and 7:18-22 (ὅρκω / ὁρκωμοσίας, τῆσ προκειμένης ἐλπίδος / κρείττονος ἐλπίδος, Ἰησοῦς / Ἰησοῦς; εἰς τὸν αἰῶνα);[17] 7:1 and 7:9-10 (ὁ Μελχισέδεκ ... σθναντήσας Ἀβραάμ / συνήτησεν αὐτῷ [Ἀβραάμ] Μελχισέδεκ);[18] 7:11 and 7:28 (τελείωσις, ιερωςύνη / ἀρχιερεῖς, νενομοθέται / νόμος);[19] 7:20-28 (ὁρκωμοσίας x2 / ὁρκωμοσίας);[20] 8:3 and 10:18;[21] 8:8-12 and 10:15-17 (the quotation from Jeremiah 31:31-34);[22] 8:7 and 8:13 (πρῶτος, δευτέρας / καινός);[23] 9:1 and 9:10 (δικαίωμα);[24] 9:11 and 9:14 (Χριστός);[25] 9:11-12 and 9:28 (Χριστός, παραγενόμενος / παραγενόμενος / ὀφθήσεται);[26] 9:15 and 9:17 (διαθήκη); 9:18-22 (χωρὶς αἵματος / χωρὶς αἱματεκχυσίας); 10:1 and 10:3 (κατ' ἐνιαυτόν / κατ' ἐνιαυτόν);[27] 10:1 and 10:14 (ταῖς αὐταῖς θυσίαις / μιᾷ ... προσφορᾷ, εἰς τὸ διηνεκὲς, οὐδέποτε δύναται ... τελειῶσαι / τετελείωκεν, τοὺς προσερχομένους / τοὺς ἁγιαζομένους);[28] 10:11 and 10:18 (προσφέρων / προσφορά); 10:27 and 10:31 (φοβερός); 11:1 and 11:7 (οὐ βλεπομένων / μηδέπω βλεπομένων);[29] 11:1-2 and 11:39-40 (μαρτυρέω, πίστις, βλεπομένων / προβλεψαμένου);[30] 11:23 and 11:27 (οὐκ ἐφοβήθησαν ... τοῦ βασιλέως / μὴ φοβηθεὶς ... τοῦ βασιλέως); 11:33 and 11:39 (διὰ πίστεως / διὰ τῆς πίστεως);[31] 12:2a and 12:16 (ἀντί, ὑπέμεινεν / ἀπέδετο);[32] 12:5 and 12:8 (υἱός);[33] 13:7 and 13:17 ('ἡγέομαι).[34]

---

17. Hughes, *Hebrews and Hermeneutics*, 21.
18. Guthrie, *Structure*, 84.
19. Guthrie, *Structure*, 84.
20. Macleod, "Literary Structure," 187.
21. Guthrie, *Structure*, 84-85, suggests that the statement of 10:18 "wraps up the discussion" begun in 8:3 regarding the need for the heavenly high priest to have something to offer.
22. Guthrie, *Structure*, 85.
23. Guthrie, *Structure*, 85-86; Macleod, "Literary Structure," 187.
24. Guthrie, *Structure*, 86.
25. Macleod, "Literary Structure," 187.
26. Guthrie, *Structure*, 86.
27. Macleod, "Literary Structure," 187-88.
28. Guthrie, *Structure*, 87.
29. Macleod, "Literary Structure," 188.
30. Guthrie, Structure, 87-88; Rhee, *Faith*, 180-221, and "Chiasm," 327-45.
31. Macleod, "Literary Structure," 188.
32. Andriessen and Lenglet, "Quelques passages difficiles," 220.
33. Macleod, "Literary Structure," 188.
34. Macleod, "Literary Structure," 188.

Scholars have also noted the presence of unusual patterns of repetition within adjacent or nearly adjacent text.[35] Examples of this include the repetition of τῶν ἀγγέλων (1:4) in 1:5; τὰ παιδία (2:13, 14); πιστός (2:17, 3:2); ἀρχιερεύς (2:17, 3:1); εἰσέρχομαι (3:19, 4:1); ὁ λόγος (4:12, 13); ἔχω (4:14, 4:15); ἐπαγγελίας (6:12) and ἐπαγγειλάμενος (6:13); ἱερεύς (7:1, 3); ἡ πρώτη (8:13, 9:1); οὐρανός (9:23, 9:24); πίστις (10:39, 11:1); κληρονόμος (11:7, 8); μαρτθρηθέντες (11:39) and μαρτύρων (12:1); ἐγώ (11:40 and 12:1); and λαλέω (12:24, 25).[36]

Some have drawn attention to the author's repeated use of key vocabulary within particular sections (e.g., πίστις, "faith," occurs twenty-four times in 11:1–40)[37] or across the discourse as a whole (e.g., κρείττων, "better").[38] A. Descamps deems such words "characteristic terms," noting, for instance, that ἄγγελος ("angel/messenger") occurs eleven times between 1:4 and 2:16, and only twice after that point in the remainder of the discourse.[39]

Several others have recognized a different kind of pattern involving repetition whereby the author of Hebrews seems to establish a connection with a text *outside* of Hebrews by making use of similar vocabulary within his text. Citing Hebrews 3 as an example of "midrashic treatment," Guthrie notes that in 3:12–19 the author takes the concepts "heart," "day," "today," "hear," "enter," "test," "rest," "unbelief," and "swear" from Psalm 95, "weaving them into a potent commentary and exhortation" of the earlier text.[40] Similarly in chapter 4, Lane suggests that the author makes use of cognate terms from both Psalm 95 and Genesis 2:2 (both LXX)

---

35. Our distinction between "non-adjacent" and "adjacent/near adjacent" text is not intended as a precise designation but serves to differentiate between the location of patterns of repetition in broad brushstrokes.

36. These represent "the main hook words in Hebrews" according to Macleod, "The Literary Structure of the Book of Hebrews," 188. Cf. Lightfoot, *Jesus Christ Today*, 49.

37. Heb 11:1, 3, 4, 5, 6, 7 x2, 8, 9, 11, 13, 17, 20, 21, 22, 23, 24, 27, 28, 29, 30, 31, 33, 39. See also the three further references in the immediate context: 10:38, 39; and 12:2.

38. Bruce, *A Commentary*, lxiii–lxiv, notes that ἀγαθός is used in its comparative form to describe a "better name" (1:4), "a better hope" (7:19), "a better covenant" (7:22), "a better ministry" (8:6), "better sacrifices" (9:23), "a better possession" (10:34), "a better country" (11:16), "a better resurrection" (11:35), "something better for us" (11:40), and "a better word" (12:24).

39. Descamps, "La Structure," 251–58, 333–38. The first occurrence of the word is located in 1:4 and its final appearance is in 2:16.

40. Guthrie, *Hebrews*, 129.

to establish an inference within his text on the basis of an "analogy of words" between the two ancient texts.[41]

Still others have drawn attention to the unusual symmetry formed by patterns of repetition which seems to operate at various levels of the text. Most famously, Vanhoye claims that the discourse as a whole (excluding 13:22–25) functions as a perfect five-part chiasm which pivots in 8:1–9:28 on the sacrifice of Christ, with Χριστὸς δέ ("now Christ," 9:11) as its center.[42] Although his macro proposal has been widely rejected as artificial, many have since claimed to detect other instances of symmetry within smaller units of text such as 1:1–4,[43] 1:5,[44] 2:1–4,[45] 3:1–6,[46] 5:1–10,[47] 12:1–2,[48] and 13:1–6,[49] and even within particular sentences in the discourse. As an example of this micro-symmetry, Vanhoye draws attention to examples of "symétrie concentrique" and "symétrie parallèle" in Hebrews 3:3 (fig. 1 below).[50]

---

41. Lane, *Hebrews 1–8*, n.p.

42. Vanhoye, *Structure*, 40a–40b. See Welch, "Chiasmus," 220, for an alternative proposal. The word "chiasm" derives from the Greek letter, Χ (chi), and denotes a "crosswise, diagonal arrangement" between clauses or sentences in which the first part corresponds with the final part, the second with the penultimate, and so on. It thus describes "an inversion of the order of the words or phrases which are repeated or subsequently referred to." Cf. Rhee, *Faith*, 14–15.

43. D. W. B. Robinson, "Literary Structure," 178–86; Meier, "Structure," 167; Ebert, "Chiastic Structure," 163–79; Ellingworth, *Hebrews*, 95; Rhee, *Faith*, 66–67; L. T. Johnson, *Hebrews*, 68.

44. Vanhoye, *La Structure*, 70; Westfall, *Discourse Analysis*, 54; and Lane, *Hebrews 1–8*, n.p.

45. Auffret, "Note," 166–79.

46. Auffret, "Essai," 380–96.

47. Ellingworth, *Hebrews*, 271, states that "the generally chiastic structure of 5:1–10 is widely recognized, but cannot be pressed in detail." Cf. Vanhoye, *La Structure*, 107–13.

48. Horning, "Chiasmus," 41. Cf. Hamm, "Faith," 272; and Man, "The Value of Chiasm," 146.

49. Vanhoye, "La Question," 121–39.

50. Vanhoye, *La Structure*, 88. Cf. Auffret, "Note sur la Structure Littérraire d'Hb II.1–4," 166–79; and Lane, *Hebrews 1–8*, n.p., who points out the "unusual word order calculated to arouse the attention" within 2:14.

Example 1: *"symétrie concentrique"*

οὗτος
παρὰ Μωϋσῆν
ἠξίωται

ὁ κατασκευάσας
τοῦ οἴκου
τιμὴν ἔχει

Example 2: *"symétrie parallèle"*

πλείονος
δόξης

πλείονα
πλείονα τιμὴν

Fig. 1.

2.3 Modern Scholarship on the Function of Repetition within Hebrews

In light of these observations, this section seeks to explore how modern scholarship has understood the function of repetition within Hebrews by summarizing and critiquing the work of Wolfgang Nauck, Albert Vanhoye, George H. Guthrie, Victor (Sung-Yul) Rhee, and Cynthia Long Westfall. While those selected are by no means the only scholars to have observed these patterns of repetition, each represents someone who has sought to account for its distinctive presence in the text in a consistent and systematic fashion. It is worth stressing once more that this chapter is not primarily a historical survey on the structure of Hebrews—despite the fact that each scholar surveyed has made a distinctive contribution in this area.[51] Rather it focuses specifically on what has been said with regard to what repetition is *doing* within the discourse.[52]

2.3.1 Wolfgang Nauck

Although brief at only six pages, Wolfgang Nauck's essay "Zum Aufbau des Hebräerbriefes" represents the first major contribution to the discussion of repetition and its function in Hebrews. Nauck proposed a tripartite structure for the discourse based on his perception of links between the "logos-hymn" of 1:2b-3 and the "sophia hymn" of 4:12-13; the hortatory material of 4:14-16 and 10:19-31; and the calls to "remember" with their associated "consequences" in 10:32ff and 13:7ff,[53]

---

51. For a good general survey of other approaches see Joslin, "Can Hebrews be Structured?," 99–129; Westfall, *Discourse Analysis*, 1–21; and Guthrie, *Structure*, 3–41.

52. For this reason, we will not be engaging in depth with Martin and Whitlark's excellent analysis of Hebrews' argument and rhetorical arrangement in light of the ancient handbooks, *Inventing Hebrews*; nor with Gelardini's synthetic approach to the same topic in *Verhärtet eure Herzen nicht*, and "Linguistic Turn," 49-50.

53. Nauck, "Zum Aufbau," 200–05, views 13:18–25 as a postscript attached when

PATTERNS OF REPETITION, STRUCTURE, AND MEANING

which he read as parallel passages surrounding each section. While not all of the details of Nauck's outline have withstood scrutiny,[54] leading some to criticize the simplicity of his approach,[55] many today view his parallels between Hebrews 4:14–16 and 10:19–31 (see below in light of minor modifications by George Guthrie) as "compelling,"[56] and his findings have proven enormously influential in shaping modern proposals on the structure of this discourse.[57]

Heb 4:14–16	Heb 10:19–23
Ἔχοντες οὖν . . .	Ἔχοντες οὖν . . .
ἀρχιερέα μέγαν	ἱερέα μέγαν
διεληλυθότα τοὺς οὐρανούς	. . . διὰ τοῦ καταπετάσματος
Ἰησοῦν	Ἰησοῦ
τὸν υἱὸν τοῦ θεοῦ	τὸν οἶκον τοῦ θεοῦ
κρατῶμεν τῆς ὁμολογίας	κατέχωμεν τὴν ὁμολογίαν
προσερχώμεθα . . . μετὰ	προσερχώμεθα μετὰ
παρρησίας . . .	παρρησίαν

For present purposes, however, Nauck's suggestion of a structuring function for repetition in Hebrews represents his most important insight.

---

the sermon was sent.

54. Guthrie, *Structure*, 81, rejects Nauck's proposal of an inclusion between 10:32 and 13:7, claiming "the only verbal parallel between the two passages involves the opening term in each—Ἀναμιμνῄσκεσθε in 10:32 and Μνημονεύτε in 13:7. Nauck is correct in suggesting that the passages are similar in form. Yet, they also share this similarity with 3:12–15; 6:9–12; and 12:4–7. These correspondences, found so far apart in the text, do not warrant the label *inclusio*." He also claims that Nauck's extension of the second passage (Heb 10:19ff.) to verse 31 "seems unwarranted," proposing instead that the second unit ends after v. 23.

55. Attridge, *The Epistle to the Hebrews*, 15, states that Nauck's divisions do not account for the intricacies of the structure and that his analysis "does little to illuminate the complex interrelationships of sections within the text"; Joslin, "Can Hebrews be Stuctured?," 109.

56. Guthrie, *Structure*, 80–81. Cf. Joslin, "Can Hebrews be Structured?," 108.

57. See Martin and Whitlark, *Inventing Hebrews*, 4; Joslin, "Can Hebrews be Structured?," 108; Westfall, *Discourse Analysis*, 13; Guthrie, *Structure*, 79, who calls these passages "the most striking use of inclusio in the book of Hebrews"; and O'Brien, *Hebrews*, 360. Although in broad agreement with Nauck's understanding of the shape of Hebrews, this study argues (in 6.3.1) that 4:14–16 and 10:19–22 are in fact better understood as the introduction and conclusion (or part thereof) of two separate sections (4:14—8:3 and 7:25—10:22) which share an overlapping boundary at 7:25—8:3.

2.3.2 Albert Vanhoye

2.3.2.1 Overview

Probably the single greatest contribution to the topic of repetition and its function in Hebrews has been made by Albert Vanhoye. Widely regarded as "the most influential and debated work ever written on the structure of Hebrews,"[58] Vanhoye's seminal *La structure littéraire de l'Épître aux Hébreux* (1963) represents an attempt to understand the structural organization of the text on the basis of five "literary devices" which he claims may be found throughout the text. Since, according to Vanhoye, nothing in Hebrews is a matter of chance, the modern scholar is able to come to an accurate assessment of structure by paying close attention to these devices and their interaction in context.[59] The key to correct interpretation then is to recognize the author's use of such techniques "without mistakes."[60] These techniques, together with a sixth added later,[61] are summarized as follows:

1. *The announcement of the Subject*: "A brief formula before each major part which presents the theme to be discussed and its principle divisions" (cf. 1:4; 2:17–18; 5:9–10; 10:36–39; 12:13).

2. *Inclusions*: The use of the same word or words at the beginning and end of the development of a subject.[62]

3. *Hook Words*: A word used at the end of one section of text and at the beginning of the next.[63]

---

58. Guthrie, *Hebrews*, 14. Cf. Joslin, *Hebrews*, 109; and Westfall, *Discourse Analysis*, 7, who notes that Vanhoye has had a profound influence on H. W. Attridge, D. A. Black, P. Ellingworth, G. H. Guthrie, and W. L. Lane among others.

59. Vanhoye, *Structure*, 20, claims that "our author is not one of those preachers who makes outlines easy by stating straightforwardly at the beginning of their sermon that they will develop three points: one, two, and three. The author of Hebrews is too much an artist to use this mathematical way of proceeding. He prefers to use structuralizing techniques which are more subtle and which rely on the insight of the listeners."

60. Vanhoye, *Structure*, 19, 20.

61. Vanhoye's later work, *Structure and Message of the Epistle to the Hebrews* (1989), includes a sixth technique which he terms "symmetrical arrangements," 76.

62. Guthrie, *Structure*, 15, notes that an "inclusion" (from the Latin *inclusio*) represents a well-documented literary technique in various ancient traditions in which the same components begin and end a unit of text.

63. Guthrie, *Structure*, 97, notes that the "hook word" represents essentially the same feature as Vaganay's *mot crochet*.

4. *Characteristic Terms*: Topically significant words which appear an unusually high number of times in a section.

5. *Alteration in the use of literary genres*: the change from one type of discourse to another (i.e. exposition and exhortation).

6. *Symmetrical Arrangements*: these describe "patterns formed from correspondences in many details."⁶⁴

2.3.2.2 The Function of Repetition in Vanhoye

As even a brief glance at his "literary devices" will show, repetition plays a highly significant role in Vanhoye's schema, serving at least four distinct functions within the discourse.

First, by forming inclusions, repetition *defines and marks out the limits of particular units* within Hebrews.⁶⁵ As such, it serves a *discontinuous* function in the text. Noting, for example, the formal parallels between τίνι γὰρ εἶπέν ποτε τῶν ἀγγέλων (1:5) and πρὸς τίνα δὲ τῶν ἀγγέλων ἔρηκέν ποτε (1:13), Vanhoye states that repetition serves to "introduce the end of the paragraph" begun previously.⁶⁶ See fig. 2 below:

Fig. 2.

Vanhoye detects over thirty such inclusions within Hebrews⁶⁷ and he recognizes their capacity to structure the text into units at multiple levels within the discourse: "it is important to note that the inclusions can be multiplied in the same context and fit into each other."⁶⁸ For example, Vanhoye suggests that the repetition of the verb προσφέρω ("I offer," 8:3 and 9:28) functions as an inclusion which bounds a unit, 8:3–9:28, containing two sub-units (8:3–9:9; 9:11–28), each of which is bounded by further inclusions based on δῶρά τε καὶ θυσίας ("gifts and sacrifices," 8:3

---

64. Vanhoye, *Structure*, 76.
65. Vanhoye, *Structure*, 76.
66. Vanhoye, *Structure*, 76.
67. Guthrie, *Structure*, 76.
68. Vanhoye, *Structure*, 77.

and 9:9) and Χριστόν ("Christ," 9:11 and 9:28) respectively. Each of these sub-units may themselves be separated into still smaller units by means of inclusions surrounding 8:2 and 8:6 (λειτοθργός / λειτοθργίας, "minister / ministry," 8:2 and 8:6), 8:7 and 8:13 (ἡ πρώτη, "the first" 8:7 and 8:13), etc.[69] This may be seen in the diagram (fig. 3) which follows:

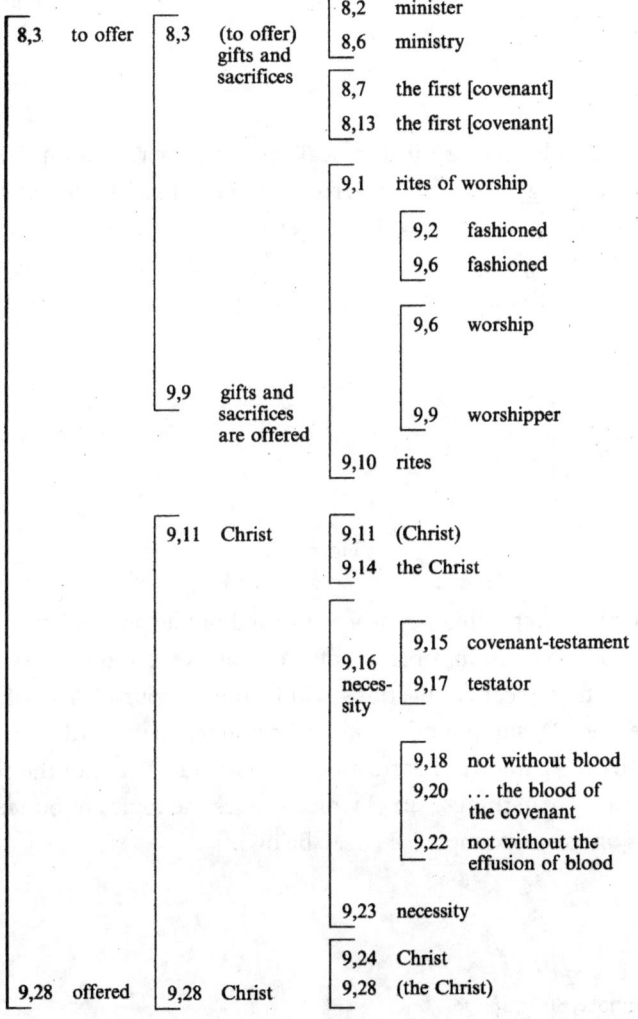

Fig. 3.

---

69. Vanhoye, *Structure*, 38–39. Cf. Vanhoye's comments regarding πίστις in 11:1, which he suggests functions as the tail member of a hook with 10:39 while also serving as the head of two inclusions: 11:1 and 7, and 11:1 and 39 (p.100).

Second, repetition *ties together various paragraphs or units* within the discourse by means of "hook words" (see fig. 4).[70] Vanhoye cites the repetition of τῶν ἀγγελων (1:4) in 1:5 as one such example which functions to join together the "exordium" (1:1–4) with the "first part" of the discourse (1:5—2:18).[71]

```
┌─────────────────────┐
│          X│X        │     Function: to link distinct units together
└─────────────────────┘
```

Fig. 4.

Vanhoye also sees a third topical function for repetition. He suggests that by using "characteristic terms," the author *builds semantic cohesion* within particular units which serves both to articulate and develop primary themes, giving to the material a "distinctive physiognomy," and to identify their limits within the text (see fig. 5 below).[72]

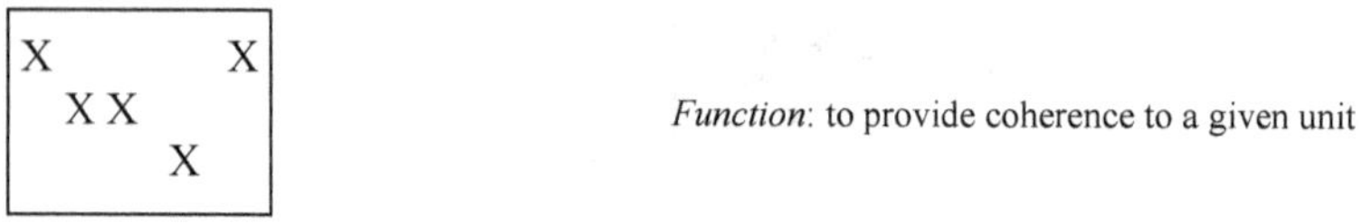

```
┌─────────────────────┐
│ X           X       │
│   X X               │     Function: to provide coherence to a given unit
│      X              │
└─────────────────────┘
```

Fig. 5.

Fourth, by repeating key words marked out as prominent by their previous location within topic announcements, repetition serves to indicate various topical connections within the discourse. According to Vanhoye, such "resumptions" relate to "announcement words which are *resumed* by the author in his treatment."[73] His translation of the phrase κατὰ πάντα ("in all things," 4:15) which echoes the topic announcement of 2:17 is one such example (see fig. 6 below).[74]

---

70. Vanhoye, *Structure*, 76.
71. Vanhoye, *Structure*, 76, 40.
72. Vanhoye, *Structure*, 76. His example of the word ἄγγελος follows Descamps, "La Structure de l'Épître aux Hébreux," 251–58; 333–38.
73. Vanhoye, *Structure*, 77.
74. Vanhoye, *Structure*, 77.

| X   X | *Function*: to re-activate a key word / topic |

Fig. 6.

2.3.2.3 Evaluation of Vanhoye

Vanhoye's greatest contribution lies in his incorporation of the insights of earlier scholars such as Thien, Gyllenberg, Descamps and Vaganay into a broad synthetic approach to the text. By pointing to features "which lie clearly present on the surface of the text,"[75] Vanhoye paved the way for a more rigorous "objective" methodology which has been followed and developed by many.[76] Consequently most scholars today would agree with his statement: "The study of structure should . . . be undertaken with no *a priori* conclusions and should begin with a search for the first series of indications. These indications allow one to make out the arrangement of the text."[77]

With regard to his understanding of the function of repetition, Vanhoye's demonstration of the role played by inclusions in defining and marking out unit boundaries has convinced the majority of researchers today that at least on occasion "inclusions do play a primary role in marking sections of Hebrews' and must therefore be considered in any assessment of the document"s structure.[78] Even if some of the details don't stand up to close scrutiny,[79] his description of their role in shaping the discourse into a series of hierarchically ordered units is compelling, especially given Vanhoye's identification of a contemporary text, *Wisdom*, in which repetition seems to function very similarly to the way he describes in Hebrews.[80] Vanhoye's categories of "hook words" and

---

75. Ellingworth, *Hebrews*, 58.

76. See Heil, *Chiastic Structures*, for example (2.3.2.6). Black, "The Problem," 174, notes: "The great merit of Vanhoye's treatment is that it shows concretely how an understanding of structural linguistics can serve the expositor." Attridge, *Hebrews*, 16, comments similarly: "In its appeal to a variety of structurally significant literary indices this analysis marks a definite advance over simple catalogues of content and artificial thematic structures."

77. Vanhoye, *Structure*, 33.

78. Guthrie, *Structure*, 76.

79. See Guthrie, *Structure*, 76.

80. *Wisdom* is believed to have been written in the 1st or 2nd century B.C. Vanhoye,

"characteristic terms" have proven similarly influential, with the latter providing the central plank for Westfall's subsequent analysis.[81] Meanwhile his observation of the capacity for repetition patterns to play *more than one role simultaneously* within the discourse, henceforth described in this study as "multifunctionality," represents an important insight which reflects the complexity of this text: "It not infrequently happens that a word which serves as a hook word performs at the same time another function: for example, though the word angels in 1,4 is only a hook word, in 1,5 the same word is used both as a hook word, joining 1,5 and 1,4, and as the beginning of an inclusion."[82]

Vanhoye's analysis is not without its difficulties, however. Many consider his overall presentation less than persuasive in light of his "assumption of symmetry in the discourse in spite of many indicators of asymmetry."[83] Vanhoye's dismissal of Hebrews 13:19 and 22-25 as unoriginal has been overturned by Spicq (1947) and Filson (1967), and few today would accept Hebrews 9:11 as the center of the discourse.[84] Scholars have also criticized Vanhoye's failure to engage adequately with Nauck's observations regarding 4:14-16 and 10:19ff.[85]

Turning to repetition itself, Vanhoye's analysis suffers from drawing too sharp a distinction between form and content. On the one hand, his detection of "topic announcements" seems to depend entirely "on the ability of the commentator to subjectively discern the flow of the author's

---

Structure, 22, plausibly claims that "all the evidence points to the fact that Hebrews is part of this same literary tradition." Cf. M. Gilbert's analysis, *Wisdom*, 22.

81. Westfall, *Discourse Analysis*, 9, comments: "The literary device of "characteristic words" is very important in recognizing discourse chunks. What he [Vanhoye] calls "hook words," or repetition of words, phrases or paraphrases in different sections, is the way authors create cohesion and texture." Cf. Macleod, "The Literary Structure of the Book of Hebrews," 188; and Gelardini, "Linguistic Turn," 55.

82. Vanhoye, *Structure*, 78.

83. Hughes, *Hebrews*, 2, comments: "Vanhoye in his detailed study seems to me to err on the side of overstatement and to find more stylistic symmetries and literary subtleties than are really present." Meanwhile Kuss, *Der Brief an die Hebräer*, 14, suggests that his arrangement says more about the modern scholar than the structure of Hebrews, while Ebert, "The Chiastic Structure of the Prologue to Hebrews," 165, dismisses as "invalid" Vanhoye's representation of the whole discourse as a chiasm. Cf. Westfall, *Discourse Analysis*, 11; Koester, *Hebrews*, 83; Joslin, "Can Hebrews be Structured?," 111.

84. Joslin, "Can Hebrews be Structured?," 110; and Westfall, *Discourse Analysis*, 10.

85. Cf. Guthrie, *Structure*, 79; and Joslin, "Can Hebrews be Structured?," 111. Since "this is one of the major questions one must confront when studying the structure of Hebrews," this omission is somewhat surprising, as Joslin notes.

argument" without reference to any "structurally-oriented data" by which such an outline might be determined.⁸⁶ On the other, his structural "backbone" apparently plays little or no role in communicating content. Individual instances of repetition are classified *either* as "topic announcements" *or* "inclusions" but never both, seemingly without justification.⁸⁷

Without objective criteria for his functional categories, many of Vanhoye's findings are open to question. How can we be certain, for instance, that the repetition of Χριστός forms an inclusion between 9:11 and 28 when the same word also appears in 9:14 and 9:24? On what basis does Vanhoye accord structural significance to one lexical connection but not to another (identical connection)?⁸⁸ Why, for example, does Vanhoye analyze 4:15—5:1 as a cluster of "resumptions" rather than as the tail member of an inclusion begun in 2:17—3:1, given the extensive linkage between the two passages?⁸⁹

Two final difficulties relate to the application of Vanhoye's functional categories to the text itself. First, while Vanhoye suggests that inclusions "define" the limits of textual units, in practice his "topic announcements" consistently occur *before* the head of various inclusions and thus lie *outside* of the boundaries of the unit they introduce.⁹⁰

---

86. Guthrie, *Structure*, 28. Cf. Westfall, *Discourse Analysis*, 9–10; and Bligh, *Chiastic Analysis*, 174, who asks, "who, for example, would suspect at first, second, or even third reading that the phrase καρπὸν εἰρηνικὸν . . . δικαιοσύνης in 12:11 indicates a major division in the argument?." As Rhee, *Faith*, 26, observes: "If the author of Hebrews had this device originally in mind [topic announcements], then it should be readily distinguishable to the readers."

87. For example, noting the large number of semantic ties between Hebrews 2:17–3:1 and 4:14–5:3 (see below), Vanhoye ἀρχιερεύς / ἀρχιερέα (2:17, 4:14) as a topic announcement, while claiming that the repetition of ἐποθρανίου in τοὺς οὐρανούς (3:1, 4:14) functions as an inclusion. This distinction seems arbitrary, however, as these roles could be reversed without difficulty.

88. Guthrie, *Structure*, 76, suggests that many of Vanhoye's "inclusions" are in fact examples of "common lexical repetition," claiming that "Vanhoye seems to err most often when he finds an inclusio built around a single word, or short phrase, the special structural function of which may be called into question" (p. 81).

89. Vanhoye, *Structure*, 83, notes the following links: "to become like," 2:17 and 4:15; "merciful," 2:17 and 4:16; "high priest," 2:17 and 4:15; "for the things of God," 2:17 and 5:1; "suffered," 2:18 and 4:15; "having been tested," 2:18 and 4:15; "he is able," 2:18 and 4:15; "to offer help," 2:18 and 4:16.

90. For instance, Vanhoye, *Structure*, 38, notes that the repetition of προσφέρω in 8:3 and 9:28 forms an inclusion which takes in "all of this section *except* for the introductory sentence 8:1–2." Italics mine.

Second, Levinsohn raises questions about the function of a number of Vanhoye's "hook words."[91]

These difficulties notwithstanding, Vanhoye's analysis of Hebrews remains the most important contribution to our topic to date. This study will build on his strengths and, by more careful attention to the criteria by which significant repetition is detected and to alternative possibilities regarding the function of repetition, overcome some of these weaknesses and criticisms.

2.3.3 George H. Guthrie

2.3.3.1 *Overview*

Approaching the text from the perspective of "discourse analysis," a relatively new discipline at the time, George H. Guthrie develops many of the insights of Vanhoye, Nauck, L. L. Neeley, and others within a three-step approach to the text.

1. Identify unit boundaries.
2. Investigate the "interrelatedness" of textual units.
3. Account for the formal connections identified in steps one and two.

In his first step, Guthrie seeks to identify unit boundaries through "cohesion shift analysis" and the detection of inclusions in the discourse. He proposes that since "cola of the same paragraph have a higher level of cohesiveness when considered together than with cola outside that paragraph,"[92] shifts from one paragraph or section to another can be tracked by observing corresponding shifts in what he terms "cohesion fields" within the discourse (i.e. genre, topic, connection, subject, pronominal reference, lexical cohesion, temporal and spatial indicators).[93] Guthrie identifies twenty-two high-level and thirty-three median-level

---

91. See Levinsohn, review of Guthrie, 183. These will be addressed with regard to Guthrie's analysis in the following section.

92. Guthrie, *Structure*, 54, follows D. A. Black in defining a colon as "a unit of grammatical structure with clearly marked external dependencies. It always has either overtly or covertly a central matrix consisting of a nominal element (subject) and a verbal element (predicate), each having the possibility of extended features. Those features which are added to either the nominal or verbal element restrict the range of reference even as they supply further information."

93. Guthrie, *Structure*, 54.

shifts,[94] together with eighteen inclusions within Hebrews, claiming that "the head and tail members of *every inclusio* correspond to a high or median-level cohesion shift."[95]

Boundaries having been identified, Guthrie next attempts to understand the "interrelatedness" of units within Hebrews by examining inclusions, evidence of a "high level of lexical and pronominal cohesion"[96] and the use of various "transition devices" to move from one to the next.[97] He claims that just as cola are grouped together to form paragraphs, so in a "macro-discourse" such as Hebrews, paragraphs are grouped together into larger "embedded discourses" (or EDs, see fig. 7 below) which combine to form a hierarchically-ordered whole.[98]

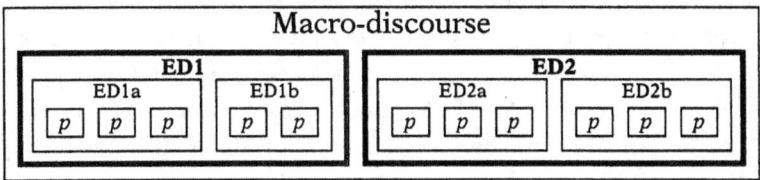

Fig. 7.

In his third and final step, Guthrie seeks to account for the formal connections discovered in step two: "It is not sufficient . . . merely to demonstrate that discourse units relate to other discourse units in the macro-structure. *Why they are arranged in their present position* stands as the ultimate question for any structural investigation."[99] He approaches his task by analyzing the relationships first between units of "exposition," then between units of "exhortation" and third between the two together, finding that the text consists of two independent but interrelated backbones that run side by side but eventually converge. The exposition proceeds according to a spatial and logical "step-by-step" progression while the exhortation forms an elaborate *chiasmus*.

94. Guthrie, *Structure*, 74.
95. Guthrie, *Structure*, 88.
96. Guthrie, *Structure*, 55–56, 90–92, claims that the presence of a similar or related lexical item in two or more units (e.g., son, chief priest and priest) demonstrates a semantic relationship between the two.
97. Guthrie, *Structure*, 57.
98. Guthrie, *Structure*, 48.
99. Guthrie, *Structure*, 57. Guthrie's italics.

2.3.3.2 *The Function of Repetition in Guthrie*

As was the case with Vanhoye, repetition serves a range of significant formal functions within Guthrie's analysis. Guthrie agrees with his predecessor that repetition plays both a "primary role" in structuring the discourse by forming inclusions which mark out unit boundaries,[100] and that it also serves to create cohesion within particular units at times.[101] However, it is Guthrie's category of "transitions" which marks his most distinctive contribution to the discussion.

Noting the difficulty modern scholars have had in identifying points of division within the text,[102] Guthrie claims that the problem stems, at least in part, from a failure to recognize the transitional nature of many of Hebrews' boundaries. He suggests that in contrast to later European conventions, the author of Hebrews frequently uses the repetition of "important lexical items strategically placed at the beginning or end of a text unit" to effect "smooth passage from one unit to the next."[103] Guthrie identifies no fewer than ten different kinds of these transitions which he addresses under two broad headings.

First, *constituent transitions* are those in which the transitional element is located in one or more of the constituents (always an introduction or conclusion) of the two units of material being joined together by the transitions.[104] These include:

- "hook words" which join together adjacent units;
- "distant hook words" which join together non-adjacent units of the same genre (see fig. 8 below);[105]

---

100. Guthrie, *Structure*, 76.
101. Guthrie, *Structure*, 90–93, 101, uses the descriptor "characteristic terms" in similar fashion to Vanhoye and he cites references to God, Jesus, the "word of God" and the word ἄγγελος as examples.
102. Guthrie, *Structure*, 21–25.
103. Guthrie, *Structure*, 95.
104. Guthrie, *Structure*, 95.
105. Guthrie, *Structure*, 97.

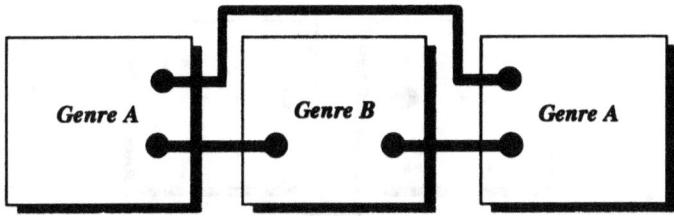

Fig. 8.

- "hooked key words" which describe "(a) a characteristic term used in the second unit and introduced in the conclusion of the first unit, (b) a characteristic term in the first unit used in the introduction of the next, or (c) a combination of the two" (see fig. 9 below)[106]. For example, Guthrie cites the repetition of ἄγγελος ("messenger") in 1:4 and 5 as an example of pattern (a). He states that while the word is linked structurally with the preceding unit (1:1–4), it also represents a "key" term which "points ahead to the main theme of the next section."[107]
- "overlapping constituents" which refer to "a passage used simultaneously as the conclusion of one block of material and the introduction to the next" (e.g., 4:14–16 and 10:19–25); and
- "parallel introductions" which describe roughly parallel statements which introduce new yet related blocks of discourse (e.g., 1:5 and 5:5; and 5:1 and 8:3).[108]

---

106. Guthrie, *Structure*, 101.
107. Guthrie, *Structure*, 101–2.
108. Guthrie, *Structure*, 101.

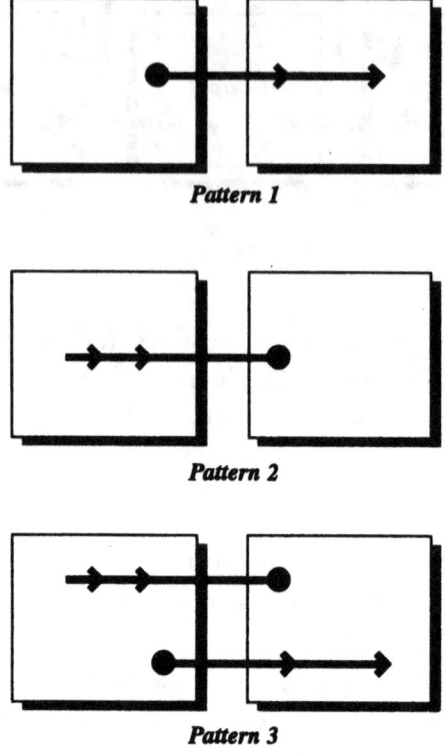

Fig. 9.

While clearly related, Guthrie's second kind of transitions, *intermediary transitions*, differ from constituent transitions in that "the unit used to make an intermediary transition belongs neither exclusively to the discourse unit which precedes it nor the one which follows, but contains elements of both."[109] Guthrie identifies three distinct categories of intermediary transitions (direct, woven and ingressive), citing 8:1–2 as an example of the first, which he claims serves to join together 5:1—7:28 and 8:3—10:18 (see fig. 10).[110]

---

109. Guthrie, *Structure*, 95–96.
110. Guthrie, *Structure*, 106–07.

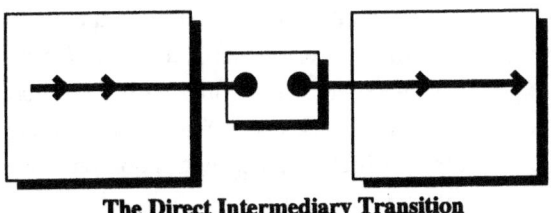

The Direct Intermediary Transition

Fig. 10.

2.3.3.3 Evaluation of Guthrie

Guthrie's discourse analysis represents a major contribution to research into Hebrews thanks primarily to its valuable methodological suggestions. His broad synthetic approach develops the best insights from previous scholarship, thereby considerably advancing the discussion. His examination of the interaction between expository and hortatory material establishes that "in every instance in Hebrews where expositional material is followed by hortatory, the hortatory utilizes semantic material from the expositional discussion."[111] Furthermore, his insistence that scholars must understand the relationship between paragraphs (in addition to that existing between words and sentences) in order to understand the text as a whole is a significant insight.

With regard to repetition, Guthrie fruitfully expands the category to include synonyms and other kinds of connections on the basis of evidence from ancient literature.[112] Moreover, his analysis of its function is significant in three ways. In the first place, it confirms Vanhoye's basic thesis that repetition can and does serve a structural function in Hebrews which must be considered in any serious attempt to understand

---

111. Guthrie, *Structure*, 140.

112. Guthrie, *Structure*, 15, notes that "variations on a strict *inclusio* include the use of a synonymous or complementary element rather than the same element," and he sees a significant structural connection between προσαγορεύω ("I designate") used in 5:10 and καθίστημι ("I appoint") in 5:1 (p. 82) as well as a "conceptual parallel" between the notion of God "speaking" (1:1) and the statement concerning the "word of God" in 4:12-13. See too Joslin, "Can Hebrews be Structured?," 120, who notes that "many of the rhetorical elements of which Guthrie writes are indeed found in the cultural milieu of Hebrews."

the meaning of the discourse.¹¹³ Second, by recognizing the capacity for links to perform *both* a formal *and* a topical role in the discourse, Guthrie avoids some of the difficulties of Vanhoye's either/or methodology and better explains what repetition is doing within the text. Third, his chapter on inclusions (chapter 5), which rejects as insufficient much of the evidence for Vanhoye's inclusions, provides pointers towards a more certain method for their identification.¹¹⁴

However, for present purposes, it is Guthrie's observation of overlap within the discourse which represents his most important insight. Guthrie repeatedly demonstrates the capacity for particular elements within Hebrews to function within *more than one context simultaneously*.¹¹⁵ In this way, he provides a plausible solution to the vexed problem of unit boundaries within this text, without retreating to the structural agnosticism of Moffatt and others.¹¹⁶

While representing a giant leap forward, Guthrie's analysis is not without a number of difficulties, however. At times his outline fails to accommodate his own findings of overlap in the text. For example, while he identifies 2:5–9; 4:14–16; 10:19–25; 8:1–2 and the "hook word" ἀγγέλων in 1:4 as portions of text which function as part of more than one unit simultaneously, he analyzes 4:14–16 and 10:19–25 as "overlapping constituents" which belong to *both* units, 2:5–9 and 8:1–2 as "intermediary transitions" which belong to *neither*, and ἀγγέλων as part of *one but not*

---

113. *Contra* Swetnam, "Form and Content," 374, who argues that hook words, characteristic terms and inclusions are "at best only secondary formal criteria for structure" in contrast to the much more secure "topic announcement," Guthrie demonstrates that such formal evidence in fact plays a primary role in determining the structure of Hebrews.

114. For example, Guthrie, *Structure*, 78, argues for an inclusion between 2:10 and 2:17–18 on the basis of a significant number of links of various kinds between the two passages and because "the tail boundary of the section finds further support from an inclusio at 3:1/ 4:1." Elsewhere (p. 77), he suggests that "where a single word, or brief phrase, is identified as the key element utilized to close out an inclusio, there should be no intervening use of that word, or the use of that word should be uniquely complementary to the opening, serving to round off the topic under discussion."

115. Commenting on the relationship between 3:1–4:16 and 4:14–16, for example, Guthrie, Structure, 82, states "if 3:1—4:16 be considered a section and 4:14–10:23 be considered a section, then an overlap presents itself. This dynamic cannot be ruled out as an impossibility."

116. For example, Guthrie, *Structure*, 104, states that the dual function of 10:19–25 provides "an explanation for why scholars such as Donald Guthrie, F. F. Bruce, and R.C.H. Lenski end the central section at 10:18, while others such as Harold Attridge and Wolfgang Nauck extend it to include 10:19 and following." Cf. Moffatt, *A Critical Commentary*, xxiii–xxiv; and Guthrie, *Structure*, 24–25.

the other.[117] This treatment seems inconsistent, however, and raises questions about Guthrie's partitioning of the text.

Scholars since Guthrie have also cast doubt on his fundamental assumption that the text in Hebrews may be meaningfully separated on the basis of genre.[118] Once the complexity of the interaction between these genres is noted, Guthrie's analysis clearly needs further refinement.[119] Others have challenged his findings of a correspondence between the location of inclusions and various cohesion shifts within the discourse,[120] while still others have questioned the objectivity of his method (i.e. cohesion shift analysis)[121] and its failure to give due consideration to the author's use of conjunctions.[122]

Perhaps the biggest difficulty with Guthrie's approach, however, lies not with his method itself but with the task he assigns it: the detection of individual unit boundaries. As its name suggests, "cohesion shift analysis" operates on the assumption that textual boundaries may

---

117. Guthrie, *Structure*, 102–3, 105–109, 96.

118. Mackie, *Eschatology and Exhortation*, 19, notes that "while some scholars have attempted to identify structural points of division between exposition and exhortation in Hebrews, it has become increasingly recognized that the two are in fact inseparable.

119. For instance, while 10:26—13:21 is undoubtedly primarily hortatory, the lengthy exposition of 11:1–40 seems to indicate that it is *more than* a "massive rolling exhortation" as Guthrie suggests (*Structure*, 141). Guthrie claims (p. 40) that the "surface structure" of the 11:1–40 is "misleading" at this point in light of Michael R. Cosby's suggestion, "Rhetorical Composition," 268, that "the use of lists of exempla was a hortatory device used extensively in the ancient world to persuade the reader to take some action." However, as Westfall, *Discourse Analysis*, 20, observes: "Guthrie goes beyond Cosby's thesis. Auditory impact does not equal exhortation." Guthrie's decision to identify 5:11—6:20 as "a hortatory section" (p. 98) is similarly questionable given the lack of any explicitly hortatory material from 6:13 onwards. On the other hand, he labels 4:14—5:10 a unit of "exposition" despite the fact that it includes the justly famous hortatory subjunctives of 4:14–16.

120. Levinsohn, review of Guthrie, 183, suggests that the fact that Guthrie allows components of inclusions to occur "close to the beginning or end of the unit rather than exactly at the beginning or end" (Guthrie, *Structure*, 15), rather weakens his findings, "especially in the case of the inclusion of Hebrews 10:1 and 10:14" whose corresponding high-level shift in fact occurs between vv. 18 and 19, with a median-level shift between vv. 10 and 11.

121. Westfall, *Discourse Analysis*, 20, criticizes Guthrie's double-counting of genre within the charting of intensity, suggesting that his analysis thereby "exaggerates and skews the detection of shifts," and claims, perhaps somewhat unfairly, that "the analysis is subject to his [Guthrie's] preconceptions about topic structure but maintains the appearance of objectivity." She is also critical of Guthrie's failure to address prominence (p. 19).

122. Levinsohn, review of Guthrie, 185.

be detected by observing "shifts" in cohesion fields within a particular text. However, while such an approach might work well for texts which contain clearly defined, distinct units with no overlap, it is less clear that boundaries can be obtained with any precision in texts such as Hebrews which seem to abound with *overlapping* transitions. Since the majority of Guthrie's functional categories (and especially his transitions) rely upon unit boundaries determined in this way, some measure of doubt must exist over his analysis of the function of repetition in Hebrews.

With regard to these functional categories themselves, some of Guthrie's inclusions seem more secure than others,[123] and he admits to "a noteworthy variation" or "anomaly" within his analysis of "distant hooks."[124] Moreover, from a topical perspective, it is not clear that many of Guthrie's "intermediate transitions," which he views as *distinct from* both neighboring units, might not be better understood as "overlapping constituents" which are *wholly integrated and inseparable* from both.[125] Guthrie also seems to argue in different directions on the basis of similar formal evidence at times. For example, noting the clear (*inclusio*-like) parallels between 5:1 and 8:3, Guthrie states: "The parallel statements found at 5:1 and 8:3 do not form an *inclusio*. The *inclusio* begun in Heb. 5:1–3 has already been shown to close at 7:26–28. Rather, 5:1 and 8:3 form a special type of transition referred to in the present study as 'parallel introductions.'"[126]

However, while 8:3 may well function as an introduction as Guthrie suggests, this in no way entails that it *cannot* also serve as part of a conclusion to the previous unit (as Guthrie proposes with regard to 4:14–16 and 10:19–25).[127] Finally, Levinsohn raises some important questions concerning a number of Guthrie's "hook words," noting:

---

123. Guthrie's suggestion of an inclusion based on the partial repetition of the quote from Jer 31:33–34 in 8:8–12 and 10:15–17 (Guthrie, *Structure*, 85) seems unlikely.

124. *Contra* his assertion that "in every instance in Hebrews where hortatory material follows exposition and in turn is followed by exposition, the author . . . uses what may be designated "distant hook words" to "jump" the hortatory section and resume his exposition" (*Structure*, 98), Guthrie identifies Heb 4:14–16 as a hortatory passage which is linked in this way to Heb 2:17–18, an expositional passage (p. 100).

125. See especially 8:1–2, which Guthrie treats separately from 7:11–28 and 8:3–6, despite clear (and perhaps even necessary) coherent relationships with both these units.

126. Guthrie, *Structure*, 85.

127. As our analysis will show (see chapter 6.3), the close proximity of 7:26–28 to 8:3 and the fact that both texts seem linked to 5:1 suggests that Heb 7:26—8:3 is better understood as a single cluster which is formally related to material at 4:14—5:1.

When Paul uses the same device, he places the hook word at the very end of the sentence that ends the first section, even if this involves postponing the hook word from its default position. For example, Galatians 3 ends with the postponed hook word κληρονόμοι, which becomes the topic of the first verses of chapter 4.

(3:29) εἰ δὲ ὑμεῖς Χριστοῦ, ἄρα τοῦ Ἀβραὰμ σπέρμα ἐστέ, κατ' ἐπαγγελίαν κληρονόμαι
(4:1) Λέγω δέ ἐφ' ὅσον χρόνον ὁ κληρονόμος νήπιός ἐστιν

In Hebrews, in contrast, some of the hook words that Guthrie mentions do not occur at the end of the sentence, and there is no evidence of postponing. This makes me question whether the writer really is making use of this device in these instances.[128]

These difficulties notwithstanding, Guthrie succeeds in providing a "coherent, though not simplistic, outline of the structure of Hebrews"[129] which agrees in broad terms with Vanhoye's presentation of a multilayered discourse made up of a hierarchically ordered group of units. This study will build on his strengths, seeking to further develop Guthrie's insight into the transitional nature of much of the material within the discourse and to better understand its function in Hebrews.

2.3.4 Victor (Sung Yul) Rhee

2.3.4.1 *Overview*

The work of Sung Yul Rhee is also worthy of mention at this point due to the distinctive role he attributes to repetition in determining the structure of Hebrews. Rhee sets out to understand the concept of "faith" in Hebrews, by means of a four-fold approach to the text involving exegesis, biblical theology, analysis of "chiasm" and what he terms "alternating structure."[130]

---

128. Levinsohn, review of Guthrie, 183. For instance, Guthrie, *Structure*, 97, reads the references to σωτηρία in 1:14 and 2:3 as "hook words" linking 2:1-4 and 1:5-14, despite the fact that the word in 2:3 occurs 33 words *after* the beginning of the unit it is supposed to introduce. Cf. similar difficulties involving references to πιστός in 2:17 and 3:2 which are separated by no fewer than 37 words, and ἐπουράνια / οὐρανόν in 9:23 and 24.

129. Joslin, "Can Hebrews be Structured?," 122.

130. Rhee, *Faith*, 12, 13, 17. By "alternating structure," Rhee refers to Vanhoye's

2.3.4.2 The Function of Repetition in Rhee

In agreement with both Vanhoye and Guthrie, Rhee claims that repetition serves to group a text into literary units by means of inclusions, to link these units together through hook words, and to create lexical cohesion within various parts of the discourse by means of characteristic terms.[131] His main contribution, however, lies in his observation of the role played by repetition in the formation of chiasms throughout the discourse. Rhee identifies over twenty-five such chiasms in Hebrews[132]—far more than previously noted—which he proposes play a crucial role with regard to the interpretation of this discourse. While noting that chiasms served a range of potential purposes in the ancient world,[133] he argues that the author of Hebrews structured his material in this way not so much "to impress readers" with a display of literary artistry as *to clarify ambiguity* within certain passages by providing parallel contexts in light of which readers might understand his intended meaning.[134] In other words, Rhee suggests that Hebrews uses parallelism primarily as "a means toward more effective communication."[135] This function may be demonstrated below with regard to Rhee's analysis of his first chiasm, 1:1–4:

---

depiction of the text as divided up into alternating units of doctrine and parenesis which are related to one another (e.g., the unit of doctrine, 1:1–14 gives way to a unit of exposition, 2:1–4). This aspect of his analysis is thus dependant on Vanhoye's results.

131. Rhee, *Faith*, 66, 110.

132. Rhee, *Faith*, 66-7, detects chiasms at 1:1-4 (p. 67-68); 2:1-4 (p. 71); 3:1-6 (p. 91); 3:12-13 (p. 98); 5:1-10 (p. 102); 7:11-19 (p. 136); 7:18-19 (p. 137); 7:20-22 (p. 138); 7:23-25 (p. 139); 7:26-28 (p. 140); 8:4-6 (p. 142); 9:11-12 (p. 146); 9:11-28 (pp. 147-48); 10:1-4 (p. 148-49); 10:5-7 (p. 150); 10:11-18 (pp. 150-51); 10:32-39 (p. 172); 10:32-34 (p. 175); 10:36-39 (p. 176); 11:1-3 (p. 211); 11:1-40 (p. 183); 11:13-17 (p. 184); 11:8-10 (p. 191); 11:20-22 (p. 192); 11:23-29 (pp. 195-96); 11:24-26 (p. 196); 11:27-29 (p. 197); 11:30-31 (p. 204); 12:1-3 (p. 225); 12:4-13 (p. 232); 12:14-29 (p. 236).

133. Cf. Miesner, "Chiasmus," 44-49; Welch, *Chiasmus in Antiquity*, 145-63; and Man, "The Value of Chiasm," 148-54.

134. Rhee, *Faith*, 13-14, follows the approach taken by Horning, "Chiasmus, Creedal Structure, and Christology in Hebrews 12:1–2," 41, with regard to their analysis of Hebrews 12:1–2 at this point. Cf. Rhee, *Faith*, 53; and Hamm, "Faith in the Epistle to the Hebrews," 280.

135. Rhee, *Faith*, 13.

A   Πολυμερῶς καὶ πολυτρόπως πάλαι ὁ θεὸς λαλήσας τοῖς πατράσιν ἐν τοῖς προφήταις ἐπ' ἐσχάτου τῶν ἡμερῶν τούτων ἐλάλησεν ἡμῖν ἐν υἱῷ

B   ὃν ἔθηκεν κληρονόμον πάντων

C   δι' οὗ καὶ ἐποίησεν τοὺς αἰῶνας

D   ὃς ὢν ἀπαύγασμα τῆς δόξης καὶ χαρακτὴρ τῆς ὑποστάσεως αὐτοῦ

C'   φέρων τε τὰ πάντα τῷ ῥήματι τῆς δυνάμεως αὐτοῦ

B'   καθαρισμὸν τῶν ἁμαρτιῶν ποιησάμενος ἐκάθισεν ἐν δεξιᾷ τῆς μεγαλωσύνης ἐν ὑψηλοῖς

A'   τοσούτῳ κρείττων γενόμενος τῶν ἀγγέλων ὅσῳ διαφορώτερον παρ' αὐτοὺς κεκληρονόμηκεν ὄνομα

Fig. 11[136]

According to Rhee, 1:1-4 represents a "chiasm at the conceptual level" which is made up of three parallel elements (A/A', B/B' and C/C') which surround the central and most important element (D). The outer sections are linked by the parallel thought of the Son's superiority to the prophets (A) and to the angels (A'), while Rhee sees a temporal connection between the appointment of the Son as heir (B) and his heavenly session (B') and between the words "created" (ἐποίησεν, C) and "sustain" (φέρων, C'). On the basis of these links, Rhee suggests that the phrase τοσούτῳ κρείττων γενόμενος (1:4) makes "more explicit" what is implied in 1:1-2 regarding the greatness of the Son, and claims that the reference to the purification of sins' in B' (καθαρισμὸν τῶν ἁμαρτιῶν) clarifies that Jesus' appointment as heir (described in B) "took place with the exaltation of Christ."[137]

2.3.4.3 Evaluation of Rhee

Rhee's study contains a number of important strengths. He seeks to identify the boundaries of units and their relationship within the text on the basis of formal evidence[138] and his analysis advances the understanding of repetition by revealing more connections within Hebrews

---

136. Rhee, *Faith*, 13.

137. Rhee, *Faith*, 67-68, claims that the contrast between "long ago" and "in these last days" implicitly suggests that God's revelation given to the new era through the Son is superior to that given to the old era through prophets. Cf. Michel, *Der Brief*, 103.

138. Rhee, *Faith*, 65 and 85, begins his investigation into each unit with good starting questions, examples of which follow: "What is the basis for the literary unit?," "Then what are the structural clues which denote that 3:1—4:16 is related to 2:5-16?."

than have been previously observed.¹³⁹ Furthermore, his suggestion of a repeated chiastic structure for Hebrews is historically plausible given that, as Welch notes, "parallelism thrived" in the ancient world and was used for "express pedagogical functions," as an aid to memorization and in service of liturgical purposes.¹⁴⁰ Most importantly, however, by seeking to interpret the topical content of the text in the light of its formal parallels (where applicable), Rhee pioneers a fresh approach to Hebrews which represents a potentially significant way by which the modern scholar might gain a better appreciation of the author's intended meaning in his discourse.¹⁴¹

Unfortunately, Rhee's approach suffers from faulty methodology in at least two ways. First, he assumes with minimal alteration both Vanhoye's analysis of genre and his unit break up, thereby inheriting the problems associated with the earlier study. Second, and more seriously, Rhee neither develops nor explains the criteria used to arrive at his findings. While he detects numerous connections within the text, he rarely accounts adequately for their significance. This is problematic since many of Rhee's links are less than obvious. For example, Rhee argues for an inclusion between 2:5–9 on the basis of the repetition of a single word ἄγγελος in 2:5 and 9, which also appears on three further occasions in the immediate context (vv. 2, 7, 16), claiming somewhat cryptically that the fact "that the author does not use the word between 2:10 and 2:15 indicates that he wants to make 2:5–9 as the sub-unit."¹⁴²

The fact that Rhee fails to provide sufficient evidence in support of his findings casts serious doubt upon his structural analysis. With the exception of his presentation of 1:1–4 (see above), few of his "chiasms" function consistently as he describes. For instance, while Rhee's chiasm at 11:1–40 contains at least one plausible connection (involving the

---

139. For example, Rhee, *Faith*, 81, 131, draws attention to repetition involving τοιοῦτος ... ἀρχιερεύς and τοιοῦτον ... ἀρχιερέα ("such a high priest," 7:26 and 8:1); βλέπω in 11:1 and 3 (pp. 210-11); and ἀδελφός and παιδίον in 2:12-13 and 2:14 (p. 17).

140. Welch, *Chiasmus in Antiquity*, 11–12, comments with regard to an example of a chiasm he detects in Ps 3:7–9 that through its structural arrangement, "each term is strengthened and fulfilled by its parallel part ... With meticulous composition, it is little wonder that this passage, and others like it, convey intense emotions and concise thoughts in a minimum number of verbal expressions."

141. This approach only works for text which stands in clear parallel relationship to other text in the discourse.

142. Rhee, *Faith*, 81.

repetition of πίστις and μαρτυρέω in 11:1–2 and 11:39–49),[143] his justification for other "parallels" seems much less convincing.[144]

Nevertheless, while some of his results seem less than secure, Rhee is to be commended for opening up an exciting new avenue of research within Hebrews. This study will further develop his insights into the relationship between formal parallelism and meaning in the discourse.

2.3.5 Cynthia Long Westfall

2.3.5.1 Overview

The most recent scholar to have made a substantial contribution to the discussion of repetition and its function in Hebrews is Cynthia Long Westfall. In her major study, *A Discourse Analysis of the Letter to the Hebrews*, Westfall adopts a four-step approach to the text, investigating cohesion patterns and shifts, topic, prominence and the relationship with the co-text.[145]

a. *Cohesion*: Westfall begins with an analysis of cohesion which examines "the choices that the author makes to create continuity" within the discourse.[146] She claims that units may be detected in Hebrews by looking horizontally at the "linear organization of the discourse" for any indications of "continuity followed by variation."[147]

b. *Topic*: Westfall next seeks to identify central sentences, topic-opening and closing sentences and "cohesive ties that appear to be semantically unrelated" within an analysis of topic, so as to gain a greater understanding of the text's "ideational" field of meaning.[148]

---

143. The lexical connections between these verses, which function as part of A and A' within Rhee's schema have been noted as significant by Calvin, *Commentary*, 263; Koester, *Hebrews*, 473; and Ellingworth, *Hebrews*, 567.

144. Rhee, "Chiasm and the Concept of Faith in Hebrews 11," 333–34, and *Faith*, 180–221, reads 11:7 (E) and 11:23–29 (E') as structural parallels "related by water experiences" despite their obvious imbalance and the complete absence of any semantic, synonymous or syntactical parallels. He also links 11:8–10 (F) with 11:20–22 (F') on the basis of their shared "forward looking aspect of faith," despite acknowledging that "as for Jacob, it is not immediately clear whether his blessing was eschatologically oriented."

145. For Westfall, *Discourse Analysis*, 80–81, "co-text" refers to text that is formally linked in some way to the text at hand.

146. Westfall, *Discourse Analysis*, 19. According to Westfall, cohesion represents a property of the text which can be formally examined.

147. Westfall, *Discourse Analysis*, 29.

148. Westfall, *Discourse Analysis*, 82–84.

c. *Prominence*: The third step involves attempting to identify the various means by which the author "highlights some element as more significant than others" with peaks in the discourse indicated by "a confluence of markedness, emphasis and discourse themes."[149] By "locating marked material," the discourse can thus be "hierarchically organized in different levels with different ranks."[150]

d. *Relationship with the Co-Text*: Westfall concludes by investigating the relationship of individual texts to their co-text. She suggests that this can provide significant clues to the author's intention as his discourse develops.

2.3.5.2 The Function of Repetition in Westfall

As part of her analysis of cohesion, Westfall broadens the category of repetition, classifying it under three main headings in light of insights drawn from modern linguistics. First and most obviously, she notes that "the various forms of repetition of lexis are widely recognized as a basis for cohesion."[151] Westfall's second category of repetition involves words and phrases which are semantically unrelated yet related in other ways. Repetition within this category includes connections made through labelling, categorization and lists,[152] identity chains formed "by noun phrases, pronouns and verbs that refer to the same person,"[153] "spatio–temporal" references, metaphors, analogy, typology and word

---

149. Westfall, *Discourse Analysis*, 85–86. This involves "locating the confluence of markedness, and/or emphasis in the unit with grammar, conjunctions, particles, deixis, interrogatives, semantic features and thematic repetition. . . . Elements that are repeated may be prominent at the level of section or discourse."

150. Westfall, *Discourse Analysis*, 31.

151. Westfall, *Discourse Analysis*, 47. These include "simple lexical repetition (leave, leaving, left), synonymy (leave, depart), antonymy (leave, arrive), hyponymy (travel, departure) and meronymy (hand, finger)."

152. Westfall, *Discourse Analysis*, 50, states: "A writer or speaker may create non-lexical categories by placing things that do not necessarily belong to the same semantic domain or scenario in the same pile or by calling them by the same name." She cites by way of example the qualifications for the office of overseer in 1 Tim 3:2–7 which, though separately unrelated, are connected by means of the list.

153. Westfall, *Discourse Analysis*, 83. These may also be formed by means of "instantial ties" of *equivalence* (you are my friends), *naming* (a poor man named Lazarus) *semblance* (everyone who hears these words will be like a man who built his house on rock). Cf. Westfall, *Discourse Analysis*, 83.

pictures,"[154] various rhetorical effects[155] and other patterns.[156] Connections can also be made, third, through the grammatical system by forming patterns of continuity followed by discontinuity with regard to tense, mood, person and number, case and voice.[157] Thus for example:

> The use of case in Heb. 11 is particularly interesting. The repetition of (by faith) creates a series of faithful action-events. The pattern is created by the repetition of the dative case as much as it is created by the repetition of lexis. The two occurrences of (according to faith) in vv. 7 and 13 should not [be, *sic*] considered part of the formulaic pattern.[158]

Westfall's approach also represents a significantly different understanding of the function of repetition from that of her predecessors. From the standpoint of cohesion analysis, Westfall proposes that while multi-functional, repetition serves the author's purpose in Hebrews in one of two basic ways:

a. by *grouping* material within the text into units or chunks; and

b. by indicating relative *prominence* within the discourse.[159]

First, Westfall states that the primary role of repetition in Hebrews is *to group together related material so as to create continuity and cohesion* within the discourse.[160] By forming "clusters and clumps," repetition unites such material into paragraphs, units and sections, and also provides information with regard to its content.[161] Westfall claims that "explicit cohesive links in the unit are the best indicators of the topic"

---

154. Westfall, *Discourse Analysis*, 54, claims that "the author's use of language creates cohesion between entities and scenarios that do not belong to the same semantic domain, and which may have no previous connection to each other."

155. Westfall, *Discourse Analysis*, 47, suggests that "cohesive ties can also involve patterns of sound and the repetition of formulas."

156. Westfall, *Discourse Analysis*, 84, notes: "Certain patterns of text organization are popular in cultures and form part of the readers, expectations of structure." These include problem-solution, goal-achievement, opportunity-taking, desire-arousal-fulfilment, gap in knowledge-filling and question-answer etc. Westfall detects the use of a number of these patterns within Hebrews.

157. Westfall, *Discourse Analysis*, 39–46.

158. Westfall, *Discourse Analysis*, 46.

159. Westfall, *Discourse Analysis*, 29.

160. Westfall, *Discourse Analysis*, 19.

161. Westfall, *Discourse Analysis*, 37, 47.

of said paragraphs, units and sections.[162] By way of example, she claims that the repetition of various verbs of speech in Hebrews 1:1–2:4[163] forms a "process chain" (see fig. 12 below) which, together with a number of other indicators, makes clear the fundamental unity of this material and marks it out as a discrete section within the discourse.[164] She notes that repetition can also create continuity across unit boundaries by forming chains of "cohesive ties" which create "interrelated packages of information" throughout the text as a whole.[165]

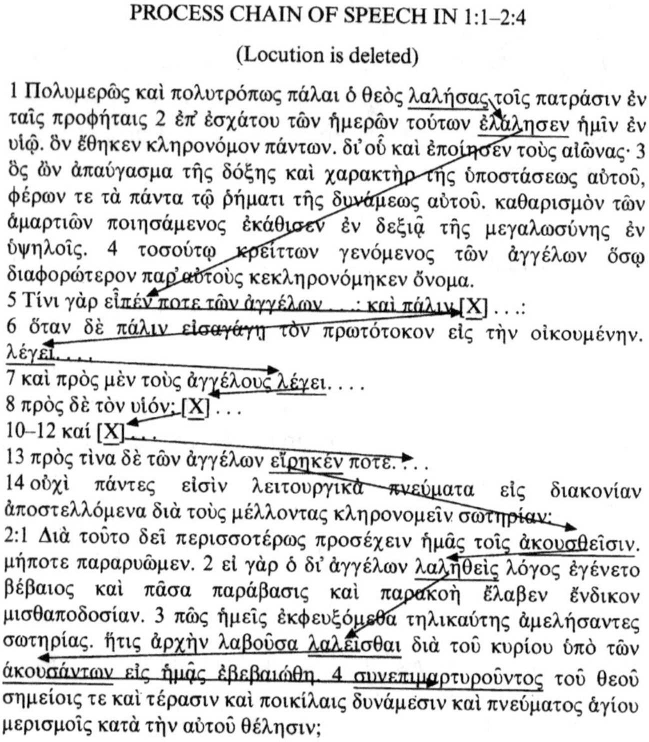

PROCESS CHAIN OF SPEECH IN 1:1–2:4
(Locution is deleted)

1 Πολυμερῶς καὶ πολυτρόπως πάλαι ὁ θεὸς λαλήσας τοῖς πατράσιν ἐν ταῖς προφήταις 2 ἐπ' ἐσχάτου τῶν ἡμερῶν τούτων ἐλάλησεν ἡμῖν ἐν υἱῷ. ὃν ἔθηκεν κληρονόμον πάντων. δι' οὗ καὶ ἐποίησεν τοὺς αἰῶνας· 3 ὃς ὢν ἀπαύγασμα τῆς δόξης καὶ χαρακτὴρ τῆς ὑποστάσεως αὐτοῦ, φέρων τε τὰ πάντα τῷ ῥήματι τῆς δυνάμεως αὐτοῦ. καθαρισμὸν τῶν ἁμαρτιῶν ποιησάμενος ἐκάθισεν ἐν δεξιᾷ τῆς μεγαλωσύνης ἐν ὑψηλοῖς. 4 τοσούτῳ κρείττων γενόμενος τῶν ἀγγέλων ὅσῳ διαφορώτερον παρ' αὐτοὺς κεκληρονόμηκεν ὄνομα.
5 Τίνι γὰρ εἶπέν ποτε τῶν ἀγγέλων   : καὶ πάλιν [X] . . .:
6 ὅταν δὲ πάλιν εἰσαγάγῃ τὸν πρωτότοκον εἰς τὴν οἰκουμένην. λέγει....
7 καὶ πρὸς μὲν τοὺς ἀγγέλους λέγει. . . .
8 πρὸς δὲ τὸν υἱόν; [X] . . .
10–12 καί [X]...
13 πρὸς τίνα δὲ τῶν ἀγγέλων εἴρηκέν ποτε . . .
14 οὐχὶ πάντες εἰσὶν λειτουργικὰ πνεύματα εἰς διακονίαν ἀποστελλόμενα διὰ τοὺς μέλλοντας κληρονομεῖν σωτηρίαν; 2:1 Διὰ τοῦτο δεῖ περισσοτέρως προσέχειν ἡμᾶς τοῖς ἀκουσθεῖσιν. μήποτε παραρυῶμεν. 2 εἰ γὰρ ὁ δι' ἀγγέλων λαληθεὶς λόγος ἐγένετο βέβαιος καὶ πᾶσα παράβασις καὶ παρακοὴ ἔλαβεν ἔνδικον μισθαποδοσίαν. 3 πῶς ἡμεῖς ἐκφευξόμεθα τηλικαύτης ἀμελήσαντες σωτηρίας. ἥτις ἀρχὴν λαβοῦσα λαλεῖσθαι διὰ τοῦ κυρίου ὑπὸ τῶν ἀκουσάντων εἰς ἡμᾶς ἐβεβαιώθη. 4 συνεπιμαρτυροῦντος τοῦ θεοῦ σημείοις τε καὶ τέρασιν καὶ ποικίλαις δυνάμεσιν καὶ πνεύματος ἁγίου μερισμοῖς κατὰ τὴν αὐτοῦ θέλησιν;

Fig. 12.

---

162. Westfall, *Discourse Analysis*, 95.

163. Namely λαλέω x4, λέγω x4 (plus 3 occurences of ellipsis), ἀκούω x2; and συνεπιμαρτθρέω x2.

164. Westfall, *Discourse Analysis*, 95–96.

165. Westfall, *Discourse Analysis*, 47, follows Halliday and Hasan, *Language*, 57, at this point. Cf. Reed, "Cohesiveness," 44.

The difference between Westfall and Vanhoye, Guthrie and Rhee at this point is significant and may be seen represented diagrammatically below (fig. 13). Where her predecessors emphasized the *discontinuous* function of repetition (i.e. repetition in Hebrews serves primarily to mark out the edges of units and define boundaries by means of inclusions), Westfall stresses its *continuous* role, claiming that the "repeating function of cohesion" is more important and criticizing Guthrie for failing to provide more of an "analysis of cohesion."[166]

i. Grouping by means of inclusion (Vanhoye, Guthrie and Rhee)

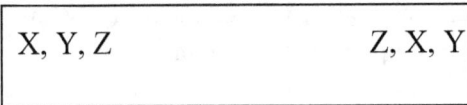

ii. Grouping by means of cohesion (Westfall)

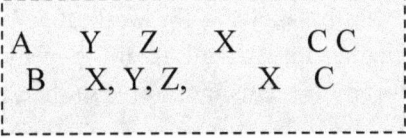

Fig. 13.

Second, Westfall claims that in addition to its horizontal function, repetition also plays a significant vertical role by marking out some parts of the text as more prominent than others. She suggests that sentences which display "unusually high levels of bonding" or connectedness might be regarded as "central." Since such sentences, which commonly function as "topic-opening" or "topic-closing" sentences, provide summaries of the material contained within the unit,[167] "a summary of the discourse can be obtained by deleting the marginal sentences and compiling the central sentences in one summary."[168]

---

166. Westfall, *Discourse Analysis*, 19. This difference is one of emphasis only, since both Vanhoye and Guthrie recognize the potential for this kind of function within Hebrews as well (e.g., "characteristic terms").

167. Westfall, *Discourse Analysis*, 83.

168. Westfall, *Discourse Analysis*, 73. Neeley, "Discourse Analysis," 28–31, argues for something similar.

2.3.5.3 Evaluation of Westfall

Without doubt Westfall makes her greatest contribution by introducing many of the principles of modern discourse analysis to the text of Hebrews.[169] As she observes:

> The application of linguistics and its research methodology to the Greek text is an exciting frontier for biblical research. It has the potential to offer a new perspective on old debates and may offer a way forward in either solving puzzles or illuminating the reason why the puzzles exist.[170]

The extensive criteria Westfall provides for identifying links is also impressive and far more comprehensive than any described by earlier approaches.[171] It is hardly surprising, therefore, that her study observes more instances of cohesion across the discourse than have been commonly noted.[172] Westfall's analysis of prominence represents a similarly welcome addition to scholarship by applying the work of S. Wallace and Porter to the text,[173] while her understanding of the relationship between exposition and exhortation seems more precise than that of either Vanhoye or Guthrie.[174]

With regard to the function of repetition, although Westfall is highly critical of Guthrie,[175] in many ways her methodology serves as a helpful supplement to his approach, recognizing more possibilities than previously considered. Her analysis of cohesion/continuity provides a counter-balance to Guthrie's investigation of discontinuity. She also

---

169. As Porter, "Discourse Analysis," 19, notes, "the distinctiveness of discourse analysis and the concern of discourse analysts is to be able to provide as comprehensive a description as possible of the various components of a given discourse, including its meaning and structure, and the means by which these are created and conveyed."

170. Westfall, *Discourse Analysis*, 20.

171. Many of these criteria have been incorporated within the methodology of this study (see chapter 3).

172. Westfall, *Discourse Analysis*, 38, notes that "a more comprehensive model that is suitable for a range of languages and cultures will consider all forms of repetition as possible bases for organizing a text."

173. Westfall, *Discourse Analysis*, 33. Wallace relates prominence to "linguistic categories such as aspect, mode, tense, voice and nominal expressions associated with verbs," while Porter applies these categories to Hellenistic Greek. Cf. Wallace, "Figure and Ground," 214; and Porter, *Verbal Aspect*, 92–93.

174. See for instance Westfall's comments regarding the break between 10:25 and 10:26 in Westfall, *Discourse Analysis*, 231.

175. Westfall, *Discourse Analysis*, 20.

develops many of Guthrie's observations regarding transitions, further demonstrating the reality of structural overlap and exploring its function in passages such as 3:1, 4:14–16, 10:19–25.[176] Westfall shows that on several occasions, sentences or small spans of sentences serve multiple structural (and other) functions in the discourse,[177] and concludes:

> The identification of the transitional nature of the commands or exhortations in Hebrews is not innovative or controversial in verses such as 2:1–4, 3:1, 4:1 and 4:11–16. The transitional nature of these verses has been formally and intuitively recognized.... Hebrews abounds with sentences and short spans that serve in this capacity, but they are generally labelled as "transitions," which indicates a somewhat marginalized function.[178]

Westfall's topical analysis, which attempts to locate formal criteria for the detection of "central" or "topic" sentences, also seems less subjective than previous attempts by Vanhoye and others, while her discussion of "cohesive ties" highlights a further way in which repetition might link together various elements of the discourse beyond individual unit boundaries.

There are, however, difficulties with Westfall's approach. Joslin criticizes her outline as less "satisfying" than Guthrie's, noting its failure to account for shifts in genre within the text and the meaning and function of specific parts of the discourse.[179] Responding to Westfall's conclusion that 5:11–6:20 amounts to "a lack of coherence (or at least disorganization) in the discourse,"[180] Joslin notes:

---

176. Westfall, *Discourse Analysis*, 111, makes a particularly strong case for a dual function for 3:1: "Though it is marked as a conclusion to the preceding co-text, it forms a sentence with a dependent clause that accomplishes a clear topic shift to the next unit in 3:2. Therefore, there is no clear break or division in the discourse at the point where two subsections are joined, but rather a smooth transition within the discourse conclusion/summary." See too her comments with regard to 8:1 (p. 190).

177. Westfall, *Discourse Analysis*, 77, states: "Sometimes one sentence or a small span of sentences can have the multiple function of concluding the preceding unit by serving as its central sentence, acting as the location of the shift or boundary, and providing the point of departure for a new unit."

178. Westfall, *Discourse Analysis*, 84, 88.

179. Joslin, "Can Hebrews be Structured?," 116, 121–22. Cf. Westfall, *Discourse Analysis*, 34.

180. Westfall, *Discourse Analysis*, 141.

G. Guthrie affirms that 5:11–6:20 forms a literary unit, and in his analysis the digression of 5:11–6:20 is purposeful and pastoral—it is meant to exhort the readers to open their ears and minds to the gravity of the situation at hand. In this reading there is no discontinuity in the argument, and rhetorically the beginning and end of this section are joined by inclusio to close out the exhortation and to prepare the readers for the different topic of the priesthood of Melchizedek.[181]

A number of Westfall's section boundaries are also questionable. While noting the relationship between the collections of subjunctives in 4:14–16 and 10:19–25, Westfall reads 4:11 and not 4:14 as the beginning of a new unit (4:11–10:25) based on her understanding of 4:11 as the beginning of a summary of the material beginning at 1:1.[182] Yet, as Joslin suggests, "the presence of the subjunctive in 4:11 (σπουδάσωμεν) might better be understood as the logical conclusion for what has been explicitly argued in 4:1–10, the κατάπαυσις of God. Westfall in her decision is unique at this point."[183]

Turning to Westfall's understanding of topic, a number of her conceptual parallels seem forced. Although Westfall is surely right in drawing attention to the "metaphoric nature of the language" used in Hebrews—especially in connection with the key hortatory material[184]—it is not clear, for example, that "let's draw near to the throne" represents a functional equivalent of "let's consider how to stimulate," or that "let's enter the rest" (4:11) is a different way of saying, "let's press on to maturity" (6:1), as she proposes.[185] Moreover, the question must be asked about the *significance* of what has been achieved through Westfall's analysis of cohesion. While her approach might succeed in demonstrating relationships between individual textual elements by means of identity and process chains, it seems unable to explain *why* these connections are where they are or *what* they are doing because of a failure to engage adequately with more straightforward grammatical connections. As J. P. Louw suggests:

---

181. Joslin, "Can Hebrews be Structured?," 119. Cf. Guthrie, *Structure*, 71, 100.

182. Westfall, *Discourse Analysis*, 140, writes, "It is generally recognized that the topic of Jesus' high priesthood is reactivated in 4:14, so that a major structural shift is often placed in the middle of the hortatory subjunctive span in 4:11–16."

183. Joslin, "Can Hebrews be Structured?," 121.

184. Westfall, *Discourse Analysis*, 137.

185. Westfall, *Discourse Analysis*, 137, acknowledges that "the connection between 4:11 and 10:24–25 is less transparent."

> In a continuous discourse it is important to maintain a clear distinction between the syntactic structure and the semantic relationships; and in order to establish a firm basis for semantic analysis, it is important to begin with the overt syntactic structure. Otherwise, one may engage in all types of fanciful intuitive judgments. Since the surface structure shows clearly how an author chose to present his message, it is this surface representation which is fundamental to a valid semantic interpretation.[186]

Perhaps most serious, however, in light of her stated interest in identifying textual units, is Westfall's failure to engage sufficiently with the strong evidence for the structural function of inclusions within the text. Following Vanhoye and Guthrie, most today would agree that, at least on occasion, repetition serves a discontinuous function by marking out unit boundaries within the text of Hebrews. Westfall, however, has very little to say on the subject. Although she observes inclusion-like features in the text,[187] and refers to observations of inclusions by others, they play a minimal role in her analysis.[188] Given that inclusions represent "viable tools which an author of the time had at his disposal,"[189] this seems a major omission.

Notwithstanding these difficulties, this study will build on Westfall's strengths by seeking to incorporate her insights into overlap within Hebrews and the role played by repetition in making certain text more prominent, as well as elements of her methodology, with the sound structural insights of previous scholarship.

---

186. Louw, *Semantics of New Testament Greek*, 115.

187. Most obviously, Westfall's macro-structure is built on the observation that "the central section of Hebrews is marked by two triads of hortatory subjunctives in 4:11-16 and 10:19-25." Westfall, *Discourse Analysis*, 188. However, she also notes at the micro-level that 2:14-18 "hangs together because of the repetition of words and phrases about sharing and similarity in vv. 14 and 17" (p. 103).

188. For instance, though noting that "the detection of an inclusion in vv. 5 and 16 and 10 and 17–18" disrupts cohesion at these points, she reads 2:5–18 as a single unit based on the fact that "the role that angels play in the determination of the topic is more of a major issue." Westfall, *Discourse Analysis*, 100.

189. Guthrie, *Structure*, 34.

2.3.6 John Paul Heil

In some ways, the conclusions presented in John Paul Heil's dissertation, *Hebrews: Chiastic Structures and Audience Response*, more closely resemble the findings of this present approach than any of the investigations discussed above. Heil argues that the repetition of words and phrases in the text reveals that Hebrews has been arranged into a series of micro chiastic units, and that the sound of particular words is of particular importance in understanding their function at times.[190] Moreover, he claims that Hebrews consists of multiple levels of discourse.[191] Beyond these similarities, however, only three of Heil's 33 units (1:1–4; 2:5–9; and 4:12–13) correspond to units we have identified[192] and his chiastic presentation of Hebrews' macro structure is also vastly different from our analysis (see chapter 7).[193]

While Heil's study focuses more squarely on repetition than previous approaches, his analysis shares several of the strengths and weaknesses of its predecessors (as follows). On the one hand, his attempt to understand the content of Hebrews in light of "salient textual details" is commendable,[194] as is the scope of his research, which spans the whole of the discourse at the micro level. On the other hand, many of Heil's parallels are (inadequately) supported by the repetition of a single word,[195] seem unbalanced and/or topically unrelated, and stand in the place of other stronger ties within the text. For example, the claim that 2:11–12 and 14–17a represent parallel components of a chiasm at 2:10–18 is based on the sole repetition of ἀδελφός ("brother," in 2:11, 12 and 17), despite the abundance of other functional equivalent terms in the immediate context (e.g., "child," "son"),[196] while the suggestion that verse 13b (C′) mirrors 13a (C) and represents the center of this chiasm obscures

---

190. Heil, *Chiastic Structures*, 4.
191. Heil, *Chiastic Structures*, 2.
192. And even these differ from ours with regard to their internal arrangement.
193. According to Heil, *Chiastic Structures*, 4, "the text of Hebrews divides itself into three micro chiastic levels. The first level divides the entire text into three main sections in a basic A-B-A′ chiastic pattern. The second level divides each of these three main sections into eleven distinct units arranged in an A-B-C-D-E-F-E′-D′-C′-B′-A′ pattern. The third level divides the first five as well as the final five units of each of these main sections into a total of six A-B-C-B′-A′ patterns." Cf. chapters five and six for our alternative presentation.
194. Heil, *Chiastic Structures*, 4.
195. For further explanation of the problem with this approach see 2.3.2.3.
196. Heil, *Chiastic Structures*, 64–5.

the more obvious symmetry between 2:12a and b (see 4.2.6bi).[197] Heil also assumes without sufficient justification that repetition functions at times as "transitional" (i.e. hook) words.[198]

More generally, Heil's apparent failure to consider and incorporate several of the key structural insights of previous scholarship is problematic and means, for example, that he makes no comment on the possibility of overlap within Hebrews. Finally, his treatment of the macro discourse is too brief (at only 11 pages) to explain the complexities of his own macro chiastic presentation, leaving the reader to wonder whether, like Vanhoye, Heil "finds more symmetries and literary subtleties than are really present."[199] These difficulties notwithstanding, Heil makes a valuable contribution to the understanding of this text and represents an important conversation partner for our micro analysis of Hebrews 1:1–3:8 in chapter 4.

2.4 Conclusions

This chapter has shown, first, that many today recognize Hebrews as a text which abounds with unusual patterns of repetition. These establish seemingly significant connections between texts within Hebrews (whether adjacent or separated by considerable distance within the discourse), and between texts in Hebrews and other external texts (e.g., Psalm 95).

It has also found, second, that scholars recognize at least four distinct functions for repetition within this discourse:

1. Whether by forming inclusions, chiasms or "clusters and clumps," repetition functions structurally to group the text into units, subsections and sections.

2. Repetition creates cohesion within the wider discourse by forming connections across unit boundaries.

---

197. Heil's suggestion (*Chiastic Structures*, 26) that καθαρισμὸν τῶν ἁμαρτιῶν ποιησάμενος (1:3) should be read as a parallel of δι' οὗ καὶ ἐποίησεν τοὺς αἰῶνας (1:2) on the basis of the repetition of ποιέω in 1:2 and 3 is similarly doubtful for two reasons. First, a closer topical parallel containing two lexical links exists between 1:2c and 1:3b (δι' οὗ / τῷ ῥήματι τῆς δὁνάμεως and τοὺς αἰῶνας / τὰ πάντα). Second, the grammar of 1:1–4 argues decisively against making any significant division between the participle, poihsa,menoj and the verb ἐκάθισεν, with the former clearly dependent on the latter.

198. Heil, *Chiastic Structures*, 74.

199. Hughes, *Hebrews*, 2.

3. Repetition serves a "vertical" role by marking out particular text as more prominent.

4. Repetition clarifies meaning in the discourse by: (a) identifying "key words" which guide readers to an understanding of theme; (b) creating parallel contexts which clarify ambiguity; and/or (c) marking out "topic sentences" which summarize the content of various portions of the text.

Third, this chapter has discovered that while many scholars have noted significant connections between *individual* words and phrases, the frequent location of such connections within what we have termed "link clusters" has been largely overlooked. Consequently, the consistency of this kind of patterning throughout the discourse has not been fully appreciated and its *combined function* left largely unexamined. This seems the likely result, at least in part, of previous approaches to the text which have sought to analyze instances of repetition *separately* from one another due to perceived differences in their function and context. With regard to function, by identifying one link as a "hook word" and another as an "inclusion," scholars have often failed to give due attention to their shared location and the possibility of a common function. Similarly, with regard to context, the imposition of somewhat arbitrary and inflexible boundaries onto the text has often meant that clusters have been split up or "de-clustered" *before* they have been properly examined *in situ* as a textual phenomenon in their own right.[200]

2.5 Questions that Remain

In light of these findings, this study will seek to address the following questions arising from the previous discussion.

First, what constitutes "significant" (as opposed to common or regularly occurring) repetition? And how might this kind of repetition be detected with confidence? Given the almost limitless number of

---

200. See for example, the discussion in chapter 4 concerning the remarkable extent of lexical repetition within 2:1–4 which has been all but overlooked within recent scholarship, seemingly because of assumptions of a unit boundary at 2:1 and 2:5, and perceptions of difference between the function of individual links.

connections within Hebrews, this remains a key question for our analysis.[201]

Second, *where* do link clusters occur within the text and *to what extent* does the author structure his material in this way?

Third, what import does the *context* in which repetition occurs have for understanding its function?

Fourth, what can be said with regard to the *combined function* of repetition within Hebrews? More specifically, *how* do link clusters function individually, in relation to one another, and to the wider discourse as a whole?

Fifth, how does Hebrews' use of link clusters shed light on meaning within this discourse?

---

201. For example, the word ἄγγελος, which appears eleven times as a noun in the first two chapters of Hebrews in 1:4, 5, 6, 7 (x2), 13, 2:2, 5, 7, 9 and 16, generates an enormous number of semantic connections involving this word in this context alone. Yet which (if any) of these connections are significant? Are some ties more important than others? And if so on what basis?

3

Questions of Methodology

3.1 Introduction

THIS CHAPTER OUTLINES A method by which link clusters may be identified and their function analyzed within Hebrews. In the first place the research is located within the wider linguistic discipline of Cohesion Analysis. Clear parameters for what will be explored are then established by investigating the different types of repetition and by carefully defining the meaning and significance of the terms, "link" and "link cluster." Following this, a four-step heuristic device is developed by which link clusters may be detected and examined.

3.2 Cohesion Analysis

3.2.1 A Brief Introduction

The analysis and understanding of "cohesiveness" has been "a central concern of discourse analysts ever since modern linguists turned their concerted attention to the study of complete discourse rather than isolated sentences."[1] According to what Porter terms the "English and Australian model" of discourse analysis, language is understood as a social semiotic consisting of networks of systems that establish meaning.[2] These systems of semantics, grammar and thematic structure

---

1. Reed, "Cohesiveness," 28.
2. Porter, "Discourse Analysis," 27. One of four schools described by Porter, the English and Australian model of discourse analysis encompasses the work of J. R. Firth, M. A. K. Halliday and R. Hasan.

combine together to create "texture" within texts, providing means by which a coherent "message" (theme) might be produced.[3] In other words, texts represent *more* than mere sequences of unrelated clauses: they are pieces of communication which demonstrate evidence of internal organization or "cohesion."

> That there is a relationship both semantically and grammatically between the various parts of a given text, and that there is some thematic (prominent) element which flows through it, allow an audience to recognize it as a cohesive text rather than as a jumble of unrelated words and sentences. On the one hand, we expect discourse to be cohesive . . . that is, its various linguistic elements should interrelate in a meaningful whole. Furthermore, certain elements must distinguish themselves as thematic (or prominent), that is, each discourse should be about something in particular, not everything in general.[4]

Cohesion Analysis, then, seeks to uncover the properties of language which contribute to the production and interpretation of cohesion within texts by investigating what Halliday and Hasan describe as *cohesive ties*. The key notion here is that in all texts, connections exist between an item at one point and an item at another point which make "at least one of the items dependent on the other for its interpretation."[5] Consequently, by enquiring into the nature and location of such connections, it is possible to gain a better understanding of the discourse as a whole since such connections "signal the author's intentions of how the discourse is grouped."[6]

Cohesive ties consist of two types: (i) *organic* and (ii) *componential*, which correspond to the (i) synchronic and (ii) diachronic dimensions of a text. "Organic ties" are syntagmatic relations which relate to the linear relationship between a linguistic unit and other words or units with which it is chained together.[7] As Silva notes, these "play the determinative role in language. While paradigmatic relations alert us to the

---

3. Halliday and Hasan, *Cohesion in English*, 2, propose that a "text" may be distinguished from a "non-text" by the presence of "texture" (i.e. that which holds clauses together and gives them unity).

4. Reed, "Cohesiveness," 30. According to Reed, cohesion is a relative concept such that "the cohesiveness of a given text should be viewed as a continuum" between strongly cohesive and completely incohesive (p. 31).

5. Eggins, *Introduction*, 88. See too Halliday and Hasan, *Cohesion in English*, 4.

6. Westfall, *Discourse Analysis*, 55.

7. Thistleton, "Semantics," 82. The italics is his.

potential for lexical expression in a particular language, this potential becomes "actualized" only when words are in fact combined with one another by a specific speaker or writer to form sentences."[8] Syntagmatic relations are signaled by prepositions, grammatical structure, and conventionalized lexical items and make up the "logical" system of natural language.[9] For instance, in the phrase, "a can of worms," the word "can" forms a syntagmatic relationship to "a" and "worms."

"Componential ties," on the other hand, represent paradigmatic relationships which describe "the relation between a word or linguistic unit and another such unit which is *not* present in the actual utterance, but which might have been chosen *in its place*."[10] Whereas organic ties generally concern logico-semantic relationships "*between clauses and paragraphs* (and phrases)," componential ties are typically semantic and "generally concern the meaningful relationships between *individual linguistic components* in the discourse (e.g., repetition of words).[11] As such, they can be used by an author to create links between non-adjacent (as well as adjacent) text. Componential ties may be established by means of "lexical repetition" and "reference" as well as through non-adjacent relations achieved through the grammatical system.[12] Thus, in the example above, the word, "worms" stands in paradigmatic relationship with "beans," "soup" or any other word which could have been slotted in, in place of "worms."

According to Halliday and Hasan, the most cohesive texts are those which are syntactically coherent and demonstrate the interaction of more than one "semantic chain" (sets of discourse lexemes which relate in expressing identity or similarity) at a time. Thus, if two or more chains interact in more than one part of the text (especially in close contexts), it is probable that the author is "on about" a similar topic.[13] Porter notes that

---

8. Silva, *Biblical Words*, 120.
9. Reed, "Cohesiveness," 33.
10. Thistleton, "Semantics," 83. The italics is his.
11. Reed, "Cohesiveness," 36.

12. Eggins, *Introduction*, 95. Each of these categories will be explained later in the chapter. Halliday and Hasan subdivide Eggin's category of "reference" into two further categories, "substitution" and "ellipsis." Meanwhile Hoey, *Patterns*, 71, connotes essentially the same thing as Eggins does by "reference" under his category, "substitution."

13. Halliday and Hasan, *Language, Context, and Text*, 57, claim that "the minimum requirement for chain interaction can be phrased as follows: for two chains x and y to interact, at least two members of x should stand in the same relation to two members of y." Reed, "Cohesiveness," 44, clarifies this as follows: "two lexical items (the same or

while chain interaction typically involves a chain of *participants* (e.g., "the Philippian Christians") and a chain of *events* (e.g., "think"), it also occurs "when one chain of participants interacts repeatedly with another chain of participants (e.g., "Paul" *says, hopes, sends* "the Philippians").[14]

3.2.2 Significant Studies

Cohesion analysis was first introduced by Halliday and Hasan's groundbreaking work, *Cohesion in English* (1976). Since then, other important writings of the subject include Brown and Yule, *Discourse Analysis* (1983), and Eggins, *An Introduction to Systemic Functional Linguistics* (1994). Given the potential value of such an approach, Reed notes that it is surprising "that there has been little discussion of New Testament cohesiveness from a modern linguistic perspective"[15] such that to the present day, Porter's paraphrase of the book of Judges holds true: "There was no agreed upon method of discourse analysis, and everyone did what was right in his own eyes."[16] Porter cites the difficulty felt by scholars in getting up to speed with modern linguistic methods together with perceptions that it may not be "worth the effort" as factors which explain this neglect.[17]

For the purposes of this study, the most important work in cohesion analysis to date is Michael Hoey's *Patterns of Lexis in Text* (1991). Drawing on the work of Hasan,[18] Winter,[19] and Phillips[20] in particular, Hoey goes beyond earlier scholarship by seeking not so much to itemize cohesive features (as, for example, Eggins does) as to observe how they combine to organize text: "Our own approach . . . is firmly based on the assumption that cohesion can only be satisfactorily understood if it is described

---

different) of the same chain must be used in conjunction with at least two other lexical items (the same or different) of another chain."

14. Reed, "Cohesiveness," 44.

15. Reed, "Cohesiveness," 29. Exceptions include Westfall's *Discourse Analysis* and Reed's own excellent article, "Cohesiveness." For summaries of the history of attempts to apply discourse analysis in general to the NT, see Westfall, *Discourse Analysis*, 22–27; Porter, "Discourse Analysis," 14–35; and Porter, "How can Biblical Discourse be Analyzed?," 107–17.

16. Porter, "How can Biblical Discourse be Analyzed?," 107. See Judges 21:25.

17. Porter, "Discourse Analysis," 29.

18. Hasan, "Coherence and Cohesive harmony," 181–219.

19. Winter, "Replacement," 95–133.

20. Phillips, *Aspects*, 1985.

functionally and taken as a piece."[21] To this end, Hoey insists on "the metaphor of the sentence" rather than the clause or word as the key unit for his analysis and is critical of Hasan's concept of the "semantic chain" because of its failure to take seriously the grammatical form of the text.

> What Hasan's notion of the chain does not do... is provide any insight into the answer to the question of the relationship of cohesion to the ways sentences connect as wholes. The entire strategy of describing text in terms of cohesive chains militates against consideration of how the sentences relate to each other as sentences.[22]

Hoey claims, following Winter, that "if cohesion is to be interpreted correctly, it must be in the context of the sentence where it occurs" and that "we are more likely to arrive at a satisfactory account of how cohesion works if we concentrate on the way repetition clusters in pairs of sentences."[23]

The first step in his approach involves detecting what he calls "bonded sentences" (sentences which demonstrate an above-average level of semantic connectedness). Hoey notes that "a single lexical repetition is not normally going to be sufficient to establish the relatedness of sentences, which are only likely to be linked in a meaningful way by a multiplicity of repetitions."[24] From here, he proposes:

> In the first place, sentences appropriately connected by repetition, however far apart, should make some sense or show some clear relationship together. Secondly, it should be possible to trace the development of a theme by bringing together the sentences that share lexis. Thirdly, it should be possible to mark off in a principled way the beginning and end of topics in text. Finally, it should be possible to place sentences on a scale of centrality or marginality according to the number of sentences they are lexically linked to.[25]

For Hoey, then, all text is organized in one of *three ways*: first, by adjacent semantic relations rooted in the grammar of the clause, *second*

---

21. Hoey, *Patterns*, 16. Both Winter and Hasan make much the same point. Cf. Winter, "Replacement," 95–133: "It is the common repeating function of much cohesion that is important, not the classificatory differences between types of cohesion."
22. Hoey, *Patterns*, 16.
23. Hoey, *Patterns*, 20.
24. Hoey, *Patterns*, 35.
25. Hoey, *Patterns*, 75.

by larger clause relations and basic text structures and patterns of organization and *third* by an "organizing relation, that holding between single sentences at distance from each other" which is "not explicable in terms of, or subsumable within, the larger organization of the text."[26] Hoey is reluctant to speak of this third type of organization as "structure." Nonetheless, he demonstrates that it represents an objective phenomenon common to all texts, which on further examination yields great insight into the thematic and topical unity of discourses.[27]

Hoey's observations regarding parallelism are of particular significance for this study. As noted previously, he proposes that the primary function of repetition is to mark out pairs of sentences as significantly related in some way. However, Hoey also argues for a second function whereby repetition "creates an environment in which other equivalences may be recognized."[28] In addition to lexical connections, he notes that in all texts:

> There are connections that only function in particular contexts between particular sentences, connections that are in no sense a permanent part of the lexical system. That such connections exist and are an important resource in the creation of text is increasingly being recognized; the question they give rise to, is how readers and listeners recognize them and are able to make use of them, given their ephemerality.[29]

Hoey labels these types of connections "instantial equivalences" (i.e. equivalences that only operate within particular texts) and suggests that the answer relates to their location within contexts tied together by repetition. He states:

> The relationship between repetition and replacement is potentially more complex than was originally suspected. Instead of analyzing pairs of sentences in terms of a single relationship between repetition (old information) and replacement (new information), we should now want to argue for a two-stage relationship, in the first stage of which repetition (as defined in this work) creates a framework for the recognition of instantial equivalences and of implied information.[30]

26. Hoey, *Patterns*, 126.
27. Hoey, *Patterns*, 26–30, 183.
28. Hoey, *Patterns*, 167.
29. Hoey, *Patterns*, 166–7.
30. Hoey, *Patterns*, 167.

Hoey's four-step analysis of the pair of bonded sentences (printed below) is included in some detail as an example of his method at this point.[31]

> 1. What is attempted in the following volume is to present to the reader a series of actual excerpts from the writings of the greatest political theorists of the past; selected and arranged so as to show the mutual coherence of various parts of an author's thought and his historical relation to his predecessors or successors; and accompanied by introductory notes and intervening comments designed to assist the understanding of the meaning and importance of the doctrine quoted.
>
> 4. I have tried rather to render the work of Aristotle, Augustine, and the rest accessible to the student, than to write a book about them; and the main object of this work will have been achieved if it serves not as a substitute for a further study of the actual works of these authors, but as an incentive to undertake it.

In the first place, links are juxtaposed (e.g., "what is attempted by me" and "I have tried"). Next, he represents as parallel any words or phrases that are necessarily implied by the text (e.g., the words, "by me" are not present in the original sentence and must be inferred by the reader to make sense of what is read). Third, any material that does not contain a link but which would be read by most readers as equivalent is also placed in parallel (e.g., "of the greatest political theorists of the past" and "of Aristotle, Augustine, and the rest"). Finally, information which is "not likely to be regarded as equivalent in the context but which is likely to be seen as related in some fashion" is also lined up. The = sign in the diagram indicates equivalence or approximate equivalence in the context, while the § sign indicates related information. Inferences are represented by italics. See fig. 14 below:

---

31. Hoey, *Patterns*, 163–66.

1		4
What is attempted *by me*	=	I have tried
In the following volume	=	*in the following volume*
[is] to present	§	to render . . . accessible
to the reader	§	to the student
a series of actual excerpts from the writings	§	the work
is to	§	is not to
present to the reader	=	*provide* the student *with*
a series of	§	a substitute for a further study of
actual excerpts from the writings	§	the actual works
of the greatest political theorists	?=	of Aristotle, Augustine, and the rest
of the past	?=	of these authors

Fig. 14.

Based on his analysis, Hoey concludes:

> The category of repetition in this and previous diagrams has been expanded to account for parallelisms of an oblique nature. In addition to the [standard] categories of repetition . . . we are also here treating as repetition items and phrases that would not have been accepted as creating links for the purposes of our analysis. Thus, for example, in [the diagram above], in addition to utilizing the paraphrase that exists between **attempted** and **tried**, which was one of the links that helped create the bond between the pair of sentences that we were investigating, we were also recognizing an equivalence between **of the greatest political theorists of the past** and **of Aristotle, Augustine, and the rest**, an equivalence which we would not have wanted to pick up in our first analysis.[32]

Hoey points out that, while demonstrable within texts, these kinds of connections cannot be located within the lexical or syntactical system but "are available to the reader or listener *because of the existence of the other less ephemeral links*."[33]

> What is being said is that when we read and write, we all recognize and produce parallels in sentences that form the basis for the interpretation of new information in the light of repeated information. This ability to produce and recognize parallels is built upon certain basic processes, most of which have been

---

32. Hoey, *Patterns*, 166. The **bold** words are his.
33. Hoey, *Patterns*, 167. The *italics* are his.

independently recognized as functioning in language production and reception.[34]

If correct, Hoey's analysis is important because it suggests that a key function of repetition is its ability to clarify meaning within a discourse through the creation of structurally parallel contexts.

3.2.3 The Approach of This Study in the Light of Cohesion Analysis

There is a considerable degree of overlap between the goals and methods of cohesion analysis (as exemplified by Michael Hoey in particular) and the approach adopted in this enquiry. First, this study seeks to identify various forms of repetition within Hebrews and makes use of categories devised by Halliday, Hasan, Yule, Brown, Eggins *et al.* Second, in agreement with Hoey, *Patterns of Lexis in Text*, it focuses not on repetition in general but rather specifically on "the way repetition clusters in pairs of sentences" within a text.[35] Third, it asks similar questions with regard to the function of particular clusters of cohesion. Finally, many of the principles discovered through cohesion analysis regarding the general function of repetition are enormously valuable and will be directly applicable to Hebrews. See, for example, Hoey's description of the nexus between the level of connectedness between sentences and their relative importance in the discourse:

> We might expect those sentences that are germane to the development of the theme(s) of a text (that is, in our terms, *central*) to make a number of connections with other sentences, while those sentences that contribute less to the development of its theme(s) (that is, marginal) we might expect to show fewer signs of connection with the rest of the text. We would expect a marginal sentence to have low information value, to be metalinguistic in nature or to offer information that is not directly needed or made much use of within the text.[36]

Hoey's concept of the "link triangle" is similarly useful. He proposes, with strong support from Phillips' study of collocation, that "if a lexical item appears for a third (or more) time in a text, it is only

---

34. Hoey, *Patterns*, 183.
35. Hoey, *Patterns*, 20.
36. Hoey, *Patterns*, 43. The italics is his.

necessary to establish a contextual connection with *one* of the previous occurrences for the item to be treated as forming a repetition link with *all* previous occurrences."[37] While some caution is needed given the significant differences between the Ancient Greek and modern English culture and language, since all texts are attempts to communicate with readers, it is not unreasonable to assume that what holds true for texts in general also holds true for *this* text.

At the same time, this study deviates from pure cohesion analysis in at least three ways relating to its goal and methods. First and most obviously, what follows does not represent a general analysis of cohesion within Hebrews. Although there are many elements which create cohesion (e.g., conjunctions), this study examines the author's use of only one type of cohesion (componential cohesion) within specific contexts (link clusters) of this text, so as to assess the particular contribution of this literary phenomenon to the form and content of the work as a whole.

The second difference relates to its starting point. This study did not arise from a decision to apply and examine a particular abstract linguistic principle to the text of Hebrews, but from *an observation* that repetition in general and the link cluster in particular seem unusually significant within *this* text. In other words, it represents more of an Aristotelian "ground up" enterprise than the Platonic "tops down" approach of modern linguistics. Such a distinction is not necessarily significant where the particular text demonstrates more-or-less conventional patterns of cohesion. However, it is crucial in this case since Hebrews seems to contain distinctive and unusual patterns of repetition which indicate the possibility that *more might be said regarding the function of repetition in Hebrews than is generally true of all texts*. For example, Hoey claims that while his analysis of links is useful for uncovering how texts are "organized," it does not reveal structure as such.[38]

> It is impossible to imagine that the nets we have generated and the bonds of which they are formed could ever be described in terms that could properly be regarded as structural. The best that could be hoped for is a system of description in which these non-structural facts coexisted with other truly structural facts.[39]

37. Hoey, *Patterns*, 57. The italics is his.

38. For more on the distinction between textual "organization" and "structure," see Hoey, *Patterns*, 26–29. Hoey rejects many structures "found" within texts by linguists and is cautious about claiming too much for his method.

39. Hoey, *Patterns*, 193. According to Hoey (p. 92), a "net" describes "the

As we have seen with regard to Hebrews, however, most scholars recognize at least some of the distinctive patterns of repetition within it as "truly structural facts" which may well allow us to make formal assessments regarding structure within this discourse. In other words, it is likely that Hoey's second and third categories of textual organization coincide to some extent in Hebrews.

Hoey is similarly and necessarily cautious in his conclusions regarding the relationship between form and content in text. He states that "it is possible to identify both marginal and central sentences with the help of the nets and to use them to create intelligible abridgements of the text" and that nets of connections "have something to tell us about the way topics are introduced and dropped in the course of a text."[40] However, since his method makes no claim to identify authorial intent, he does not press any connections he finds too far. Any coherence discovered may be deliberate. Equally, however, it may represent an "accident" of the writing process or a reflection of the mind of the reader. In this way Hoey differentiates between two types of claims—the "strong" and the "weak"—for all texts. According to the weak claim, "each bond marks a pair of sentences that is semantically related in a manner not entirely accounted for in terms of its shared lexis."[41] According to the strong claim, "because of the semantic relation referred to in the weak claim, each bond forms an intelligible pair in its context."[42] He proposes:

> What the weak claim suggests is that the co-occurrence of a certain number of repetitions (the requisite number varying from text to text but, as we have seen, frequently three) is not a matter of chance, and that it will always be possible to interpret the two sentences in a manner that derives directly from the meaning of the sentences in the larger text. What the strong claim suggests is that the co-occurrence of the requisite number of repetitions is sufficient to compel a reading of the pairs as intelligible; in other words, bonded sentences make sense together in their content without the intervening text. The weak claim appears to be true of virtually all bonds; the strong claim is true of a large proportion of them.[43]

---

interconnection of bonded sentences."

40. Hoey, *Patterns*, 124.
41. Hoey, *Patterns*, 125.
42. Hoey, *Patterns*, 126.
43. Hoey, *Patterns*, 126.

In the case of Hebrews, however, the careful and consistent arrangement of repetition patterns within link clusters strongly suggests (it will be argued) that our author *intends* for his readers to read sentences and parts of sentences joined in this way together. Consequently, the analyst can be far more confident than even Hoey's "strong claim" allows of a meaningful relationship between them.

The third difference between this approach and cohesion analysis is that it will supplement modern linguistic methods with insights gained from the study of ancient literature where relevant.[44] Since virtually all scholars recognize that Hebrews seems to utilize certain forms in line with particular literary conventions of the day (e.g., inclusions), it is reasonable to seek to understand their function in the light of this evidence.

3.3 Types and Forms of Repetition to be Examined

Having located our study within the field of contemporary Cohesion Analysis, the second task involves determining exact parameters for what will be here explored. As stated previously, the focus of this investigation is the link cluster and its distinctive function within the text of Hebrews. This raises two questions of definition which must be addressed before we can proceed any further:

1. Under what circumstances can we reasonably speak of two or more textual elements being tied together? In other words, what constitutes a link?
2. What is a link cluster?

3.3.1 What constitutes a link?

While there is a multiplicity of ways by which an author might establish a connection between particular words and phrases in his or her discourse, links represent repetitive ties within a text which may be

---

44. General works consulted include Robbins, *Exploring the Texture of Text*; Berger, "Rhetorical Criticism," 390–96; Porter, *Rhetoric and the New Testament*; Ryken, *The Literature of the Bible*; Stamps, "Rhetorical and Narratological Criticism," 219–40; Löhr, "Reflections of Rhetorical Terminology in Hebrews," 199–210; Kennedy, *Rhetorical Criticism*; and Welch, *Chiasmus in Antiquity*. Other works more specifically related to Hebrews include deSilva, *A Socio-Rhetorical Commentary*; and Cosby, *The Rhetorical Composition and Function of Hebrews 11*.

grouped under five broad categories as follows: lexical relations, reference relations, grammatical relations, phonological relations, and inter-textual relations.

1. Lexical Relations

Relations between various forms of lexis represent "the dominant mode of creating texture" (i.e. the organization of text).[45] The following four basic categories of lexical relations reflect those found in Hasan, but have been modified slightly in light of Silva and Westfall.[46]

a. LEXICAL REPETITION

First, and most obviously, the repetition of a particular lexical item is a basis for cohesion.[47] Hoey subdivides lexical repetition into two further categories, "simple lexical repetition" (i.e. leave, leave) and "complex lexical repetition" which occurs when "two lexical items share a lexical morpheme, but are not formally identical" (i.e. leave, leaving).[48]

In addition to repetition, linguists also recognize various other kinds of "sense relations" which exist between words in a text based on similarity, opposition and non-semantic relations of field.[49]

---

45. Hoey, *Patterns*, 11, is critical of Halliday and Hasan, *Cohesion in English*, for its relatively brief treatment of the subject, claiming that lexical cohesion "is the single most important form of cohesive tie, even in terms of Halliday and Hasan's own sample analyzes at the end of the 1976 book" (p. 9).

46. Hasan, "Coherence and Cohesive harmony," 202. Cf. Silva, *Biblical Words*, 118–33; and Westfall, *Discourse Analysis*, 22–87.

47. Halliday and Hasan, *Cohesion in English*, 278.

48. Hoey, *Patterns*, 55–56, warns against "assuming that complex repetition is just simple repetition with knobs on." The distinction he makes between these forms of repetition is not overly significant for our investigation into clusters, however, since any complex repetition that occurs within such clusters must—by definition—share a common context, even if, in the language as a whole, the items have quite different collocational profiles.

49. Silva, *Biblical Words*, 118, terms his category of "opposition," "oppositeness." Cf. Thistleton, "Semantics," 90, who contrasts "opposition" with "synonymy."

b. SIMILARITY

Synonymy and contiguous relations are sense relations which arise from different degrees of similarity.[50] Absolute synonymy exists where words have the exact same range of sense, connotation, and habitual collocation. Instances of this are rare since their redundancy usually causes one or other of the words to undergo semantic change or fall into disuse.[51] At the other end of the spectrum, the relation of "contiguity" (or "improper" synonymy) is where the meaning of words is closely associated, but there is no overlap. For example, while the words "walk" and "run" share some features and can be collocated with similar nouns, they cannot be substituted without changing the meaning of the sentence. Between these extremes lies the relation of "proper" synonymy, by which "words may possess a true identity of meaning in some or all senses of a word, but will be interchangeable only in some contexts" (e.g., "book" and "volume").[52] As applied to NT Greek, Smith suggests that διδάσκω and κατηχέω represent proper synonyms since both words can be "glossed" with the English words "teach" or "instruct" and are considered core "teaching" vocabulary. By contrast, the relationship between διδάσκω and προφητεύω is one of contiguity for while both involve the (usually verbal) transmission of information, and may have the purpose and/or result that addressees learn, they may not be substituted with one another without changing the meaning of the sentence.[53] The difference between proper and improper synonymy may be seen diagrammatically below (see fig. 15).[54]

---

50. According to Eggins, *Introduction*, 102, synonymy exists when "two words essentially restate each other." Hasan's category heading, "synonymy" is unduly narrow at this point as synonymy is included within this general category. Hasan, "Coherence and Cohesive Harmony," 202.

51. Cotterell and Turner, *Linguistics*, 159. Porter, *Studies*, 71.

52. Cf. Cotterell and Turner, *Linguistics*, 159; Hoey, *Patterns*, 62; and Silva, *Biblical Words*, 122, who notes Archbishop Trench's description of synonyms as "words of like significance in the main; with a large extent of ground which they occupy in common, but also with something of their own, private and peculiar, which they do not share with one another."

53. Smith, *Scholastic Communities*, 5.

54. Silva, *Biblical Words*, 126.

PATTERNS OF REPETITION, STRUCTURE, AND MEANING

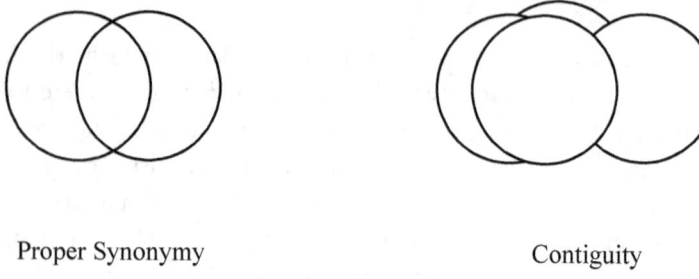

Proper Synonymy   Contiguity

Fig. 15.

A further relation, the "inclusive" relation, may be observed by stretching the notion of similarity to its limits.[55] Inclusive relations are those in which one term *includes* the other as a subset within it and occur when two (or more) lexical items are related either "through classification or sub-classification" (hyponymy) or as parts of a greater whole (meronymy).[56] Thus with regard to the former, there is a hyponymic relationship between the words "jaundice" and "illness" in that the latter *includes* the former as a subset within it. "Jaundice" is a "hyponym" of "illness," while "illness" represents the "superordinate" of "jaundice." Relations can also exist between two hyponyms from the same superordinate class and are referred to as "co-hyponymy" (e.g., "jaundice" and "pneumonia"). With regard to the latter, "meronymy" describes a different kind of inclusive relationship which is based on composition.[57] Meronymy occurs when two words are related as whole to part (or vice versa) and describes, for example, the relationship between "hand" and "finger." "Co-meronymy" occurs when two lexical items are related by both being parts of a common whole (e.g., "arteries" and "veins" to "the circulation system").[58]

The relationship between synonymy and hyponymy may be seen represented diagrammatically below (see fig. 16).[59]

---

55. Silva, *Biblical Words*, 126.
56. Eggins, *Introduction*, 102.
57. Eggins, *Introduction*, 102.
58. Eggins, *Introduction*, 102.
59. Silva, *Biblical Words*, 127.

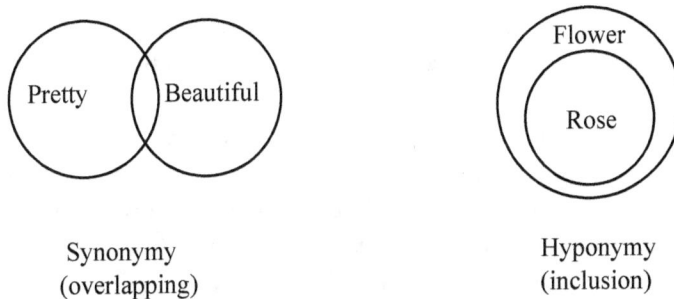

Fig. 16.

Although unnamed, Hoey and Eggins recognize the possibility of a final type of relation of similarity which exists between lexical strings consisting of more than one word. Thus although not strictly synonymous,[60] there are clear similarities between the word, "baby," and the phrase, "human infant," as there are between the word, "embrace" and the more complex lexical string, "have a cuddle."[61] Links of this kind may also occur through the processes of "lexical expansion" or "lexical reduction."[62] So "modern reader" may be easily reduced to "reader" without significant loss of meaning. For the purpose of this analysis, in cases where two or more lexical items combine to express a single piece of content which links with another word or phrase, they will be treated as a single item.

At this point, it is worth addressing a potential difficulty that exists for students of NT Greek. Given the gap between the modern reader for whom Ancient Greek is not their first language and the culture in which Hebrews was first produced, how can we be sure that our understanding of the relationship between particular words (and phrases) is the same as that held by the author and his readers? How might we safeguard against seeing connections where they did not exist and missing others which did? While a full investigation into this important issue lies beyond the scope of this book, it is suggested that a reasonable degree of objectivity is achievable in two ways. First, this study will draw upon work already done in this field that represents something of an

---

60. Synonyms are relations which exist between individual words.
61. Eggins, *Introduction*, 103.
62. Hoey, *Patterns*, 171.

"industry standard." Louw and Nida's *Greek-English Lexicon of the New Testament based on Semantic Domains* (L-N) classifies the "meanings of New Testament vocabulary into domains and sub-domains," each of which consist of groups of words that have associated meanings.[63] Consequently, differences and similarities between words within a domain are made clear, with the semantic range of a particular word indicated by the variety of domains/sub-domains within which it occurs. Although neither exhaustive nor infallible,[64] this lexicon represents an important tool for the analysis of cohesion.

Second, and more importantly, however, this study will pay particular attention to context. Since as Thistleton suggests "most so-called synonyms are context-dependent,"[65] the identification of particular words as synonyms *must be based upon the observation of their use in context* (whether the New Testament, Hebrews as a whole or as part of particular clusters within the text). Context is the key to determining whether relations can reasonably be thought to exist between words.[66] As Silva rightly notes, "the closer contextual levels should take priority in interpretation": whereas "broader theological concerns are not to be set aside in the exegetical process."[67] Most of the synonymous links identified in this study

---

63. The grouping together of words in NT Greek into related semantic domains is a relatively recent phenomenon which stems from James Barr's seminal work of 1961, *The Semantics of Biblical Language*. Barr, *Semantics*, 234, describes a new approach to word studies using semantic fields which recognized the priority of synchronic factors in determining the meaning of words: "This procedure would be to group the words in groups each representing a related semantic field, e.g., the "holy" group with its chief representatives in ἅγιος and ἁγνός and ἱερός. Within a general field thus loosely defined one word would be made to mark off the semantic oppositions between one word and another as precisely as possible; and from this to proceed to special context and word-combinations in which each word occurred—bringing in, of course, the words from outside the loosely defined field freely." Other important works on this subject include *The New International Dictionary of Theology* edited by Colin Brown in 1976, which rejected the alphabetic ordering of "root words" used in *TDNT*, grouping words instead in semantically related categories; Silva, *Biblical Words*,18–22, for criticisms of Barr's approach and its influence on later scholarship; and Downing, "Ambiguity, Ancient Semantics, and Faith," 139–62.

64. Smith, *Scholastic Communities*, 3, criticizes Louw and Nida's *Greek-English Lexicon* "for not considering extra-Biblical word use, for basing domains on English categories and grouping words on the basis of glosses in languages other than NT Greek, and for drawing word definitions from existing lexical resources, without the fresh consideration of discourse contexts suggested by Barr."

65. Thistleton, "Semantics," 92.

66. Cf. Carson, *Exegetical Fallacies*, 44–54; Thistleton, "Semantics," 92–93.

67. Silva, *Biblical Words*, 136.

are widely recognized and will not need to be established. In controversial cases, however, where context clearly indicates that the author is placing a word or phrase in the same category as another, semantic domains may need to be extended beyond those recognized by L-N.

c. Opposition

The third type of lexical relation, opposition, occurs in cases where words "encode a contrast relationship" with one another.[68] Words related in this way share at least one major semantic feature and therefore belong to the same semantic field yet have a form of opposition in their meanings.[69] The two basic types of relations are "opposition by scale" and "opposition by cut."[70] Antonymy (leave, arrive) is "opposition by scale," and occurs where "the relation between the two words is gradable or relative, indicating explicit or implied comparison."[71] Complementarity is a form of "opposition by cut," and involves a "two-way exclusion" where "the denial of one involves the assertion of the other" (e.g., the relationship between the words, "man" and "woman," or "single" and "married").[72] To these may be added the relation of converseness by which non-gradable opposition arises from facts other than the meaning of the words themselves. Thus in Romans 11:6, Paul sets the word "by grace" in opposition to "by works" by his statement "if it is by grace, it is no longer on the basis of works."[73] As was observed to be the case with similarity, so the relation of opposition may also occur between lexical strings consisting of more than one word. Thus, it seems likely that there is a link of opposition within Hebrews

---

68. Eggins, *Introduction*, 102.

69. Beekman and Callow, *Translating*, 295, suggest that the negation of the same word or a synonym represent two of five potential ways to establish a "relation of contrast" between two propositions, all of which involve at least one point of similarity and at least two points of difference: "1. negation of the same predicate; e.g., He sings in his bath, but I don't (sing in my bath); he is clever, but I am not. 2. negation of synonyms; e.g., Bill came yesterday, but John didn't arrive; he is healthy, but I am not well. 3. negation implied by antonyms: e.g., He stayed, but I left; he is strong, but I am weak. 4. negation implied by difference of degree; e.g., He doesn't eat as quickly as I do; he isn"t as heavy as I am. 5. negation of an alternative; e.g., He fell into the lake, not the river; he wasn't first in the race, he was second."

70. Thiselton, "Semantics," 90, 103, fn. 71.

71. Smith, *Scholastic Communities*, 6.

72. Halliday and Hassan, *Cohesion in English*, 285. Cf. Thiselton, "Semantics," 92-93; and Cruse, *Meaning in Language*, 166–67.

73. Thistleton, "Semantics," 92.

between the dual imperatives, "pay attention" (κατανοήσατε, 3:1) and "do not harden your hearts" (μὴ σκληρύνητη σκληρύνητε τὰς καρδίας ὑμῶν, 3:8) in that both expressions seem to convey a very similar sentiment in opposite ways. Once more context is determinative at this point.

d. NON-SEMANTIC RELATIONS OF FIELD

The final type of lexical relationship to be considered derives from the observation that there are certain relations between words which do not belong to the same semantic domain and may have no previous connection to each other. Eggins notes as an example, "if you read the word *mouse* in a text, you will not be surprised to come across the words *cheese, white, squeak, tail,* or *rodent* in nearby text, while you would be much more surprised to come across the words *thunderstorm, bark* or *ironing board*."[74] Connections of this sort may operate between an action and the "doer" of that action (doctor-operate; baby-cry; dog-bark); an action/process and the participant effected by that action (smack-child; eat-dinner; play-piano); an event/process and the typical location in which it takes place (operation-hospital; transaction-bank) and between individual lexical items and the composite group they form (blood-donor; blood-transfusions).[75] Eggins notes that sometimes two or more lexical items may function to express a single piece of lexical content (baby-human infant; embrace-have a cuddle).[76] Such cases will be treated as a single item for the purpose of our analysis.

While it is easy to recognize the reality of such connections, it is harder to account for them in any coherent way.[77] A. J. Sanford and

---

74. Italics original. Eggins, *Introduction*, 101. Cf. Westfall, *Discourse Analysis*, 43.

75. Eggins, *Introduction*, 102, 103.

76. Eggins, *Introduction*, 103.

77. Halliday and Hasan's original category of "Collocation" which includes a "ragbag" of such relations is certainly problematic as Hoey, *Patterns*, 7–8, points out, criticizing both their misuse of the meaning of the word "collocation" and their failure to analyze the various relations in any real sense. "Intuition is certainly an unreliable guide." However, there are also difficulties with Eggins" approach which labels such links as "expectancy relations" since she fails to explain why such expectations exist between particular words beyond the general observation that they "relate "upwards" to the field dimension of the context." Eggins, *Introduction*, 105. Clearly such relations do not only exist in the minds of individual readers (as could be tested by collocation). However, it is possible to conceive of a reader who would not recognize a connection between Eggins" example of "mouse" and "squeak" for example (perhaps an "English as a Second Language" reader who has not grown up on a diet of western children's

S. C. Garrod's category of *scenario* is of considerable value at this point, however. Sanford and Garrod suggest that readers recognize connections such as those described above when they understand both words within particular "domains of reference" or scenarios. On the basis of studies into Artificial Intelligence, they conclude: "There is little doubt that general expectations about people's behavior limit the information that is typically retrieved from memory."[78] According to this view, scenarios include certain "role" slots (e.g., a restaurant includes a waiter, food, tables and chairs) and display a particular register (specialized language used in a certain situation) and are potentially activated when a text refers to "a specific partial description of an element of the scenario itself."[79]

With regard to Hebrews, caution must be exercised when identifying links achieved through scenarios for similar reasons to those already given relating to the gap between the original human author and the modern reader. Scenarios are not always immediately recognizable and patterns of words and phrases can generate more than one potential candidate, leading to significant distortion if the wrong one is chosen.[80] Clearly, context plays a major role once more at this point.[81] Nonetheless, we may be reasonably certain that we have correctly identified relations of field between particular words and phrases when similar relations also occur within other texts related to Hebrews in some way. For example, it is likely that the semantically dissimilar titles Χριστός ("Christ") and υἱὸς [τοῦ θεοῦ] ("Son [of God]") are in fact closely related in Hebrews given that both represent titles for the King of Israel in the LXX. Other scenarios which have been previously noted in this text include those relating to athletic competition and cultic worship,[82] the latter of which

stories).

78. Sanford and Garrod, *Understanding Written Language*, 130.

79. Sanford and Garrod, *Understanding Written Language*, 129.

80. For example, Sanford and Garrod, *Understanding Written Language*, 130, recognize that "the riders lined up" may connote both "horse-racing" or a fox hunt, while the sentence "Barry was feeling hungry" takes on quite a different meaning depending on whether the scene is the dinner table or the Alaskan wilderness following a plane crash.

81. Brown and Yule, *Discourse Analysis*, 261–66, note that unlike all other categories of lexical relations examined thus far, scenarios do not result from the relationship between particular lexical items alone but are "context-dependent" and "text-specific." Thus while "tyre" is linked to "car" by the relation of composition, no such lexical relation exists between "beer" and "picnic supplies" even though the words may be linked within a particular domain of reference.

82. Westfall, *Discourse Analysis*, 84.

forms potentially significant links between the otherwise unrelated words, "curtain," "high priest," and "sacrifice."

2. Relations of Reference

The second type of repetition, reference, occurs "whenever one of a small class of items "stands in for" an earlier item in the text," creating a link between the two.[83] Unlike lexical links, these "depend entirely on other items for their interpretation and have no definitional meaning in themselves. They are grammatical members of closed systems and not lexical items" which substitute for words and phrases and form identity chains within the text.[84] For instance, in the following pair of sentences, "I caught the snake by its tail. It bit me," the word "it" stands in for "the snake" and refers back to it such that the reader/listener needs to retrieve the identity of that item from context in order to follow the text.[85] The relation of reference may be established through personal pronouns (he, she, it), demonstrative pronouns (this, that, these) and other substitution links (e.g., the first one, another one; so; the same, different etc)[86] which can refer either backwards (anaphorically) or forwards (cataphorically) within the text.[87]

3. Non-adjacent Relations achieved through the Grammatical System

A third type of repetition considered within this study is that achieved through the grammatical system of the text in one of three ways.

---

83. Hoey, *Patterns*, 5, includes "Reference" within his category of *substitution* links which also contains "ellipsis" ("when what stands in for the earlier item is nothing at all"). Cf. Halliday and Hasan, *Cohesion in English*, 279, who note that "the boundary between lexical cohesion of the type we are calling REITERATION, and grammatical cohesion of the REFERENCE type, is by no means clear cut." The capitalization is theirs.

84. Hoey, *Patterns*, 71; Westfall, *Discourse Analysis*, 83.

85. Eggins, *Introduction*, 96. Eggins distinguishes between "homophoric" reference in which the substituting item may be retrieved from the general context of culture; "exophoric" reference, in which it may be found within the immediate situation and "endophoric" reference in which it is retrieved from within the text.

86. Hoey, *Patterns*, 71–74.

87. Eggins, *Introduction*, 97.

QUESTIONS OF METHODOLOGY

a. String Repetition

First and most obviously, grammatical links may be established through the exact or near exact repetition of material within a new context in the discourse. Such "string" repetition represents more than the sum of its parts (i.e. a collection of individual semantic links) and is of particular significance in Hebrews which frequently quotes (and re-quotes) material from both without (e.g., Heb 2:6–8 represents a direct quotation from Ps 8:4–6) and within (e.g., 5:1 and 8:3) the discourse. See, for example, the variations of the same basic phrase εἰσελεύσονται εἰς κατάπαυσίν μου ("they will not enter my rest") in 3:18, 19, 4:1, 3 x2, 5, 6 x 2, 10, and 11) which tie these sentences back to the quotation from Psalm 95 in Hebrews 3:7–11 (εἰ εἰσελεύσονται εἰς τὴν κατάπαυσίν μου). As with lexical repetition, string repetition can be used to establish relationships of identity (e.g., 3:11 and 4:5), similarity (e.g., 3:11 and 3:18, μὴ εἰς τὴν κατάπαυσιν αὐτοῦ), and opposition (εἰσερχόμεθα γὰρ εἰς [τὴν] κατάπαυσιν, "for we will enter into Rest," 4:3).

In the absence of strong external evidence to the contrary, cases of repetition with variation involving strings taken from the LXX will be assumed to reflect authorial intent rather than differences of source material or scribal carelessness.[88]

b. Syntactic Equivalences

Hoey observes that texts also frequently demonstrate what he calls "syntactic equivalences" which "are used to establish parallelisms between bonded sentences"[89] by "repetition of the same syntactical structure,"[90]

---

88. This pragmatic assumption is based on widely acknowledged observations regarding the author's literary skill and the findings of a number of important studies into Hebrews' use of Scripture which demonstrate both that the author uses the LXX as his source material and that he freely modifies his material by making "textual alterations that parallel many hermeneutical practices of the first century . . . to guide the reader concerning the truth about the Son." Bateman, *Early Jewish Hermeneutics*, 145–47. Cf. also Kistemaker, "Psalm Citations"; Gheorghita, *The Role of the Septuagint*; Tönges, "Jesus-Midrash," 95; Guthrie, "Hebrews," 919–96; and Bruce, *Hebrews*, 331–36.

89. Hoey, *Patterns*, 171. Westfall's comments regarding the two groups of three hortatory subjunctives (highly marked moods) in 4:14–16 and 10:19–25 represent a functional description of this phenomenon. Westfall, *Discourse Analysis*, 41–42. She suggests that "when either subjunctive or imperative verbs appear as a cluster in independent clauses, it creates a unit based on a grammatical span in the text."

90. Black, "Hebrews 1:1–4," 189.

or superficially unlike yet related strings. For example, there is a form of grammatical parallelism which is evident between the discourse chains "the skill of surfing" and "surfing as a skill" but not between "the wit of Oscar Wilde" and "Oscar Wilde as a wit," nor "the grounds of the palace" and "the palace as grounds."[91] Once more, a careful analysis of context is necessary to avoid seeing superficial structural connections as more important than they are in fact.[92]

c. Various Patterns of Text Organization

In addition, "certain patterns of text organization are popular in cultures and form part of the readers" expectations of structure"[93] thereby joining different parts of a text together. These patterns include problem-solution, goal-achievement, opportunity-taking, desire-arousal-fulfilment, gap in knowledge-filling and question-answer.[94] Westfall claims to detect a number of these kinds of patterns within Hebrews (for instance, question and answer form).[95]

4. *Phonological Relations*

"Phonological relations" describe a fourth kind of way by which an author might establish significant connections within a discourse. Stemming from observations regarding the oral rather than literary dimension to the work, these refer to connections made through similarities in the *sound* of particular words and phrases which would have been noted by the original audience. For example, the euphony between the verbs within the phrase ἔμαθεν ἀφ' ὧν ἔπαθεν ("he learned from the things he

---

91. Hoey, *Patterns*, 171.

92. Thistleton, "Semantics," 96, cites Jesperen's example of the phrases, "the doctor's arrival" and "the doctor's house," which although superficially parallel, are in fact structurally distinct, resulting from two different "transforms" ("the doctor arrived" and "the doctor has a house").

93. Westfall, *Discourse Analysis*, 84.

94. Beekman and Callow's categories of "support propositions which argue" are also helpful here in outlining other possible connections (e.g., reason-result, means-purpose, means-result, and grounds-conclusion. Beekman and Callow, *Translating*, 301–09.

95. Westfall, *Discourse Analysis*, 84, claims that "in certain genres, such as novels, retrospective clues and the suspense of deferred answers are recognized and appreciated."

suffered," 5:8) establishes a non-semantic rhetorical connection or play-on-words known as *parechesis*.[96] Different kinds of phonological connections can also be established through the repetition of parts of certain words in different contexts. See, for instance, the three-fold use of the prefix ἀνα ("again") in 6:1-6,[97] a context which also includes two uses of πάλιν ("again," 6:1, 6) and its near opposite ἅπαξ (6:4); and the six-fold repetition of the κατά sound in Hebrews 7:15-17 (see below):

> Καὶ περισσότερον ἔτι **κατά**δηλόν ἐστιν εἰ **κατὰ** τὴν ὁμοιότητα Μελχισέδεκ ἀνίσταται ἱερεὺς ἕτερος ὃς οὐ **κατὰ** νόμον ἐντολῆς σαρκίνης γέγονεν ἀλλὰ **κατὰ** δύναμιν ζωῆς ἀ**καταλ**ύτου μαρτυρεῖται γὰρ ὅτι Σὺ ἱερεὺς εἰς τὸν αἰῶνα **κατὰ** τὴν τάξιν Μελχισέδεκ

While observed and analyzed within parts of the discourse,[98] Hebrews' frequent use of such rhetorical connections, which are not easily translated, remains largely unexplored.

5. *Intertextual relations*

The final type of repetitive tie to be considered by this study, "intertextual relations," refer to connections established between texts which arise from a common dependence on the same extra-textual material. This type of connection may be subsumed and analyzed within the category of "string repetition" (category 3a) at times. For example, the shared dependance of both Hebrews 8:8-12 and 10:16-17 on Jeremiah 31:31-34, which establishes an inter-textual connection between these texts, is clear from their quotation of the same lexical strings from the LXX text. However, this is not always the case. For example, an examination of the vocabulary used in Hebrews 2:16 and 3:1 strongly suggests a shared dependence on Isaiah 41:8, despite the absence of common material cited.[99]

---

96. Lane, *Hebrews 1-8*, n.p. cites Coste, "Notion grecque," 485, noting that the phrase "has a long history in Greek literature" stemming from the phonetic similarity of the verbal roots, and that "the play on words is relatively common in Philo, who applies it to the young and the foolish who must learn from what they endure (e.g., *On Flight and Finding* 138). From this perspective the application of the conventional proverb to Jesus is daring." Cf. Ebert, "Chiastic Structure," 174.

97. Cf. ἀναστάσεως (6:2); ἀνακαινίζειν and ἀνασταθροῦντας (6:6).

98. Cf. Cosby, *Rhetorical Composition*, and "Rhetorical Composition," 257-73.

99. Cf. 4.2.7c.

6. *Summary*

In summary then, a link is a repetitive tie which exists between two items in a text and which may be classified under five headings. First, lexical relations describe links formed between individual words and include lexical repetition, similarity, opposition, and non-semantic connections based on field/scenario. Links may also be established, second, by means of reference in which one of a small class of items (pronouns, demonstratives etc) stands in for another item. Connections can be made in various other ways through, third, the grammatical system, fourth, similarities in the sound of particular words and phrases, and, fifth, a shared dependance on the same extra-textual material.

3.3.2 What Is a Link Cluster?

In light of the above, a "link cluster" may be defined as two sentences or larger semantic units within the text of Hebrews which demonstrate a higher degree of linkage than would be expected from common lexical repetition. Hoey describes essentially the same feature using different terminology: "A bond is a connection that exists between a pair of sentences of above-average number of links."[100] While the number of connections required is not absolute, Hoey claims that it does not vary greatly from text to text and that "any two sentences are connected as packages of information if they share at least three points of reference."[101] He explains:

> The reason for this [choice of number] is practical: if less than three repetitions are treated as establishing a significant connection, then virtually every sentence will be connected to virtually every other sentence, and that is not going to tell us anything interesting about the function of cohesion except that it is pervasive.[102]

---

100. Hoey, *Patterns*, 83.

101. Hoey, *Patterns*, 36, 160. Hoey's findings are based on his analyzes of a wide range of texts. He also cites, in further support, Phillips, *Aspects*, 162–63, whose 1985 study of collocation in longer book-length texts comes to similar conclusions: "A conservative criterion would, then, be to require that chapters must be connected by a minimum of three . . . links in order to qualify as significantly related."

102. Hoey, *Patterns*, 36.

For present purposes, sentences and larger textual units will be deemed clusters when joined by *three or more* links. Sentences linked in this way may be located in close proximity to one another (adjacent) or span large portions of text.

One of the problems with repetition-in-structure that has previously been identified (2.5, question one) is how to demonstrate a "significant" link beyond normal common lexical repetition. This problem is avoided, however, by limiting our investigation to link clusters since such clusters show convincing evidence of textual organization and therefore significance.[103]

3.4 Collection and Analysis of Data

This study will follow a synthetic four-step approach to the text which combines the insights derived from the main structural approaches to Hebrews (discussed earlier) with some of the goals, methods and results of modern linguistic cohesion analysis:

1. Identify link clusters within the text.
2. Examine the location of links within each cluster for evidence of any potential structuring function for repetition.
3. Seek to understand the topical function of repetition within individual clusters.
4. Seek to understand the relationship between link clusters within the discourse as a whole.

1. Identify link clusters within the text.

The first step involves correctly locating and identifying clusters of links (both intertextual and intratextual) by carefully reading the text in linear fashion from the beginning without any presuppositions concerning semantic structure and unit break up.[104] Where an individual link is noted

---

103. Hoey, *Patterns*, 56.

104. The decision to proceed independently of scholarly opinion regarding structural boundaries is not so much an expression of willful defiance as a response to the lack of any firm consensus of opinion regarding unit boundaries throughout the text and the fact that such boundaries have on occasion obscured the detection of link clusters.

between a pair of sentences, whether within or without Hebrews, especially when the links are strong and obvious (see below), further investigation will follow to determine whether or not that link is part of a cluster and thus relevant to this study. All links not found to be part of clusters will be excluded from further analysis at this point. On the other hand, links deemed to be of potential significance yet not relevant to a particular context will be passed over for further analysis down the track.[105]

Since, in agreement with Hoey, it is assumed that "links vary in weight,"[106] greater significance will be attached to some links than others. In broad terms, those achieved through lexical relations and the grammatical system will be thought to be stronger than those established by means of reference.[107] More specifically, connections which will be held to be relatively "strong" include:

a. links between infrequently occurring words and phrases. For instance, εὐαγγελίζω ("I preach the Gospel") occurs twice only in Hebrews in 4:2 and 4:6.

b. the re-occurrence of identical, similar or contrasting phrases in the text. See for example, the extraordinary number of "variations" of the theme, εἰσελεύσονται εἰς τὴν κατάπαυσιν in 4:1-11 mentioned earlier (4:1, 3 x2, 5, 6 x 2, 10, 11).

c. words and phrases which, while syntactically unlike, clearly express similar or opposite meanings. Thus, the phrase γεύσηται θανάτου ("he [Jesus] might taste death," 2:9) is closely related to the equally experiential statement αὐτὸς . . . μετέσχεν τῶν αὐτῶν ("he [Jesus] has shared these (i.e. blood and flesh, in context)," 2:14).

d. words and phrases which are held together by parallel grammatical constructions. Thus, although superficially unlike, the prepositional phrases beginning ἐν τῷ (3:12) and διά + accusative both depict "unfaithfulness" as the cause of Israel's failure to enter God's Rest.[108]

105. See, for example, comments on the clear parallels within 1:1-2 in 4.2.1.

106. Hoey, *Patterns*, 83.

107. Pace Hoey, *Patterns*, 83-84. Hoey ranks the different kinds of repetition in decreasing order of importance as follows: simple lexical repetition, complex lexical repetition, simple mutual paraphrase, simple partial paraphrase, antonymous complex paraphrase, other complex paraphrase, substitution, co-reference, ellipsis. While acknowledging (p. 83) that "the low placings of substitution and ellipsis are likely to be challenged," he insists that "it makes sense to give top priority to lexical links over grammatical links."

108. The first represents an instrumental dative, while διά + accusative is here

On the other hand, repetition involving the most commonly occurring words such as καί, the definite article, and the most common prepositions will not be considered *except* in contexts where their unusually high frequency indicates a particular significance.[109] While this kind of differentiation is of some value, attempting to gain greater precision regarding the relative significance of each kind of link need not concern us to any great extent since *it is the number of such links in combination within clusters* rather than their generic kind that matters for the purposes of this study.

It is also worth saying a word about ambiguity at this juncture. This approach seeks to proceed inductively by drawing attention to connections which exist within the text itself. Given the considerable evidence of overlap noted in the previous chapter, the possibility that particular words, phrases or whole clusters may function in more than one way simultaneously must be taken seriously. Since context is the key to understanding meaning, where a word functions within more than one context, the possibility exists that it might have more than one meaning. Consequently, we must not go further than the text allows in attempting to resolve it one way or the other.[110] A similar point may be made with regard to Greek grammatical structure. As J. P. Louw observes, the tendency of Ancient Greek writers to combine virtually all colons together in various ways means that "from a purely formal standpoint (based on analogies in present-day European languages) a sentence would be enormously long and involved."[111] However, the inherent flexibility of Greek grammar (or what Louw terms "surface structure") provided opportunities for ancient authors to do more than one thing simultaneously within texts, opportunities which were frequently exploited to produce more than one level of meaning ("deep structure"). Louw states:

> It is essential to realize that in continuous discourse the multiple relationships are often highly complex and must often be stated in terms of multiple dimensions. It is therefore impossible to treat such structures as amenable to fixed sets of rules. Different alternatives must be considered on the basis of degrees of

---

meant to be read in a causal sense. Cf. Wallace, *Greek Grammar*, 742.

109. See for example the prominence of markers of location, especially "within" and "without" in 3:11–4:1.

110. Thistelton, "Semantics," 97. See too Silva, *Biblical Words*, 149–55, on "deliberate ambiguity"; and Downing, "Ambiguity, Ancient Semantics, and Faith," 139–62.

111. Louw, *Semantics*, 100.

probability, and this is particularly true of stylistic features in which the subtle and often multidimensional factors make any rigid analysis quite impossible.[112]

Hebrews contains many such instances of grammatical ambiguity which, it will be argued, are often quite deliberate and allow for more than one possible interpretation of the text without descending to meaningless subjectivism. Clearly, this ambiguity must be approached cautiously lest the scholar fall into the trap of engaging in "all types of fanciful intuitive judgements."[113] Nevertheless, it is possible to make judgements regarding the function(s) of particular grammatical constructions which are more than mere speculation, and represent a property of the text itself, by reading them in light of their literary context (properly understood).

2. Examine the location of links within each intratextual link cluster for evidence of any potential structuring function for repetition.

Having identified an intratextual cluster of links (as defined above), the second step involves examining the *location* of individual links within each cluster so as to better understand their inter-relatedness. It seeks:

a. to ascertain whether the present position of repetition within clusters represents an accident of the writing process (i.e. what Hoey terms "organizing relations") or evidence of an author's careful and deliberate arrangement of his material (i.e. what Hoey terms "structure");[114]

b. (if the latter) to determine *if* and (if so) *how* repetition serves to delineate the unit's boundaries and establish parallel contexts within the cluster.

Further evidence from modern scholarship regarding unit boundaries and the grammatical relations within clusters will also be considered at this stage where relevant.

---

112. Louw, *Semantics*, 104. Cf. Beekman and Callow's observations of "multifunctionality" within texts, *Translating the Word of God*, 270.

113. Louw, *Semantics*, 115.

114. Hoey, *Patterns*, 26–29.

3. Seek to understand the topical function of repetition within individual link clusters

An attempt is then made to understand the topical function of repetition within individual link clusters by seeking:

a. to provide a coherent topical explanation for any formal connections between linked sentences or parts thereof in light of Hoey's observation that "sentences appropriately connected by repetition, however far apart, should make some sense or show some clear relationship together":[115]

   i. Do link clusters serve to unite material into paragraphs (i.e. units which are cohesive in terms of "scope and topic")?[116]

   ii. Can formally related elements within paragraphs be read together in a meaningful way? And if so, what insight does this contribute to the meaning of the paragraph?

   iii. In cases of repetition which involve quotations or allusions to an earlier text (e.g., Heb 1:8–9 rests on LXX Ps 44:7–8), what light does this repetition shed upon the meaning and function of that text within its new context?

b. to distinguish between material which is formally marked as more (and less) prominent by means of repetition. What are the key words, phrases and ideas in this unit? Conversely, which words, phrases and concepts are less important in this context?

c. to identify words and phrases seemingly held together in parallel relations by the context, so as to understand the reason they have been brought together in this way. Is there an "instantial equivalence" at this point?[117] And if so, what light does it shed on meaning?

---

115. Hoey, *Patterns*, 75.

116. This more technical definition of paragraph corresponds with Louw's terminology in *Semantics*, 98. Cf. Beekman and Callow, *Translating*, 272, who describe much the same entity by the label, "proposition": "A *proposition* is a grouping of concepts, again with one of the concepts central, that is, nuclear. It is a unit of communication, that is, it affirms, denies, questions, or commands something." Elsewhere (p. 249) they note: "The basic criterion is that a section or a paragraph, deals with only one theme. If the theme changes, then a new unit has started.... What gives a section or paragraph its overall coherence as a semantic unit is the fact that one subject matter is being dealt with."

117. According to Hoey, *Patterns*, 166, an instantial equivalence represents an equivalence that only operates for this text.

4. Seek to understand the relationship between link clusters in the discourse as a whole.

Arising out of the third stage, and as an extension of it, the fourth step investigates the function of the link cluster as a discrete unit within its wider context. This involves finding answers to the following questions.

   a. How do intratextual link clusters relate with other clusters at *the same* discourse level?
   b. Assuming for the moment that Hebrews might be thought of as a hierarchically structured text which operates at numerous levels (as Vanhoye, Guthrie, Rhee and Westfall suggest), how do intratextual link clusters relate with other clusters at *different* discourse levels?
   c. What does the interaction of various clusters reveal about the organization of Hebrews as a whole? In other words, how do link clusters "fit together" as part of the one coherent whole?

Of particular interest for our enquiry is the question of whether macro link clusters might reasonably be understood to function as "topic" sentences within the discourse.[118] Virtually all would agree with Vanhoye that, if detectable, topic sentences would represent the "most important" structural device for conveying meaning in Hebrews since, by their nature, such sentences unite together the information they summarize.[119] However, do they in fact function in this way?

What distinguishes this present approach from earlier ones is the attempt to locate topic sentences on the basis of *both* form *and* content. With regard to form, earlier "conceptual" approaches such as Vanhoye's rely upon the ability of the commentator to discern the structure of the text on the basis of content alone. In contrast, this study limits its inquiry to text which has been formally marked out as prominent by only considering sentences which have been significantly bonded together through repetition. With regard to content, Westfall notes:

> Approaching the discussion of topic with well-defined criteria is an important consideration in the debate of the structure of Hebrews and essential to determining the meaning and message.[120]

---

118. Cf. Westfall, *Discourse Analysis*, 83 and 113.
119. Vanhoye, *Structure*, 20. Cf. Westfall, *Discourse Analysis*, 73.
120. Westfall, *Discourse Analysis*, 85.

For the purposes of this study, a word, phrase or sentence may be identified as a *topic sentence* when each of the following three conditions is fulfilled.

1. It is clearly *discontinuous* (i.e. semantically or conceptually new) in some way with immediately preceding material. Levinsohn observes that "the presence or absence of a (fronted) point of departure has a major part to play in determining the validity of potential evidence."[121] Similarly, Beekman and Callow note that since the basic criterion of a section or a paragraph is that it deals with only one theme: "if the theme changes, then a new unit has started.... What gives a section or paragraph its overall coherence as a semantic unit is the fact that one subject matter is being dealt with."[122]

2. It occurs *at or near the end of a previous unit*.[123]

3. There is *demonstrable continuity* with the material which it "introduces" or "concludes." Proximity to the beginning of a unit is not enough to identify the function of a word or phrase as an "introduction" or "conclusion." There must be some form of coherence evident between the marked material and the other material to which it is related.[124]

3.5 Conclusions

This chapter has sought to establish responsible parameters for the enquiry into the function of link clusters within Hebrews by:

a. outlining the relationship between this approach and that of modern cohesion analysis;

b. discussing the types and forms of repetition to be examined and carefully defining what is meant by the terms "link" and "link cluster";

c. describing the four-step approach to the text which will be employed in the following chapters of this analysis.

121. Levinsohn, "Review," 191.
122. Beekman and Callow, *Translating*, 249, 191,
123. Given the possibility of overlap, "at or near the end" does not necessarily mean "after."
124. Cf. Swetnam, "Form and Content," 369, who notes: "Rather than establish form on purely formal principles it would seem preferable to establish form on formal principles but in the light of content, just as content should be studied on the basis of content but in the light of form."

4

Micro Link Clusters in Hebrews 1:1—3:8

4.1 Introduction

THIS CHAPTER REPRESENTS AN examination into the first seven intratextual micro link clusters in Hebrews (1:1–4; 1:3–6; 1:7–14; 2:1–4; 2:5–9; 2:8–17; 3:1–8) in light of the first three steps of the method outlined in the previous chapter. Although intertextual clusters will also be identified and examined for the insight they provide into the meaning of this material, the chief focus of this chapter is to identify the location of link clusters between texts *within* Hebrews by itemizing connections so as to come to an understanding of their function and contribution to the structure and meaning of this discourse. It will demonstrate:

> *first*, that Hebrews consistently uses link clusters to unite the text into a series of overlapping concentric units, which consist of two or more pairs of balanced parallel phrases;
>
> *second*, that link clusters function topically to indicate coherent relationships between texts, both within Hebrews and with various LXX texts, thereby allowing readers/hearers to understand the author's intended meaning and particular emphasis with increased precision by reading these texts together;
>
> *third*, that by forming parallel contexts in this way, link clusters also establish environments in which instantial equivalents might be

recognized,[1] thereby further clarifying the meaning of ambiguous words and phrases in the discourse;

fourth, that link clusters serve a "vertical" role by marking out particular words and phrases as more prominent and therefore central to the author's purpose than others;

fifth, that by paying attention to (a), (b), (c) and (d), the reader/hearer is able to arrive at a precise understanding of the topic of each paragraph.

Each cluster will be analyzed in turn by means of the approach (outlined below) with specific exegetical findings and inferences presented as they are discovered along the way:

1. Identify link clusters by observing significant repetition (previously unobserved and observed) in the text.
2. Seek to ascertain the function of each link cluster by:
    i. observing the location of repetition within it so as to identify formally related words, phrases, clauses and sentences;
    ii. examining texts linked in this way for evidence of coherence between them which might allow us to understand their meaning together (e.g., A in light of A' and ABC in light of C'B'A');
    iii. identifying instantial equivalents within parallel contexts;
    iv. identifying its most and least prominent material, as indicated by repetition; and
    v. summarizing its topic in light of i–v.

4.2 Link Clusters in Hebrews 1:1—3:8

4.2.1 Hebrews 1:1–4

a. Introduction

Though justly famous for its elegant form and prominent position at the head of the discourse, important questions remain with regard to Hebrews 1:1–4 relating to the meaning in context of a number of

---

1. As defined by Hoey, *Patterns*, 166–67, an "instantial equivalent" is an equivalence between word and/or phrases which only operates within particular texts (cf. 3.2.2).

its words and phrases (especially τοὺς ἀγγέλους and ὄνομα in 1:4), the relationship between its component parts (e.g., between the events described in 1:2b and 1:3d), and the topical significance of the comparison between Jesus and οἱ ἄγγελοι in 1:2, his appointment as heir in 1:2, and 1:1–4 as a whole. This section will address these questions and seek to clarify the topic of this material with new evidence garnered from an investigation into the location and inter-connectedness of repetition patterns in Hebrews 1:1–4.

b. Significant repetition previously observed in Hebrews 1:1–4

The first example of significant repetition within Hebrews occurs within the first sentence of the text (1:1–2).[2] As Black and others have noted, the lexical repetition of λαλήσας in ἐλάλησεν, together with four relations of opposition regarding the timing (πάλαι / ἐπ ἐσχάτοθ τῶν ἡμερῶν τούτων), recipients (τοῖς πατράσιν / ἡμῖν), agents (ἐν τοῖς προφήταις / ἐν υἱῷ) and ways (πολθμερῶς καὶ πολυτρόπως / [implied] one way) of God's address reveal these opening clauses to be "completely parallel syntactically."[3] However, while almost certainly deliberate and deserving of further examination, the repetition in Hebrews 1:1–2a does not constitute a link cluster for the simple reason that the opening clause πολυμερῶς καὶ πολυτρόπως πάλαι ὁ θεὸς λαλήσας τοῖς πατράσιν ἐν τοῖς προφήταις is syntactically dependent on the second.[4] In other words, we do not have here a relationship of repetition between two *sentences* but rather between two related clauses within the one sentence.[5]

With this in mind, the first link cluster proper in Hebrews spans 1:1–4. Lexical repetition noted by others in this portion of text includes:

---

2. This is true regardless of whether this sentence is taken to end after υἱῷ (1:2), αἰῶνας (1:3), δόξης (v3), αὐτοῦ (1:3), ὄνομα (1:4) or σε (1:5).

3. Black, "Hebrews 1:1–4," 177, 189. See too Ellingworth, *Hebrews*, 91; Adam, *The Majestic Son*, 18; Guthrie, *Hebrews*, 46; O'Brien, *Hebrews*, 47–48. For discussion of the textual variant τοῖς πατράσιν ἡμῶν, see Ellingworth, *Hebrews*, 92.

4. The participle λαλήσας clearly stands in a dependent relationship with the indicative verb ἐλάλησεν, meaning that it cannot be read as an independent sentence. Wallace, *Greek Grammar*, 651–53, notes in agreement with Brookes and Winbery's assessment that "if a participle can be identified as dependent (i.e., if it can at all be attached to a verb), it should be so considered."

5. We will consider the function of this kind of repetition in chapter 6.

- the reflection of the relatively rare noun κληρονόμος ("heir," 1:2) in the verb κεκληρονόμηκεν ("he has inherited," 1:4);[6] and
- the two forms of the verb ποιέω in 1:2 and 3 respectively.[7]

Important relationships have also been detected between a number of semantically unlike phrases in this section.

a. Although superficially dissimilar, many have observed parallels between ὃς ὢν ἀπαύγασμα τῆς δόξης ("who is the radiance of the Glory," 1:3a) and χαρακτὴρ τῆς ὑποστάσεως αὐτοῦ ("the imprint of his substance," 1:3b), with both representing metaphorical images which depict both unity and distinction between the Father and the Son;[8]

b. Scholars have also drawn attention to similarities between the clause in 1:2b, ὃν ἔθηκεν κληρονόμον πάντων ("whom he appointed the heir of all") and the description of the Son's heavenly session in 1:3d, ἐκάθισεν ἐν δεξιᾷ τῆς μεγαλωσύνης ἐν ὑψηλοῖς ("He sat down at the right hand of the Majesty in the Heights").[9] Both statements (i) reflect messianic Psalms (2:8 and 110:1 respectively),[10] (ii) involve

---

6. The word κληρονόμος appears only 3x in Hebrews (1:2; 6:17 and 11:17), while the verb κληρονομέω occurs 4x in 1:4; 1:14; 6:12 and 12:17. Cf. Ebert, "Chiastic Structure," 170-71; Meier, "Structure," 187, and "Symmetry," 522; Ellingworth, *Hebrews*, 95; and Rhee, *Faith*, 66-67.

7. Ebert, "Chiastic Structure," 170-71; Meier, "Structure," 187, and "Symmetry," 522.

8. Lane, *Hebrews 1-8*, n.p., suggests "the arrangement of the two members of the first clause in synonymous parallelism is intentional. They are meant to say the same thing." Johnson, *Hebrews*, 68-69, observes that in combination both phrases "clearly and overwhelmingly assert the divine status of the Son." Cf. Ebert, "Chiastic Structure," 167; Guthrie, *Hebrews*, 48; and Ellingworth, *Hebrews*, 95. Cf. Heil, *Chiastic Structures*, 31, who finds in this verse a reference to Wisdom 7:25-26.

9. Lane, *Hebrews 1-8*, n.p., proposes a relationship between the larger phrase καθαρισμὸν . . . ποιησάμενος ἐκάθισεν ἐν δεξιᾷ and 1:2b, while Ellingworth, *Hebrews*, 95, links both ideas under the one heading, "enthronement." Cf. Ebert, "Chiastic Structure," 172-74; Meier, "Structure," 176.

10. Ebert, "Chiastic Structure," 172-74, notes that while not a word-for-word quotation, the connection between Psalm 2 and Heb 1:2 is "commonly recognized," finding further evidence in the recurrence of these two Psalms at the beginning and end of the catalogue of quotations in 1:5-14 and in Heb 5:5 and 6. "It is clear that these two psalms were linked in the writer's mind." Meanwhile, Lane, *Hebrews 1-8*, n.p., says of 1:3, "the declaration that the Son has been exalted to a position at God's right hand bears an unmistakable allusion to Ps 110:1, for this is the only biblical text that speaks of someone enthroned beside God." Cf. Meier, "Structure," 184.

the same two participants (the Father and the Son), and (iii) seem likely to describe the same event—the "enthronement" of the Son—viewed from different perspectives.[11] Moreover, in each case, (iv) the author's use of the aorist views this event as a completed whole.[12] Ebert also notes that "the inversion of the two consonants θ and κ in these parallel verbs is a happy coincidence" which allows the author to create "a balance of sound between the two corresponding verbs ἔθηκεν and ἐκάθισεν."[13]

c. Others have identified a connection between δι' οὗ καὶ ἐποίησεν τοὺς αἰῶνας ("through whom also he made the universe," 1:2) and φέρων τε τὰ πάντα τῷ ῥήματι τῆς δυνάμεως αὐτοῦ/ ("and bearing all things by the word of his power," 1:3) based on the fact that both clauses (i) contain similarly nuanced verbs and (ii) emphasize the Son's causal role (δι' οὗ / τῆς δυνάμεως αὐτοῦ) with regard to his (iii) "action in the universe."[14]

c. *Potentially significant repetition previously unobserved in Hebrews 1:1–4*

Potentially significant yet previously unobserved connections within this text include the lexical repetition of the relatively common adjective πᾶς (πάντων, 1:2; πάντα, 1:3),[15] and the synonymous (or near synonymous) relationship between:

- τοὺς αἰῶνας (1:2), πάντων (1:2), and τὰ πάντα (1:3), which seem likely to function in present context as references to the totality of created existence (i.e. "the world," "the universe"); and

11. Ellingworth, *Hebrews*, 95, reads both as references to the Son's "enthronement." In the first, the Son is the grammatical object of the Father's action (ὃν ἔθηκεν), while in the second, he represents the subject and agent of the verb (ἐκάθισενεν), with the Father appearing as indirect object.

12. By means of the aorist, the event is described as a whole, in summary fashion, without interest in its internal workings. Wallace, *Greek Grammar*, 753; Meier, "Structure," 177.

13. Ebert, "Chiastic Structure," 174.

14. *Pace* Ellingworth, *Hebrews*, 95, 100; and Rhee, *Faith*, 66–68. *Contra* Ebert, "Chiastic Structure," 171.

15. Unless stated otherwise, comments regarding the relative frequency or otherwise of particular words and phrases in chapters four to seven refer to their use within Hebrews.

- τῆς δόξης and τῆς μεγαλωσύωης (1:3), which both convey the idea of "high status or rank"[16] and may be translated as "majesty" or "glory."

Further links of similarity may be detected between:

a. the phrase τῆς μεγαλωσύωης ἐν ὑψηλοῖς ("the Majesty in the Heavens," 1:3) and ὁ θεός ("God," 1:1), with both functioning as descriptors of the same divine being. It is possible that τῆς δόξης (1:3) should also be read in similar fashion as a reference to God ("the Glorious One") rather than to an abstract quality, "glory";[17]

b. πολθμερῶς καὶ πολυτρόπως (1:1), which only occurs here in Hebrews, and διαφορώτερον (1:4; cf. 8:6 and 9:10). While many translate διαφορώτερον as "more excellent" (or its near equivalent) due to the grammatical link with κρείττων,[18] Chrysostom paraphrases πολθμερῶς καὶ πολυτρόπως, read together, as διαφορώτερον;[19]

At this point, it should be stated once more that while some of the connections described above seem likely to be of significance in some way or another, no judgment has yet been made in this regard. We have simply been assembling evidence of *possible* connections which come from the text so as to examine their combined significance. Having completed our inventory (step 1 of our method), however, we are now in a position to proceed with our investigation into the location and function of repetition in this part of the text (i.e. steps 2 and 3).

d. *The location and formal function of repetition in Hebrews 1:1-4*

The frequency and strength of connections observed represents strong formal evidence which suggests that the first link cluster (1:1-4), functions as a closely united and coherent literary unit.[20] This proposal, which

---

16. Louw and Nida, *Greek-English Lexicon*, n.p.

17. Taken this way, the article functions as a substantiver. Wallace, *Greek Grammar*, 733.

18. Ellingworth, *Hebrews*, 104; Johnson, *Hebrews*, 74; Guthrie, *Hebrews*, 50. The word is most commonly rendered as "different, varied" (Louw and Nida, *Greek-English Lexicon*, n.p.) or "different, diverse, of varying kinds" (Friberg, *Analytical Lexicon*, n.p.).

19. Cf. Ellingworth, *Hebrews*, 91.

20. Cf. Hoey's "strong claim," *Patterns*, 126.

is consistent with the views of most scholars,[21] is further supported by the absence of any clear connections with material in the following verses and by an examination of its grammar. Hebrews 1:1–4 forms a single, multi-clause sentence whose second half is syntactically dependent on the first.[22] A clear shift of subject from the Father to the Son occurs following ὅς in 1:3 which divides the unit into two parts (vv. 1–2 and 3–4) and affects a subtle shift in content from "theo-logy" to "christo-logy."[23]

Before turning to investigate its content, however, more needs to be said regarding the precise *location* of repetition within this cluster. Based on Michael Hoey's findings regarding repetition patterns within coherent written texts, we might expect to find within Hebrews 1:1–4 a considerable number of connections which are "unevenly distributed" between pairs of sentences,[24] reflecting the "organizing relations" which arise as part of the writing process.[25] In Hoey's example below (fig. 17), which reflects the conventional pattern, each of the five sentences in the paragraph is connected to a varying degree with each of the other sentences in its immediate literary context. Sentence 1 has most links with Sentences 2 and 5 (four each) and least with Sentence 3.[26]

---

21. Westfall, *Discourse Analysis*, 89; Guthrie, *Hebrews*, 45; Vanhoye, *Structure*, 80; Rhee, *Faith*, 67; Black, "Hebrews 1:1–4," 175; Ebert, "Chiastic Structure," "Chiastic Structure," 163; Westfall, *Discourse Analysis*, 89; and Heil, *Chiastic Structures*, 26.

22. Guthrie, *Hebrews*, 45; Johnson, *Hebrews*, 64; Westfall, *Discourse Analysis*, 90; and Meier, "Structure," 171.

23. Meier, "Symmetry," 527, notes that "by a carefully constructed slant in the movement of thought and language, the theo-logy gradually becomes christo-logy." Cf. Vanhoye, *La Structure*, 65–68; and Black, "Hebrews 1:1–4," 183.

24. Hoey, *Patterns*, 118.

25. Hoey, *Patterns*, 26–29.

26. Hoey, *Patterns*, 37.

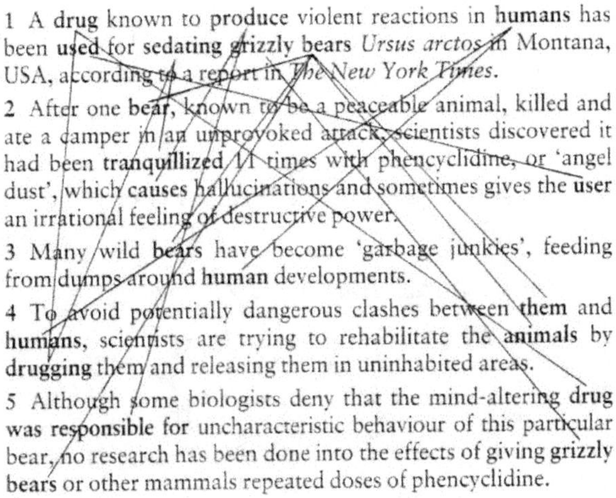

1 A drug known to produce violent reactions in humans has been used for sedating grizzly bears *Ursus arctos* in Montana, USA, according to a report in *The New York Times*.
2 After one bear, known to be a peaceable animal, killed and ate a camper in an unprovoked attack, scientists discovered it had been tranquillized 11 times with phencyclidine, or 'angel dust', which causes hallucinations and sometimes gives the user an irrational feeling of destructive power.
3 Many wild bears have become 'garbage junkies', feeding from dumps around human developments.
4 To avoid potentially dangerous clashes between them and humans, scientists are trying to rehabilitate the animals by drugging them and releasing them in uninhabited areas.
5 Although some biologists deny that the mind-altering drug was responsible for uncharacteristic behaviour of this particular bear, no research has been done into the effects of giving grizzly bears or other mammals repeated doses of phencyclidine.

Fig. 17.

What we actually find in Hebrews 1:1-4, however, is a startlingly different pattern of repetition. Leaving aside for now the cluster of links noted earlier in 1:1-2 (to which we will return in 7.2), three things stand out. First, the clear majority of connections within this unit *occur on one side or other of a midpoint* which occurs between τῆς δόξης and καί in verse 3, dividing the unit into two halves. Second, both halves *contain 36 words* (see below).[27]

Heb 1:1-3a

Πολυμερῶς καὶ πολυτρόπως πάλαι ὁ θεὸς λαλήσας τοῖς πατράσιν ἐν τοῖς προφήταις ἐπ' ἐσχάτου τῶν ἡμερῶν τούτων ἐλάλησεν ἡμῖν ἐν υἱῷ ὃν ἔθηκεν κληρονόμον πάντων δι' οὗ καὶ ἐποίησεν τοὺς αἰῶνας ὃς ὢν ἀπαύγασμα τῆς δόξης

Heb 1:3b-4

καὶ χαρακτὴρ τῆς ὑποστάσεως αὐτοῦ φέρων τε τὰ πάντα τῷ ῥήματι τῆς δυνάμεως δι' αὐτοῦ καθαρισμὸν τῶν ἁμαρτιῶν ποιησάμενος ἐκάθισεν ἐν δεξιᾷ τῆς μεγαλωσύνης ἐν ὑψηλοῖς τοσούτῳ κρείττων γενόμενος τῶν ἀγγέλων ὅσῳ διαφορώτερον παρ' αὐτοὺς κεκληρονόμηκεν ὄνομα

27. For the purposes of this analysis, the wording of NA28 is assumed to be accurate at this point. In the interests of avoiding confusion, not all connections listed have been included.

Third, when viewed as a whole, the location of and relationship between its clauses suggests that Hebrews 1:1–4 has been *artfully composed to form a seven-part chiasm* (1:1–2a, 2b, 2c, 3a and 3b, 3c, 3d and 4; see below).[28]

    A. ¹:¹ Πολυμερῶς καὶ πολυτρόπως πάλαι ὁ θεὸς λαλήσας τοῖς πατράσιν ἐν τοῖς προφήταις ² ἐπ' ἐσχάτου τῶν ἡμερῶν τούτων ἐλάλησεν ἡμῖν ἐν υἱῷ

        B. ²ᵇ <u>ὃν ἔθηκεν κληρονόμον πάντων</u>

            C. ²ᶜ δι' οὗ καὶ ἐποίησεν τοὺς αἰῶνας

                D. ³ᵃ ὃς ὢν ἀπαύγασμα τῆς δόξης

                D′. ³ᵇ καὶ χαρακτὴρ τῆς ὑποστάσεως αὐτοῦ

            C′. ³ᶜ φέρων τε τὰ πάντα τῷ ῥήματι τῆς δυνάμεως αὐτοῦ

        B′. ³ᵈ καθαρισμὸν τῶν ἁμαρτιῶν ποιησάμενος <u>ἐκάθισεν ἐν δεξιᾷ τῆς μεγαλωσύνης ἐν ὑψηλοῖς</u>

    A′. ⁴τοσούτῳ κρείττων γενόμενος τῶν ἀγγέλων ὅσῳ διαφορώτερον παρ' αὐτοὺς κεκληρονόμηκεν ὄνομα

Though not every word or phrase in our outline occurs in exactly the mirror location of its partner word or phrase,[29] the fact that *most do* is significant: such symmetry is unlikely to be accidental. Further evidence in favor of design may also be seen in the author's choice and use of a similar group of words and phrases in both 1:1–2 and 1:3b–4 *even when their referents are different and/or the same idea could be more naturally expressed without them.* Ebert notes, for example, that "in verse 3c the author appears to have deliberately used the periphrastic καθαρισμόν . . . ποιησάμενος, combining the participle with the adjective, rather than using the simple verb καθαρίζω" so as to form a lexical connection with ἐποίησεν in 1:2.[30] He claims that this "verbal parallel

---

28. Although comprised of topically parallel elements, 1:3a is treated together as a single component, D, on the basis that καὶ χαρακτὴρ τῆς ὑποστάσεως αὐτοῦ/ is grammatically dependent on ὃς ὢν ἀπαύγασμα τῆς δόξης, while the symmetry is reflected in the numbering (D and D′).

29. ἐποίησεν occurs in C while ποιησάμενος occurs in B′; πάντων occurs in B, while τὰ πάντα may be found in C′; and κληρονόμον comprises part of B while κεκληρονόμηκεν occurs in A′.

30. Ebert, "Chiastic Structure," 171.

based on the word ποιέω is not accidental," nor is it merely a matter of style, but serves the author's purpose by establishing a significant formal connection between these texts.³¹ There is thus good evidence that repetition plays a significant structuring role within Hebrews 1:1-4 by establishing formal connections between phrases within the text.

While this study is certainly not the first to suggest that Hebrews 1:1-4 has been patterned as a chiasm,³² the fresh methodological approach of this study confirms these previous observations as well as yielding a presentation which differs from earlier versions with regard to its internal arrangement.³³ Clearly, the ideational content of the text must be considered before any further conclusions are drawn.

e.   The topical function of repetition in Hebrews 1:1-4

While the overall topical coherence of 1:1-4 is widely acknowledged, the relationship between its parallel components and between each of its halves has not often been considered in seeking to determine the meaning of this unit. Both A and A' feature (a) a contrast between (b) various of God's messengers (τῶν αγγέλων and τοῖς προφήταις) and (c) the Son, which involves (d) unusual yet related terminology (πολθμερῶς καὶ πολυτρόπως and διαφορώτερον). Meanwhile, as noted previously (cf.

---

31. Ebert, "Chiastic Structure," 171. Cf. the repetition of the striking κληρονομέω which functions similarly by establishing a lexical link with κληρονόμος in 1:2.

32. Cf. Robinson, "Literary Structure," 178-86; Ebert, "Chiastic Structure," 170; Ellingworth, *Hebrews*, 95; Guthrie, *Hebrews*, 55; Rhee, *Faith*, 66-67; and Heil, *Chiastic Structures*, 26.

33. Our findings most closely resemble those of Rhee, *Faith*, 66-67 (cf. 2.3.4.3), with the only difference relating to our observations of a further symmetrical relationship within the central component of the chiasm (i.e. D). Ellingworth's proposal (*Hebrews*, 95) excludes our parallels, A and A', yet corresponds on all other points. Alternatively, Lane's outline, *Hebrews 1-8*, n.p., matches ours with regard to A and B (and thus A' and B'), but differs in its understanding of the center of the chiasm: Lane sees a correspondence between δι' οὗ καὶ ἐποίησεν τοὺς αἰῶνας (1:2), and ὃς ὢν ἀπαύγασμα ... καὶ χαρακτὴρ ... φέρων τε τὰ πάντα (1:3), reading both as "statements descriptive of divine Wisdom in the theology of Alexandrian Judaism." Ebert's proposal, "Chiastic Structure," 170, which resembles that of Heil, *Chiastic Structures*, 26, meanwhile, differs from ours (i) by linking together 1:2c and 1:3d as C and C' respectively on the basis of the repetition involving ἐποίησεν and ποιησάμενος, and the creation/redemption motif in the LXX (e.g., Ps 95); and (ii) by reading 1:3a-c together as its center (D). Finally, Meier, "Structure," 168-89, suggests that "the seven designations in 1,2b-4 form a definite ring pattern, moving from exaltation back through creation to preexistence and forward again through creation to exaltation."

4.2.1b), B and B' represent twin descriptions of this Son's appointment as heir of all,[34] C and C' emphasize his activity within the universe at two distinct chronological eras,[35] while the statements in D and D' essentially "say the same thing."[36]

When read together, the first half of the unit states that where once God spoke "long ago" through prophets, he has now spoken "at the end of these days" through the Son: the heir (B) and creator of all (C), the very radiance of "the Glory" himself (D). In context, B, C and D represent statements which elucidate the greatness of this speaker in terms of his future role, past work of creation, and eternal identity. Their main purpose appears to be not so much to define the Son's ontological relationship with his Father—though this is done implicitly—as to stress "the divine-revelatory capacity" of this Son.[37] It is also pertinent to note that the contrast between the Father's speech at the *beginning* and *end* in A is reflected in the Son's active role at the *end* (B) and *beginning* (C).[38] This is hardly surprising given the Son's identity.[39]

Having moved "backwards," as Meier observes, "our author will ultimately move forward again [in verses 3-4] to exaltation" in the relative clause beginning with ὅς.[40] By covering similar content, each component (i.e. D', C', B', and A') thus functions to further clarify and amplify the *meaning* of the earlier statements in three important ways.

---

34. The claim by some scholars (cf. Ebert, "Chiastic Structure," 170–71; and Heil, *Chiastic Structures*, 26) that καθαρισμὸν τῶν ἁμαρτιῶν ποιησάμενος (1:3) should be read as a parallel of δι' οὗ καὶ ἐποίησεν τοὺς αἰῶνας (1:2) on the basis of the repetition of ποιέω in 1:2 and 3 is doubtful for two reasons. First, a closer topical parallel containing two links exists between 1:2c and 1:3b; and second, the grammar of 1:1–4 argues decisively against making any significant division between the participle, ποιησάμενος and the verb ἐκάθισεν, with the former clearly dependent on the latter.

35. Against the suggestion made by Ebert, "Chiastic Structure," 171, that 1:3b is better understood as a parallel of 1:3a, 1:3a is about who the Son *is*, while 1:3b is about what he *does* (as is 1:2c). Ebert's understanding results in a somewhat unbalanced and asymmetrical center to his chiasm.

36. Lane, *Hebrews 1–8*, n.p.

37. Ebert, "Chiastic Structure," 177.

38. Noting the retrogressive chronology in 1:2, Meier, "Structure," 178, quips: "Our author is apparently proclaiming the Son to be, not the Alpha and the Omega, but the Omega and the Alpha."

39. Meier, "Structure," 182, attempts to read B, C and D as descriptive of the Son's life and work at three distinct time periods (the future, the past, and "the timeless pre-existence of the Son with God"). However, D speaks not only about what the Son *was*, but who he now *is* (ὤν).

40. Meier, "Structure," 178–79.

First, the unusual expression τῷ ῥήματι τῆς δυνάμεως ("by the word of his power") reintroduces and reinforces the earlier ideas in C concerning the personal involvement (δι' οὗ) of this Divine Son in relation to the universe (τὰ πάντα), making more specific *the way* in which he is actively involved in his world (i.e. τῷ ῥήματι, "through his word," 1:3).

Second, the *significance* for the author of the Son's appointment as heir, described in B, is made clear in both B' and A'. For since, having made atonement for sins, the Son has already "sat down" at the Father's right hand, he has even now "become greater" than all previous messengers of God.

Finally, the fact that this recently acquired greatness is *directly proportional* to the extent to which the Son's name "surpasses" and/or "differs from" theirs (τοσούτῳ κρείττων . . . ὅσῳ, "by as much greater as," A') makes clear the topical import of 1:1-2: that by communicating ἐν υἱῷ, God has now spoken *in a different and far more significant way than ever before*. While Ellingworth claims, against the syntax, that the meaning of verse 4 is best understood as "the Son is greater than angels because God has given him a higher status than theirs,"[41] Jesus' relative greatness in comparison to the ἄγγελοις is indeed presented as directly proportional to the greatness of his name in contrast to theirs in this context *for* (γάρ, 1:5) both depend equally upon the testimony of God. Jesus' name is greater than that of αγγέλων because God has uniquely addressed him as Son. Similarly, he himself has become greater for the very same reason. Understood this way, what is stated implicitly in verses 1-2 is made explicit in reverse order in verses 3-4.[42]

In summary, then, our analysis of topic has found clear and demonstrable evidence of coherence both between the two halves of this unit and between each of the formal parallels within it (A / A', B / B', C / C', D / D'), which, when these texts are read together, serves to magnify the extraordinary significance of what God has done by speaking to us through his Son.

---

41. Ellingworth, *Hebrews*, 104.

42. Rhee, *Faith*, 68, argues for a similar understanding from different grounds, claiming that "the contrast between the old and the new era by the temporal indicators, "long ago" (πάλαι) and "in these last days" (ἐπ'ἐσχάτου τῶν ἡμερῶν τούτων), implicitly suggests that God's revelation given to the new era through the Son is superior to that given to the old era through prophets."

f.   Further implications for meaning in light of the parallelism within Hebrews 1:1-4

As discussed in the previous chapter, Hoey demonstrates that an important function of repetition is its capacity to create "an environment in which other instantial equivalences may be recognized."[43] In other words, by establishing parallels between pairs of sentences, repetition serves to alert readers to further connections which, while not generally true for all texts, hold true for particular texts. Armed with this insight, three further concluding observations can be made in the light of our analysis of formal and topical parallelism in Hebrews 1:1-4.

First, and perhaps most importantly, although the key word ἄγγελος, which occurs eleven times in the first two chapters, has almost invariably been translated as "angel," leading to all kinds of scholarly speculations regarding the background of this text,[44] the parallelism between A and A' (1:1-2 and 1:3c-4) indicates that the reference to οἱ ἄγγελοι in 1:4 is best understood as an instantial equivalent of the "many ways and means" (πολυμερῶς καὶ πολυτρόπῳ, 1:1) by which God has spoken to the Fathers in the past. Understood in this light, the relationship between "οἱ ἄγγελοι" and the various other means of communication described in verse 1 corresponds with and contrasts to that between the description of the Son in verses 3-4 and the word υἱῷ (1:1),[45] making clear that the emphasis at this point *rests more upon their role as messengers* than on their supernatural nature. For, in this context at least, οἱ ἄγγελοι *includes* τοὺς προφήτας ("the prophets," 1:1) and all the former human agents of God's communicative activity (e.g., Moses and David; see 2:2-4).[46]

---

43. Hoey, *Patterns*, 167.

44. See, for example, Hughes, *Hebrews*, 51-52, who reads the comparison between Christ and the angels as evidence "that those to whom this letter was sent were entertaining, or being encouraged to entertain, teaching which elevated angels, or particular angels, to a position which rivaled that of Christ himself." Cf. Guthrie, "New Testament Exegesis," 593; Heil, *Chiastic Structure*, 33; and Lane, *Hebrews 1-8*, n.p.

45. Cf. Guthrie, "New Testament Exegesis," 593, who finds a "structural parallel" between the reference to τοῖς προφήταις in 1:1 and οἱ ἄγγελοι in 1:4.

46. *Contra* Guthrie, "New Testament Exegesis," 593, and Lane, *Hebrews 1-8*, n.p., who read οἱ ἄγγελοι and τοῖς προφήταις as two *distinct* if related groups (angels and prophets), Hebrews' use of the term in 1:4 makes clear that the latter is included within the former, such that the *same* group is contrasted with the *same* person (the Son) in both A and A'."

This understanding is further supported by the common use of the word in the LXX[47] and by the definite article in 1:4, which makes clear that, whatever it might mean, the mention of ἄγγελοι is not a "brand-new entity" that initiates a new topic but relates instead to an earlier reference in the text.[48] In other words, τῶν ἀγγέλων in 1:4 means "the *previously referred to* ἀγγέλων." For these reasons, ἄγγελος will be translated hereafter as "messenger" not "angel," even when a heavenly referent is clearly on view (as, for instance, in 2:16).[49]

Second, the parallelism between 1:1-2 and 1:3c-4 (and especially the distinctive repetition of the noun κληρονόμος / κληρονομέω) also makes clear that the unspecified inherited "name" (ὄνομα) of 1:4 is that of "Son" (υἱός, 1:2).[50] As Ebert observes, "it is only in these two extremes of the structure that the Son is explicitly mentioned"[51] and the subsequent context (v. 5) also speaks for this identification: The γὰρ of 1:5 marks τίνι γὰρ εἶπεν ποτε as support material which provides the evidential basis for the claim of 1:4. In other words, *because* the Father calls the Son "Son" in Psalm 2, the author is able to draw the inference regarding the distinctive superiority of his name relative to that of all other messengers.

A potential objection to this interpretation is raised by Ellingworth, who claims that since "sonship is spoken of as a permanent attribute of Christ," it cannot function as "a title which is given or acquired at the time of his exaltation" as would be required.[52] However, Guthrie points out that "it seems clear from the Dead Sea Scrolls that the concept of the Messiah as God's Son was an aspect of Jewish thinking even prior to the

---

47. For just a few of the many unambiguous references to human (i.e. non-supernatural) ἄγγελοι in the LXX, see Num 20:14; Josh 7:22; Judg 6:35; 7:24; 9:31; 11:12, 13, 14, 17, 19; 1 Sam 11:3, 4, 7, 9 (x2); 16:9; 19:11, 14, 16, 20 (x2), 21; 23:27; 25:14.

48. Westfall, *Discourse Analysis*, 91.

49. The difficulty in translating ἄγγελος relates to the fact that in modern English, unlike Biblical Greek, an "angel" does not normally refer to a human being, while the word "messenger" does not typically carry with it connotations of a divine being. As Guthrie, "New Testament Exegesis," 593, recognizes, they function as "a reference point from which to magnify both the exaltation and incarnation of the Son."

50. *Pace* Mackie, "Confession," 116; Michel, *Der Brief an die Hebräer*, 105; Attridge, *Hebrews*, 47; Vanhoye, *Structure*, 189; and Meier, "Structure," 187, and "Symmetry," 522. *Contra* Johnson, *Hebrews*, 73, who argues for a more general understanding of κύριος; Guthrie, "Hebrews' Use of the Old Testament," 274, and Heil, *Chiastic Structure*, 33.

51. Ebert, "Chiastic Structure," 174.

52. Ellingworth, *Hebrews*, 105. Cf. Meier, "Structure," 187.

Christian era."⁵³ He also notes that within early Christian literature, "the title itself, as used by other characters in the divine drama, is often closely associated with the title "Christ" (i.e., Messiah; see Matt. 16:16; 26:63; Mark 8:29; Luke 4:41; John 11:27; 20:31)" and that both "Psalm 2:7 and 2 Sam 7:14 had been adopted in earliest Christianity as pointing to the enthronement of Messiah."⁵⁴

Thus Hebrews teaches in 1:1-4 that "God the Son" (a permanent ontological reality) *has become even greater than he was already* by being named "the Son of God" (i.e. the Christ/ King) in fulfilment of Psalm 2:7 (cf. Rom 1:4) following his work of atonement.

Third, given its connection with πολυμερῶς καὶ πολυτρόπως in 1:1, it seems best to render διαφορώτερον (1:4) as "more outstanding"⁵⁵ or even "to be distinguished from"⁵⁶ rather than "greater" in this context, so as to make clear the *distinctiveness* of Jesus' "name" as Son as well as its relative superiority to the "name" of the messengers/prophets.

Turning attention now to a consideration of prominence, the repeated references to the Son throughout 1:1-4,⁵⁷ together with the emphasis on his role as God's ultimate agent of revelation at both the center (D) and extremes (A/A') of the unit suggests the relative importance of this material.⁵⁸ On the other hand, the absence of any obvious parallels suggests that the recipients of God's address (to the fathers, to us) and the clause καθαρισμὸν τῶν ἁμαρτιῶν ποιησάμενος (1:3) are less prominent here. This raises questions about what such material is "doing" in the text at this point, which will be addressed in a subsequent chapter (see 5.3.5). The unit may be translated as follows:

> A. ¹:¹ While God spoke long ago in many ways and places to the Fathers by the Prophets, ² in the last of these days, he has spoken to us by the Son,
>
> B. whom he appointed as the heir of all,

---

53. Guthrie, *Hebrews*, 68, notes that in 4Q Florilegium, 2 Samuel 7:14 is given explicit messianic application.

54. Guthrie, *Hebrews*, 68.

55. Ellingworth, *Hebrews*, 105.

56. Johnson, *Hebrews*, 74.

57. Cf. the following: υἱῷ ὃν ... δι' οὗ ... ὃς ὢν ... φέρων ... τῆς δυνάμεως αὐτοῦ καθαρισμὸν ... ποιησάμενος ἐκάθισεν ... τοσούτῳ κρείττων γενόμενος.

58. Ebert, "Chiastic Structure," 177, 167, quotes Radday, *Chiasmus in Antiquity*, 51, who claims that Biblical authors "placed the main idea, the thesis, or the turning point of each literary unit at its center."

C. through whom he also made the universe.

   D. ³ He being the image of the Glory.

   D'. And the exact imprint of his substance.

   C'. And bearing all things by the word of his power,

   B'. having made atonement for sins, he sat down at the right hand of the Majesty in the Heavens,

A'. ⁴ having become greater than the messengers by as much as the name he has inherited stands out from theirs.

g. *Summary of Findings*

In addition to itemizing occurrences of repetition noted by previous scholarship, our analysis of repetition patterns in 1:1–4 represents fresh evidence which:

a. identifies a number of previously unobserved significant connections within this part of text (πᾶς in 1:2 and 3; τοῦς αἰῶνας (1:2); πάντων (1:2) and τὰ πάντα (1:3); τῆς δόξης and τῆς μεγαλωσύνης (1:3); ὁ θεός (1:1) and τῆς μεγαλωσύνης ἐν ὑψηλοῖς (1:3); πολθμερῶς καὶ πολυτρόπως (1:1) and διαφορώτερον (1:4);

b. demonstrates that repetition serves an important structural function in this context by uniting the text into a unit comprised of a series of balanced parallel phrases;

c. confirms previous presentations of Hebrews 1:1–4 as a concentric semantic unit;

d. clarifies with greater precision the coherent topical relationship between its component parts, showing:

- the significance of 1:1–2b, namely, that by revealing himself through the Son and heir, God has now spoken in a different and far more significant way than ever before;

- that verses 2b and 3d represent parallel descriptions of the same event, the Son's enthronement in fulfilment of Psalm 110:1, which serve to emphasize his exalted status above the ἄγγελοι.

- that 1:2c and 1:3c (C and C') and 1:3a and b (D and D') serve to summarize the Son's activity with regard to the universe and to emphasize the unity (and distinction) he shares with his Father respectively.

e. identifies οἱ ἄγγελοι (1:4) as an instantial equivalent of τοὺς προφήτας (1:2) in this context, and the title "Son" (υἱός) in 1:2 as the "name" (ὄνομα) of 1:4.

f. leads us to conclude that the Son's role as *God's final and supreme agent of revelation* represents the topic of 1:1–4.

4.2.2 Hebrews 1:3–6

a. Introduction

Scholars have identified three main problems in Hebrews 1:3–6 which relate to (i) the determination of opening (and closing) boundaries for the unit which follows 1:1–4, (ii) the precise location of its source material, and (iii) the meaning and significance of the cryptic verse 6a, both in its parts (πάλιν, εἰσαγάγῃ, τὸν πρωτότοκον, εἰς and τὴν οἰκοθμένην)[59] and as a whole.[60] The identification of an intratextual link cluster at Hebrews 1:3–6 represents fresh evidence which, together with an examination of several inter-textual clusters between Hebrews 1:6 and various LXX texts, sheds new light on each of these problems and the meaning of the unit as a whole.

b. Significant repetition previously observed in Hebrews 1:3–6

Leaving aside any potential connections within 1:3c–4 for similar reasons to those mentioned in our analysis of 1:1–5 (see 4.2.1a), the second intratextual link cluster in Hebrews occurs between 1:3–6. Significant repetition previously observed includes the following syntactically equivalent or nearly related phrases:

---

59. As many have noted, the verse contains unusual language: εἰσαγάγῃ occurs only once in the NT, while πρωτότοκον and τὴν οἰκουμένην occur three (1:6; 11:28; 12:23) and two (1:6 and 2:5) times respectively in Hebrews.

60. The comment by O'Brien, *Hebrews*, 68, that the first part of the verse "is rather ambiguous in meaning" reflects the general consensus of opinion at this point.

a. As several have noted,[61] the first part of the quotation of 2 Samuel 7:14/1 Chronicles 17:13 and the second part of the quotation from Psalm 2:7 express exactly the same content with differences accounted for by tense (present as opposed to future) and person (i.e. 2nd as opposed to 3rd person). This relationship may be seen clearly in the table below (in which word order has been altered to highlight the parallels):

Heb 1:5a	What God says *to* the Son	σύ	εἶ	υἱός μου
Heb 1:5d	What God says *about* the Son	καὶ αὐτὸς	ἔσται	μοι εἰς υἱόν

b. In similar fashion, the second part of the same quotation from 2 Samuel 7:14/1 Chronicles 17:13 in 1:5a mirrors the first part of the quotation from Psalm 2:7 in 1:5d.[62] The difference relates to emphasis: where Psalm 2 stresses the beginning of this new relationship between the Father and the Son by means of the emphatic perfect tense ("I have given birth to you"), 2 Samuel 7:14/1 Chronicles 17:13 makes clear its ongoing implications ("I will be a Father to him"):

Heb 1:5a	What God says *to* the Son	ἐγώ	σήμερον γεγέννηκά	σε
Heb 1:5d	What God says *about* the Son	ἐγώ	ἔσομαι εἰς ... πατέρα	αὐτῷ

c. Ellingworth notes a further connection between the statement ἐκάθισεν ... κεκληρονόμηκεν ὄνομα (1:3-4) and the (near) quotation from the LXX in Hebrews 1:6 προσκυνησάτωσαν αὐτῷ πάντες ἄγγελοι θεοῦ which he suggests effectively "subordinates the angels to Christ."[63]

---

61. Cf. Vanhoye, *La Structure*, 70; Westfall, *Discourse Analysis*, 54; Ellingworth, *Hebrews*, 113; and Heil, *Chiastic Structures*, 37.

62. Ellingworth, *Hebrews*, 113; and Heil, *Chiastic Structures*, 37.

63. Ellingworth, *Hebrews*, 116. Cf. Guthrie, *Hebrews*, 69, who similarly observes that 1:6 implies the angels' "subordination to the Son"; and Johnson, *Hebrews*, 78, who states that whether Psalm 96:1 or Deuteronomy 32:43 stand behind the quotation of verse 6, "either passage would suggest to the hearers of Hebrews multiple links to the enthronement of the Son at the right hand of the majesty on High (Heb 1:3)."

d. Scholars have also drawn attention to a number of intertextual connections between Hebrews 1:6a and various LXX texts. Following Andriessen, most read Hebrews 1:6a as an echo of Deuteronomy 6:10/11:29, which speaks of Israel"s entrance into the promised land (see below), in light of the formal verbal similarities between these texts:[64]

Heb 1:6 ὅταν δὲ πάλιν εἰσαγάγῃ τὸν πρωτότοκον εἰς τὴν οἰκουμένην
"and when again he leads up the firstborn into the world"

Deut 6:10/11:29 καὶ ἔσται ὅταν εἰσαγάγῃ σε κύριος ὁ θεός σου εἰς την γῆν
"and when he the Lord your God will lead you up into the land"

Others have detected a second allusion to Psalm (LXX) 88:28 in the reference to Jesus as τὸν πρωτόκον ("the firstborn") within the same verse.[65] While Andriessen dismisses this proposal as unnecessary,[66] the clear thematic resonance between this Psalm and the immediate context of Hebrews (and therefore Psalm 2, 2 Samuel 7 and Psalm 110) argues in its favor: In its original context, ὁ πρωτόκος describes the prophesied Davidic king, who would be lifted up *beyond* all the rulers of the earth and whose righteous throne would be established forever. Further support for this connection may also be seen in the remarkable collocation between the language used in Hebrews 1 (and 1:6 in particular) and the earlier messianic prophecy. Significant words common to both include:

- ὁ πρωτόκος ("the firstborn," Ps [LXX] 88:28; Heb 1:6), which occurs only in this context within the LXX in reference to a prophesied messianic figure;[67]
- οἰκοθμένη ("world," Ps [LXX] 88:12; Heb 1:6);

---

64. Andriessen, "La teneur," 295–97. Cf. Lane, *Hebrews 1–8*, n.p.; and Heil, *Chiastic Structures*, 39.

65. Lane, *Hebrews 1–8*, n.p. and Attridge, *Hebrews*, 56.

66. Andriessen, "La teneur," 295–97, claims that the replacement of σε with τὸν πρωτόκον simply reflects the tradition that Israel is Yahweh's firstborn son (cf. Exod 4:22), such that the component parts of Hebrews 1:6 may all be found in Deuteronomy.

67. The word πρωτόκος is frequently used in the LXX (130 times), mostly in genealogies and historical narratives. In the New Testament, the word always refers in the singular to Jesus Christ (Col 1:15, 18; Rom 8:29; Rev 1:5). Cf. Meier, "Structure," 510.

- ἔλαιον ("oil," Ps [LXX] 88:21; 44:8; Heb 1:9);

- ὑψηλός ("high," Ps [LXX] 88:28; cf. its verbal cognate ὑψόω ("I exalt"), Ps [LXX] 88:14, 17, 18, 20, 25, 43; Heb 1:3);

- αἰών ("age," Ps [LXX] 88:2,3,5, 29, 30 [x2], 37, 38, 53; Heb 1:2, 8 [x2]);

- δικαιοσύνη ("righteousness," Ps [LXX] 88:15, 17; Heb 1:9 [Ps 44:8];

- ὄνομα ("name," Ps [LXX] 88:13, 17, 25; Heb 1:4);

- σωτηρία ("salvation," Ps [LXX] 88:27; Heb 1:14);

- υἱός ("son," Ps [LXX] 88:7, 23, 31, 48; Heb 1:2, 5 [x2], 8);

- χρίω ("I annoint," Ps [LXX] 88:21; Hebrews 1:9); and

- τίθημι ("I appoint," Ps [LXX] 88:20, 26, 28, 30; Heb 1:2, 13; Ps 110:1.

More broadly, like Psalm (LXX) 88, Hebrews 1 describes this "firstborn" as an individual who (a) has been anointed by God with "oil" (ἔλαιον, Ps [LXX] 88:21; Heb 1:9), (b) relates to God as his Father (πατηρ μου, Ps [LXX] 88:27; Heb 1:5), (c) possesses an eternal and righteous "throne" (θρόνος, "throne," Ps [LXX] 88:5, 15, 30, 37, 45; Hebrews 1:8 [Ps (LXX) 44:7]), and (d) has been exalted over all others (Ps [LXX] 88:28; Heb 1:9 [Ps 44:8]). Taken together, these formal and topical connections strongly suggest that Hebrews 1:6a should be understood in light *not only* of Deuteronomy 6:10/11:29 but also Psalm (LXX) 88.

e. Finally, most recognize Hebrews 1:6b as a composite of two LXX quotations, Psalm 96:7 and Deuteronomy 32:43 which also corresponds exactly with text from Odes 2:43 (see below with differences highlighted in bold):[68]

---

68. Cf. Kistemaker, "Psalm Citations," 22–23; Gheorghita, *The Role of the Septuagint in Hebrews*, 40–43; and Bateman, *Early Jewish Hermeneutics*, 142–44. Kistemaker claims that the "obvious conclusion" to be drawn from the correspondence between Hebrews and the book of Odes is that "the quotation has been part of the Hymn of Moses (Odes), which was securely incorporated in the liturgy of the Church," 22–23. Cf. Moffatt, *Hebrews*, 11. Against this, however, Gheorghita (p. 42) suggests that "considerations of origins, availability and probable Christian editing of this hymn-compilation make one hesitant to decide in its favour."

Heb 1:6b	καὶ προσκυνησάτωσαν αὐτῷ πάντες ἄγγελοι θεοῦ
	"and let all the messengers of God worship him"
Odes 2:43	καὶ προσκυνησάτωσαν αὐτῷ πάντες ἄγγελοι θεοῦ
	"and let all the messengers of God worship him"
Ps 96:7	**προσκυνήσατε** αὐτῷ πάντες οἱ ἄγγελοι **αὐτοῦ**
	"Worship him all his messengers!"
Deut 32:43	καὶ προσκυνησάτωσαν αὐτῷ πάντες **υἱοὶ θεοῦ**
	"and let all the sons of God worship him"

c. *Potentially significant repetition previously unobserved in Hebrews 1:3–6*

In addition to the repetition described above, there are at least six further significant lexical links in 1:3–6 between:

- ἄγγελοι (1:4, 5, 6);
- εἶπεν / λέγει (1:5 and 6);[69]
- υἱός / υἱόν (1:5 x2);
- μου /μοι (1:5 x2);
- εἶ / ἔσομαι, ἔσται all in reference to the Son (1:5 x2); and ἐγώ / ἐγώ (1:5 x2).[70]

Further connections include:

- the relationship of field existing between the relatively uncommon (in this text) γεγέννηκα ("begotten," 1:5) and τὸν πρωτότοκον ("first-born," 1:6),[71] both of which are also linked to the references to υἱός; and
- the same connection seen in the first unit between τῆς μεγαλωσύνης ἐν ὑψηλοῖς (1:3) and θεοῦ (1:6), now in reverse order.

69. The speaker is the same in each case as is the object of his address (the Son, who is first addressed directly (συ ... σε) and then indirectly (αὐτῷ ... αὐτός).

70. ἐγώ is used only seven times in Hebrews, always in reference to God's self address.

71. γεγέννηκα occurs on 3 other occasions in Hebrews while Ellingworth, *Hebrews*, 117, notes that πρωτότοκον appears twice more (11:18; 12:23) yet "is not applied elsewhere to Christ."

There is also an example of what Hoey terms "hidden parallelism" between the clause τίνι . . . εἶπέν ποτε τῶν ἀγγέλων (1:5a) and the word πάλιν (1:5b), with the second term replacing, and functioning as an exact equivalent of, the earlier phrase.[72] When what is implied is made explicit (see diagram below), the context makes clear that both quotations in verse 5 function as part of a pair of rhetorical questions[73] which support the author's thesis regarding the Son's greatness by together asserting that *"there is no angel to whom God has said . . . !"*[74]

Heb 1:5a	γὰρ τίνι εἶπέν ποτε τῶν ἀγγέλων	υἱός μου εἶ σύ
	"for to which of the messengers has he ever said"	'you are my son'
Heb 1:5b	καὶ [τίνι εἶπέν ποτε τῶν ἀγγέλων]	ἐγὼ ἔσομαι αὐτῷ εἰς πατέρα
	"and [to which of the messengers has he ever said]"	'I will be a father to him'

The picture which emerges clearly shows that, like 1:1–4, 1:3–6 contains significant repetition. It now remains for us to examine the location of repetition within this cluster for evidence of a combined structural function.

d. The location and formal function of repetition in Hebrews 1:3–6

Once again, the location of repetition in this portion of the text is unusual. The overwhelming majority of connections occur on one side or other of a midpoint located in 1:5, splitting the cluster into two broadly balanced halves (see below). The first half contains 36 words, the second, 29.

^{1:3d} καθαρισμὸν τῶν ἁμαρτιῶν ποιησάμενος <u>ἐκάθισεν ἐν δεξιᾷ τῆς μεγαλωσύνης ἐν ὑψηλοῖς</u> ⁴ <u>τοσούτῳ κρείττων γενόμενος τῶν ἀγγέλων</u> ὅσῳ διαφορώτερον παρ' αὐτοὺς κεκληρονόμηκεν ὄνομα

---

72. Hidden parallelism involves "words or phrases necessarily implied by the text" which "must be inferred by the reader if he or she is to make any sense of what is being read." Hoey, *Patterns*, 104.

73. In context, καί functions here to introduce the second rhetorical question which relates back to the conjunction, γάρ, in 1:5a.

74. Cf. Guthrie, *Hebrews*, 68; and Beekman and Callow, *Translating the Word of God*, 229–48.

⁵ τίνι γὰρ εἶπέν ποτε τῶν ἀγγέλων <u>υἱός μου εἶ σύ ἐγὼ σήμερον γεγέννηκά σε</u>

καὶ πάλιν <u>ἐγὼ ἔσομαι αὐτῷ εἰς πατέρα καὶ αὐτὸς ἔσται μοι εἰς υἱόν</u>
⁶ ὅταν δὲ πάλιν εἰσαγάγῃ τὸν πρωτότοκον εἰς τὴν οἰκουμένην λέγει καὶ <u>προσκυνησάτωσαν αὐτῷ πάντες ἄγγελοι θεοῦ</u>

More than this, however, there is again clear evidence here that particular words, phrases and clauses have been carefully selected and located by the author within his text so as to group together related material into a series of balanced parallel phrases. Words such as υἱός, ἐγώ, and μου/μοι (each of which occur twice in 1:5) do not seem to function in this context as "catchwords," which join together separate units of discourse,[75] but serve instead, together with other types of repetition, to mark out parallel clauses *within* this material, thereby revealing Hebrews 1:3-6 as a single, tightly bound and symmetrical unit which overlaps with the previous unit, 1:1-4 (see below).[76]

A. ³ᵈ καθαρισμὸν τῶν ἁμαρτιῶν ποιησάμενος <u>ἐκάθισεν ἐν δεξιᾷ τῆς μεγαλωσύνης ἐν ὑψηλοῖς</u> ⁴ <u>τοσούτῳ κρείττων γενόμενος τῶν ἀγγέλων</u> ὅσῳ διαφορώτερον παρ' αὐτοὺς κεκληρονόμηκεν ὄνομα

B. ⁵ τίνι γὰρ εἶπέν ποτε τῶν ἀγγέλων <u>υἱός μου εἶ σύ ἐγὼ σήμερον γεγέννηκά σε</u>

B'. καὶ πάλιν <u>ἐγὼ ἔσομαι αὐτῷ εἰς πατέρα, καὶ αὐτὸς ἔσται μοι εἰς υἱόν</u>

A'. ⁶ ὅταν δὲ πάλιν εἰσαγάγῃ τὸν πρωτότοκον εἰς τὴν οἰκουμένην λέγει καὶ <u>προσκυνησάτωσαν αὐτῷ πάντες ἄγγελοι θεοῦ</u>

75. Guthrie, *Hebrews*, 67.

76. Noting their semantic and conceptual similarity, Lane, *Hebrews 1-8*, n.p., and Heil, *Chiastic Structures*, 37, propose that the two quotations in 1:5 have been arranged so as to form a chiasm (A B B' A'). See Lane's version below, to which Heil adds a third element, C, "and again"):

A You are my Son;
   B today I have become your Father.
   B´ I will be his Father,
A´ and he will be my Son.

However, while the clauses are semantically similar, both these representations give insufficient weight to the presence in the text of the hidden parallelism involving καὶ πάλιν, which both interrupts the symmetry and suggests the likelihood of a stronger connection between 1:5a and 1:5b as a whole.

The suggestion that 1:3-6 forms a literary unit is certainly novel, with most scholars understanding 1:5-14 as the second unit of the text[77] based on (i) its location following 1:1-4, (ii) perceived similarities between the form and content of the LXX citations within this material,[78] (iii) the "inclusion" between 1:5 and 1:13,[79] and (iv) Vanhoye's observation that 1:5 contains "new" material which directs the course of the discourse from here (e.g., "the name").[80]

Against the conventional view (and in favor of our suggestion above), however, the following points can be made. First, as Westfall acknowledges, the common division of 1:1-2:4 into three unrelated units (1:1-4, 1:5-14 and 2:1-4) "has historically presented a puzzle in coherence, cohesion and the role of prominence."[81] Specifically, there is a "perception that 1:5-14 (or 1:4-15) does not logically flow from the first four verses" as would be required by the γάρ of 1:5.[82] Second, while the evidence of a connection between 1:5 and 1:13 is undeniably strong, the connection between τίνι . . . εἶπέν ποτε τῶν ἀγγέλων (1:5a) and the word πάλιν (1:5b), which is further supported by the close topical correspondence between Psalm 2:7 and 2 Samuel 7:14/1 Chronicles 17:13 (cf. previous discussion in 4.2.2b), *seems at least as strong*. Indeed, this study will demonstrate that *both* these connections play important structuring roles at different levels of the discourse.[83] Third, from a topical perspective, although 1:5 contains new material as Vanhoye suggests, on closer inspection, this material clearly begins

---

77. Westfall, *Discourse Analysis*, 89, 91; Guthrie, *Hebrews*, 45 and *Structure*, 144; Vanhoye, *Structure*, 80-81; Rhee, *Faith*, 67; Johnson, *Hebrews*, 81; Ellingworth, *Hebrews*, 109, 120; and Heil, *Chiastic Structures*, 36.

78. Following Meier, "Structure," 169, Westfall, *Discourse Analysis*, 91, notes that within her second sub-unit, 1:5-14, "the seven Old Testament projections/quotations form a close set of parallel relationships, not only because of the stylistic similarity of the quotations and their relationship to 1:1-4, but also through the similarity of the formulaic repetition of the process in the main discourse that joins them together."

79. Guthrie, *Structure*, 77, reads 1:5 and 1:13 as head and tail members of an inclusion based on the "close approximation of the same question" in both verses and their quotation of a Psalm (Ps 2:7 and Ps 100:1 respectively). Cf. Ellingworth, *Hebrews*, 108.

80. Vanhoye, *Structure*, 23-24, sees 1:5 as the beginning of two units at different levels of discourse, 1:5-2:18 and 1:5-14.

81. Westfall, *Discourse Analysis*, 89.

82. Westfall, *Discourse Analysis*, 89.

83. Cf. 5.3.2 and the further connections proposed between 1:7 and 13 (in 4.2.3) and 1:13 and 2:5 (in 4.2.4).

before verse 5, as many have acknowledged.[84] Guthrie, for example, observes that while "structurally" related to 1:1-4, the semantic content of verses 3-4 "also points ahead to the main theme of the next section on the Son's superiority to the angels."[85]

For these reasons, it is proposed that 1:3d-4 serves at least two roles in this text, functioning both as part of the conclusion to 1:1-4 and the introduction to 1:3-6.[86]

e. The topical function of repetition in Hebrews 1:3-6

Turning to topic, as with the previous unit (1:1-4), the formal parallels identified in 4.2.2c display a considerable degree of coherence when read together.

While the overlap in meaning between the statements in 1:5 (B and B') has been widely recognized,[87] few have observed the coherence which also exists between 1:3-4 and 1:6 (A and A' in our arrangement).[88] Both represent sentences which (a) emphasize the relative *greatness* of (b) the Son in comparison to (c) τῶν ἀγγέλων, and which (d) rest upon God's speech as recorded in various messianic Psalms. In the first, this greatness is presented as proportional to the extent to which the Son's "name," revealed subsequently as υἱός in 1:5 (Ps 2:7), surpasses theirs. In the second, it is seen in the command to worship given to the messengers in Ps 96:7 (LXX) and Deut 32:43. Furthermore, in both cases (e), this relative greatness is depicted not as timeless reality but as having begun at a particular moment in association with a *particular event*. In 1:3-4, the Son "became greater" when he sat down, "having made atonement for sins" (καθαρισμὸν τῶν ἁμαρτιῶν ποιησάμενος). The relationship

---

84. Westfall, *Discourse Analysis*, 89, notes a significant minority including Delitzsch, Nida, Hughes, and Strobel, who argue for a unit division following 1:3 on the basis of strong cohesive ties with what follows. Cf. Johnson, *Hebrews*, 72; Ellingworth, *Hebrews*, 53; and Lane, *Hebrews 1-8*, n.p.

85. Guthrie, *Structure*, 102.

86. Since the phrase καθαρισμὸν τῶν ἁμαρτιῶν ποιησάμενος most naturally attaches to the main verb ἐκάθισεν in 1:3, it is likely that this represents the start of the unit.

87. Meier, "Symmetry," 506, claims "it is difficult to see what 2 Sam 7:14 really contributes to the argument except a deft inclusion," while Lane, *Hebrews 1-8*, n.p., notes, "The first and last lines concern sonship and frame the second and third lines, which speak of paternity." Cf. Ellingworth, *Hebrews*, 113.

88. Ellingworth's comments on the relationship between the Son's heavenly session and the quotation of 1:6 (cf. 4.2.2ac) represent a notable exception.

between the aorist participle and the main verb ἐκάθισεν establishes that the acts of purifying and sitting were temporally sequential ("*after* he had made purification he sat down").[89] Similarly, the exaltation of the Son in 1:6, which begins with the Father's call to worship, occurs "when" or "after" (ὅταν) the entry of the firstborn into the (heavenly) world (πάλιν εἰσαγάγῃ τὸν πρωτόκον εἰς τὴν οἰκοθμένην).

In light of these many formal and topical connections (above), it is likely that 1:3-4 and 1:6 both describe essentially the *same event* from two different perspectives.

The first half of the unit (1:3c-5a) comprises an assertion (A) accompanied by evidence (B) which makes the four-step claim that:

1. having made atonement for sins,

2. Jesus sat down, having become greater than the other messengers

3. *by as much as* his name is greater than theirs

4. *for* (γάρ) God only speaks to one person as Son in Psalm 2:7.

While Jesus' claim to greatness is primarily based on the Father's testimony in 1:5, as noted earlier (see 4.2.1e), the fact that mention of this greatness is also grammatically linked to the Son's atoning work of 1:3 suggests that the participle expresses more than a temporal relationship at this point. In this sense, not only did Jesus become greater than the messengers *after* he made atonement for sins, he became greater, in part at least, *because of* this completed atoning work (cf. Isa 53:10-12; Phil 2:6-11). 1:5b-6, meanwhile, covers much the same ground again in reverse order. It begins by asking virtually the identical question in 1:5b as in 1:5a (B') before once more affirming the Son's superiority over the messengers in 1:6 (A').[90]

There is thus clear and demonstrable evidence of coherence both between the two halves of this unit and between the formally parallel clauses within it (A / A', B / B') which, when read together, emphasizes the Son's incomparable superiority over the messengers.

---

89. Lane, *Hebrews 1-8*, n.p.; so too Meier, "Structure," 185.
90. Cf. following discussion on the meaning of this ambiguous verse in 4.2.2e.

f.   Further implications for meaning in light of the parallelism within Hebrews 1:3–6

As with the previous chapter, the discovery of parallelism within 1:3–6 (established through both intratextual and intertextual link clusters) is also of considerable significance in identifying a number of "instantial equivalents" in this context and thereby further clarifying its meaning.

First, in view of the evident parallelism between A and A' and its clear links to the LXX (Deuteronomy 6:10/11:29 and Psalm 88:27), the ambiguous ὅταν δὲ πάλιν εἰσαγάγῃ τὸν πρωτότοκον εἰς τὴν οἰκουμένην (1:6a) is best understood *not* as a reference to Jesus' incarnation (i.e. ἡ οἰκουμένη = the world) but as a *further description of his enthronement* described in Hebrews 1:3b–4 from a different perspective. In this sense, πάλιν in 1:6 functions not as a reference to the "re-introduction" of the Son into the world, as some have argued,[91] but as clarification that 1:6a represents a return to an earlier topic. In other words, having already spoken of the Son's exaltation in 1:4, the author speaks "again" (πάλιν) of this moment as the time when God led his Son, "the Firstborn" (ὁ πρωτότοκος), into "the heavenly world of eschatological salvation" (ἡ οἰκοθμένη, cf. 2:5)[92] to be worshipped and glorified by the "οἱ ἄγγελοι."

When read together in this way, 1:3d and 1:6a thus make clear that the Son's exaltation occurred *after* his having made atonement for sins on the cross when he was led as the Firstborn into the heavenly land. For *at that moment*, the Father named Jesus as the Son, the prophecies of Psalms 110:1, 2:7, 88:28 and 2 Samuel 7:14/1 Chronicles 17:13 were fulfilled, and Jesus *became greater* than all other messengers.

Second, the echo of Deuteronomy 6:10/11:29 in verse 6a also strongly suggests the beginning of a typological relationship between Jesus' entry into Heaven as "my Son" (υἱός μου, cf. Heb 1:5/Ps 2:7), "the firstborn" (ὁ πρωτότοκος, Heb 1:6) and the entry of "my firstborn son Israel" (cf. υἱὸς πρωτότοκός μου Ισραηλ, Ex 4:22) into the land of Canaan. Though faint at this stage, this connection is expanded further in 2:10 and 12:2 by the description of Jesus as a "pioneer leader" (ἀρχηγός, 2:10) like Moses, and by the discussion of rest in chapters 3 and 4.

---

91. Cf. Michel, *Der Brief*, 113; Andriessen, "La teneur," 296–97, 299–300; Vanhoye, *Structure*, 80.

92. Lane, *Hebrews 1–8*, n.p. Cf. Caneday, "The Eschatological World," 28; Guthrie, *Hebrews*, 66, and "Hebrews," 927; and Johnson, *Hebrews*, 79, who translates οἰκουμένη as "the realm of the divine presence."

Third, by bringing together Psalm (LXX) 96:7 and Deuteronomy 32:43 in 1:6b, the author makes clear that the ἄγγελοι of 1:4 and 6 should be understood as equivalent to the υἱοὶ θεοῦ ("sons of God") in this context, referring more precisely to heavenly messengers (i.e. angels) than in the previous context.[93]

The key words and phrases, as revealed by repetition, relate to the Son's identity as Son/firstborn, his relative greatness in comparison with the messengers and the speech of God. The main point of the unit is that, having sat down at God's right hand, Jesus has *become far greater* than all God's messengers.[94] For out of all the myriads of ἄγγελοι/υἱοὶ θεοῦ, God has only ever addressed Jesus as "my son" (υἱός μου)/the "firstborn" (ὁ πρωτότοκος) when he sat down at his right hand, having completed his work of atonement.

The unit can be translated as follows:

- A. ^{1:3c} Having made atonement for sins, he is seated at the right hand of the Majesty in the Heights, ⁴ having become as much greater than the messengers as the name he has inherited stands out from theirs.

- B. ⁵ For to which of the messengers did he ever say "you are my Son, today I have begotten you"?

- B'. And again: "I will be to him as a father, and he will be to me as Son."

- A'. ⁶ And again, when he leads up the Firstborn into the Heavenly world, he says: "Let even all the messengers of God worship him" (1:5-6).

g. Summary

In addition to itemizing occurrences of significant repetition noted by previous scholarship, this analysis of repetition patterns in 1:3-6:

a. identifies a number of significant yet previously unobserved connections within this part of the text (ἄγγελοι (1:4, 5, 6); εἶπεν / λέγει (1:5, 6); υἱός / υἱόν (1:5, 6); μου / μοι (1:5, 6); μου / μοιεῖ / ἔσομαι,

---

93. The clear heavenly context in both 1:3-4 and 1:6 lends further support to this reading.

94. Note the occurrence of three "great" words in the immediate context (τῆς μεγαλωσύνης; κρείττων; διαφορώτερον, 1:3-4).

ἔσται (1:5); ἐγώ (1:5, 6); γεγήννκα (1:5), τὸν πρωτόκον (1:6) and υἱός (1:5); τῆς μεγαλωσύνης ἐν ὑψηλοῖς (1:4) and θεοῦ (1:6); and τίνι ... εἶπέν ποτε τῶν ἀγγέλων (1:5a) and πάλιν (1:5b);

b. strengthens with fresh formal evidence the suggestion that Psalm (LXX) 88:28 (as well as Deuteronomy 6:10/11:29) lies behind Hebrews 1:6;

c. reveals that 1:3–6 contains far more intertextual connections than are commonly acknowledged, which play a significant role in determining its meaning;

d. demonstrates that repetition also serves an important structural function in this context by marking out 1:3–6 as a concentric and coherent textual unit consisting of four parts, each of which rests upon distinct messianic testimonies ([LXX] Pss 110:1; 2:7; 88:28; and 2 Sam 7:14/1 Chr 17:13);

e. clarifies with greater precision the coherent topical relationship between its component parts, showing:

- that both 1:3–4 and 1:6 (A and A') emphasize the relative *greatness* of the Son in comparison to "οἱ ἄγγελοι";
- that in each case, this claim to greatness is based upon the Father's having spoken to/about the Son by the name "Son" (υἱός, 1:5);

f. identifies the ambiguous 1:6 as a parallel account of the Son's exaltation recorded in 1:3–4 which describes "again" (πάλιν) Jesus' entry into the "heavenly world" (οἰκουμένη) in fulfilment Psalm (LXX) 88:28 using language evocative of Israel's entry into the promised land;

g. concludes that the topic may best be understood as: Having sat down at God's right hand, Jesus, who bears the name "Son" (υἱός), *has become far greater* than all God's messengers.

4.2.3 Hebrews 1:7–14

a. Introduction

Following Meier, Hebrews 1:7–14 is most commonly read as a united "scriptural catena" of quotations (beginning at verse 5) assembled in support of the author's main point in 1:1–4.[95] In spite of this agreement, however, scholars have found difficulty in determining this unit's boundaries, explaining the author's choice and use of particular LXX texts and their meaning within their new context, and accounting for the seemingly deliberate alterations to these texts from their original context. Specifically, scholars have failed to account with precision for:

1. the meaning of the quotation from Psalm 103:4 (LXX) in Hebrews 1:7;[96]
2. the extent and function of the quotation from Ps 44:7–8 (LXX) in Hebrews 1:8–9. While most read verses 8–9 as a series of affirmations regarding the divinity, eternity and Royal status of the Son,[97] this reading makes it "difficult to see why the writer extended the quotation of Ps 45:6 to include v 7";[98]
3. various alterations to the LXX versions of the Psalms quoted in Hebrews 1:7–14 (Pss 103:4, 44:7–8, and 101:26–28)[99] which are listed as follows:

    - Where Psalm 103:4 (LXX) speaks of a "flaming fire," πῦρ φλέγον, Hebrews refers to "flames of fire," πυρὸς φλόγα (the accusative πῦρ is replaced by the genitive πυρός, while the plural noun φλόγα replaces the singular participle φλέγον)(see below);[100]

---

95. Meier's two articles on the structure, form, and meaning of the first chapter of Hebrews ("Structure and Theology" and "Symmetry and Theology") have been particularly influential in shaping the scholarly understanding of this section of the text. Cf. Vanhoye, *Structure*, 80–81; Guthrie, *Hebrews*, 45, and *Structure*, 144; Rhee, *Faith*, 67; Westfall, *Discourse Analysis*, 89, 91; Johnson, *Hebrews*, 81; Ellingworth, *Hebrews*, 109, 120.
96. Cf. Ellingworth, *Hebrews*, 120; and Meier, "Structure," 511–12.
97. Cf. Johnson, *Hebrews*, 79; Guthrie, *Hebrews*, 70; Calvin, *Commentary*, 45–46.
98. Lane, *Hebrews 1–8*, n.p.
99. Meier, "Symmetry," 513, claims that "both the MT and the LXX forms of Ps 45:6–7 (vv. 7–8 in the MT; LXX Ps 44:7–8) bristle with problems of text and interpretation." Cf. Kistemaker, "Psalm Citations," 20–29; and Gheorghita, *The Role of the Septuagint in Hebrews*, 40–42.
100. Although Ellingworth, *Hebrews*, 121, rejects the suggestion that φλόγα be read as an accusative plural as "unnecessary and unconvincing," the modification (i) is clearly original; (ii) almost certainly deliberate (cf. Tönges, "The Epistle to the Hebrews as a 'Jesus-Midrash,'" 95); (iii) consistent with similar modifications of LXX texts throughout Hebrews 1–4 (e.g., 3:10, this generation); and (iv) allows for a reading which better reflects the concerns of Hebrews. Ellingworth's own theory—that the change is explained by the author's desire to be more "current"—seems unlikely given Hebrews' apparent lack of concern for this throughout the rest of the text where

- In place of ῥάβδος εὐθύτος ἡ ῥάβδος (Ps 44:7), Hebrews 1:8 reads καὶ ἡ ῥάβδος τῆς εὐθύτος ῥάβδος;[101]
- Hebrews 1:10–12 changes the word order and adds καί to the beginning of the quotation from Ps 101:26–28, replaces ἀλλάξεις with the closely related ἑλίξεις, and repeats the phrase ὡς ἱμάτιον in verse 12.

This section seeks to address these difficulties with fresh evidence arising from an investigation into repetition patterns within Hebrews 1:7–14.

b. Significant repetition previously observed in Hebrews 1:7–14

The third link cluster in Hebrews occurs between 1:7–14. Lexical connections noted by others in this section include the recurrence of the relatively infrequent terms, πνεύματα (1:7 and 14) and λειτουργούς/ λειτρουργικά (1:7 and 14) in close proximity to one another.[102]

More broadly:

a. Lane observes that verses 8–9 and 13 are linked together by a whole raft of terms, phrases and ideas which relate to expectations concerning the Messiah/Christ from the LXX;[103]

b. Guthrie identifies 1:14 as "the author's recapitulation of, and further comment" on his statement regarding "οἱ ἄγγελοι" in 1:7;[104] and

c. Meier detects a "general symmetry between the movement of thought" in the Christological designations of Hebrews 1:2b–4 and the seven LXX citations he finds in 1:5–14

---

original forms are often maintained, and he fails to account adequately for the meaning of the quotation within its new surroundings (p. 121).

101. Lane, *Hebrews 1–8*, n.p., dismisses theses differences as "minor details."

102. Vanhoye, *Structure*, 81, reads this pair of links as an inclusion. The word πνεῦμα appears in plural form on only four occasions in Hebrews (1:7; 1:14; 12:9; 12:23) out of a total of twelve occurences. Meanwhile λειτουργός appears as a noun on only one other occasion (8:2), while the adjective λειτοθργικός is a *hapax legomenon* in the NT. The related noun λειτουργία may also be found in 8:6; 9:21; and 10:11.

103. Lane, *Hebrews 1–8*, n.p., labels both Pss 44:7–8 and 110:1 as "messianic testimonies." These will be explored in more detail in 4.2.3b.

104. Guthrie, *Hebrews*, 69, and *Structure*, 144. This insight is neither developed nor reflected in Guthrie's structural outline.

(Exaltation—Creation—Pre-existence—Creation—Exaltation).[105] Although he also finds a thematic connection between 1:7 and 1:10-12 involving "creation,"[106] this connection seems questionable given that a different agent is on view in each case (God the Father / God the Son)[107] and that, as Guthrie recognizes, verse 7 may be better understood, in the light of verse 14, to make quite a different point.[108]

c. *Potentially significant repetition previously unobserved in Hebrews 1:7-14*

To the links noted above may be added many other examples of potentially significant repetition in this section which have gone largely unnoticed. Further lexical repetition includes:

- τοὺς ἀγγέλους . . . τοὺς ἀγγέλους / τῶν ἀγγέλων (1:7 and 13);
- λέγει / εἴρηκεν (1:7 and 13);
- πρός . . . πρός / πρός (1:7, 8, and 13);[109] and
- the phrase ὡς ἱμάτιον ("as a garment," 1:11, 12), the second occurrence of which appears to be a deliberate addition to the Psalm 101 citation (cf. Ps 101:27 LXX).

There is also a relationship of contrast between the references to Jesus' hands in 1:10 (τῶν χειρῶν σου, "your hands") and God's "right hand" (ἐκ

---

105. Meier, "Symmetry," 529, acknowledges that "the parallel is not a perfect one-to-one correspondence of each designation to the numerically equivalent citation; it is rather a general correspondence in the themes and movement of thought." See Westfall, *Discourse Analysis*, 91, who claims that "the seven Old Testament projections/quotations form a close set of parallel relationships, not only because of the stylistic similarity of the quotations and their relationship to 1:1-4, but also through the similarity of the formulaic repetition of the process in the main discourse that joins them together"; and Rhee, *Faith*, 69-70.

106. Meier, "Symmetry," 523.

107. See comments on vv. 10-12 in 4.2.4d.

108. Guthrie, *Hebrews*, 69, and *Structure*, 144. See further discussion on this in 4.2.4d.

109. Even though the preposition πρός serves as the building block of a parallel grammatical construction (see following), the fact that it is repeated in the later sentence qualifies it also as an instance of lexical repetition.

δεξιῶν μου, 1:13), and between both and Jesus' feet on the other (τῶν ποδῶν σου, 1:13).

More broadly, 1:7–14 contains a number of parallel or closely related phrases:

a. The grammatical construction of 1:7–8 is similar to that used in 1:13, featuring lexical repetition involving πρός, τοὺς ἀγγέλους, and τοὺς ἀγγέλους λέγει as well as agreement with regard to the agent and object of address.

> Heb 1:7–8 πρὸς μὲν τοὺς ἀγγέλους λέγει . . . πρὸς δὲ τὸν υἱόν
> "to the messengers he says on the one hand . . . but to the son"
>
> Heb 1:13 πρὸς τίνα δὲ τῶν ἀγγέλων εἴρηκέν ποτε
> "and to which of the messengers has he ever said"

This connection is further strengthened when the immediate context of verse 14, utilizing οὐχί as it does, is considered. The question, "are not they all" expects the readers to agree with the author's designation of the messengers as "ministering spirits" based on his earlier quotation in 1:7. Taken together, then, 1:7–8 represents a pair of statements about the messengers and the Son which correspond to a pair of rhetorical questions about the Son and the messengers in 1:13–14.[110] Interestingly, though the form of 1:13 is similar to 1:7, which describes the messengers, it functions together with 1:8–9 in context to make a statement *about the Son*: God has never said such things about the messengers (but he has about the Son).

1:7	statement about the messengers
1:8	statement to the Son
1:13	question about the Son
1:14	question about the messengers

b. God's "making" the messengers to be servants (ὁ ποιῶν τοὺς ἀγγέλους . . . λειτουργούς, 1:7) and his "sending" them out for service (εἰς

---

110. The μέν . . . δέ construction of 1:7–8 makes clear the close connection between the two (on the one hand . . . on the other hand), while the rhetorical question of 1:14 (which expects the answer, "yes") flows from the rhetorical question of 1:13 (which expects the answer, "none of them").

διακονίαν ἀποστελλόμενα, 1:14),[111] are also closely related. Against Buchanan's attempt to draw a sharp distinction between the types of service on view here, "it is possible to think of διακονίαν as merely reinforcing the synonym λειτουργικά, or preparing for its meaning to be developed in the rest of the sentence."[112]

c. In addition to their general thematic similarity, the quotations from Psalm 44:7-8 (LXX) and 110:1 in Hebrews 1:8-9 and 13 also share a number of specific points of connection as follows:

   i. The reference to the Son's "throne" (ὁ θρόνος σου, 1:8) relates to both the divine command to "sit at my right hand" (κάθου ἐκ δεξιῶν μου 1:13) and

   ii. to the "footstool under your feet" (ὑποπόδιον τῶν ποδῶν σου, 1:13) as part of a matched set;[113]

   iii. Both Psalm 44:7-8 (LXX)/Hebrews 1:8-9 and Psalm 110:1/Hebrews 1:13 employ related terminology, ἔχρισεν θῶ (1:9) and θῶ (1:13), to describe the Father's "appointment" of the Son as Christ on the one hand and the placement of his enemies under his feet on the other.[114]

   iv. Although superficially unalike, there is a close relationship between the time references mentioned in 1:8 and 13 (εἰς τὸν αἰῶνα τοῦ αἰῶνος / ἕως ἂν) which both refer to the duration of the Son's rule and effectively describe it as eternal.[115]

---

111. In each case, God is the unchallenged agent whose will determines all things. Moreover, by describing the "sending out" of the messengers, the second phrase further clarifies the nature of this service for by "sending" his angels out to serve, he is effectively making them his servants.

112. Ellingworth, *Hebrews*, 133, 120. Cf. Guthrie, *Hebrews*, 69, who notes that these descriptions "imply their subordination to the Son."

113. Cf. Sanford and Garrod, *Understanding Written Language*, 130.

114. In the present context, ἔχρισεν conveys the meaning "to assign a person to a task . . . to anoint, to assign, to appoint," Louw and Nida, *Greek-English Lexicon*, n.p., and describes "God's activity in appointing someone to an office, function, or privilege," Friberg, *Analytical Lexicon*, n.p. Friberg also notes that in connection with a double accusative, τίθημι can mean "to *establish, appoint, make* someone something, *destine* someone to or for something (Acts 13.47; Rom 4.17)."

115. The permanence of the Son's rule in 1:13 is made clear by the fact that having placed "his enemies under his feet," there is no possibility of any further challenge to God's authority. Ellingworth, *Hebrews*, 131, notes that ἕως ἂν + aorist subjunctive is used "of a punctiliarly conceived future event preceded in time by the action of the main clause."

v. Although frequently overlooked, the references in Ps 44 (LXX) to the *symbols* (the Throne and Scepter) and *moral prerequisites* for the Son's role as Judge ("you have loved righteousness and hated wickedness . . . therefore,"[116] 1:9) seem related by the scenario of eschatological messianic judgment to the statement in 1:13 about God's future placement of the "enemies" under the feet of the Son.[117]

Taken together, these connections suggest that the quotation from Psalm 110:1 is perfectly suited to serve as a mirror of Psalm 44, reflecting each of its main points.

d. Conversely, the statements καί σὺ κατ' ἀρχάς, κύριε, τὴν γῆν ἐθεμελίωσας καὶ ἔργα τῶν χειρῶν σού εἰσιν οἱ οὐρανοί (1:10) and καὶ πάντες ὡς ἱμάτιον παλαιωθήσονται καὶ ὡσεὶ περιβόλαιον ἑλίξεις αὐτούς (1:11–12) function in the present context as closely related contrasting chronological bookends for the Son's work with regard to the universe, emphasizing first his work at the beginning, then at the end.

  i. The reference to πάντες (1:11) and its corresponding partner αὐτοὺς in 1:12 represents a more succinct version of τὴν γῆν . . . καὶ . . . οἱ οὐρανοί ("the earth . . . and . . . the heavens," 1:10) and thus connotes "all things."

  ii. The emphasis throughout is upon the Son's "handiwork" (cf. ἔργα τῶν χειρῶν σού, 1:10), making clear that the same hands which once "laid the foundations" of the created reality would one day "roll up" that created reality forever.[118]

  iii. Interestingly, ἑλίξεις, which represents an alteration from the LXX's ἀλλάξεις ("you will change"), enjoys *both* a link of similarity with the phrase ἔργα τῶν χειρῶν σού ("the works of your hands," 1:10) *and* a relationship of opposition with the phrase, ἐθεμελίωσας ("you founded," 1:10).

---

116. διὰ τοῦτο makes clear that the Son's appointment is "because of this" (i.e. rests upon this basis). NB in context, "this" probably includes his "uprightness," metaphorically depicted as a sceptre in v. 8.

117. Cf. Sanford and Garrod, *Understanding Written Language*, 130.

118. The word ἑλίξεις ("to roll up") whether in reference to clothing or a scroll signifies "pack up time," i.e. the end of a span of useful activity. Louw and Nida, *Greek-English Lexicon*, n.p.

These connections are demonstrated below:

	Heb 1:10	Heb 1:11-12
The Son's Work	"You... Lord, laid the foundations" σὺ... κύριε τὴν γῆν ἐθεμελίωσας	"You will roll them up as a cloak" ὡσεὶ περιβόλαιον ἑλίξεις αὐτούς
Object	"the earth... and... the heavens" τὴν γῆν... καὶ... οἱ οὐρανοί	all things... them πάντες... αὐτούς
Time	"in the beginning" (past) κατ' ἀρχάς	at the end (future), things having "grown old" (παλαιωθήσονται) and requiring a change

e. There is also a clear link between the matched pair of sentences in 1:11 and 1:12, both of which use a similar grammatical construction (αὐτοὶ ἀπολοῦνται, σὺ δέ / καὶ ἀλλαγήσονται σύ δέ). Both sentences contrast the Son's eternal nature with the impermanent duration of the universe, with the second representing *an expansion* which clarifies the meaning of the first. In this way the future "destruction" of the heavens and the earth spoken of briefly in 1:10 is likened to the changing of a garment (ὡς ἱμάτιον, 1:12), while the implications of the fact that the Son "remains" are further expounded in 1:12 in terms of his lack of change and eternal existence ("your years do not end").

Heb 1:10	αὐτοὶ ἀπολοῦνται "they will perish"	σὺ δὲ διαμένεις "but you remain"
Heb 1:12	ὡς ἱμάτιον καὶ ἀλλαγήσονται "they will be changed as a garment"	σὺ δὲ ὁ αὐτὸς εἶ καὶ τὰ ἔτη σου οὐκ ἐκλείψουσιν "but you are the same *and your years will not end*"

The picture which emerges reveals that 1:7-14 contains far more significant repetition within it than has been previously noted. It now remains for us to examine the location of repetition within this cluster for any evidence of a combined structural function.

d. The location and formal function of repetition in Hebrews 1:7-14

Although 1:5-14 is commonly read as a unit,[119] the repetitive ties between 1:7-14 (and between 1:7-8 and 1:13-14 in particular) suggest that this material is better understood as a carefully arranged concentric unit which follows on from 1:3-6.[120] This proposal is further strengthened by the observation that 1:7-8 shares a number of formal similarities with the beginning of both the previous two units (and indeed each of the eight units herein examined) which suggests, as will be argued in chapter 5, that it functions as a "topic marker" in this context.[121] The majority of significant connections occur on one side or other of a midpoint following verse 11a, splitting the cluster into two halves which may be further subdivided into three matched pairs of sentences (A, A'; B, B'; C, C'). The unit begins with the καί of verse 7 and ends after the mention of salvation in 1:14, as seen by the lack of any direct relationship with the following material (i.e. 2:1ff.).

> A. 1:7 καὶ πρὸς μὲν τοὺς ἀγγέλους λέγει <u>ὁ ποιῶν τοὺς ἀγγέλους αὐτοῦ πνεύματα καὶ τοὺς λειτουργοὺς αὐτοῦ πυρὸς φλόγα</u>
>
> > B. 8 πρὸς δὲ τὸν υἱόν <u>ὁ θρόνος σου ὁ θεὸς εἰς τὸν αἰῶνα τοῦ αἰῶνος</u> καὶ ἡ ῥάβδος τῆς εὐθύτητος ῥάβδος τῆς βασιλείας σου 9 ἠγάπησας δικαιοσύνην καὶ ἐμίσησας ἀνομίαν διὰ τοῦτο ἔχρισέν σε ὁ θεὸς ὁ θεός σου ἔλαιον ἀγαλλιάσεως παρὰ τοὺς μετόχους σου
> >
> > > C. 10 καί σὺ κατ' ἀρχάς κύριε τὴν γῆν ἐθεμελίωσας καὶ ἔργα τῶν χειρῶν σού εἰσιν οἱ οὐρανοί αὐτοὶ 11 <u>ἀπολοῦνται σὺ δὲ διαμένεις</u>

---

119. See Meier, "Structure," 169; Vanhoye, *Structure*, 80-81; Guthrie, *Hebrews*, 45, and *Structure*, 144; Westfall, *Discourse Analysis*, 89, 91; Johnson, *Hebrews*, 81; Ellingworth, *Hebrews*, 109, 120.

120. See 4.2.2c for discussion of the problems associated with the conventional understanding. Cf. Heil's alternative proposal, *Chiastic Structures*, 35.

121. See 5.2 for further discussion on these formal similarities and their suggested function. Lane, *Hebrews 1-8*, n.p., recognizes these verses as a "new formula of introduction" which "introduces the second set of contrasting statements concerning the angels and the Son" (i.e. 1:7-8).

C'. καὶ πάντες ὡς ἱμάτιον παλαιωθήσονται ¹² καὶ ὡσεὶ περιβόλαιον ἑλίξεις αὐτούς ὡς ἱμάτιον καὶ <u>ἀλλαγήσονται σὺ δὲ ὁ αὐτὸς εἶ καὶ τὰ ἔτη σου οὐκ ἐκλείψουσιν</u>C

B'. ¹³ πρὸς τίνα δὲ τῶν ἀγγέλων εἴρηκέν ποτε <u>κάθου ἐκ δεξιῶν μου</u> ἕως ἂν θῶ τοὺς ἐχθρούς σου ὑποπόδιον τῶν ποδῶν σου

A'. ¹⁴ <u>οὐχὶ πάντες εἰσὶν λειτουργικὰ πνεύματα εἰς διακονίαν ἀποστελλόμενα</u> διὰ τοὺς μέλλοντας κληρονομεῖν σωτηρίαν

e. *The topical function of repetition in Hebrews 1:7–14*

The observation of parallelism in the previous sections (4.2.3a and b) is instructive at this point again in identifying relationships of coherence within 1:7–14 and clarifying with greater precision the meaning of the unit, in its parts and as a whole, thereby providing solutions to at least some of these difficulties.

This may be seen, first, with regard to the modified quotation from (LXX) Psalm 103 about οἱ ἄγγελοι in 1:7 (A), which would have been "quite familiar to Jewish ears," being used in the liturgy of the Synagogue on Friday evening and the Sabbath morning.[122] In its original context, the word πνεύματα almost certainly means "winds" ("He makes the winds his messengers"). Recognizing that in Hebrews 1:7 the phrase is clearly a statement about "οἱ ἄγγελοι" rather than πνεύματα,[123] the majority of commentators render it, "he makes the angels spirits."[124] However, a different picture emerges when 1:7 is read in connection with its partner text (1:14, A'), and as part of a contrast with the Son in B / B'. In verses 7–8 the angels are described as "servants" and "spirits" in contrast to the messianic Son who is addressed as "God" and given his own throne "forever." The same two words appear once more in 1:14 (A'), now fused together into a single statement λειτουργικὰ πνεύματα in a context once

---

122. Kistemaker, "Psalm Citations," 23. Cf. Werner, *Sacred Bridge*, 150.

123. Both alternatives are grammatically possible since τοὺς ἀγγέλους and πνεύματα are both accusatives which can function as the object of God's activity of "making." However, the context makes clear that while the same form of words is used, a different meaning to the Psalmist is intended in Hebrews. See the parallel statement in 1:14 which *cannot* function as a statement about πνεύματα (οὐχὶ πάντες εἰσὶν λειτουργικὰ πνεύματα).

124. Cf. Ellingworth, *Hebrews*, 120.

more involving an (implied) contrast with the Son in terms of his messianic greatness and longevity (B'). For the Son will sit on the throne "until all his enemies are under his feet," while they are but πνεύματα. Thus the contrast in both cases seems to be one involving *status* (the Son / servants) and *permanency* ("forever" / transitory "winds").[125] This strongly suggests that the words λειτουργικὰ πνεύματα should be taken as a summary statement not only of Ps 104:4 but of the author's main point about the messengers and the Son in 1:7-9. Namely, while God says that the Son is both God and King, he speaks of the messengers as *only* servants. While God says that the Son will rule forever, he says that they will flicker out like the winds/breath.

Similarly, the close relationship between B and B' makes clear, when read together, that the main reason for the author's inclusion of the lengthy quotation from Ps 44:7-8 (LXX) is found in its final clause, ἔχρισέν σε . . . παρὰ τοὺς μετόχους σου (1:9b). The point is not simply that the Son is the divine Christ who will rule for all time.[126] Rather it is that in as much as he alone has been appointed as divine Christ, *the Son's anointing is superior to that of "*οἱ ἄγγελοι,*"* "going beyond that of his companions."[127] For God has only ever spoken to one person (and certainly to no angel) in such an exalted way (1:13).[128] Thus, the messianic testimony of 1:8 serves its main purpose by continuing the contrast between the Son and the messengers.

Third, both C and C' serve to further develop the reference to the Son's eternal nature introduced by the quotation from (LXX) Psalm 44 as the basis for a further contrast of *duration*, this time not with the messengers but with the whole of creation: While the heavens and the earth—which the Son created and will one day "roll up"—will grow old and pass away, the Son is, was, and will be the same forever (σὺ δὲ διαμένεις, 1:11; ὁ αὐτὸς εἶ καὶ τὰ ἔτη σου οὐκ ἐκλείψουσιν, 1:12).

---

125. For further evidence of this second contrast, see comments on πυρὸς φλόγα in 1:7.

126. So Johnson, *Hebrews*, 79; Guthrie, *Hebrews*, 70; and Calvin, *Commentary*, 45-46.

127. τοὺς μετόχους is best understood within Hebrews as a further reference to the angels.

128. The emphasis on God's appointment of his Son at his exaltation in these verses argues against Meier's reading of v. 8 as a reference to "the eternal rule which the preexistent Son has exercised from all eternity" (Meier, "Symmetry," 515), casting doubt on his detection of a chronological link between 1:8 and 1:3a on the basis of "preexistence" (p. 523).

As may be seen below, the addition of ὡς ἱμάτιον ("like a garment"), which is repeated from verse 11, before καὶ ἀλλαγήσονται ("and they will be changed," v. 12b), keeps the imagery of clothing in view and serves to unite the ideas of growing old and being put away (vv. 11c–12b) into a single thought which functions as a contrast to the Son who always remains "the same" (ὁ αὐτός, 1:12c; cf. 1:11a–b). It is this eternal nature which forms the necessary pre-condition for the statement in (LXX) Psalm 44:7–8 about the Son's eternal reign (1:8, "your throne, O God, is forever and ever"). Although subtle, the second change from the original, κατ' ἀρχάς σύ ("in the beginning, you," LXX 101:26) to καί Σὺ ("and you," Heb 1:10) is similarly significant because it explicitly links the testimony of (LXX) Psalm 101 with the earlier quotation from Psalm 44, revealing the author's understanding that both represent statements made by God *to the Son* (πρὸς δὲ τὸν υἱόν, 1:8).[129] This is a surprising twist in the case of the second quotation, given that in its original context, these words most obviously refer to God himself.

Psalm 101:26–28

κατ' ἀρχὰς τὴν γῆν σύ κύριε ἐθεμελίωσας καὶ ἔργα τῶν χειρῶν σού εἰσιν οἱ οὐρανοί αὐτοὶ ἀπολοῦνται σὺ δὲ διαμένεις καὶ πάντες ὡς ἱμάτιον παλαιωθήσονται καὶ ὡσεὶ περιβόλαιον ἀλλάξεις αὐτοὺς καὶ ἀλλαγήσονται σὺ δὲ ὁ αὐτὸς εἶ, καὶ τὰ ἔτη σου οὐκ ἐκλείψουσιν

Heb 1:10–12

καί σὺ κατ' ἀρχάς κύριε τὴν γῆν ἐθεμελίωσας, καὶ ἔργα τῶν χειρῶν σού εἰσιν οἱ οὐρανοί αὐτοὶ ἀπολοῦνται σὺ δὲ διαμένεις καὶ πάντες ὡς ἱμάτιον παλαιωθήσονται καὶ ὡσεὶ περιβόλαιον ἑλίξεις αὐτοὺς ὡς ἱμάτιον καὶ ἀλλαγήσονται σὺ δὲ ὁ αὐτὸς εἶ καὶ τὰ ἔτη σου οὐκ ἐκλείψουσιν

There is also a high degree of cohesion between the two halves of the unit, with 1:11b–14 (A'–C') providing a context which in each case further clarifies the meaning of 1:7–11a (A–C). The first half claims that in comparison to the messengers described as transitory servants (A), God has spoken of the Son *both* as divine eternal King, whose appointment goes far beyond all others (B) *and* as founder of the universe

129. In context, καί ultimately functions to link back to λέγει in v7 as follows: about the angels he says... (1:7); but to the Son (he says)... (1:8), "and (he also says)." Cf. Gheorghita, *The Role of the Septuagint in Hebrews*, 44; and Bateman, *Early Jewish Hermeneutics*, 130–35. The indirect nature of the quotations *about* the angels in A / A' in comparison to God's direct address *to* the Son in B / B' and C / C' is also interesting and implies a further contrast between their relative importance. For whereas God has spoken about the messengers, he has spoken to the Son.

(C). Meanwhile, following discussion of God's designation of the Son as the one who never changes and will one day bring an end to creation (C'), the author enquires regarding the existence of any royal testimony similar to Psalm 110:1 spoken in relation to the messengers (B'), before indirectly answering his question in the negative with another question clarifying their diminished status and nature (A').

Thus, our analysis of topic has found clear and demonstrable evidence of coherence between each of the formal parallels within the unit (A / A', B / B', C / C', and ABC and C'B'A') which combine to provide additional testimony in support of the author's claim regarding the Son's greatness in the previous unit.

f. Further implications for meaning in light of the parallelism within Hebrews 1:7–14

The identification of parallelism within 1:7–14 is also of assistance in clarifying the meaning of a number of ambiguous words and phrases within it.

First, in light of the importance of the Psalm to the original audience of Hebrews[130] and the clear parallelism between Hebrews 1:7 and 1:14, the replacement of πῦρ φλέγον ([LXX] Ps 103:4) with πυρὸς φλόγα (Hebrews 1:7) almost certainly represents a deliberate alteration to the LXX text which serves to clarify and drive home the author's emphasis upon *the transient and insubstantial nature* of the angels as expressed primarily by their description as πνεύματα ("winds"). In other words, just as εἰς διακονίαν ἀποστελλόμενα (1:14) functions together with λειτουργικά to accentuate their inferior serving status (see 4.2.3b), so the description of the angels as "flames" reinforces the contrast between their temporality and the Son's "foreverness" (εἰς τὸν αἰῶνα τοῦ αἰῶνος) in 1:8. The different functions played by material in 1:7 and 14 may be seen in the diagram below:

	Common material 1	Common Material 2	Unique material
Heb 1:7	πνεύματα	τοὺς λειτουργοὺς αὐτοῦ	πυρὸς φλόγα (related to 1)
Heb 1:14	πνεύματα	λειτουργικά	εἰς διακονίαν ἀποστελλόμενα (related to 2)

---

130. See Kistemaker, "Psalm Citations," 23.

Second, the parallelism within 1:7–14 as a whole suggests the possibility that the replacement of ἀλλάξεις (Psalm 101:27) with the synonymous ἑλίξεις (1:12) might be explained, at least in part, by the author's desire to mitigate against his hearers/readers perceiving a formal symmetry he does not intend within 1:12.[131] Alternatively, it may stem from a desire to create a further extra-textual connection between Hebrews 1:12 and Isaiah 34:4, a passage which explicitly describes the eschatological judgment of the LORD, thereby further developing this theme (cf. Hebrews 1:3, 8).[132]

Read as a whole, the key words and concepts relate to the Father's contrasting testimony to/about the angels and the Son, his superior status as messianic judge, his work with regard to the universe and especially his eternal nature. Conversely, references to "enemies" and to "those about to inherit salvation" in verses 13–14 do not play a significant function within this context.[133] The topic of 1:7–14 may be summarized as:

God's word spoken in the LXX reveals the superiority of the Son over the angels in terms of his kingly status, eternal nature and unique role with regard to creation.

The unit is translated as follows:

A. ¹:⁷ And about the messengers on the one hand, he says: "He makes his messengers winds and servants of him, flames of fire."

B. ⁸ But to the Son he says, "Your throne, O God, is forever. And the scepter of uprightness is the scepter of your Kingdom. ⁹ You love righteousness and hate lawlessness. Therefore God, your God, has anointed you with the oil of joy beyond your companions."

---

131. In association with the twin references to ὡς ἱμάτιον in 1:11 and 12, the Psalm's original repetition (ἀλλάξεις / ἀλλαγήσονται; παλαιωθήσονται and ἀλλαγήσονται) might have suggested a division between αὐτούς and ὡς ἱμάτιον in 1:12. By changing the word, however, the connection is weakened and a potential danger averted.

132. ἐλίσσω appears only four times in verbal form within canonical material (Job 18:8; Isa 34:4; Heb 1:12; Rev 6:14), twice in contexts of end-time judgement (Isa 34:4; Rev 6:14). Cf. Bateman, *Hermeneutics*, 139–40.

133. *Pace* Ellingworth, 131, "Hebrews offers no exegesis of the second line of the quotation, except indirectly via Ps. 8 in Heb. 2:8f. It is therefore misconceived to ask who, for the author of Hebrews, are the "enemies" in the quotation."

> > C. ¹⁰ And "You, Lord, founded the earth in the beginning, and the Heavens are the works of your hands. ¹¹ They will perish but you remain.
>
> > C'. "And all things will wear out like clothing ¹² and like a coat you will roll them up and they will be exchanged like a garment. But you are the same and your years will not end."
>
> > B'. ¹³ And to which one of the messengers has he ever said: "Sit at my right hand until I make your enemies a footstool for your feet"?
>
> A'. ¹⁴ Are not they all ministering spirits sent out to serve those about to inherit salvation? (1:13–14)

g. *Summary of findings*

This analysis of the link cluster at Hebrews 1:7–14:

a. identifies a large number of previously unobserved yet significant instances of repetition: τοὺς ἀγγέλους; τοὺς ἀγγέλους / τῶν ἀγγέλων (1:7 and 13); λέγει / εἴρηκεν (1:7 and 13); πρός (1:7, 8 and 13); ὡς ἱμάτιον (1:11, 12); and more broadly between 1:7–8 and 1:13–14; 1:8–9 and 1:13; and 1:10–11a and 1:11b–12;

b. demonstrates that repetition serves an important structural function in this context by marking out 1:7–14 as a concentric and coherent textual unit consisting of six related parts (A, A'; B, B'; C, C');

c. clarifies with greater precision the coherence between its parts and within the unit as a whole, showing:

- that 1:7–8 and 13–14 (A/A') and 1:8–9 and 1:13 (B/B') function as twin pairs of statements which contrast the *status* (the King / servants) and *permanency* ("forever" / transitory "winds") of the Son in relation to the angels on the basis of testimony from (LXX) Psalms 44, 103 and 110;

- that 1:10–11a and 1:11b–12 (C/C') represents a second contrast between the eternal nature of the Son as creator and the impermanent nature of his creation.

d. shows with regard to his use of the LXX that the author frequently brings out *new meanings from old forms of words* by (i) introducing subtle yet significant variations to his source material and (ii) utilizing certain pre-existing textual features to his own advantage (e.g., the parallelism within Psalm 101:26-28) thereby clarifying his interpretation. More specifically, in this context:

- Psalm 103:4 testifies to the relative inferiority of the "οἱ ἄγγελοι" in comparison with the Son;
- Psalm 44:7-8 emphasizes the relative superiority of the Son's messianic anointing in comparison to the "οἱ ἄγγελοι"; and
- Psalm 101:26-28 praises the Son as the unchanging creator of all things.

e. concludes that the topic of 1:7-14 might best be understood as: God's word reveals the superiority of the Son over the angels in terms of his kingly status, eternal nature and unique role with regard to creation.

4.2.4 Hebrews 2:1-4

a. Introduction

While the unity and prominence of 2:1-4 has been widely recognized, scholars have failed to appreciate the full extent of the connections within this text. Consequently, many parallels have been overlooked, which has resulted in several key words and phrases being misunderstood (ὁ δι' ἀγγέλων λαληθεὶς λόγος in 2:2; ἥτις ἀρχὴν λαβοῦσα λαλεῖσθαι διὰ τοῦ κυρίου, 2:3; and ἀκουσάντοι, 2:3) and the unit as a whole being viewed as a "digression" which "momentarily interrupts the flow of the exposition"[134] rather than as the culmination of the first main movement in Hebrews. The identification of a link cluster between 2:1-4 provides new evidence on the meaning and significance of these words and phrases (above) and, more generally, of the unit as a whole.

---

134. Following Synge, Ellingworth, *Hebrews*, 147, refers to 2:1-4 as a "digression," while Lane, *Hebrews 1-8*, n.p., suggests that 2:1-4 "momentarily interrupts the flow of the exposition." Cf. Johnson, *Hebrews*, 89.

b. Significant repetition previously observed in 2:1-4

The fourth link cluster in Hebrews occurs between 2:1-4.[135] Significant repetition previously observed in 2:1-4 includes the following lexical links:

- βέβαιος / ἐβεβαιώθη (2:2 and 3);[136]
- τοῖς ἀκουσθεῖσιν / τῶν ἀκουσάντων (2:1 and 3);[137]
- λαληθείς / λαλεῖσθαι and λαλοῦμεν (2:2 and 3);[138] and
- ἡμᾶς / ἡμεῖς, ἡμᾶς (2:1, 2:3—x2).[139]

Vanhoye also draws attention to the contrast between the agents of God's address involving λαλέω (2:2, 3), expressed in each case through matched passive participles featuring διά + genitive: δι' ἀγγέλων ("through messengers") and διὰ τοῦ κυρίου ("through the Lord").[140]

c. Potentially significant repetition previously unobserved in Hebrews 2:1-4

In addition to these links, there are many other instances of potentially significant repetition in 2:1-4. Indeed, the connections within this section of text are astonishing in their range, frequency, variety and location. Further lexical links may be found between:

- ἔλαβεν (2:2) and λαβοῦσα (2:3);[141] and
- πνεύματα (1:14) and πνεύματος (2:4).[142]

---

135. See 4.2.4c for discussion of its boundaries.

136. Vanhoye, *La Structure*, 76; Rhee, *Faith*, 71-72. Cognates of this word occur in 3:14, 6:19, 9:17 and 13:9.

137. Vanhoye, *La Structure*, 76; Westfall, *Discourse Analysis*, 94. The word occurs 8 times in Hebrews in 2:1, 3; 3:7, 15, 16; 4:2, 7; and 12:19.

138. Vanhoye, *La Structure*, 76; Guthrie, *Structure*, 97; Rhee, *Faith*, 71-72; and Westfall, *Discourse Analysis*, 94. Each scholar sees significance only in the first two occurrences of the word in 2:2 and 2:3.

139. Vanhoye, *La Structure*, 76. These references represent the first mention of the letter's recipients since 1:2.

140. Vanhoye, *La Structure*, 76.

141. The word appears 17 times in Hebrews, 6 of which occur within chapter 11 (11:8, 11, 13, 29, 35, 36).

142. To these may be added connections between εἰς / εἰς (1:14 and 2:3); διά (δι') + genitive (2:2 and 3); διά + accusative in 1:14, 2:1; οὐχί / οὖν (1:14 and 2:5); and γάρ (2:2 and 5).

Moreover, although representing different parts of speech (adverb, adjective respectively), there is a likely connection between περισσοτέρος in 2:1 and τηλικαύτης in 2:3. Louw and Nida list both under the domain, "More than, Less than (Comparative Degree)," stating that the first term refers to "a degree which is considerably in excess of some point on an implied or explicit scale of extent—'very great, excessive, extremely, emphatic, surpassing, all the more, much greater,' while the second relates to 'a degree which is comparable to some other expression of degree.'"[143]

There is also a relation of opposition between the command to "pay attention," τροσέχειν (2:1) and the verbs παραρυῶμεν (denoting "to drift away from one's course," also 2:1) and ἀμελήσαντες ("neglecting," 2:3). Lane notes that προσέχειν and παραρυῶμεν represent "nautical terms which reflect a Hellenistic idiom," translating the former as "to hold a ship toward port."[144] Consequently, by calling on his hearers to "pay attention ... lest we drift" (προσέχειν ... μήποτε παραρυῶμεν, 2:1), the author is urging the exact opposite action to that described by the word ἀμελήσαντες.

More broadly, 2:1-4 contains at least a couple of other nearly related phrases:

a. ὁ δι' ἀγγέλων λαληθεὶς λόγος ("the word spoken through messengers," 2:2) and both τηλικαύτης ἀμελήσαντες σωτηρίας ἥτις ἀρχὴν λαβοῦσα λαλεῖσθαι διὰ τοῦ κυρίου ὑπὸ τῶν ἀκουσάντων ("so great salvation which was first received spoken through the Lord by those who heard," 2:3) and συνεπιμαρτυροῦντος τοῦ θεοῦ σημείοις τε καὶ τέρασιν καὶ ποικίλαις δυνάμεσιν καὶ πνεύματος ἁγίου μερισμοῖς κατὰ τὴν αὐτοῦ θέλησιν ("God having added testimony by both signs and wonders and by diverse powers and gifts of the Holy Spirit according to his will," 2:4) with each describing overlapping acts of divine communication.

b. the phrase πᾶσα παράβασις καὶ παρακοὴ ἔλαβεν ἔνδικον μισθαποδοσίαν ("and every transgression and disobedience has received just retribution," 2:2) can be conceived as a plausible summary description

---

143. Louw and Nida, *Greek-English Lexicon*, n.p. Lane, *Hebrews 1-8*, n.p., observes that in Koine Greek there was a decline in the use of the superlative form, with the comparative pressed into service to take its place. "The comparative adverb περισσοτέρως illustrates this tendency and probably carries an elative force not only here but whenever it occurs in the NT."

144. Lane, *Hebrews 1-8*, 37. Cf. Johnson, *Hebrews*, 86; Guthrie, *Hebrews*, 84; and Westcott, *Hebrews*, 36-37.

of the "so great salvation" of 2:3 (τηλικαύτης ... σωτηρίας) from the perspective of its recipients.

In summary, though many different connections have been observed by scholars in 2:1-4, the combined force of their presence within this location has not been fully appreciated. Vanhoye notes many of the lexical links between 2:1-2 and 2:3 (with the exception of λαμβάνω in 2:2 and 2:3);[145] Guthrie fails to mention lexical connections which play no role in his structural outline (e.g., λαμβάνω in 2:2 and 2:3), βέβαιος (2:2, 2:3), and ἀκούω (2:1, 2:3);[146] meanwhile Westfall observes only the more general connection between the references to λαλέω (2:2, 2:3) and ἀκούω (2:1, 2:3) which form part of a "process of speaking" chain beginning in 1:1.[147]

It now remains for us to examine the location of repetition within this cluster for any evidence of a combined structural function.

d. The location and formal function of repetition in Hebrews 2:1-4

When viewed together, the evidence of symmetry is unmistakable in 2:1-4, with the majority of connections occurring on one side or other of a midpoint at 2:3a. This may be seen most clearly with regard to 2:1-3 (below).

Heb 2:1-2	Heb 2:3
περισσοτέρως	τηλικαύτης
προσέχειν ... μήποτε παραρυῶμεν	ἀμελήσαντες
ἡμᾶς	ἡμεῖς ... ἡμᾶς
τοῖς ἀκουσθεῖσιν	τῶν ἀκουσάντων

145. Vanhoye, *La Structure*, 75-76; and *Structure*, 80-83.

146. Guthrie, *Structure*, 97 and 103, identifies links as significant on the basis of his perception of their function. He proposes that the repetition of σωτηρία serves as a "hook word" linking 1:5-14 with 2:1-4; λαλεῖσθαι and λαλοῦμεν function similarly to join 2:1-4 with 2:5-9; τῶν ἀγγέλων (1:14) and ἀγγέλων (2:2) represent "hooked key words" which aid the connection between the two sections, while μέλλοντας / μέλλουσαν and τῶν ἀγγέλων / ἀγγέλοις (1:13 and 2:5) function as distant hook words joining together 1:5-14 and 2:1-4.

147. Westfall, *Discourse Analysis*, 94.

Heb 2:1-2	Heb 2:3
λαληθεὶς	λαλεῖσθαι
δι' ἀγγέλων	διὰ τοῦ κυρίου
ἐγένετο βέβαιος	ἐβεβαιώθη
ἔλαβεν	λαβοῦσα

As with Hebrews 1:1-4 (see 4.2.1d), the likelihood that this symmetrical arrangement reflects authorial design is strengthened by an examination of the author's use of this vocabulary which reveals that virtually the same collection of words is used in 2:3 as in 2:1-2, *even when their referents are clearly different or their inclusion requires the use of a grammatically awkward construction* which cannot easily be explained on topical grounds. For example, the reference to τοῖς ἀκουσθεῖσιν in 2:1 describes an object ("the things heard").[148] In 2:3, however, the same lexical item is used to depict a group of people who have heard and passed on that object to others (τῶν ἀκουσάντων, "those who heard").[149] Commentators have also described as both unusual[150] and "awkward"[151] the author's use of the periphrastic phrase λαβοῦσα λαλεῖσθαι (2:3), which corresponds with ἔλάβεν in 2:2, instead of a more straightforward alternative. Given the consummate skill of the author, this distinctive use of repetition is unlikely to reflect poor style but represents instead further evidence that the author's choice of particular words is guided at times by a desire to forge lexical (and other kinds of) connections within the text.[152]

This, then, together with the formal evidence assembled above, suggests *pace* the majority of scholars that Hebrews 2:1-4 constitutes a concentric textual unit.[153] Grammatically, God's testimony regarding

---

148. Ellingworth, *Hebrews*, 136, claims that the reference "must be grammatically neuter, 'to what we have heard.'" Cf. Guthrie, *Structure*, 84; and Vanhoye, *Structure*, 81.

149. This change in meaning is reflected in the shift from the dative neuter to the masculine genitive plural participle.

150. Ellingworth, *Hebrews*, 140, notes that while found in secular literature from the 2nd Century BC onwards, the phrase λαβοῦσα λαλεῖσθαι is "not found elsewhere in the Greek Bible."

151. O'Brien, *Hebrews*, 88.

152. See Ebert's comments, "Chiastic Structure," 171, on the use of καθαρισμὸν ... ποιησάμενος in 1:3.

153. Vanhoye, *Structure*, 81; Johnson, *Hebrews*, 85; Ellingworth, *Hebrews*, 134; Guthrie, *Structure*, 144; Westfall, *Discourse Analysis*, 93; and Heil, *Chiastic Structures*, 53.

the Son's greatness relative to the messengers (cf. 1:13-14) functions as the inferential basis (διὰ τοῦτο) for the call to action of 2:1.[154] Following this, the γάρ of 2:2 and 2:5 marks out 2:2-4 as support material which further explains the need for action.[155] More specifically, 2:2-3 represents the explanation while 2:4 provides further clarification of how the great salvation "has been established for us by those who heard."[156]

With regard to its internal arrangement, the material in 2:1-3 has proven challenging to modern commentators.[157] The chief difficulty lies in knowing what to do with the clearly prominent phrase πῶς ἡμεῖς ἐκφευξόμεθα τηλικαύτης ἀμελήσαντες σωτηρίας in 2:3a. Representing, as it does, part of a first class condition joined by means of a εἰ . . . πῶς construction and which cannot meaningfully be separated, 2:3a must be left attached to εἰ γάρ in 2:2. At the same time, however, 2:3a also clearly belongs with what follows (2:3-4), as is evidenced by the dependence of ἥτις in 2:3 upon the word σωτηρίας. Thus, the syntax argues against making any break between this material. On the other hand, the extensive formal symmetry between 2:1-2 and 2:3 seems to demand further partitioning than would be the case were we to take 2:1-3 as a single unit.

---

154. Διὰ τοῦτο "is a prepositional idiom that functions as an inferential conjunction and signals a conclusion based on grounds that have been provided in the preceding co-text." Westfall, *Discourse Analysis*, 93. See further discussion for precisely which co-text is on view here.

155. Cf. Johnson, *Hebrews*, 89; and Westfall, *Discourse Analysis*, 95.

156. The dependent participle συνεπιμαρτυροῦντος which ties to the clause ἥτις . . . ἐβεβαιώθη (2:3) explains the means by which this salvation has reached us.

157. Vanhoye, *La Structure*, 76-77, describes these verses as "une symétrie concentrique." However, while the first four of his parallel "membres" are convincing (ἡμᾶς / εἰς ἡμᾶς; τοῖς ἀκουσθεῖσιν / τῶν ἀκουσάντων; δι' ἀγγέλων / διά τοῦ κυρίου; and λαληωείς / λαλεῖσθαι), (i) his inner links are questionable (παράβασις / ἀμελήσαντες; μισθαποδοσίαν /ἐκφευξόμεθα), (ii) he omits other material which does not fit the arrangement and (iii) his analysis fails to account adequately for the location both of what he terms "la seule exception" (repetition involving βεβαιόω in 2:2, 3) and a further "exception" (the repetition of λαμβάνω in 2:2 and 2:3), which he fails to observe. Alternatively, Rhee, *Faith*, 71-72, reads 2:1-4 as a five-part chiasm on the basis of his perception of parallelism between A which stresses the "importance of paying closer attention to what the readers have heard" and A' which "explains the reason for it," and "the idea of confirmation" in B and B' as expressed through the words βεβαιόω and λαλέω in 2:2, 3. Rhee's analysis better accounts for the placement of βεβαιόω than Vanhoye's, and his identification of parallelism between 2:2a and 2:3 is supported by our detection of a number of other strong links between these clauses (i.e. δι' ἀγγέλων / διὰ τοῦ κθρίου; λαμβάνω; and ἡμᾶς). See too Heil's similar presentation (to Rhee's) in *Chiastic Structures*, 48.

For this second reason, 2:3a is depicted below as D, such that it *properly belongs to both halves of the unit* in recognition of this overlap.[158]

A. ²:¹ Διὰ τοῦτο δεῖ περισσοτέρως προσέχειν ἡμᾶς τοῖς ἀκουσθεῖσιν μήποτε παραρυῶμεν ² εἰ γὰρ ὁ δι' ἀγγέλων λαληθεὶς λόγος ἐγένετο βέβαιος καὶ πᾶσα παράβασις καὶ παρακοὴ ἔλαβεν ἔνδικον μισθαποδοσίαν

B. ³ πῶς ἡμεῖς ἐκφευξόμεθα τηλικαύτης ἀμελήσαντες σωτηρίας

A'. ἥτις ἀρχὴν λαβοῦσα λαλεῖσθαι διὰ τοῦ κυρίου ὑπὸ τῶν ἀκουσάντων εἰς ἡμᾶς ἐβεβαιώθη ⁴ συνεπιμαρτυροῦντος τοῦ θεοῦ σημείοις τε καὶ τέρασιν καὶ ποικίλαις δυνάμεσιν καὶ πνεύματος ἁγίου μερισμοῖς κατὰ τὴν αὐτοῦ θέλησιν;

e. *The topical function of repetition in Hebrews 2:1-4*

The topical relationship between the unit's parts is also less than straightforward. In addition to sharing much the same vocabulary, both A (2:1-2) and A' (2:3b-4) emphasize the *establishment* (cf. ἐγένετο βέβαιος / ἐβεβαιώθη) of a message of salvation and contain a matched contrast between the agents of its transmission (δι' ἀγγέλων and διὰ τοῦ κυρίου respectively). Moreover, when read together with B, as the grammar requires, both seem designed to strengthen the implicit appeal within the question of 2:3a to *not neglect* the great salvation won for "us" in Christ in view of the impossibility of escape for those who do. In 2:1-2 (A), this is achieved by means of a two-part conditional statement which supports the appeal to "pay much closer attention"[159] by making clear the impossibility of escape for those who fail to do so (*How if this + this?*). The grammatical construction reveals that the second phrase is dependent on the εἰ in 2:2, suggesting that the second clause is related to and flows as an inference from the first. The logic may be expressed as follows:

> *If* the word spoken through messengers has come into effect (and it has), so that every transgression has received just reward (which it has),

---

158. For discussion on the location and function of 1:3 within 1:1-4 see 4.2.1d.

159. As most recognize, 2:1 represents more than a statement about the necessity of a particular action, functioning as a "logical imperative" to "pay much closer attention" to what we have heard. Cf. Lane, *Hebrews 1-8*, 37; and Westfall, *Discourse Analysis*, 93.

Then we will certainly not escape if we neglect this much greater salvation!

Meanwhile, the two-part statement of A', which further describes the "great salvation" of 2:3a, seems similarly calculated to elicit a response from "us" by amplifying the urgency of our need to respond: *We must act now* in view of the greatness of the one who first spoke this salvation ("the Lord") and especially in light of its present fulfillment.[160]

Clearly then, a close relationship exists between 2:1-2 and 2:3b. Yet what can be said about its precise nature? The answer to this question depends on one's understanding of the relationship between ὁ δι' ἀγγέλων λαληθεὶς λόγος (2:2) and ἥτις ἀρχὴν λαβοῦσα λαλεῖσθαι διὰ τοῦ κυρίου (2:3b). Are these *two separate entities*: "the word spoken through messengers" on the one hand and "the great salvation spoken through the Lord" on the other, which have now *both* been established? Or are they in fact twin descriptions of the *same entity*: the established word of salvation, spoken by both messengers and the Son?

Heb 2:2   ὁ δι' ἀγγέλων λαληθεὶς λόγος

"the word spoken through messengers"

Heb 2:3   ἥτις ἀρχὴν λαβοῦσα λαλεῖσθαι διὰ τοῦ κυρίου

"[great salvation,' 2:3a] which from the beginning was spoken through the Lord"

Virtually all modern commentators read ὁ δι' ἀγγέλων λαληθεὶς λόγος in this first way as a reference to the Law of Moses.[161] Understood in this way, the word βέβαιος is taken variously to mean "valid,"[162] "binding,"[163] "secure"[164] and even "attested"[165] and 2:2 is understood to function as

---

160. The dependence of λαβοῦσα λαλεῖσθαι upon the aorist indicative ἐβεβαιώθη makes clear that the chief idea here relates to the present status of "establishment" of this Salvation.

161. Vanhoye, *La Structure*, 75; Ellingworth, *Hebrews*, 134, 138, notes Origen's equation of λόγος with νόμος favorably, claiming that the phrase "refers in rather general terms to the circumstances in which the Mosaic Law was given." Cf. Johnson, *Hebrews*, 87; Guthrie, *Hebrews*, 84; and Heil, *Chiastic Structures*, 50.

162. Ellingworth, *Hebrews*, 138.

163. Guthrie, *Hebrews*, 84.

164. Johnson, *Hebrews*, 87.

165. Eisenbaum, "Locating Hebrews," 227-28, notes that "the Greek word generally means to confirm, establish, secure, or guarantee."

part of an *a fortiori* contrast between the "less great" word of the Law and the "much greater" one spoken through Jesus. The point then is that since those who tried to escape the Law received full punishment for their sins (this being proof of its "confirmation"/ "establishment"), there can be no hope of escape for any who neglect the much greater "word."[166]

There are significant problems with this interpretation, however. First, that the phrase, ὁ δι' ἀγγέλων λαληθείς, is a reference to the "Law of Moses" is nowhere made clear and could equally refer to any or "all of God's former revelation."[167] Second, the reading rests upon two further problematic assumptions: (i) that angels were responsible for "speaking" the Law to Israel, despite no clear LXX attestation of this fact,[168] and (ii) that τηλικαύτης serves to make a comparison between the greatness of Jesus' salvation *in comparison with the Law*, when context suggests a proportional relationship between the greatness of this salvation and the extent to which we must pay attention (as evidenced by the connection noted earlier between περισσοτέρως in 2:1 and τηλικαύτης in 2:3).[169] Even without these difficulties, such a reading does not fit easily with its pre- or proceeding context: The reference to the Law seems to jump out without clear relationship to the point of chapter 1 before disappearing again without a trace.[170] Consequently, the exhortation of 2:1 is based

166. Cf. Ellingworth, *Hebrews*, 139; Guthrie, *Hebrews*, 84; Johnson, 87. Buchanan, *Hebrews*, 24; Bruce, *Hebrews*, 68; Westfall, *Discourse Analysis*, 94; Rhee, *Faith*, 73; and Heil, *Chiastic Structures*, 52.

167. Johnson, *Hebrews*, 87.

168. O'Brien, *Hebrews*, 84-85, claims to find "biblical warrant in Deuteronomy 33:2 (LXX)": "The Lord came from Sinai; . . . at his right hand were angels with him." However, this goes beyond what the text actually says and seems contradicted by Exodus 19:25–20:1 which speaks of Moses alone. Ellingworth, *Hebrews*, 138, meanwhile, claims that the "belief that angels acted as intermediaries in the giving of the Law to Moses is well attested in the NT" yet the texts he cites in support of this view are doubtful. Acts 7:38 and 53 are both ambiguous: While an angel certainly spoke to Moses at Mount Sinai, it is not clear that God spoke the law through him. Similarly, while the reference in Galatians 3:19 to the Law as διαταγείς δι' ἀγγέλων ἐν χειρὶ μεσίτου ("having been ordained through messengers by the hand of a mediator") makes clear that ἄγγελοι were involved in its transmission, the same text that it was "spoken" by Moses (the mediator) alone. For non-canonical support for the idea of an angelic mediation of the Law, see *Jubilees* 1:27, 29; 2:1; and Josephus, *Antiquities* 15.136.

169. Cf. Johnson, *Hebrews*, 89.

170. The contrast between the Law and the Salvation brought by Jesus is not picked up again until chapter 8. On the other hand, exactly this contrast between Law and Christ's salvation seems to be made in 10:26–31. Ellingworth's warning "not to read back a later stage of the argument on to the present verse" seems appropriate here. *Hebrews*, 165.

not on the argument of the chapter to this point but upon a seemingly tangential point from *outside the text*. Fourth, the assumption of a distinction between the word of the messengers and that of the Son seems contradicted by the fact that in its present context "what we have heard" (2:1) clearly includes *both* the word of the Son *and that of the messengers* (1:1–14, especially 1:14). For "all of these" (e.g., Moses, the Psalmist, Isaiah) are ministering spirits, sent out to serve *us* (i.e. "those about to inherit," 1:14), through whom God *continues to testify* to his will (2:4), and to whom we must listen if we desire to experience this salvation.[171] Fifth, the fact that neither μισθαποδοσία nor παρακοή appears in the LXX, and that παράβασις occurs once only in an unrelated context, (LXX) Ps 100:3, represents further evidence against reading 2:2 as a reference to specific events from Israel"s history given Hebrews' tendency to use similar vocabulary to relevant LXX texts when describing such events. Finally and perhaps most importantly, whatever else it might be, the Mosaic Law is most certainly *not* a "word of salvation" in the mind of Hebrews' author, as such a reading requires (see 7:19, 28; 8:5ff etc).

If, on the other hand, "the word spoken through messengers" (2:2) functions as a parallel reference to "the great salvation" of 2:3, the meaning of 2:1–3 is completely different. For rather than referring to two "establishments" (2:2 and 3) of two distinct messages at two different times (the Mosaic era / the first century AD), these verses speak of *a single establishment* of the one message of salvation spoken through two groups (the Son—via the apostles—and the messengers). In other words, the point of difference relates not to the *content* of the message but rather to the means and timing of its transmission.[172]

Read this way, the word βέβαιος in both 2:2 and 2:3 is used to describe the coming into existence in real time and space of that which had previously only been spoken of in anticipation, God's plan of salvation.[173] 2:2 does not describe the fulfilment of the angelic word of

---

171. This understanding is consistent both with its immediate context (chapter 1 having outlined some of this testimony for us) and wider context (i.e. "we" don't just listen to Jesus' earthly testimony but to the whole OT which is living and active etc, cf. 4:11–14).

172. For additional evidence in support of this reading, see Hebrews' treatment of Jer 31:31–34 in 8:1–13 and 10:15–18 in which the author assumes that Jeremiah spoke in anticipation of the great salvation which would be fulfilled at a later date by Jesus. See too 1 Pet 1:10; Rom 1:2, 15:8 for other NT support.

173. Cf. Heb 9:17 where the word is clearly used to describe the coming into effect of a διαθήκη ("covenant").

judgement which occurred at Sinai but makes clear that *God's promised salvation has now come into effect through the life, death, and resurrection of Jesus*. The point assumed true for the sake of argument (εἰ) is that since the Son has been enthroned as Lord of all, having completed his work of atonement, (i) God has now established the word of salvation spoken previously by messengers, such that (ii) every human sin *has received "due payment,"* requiring no further atonement. The difference between these two positions is outlined below:

Heb 2:2   εἰ γὰρ ὁ δι' ἀγγέλων λαληθεὶς λόγος ἐγένετο βέβαιος καὶ πᾶσα παράβασις καὶ παρακοὴ ἔλαβεν ἔνδικον μισθαποδοσίαν

Reading 1   For if the word (of warning) spoken δι' ἀγγέλων (at Sinai) came to pass so that every transgression and disobedience received just retribution etc.

Reading 2   For if the word (of salvation) spoken δι' ἀγγέλων *has been established* and every transgression and disobedience *has received just recompense* (through Christ's atoning sacrifice) etc.

This means that the phrase ἥτις . . . εἰς ἡμᾶς ἐβεβαιώθη ("which . . . has been established for us," 2:3) ought not to be read in connection with ὑπὸ τῶν ἀκουσάντων (2:3), as commonly understood,[174] as though "those who heard" represent the agents of this confirmation. Rather, it functions as a further modification of the participial phrase ἥτις ἀρχὴν λαβοῦσα λαλεῖσθαι διὰ τοῦ κυρίου ὑπὸ τῶν ἀκουσάντων (2:3), clarifying the way this salvation has been received ("by those who heard [Him]," i.e. most likely through and by the apostles). As such, it represents a second statement about salvation itself rather than about the method of its communication.

Such an interpretation fits well within the flow of argument in Hebrews chapter 1 and the theology of the book as a whole (e.g., chapters 9–10), and with the meaning of the word βέβαιος and its cognate βεβαιόω as used elsewhere in the NT. In Romans 15:8, for instance, the word is used to describe the coming of Christ "in order to confirm/fulfil the promises of the fathers" (εἰς τὸ βεβαιῶσαι τὰς ἐπαγγελίας τῶν πατέρων). Similarly, in 2 Peter 1:19, "the prophetic word" (τὸν προφητικὸν λόγον) is described as "more certain/sure" (βεβαιότερον) in the light of Christ's having come with power, as witnessed by the apostles (2 Pet 1:16). Peter's

---

174. Cf. Ellingworth, *Hebrews*, 141.

point is not that the reliability of the prophetic Word of God was somehow in doubt (*less sure*) before its fulfilment in Christ—such a thought would be anathema to the faithful Israelite (cf. Ps 119, Isa 55:10–11)—rather, the comparative βεβαιότερον indicates that what was once only spoken of *in anticipation* has now come to pass in concrete human existence.

In light of all this, ἥτις ἀρχὴν λαβοῦσα λαλεῖσθαι διὰ τοῦ κυρίου ὑπὸ τῶν ἀκουσάντων ("which, having been first received spoken through the Lord by those who heard, has been established for us," 2:3b) functions together with its partner phrase (2:1–2) to clarify meaning in three ways:

1. by making explicit the *content* of "the things heard" (τοῖς ἀκουσθεῖσιν, 2:1) and "the word spoken by messengers" (δι' ἀγγέλων λαληθεὶς λόγος, 2:2; cf. 1:1–2, 4) as the "so great salvation" (τηλικαύτης ... σωτηρίας) which has been "established for us" (εἰς ἡμᾶς ἐβεβαιώθη);

2. by identifying the Son as the original *source* of apostolic communication. For "that which was received" by those who heard came first "through the Lord" (διὰ τοῦ κυρίου, 2:3).[175]

3. by explicitly identifying "us" as the *intended recipients* of God's communicative and saving activity through his Son.[176]

Read together in linear fashion, the unit begins with the preacher's conclusion to his argument of the first chapter: "Because of this" (διὰ τοῦτο),[177] he warns, we *the heirs* must pay much closer attention to "what we have heard." For if what was spoken through the messengers has now been established and every transgression and disobedience received its due penalty (A), how will we escape if we neglect such a great salvation (B)? By this reading, the call for a response is grounded in the fact that salvation has been established such that all sin has been conclusively dealt with. There can be no hope for those who fail to respond appropriately, since the one who drifts from this message is effectively choosing

---

175. Guthrie, *Hebrews*, 85; Ellingworth, *Hebrews*, 141; and Heil, *Chiastic Structures*, 52.

176. While clearly implied in 2:1, in its present context, 2:3 makes clear that this great salvation has been "established for us" (εἰς ἡμᾶς ἐβεβαιώθη).

177. While most scholars read διὰ τοῦτο as an inferential reference, which ties back either to the argument of the first chapter (cf. Ellingworth, *Hebrews*, 135; Johnson, *Hebrews*, 86), or to the string of LXX texts in 1:5–14 (so Guthrie, *Hebrews*, 83; and Heil, *Chiastic Structures*, 49), the exhortation is also connected to the assertions made by means of the twin rhetorical questions of 1:13–14 and the fact that the word spoken by the messengers, τοῖς ἀκουσθεῖσιν ("what we have heard," 2:1), has been spoken by God for the sake of this salvation (1:14).

to remain in their "transgressions and disobedience" and faces only "the fearful expectation of judgment" (10:26).

Meanwhile, the second half of the unit (B', A') makes virtually the same point again for slightly different (though related) reasons. The question of 2:3 functions here as an implicit warning not to neglect the salvation which has been heard spoken (B). While mention is made once more of the "established" status of God's great salvation (2:3), the appeal is made primarily on the basis of its *surpassing greatness* (τηλικοῦτος) at this point, a greatness which corresponds directly with the greatness of its speaker. For, the preacher warns, by neglecting the word of salvation, the hearer rejects not only "messengers" but ultimately "the Lord" (τοῦ κυρίου, 2:3), "God" (τοῦ θεοῦ, 2:4) and "the Holy Spirit" (πνεύματος ἁγίου, 2:4) who stand together as one Triune God behind this word. Any hope of future escape must therefore be extinguished.

Read as a whole in its immediate context, Hebrews 2:1-4 thus describes three distinct "stages of salvation" which may be summarized in reverse chronological order below:

1. We are "about to inherit" salvation (1:14; 2:5),
2. which has been "established" for us (2:2; 2:3),
3. having been announced "through messengers" in the past (1:14; 2:2).

f. Further implications for meaning in light of the parallelism within Hebrews 2:1-4

The identification of clear and demonstrable coherence between the formal parallels within 2:1-4 is once again of further assistance in clarifying the meaning and significance of ambiguous words and phrases in this context in one further way.

Although Hebrews 2:3 is almost universally cited as evidence which reveals the author as a "second-generation Christian" who received his understanding from the apostles (and therefore not Paul), this conclusion is seriously flawed.[178] If ἐβεβαιώθη functions in relation

---

178. According to Ellingworth, *Hebrews*, 7, "the single most striking piece of internal evidence against Pauline authorship of Hebrews is the author's explicit statement that the message which began with Jesus ὑπὸ τῶν ἀκουσάντων εἰς ἡμᾶς ἐβεβαιώθη (2:3); in other words, that the author and his readers received the gospel indirectly. This need

to σωτηρία rather than τῶν ἀκουσάντων as we have described, the verse provides us with *no evidence regarding the author of Hebrews one way or the other*, casting serious doubt on what has hitherto been regarded as a secure "fact."

Key words and concepts marked out by repetition include the Triune God's "received" and "heard" testimony about salvation; its present "established" state; and implications for "us." The prominent location of 2:3a at the center of the chiasm and its grammatical connectedness with both halves of the unit indicates the particular importance of the material in B for the unit as a whole.[179]

The topic of Hebrews 2:1–4 may be summed up and translated as follows: We must pay as much more attention to the word of salvation which we have heard has been established for us, for we will not escape if we fail to do so.

> A. ²:¹ Because of this, it is necessary for us to pay much closer attention to what we have heard lest we drift. ² For **if** the word spoken through messengers has been established and every transgression and sin received due penalty
>
>> B. ³ **How will we escape if we neglect such a great salvation?**
>
> A′. . . . which, having been first received spoken through the Lord by those who heard, has been established for us, ⁴ God adding his testimony with signs and wonders and various kinds of powers and distributions of the Holy Spirit according to his will.

g. Summary of findings

This analysis of the link cluster at Hebrews 2:1–4:

---

not mean that they were Christians of the second or a later generation (see p. 30), but it is in sharp contrast with Paul's claim (Gal 1:1, 12) that he received his commission directly from the risen Lord."

Cf. Calvin, *Hebrews*, 1; Guthrie, *Hebrews*, 85; Johnson, *Hebrews*, 88; Ellingworth, *Hebrews*, 7; O'Brien, *Hebrews*, 5; and Vanhoye, *Situation du Christ*, 49.

179. *Pace* Rhee, *Faith*, 71–72.

a. paints a far more comprehensive picture of the extent of connectedness within this part of the text than has been previously identified, synthesizing the observations of previous scholarship;

b. demonstrates that intratextual connections within this context serve to mark out 2:1–4 as a three-part concentric and coherent textual unit whose central component (B) is revealed as especially prominent both by its location and grammatical connectedness both forwards and backwards;

c. reveals considerable topical coherence between both halves of the unit and the formal parallels within it which clarifies:

   - that the implicit appeal of 2:1 functions *not* as a digression *but* as the direct and urgent application of the topical content both of Hebrews 1 as a whole;
   - that ὁ δι' ἀγγέλων λαληθεὶς λόγος ("the word spoken through messengers") in 2:2 functions not as a reference to the Mosaic Law but as a parallel reference to the "great salvation" of 2:3, announced in advance by the Prophets, which has now "has been established" (ἐγένετο βέβαιος) for us;
   - that βέβαιος in both 2:2 and 2:3 describes the "establishment" in real time and space of God's long-anticipated salvation rather than the "confirmation" of the message;
   - that ἀκουσάντοι (those who heard," 2:3) represents the apostles in this context; and consequently;
   - that 2:3 does *not* rule out Pauline authorship as has been almost universally assumed.

d. concludes that the unit functions as the culmination of the preceding discourse whose topic might be summarized as follows: We must pay much more attention to the word of salvation which has now been established for us, for we will not escape if we fail to do so.

4.2.5 Hebrews 2:5–9

a.   Introduction

While 2:5–9 is universally recognized as a coherent textual unit,[180] problems of understanding remain with regard to the function of γάρ in 2:5, whose inferential character has been largely disregarded by modern scholars,[181] the precise relationship between Jesus and the ἄνθρωπος/υἱὸς ἀνθρώπου of (LXX) Psalm 8:5, and the meaning, significance and topic of the unit as a whole.[182] This section seeks to address these difficulties with fresh evidence arising from an investigation into the relationship between repetitive ties within the link cluster at Hebrews 2:5–9 and to clarify with greater precision many other aspects of meaning within this unit.

b.   Significant repetition previously observed in Hebrews 2:5–9

The next link cluster occurs at 2:5–9. As many have observed, verses 7–8a are related in a general sense to 8b–9, with the latter comprising "an elaboration" on the quotation from (LXX) Psalm 8:5–7 which contains many of the same words and phrases.[183]

---

180. See Vanhoye, *Structure*, 79; Guthrie, *Structure*, 28; Rhee, *Faith*, 81; Neeley, "Discourse Analysis," 141; Ellingworth, *Hebrews*, 50; Johnson, *Hebrews*, 85; and Westfall, *Discourse Analysis*, 299.

181. Johnson, *Hebrews*, 89, notes that "translators and commentators tend to slight the inferential character of the γάρ ("for") in verse 5, rendering it as "now," as though Hebrews was simply picking up the thread that had been dropped in 1:14 (see NRSV, Attridge, Lane, Koester, Ellingworth). Cf. Westfall, *Discourse Analysis*, 101; and Mora, *La Carta a los Hebreos como Escrito Pastoral*, 146–49, who argues that γάρ in this context does not necessarily signal a direct explanation of the co-text that directly precedes it.

182. According to Lane, *Hebrews 1–8*, n.p., 2:5–9 makes the point that "Jesus' condescension to be made "lower than the angels" (v 9) does not call into question his transcendent dignity." Guthrie, *Hebrews*, 96, and *Structure*, 63–4, meanwhile, suggests that "the key to understanding this text lies in its role as a transition"; by introducing Ps 8:5–7 into the discussion, he resumes his exposition on Christ (interrupted in 1:14), moving from consideration of his exalted to his incarnate state. Finally, O'Brien, *Hebrews*, 92, claims that 2:5–9 functions together with 2:10–18 to "clarify the relationship of the Son to the angels" and that at 2:5 the "center of attention shifts to his incarnation and earthly ministry." Yet none of these readings pay sufficient attention to what the author says he is talking about in 2:5 (the subjection of the world-to-come) and discussion about Jesus' incarnation is not in fact the "center of attention" until at least verse 8c.

183. Westfall, *Discourse Analysis*, 101. Cf. Guthrie, *Hebrews*, 96; Johnson, *Hebrews*, 85; Ellingworth, *Hebrews*, 143–44; and Lane, *Hebrews 1–8*, n.p., who sees this as a

More specifically, scholars have drawn attention to:

- the "wordplay" involving ὑποτάσσω, which occurs four times within these verses in 2:5 and 2:8 (x3) and then not again until 12:9, serving to create cohesion within the paragraph;[184] and
- the repetition of ἄγγελος (in 2:5, 9), which has been understood (like ὑποτάσσω) to function as an inclusion by some.[185]

c. *Potentially significant repetition previously unobserved in Hebrews 2:5-9*

Other connections additional to those above include:

- the six-fold repetition of the masculine singular personal pronoun, αὐτός (2:6 [x2]; 2:7 [x2]; 2:8 [x2]),[186] and
- repetition associated with the vocabulary from Psalm 8 (discussed in detail later).

More broadly:

- the phrase ὑποκάτω τῶν ποδῶν αὐτοῦ ("under his feet," 2:8) represents the functional opposite of αὐτῷ ἀνυπότακτον ("insubordinate to him," 2:8b).
- Psalm 8's statement about God's attitude to Man[187] as reflected in the verbs μιμνήσκῃ and ἐπισκέπτῃ ("he should remember," "he should shepherd/take care of") apparently contrasts sharply with the actual experience of the Man, Jesus, who endured "the suffering of death" (τὸ πάθημα τοῦ θανάτου, 2:9).

---

typical expression of "Midrashic commentary."

184. Guthrie, *Structure*, 63; and O'Brien, *Hebrews*, 92-93.

185. See Rhee, *Faith*, 81, who follows Vanhoye, *Structure*, 82, in reading both ἄγγελος and ὑποτάσσω as markers of an inclusion spanning these verses; Neeley, "Discourse Analysis," 79; and O'Brien, *Hebrews*, 92. Alternatively, Guthrie, *Structure*, 76, labels Vanhoye's inclusion as "questionable" at this point.

186. Although the word is extremely common throughout Hebrews, its concentration within this unit is notable given that in each case the referent is the same.

187. The decision to render ἄνθρωπος as "Man" throughout this unit, rather than the more gender neutral "person" or "humanity," rests upon our understanding of its meaning in this context as humanity in general as represented and fulfilled ultimately by the particular man Jesus Christ.

2:5–9 also contains several closely related phrases and/or grammatical constructions:

a. There are a large number of connections between the statements of 2:5 and 2:8–9.

   i. Both speak of the same event, God's subjection of all things to a particular individual or group. In context, the phrase τὴν οἰκουμένην τὴν μέλλουσαν ("the universe to come," 2:5) stands in metonymic relation to τὰ πάντα ("everything," 2:8c), since the latter includes the former.[188]

   ii. Both describe this event using the aorist (ὑπέταξεν, 2:5; ὑπέταξας, ὑποτάξαι, and ὑποτεταγμένα in 2:8) which depicts the subjugation in summary form as a whole.

   iii. The individual in focus in both cases represents ἄνθρωπος not ἄγγελος.

   iv. Both make use of a grammatically similar construction to set up contrasts between the messengers and Man in 2:5–6 (οὐ ... ἀγγέλοις ... δέ ... ἄνθρωπος / "not ... the messengers ... but ... man") and between what we do and do not yet see (νῦν δὲ οὔπω ὁρῶμεν ... δὲ ... βλέπομεν).

   v. Both make use of time references, μέλλουσαν ("about to come," 2:5) and νῦν ("now," 2:8), which refer to essentially the same period of time, the present: i.e. that span of time which occurs *after* God's subjection of all things to his Son and *before* the "appearance" of the world-to-come. The difference between the terms is one of emphasis, with the former stressing the imminence (i.e. "about-to-happenness") of the prophesied future in contrast to the latter, "but now not yet," which stresses the gap between present and future (the fact that now is not yet).

   vi. Lastly, both rest upon the same text of Scripture, Psalm 8:4–6, for support. In 2:5 this is made explicit by the statement, διεμαρτύρατο δέ πού τις λέγων ("but someone somewhere has testified, saying"),[189] while the dependence of 2:8–9 upon this

---

188. This is made explicit by the supporting comment of v. 8.

189. The ambiguous phrase πού τις ("someone somewhere," v. 5), described as almost "perversely vague" by Ellingworth, *Hebrews*, 147, is probably employed so as to avoid drawing attention away from the main point here. Details of exactly who said what, where and when are irrelevant to the author: what matters is that God has in fact

same Psalm is similarly clear in the vocabulary used in these verses.

b. The phrase ἠλάττωσας αὐτὸν βραχύ τι παρ' ἀγγέλους (2:7) corresponds to τὸν δὲ βραχύ τι παρ' ἀγγέλους (2:9), with the latter differing from the former by the insertion of τὸν ... Ἰησοῦν in place of αὐτόν, and the recasting of the aorist participle, ἠλάττωσας (2:7), in the perfect tense (ἠλαττωμένον, 2:9).

Heb 2:7	αὐτόν	ἠλάττωσας	βραχύ τι παρ' ἀγγέλους
Heb 2:9	τὸν ... Ἰησοῦν	ἠλαττωμένον	βραχύ τι παρ' ἀγγέλους

c. In much the same way, the phrase δόξῃ καὶ τιμῇ ἐστεφάνωσας αὐτόν (2:7) has been altered to become τὸν ... Ἰησοῦν ... δόξῃ καὶ τιμῇ ἐστεφανωμένον (2:9), by the replacement of αὐτὸν with τὸν ... Ἰησοῦν and the aorist participle, ἐστεφάνωσας, with the perfect participle, ἐστεφανωμένον (2:9). See diagram below:[190]

Heb 2:7	αὐτόν	δόξῃ καὶ τιμῇ ἐστεφάνωσας
Heb 2:9	τὸν ... Ἰησοῦν	δόξῃ καὶ τιμῇ ἐστεφανωμένον

d. *Contra* Heil, who argues for a parallel between 8a–b and 8c,[191] the Psalmist's statement regarding the action of God in 2:8a πάντα ὑπέταξας ὑποκάτω τῶν ποδῶν αὐτοῦ is better understood to mirror the author's own statement of 2:8b ἐν τῷ γὰρ ὑποτάξαι οὐδὲν ἀφῆκεν αὐτῷ ἀνυπότακτον, with the second representing a slight expansion, amplification and clarification of the meaning of the first using opposite terminology.[192]

In summary, this survey of repetition patterns in 2:5–9 has found many more instances of significant repetition than have been noted previously.

---

given testimony that he has not subjected the future world to the angels. Ellingworth rightly rejects Synge's suggestion that the author "has no idea where his citations come from," noting that "the author normally pays careful attention to the context of his quotations." Cf. Johnson, *Hebrews*, 89.

190. Word order has been changed here to make the similarities and differences obvious.

191. Heil, *Chiastic Structures*, 55, reads 8a–b and 8c as B and B' respectively.

192. While the person system is different in each case with the first representing direct address in comparison to the 3rd person indirect address, the subject is clearly God in each case.

It now remains for us to examine the location of this repetition for any evidence of a combined structural function.

d. The location and formal function of repetition in Hebrews 2:5-9

Once more, the location of repetition is significant in 2:5-9, serving both to confirm the conventional understanding of this text as a paragraph[193] and to indicate its structural arrangement. The majority of links occur on one or other side of a midpoint located after αὐτοῦ in 2:8a, splitting the cluster into two balanced halves consisting of 45 and 43 words respectively (2:5-8a and 2:8b-9), which may be further sub-divided into two pairs of matched components (A/A' and B/B') which together form a four-part chiasm similar to 1:3-6 (cf. 4.2.2c). This may be seen below:

A. ²:⁵ οὐ γὰρ ἀγγέλοις ὑπέταξεν τὴν οἰκουμένην τὴν μέλλουσαν περὶ ἧς λαλοῦμεν ⁶ διεμαρτύρατο δέ πού τις λέγων· Τί ἐστιν ἄνθρωπος ὅτι μιμνῄσκῃ αὐτοῦ ἢ υἱὸς ἀνθρώπου ὅτι ἐπισκέπτῃ αὐτόν; ⁷ ἠλάττωσας αὐτὸν βραχύ τι παρ' ἀγγέλους δόξῃ καὶ τιμῇ ἐστεφάνωσας αὐτόν

B. ⁸ <u>πάντα ὑπέταξας ὑποκάτω τῶν ποδῶν αὐτοῦ</u>

B'. <u>ἐν τῷ γὰρ ὑποτάξαι οὐδὲν ἀφῆκεν αὐτῷ ἀνυπότακτον</u>

A'. νῦν δὲ οὔπω ὁρῶμεν αὐτῷ τὰ πάντα ὑποτεταγμένα ⁹ τὸν δὲ βραχύ τι παρ' ἀγγέλους ἠλαττωμένον βλέπομεν Ἰησοῦν διὰ τὸ πάθημα τοῦ θανάτου δόξῃ καὶ τιμῇ ἐστεφανωμένον ὅπως χάριτι θεοῦ ὑπὲρ παντὸς γεύσηται θανάτου

The unit's start boundary is relatively easy to identify since: (i) 2:5 clearly introduces new material relating to God's testimony regarding his subjection of the world-to-come to ἄνθρωπος; (ii) there are no other clear links between 2:4 and the material that follows; and (iii) the phrase περὶ ἧς λαλοῦμεν by which the author "steps out of the discourse" to address the reader directly, seems designed to alert him to the new topic at hand. This indicates that 2:5 functions as transitional material which belongs both to 2:1-4 and 2:5-9.

---

193. See Vanhoye, *Structure*, 79; Guthrie, *Structure*, 28; Adam, *The Majestic Son*, 12; Rhee, *Faith*, 81; Neeley, "Discourse Analysis," 141; Ellingworth, *Hebrews*, 50; Johnson, *Hebrews*, 85; Westfall, *Discourse Analysis*, 299; and Heil, *Chiastic Structures*, .

The γάρ of 2:5 also makes clear the likelihood that the material which follows functions as support material for the former unit 2:1-4. Against the majority who understand γάρ to function by joining together the two chains of LXX citations (1:5-13 and 2:6-16) after the "digression" of 2:1-4,[194] the inferential character of this conjunction suggests "that the resumption of the contrast with the angels is not merely a return to the prior subject but builds on the exhortation in 2:1-4, providing further support for the necessity of paying attention to the great salvation announced to those hearing this discourse."[195]

e. The topical function of repetition in Hebrews 2:5-9

As with each of the units previously examined, repetition functions once again within 2:5-9 to indicate coherence between its formally related parts, clarifying meaning in a number of important ways. On its own, 2:5-8a might be understood as a general statement about Man's future rule with a proof text (2:6-8a) attached for support. When read in light of its formal partner, 2:8b-9, however, the text makes clear that the author's primary concern lies with the relative position of ἄγγελοι and ἄνθρωπος in light of God's testimony in Psalm 8 regarding the world-to-come.[196]

The differences between A and A' are also significant in clarifying meaning in a number of ways. First, when read together with 2:8, 2:5 makes clear that from the author's perspective, the subjection of all things spoken of in Psalm 8 has *already occurred*.[197] While the use of the aorist ὑπέταξεν in 2:5, although suggestive, is not determinative in and of itself, the comment that "we don't yet see" all things in subjection to Jesus (νῦν δὲ οὔπω ὁρῶμεν) only makes sense if this event has already happened. For only then would it be reasonable to expect that one *might possibly see* such a thing in the present.[198]

---

194. See Lane, *Hebrews 1-8*, n.p., who follows Moffatt in arguing for "the idiomatic translation" of γάρ in the sense of "now"; Guthrie, *Hebrews*, 96; Rhee, *Faith*, 80-81; and O'Brien, *Hebrews*, 93.

195. Johnson, *Hebrews*, 89. Cf. Westfall, *Discourse Analysis*, 95.

196. While noting the similarities between 1:13 and 2:5, Ellingworth's assessment, *Hebrews*, 144, that verse 5 "introduces no new thought" misses the fact that the verse also introduces a new point of departure relating to the future universe (τὴν οἰκουμένην τὴν μέλλουσαν), the importance of which is emphasized by the epexegetical περὶ ἧς λαλοῦμεν.

197. Pace Guthrie, *Hebrews*, 99

198. While both 2:5 and 8 affirm the same truth—that Man and not ἄγγελοι has

Second, by substituting τὸν and Ἰησοῦν (2:9) in place of (LXX) Psalm 8:5's αὐτόν and αὐτόν (cf. 2:7), the author makes clear his understanding that these statements function *not* as descriptions of humanity's place within the created order, as in their original context,[199] but as prophecies which relate specifically to Jesus.[200] This reading is further supported by the word order in 2:9, for by separating τὸν and Ἰησοῦν, the author attaches both clauses in 2:7 which refer to αὐτόν to Jesus, such that he fulfills both categories as the representative man.[201]

Ps 8:5 / Heb 2:7	ἠλάττωσας αὐτὸν βραχύ τι παρ' ἀγγέλους	δόξῃ καὶ τιμῇ ἐστεφάνωσας αὐτόν
Heb 2:9	τὸν δὲ βραχύ τι παρ' ἀγγέλους ἠλαττωμένον βλέπομεν	Ἰησοῦν ... δόξῃ καὶ τιμῇ ἐστεφανωμένον

Third, by recasting the pair of aorist participles in 2:7 (ἠλάττωσας, ἐστεφάνωσας) as perfect participles in 2:9 (ἠλαττωμένον, ἐστεφανωμένον), the author emphatically announces that what was once prophesied yet unfulfilled *has now occurred* in history. For Jesus, the man spoken of in Psalm 8, has been both made lower than the angels and crowned with glory and honor.

Fourth, the phrase διὰ τὸ πάθημα τοῦ θανάτου ("because of the suffering of death," 2:9) functions to further clarify *the reason* for Jesus'

---

been given all authority—the second statement draws attention to the fact that our perception of reality seems to contradict this. For we see Man (Jesus) made lower than the ἀγγέλους (παρ' ἀγγέλους ἠλαττωμένον βλέπομεν Ἰησοῦν, 2:9). Hebrews claims that the reason for this discrepancy relates not to reality itself (i.e. that Jesus is not yet Lord) but to our perception of this reality (we don't yet see this).

199. The "natural" reading of the Psalm views verse 6 in the light of Genesis 1 and 2 as a reference to humanity's place within the created order: slightly lower (ἠλάττωσας) than the angels, yet above the rest of Creation (πάντα ὑπέταξας ὑποκάτω τῶν ποδῶν αὐτοῦ). Cf. Westfall, *Discourse Analysis*, 101. Cf. Johnson, *Hebrews*, 90.

200. Lane, *Hebrews 1–8*, n.p., criticizes previous attempts to read υἱὸς ἀνθρώπου as a reference to Jesus in light of the Son of Man Christology of the Gospels on the grounds that in every case, Jesus' self-designation is articular. Cf. Bruce, *Hebrews*, 73; and Peterson, *Hebrews and Perfection*, 52. While this criticism is well founded, Lane's claim that the author "shows no interest in the initial lines of the quotation" is contradicted by the parallelism between Hebrews 2:5-7 and 8c-9, which clearly marks out Jesus (τόν Ἰησοῦν) as an instantial equivalent of the ἄνθρωπος/υἱὸς ἀνθρώπου (later referred to as αὐτόν), making clear that he, rather than humanity in general, is indeed both "the Man" and "Son of Man" in whom "we see" fulfilled the words spoken by the Psalmist.

201. Ellingworth, *Hebrews*, 153, claims: "the main point of the sentence appears to be that Jesus has already fulfilled the two lines of the psalm which are symmetrically placed on either side of the focal βλέπομεν Ἰησοῦν."

coronation.²⁰² While Johnson reads the phrase in connection with Jesus' "being made lower" (ἠλαττωμένον),²⁰³ (i) διά + accusative does not commonly function to convey "manner" as Johnson's reading requires; (ii) one wonders why διά + genitive is not employed instead which would make this meaning far clearer; and (iii) the word order, which places βλέπομεν Ἰησοῦν between ἠλαττωμένον and διὰ τὸ πάθημα τοῦ θανάτου suggests that both dependent participles are modified by two-part clauses, βραχύ τι παρ' ἀγγέλους and δόξῃ καὶ τιμῇ ἐστεφανωμένον respectively. Thus we find here an explicitly *causal* connection between the suffering and glorification of the Christ—Jesus was crowned precisely *because* he suffered death—which reflects "the same sequential pattern of humiliation and exaltation found in Heb 1:3c" (cf. Isa 53:10-12; Phil 2:6-11).²⁰⁴

Finally, the unmatched clause ὅπως χάριτι θεοῦ ὑπὲρ παντὸς γεύσηται θανάτου functions in this context to provide the author's understanding of the express intention behind the Psalmist's prophecy of Psalm 8:5-7 as a whole, now fulfilled in Christ: Jesus was "lowered" and "crowned" because of suffering "so that by the grace of God he might taste death for all."²⁰⁵

Meanwhile, B' functions together with B to clarify the main point made by the author's quotation of Psalm 8:4-6: that God's subjection of πάντα ("everything") includes *even* the universe-to-come (τὴν οἰκουμένη, 2:5). Westfall claims that "Jesus is depicted as fulfilling all of the quotation except for the final subjugation of all things."²⁰⁶ However, the explanatory clause of 2:8b (introduced by γάρ) allows for no such exceptions. For "when" (ἐν τῷ)²⁰⁷ he subjected all things, he (God) left nothing unsubject to him (Jesus):²⁰⁸ In other words, πάντα means

---

202. *Pace* Ellingworth, *Hebrews*, 155; Vanhoye, *Structure*, 82; and Guthrie, *Hebrews*, 100,

203. Johnson, *Hebrews*, 91.

204. Lane, *Hebrews 1-8*, n.p.

205. *Pace* Ellingworth, *Hebrews*, 155; and Attridge, *Hebrews*, 69.

206. Westfall, *Discourse Analysis*, 102.

207. ἐν τῷ is rendered as "when" rather than "in" or "with respect to" (cf. Guthrie, *Hebrews*, 96) in this context in light of the fact that time seems especially important within the unit. This may be seen especially in the author's overall interpretation of the "timeless" Psalm in the light of the historical events of Jesus, but also in his use of a number temporal markers throughout (μέλλουσαν; βραχύ,; νῦν δὲ οὔπω; βραχύ).

208. In its context, the statement γὰρ . . . οὐδὲν ἀφῆκεν αὐτῷ ἀνυπότακτον refers specifically to the world-to-come. Guthrie, *Structure*, 97, ignores the inferential conjunction, γάρ, and so misses the point here.

πάντα: While we might not see it yet, God has already placed all things (present and future) under the feet of his Son (cf. 1:2).[209]

When read together in linear fashion, the first half of the unit (A and B) quotes Psalm 8 as supporting prophetic testimony for the author's assertion that Man (ἄνθρωπος / υἱὸς ἀνθρώπου) rather than angels will one day rule the world-to-come.[210] The Psalm affirms God's care for him before promising (a) the temporary diminution of his status relative to angels, (b) his crowning with glory and honor and (c) his eventual position of universal and eternal authority. The second half (B', A'), meanwhile, covers more or less the same content from the perspective of its having been *fulfilled in chronological sequence* by Jesus, "the Man" (ἄνθρωπος), "the Son of Man" (υἱὸς ἀνθρώπου). The author testifies that even now, while not yet perceptible, (c) all things (including the world-to-come) are indeed under Jesus' feet, the one who has been both (a) made lower than angels and (b) crowned with glory and honor because of his suffering. Thus, the unit as a whole reveals the author's interest in showing how *every part* of the promise of Psalm 8 has been fulfilled by Jesus.

In summary, our analysis of topic has found clear and demonstrable evidence of coherence both between the two halves of this unit (2:5-9) and between the formally parallel clauses within it (A / A', B / B'), with the author's strikingly original reading of Psalm 8 both proving his central thesis that Jesus has indeed been given all authority and introducing new thematic material regarding the Son's "lowering" which will be addressed in the following units (2:8c-18 and 2:16-3:2). While praise for the literary genius of the author to the Hebrews is hardly new, his mastery of ambiguity is clear in the way he creates suspense by deferring the meaning of the unit and function of the LXX quotation within it until the identification of Jesus as the Man/Son of Man in 2:9.[211]

---

209. So Guthrie, *Hebrews*, 99. See 1 Cor 15:27 in which Paul makes use of the same LXX material to prove Christ's authority over death.

210. Ellingworth, *Hebrews*, 143, notes that "one expects a contrasting phrase" following οὐ γὰρ ἀγγέλοις (2:5) yet concludes that "no contrast is expressed" by the phrase which is "not particularly emphatic." However, οὐ γὰρ ἀγγέλοις is better understood in association with 2:6-8 (and especially verse 8) to make the point that God has not subjected the world-to-come to messengers, *but* (δέ) he has done this with regard to Man, as Psalm 8 testifies.

211. Lane, *Hebrews 1-8*, n.p., observes that "the repetition with variation in form is rhetorically effective. It introduces an element of suspense, which is not relieved until the emphatic deferred statement of verse 9, "but . . . we see Jesus." Cf. Ellingworth, *Hebrews*, 143, who claims similarly that "the author's thought only becomes fully explicit with Ἰησοῦν, v. 9"; and Johnson, *Hebrews*, 90.

f.   Further implications for meaning in light of the parallelism within Hebrews 2:5-9

Several further conclusions can be drawn with regard to the meaning of particular words in light of the parallelism identified above.

First, the repetition of βραχύ in 2:9 makes clear the author's understanding that the word in 2:7 functions as a time reference ("for a little while") rather than a qualifier of degree (i.e. "a little lower"). For while Jesus was not made "a little" lower than the angels in any lasting sense, he was indeed made lower "for a while."[212]

Second, the key word from Psalm 8 πάντα is understood by the author of Hebrews in different ways within this context. As discussed already, the word clearly means "all things" in 2:8. However, within the phrase ὑπὲρ παντός (2:9), the word also carries the sense of "everyone" for Jesus did not undergo suffering on behalf of jellyfish (for example). This suggests a certain element of playfulness in the author's method, which delights in bringing out unexpected meaning from words and phrases, especially those taken from the LXX, and inserting them into a new and different context.

The observation of parallelism within this material is also of assistance, third, in deciding with regard to the more contentious textual variants in verses 7 and 8,[213] with the lack of any obvious corresponding parallel to the longer reading of 2:7 (αὐτόν καὶ κατέστησας αὐτον ἐπὶ τὰ ἔργα τῶν χειρῶν σου) supporting Metzger's decision to read it as "the result of scribal enlargement of the quotation (Psalm 8:7)."[214] Similarly, the lack of a corresponding reference to αὐτῷ in the first part of verse 8 together with the high frequency of the word throughout this section and its absence in the earliest Greek witnesses makes it likely that this too is a later addition.[215]

---

212. *Pace* Lane, *Hebrews 1-8*, n.p., who notes that "in Ps 8 it is almost certainly qualitative... The understanding of the writer to the Hebrews, however, is made clear when this portion of the quotation is taken up in v 9." He notes that "this has been the dominant understanding of the expression ever since the Humanist Controversy between Erasmus and the Parisian humanist Jacobius Faber Stapulensis." Cf. Ellingworth, *Hebrews*, 154.

213. See Ellingworth, *Hebrews*, 155-57, for further discussion on the textual variant χωρὶς θεοῦ in 2:9.

214. Metzger, *A Textual Commentary*, 594.

215. Metzger, *A Textual Commentary*, 594.

The key ideas, based on repetition, relate to God's subjugation (4x ὑποτάσσω, ὑποκάτω τῶν ποδῶν αὐτῶν ποδῶν αὐτοῦ, ἀωυπότακτον) of "all things" under the feet of the Son (ἄωθρωπος/υἱὸς ἀνθρώπου/αὐτός x6). On the other hand, the themes of "sight," suffering and death and the purpose for Jesus' being lowered (ὅπως χωρὶς θεοῦ ὑπὲρ παντὸς γεύσηται θανάτου) are shown to be less significant here. Taken together, the topic of the unit may be outlined as follows: Having been made lower than the angels, then glorified, Jesus the Man has been given all authority now and for evermore, as prophesied by the Psalmist in Psalm 8.

The unit is translated as follows:

- A. ²:⁵ For he has not subjected the world to come, about which we speak, to angels. ⁶ But someone has testified somewhere, saying: "What is man that you remember him? Or the Son of Man that you shepherd him? ⁷ You have made him lower than the messengers for a while. And you have crowned him with glory and honor."

- B. ⁸ You have placed all things under his feet.

- B'. For when he subjected all things, he left nothing unsubject to him.

- A'. But now we don't yet see everything subject to him. ⁹ But we see him who was made lower than angels for a while, Jesus, crowned with glory and honor because of the suffering of death, so that by the grace of God he might taste death for all.

f. Summary of findings

This analysis of the link cluster at Hebrews 2:5–9:

a. identifies many more instances of significant repetition than previously noted within this portion of text, clarifying with greater precision the nature of the connections between 2:5–8a and 2:8b–9;

b. confirms the general understanding of Hebrews 2:5–9 as a textual unit, shedding new light on its internal symmetrical arrangement (A, B, B', A');

c. reveals the topical coherence which exists between formally linked material within it (A, A'; B, B') and how by structuring his material in the way he has, the author achieves an astonishing amount using a brilliant economy of words. With regard to his reading of Psalm 8, the author:

- interprets the Psalm in a radical new fashion as messianic prophecy rather than as a hymn of praise to Humanity's place in creation;
- presents the prophecy as having been fulfilled in its entirety *chronologically* in three stages by the Man/Son of Man, Jesus, who was "lowered," "glorified" and now rules all things;
- clarifies with precision that βραχύ in 2:7 functions as a time reference ("for a little while") rather than a qualifier of degree (i.e. "a little lower"); and
- depicts Jesus' suffering as the cause of his glorification.

This allows Hebrews' author:

- to present Jesus' present superiority over οἱ ἄγγελοι (the previous main point) as fulfillment of Scripture; and also
- to introduce the new point of departure in the discourse—the "humbling" and death of Jesus which becomes central in the next unit—as fulfillment of Scripture.

d. offers fresh evidence which assists in determining which of the textual variants in verses 7 and 8 (and respectively) is more likely to be original;

e. concludes that the topic of 2:5–9 may be summarized as follows: While we might not yet see it, having been made lower than the angels, then glorified, Jesus, "the Man" has been given all authority now and for evermore, as prophesied by the Psalmist in Psalm 8.

4.2.6 Hebrews 2:8c–18

a. Introduction

Scholars have identified at least seven difficulties in 2:8c–18 concerning (i) the detection of unit boundaries within this material, (ii) the function of γάρ in 2:10, (iii) the reason for the many alterations to the LXX versions of Psalm 22 and Isaiah 8:17,[216] (iv) the meaning and significance of

---

216. These include the (seemingly deliberate) replacement of διηγέομαι in Ps (LXX)

the LXX texts in verses 11–13 (and verse 13a/Isa 8:17 in particular), (v) the meaning of a number of key words and phrases (ἀπχηγός, πρέπω and τελειόω [2:10], εἷς [2:11]), (vi) the relationship between its component parts (e.g., 2:9–10 and 2:14–18, which both seem to explain the reason for Jesus' earthly mission) and (vii) its overall coherence.[217] The identification of a link cluster between 2:8c–18 reveals many more parallels within this material than have been previously recognized, mark out 2:8c–18 as a concentric unit, shed light on many of these difficulties, and clarify the coherence operant within it.

b. Significant repetition previously observed in Hebrews 2:8c–18

The sixth link cluster in Hebrews occurs between 2:8c–18. Lexical repetition deemed significant by previous scholarship within (or in close proximity to) these verses includes:

- the reprise of παιδίον in 2:13, 14;[218]
- the recurrence of ἀδελφός ("brother") in 2:11, 12 and 17;[219]
- the link between the noun παθημάτων (2:10) and the verb πέπονθεν (2:18);[220] and
- καὶ πάλιν and ἐγώ in 2:13.[221]

Several have also noted correspondences between:

21:23 with ἀπαγγελῶ in Heb 2:12, the insertion of πάλιν twice within the quotation from Isaiah 8:17–18 (between καί and πεποιθώς and between αὐτῷ and ἰδού) and the reversal of the word order πεποιθὼς ἔσομαι.

217. Scholars have found difficulty in explaining what this material is about. Cf. Rhee, *Faith*, 84, whose suggestion that "the theme of the humanity of Christ is emphasized through the idea of solidarity between the Son and humankind," while undoubtedly true, seems to underplay the importance of the idea of Christ's death for all (2:9, 17); Westfall, *Discourse Analysis*, 299, who summarizes the content of 2:5–18 as "Jesus is a merciful and faithful high priest"; and Heil, *Chiastic Structures*, 74–75.

218. Vanhoye, *Structure*, 82–83, claims that repetition of the word παιδίον, which occurs only in 2:13 and 14, functions as a pair of "hook words" linking together 2:10–13 and 2:14–18.

219. Heil, *Chiastic Structure*, 65.

220. Guthrie, *Structure*, 78; and Heil, *Chiastic Structures*, 65.

221. Heil, *Chiastic Structure*, 65.

- ἔπρεπεν ("it was fitting," 2:10) and ὤφειλεν ("he was obligated," 2:17), with both likely to share the same rhetorical background;[222]
- υἱοί ("sons," 2:10) and ἀδελφοί ("brothers," 2:17), which both describe the "objects of salvation" in this context;[223] and
- the instrumental phrases, διὰ παθημάτων ("through sufferings," 2:10) and διὰ τοῦ θανάτου ("through death," 2:14).[224]

More broadly, scholars have drawn attention to similarities between:

a. the statements in verses 10 and 17-18, which describe the Son's "development" in different ways (using the verbs τελειῶσαι and γένηται)[225] and contain an "alliterative link" involving ἀρχηγός and ἀρχιερεύς;[226]

b. the "programmatic statements" of verses 10-11a (taken as a whole) and the material in verses 14-15 which develop many of these ideas.[227]

c. the two halves of the quotation from Psalm (LXX) 21:23 in Hebrews 2:12.[228] While noting this parallelism, Ellingworth dismisses its significance in Hebrews, commenting that there is no evidence "of the author's desire to preserve Hebrews' parallelism in quotation for its own sake."[229]

---

222. Cf. Guthrie, *Structure*, 77; Rhee, *Faith*, 81; Ellingworth, *Hebrews*, 158; O'Brien, *Hebrews*, 102; and Löhr, "Reflections of Rhetorical Terminology in Hebrews," 204-05, who identifies "pagan Hellenistic theology and philosophy" as the likely background to both words in Hebrews.

223. Guthrie, *Structure*, 77-78 and 102.

224. Johnson, *Hebrews*, 100, claims that διὰ τοῦ θανάτου in 2:14 "matches" διὰ παθημάτων in 2:10. However, the plural nature of παθημάτων suggests that while Christ's death is certainly included within and represents the ultimate expression of the "sufferings" referred to in 2:10 (see the mention of τὸ πάθημα τοῦ θανάτου in 2:9), more is on view in than Jesus' death alone, such that the second phrase *includes* the first.

225. Guthrie, *Structure*, 77-78. See too Ellingworth, *Hebrews*, 180, who claims that the latter describes "old ideas with fresh language" which "throws light on" and strengthens the former statement (p. 153); Attridge, *Hebrews*, 95; and Heil, *Chiastic Structures*, 64.

226. Heil, *Chiastic Structures*, 65.

227. Ellingworth, *Hebrews*, 170. Alternatively, Heil, *Chiastic Structures*, 64, argues for a connection between vv. 11-12 and 14-16.

228. Ellingworth, *Hebrews*, 167; and Heil, *Chiastic Structures*, 69.

229. Ellingworth, *Hebrews*, 167.

d. some of the material within 2:14-15 (cf. fig. 18).²³⁰

```
A   Since the children
  B   Shared a common human nature
A'  he too likewise                          Parallel symmetry
  B'  shared the same humanity

  C   in order that by death
    D   he might break the power
    D'  of the one who held the power        Concentric symmetry
  C'  of death

  E   and that he might liberate those
    F   who from fear of death               Concentric symmetry
    F'  throughout their lives
  E'  were held in a state of bondage
```

Fig. 18.

Ellingworth also draws attention to Hebrews' use of a significant number of distinctive words and phrases from Isaiah 41:8-10 within 2:13ff. ²³¹ These intertextual links may be seen in diagrammatic form below:

Isa 41:8-10	Heb 2:13ff.
παῖς	τὰ παιδία (vv. 13, 14)
σπέρμα Αβρααμ	σπέρματος Ἀβραὰμ (v. 16)
ἀντελαβόμην	ἐπιλαμβάνεται (v. 18 [x2])
φοβοῦ	φόβῳ (vv. 15)
ἐβοήθησα	βοηθῆσαι (v. 18)

---

230. Cf. Vanhoye, *La Structure*, 80-81; and Lane, *Hebrews 1-8*, n.p. The diagram represents Lane's translation of Vanhoye's observations. There are difficulties with several of these parallels, however. For example, the similarity between D and D' also seems less than obvious in the Greek (καταργήσῃ / τὸν τὸ κράτος ἔχοντα τοῦ θανάτου) than either scholar suggests. Cf. Heil, *Chiastic Structures*, 71.

231. According to Ellingworth, *Hebrews*, 176, the re-appearance of a number of these allusions within the final quotation of the discourse (13:5ff) indicates that "the importance of this allusion is not limited to the present passage." Cf. Koester, *Hebrews*, 232; and O'Brien, *Hebrews*, 117.

The connection between these texts is further strengthened by the identification of three additional instances of lexical repetition, previously unobserved (below):

Isa 41:8–10	Heb 2:13ff.
ἐκάλεσά, (v. 9)	κλήσεως (3:1)[232]
ἐγώ (v. 10)	ἐγώ (v. 13 [x2])
ὁ θεός (v. 10)	ὁ θεός (v. 13)

c. *Potentially significant repetition previously unobserved in Hebrews 2:8c–18*

To the connections described above may be added a raft of other previously unobserved connections within this section of text. There are at least four further instances of significant lexical repetition:

- the five-fold references to θάνατος (out of a total of ten occurrences in Hebrews);[233]
- the eight-fold occurrence of πᾶς in various forms;[234]
- θεοῦ, θεοῦ/ and τὸν θεόν in 2:9, 13 and 17; and
- the mention of ἀγγέλους in 2:9 and 16.[235]

In addition to these:

---

232. The echo of ἐκάλεσα (Isa 41:9) in κλήσεως (Heb 3:1) is particularly illuminating in clarifying the meaning of the ambiguous phrase κλήσεως ἐπουρανίου μέτοχοι (cf. discussion in 4.2.7b).

233. θανάτου and θανάτου (2:9); του θανάτου (2:14 x2); and θανάτου (2:15). To these may be added the reference to παθημάτων which, as noted previously (4.2.6a), includes the concept of death in this context.

234. τὰ πάντα x 2 (2:8); παντός (2:9), τὰ πάντα x2 (2:10), πάντες (2:11), παντός (2:15) and πάντα (2:17). Although the word is relatively common in Hebrews, the number of references suggests a special significance for πᾶς in shaping the cohesion of this portion of text. The next reference in the discourse occurs in a context in which it has a completely different meaning (3:4).

235. The reference to ἄγγελοι in 2:16 constitutes the final reference in Hebrews until chapter 12. Further lexical repetition also occurs between: μου / μοι (2:12 and 13); σου / σε (2:12); ἀδελφούς ("brothers" in 2:11,12); οὐκ and οὐ (2:11 and 16); πάλιν (2:13 and 14); διά + accusative (2:10, 11); αὐτός in singular form (2:10, 13 and 14) and ἐγώ (2:13 and 14).

- ὁρῶμεν (2:8), βλέπομεν (2:9) and ἰδού (2:13) are similar verbs of perception which each have Jesus as their object;[236]
- the reference to "life" in 1:15 (τοῦ ζῆν) functions as an antonym to the numerous references to "death" discussed previously; and
- the phrase τὸ πάθημα τοῦ θανάτου ("the suffering of death), mentioned in 2:9 in relation to Jesus, finds its likely contraction in the reference to Jesus' death of 2:14 (cf. διὰ τοῦ θανάτου) and πέπονθεν in 2:18, with the first mention emphasizing the nature of the experience for Jesus.

More broadly, 2:8-18 contains a vast matrix of words and phrases which describe in various ways a group (or groups) of people, many of which represent common descriptors of God's people in the LXX.[237] These include παντός in 2:9 ("everyone"); υἱούς ("sons," 2:10); οἱ ἁγιαζόμενοι ("those being sanctified," 2:11); ἀδελφούς ("brothers," 2:11 and 17); τοῖς ἀδελφοῖς μου ("my brothers," 2:12); ἐκκλησίας ("gathering," 2:12); τὰ παιδία ἅ μοι ἔδωκεν ὁ θεός ("the children God has given to me," 2:13); τὰ παιδία ("the children," 2:14); τούτους ὅσοι φόβῳ θανάτου διὰ παντὸς τοῦ ζῆν ἔνοχοι ἦσαν δουλείας ("those who were formerly bound to slavery by fear of death throughout their lives," 2:15); σπέρματος Ἀβραάμ ("the seed of Abraham," 2:16);[238] τοῦ λαοῦ ("the people," 2:17); and τοῖς πειραζομένοις ("those being tested," 2:18). To these may be added the first and second person plural forms of the verbs ὁρῶμεν, βλέπομεν and ἰδού (2:8, 9 and 13; cf. 1:2; 2:1-3), and αὐτῶν ("their" in reference to salvation, 2:10).

While the sheer frequency of these references alone indicates that people play a key role within this material (see below, marked out in **bold**), the grammatical connections between them make clear that each refers to *the same group of people*.[239] In this way the present readers of

---

236. Cf. Jesus (αὐτῷ, 2:9; τὸν ... Ἰησοῦν (2:10); ἐγώ (2:13). As commentators have noted, this third reference represents a likely divine allusion.

237. E.g., υἱούς, ἀδελφούς, ἐκκλησίας, τά παιδία, and σπέρματος Ἀβραάμ. Cf. Ellingworth, *Hebrews*, 159.

238. The link between Isaiah 41:8-10 and Hebrews 2 makes clear, *pace* Ellingworth, *Hebrews*, 177, that "whatever the precise meaning of σπέρμα Ἀβραάμ here, it is clearly something more concrete than 'human nature,'" and describes a group of people. Cf. further discussion on its meaning in 4.2.7b.

239. The reference to παντός in 2:9 is linked with and made more precise in the phrase, πολλοὺς υἱούς ("many sons"), which also shares a substitutional relationship with οἱ ἁγιαζόμενοι in verse 11. The γάρ in 2:11 indicates that v. 11a functions as support for 2:10, explaining why it was fitting for God to perfect his Son so as to lead "many sons" into glory. The answer indicates a clear correspondence between these sons and "those

Hebrews are characterized as a people whose identity is linked with God's people in the LXX, who once were enslaved by the fear of death, but have now been set free from the Devil's clutches by Jesus' death on their behalf (in fulfilment of the Scriptures).

Νῦν δὲ οὔπω **ὁρῶμεν** αὐτῷ **τὰ πάντα** ὑποτεταγμένα τὸν δὲ βραχύ τι παρ' ἀγγέλους ἠλαττωμένον **βλέπομεν** Ἰησοῦν διὰ τὸ πάθημα τοῦ θανάτου δόξῃ καὶ τιμῇ ἐστεφανωμένον ὅπως χωρὶς θεοῦ ὑπὲρ **παντὸς** γεύσηται θανάτου ἔπρεπεν γὰρ αὐτῷ δι' ὃν **τὰ πάντα** καὶ δι' οὗ **τὰ πάντα πολλοὺς υἱοὺς** εἰς δόξαν ἀγαγόντα τὸν ἀρχηγὸν τῆς σωτηρίας **αὐτῶν** διὰ παθημάτων τελειῶσαι ὅ τε γὰρ ἁγιάζων καὶ οἱ ἁγιαζόμενοι ἐξ ἑνὸς πάντες δι' ἣν αἰτίαν οὐκ ἐπαισχύνεται **ἀδελφοὺς αὐτοὺς** καλεῖν λέγων Ἀπαγγελῶ τὸ ὄνομά σου **τοῖς ἀδελφοῖς μου** ἐν μέσῳ **ἐκκλησίας** ὑμνήσω σε καὶ πάλιν Ἐγὼ ἔσομαι πεποιθὼς ἐπ' αὐτῷ καὶ πάλιν **Ἰδοὺ** ἐγὼ καὶ **τὰ παιδία ἅ μοι ἔδωκεν ὁ θεός** ἐπεὶ οὖν **τὰ παιδία** κεκοινώνηκεν αἵματος καὶ σαρκός καὶ αὐτὸς παραπλησίως μετέσχεν τῶν αὐτῶν ἵνα διὰ τοῦ θανάτου καταργήσῃ τὸν τὸ κράτος ἔχοντα τοῦ θανάτου τοῦτ' ἔστι τὸν διάβολον καὶ ἀπαλλάξῃ **τούτους ὅσοι φόβῳ θανάτου διὰ παντὸς τοῦ ζῆν ἔνοχοι ἦσαν δουλείας** οὐ γὰρ δήπου ἀγγέλων ἐπιλαμβάνεται ἀλλὰ **σπέρματος** Ἀβραὰμ ἐπιλαμβάνεται πιστὸς ἀρχιερεὺς τὰ πρὸς τὸν θεόν εἰς τὸ ἱλάσκεσθαι τὰς ἁμαρτίας **τοῦ λαοῦ** ὅθεν ὤφειλεν κατὰ πάντα **τοῖς ἀδελφοῖς** ὁμοιωθῆναι ἵνα ἐλεήμων γένηται καὶ ἐν ᾧ γὰρ πέπονθεν αὐτὸς πειρασθείς δύναται **τοῖς πειραζομένοις** βοηθῆσαι

Hebrews 2:8c–18 also contains four periphrastic constructions which form relations of similarity and contrast between Jesus, God the Father, the Devil, and the people in contexts relating to authority (see below): Although the Jesus we see is apparently "lower" than the angels (2:9), he is in fact Lord of all (2:8c). Meanwhile all people are "for" God—ie they belong to him (δι' ὅν) while the Devil is the one "with authority of death."[240] Although the author makes use of this formal device on other occasions throughout Hebrews (e.g., τὸν ἔχοντα τὰς ἐπαγγελίας εὐλόγηκεν in 7:6), the high concentration of these constructions at this point and their thematic similarity is noteworthy, and serves to build cohesion within this material.

Jesus	τὸν δὲ βραχύ τι παρ' ἀγγέλους ἠλαττωμένον ... Ἰησοῦν (2:9)
God, the Father	αὐτῷ δι' ὃν τὰ πάντα καὶ δι' οὗ τὰ πάντα (2:10)
The Devil	τὸν τὸ κράτος ἔχοντα τοῦ θανάτου (2:14)
The People	τούτους ὅσοι φόβῳ θανάτου διὰ παντὸς τοῦ ζῆν ἔνοχοι ἦσαν δουλείας (2:15)

---

being sanctified." Both of these terms are also further related to the labels ἀδελφοῖς μου and ἐκκλησίας (both in 2:12), since Jesus' "perfection" as τὸν ἀρχηγόν means that he now thinks of these "sons" as "my brothers," announcing God's name among them (ie within "the assembly"). Verse 13b serves in context as a summary of this solidarity between Jesus and this group, replacing all previous terms with the new familial term, τὰ παιδία ("the children"). Finally, the highly significant term, the "seed of Abraham," stands in place of the entire group described above.

240. To avoid confusion, the author clarifies the referents of the first and third respectively.

To this list may be added grammatical connections between:

a. various expressions of purpose involving ὅπως in 2:9, ἵνα (and possibly καί) in 2:14, 15, ἵνα and εἰς τό in 2:17, and (arguably) the participle, ἀγαγόντα in 2:10;[241]

b. the causal constructions, δι' + accusative in 2:10 and 11 (δι' ὃν, δι' ἣν αἰτίαν ("because of whom," "for which reason"), ὅθεν (2:17) and (possibly) ἐπεί in 2:14;[242]

c. contrasts set up by νῦν δὲ οὔπω ... δέ ("but now not yet ... but," 2:8 and 9) and δήπου ... ἀλλά ("surely not ... but," 2:16) which, while topically distinct, both make mention of ἀγγέλους.

Most striking, however, are the numerous connections between small and large sections of 2:8c–18, some of which involve combinations of the links already described. These are itemized below.

a. The phrase νῦν δὲ οὔπω ὁρῶμεν αὐτῷ τὰ πάντα ὑποτεταγμένα (2:8c) is related to the purpose statement regarding Jesus' earthly mission (ἵνα ... καταργήσῃ τὸν τὸ κράτος ἔχοντα τοῦ θανάτου ... καὶ ἀπαλλάξῃ τούτους ὅσοι φόβῳ θανάτου διὰ παντὸς τοῦ ζῆν ἔνοχοι ἦσαν δουλείας (2:14–15) in the following ways.

  i. As noted previously (cf. 4.2.6a), both indirectly affirm the Son's present universal authority.[243] The aorist participle of 2:8, ὑποτεταγμένα, which views the subjugation of all things in summary fashion, makes clear in its context that despite what we "see," all things have been subjected "to him" (αὐτῷ, i.e. Jesus) in fulfilment of Psalm 8.[244] Much the same state of affairs also seems to be envisaged in 2:14, flowing as a consequence from the Son's having "rendered powerless" (καταργήσῃ)[245]

---

241. Johnson, *Hebrews*, 95, comments: "The participle ἀγαγόντα can be connected either to God or to the Son, and as a circumstantial participle it can serve several syntactical functions. I attach the phrase to God and translate it as an occasional clause, 'in leading', but it could just as legitimately be translated as a purpose clause, 'in order to lead.'"

242. Although the phrase ἐν τῷ in 2:8 can also function causally, context rules against it on this occasion.

243. Cf. Guthrie, *Hebrews*, 99, 110, who notes that 2:8 shares the same "perspective on the inaugurated rule of the Son" as the purpose statement in 2:14.

244. See previous comments in 4.2.5d on the Son's fulfilment of Ps 8:4–6 as a whole.

245. Gingrich, *Greek Lexicon*, n.p., translates καταργέω as "render powerless." Alternatively, Newman, *Greek-English Dictionary*, n.p., translates the word as "render

his ultimate rival, the one who once had authority (τὸν τὸ κράτος ἔχοντα).[246]

ii. A further connection also exists between ὑποτεταγμένα ("having been subjected," 2:8c) and the description of those liberated by the Son as ἔνοχοι ἦσαν δουλείας ("those who were bound to slavery, 2:15).[247]

b. The description of Jesus' "having been made lower than angels" (παρ' ἀγγέλους ἠλαττωμένον, 2:9) is linked with the statements κεκοινώνηκεν αἵματος καὶ σαρκός ("He has experienced blood and flesh," 2:14) and κατὰ πάντα τοῖς ἀδελφοῖς ὁμοιωθῆναι ("to be made like his brothers in every way," 2:17). The exact nature of these connections depends on whether the clause which follows the statement in 2:9, διὰ τὸ πάθημα τοῦ θανάτου, is meant to link with the preceding or subsequent statement. If the former, then the lowering on view is directly tied to Jesus' experience of death, so that the emphasis of 2:14 is upon Jesus' sharing of αἵματος ("blood"). If, however, the latter is true, as seems more likely,[248] then both verses 9 and 14 describe a lowering which is *separate to*

---

ineffective," while Friberg, *Analytical Lexicon*, n.p., proposes "release by removal from a former sphere of control *free from*." While ἵνα ... καταργήσῃ ("in order ... that he might nullify") can be read as an unfulfilled condition (i.e. the Devil has not yet been nullified so that he still *has* authority, ἔχοντα), Ellingworth, *Hebrews*, 173, states: "realized and unrealized elements in eschatology are held in tension, as in the author's use of Ps. 110:1 (Heb. 1:13; 10:12f.). The one who has power over death is himself reduced to impotence, but death itself is not yet destroyed (cf. 1 Cor. 15:26, 54ff.)."

246. The description of the Devil as "the one who had authority over death" is emphatic and makes clear both the nature of Satan's authority (over death) and the reason Jesus came to earth: in order to seize back control over death, thereby liberating those held in slavery by the Devil through their fear of death. As such, verse 14 represents the ultimate application and proof of what we do not yet "see" (νῦν δὲ οὔπω ὁρῶμεν, 2:8c): for *even* the devil, who once held extraordinary power, has been stripped of his power by the Son.

247. As Johnson, *Hebrews*, 101, notes, "Hebrews uses a particularly powerful expression [in 2:15]. The adjective *enochos* itself suggests 'being bound' (Aristotle, Metaphysics 1009B) or 'subject to' (Plato, Laws 869B). In combination with the substantive *douleia*, it creates the phrase 'being bound to slavery.'" The use of two such similar words is particularly emphatic here and creates a contrast between the previous experience of this group (slaves of Satan) and their present experience as servants of the Son.

248. *Pace* Ellingworth, *Hebrews*, 155; Vanhoye, *Structure*, 82; Guthrie, *Hebrews*, 100; and Lane, *Hebrews 1-8*, n.p., who notes that the phrase αἵματος καὶ σαρκός represents "an established Jewish (though not OT) term for man, whether as individual or species, in his creatureliness and distinction from God." Cf. Louw and Nida, *Greek-English Lexicon*, n.p.

and *precedes* Jesus' death, referring most obviously to his incarnation. Read in this way, both 2:9 and 14 are closely related to the purpose statement in 2:17a. For having "been made lower" than angels (2:9), i.e. having *suffered and died as a man* (2:14), Jesus has truly "become like" his brothers "in every way" in fulfilment of 2:17: κατὰ πάντα τοῖς ἀδελφοῖς ὁμοιωθῆναι.

c. A similarly close relationship also exists between the purpose statements of 2:9c and 17c (see below), both of which (i) refer indirectly yet explicitly to God (θεός), (ii) follow statements related to Jesus' "lowering" and (iii) describe Jesus' death as having been undertaken purposefully (ὅπως / ἵνα ... εἰς) to offer (iv) an atoning sacrifice of himself (γεύσηται θανάτου, τὸ ἱλάσκεσθαι τὰς ἁμαρτίας) (iv) on behalf of "the people" (ὑπὲρ παντός, εἰς τὸ ἱλάσκεσθαι τὰς ἁμαρτίας τοῦ λαοῦ). In 2:9, Jesus was made lower and crowned through suffering and death "so that" (ὅπως)[249] by the grace of God he might taste death "on behalf of all" (ὑπὲρ παντός).[250] Ellingworth notes that the final phrase "is emphatic by its place in the clause."[251] Meanwhile, verse 17 insists that Jesus became like his brothers in every way "so as to atone for the sins of the people" (2:17), a reference which in Hebrews can only refer to his once-for-all death on the cross (cf. 9:11–14; 10:1–10).

Heb 2:9   ὅπως χωρὶς θεοῦ ὑπὲρ παντὸς γεύσηται θανάτου
          "so that by the grace of God he might taste death for all"

Heb 2:17 εἰς τὸ ἱλάσκεσθαι τὰς ἁμαρτίας τοῦ λαοῦ
          "in order to atone for the sins of the people"

Read together, verse 9c emphasizes the gracious intent behind Christ's suffering and death, while verse 17 makes clear the sense

---

249. *Pace* Ellingworth, *Hebrews*, 155, ὅπως is best understood in relation to v. 9 as a whole: "all this (the humiliation and the exaltation) took place in order that, within God's gracious purpose, Jesus might experience death on behalf of everyone." *Contra* Attridge, *Hebrews*, 76.

250. *Contra* Ellingworth, *Hebrews*, 157, who translates παντός as a neuter plural, "everything." Cf. Mark 10:45; 14:24; Luke 22:20; 1 Cor 11:24; John 6:51; 11:50-51; Rom 5:8; 8:34; 1 Cor 1:13; 15:3; Gal 1:4; 2:20; Titus 2:4; and 1 Thess 5:10.

251. Ellingworth, *Hebrews*, 157.

in which Christ died "for the sake of" others (now described as τὸν λαόν): namely, that he might "make propitiation" for their sins.[252]

d. The strongly experiential verb γεύσηται ("he might taste," 2:9) is also linked to the similar indicative verbs of 2:14, κεκοινώνηκεν and μετέσχεν, which both connote ideas of "sharing in" and "experiencing."[253]

e. In both 2:9-10 and 14-16, Jesus' experience of human suffering is described within the context of a mission to rescue the same group of people, fulfilled through his death. The same logical sequence of events is described in both instances (cf. fig. 15 below). In 2:9, Jesus became a man "so that *he* might taste death for all" (ὅπως . . . ὑπὲρ παντὸς γεύσηται θανάτου, 2:9), and fulfil God's plan to "lead many sons into glory" (πολλοὺς υἱοὺς εἰς δόξαν ἀγαγόντα, 2:10). Similarly, 2:14 claims *because* (ἐπεί)[254] share in flesh and blood, Jesus also partook of these in the same way "*so that* through death he might deliver" those who were formerly enslaved (ἵνα διὰ τοῦ θανάτου . . . ἀπαλλάξῃ, 2:14-15). Grammatically, the καί of verse 15 indicates that the clause beginning ἀπαλλάξῃ functions as the second of two clauses which express the purpose behind Christ's death (i.e. ἵνα διὰ τοῦ θανάτου καταργήσῃ . . . καὶ [ἵνα] ἀπαλλάξῃ).

---

252. "To make propitiation" is to be preferred over "to make expiation," because this is the usual meaning of the verb and its cognates not only in secular usage but in the LXX. Morris, *Apostolic Preaching*, 125-60

253. Louw and Nida, *Greek-English Lexicon*, n.p. recognizes "a figurative extension of meaning" for γεύμαι as "to experience, probably focusing on personal involvement." Meanwhile Lane, *Hebrews 1-8*, n.p., comments with regard to 2:14 that "the meaning of the two roots is virtually synonymous; both describe a full participation in a shared reality." Cf. Campbell, "κοινωνία," 353, 355, 363; and Ellingworth, *Hebrews*, 171, who suggests that μετέχω is "perhaps used for variety" in this context. Louw and Nida, *Greek-English Lexicon*, n.p., also note that μετέσχεν and γεύσηται are further connected by their common collocation in contexts involving food.

254. *Contra* Ellingworth, *Hebrews*, 170, who claims that ἐπεί "is only incidentally related to exegesis," the word plays a crucial function marking the cause for Jesus' action.

PATTERNS OF REPETITION, STRUCTURE, AND MEANING

	Heb 2:9-10	Heb 2:14-16
Beneficiaries	ὑπὲρ παντὸς πολλοὺς υἱοὺς	τὰ παιδία τούτους ὅσοι φόβῳ θανάτου διὰ παντὸς τοῦ ζῆν ἔνοχοι ἦσαν δουλείας οὐ ... ἀγγέλων ... ἀλλὰ σπέρματος Ἀβραάμ
Purpose 1	ὅπως ... γεύσηται θανάτου	διὰ τοῦ θανάτου
Purpose 2	πολλοὺς υἱοὺς εἰς δόξαν ἀγαγόντα	καὶ ἀπαλλάξῃ τούτους

When read together, it seems highly likely that both statements describe two sides of the *same* act of rescue, the first emphasizing its ultimate destination, the second, its starting point; the first, the work of the Father, the second, the work of the Son. Consequently, although lexically unrelated, 2:15 is best understood as an expansion of σωτηρίας αὐτῶν ("their salvation," 2:10), which adds content about the nature of the rescue affected by Jesus.[255] The point, then, is clear:

Jesus became a man *so that*
    1. he might die (for people) and
    2. thereby deliver them *from* slavery *into* glory

f. Both 2:9-10 and 14-17 also speak of an additional purpose for the Son's experience of human suffering and death in terms of *what it achieved for Jesus*. In 2:10, Jesus suffered because God deemed it "fitting" (ἔπρεπεν) for him to do so *in order to lead* (ἀγαγόντα)[256] many sons into glory as the "pioneer leader of their Salvation" (τὸν ἀρχηγὸν τῆς σωτηρίας αὐτῶν, 2:10). Had he not done so, Jesus would not have been "perfect" (i.e. fully equipped) for the task.[257] Similarly, in 2:17 the author claims that Jesus "was obligated" (ὤφειλεν) to become like his brothers "in order that he might become" (ἵνα ... γένηται) "a merciful ... and faithful high priest with reference

---

255. Johnson, *Hebrews*, 101, suggests that "Hebrews here adds 'liberation' to his glossary of terms expressing the Son's work for his fellow humans ... a list that already includes 'salvation,' 'sanctification,' 'bringing to glory,' and 'the world to come.'"

256. The adverbial aorist participle ἀγαγόντα is understood here in a telic sense, expressing purpose.

257. Lane observes, "the "perfection" of Jesus in this context (cf. 5:8-9; 7:28) has functional implications. The emphasis falls on the notion that he was fully equipped for his office."

to God to make atonement for the sins of the people" (ἐλεήμων ... καὶ πιστὸς ἀρχιερεὺς τὰ πρὸς τὸν θεόν εἰς τὸ ἱλάσκεσθαι τὰς ἁμαρτίας τοῦ λαοῦ, 2:17). Once more, had Jesus not suffered/become fully human, he *could not* have completed the task assigned to him by God.

g. There is also a considerable degree of similarity between the statement ὅ τε γὰρ ἁγιάζων καὶ οἱ ἁγιαζόμενοι ἐξ ἑνὸς πάντες (2:11a) and the quotation from Isaiah 8:18 in 2:13b ἰδοὺ ἐγὼ καὶ τὰ παιδία ἅ μοι ἔδωκεν ὁ θεός.

   i. Both statements emphasize the closeness of the relationship between Jesus and his people while simultaneously making clear his superiority over them. In verse 11, the author's use of the grammatical construction (τε ... καί, "both... and") and same root word for both (ὁ ἁγιάζων and οἱ ἁγιαζόμενοι, cf. 2:18) brings Jesus and the people together as part of the same process and plan of God, while making clear the vastly different roles played by each within that plan: Where Jesus is the active agent of sanctification, "the Sanctifier," a title which always refers to "the Lord" (κύριος) in the LXX,[258] they are the passive recipients and beneficiaries of his work. Similarly, the exhortation from Isaiah 8:18 calls on readers to "behold again" (cf. ἰδοὺ ἐγώ)[259] Jesus standing *with* the children (τὰ παιδία). At the same time, however, his relative superiority is made clear by the statement that they have been "given" to him (ἔδωκεν) by God.

   ii. Both involve the same (two or) three participants in the same order (see below). That Jesus (ἐγώ) is "the Sanctifier" (ὁ ἁγιάζων) and that "those being sanctified" (οἱ ἁγιαζόμενοι) represent the same people as "the children" (τὰ παιδία) in verse 13 is clear. If (as seems likely) the ambiguous reference to ἑνός is masculine and refers to God,[260] then a third parallel presents

---

258. Cf. Ex 31:13; Lev 20:8; 21:8, 15, 23; 22:9, 16, 32; Ezek 20:12; and 37:28. Hebrews thus makes clear that Jesus' mission represents the fulfilment of the promise of Ezekiel 37:28.

259. In view of the importance of "sight words" in this unit, it is not impossible, nor even unlikely that πάλιν functions in connection with the command to "behold!" (ἰδού), rather than as a reference back to λέγων (2:12) as per Ellingworth, *Hebrews*, 168; Johnson, *Hebrews*, 94.

260. While the adjective ἑνός ("one") in 2:11 may be either masculine or neuter, Guthrie, *Hebrews*, 108, notes that most commentators, both ancient and modern, have read it as a masculine reference to God the Father and suggests that "the emphasis

itself between "the One" spoken of in 2:11 and the reference to "God" (ὁ θεός) in 2:13, *which occurs in exactly the same location* within their respective clauses.

| Heb 2:11 | ὁ ἁγιάζων | καὶ οἱ ἁγιαζόμενοι | ἐξ ἑνὸς πάντες |
| Heb 2:13 | ἐγὼ | καὶ τὰ παιδία | ἅ μοι ἔδωκεν ὁ θεός |

iii. If ἑνός is taken as a reference to God, both verses 11a and 13b also reveal the Father as the "First Cause" in each case. In verse 11, Lane observes that "despite the qualitative difference between Jesus and the people of God, they share a unity based upon their common origin. The πάντες is clearly inclusive of both parties mentioned in verse 11, the one who consecrates and those who are being consecrated."[261] Much the same content is also conveyed by the quotation from Isaiah: "God has given the children to me" (2:13), which makes clear that Jesus' presence with the children rests upon his Father's gift.

h. Finally, the modified quotation from (LXX) Ps 21:23 functions in the present context (2:12) as part of a *pair of functionally equivalent statements*:[262]

　　i. τὸ ὄνομά σου ("your name") stands in synonymous parallelism with σε ("you");[263]

　　ii. τοῖς ἀδελφοῖς μου ("my brothers") and the ἐκκλησία ("the gathering") refer to the same group of people; and

　　iii. the verbs ἀπαγγελῶ ("I will announce") and ὑμνήσω ("I sing a hymn, I sing a song of praise"), which represents an alteration to the LXX text, share a common emphasis involving the declaration of God's praises.[264]

---

in the context on sonship in relation to God supports this choice." Cf. Ellingworth, *Hebrews*, 165–65. Alternatively, Johnson, *Hebrews*, 97–98, the NIV, and ESV read it as a neuter reference to "a common source" (i.e. Abraham), "one family" and "one origin" respectively.

261. Lane, *Hebrews 1–8*, n.p.

262. Contra Heil, *Chiastic Structures*, 64, who argues for a parallel between verse 13a and b on the basis of repetition of καὶ πάλιν and ἐγώ.

263. Ellingworth, *Hebrews*, 168.

264. Louw and Nida, *Greek-English Lexicon*, n.p. Friberg, *Analytical Lexicon*, n.p., lists among the range of meanings of ἀπαγγελῶ, "announcing something *proclaim, declare*," "acknowledging something publicly *confess*." Cf. LXX Ps 70:17 and 88:2 which

	Heb 2:12a	Heb 2:12b
Agent and action	ἀπαγγελῶ	ὑμνήσω
Object	τὸ ὄνομά σου	σε
Location	τοῖς ἀδελφοῖς μου	ἐν μέσῳ ἐκκλησίας

The picture which emerges shows that 2:8c–18 contains many more instances of significant repetition than have been previously observed. It now remains for us to examine the location of this repetition for evidence of a combined structural function.

d. The location and formal function of repetition in Hebrews 2:8c–18

Based purely on lexical repetition, the extent of this cluster is harder to discern than those examined already. This seems due to a combination of factors including the presence of a number of strong connections within 2:8c–10 (which potentially obscure the wider connections),[265] the length of this cluster, the complexity of the inter-relatedness of material in 2:8c–9 and 2:14–17, and the fact that the majority of connections here have been achieved using non-lexical forms of repetition. On closer examination, however, the location of the repetition in 4.2.6a and b conforms to the pattern seen in each of the five link clusters examined to this point.

The majority of significant connections occur on one or other side of a midpoint which occurs after ἀδελφοῖς μου in verse 12, splitting 2:8c–18 into two halves comprised of 84 and 99 words respectively which may be further subdivided into ten smaller parallel components.[266] This suggests, then, (i) that 1:13—2:5 represents a concentric unit whose boundaries overlap with 2:5–9, (ii) that 2:8c–9 represents transitional material

---

both involve declaring particular "excellencies" of God.

265. Lexical repetition within 2:8–10 includes the five-fold repetition of πᾶς (τὰ πάντα x 2 (2:8); παντός (2:9), τὰ πάντα x2 (2:10); διά + genitive x 2; θανάτου x 2; πάθημα and παθημάτων (2:9 and 10); and δόξῃ (2:9 and 10). Cf. also the synonyms of sight in 2:8 and 9 which both relate to the same object, Jesus (ὁρῶμεν αὐτῷ and τὸν ... βλέπομεν, "we see") and the broader conceptual link between the phrase "by the grace of God he might taste death for all" and the notion of "their salvation." We will examine these connections further in chapter 5.2.

266. Heil, *Chiastic Structures*, 64–5, reads 2:10–18 as a six-part chiasm as follows:

shared with 2:5–9, and (iii) that the author's careful arrangement of his material *works with not against* the parallelism within Psalm (LXX) 21:23.

- A. ²:⁸ᶜ νῦν δὲ οὔπω ὁρῶμεν αὐτῷ τὰ πάντα ὑποτεταγμένα τὸν δὲ βραχύ τι παρ' ἀγγέλους ἠλαττωμένον ⁹ βλέπομεν Ἰησοῦν διὰ τὸ πάθημα τοῦ θανάτου δόξῃ καὶ τιμῇ ἐστεφανωμένον <u>ὅπως χωρὶς θεοῦ ὑπὲρ παντὸς γεύσηται θανάτου</u>

  - B. ¹⁰ ἔπρεπεν γὰρ αὐτῷ, δι' ὃν τὰ πάντα καὶ δι' οὗ τὰ πάντα <u>πολλοὺς υἱοὺς εἰς δόξαν ἀγαγόντα τὸν ἀρχηγὸν</u> τῆς σωτηρίας αὐτῶν διὰ παθημάτων τελειῶσαι

    - C. ¹¹ ὅ τε γὰρ ἁγιάζων καὶ οἱ ἁγιαζόμενοι ἐξ ἑνὸς πάντες

      - D. δι' ἣν αἰτίαν οὐκ ἐπαισχύνεται ἀδελφοὺς αὐτοὺς καλεῖν

        - E. ¹² λέγων ἀπαγγελῶ τὸ ὄνομά σου τοῖς ἀδελφοῖς μου

        - E'. ἐν μέσῳ ἐκκλησίας ὑμνήσω σε

      - D'. ¹³ καὶ πάλιν ἐγὼ ἔσομαι πεποιθὼς ἐπ' αὐτῷ

    - C'. καὶ πάλιν ἰδοὺ ἐγὼ καὶ τὰ παιδία ἅ μοι ἔδωκεν ὁ θεός

  - B'. ¹⁴ ἐπεὶ οὖν τὰ παιδία κεκοινώνηκεν αἵματος καὶ σαρκός καὶ αὐτὸς παραπλησίως μετέσχεν τῶν αὐτῶν ἵνα διὰ τοῦ θανάτου καταργήσῃ τὸν τὸ κράτος ἔχοντα τοῦ θανάτου τοῦτ' ἔστιν τὸν διάβολον ¹⁵ <u>καὶ ἀπαλλάξῃ τούτους ὅσοι φόβῳ θανάτου διὰ παντὸς τοῦ ζῆν ἔνοχοι ἦσαν δουλείας</u>

A verse 10
B verse 11–12
C verse 13a
C' verse 13b
B' verse 14–17a
A' verses 17b–18

Against this reading, however, Heil's parallels B and B' are formally unbalanced, topically unrelated, and based on the repetition of a single word ἀδελφός ("brother") in 2:11, 12 and 17, despite the abundance of functional equivalents in this context (e.g., "child," "son"). His suggestion that verse 13b (C) mirrors 13a (C') and represents the center of the chiasm also obscures the more obvious symmetry noted previously between 2:12a and b (cf. 4.2.6bi). Cf. Swetnam, *Jesus and Isaac*, 131, for an earlier related alternative.

Α'. ¹⁶ οὐ γὰρ δήπου ἀγγέλων ἐπιλαμβάνεται ἀλλὰ σπέρματος Ἀβραὰμ ἐπιλαμβάνεται ¹⁷ ὅθεν ὤφειλεν κατὰ πάντα τοῖς ἀδελφοῖς ὁμοιωθῆναι ἵνα ἐλεήμων γένηται καὶ πιστὸς ἀρχιερεὺς τὰ πρὸς τὸν θεόν <u>εἰς τὸ ἱλάσκεσθαι τὰς ἁμαρτίας τοῦ λαοῦ</u> ⁹ ἐν ᾧ γὰρ πέπονθεν αὐτὸς πειρασθείς <u>δύναται τοῖς πειραζομένοις βοηθῆσαι</u>

The suggestion that 2:8c-18 functions as a textual unit is certainly unusual. Some argue for a unit at 2:5-16/18 on the basis of perceptions of an inclusion between οὐ γὰρ ἀγγέλοις (2:5) and οὐ γὰρ δήπου ἀγγέλων (2:16).[267] Others find a unit between 2:10-18 in view of the location of this material between its neighbors (typically understood as 2:5-9 and 3:1-6) and perceived formal and thematic links between 2:10 and 2:17-18.[268] Neither proposal is without its difficulties, however. With regard to the first, although the suggestion of an inclusion between 2:5 and 2:16 is plausible, the word ἀγγέλων in 2:16 ties equally easily to ἀγγέλους in 2:9, and the formal similarities between 2:8-9 (νῦν δὲ οὔπω . . . δὲ) and 2:16 (οὐ γὰρ δήπου . . . ἀλλά) are at least as strong as those between 2:5 and 2:16 (see 4.2.6b). Meanwhile, those who advocate a break between 2:9 and 2:10 fail to account meaningfully for the presence in the text of the conjunction γάρ ("for") in verse 10,[269] separate material which is widely acknowledged to be closely related in terms of topic, [270] and ignore the evidence which suggests a more prominent role for 2:9.[271]

267. Adam, *The Majestic Son*, 12; Ellingworth, *Hebrews*, 143; Westfall, *Discourse Analysis*, 100; and Rhee, *Faith*, 81, argue for a unit spanning 2:5-18. Vanhoye, *Structure*, 82, meanwhile, finds one between 2:5-16.

268. Ellingworth, *Hebrews*, 157-58; Johnson, *Hebrews*, 93; Attridge, *Hebrews*, 78. and Rhee, *Faith*, 81, many of whom make a further subdivision between 2:10-13 and 2:14-18.

269. Guthrie, *Structure*, 144; Lane, *Hebrews 1-8*, n.p., and Rhee, *Faith*, 81, leave γάρ untranslated and understand it in general terms as a connective which joins together the units, 2:5-9 and 2:10-18, without specific reference to its explanatory nature. Cf. Westfall, *Discourse Analysis*, 102; and Heil, *Chiastic Structures*, 64.

270. Guthrie, *Structure*, 102, claims that "the seam between Hebrews 2:5-9 and 2:10-18 presents a special challenge to the analyst" since, as many have recognized, verses 2:10ff. build immediately on material in verse 2:9. Cf. Johnson, *Hebrews*, 93; Ellingworth, *Hebrews*, 158, who states that "v. 10 is also closely linked with v. 9, . . . v. 9 has already moved beyond Ps. 8 by introducing the theme of Christ's death, and v. 10 begins to reflect (ἔπρεπεν) on this event, as the following passage will do more fully"; Lane, *Hebrews 1-8*, n.p., who outlines "a series of correspondences" which demonstrate cohesion between vv. 9 and 10; Westfall, *Discourse Analysis*, 102; and O'Brien, *Hebrews*, 102.

271. According to Westfall, *Discourse Analysis*, 109, the description of Jesus in vv. 9-10 is "the most heavily marked grammatically."

Thus, while novel, the suggestion of a unit at 2:8c–18 is not inconsistent with many observations of previous scholarship and better reflects the formal evidence of repetition outlined above (4.2.6a–c). The unit begins with the emphatic νῦν δέ ("but now") of 2:9[272] and ends after 2:17, as evidenced by the absence in the material which follows of any further reference to the key words πᾶς, ἄγγελος, and θάνατος which have been so prominent to this point,[273] the fact that 2:18 represents "re-repetition" of 2:17,[274] and the introduction of thematically new material which points forward.[275]

d. The topical function of repetition in Hebrews 2:8c–18

Turning now to the question of topic, there is once again clear evidence of coherence within 2:8c–18, not only between the halves of the chiasm but also between each pair of constituents.

Both A–B and B'–A' function together to explain the purpose for Jesus' mission to earth.[276] In 2:8–9 (A), the author wards off any potential objection to what he has said previously regarding Jesus' fulfilment of Psalm 8 (2:5) by stating that while we "don't yet see" (οὔπω ὁρῶμεν, 2:8c) Jesus as Universal Lord, "nonetheless . . . we do see" (δὲ . . . βλέπομεν, 2:9)[277] him who has been made lower than angels *so that* (ὅπως) by God's grace "He might taste death for all" (ὑπὲρ παντὸς γεύσηται θανάτου).

The γάρ in 2:10 indicates that this verse serves as support material which further explains verse 9. Yet what is the precise relationship

---

272. Westfall, *Discourse Analysis*, 106.

273. The word pa/j does not recur until 3:4 in a very different context, while θάνατος appears next in 5:7; and ἄγγελος not until chapter 12.

274. Cf. 4.2.7 for further discussion on this.

275. E.g., Jesus' capacity to "help" and the theme of "testing" which becomes prominent in the next unit. This suggests, *contra* Guthrie, *Structure*, 77–78 and 102, that the echo of παθημάτων (2:10) in πέπονθεν (2:18), is insignificant in this context.

276. Although A and B (and B' and A') are here treated together, the decision to view vv. 8c–10 and 14–17 as comprised of two pairs of components is based on the observation that A/A' is particularly concerned with the ultimate purpose for Jesus' mission—his sin-bearing death for others—in contrast to B/B' which focuses more on the implications of his mission for him and for "us."

277. The contrastive δέ is emphatic. Yes, the author concedes, we might not yet see all that Psalm 8 spoke of. But we have seen much of it fulfilled already. Meanwhile, the use of the verb βλέπομεν ("we see") is clearly metaphorical at this point, describing not what we can physically perceive but rather what we have seen and continue to see of Jesus in the testimony about him in Scripture.

between these verses? Ellingworth suggests that the conjunction connects with verse 9 as a whole, making clear that "Jesus' humiliation and death, together with his exaltation, have their right and proper place in God's purpose ὑπὲρ παντός."[278] However, γάρ seems to function more specifically than this by introducing the reason Jesus had to become human and die "for the sake of" (ὑπέρ) his people. In answer to the unspoken question, "why was it necessary for Jesus to "become lower" and taste death for others?," the author explains: *For* God thought it "fitting" (ἔπρεπεν) "to perfect/equip" (τελειῶσαι) Jesus, the "pioneer leader of their Salvation" (τὸν ἀρχηγὸν τῆς σωτηρίας αὐτῶν),[279] "through sufferings" (διὰ παθημάτων) so that he might lead many sons into glory. The point, then, is that Jesus suffered and died in part so that he might be fully equipped as τὸν ἀρχηγὸν who would lead many Sons into glory.[280]

Meanwhile, in B′ and A′, the author makes use of many of the same (or similar) formal elements as in A and B, now completely reconfigured, to make much the same point again. Following mention of τὰ παιδία in the quote from Isaiah 8:18 (in 2:13b), the author explains in verse 14 that it was because of these children that Jesus shared humanity like this *so that* (ἵνα) "through death" (διὰ τοῦ θανάτου)[281] he might claim ultimate authority and so deliver those formerly enslaved (v. 15). For (γάρ), he explains in verse 16, it is "surely not" (δήπου) ἀγγέλους that he helps, but the "Seed of Abraham." "Therefore" (ὅθεν, v. 17) it was necessary for him to become like his brothers, in order to become a merciful and faithful high priest and make atonement for the sins of the people. In its context γάρ in verse 16 functions not as a (somewhat redundant) reminder that God has not sent Jesus for the sake of angels,[282] but to clarify the need for

278. Ellingworth, *Hebrews*, 158.

279. Cf. 4.2.6e for discussion on the meaning of ἀρχηγός in this context.

280. Against any suggestion of an ethical dimension to the perfection of Jesus (as in Johnson, *Hebrews*, 96, for example), Lane, *Hebrews 1-8*, n.p., notes that τελειόω "has functional implications here," with the emphasis falling on the notion that Jesus was fully equipped for his office. Cf. Guthrie, *Hebrews*, 108, who observes similarly that "perfection in Hebrews has to do with fully completing a course, making it to the end of God's plan"; Ellingworth, *Hebrews*, 161-63; and Peterson, *Hebrews and Perfection*, 49-73.

281. As mentioned previously, Johnson, *Hebrews*, 100, notes that the instrumental phrase διὰ τοῦ θανάτου in 2:14 matches διὰ παθημάτων in 2:10, although the plural nature of the "sufferings" (παθημάτων) indicates that more is on view in than Jesus' death alone.

282. Cf. Guthrie, *Hebrews*, 11; and Ellingworth, *Hebrews*, 179, who notes that it is a literary expression indicating information which the author supposed his readers to

Jesus to share in flesh and blood in order to help/ seize (ἐπιλαμβάνεται) them. Because God was interested in saving men (not ἀγγέλους), Jesus had to *become like a man* in order to do so.

Thus, both A–B and B′–A′ explain the ultimate purpose for Jesus' earthly mission in terms of his death "for the sake of everyone" (ὑπὲρ παντός, 2:9). In other words, Jesus suffered and died so as to fittingly lead many sons from bondage into glory as their Savior. The difference between them is one of emphasis: where A focuses on what Jesus' suffering and death achieved *for Jesus*,[283] attention in A′ seems directed more towards what this death means *for others*.[284] "For" (v. 18) "because he himself suffered (death), being tested, he is able to help those being tested."

The assertion made in C (v. 11a) is also closely related to the quotation in C′ (v.13b), with the latter seeming to function in this context as Scriptural evidence which "confirms" the former. The syntax indicates that both phrases locate the ultimate cause of the Son's mission (described in A/A′ and B/B′) in the will of God. The γάρ of verse 10 indicates "a close connection with what precedes," which "deepens the argument of v. 10, rather than drawing a conclusion from it."[285] As such, verse 11 provides further clarification concerning the reason God saw the "perfection" of his ἀρχηγός through suffering as "fitting." *For* both the Sanctifier and those being sanctified are "all from the One" (ἐξ ἑνὸς πάντες), i.e. united by their common participation within God's will.[286] In other words, since Jesus and the people are joined together by their co-participation within God's plan of salvation, God deemed it appropriate to express this connection by making his Son like them in every way through suffering. Meanwhile, in C′ the voice of Jesus himself directly addresses readers to "see again" the fact that he stands with his people, now addressed as τὰ παιδία ἅ μοι ἔδωκεν ὁ θεός ("the children God gave to me").[287] The second part of this phrase reveals once more that this solidarity is part of

---

have already: "of course," "as you know," and even "obviously."

283. "Through sufferings," God perfectly equipped his Son as τὸν ἀρχηγὸν so that he might fittingly lead many sons into glory.

284. i.e. Jesus tasted death so that "through death" he might nullify the Devil and deliver/help the previously enslaved Seed of Abraham as their High Priest, atoning for their sins.

285. Ellingworth, *Hebrews*, 163.

286. Cf. Johnson, *Hebrews*, 96.

287. Cf. Johnson, *Hebrews*, 98, who suggests "we are intended to hear the declarations from Ps 21:23 and Isaiah 8:17–18, therefore, as statements of the Son, the "pioneer of salvation."

God's will, for no less a one than God himself has "given" the children to Jesus.[288] Flowing on as an inference from this will (οὖν, "therefore," 2:14), the author states that Jesus had to experience blood and flesh so that he might end their enslavement and lead them as one of them.

Finally, D and E and E' and D' represent functionally equivalent statements which together serve as proof texts for the claim of 2:11 that Jesus is not ashamed to call God's people his brothers.[289]

The first half of the unit makes clear that Jesus suffered as a man so as to lead many sons into glory through his death "on behalf of all" (A and B). *For*, the author explains in verse 11, God thought it "fitting" that Jesus, "the Sanctifier" (ὁ ἁγιάζων) should resemble "those sanctified" (οἱ ἁγιαζόμενοι), reflecting their common participation within the will and purpose of God (ἐξ ἑνὸς πάντες) (C). "For this reason" (δι' ἣν αἰτίαν), i.e. *because* Jesus' humiliation and identification constituted part of God's plan to lead many sons into glory,[290] the author insists that Jesus is not ashamed to call those being sanctified his brothers (D), as seen by what he says in (LXX) Ps 21:23 (E).[291]

Meanwhile, the second half begins with the voice of Jesus speaking through Scripture to affirm his identification with his people (E'), confirm his lack of shame about this identification (D'), and to call on readers to "see again" this solidarity as part of God's wider plan to hand over authority for the children to Jesus (C'). In light of this, the author sums up his main point once more by affirming once more that it was because of the children that God sent his Son into the world to share flesh and blood, thereby releasing the slaves "through death" (διὰ τοῦ θανάτου, B') and helping the Seed of Abraham by atoning for their sins (A').

---

288. The aorist ἔδωκεν, which views the action as a whole, indicates that the author is not interested in the details of when this "giving" occurred but rather in the fact that God's plan for the children is that they should belong his Son, Jesus.

289. Cf. 4.2.6e for further discussion on the topical relationships within verses 11–13.

290. In context, the phrase δι' ἣν αἰτίαν indicates that v. 11b represents a statement about Jesus' lack of shame regarding his relationship with his "brothers" (ἀδελφούς, 2:11) which arises as a *result* from the preceding material (δι' ἣν αἰτίαν, "for this reason"). If, as Johnson, *Hebrews*, 97–98 suggests, ἐξ ἑνὸς πάντες in 2:11a means "all from one stock," Jesus lack of shame about standing with humanity is due to the fact that he too is a human. However, if we are correct in seeing the reference to ἑνός as a reference to God, then the reason the Son relates to the fact that, by standing with humanity, he is carrying out God's great plan of Salvation for them (i.e. vv. 10–11).

291. See deSilva, *Despising Shame*, regarding the shamefulness of God's Son becoming a suffering human.

e. *Further implications for meaning in light of the parallelism within Hebrews 2:8c–18*

The evidence of formal parallelism within 2:8c–18, together with the clear coherence between such material, is of further assistance in clarifying meaning by marking out the following instantial equivalents.

In view of the multiple connections between 2:8c–10 and 14–17, it seems highly likely, first, that the author intends his readers to understand the intriguing and much-considered description of Jesus as τὸν ἀρχηγὸν τῆς σωτηρίας αὐτῶν (2:10) in light of his later identification as "high priest" (ἀρχιερεύς, 2:17). In this sense, while the word ἀρχηγός undoubtedly carries with it the notion of Jesus as "champion" in the classical tradition as Lane suggests,[292] its primary meaning lies in its representation of Jesus as the "pioneer leader/ initiator/first cause" of salvation, who brought in forgiveness of sins through his offering of a perfect sacrifice for sins.[293]

The same set of parallels also serves to strengthen, second, Peterson's suggestion that Jesus' "perfection" in 2:10 should be understood as involving "a whole sequence of events: his proving in suffering, his redemptive death to fulfil the divine requirements for the perfect expiation of sins and his exaltation to glory and honor."[294]

Third, the obscure phrase from Isaiah 8:17 quoted in Hebrews 2:13 is universally read as a statement about the Son's trust in God ("I will trust in

---

292. Lane, *Hebrews 1–8*, reads ἀρχηγός as "the champion who secures their salvation," suggesting that the author borrows the cult figure of the "divine hero" from the Hellenistic world (e.g., Hercules).

293. Further evidence in support of this suggestion is provided by Heil, *Chiastic Structures*, 67, who observes that "the alliteration between God's "leading" (ἀγαγόντα) and the term "initiator" (ἀρχηγός) lends a connotation of "leader" to the word here translated as "initiator" (2:10). On the other hand, the wordplay between the term "perfect" (τελειῶσαι), with its connotation of "bringing to an end," "finishing," or "completing," highlights the connotation of "initiating" or "beginning" present in the term ἀρχηγόν, which, through the combined effect of the alliteration and wordplay, acquires a sense of "initiating leader." The Jesus "perfected" through the suffering of death on behalf of all human beings (2:9) is thus the "Son" who serves as both the "initiator" and "leader" for the many "sons," including the audience." It is also interesting to note that in its only other appearance in Hebrews (12:2), ἀρχηγός appears once again in close association with the same word τελειωτής (now in noun form) suggesting a similar meaning in this later context. Cf. O'Brien, *Hebrews*, 104-07. And also that Moses is described as an ἀρχηγός in the book of Numbers, which plays such a key influence on the vocabulary and language in Hebrews.

294. Peterson, *Perfection*, 67.

him") in light of its original context where ἐπ' αὐτῷ refers to God.[295] Such a translation (i) presents a puzzle in coherence, however, since the rest of the unit says nothing about the Son's faith, (ii) requires a somewhat abrupt shift from the Son's direct address *to* his Father in verse 12 in the second person (ἀπαγγελῶ τὸ ὄνομά σου ... ὑμνήσω σε) to his speech *"about* him" in the third person (ἐπ' αὐτῷ, v. 13),[296] and (iii) fails to account adequately for the alterations made to the LXX text (see below).[297]

Isa 8:17-18	καὶ	πεποιθὼς ἔσομαι ἐπ' αὐτῷ		ἰδοὺ ἐγὼ καὶ τὰ παιδία ἅ μοι ἔδωκεν ὁ θεός
Heb 2:13	καὶ πάλιν	ἐγὼ ἔσομαι πεποιθὼς ἐπ' αὐτῷ	καὶ πάλιν	ἰδοὺ ἐγὼ καὶ τὰ παιδία ἅ μοι ἔδωκεν ὁ θεός

While the presence of the first πάλιν ἐγώ may be explained relatively easily as a textual marker which puts the words of the ancient prophet on the lips of Jesus,[298] the second καὶ πάλιν in verse 13 *separates text which is clearly undivided* in the LXX. This suggests both that this verse functions differently in Hebrews from its function within its original context and that the author seeks to make *two distinct points in verse 13a and b* since "he was under no obligation to quote the first line at all" (see below).[299]

Heb 2:13a   καὶ πάλιν ἐγὼ ἔσομαι πεποιθὼς ἐπ' αὐτῷ

Heb 2:13b   καὶ πάλιν ἰδοὺ ἐγὼ καὶ τὰ παιδία ἅ μοι ἔδωκεν ὁ θεός

---

295. Ellingworth, *Hebrews*, 169. Lane, *Hebrews 1–8*, suggests the phrase serves "to stress that Jesus identifies himself with the community of faith in his absolute trust and dependence upon God," and "prepares for the description of Jesus as trustworthy (πιστός) in v. 17"; while Westfall, *Discourse Analysis*, 103, develops "the necessity of trust in God and expresses a semantically related concept of having the same relationship with God as other humans." Cf. Guthrie, *Hebrews*, 110; Johnson, *Hebrews*, 99; and Heil, *Chiastic Structures*, 69.

296. *Contra* Ellingworth, *Hebrews*, 169, who views this shift as "unimportant for the author's purpose."

297. While the words from Isa 8:17 may also be found in Isa 12:2 and 2 Sam 22:3, leading some to read v. 13 as comprised of two unrelated quotes, it is more likely that the verse represents a single, modified version of the one quotation.

298. *Pace* Johnson, *Hebrews*, 99; Ellingworth, *Hebrews*, 168.

299. Ellingworth, *Hebrews*, 169. Cf. Guthrie, "Hebrews," 950.

Read in light of its partner phrase (11b), as indicated by the overall parallelism within this material, αὐτός means "this" and verse 13b ceases to be *about* God at all, functioning instead as a prophetic statement which supports the author's assertion that Jesus "is not ashamed" to call them brothers (οὐκ ἐπαισχύνεται). In this sense, we hear Jesus himself declare in the words he spoke long ago through Isaiah (cf. 2:3): "I will be convinced/certain/persuaded *about this*."[300]

C.   δι' ἣν αἰτίαν οὐκ ἐπαισχύνεται ἀδελφοὺς αὐτοὺς καλεῖν
      "because of which reason he is not ashamed to call them brothers"

C'. καὶ πάλιν ἐγὼ ἔσομαι πεποιθὼς ἐπ' αὐτῷ
      "and again I will be persuaded about this"

Fourth, while many scholars have spoken in general terms about the function of verses 11–13 within the text of Hebrews,[301] a precise understanding of the relationships within these verses and between verses 11–13 has proven elusive to this point. In light of formal parallels established through repetition, however, verses 11–13 is revealed as a carefully and symmetrically arranged network of texts comprised of two assertions which are supported by four evidential statements spoken by Jesus in words taken from the LXX. As may be seen in the diagram below (fig. 16) verse 11a (Assertion 1) is supported by 13b (Evidence 1), while 11b (Assertion 2) is evidenced both by the parallel statements of verse 12 from (LXX) Psalm 21:23 (Evidence 3a and b) and "again" (πάλιν) by Isaiah 8:17a. The subtle difference in function between verse 12 and 13a (Evidence 3a and b and Evidence 2) may be seen in the fact that where verse 13a directly supports the claim that Jesus is not ashamed to call those he rescues brothers (v. 11b) by restating

---

300. Ellingworth, *Hebrews*, 329, notes that in its passive form, the word πείθω describes a "state of having been convinced."

301. For example, Ellingworth, *Hebrews*, 170, comments: "The programmatic statements of vv. 10–11a are first provided with a scriptural basis (vv. 11b–13); then developed in vv. 14–15 in language largely atypical of Hebrews, but perhaps traditional and familiar to the first readers." See too Johnson, *Hebrews*, 98–99, who claims that vv. 12–13 "supports the association among the Son and his brothers" without going into detail. Cf. Guthrie, *Hebrews*, 110; Lane, *Hebrews 1–8*, n.p., who claims that "the pattern of quotation and explanation is characteristic of homiletical midrash and here serves to emphasize Jesus' solidarity with the human family"; Westfall, *Discourse Analysis*, 100; and Heil, *Chiastic Structures*, 65.

it using other words, verse 12 provides hearers with statements which indirectly lead to the same conclusion.

Assertion 1   ὅ τε γὰρ ἁγιάζων καὶ οἱ ἁγιαζόμενοι ἐξ ἑνὸς πάντες (v. 11a)
"For he who sanctifies and those being sanctified are both from the same one."

   Assertion 2   δι' ἣν αἰτίαν οὐκ ἐπαισχύνεται ἀδελφοὺς αὐτοὺς καλεῖν (v. 11b)
"Because of which, he is not ashamed to call them brothers"

      Evidence 3a   λέγων ἀπαγγελῶ τὸ ὄνομά σου τοῖς ἀδελφοῖς μου (v. 12a)
"saying "I will proclaim your name among my brothers,""

      Evidence 3b   ἐν μέσῳ ἐκκλησίας ὑμνήσω σε (v. 12a)
"in the midst of the gathering I will praise you."

   Evidence 2   καὶ πάλιν ἐγὼ ἔσομαι πεποιθὼς ἐπ' αὐτῷ (v. 13a)
And again, "I will be certain about this!,"

Evidence 1   καὶ πάλιν ἰδοὺ ἐγὼ καὶ τὰ παιδία ἅ μοι ἔδωκεν ὁ θεός (v. 13b)
"and look again! I and the children God has given to me."

When viewed together, the careful arrangement of these citations makes clear the importance to the author of the fact that Jesus is "not ashamed" by his experience of suffering humanity but rejoices in the fraternal relationship he shares with the people of God.

Fifth, while previous scholarship has failed to account adequately for the replacement of διηγέομαι in Psalm (LXX) 21:23 with ἀπαγγελῶ in Hebrews 2:12,[302] the clear parallelism between 2:12a and b indicates that the reason for this change probably relates to the subtle yet significant shift in emphasis it effects from *the comprehensiveness* of the act of speech[303] to its proclaimed nature. In this way, the link between the verses in 12a and b is strengthened and *the inherent parallelism within 12a is made clearer still*, thereby serving the author's symmetrical purpose for this material in its new context.[304] In light of this, τοῖς ἀδελφοῖς μου should be interpreted in the light of its partner phrase ἐν μέσῳ ἐκκλησίας in a locative sense as a dative of sphere ("among my brothers") rather

---

302. Ellingworth, *Hebrews*, 168, rightly dismisses the suggestions of Michel (that the replacement occurs because of previous references to angels) and Vanhoye (that the author found διηγήσομαι τὸ ὄνομά σου harsh, since "one does not relate a name") as "strained" and "unconvincing." Cf. Guthrie, *Hebrews*, 109.

303. Louw and Nida, *Greek-English Lexicon*, n.p., translate διηγήομαι as "to inform, to relate, to tell fully."

304. The replacement of διηγήομαι with ἀπαγγελῶ in Hebrews 2:12 thus represents strong evidence of the author's desire to preserve and even reinforce the parallelism in the quotation for his own literary purposes.

than as a dative of destination ("to my brothers"), so that both statements emphasize *Jesus' present location among his people*.³⁰⁵

Sixth, the fact that Hebrews' use of παντός in 2:15 is neither necessary nor easily explained in terms of thematic emphasis suggests that, like λαβοῦσα λαλεῖσθαι in 2:3 (see 4.2.4c), its main function within the text is to strengthen the formal connection between verse 15 and verses 8–10 (cf. τὰ πάντα in 2:8, 10 (x2).

Finally, in addition to its formal role previously described, the repetition of πάλιν in 1:13 seems to serve an important literary/rhetorical function within this text, as in 1:5 and 6, by marking out the moment of transition from one component of the chiasm to the next (C' to B' and B' to A' respectively) thereby assisting the reader/hearer to understand the form of the discourse.³⁰⁶

As seen by repetition, the key words and concepts relate to what "we see" now with regard to Jesus, his willing identification and solidarity with his people, and particularly the *purpose* for his earthly life and death.

The five-fold repetition of the word θάνατος³⁰⁷ is particularly emphatic and marks out "death" as the key term in this material (i.e. A and B, B and A). On the other hand, while mentioned twice (in 2:7 and 2:16) the ἀγγέλους are much less prominent in this context than previously. The theme of the unit may be outlined as follows: We see that Jesus was made lower than the angels so as to suffer and die as a human for all humanity and so "fittingly" lead many Sons into glory in accordance with the will of God. Consequently, he is not ashamed to call us his brothers.

The unit may be translated as follows:

> A. ²:⁸ᶜ But now, we don't yet see all things subject to him. ⁹ But we see him who was made lower than the messengers for a little while, Jesus, crowned with glory and honor through the suffering of death so that by the grace of God he might taste death for everyone.
>
> B. ¹⁰ For it was fitting for him for whom and through whom are everyone to perfect the pioneer of their

---

305. *Pace* Guthrie, *Hebrews*, 109, "the phrase "in the presence of the congregation" places emphasis on Jesus' location in our midst on earth, where we are "lower than the angels," constituting a reference to his incarnation.

306. *Contra* Heil, *Chiastic Structures*, 65, who reads the repetition of καὶ πάλιν in 2:13 as one of the parallels within his central section C/C'."

307. τοῦ θανάτου and θανάτου (2:9); τοῦ θανάτου (2:14 x2); and θανάτου (2:15).

salvation through suffering, so as to lead many sons into glory.

    C. ¹¹ For he who sanctifies and those being sanctified are both from the same one.

        D. Because of which, he is not ashamed to call them brothers,

            E. ¹² saying: "I will proclaim your name among my brothers."

            E'. "In the midst of the gathering I will praise you."

        D'. ¹³ And again, "I will be certain about this!"

    C'. And look again! I and the children God has given to me.

B'. ¹⁴ Therefore, because the children have experienced blood and flesh, he also partook of these in this way in order that through death he might nullify the one with authority ¹⁵ and deliver those who through fear of death were slaves throughout all of life.

A'. ¹⁶ For surely it is not angels that he helps, but the seed of Abraham! ¹⁷ Therefore he had to become like his brothers in every way, in order that he might become a merciful and faithful high priest so as to make atonement for the sins of the people. For because he himself has suffered, having been tested, he is able to help those who are being tested.

f.   Summary of findings

This analysis of the link cluster at Hebrews 2:8c–18:

a. uncovers a large number of previously unobserved yet significant connections within the text;

b. demonstrates that through repetition, the author marks out 2:8c–18 as a concentric textual unit which consists of five pairs of matched parallel components (A, A'; B, B'; C, C'; D, D'; and E, E'), and displays a high degree of topical coherence between its formally linked material;

c. identifies 2:8c–10 as transitional material which belongs to both 2:5–9 and 2:8c–18;

d. provides fresh insight in light of this parallelism into the meaning of various words and phrases by showing:

- that ἀρχηγός (2:10) means "pioneer leader" in this context;
- that the verb τελειόω ("I perfect," 2:10) is used to describe the process involving suffering, death and exaltation in its entirety by which Jesus was equipped to fulfil his role for us;
- that ἑνός in verse 11 is best understood in light of as a reference to God (cf. αὐτῷ; and ὁ θεός); and
- that πάλιν in verse 13 marks out the moment of transition from one component of the chiasm to the next (C' to B' and B' to A' respectively) thereby assisting the reader/hearer to understand the form of the discourse;

e. shows with regard to the author's use of the LXX:

- that the replacement of διηγέομαι in Ps (LXX) 21:23 with ἀπαγγελῶ in Heb 2:12 serves to strengthen the latent symmetry within this verse;
- that the insertion of καὶ πάλιν twice within the quotation from Isaiah 8 in 2:13 serves both a formal and topical function in the discourse. First, it makes clear that the verse makes two distinct points in its new context corresponding to 11a and b respectively. Second, it indicates the author's understanding of transition points between component parts of his chiasm;
- that αὐτῷ in 2:13 should be translated as "this" not "him" in this context;
- that, taken together, verses 11–13 have been carefully and chiastically arranged into a series of assertions and supporting pieces of evidence, each of which is presented as spoken by Jesus, thereby proving that he rejoices in the fraternal relationship he enjoys with the people of God;
- that, once again, in these ways the author brings out new meanings from old forms of words;

f. clarifies with greater precision that 2:8c–18 serves as a brilliant summary of the author's understanding *both* of God's plan and purpose for the earthly incarnation of his Son *and* the theological identity of those to whom Hebrews is addressed. With regard to the former, Jesus became a man so as to:

1. experience human existence completely (including suffering) and thereby be "perfectly equipped" as pioneer leader/high priest to save humanity.
2. die as a man "on behalf of everyone."
3. defeat Satan and overthrow his authority over death.
4. release those previously held captive (ie everyone).
5. fittingly lead them into glory as one of them.

With regard to the latter, "we" (2:8c–9; cf. 1:2; 2:1–3) represent a "gathering" (ἐκκλησία) of people, "the Seed of Abraham," and "the children," who once were enslaved by the fear of death, but have now been set free from the Devil's clutches by Jesus' death "for us," his "brothers," and who will one day be led by the Son as "sons" into God's glory.

g. concludes that the topic of 2:8c–18 might best be understood as: We see that Jesus was made lower than the angels so as to suffer and die as a human for all humanity and so "fittingly" lead many sons into glory in accordance with the will of God. Consequently, he is not ashamed to call us his brothers.

4.2.7 Hebrews 3:1–8

a. Introduction

While the majority of modern scholars consider Hebrews 3:1–6 to be a textual unit in recognition both of the unity within this material and its "unusual importance" within its wider context,[308] this understanding results in "some of the most difficult structural challenges in the discourse."[309] According to some, the inferential adverb ὅθεν ("whence/therefore") suggests that 3:1 "is not really a new start" but an inference

---

308. Lane, *Hebrews 1–8*, n.p.; Cf. Vanhoye, *Structure*, 83; Ellingworth, *Hebrews*, 194; Johnson, *Hebrews*, 104; Adam, *The Majestic Son*, 43; Guthrie, *Structure*, 144; Westfall, *Discourse Analysis*, 299; O'Brien, *Hebrews*, 126; and Heil, *Chiastic Structures*, 76.

309. Westfall, *Discourse Analysis*, 115.

based on what has been said previously.³¹⁰ Others have struggled to account for the coherence between 3:1–6 and 3:7ff.,³¹¹ and within 3:3–6 (and especially verse 4),³¹² while still others have found it hard to explain the place of this material within the wider discourse: most read it as "looking forward," some assert that it relates backwards, with others arguing that it does both.³¹³

Given these difficulties, it is perhaps unsurprising that many other questions of meaning remain as yet unresolved, relating to:

- the identity of the "builder" in verse 4;
- the purpose of this verse;
- the identity of the owner of the "house" (vv. 3–6) and the "voice" of 3:7 (i.e. who is αὐτός in 3:2 [x2], 3, 5 and 6?);
- the relationship between the contrasts involving Jesus and Moses in verses 2–3 and 5–6;
- the identity of the LXX texts which function as background material to 3:2 and 3:5 and their significance within their new context;
- the function of material quoted from Psalm 95 in its new context (i.e. v. 7ff.); and
- the topic of this material as a whole.

This section will address these questions with new evidence from an investigation into the location and interconnectedness of repetition within this material, demonstrating that Hebrews 3:1–8 is better understood

---

310. Johnson, *Hebrews*, 106. Cf. Westfall, *Discourse Analysis*, 111, who criticizes Guthrie for making a break between 2:18 and 3:1, claiming that he "misses the semantic weight of inferential conjunctions such as ὅθεν." Cf. Guthrie, *Structure*, 65–66, who identifies a "high level shift" between 2:18 and 3:1.

311. Westfall, *Discourse Analysis*, 116, claims that "if 3:1–6 is about Jesus' superiority to Moses, the transition to the projection of Psalm 95 [in 3:7ff.] lies somewhere between abrupt and non-existent." Cf. Ellingworth, *Hebrews*, 213, who states that 3:7 "does not follow smoothly on 3:6."

312. Johnson, *Hebrews*, 108, for example, comments with regard to verses 3–6: "here is where the argument, though transparent enough in its intention becomes murky in its details," while several others have labelled verse 4 as a "parenthesis" on the basis of "unresolved tension in the logic" of verses 3 and 4. Cf. Moffatt, *Hebrews*, 40–43; Spicq, *Hébreux*, vol. 2, 66–68; Buchanan, *Hebrews*, 57–58; and Attridge, *Hebrews*, 104, who claims that v. 4 "does not contribute directly to the argument."

313. Westfall, *Discourse Analysis*, 115. Cf. Swetnam, "Hebrews 1, 1–3, 6," 58.

as a formally interconnected and coherent textual unit, and offering a range of fresh insights into the text.

b. Significant repetition previously observed in Hebrews 3:1-8

Scholars have found significance in a large number of connections within this section of text. Lexical repetition noted previously includes:

- οἶκος ("house," 3:2, 3:3, 3:4, 3:5, 3:6 x2), which occurs six times in this context;[314]
- κατασκευάζω ("I build," 3:3, 3:4 x2);[315]
- ἡμῶν ("our," 3;1) and ἡμεῖς ("we," 3:6);[316]
- πιστός ("faithful," 3:2 and 5);
- Μωϋσῆς ἐν [ὅλῳ] τῷ οἴκῳ αὐτοῦ ("Moses in [the whole of] his house," 3:2), Μωϋσῆν (3:3) and Μωϋσῆς ... ἐν ὅλῳ τῷ οἴκῳ αὐτοῦ ("Moses in the whole of his house," 3:5);[317]
- πᾶς ("every") and πάντα ("all") in 3:4.[318]

Several have also drawn attention to a wider form of parallelism between two pairs of matched phrases, 3:2 and 3:5,[319] and 3:4a and b respectively (see below).[320]

---

314. Lane, *Hebrews 1-8*, n.p.; and Ellingworth, *Hebrews*, 196.

315. Cf. Heil, *Chiastic Structures*, 77, who translates κατασκευάζω as "I furnish." This repetition is obscured in the Vulgate's translation of the first instance as *fabricatur* ("make") and the second as *creavit* ("create").

316. Heil, *Chiastic Structures*, 76, claims that the repetition of ἡμῶν and ἡμεῖς establishes the parallels between A (3:1) and A' (3:6) within his chiasm.

317. Heil, *Chiastic Structures*, 76.

318. Cf. Rhee, *Faith*, 91; and Ellingworth, *Hebrews*, 205.

319. Cf. Johnson, *Hebrews*, 107; Auffret, "Essai sur la Structure Littéraire," 384; Hanson, "Christ in the Old Testament," 394-96; Rhee, *Faith*, 91; and Lane, *Hebrews 1-8*, n.p.

320. Ellingworth, *Hebrews*, 205, claims that that "the structure of the verse [3:4] is generally symmetrical" and that this, together with the identical word order and lexical repetition involving πᾶς and κατασκευάζω "provides a firm basis of comparison" between these texts. Vanhoye, *La Structure*, 88, also claims to discern two further examples of micro-symmetry in the word order of 3:3, labelling the first an example of "symétrie concentrique" and the second, "symétrie parallèle" (see below). His omission of δόξης from his example of "symétrie concentrique" makes his first example less convincing, however, since the present word order could easily have been rearranged if

PATTERNS OF REPETITION, STRUCTURE, AND MEANING

Heb 3:2   πιστὸν ὄντα τῷ ποιήσαντι αὐτὸν ὡς καὶ Μωϋσῆς ἐν [ὅλῳ] τῷ οἴκῳ αὐτοῦ
"being faithful to the one who appointed him as also Moses was in [the whole of] his house"

Heb 3:5   καὶ Μωϋσῆς μὲν πιστὸς ἐν ὅλῳ τῷ οἴκῳ αὐτοῦ
"and Moses on the one hand was faithful in the whole of his house"

Heb 3:4a   πᾶς γὰρ οἶκος κατασκευάζεται ὑπό τινος
"for every house is built by someone"

Heb 3:4b   ὁ δὲ πάντα κατασκευάσας θεός
"but God is the builder of all things"

Finally, the common dependence of both Hebrews 3:2 and 3:5 on texts from the LXX has also been widely recognized, though there is some disagreement regarding the precise identity of this background material (see the various options below).

Num 12:7   οὐχ οὕτως ὁ θεράπων μου Μωϋσῆς ἐν ὅλῳ τῷ οἴκῳ μου πιστός ἐστιν
"Not so with my servant Moses. He is faithful in all my house"

1 Chron 17:14   καὶ ἀναστήσω ἐμ αυτῷ ιερέα πιστόν ... καὶ οἰκοδομήσω αὐτῷ οἶκον πιστόν
"And I will raise up for myself a faithful priest ... and I will build him a faithful house"

1 Sam 2:35   πιστώσω αὐτὸν ἐν οἴκῳ μου
"I will make him [the "Son" and "seed of David"] faithful in my house"

Heb 3:2   πιστὸν ὄντα τῷ ποιήσαντι αὐτόν ... ἐν τῷ οἴκῳ αὐτοῦ
"[who] was faithful to the one who appointed him ... in his house"

Heb 3:5   καὶ Μωϋσῆς μὲν πιστὸς ἐν ὅλῳ τῷ οἴκῳ αὐτοῦ ὡς θεράπωνa "and Moses on the one hand was faithful in the whole of his house as servant"

---

this symmetry was intended by the author.

E.g., 1   οὗτος   ὁ κατασκευάσας   E.g., 2   πλείονος   πλείονα
         παρὰ Μωϋσῆν   τοῦ οἴκου αὐτόν   δόξης   τιμὴν
         ἠξίωται   τιμὴν ἔχει

While 3:2 is most commonly read as an "anticipation" of the explicit citation of Numbers 12:7 in Hebrews 3:5,[321] the absence of ὅλῳ is well attested and the arguments advanced for its being a deliberate omission "fail to explain why ὅλῳ should not have been omitted in verse 5 also, where emphasis on Moses would seem even more out of place."[322] Moreover, Lane demonstrates that the verse is better thought of as an "interpenetration" of two formally similar texts, (LXX) 1 Chronicles 17:14 and 1 Samuel 2:35 (as may be seen below)[323] in light of the fact that 3:2 reflects *both meanings* of the verb πιστόω used in 1 Chronicles.

> The verb πιστοῦν in the active voice means "to make πιστός (faithful, reliable)" or "to appoint." The double meaning "appointed/faithful" is reflected in the form of the allusion in 2a, "faithful to the one who appointed him in his house."[324]

c. *Potentially significant repetition previously unobserved in Hebrews 3:1–8*

To the list of links above may be added a large number of other significant yet unobserved connections within this portion of the text. Additional repetition includes:

- the reprise of ἅγιοι (3:1) in 3:7 (ἅγιον);
- the somewhat cryptic references to αὐτός in 3:2 (x2), 3, 5 and 6 (cf. also οὗτος in 3:3);[325]

---

321. Johnson, *Hebrews*, 107, claims that "the author anticipates the citation [of Numbers 12:7 in 3:5] by stating that Jesus was faithful to the one who made him." Cf. Attridge, *Hebrews*, 104; Ellingworth, *Hebrews*, 201; Guthrie, *Hebrews*, 127; Johnson, *Hebrews*, 107; and O'Brien, *Hebrews*, 131.

322. Ellingworth, *Hebrews*, 201-02. Cf. Attridge, *Hebrews*, 104. *Contra* Johnson, *Hebrews*, 105; and Metzger, *A Textual Commentary*, 594-95, who grades the decision to include ὅλῳ as a "C" (indicating "that the Committee had difficulty in deciding which variant to place in the text," 14) and claims that: "Both external evidence and transcriptional probabilities are singularly difficult to evaluate.... In the face of such a balance of possibilities, a majority of the Committee thought it best to include ὅλῳ in the text, but to enclose it within square brackets in order to express doubt whether it belongs there." Its inclusion is likely explained by its "having been conformed to the text of verse 5 and/or of Numbers 12.17 LXX."

323. Lane, *Hebrews 1-8*, n.p. Cf. Guthrie, "Hebrews," 957.

324. Lane, *Hebrews 1-8*, n.p., who also notes that 1 Chronicles 17:12-14 has been alluded to once in Hebrews already (in 1:5b), indicating its importance to the author of Hebrews. Cf. D'Angelo, *Moses*, 74-75, 78, 91-92.

325. Less obviously significant is the lexical repetition involving πλείονος (3:3 x2);

There are also a number of further connections between clauses within 3:1-8:

a. 3:1 is linked with 3:7-8 in a number of important ways.

   i. A relationship of similarity seems likely between the "heavenly call" of v. 1 (κλήσεως ἐπουρανίου) and "His voice" of v. 7 (τῆς φωνῆς αὐτοῦ), irrespective of whether "He" is God the Father or Jesus, since both speak from Heaven;

   ii. The inferential conjunction διά + the imperatival phrase μὴ σκληρύνητε τὰς καρδίας ὑμῶν ("Do not harden your hearts," 3:7) functions as a rough syntactic equivalent of the causal adverb ὅθεν + the imperative κατανοήσατε (3:1).[326] The use of an inferential conjunction in both cases indicates that both exhortations flow from what has been previously argued;[327]

   iii. Despite formal differences of expression, both κατανοήσατε and μὴ σκληρύνητε represent non-auditory metaphors which relate to other senses (sight and touch) and seem to call for a similar response:

κατανοήσατε	"Pay attention!"
μὴ σκληρύνητε	"Do not harden (your hearts)!"

   iv. Both of these exhortations also occur in contexts which stress the *imminence* of the message which has been heard. In 3:1 the "holy brothers" who must pay attention to Jesus are described as "those who presently share/participate in a heavenly call" (κλήσεως ἐπουρανίου μέτοχοι).[328] Meanwhile in 3:7,

---

ἐν (3:2, 5, 8x2); γάρ (2:18, 3:3 and 4); ὡς x 3; κατά (x2, 3:3 and 3:8) and ἐάνπερÐ (3:6,7).

326. Friberg, *Analytical Lexicon to the Greek New Testament*, n.p., suggests that ὅθεν can function as an expression of cause: "for which reason, because of which."

327. *Contra* Guthrie, *Hebrews*, 125, who claims with regard to 3:1 that here as elsewhere "the author often follows a distinct pattern in his exhortations—setting forth the *exhortation* itself and then its *basis* or *grounds*"; and O'Brien, *Hebrews*, 131, who states that "as yet no precise reason is given" as to why to heed the appeal of 3:1, Jesus' newly acquired capacity to help (2:18) serves as the primary basis for the exhortation of 3:1, with further reasons given in verses 3-4 (as seen by the function of γάρ in 3:3 and 3:4). Meanwhile, the appeal of 3:7 seems based on the relative greatness of Jesus in comparison to Moses together with the fact that our participation in him depends upon our response.

328. See previous discussion on the meaning and emphasis of this phrase in 4.2.7b.

the immediacy of the Spirit's address is emphasized in 3:7 by the use of the present tense regarding God's speech (λέγει), irrespective of whether σήμερον is read in connection with λέγει to describe what the Holy Spirit "says today," or as a part of a quotation from Ps 95 ("Today, if you hear his voice, do not harden your hearts!");

b. Though the parallelism between 3:2-3 and 3:5-6 has been noted to some degree (cf. 4.2.8a), the extent of "connectedness" between these clauses and their combined significance not been fully appreciated and is worthy of closer consideration.

Heb 3:2
πιστὸν ὄντα τῷ ποιήσαντι αὐτὸν ὡς καὶ Μωϋσῆς ἐν τῷ οἴκῳ αὐτοῦ πλείονος γὰρ οὗτος δόξης παρὰ Μωϋσῆν ἠξίωται καθ' ὅσον πλείονα τιμὴν ἔχει τοῦ οἴκου ὁ κατασκευάσας αὐτόν

Heb 3:5-6a
καὶ Μωϋσῆς μὲν πιστὸς ἐν ὅλῳ τῷ οἴκῳ αὐτοῦ ὡς θεράπων εἰς μαρτύριον τῶν λαληθησομένων Χριστὸς δὲ ὡς υἱὸς ἐπὶ τὸν οἶκον αὐτοῦ

i. The clause πιστὸν ὄντα τῷ ποιήσαντι αὐτὸν ὡς καὶ Μωϋσῆς ἐν [ὅλῳ] τῷ οἴκῳ αὐτοῦ (3:2a) is formally related to 3:5-6a in a number of ways. Both (a) make use of the subordinating conjunction ὡς within (b) a comparison between Jesus and Moses, (c) relating to their faithfulness (d) "within [the whole of] his house" (ἐν [ὅλῳ] τῷ οἴκῳ αὐτοῦ). At the same time, the topical difference between the two passages is made clear by the distinctly different function of ὡς in each context.[329]

ii. The statement πλείονος γὰρ οὗτος δόξης παρὰ Μωϋσῆν ἠξίωται in 3:3 and the contrast between Jesus and Moses in verses 5-6 (described above) *both emphasize the Son's superiority over Moses.*

---

329. In 3:2, ὡς is used to compare Jesus' faithfulness with Moses: "He was faithful ... like Moses also was" (πιστὸν ὄντα ... ὡς καὶ Μωϋσῆς). In 3:6a, meanwhile, the faithfulness of both men is assumed with minimal repetition by means of a μὲν ... δέ construction. The emphasis is now upon the particular *role* carried out by both faithful men: for his part, Moses was faithful "as a servant for a testimony to the things that would be spoken" (ὡς θεράπων εἰς μαρτύριον τῶν λαληθησομένων), where Jesus was faithful "as the Son upon his house" (υἱὸς ἐπὶ τὸν οἶκον αὐτοῦ).

In verse 3 this superiority is explicitly affirmed by the statement: "He is worthy of much more glory than Moses," while in verses 5-6 it is *illustrated* in terms of Jesus' *role* and *position* relative to Moses in connection with "his house."[330] With regard to his role, where Moses was appointed as "servant in order that he might testify to the things that would be spoken" (ὡς θεράπων εἰς μαρτύριον τῶν λαληθησομένων), Jesus was named "Son," the fulfilment of that previously spoken prophetic word. Interestingly, this description of Moses" role makes him a model example of a "messenger" (ἄγγελος, cf. chapter 1, 2:2), further confirming our understanding of the meaning of the word in these earlier contexts.[331] Similarly, with regard to his *position*, where Moses is described as a servant "*within* his house" (ἐν [ὅλῳ] τῷ οἴκῳ αὐτοῦ), Jesus is spoken of as the Son "*over*" (ἐπὶ) it.[332] The function of these verses is thus very similar such that when read together they make a closely related point to the statements in 1:3 and 1:6 which contrast the unparalleled greatness of Jesus with that of the messengers (see 4.2.2d).[333]

 iii. The reference to τῷ ποιήσαντι αὐτὸν ὡς καὶ Μωϋσῆς ("to the one who appointed him as also Moses") in verse 2 is also connected to verses 5-6, with the latter clauses functioning to expand and clarify the nature of this appointment as Son and servant respectively.

 iv. Finally, both 3:3 and 3:6 contain metaphors which describe a relationship between Jesus and his people. In 3:3, Jesus is "the builder (ὁ κατασκευάσας) "of the house" (τῷ τοῦ οἴκου) while in 3:6, he is the "Christ" (Χριστός) who sits "as Son upon his house" (ὡς υἱὸς ἐπὶ τὸν οἶκον αὐτοῦ, 3:6).

c. Though the relationship between Hebrews 3:2, 1 Chronicles 17:14 and 1 Samuel 2:35 (and also Numbers 12:7/Hebrews 3:5) has been

---

330. Lane, *Hebrews 1-8*, n.p.

331. Cf. Lane, *Hebrews 1-8*, n.p., who notes that "by defining Moses" service in this way, the writer indicates that Moses" status as servant corresponds to that of the angels, who are servants to the heirs of salvation."

332. Heil, *Chiastic Structures*, 83, notes that the phrase depicts Jesus as "eternally enthroned over the "house" of God as "Son," God's "firstborn" (1:6) with the right of inheritance, indeed the "heir" of all things (1:2)."

333. 1:4 explicitly affirms Jesus' superiority over τῶν ἀγγέλων, while 1:6 illustrates the point in terms of their reverent posture towards him.

recognized,[334] the strength and significance of the connections with 1 Chronicles and 1 Samuel 2 have not been fully appreciated. Lexical connections between 1 Chronicles 17:12-14 and Hebrews 2:16-3:6 include:

I Chron 17:12-14	Heb 3:1-6
οἶκος x 2	οἶκος x 6
αὐτὸς οἰκοδομήσει μοι οἶκον	ὁ κατασκευάσας αὐτόν [τὸν οἶκον]
υἱός	υἱός
πιστώσω αὐτὸν	πιστὸν ὄντα τῷ ποιήσαντι αὐτὸν [i.e. θεός]
ἐν οἴκῳ μου	ἐν οἴκῳ αὐτοῦ
αὐτός x 8	αὐτός x 6

Further correspondences may also be identified between the form and content of these texts, both of which:

- refer to an οἶκος ("house") consisting of a group of people;[335]
- use υἱός ("Son") to describe a specific *role* connected with the building of this house rather than as a descriptor of an individual (cf. 1:4-5);[336]
- employ the singular masculine personal pronoun αὐτός an unusually large number of times (8 x in Chronicles and 5 in Hebrews 3:1-6);
- contain overt messianic overtones.[337]

Similar kinds of connections also exist between Hebrews 3:2 (and its immediate context) and 1 Samuel 2:35. Significant vocabulary shared by both texts includes: οἶκος ("house"); οἰκοδομέω ("I build a house");

334. Cf. Lane, *Hebrews 1-8*, n.p.

335. In 1 Chronicles 17, μοι οἶκον ("my house," vv. 12, 14) is closely linked with "His Kingdom" (τὴν βασιλείαν αὐτοῦ, vv. 11, 14), while in Hebrews 3:6, "*we* are his house" (οὗ οἶκός ἐσμεν ἡμεῖς).

336. In 1 Chronicles 17, God promises that "the seed" (of David) who will build his house will be to me "as a Son to me" (μοι εἰς υἱόν). Similarly, Heb 3:6 describes Christ's faithfulness "*as* Son over his house" (ὡς υἱὸς ἐπὶ τὸν οἶκον αὐτοῦ).

337. Cf. the twin references to βασιλεία ("Kingdom," v. 11 and 14) and ὁ θρόνος ("the throne," v.12 and 14) in 1 Chronicles 17 and the description of Jesus as Χριστὸς who rules as υἱὸς ἐπὶ τὸν οἶκον αὐτοῦ in Hebrews 3:6.

πιστός x 2 ("faithful"); Χριστός ("Christ"); πᾶς x 2 ("every"); ποιέω ("I make"); αὐτός ("he"); ἡμέρα ("day," cf. 3:8); and καρδία ("heart," cf. 3:9). More broadly:

i. both 1 Samuel 2:35 and Hebrews 3:2 describe God's appointment (cf. ἀναστήσωα / τῷ ποιήσαντι αὐτὸν) of a faithful priest (ἱερεύς / ἀρχιερεύς) in association with an οἶκος;

ii. the puzzling topical shift from discussion regarding Jesus as housebuilder (3:2-6) to the exhortation to listen to his voice (3:7) seems likely to reflect the two parts to the promise of 1 Samuel 2:35 that God would raise up, first, a faithful priest (ἱερέα πιστόν) and, second, a "faithful house" (οἶκον πιστόν). For having emphatically announced Jesus' "faithfulness" to his priestly appointment (3:2-4), Hebrews calls on his "house" itself (i.e. "us," 3:6) to be faithful (3:7ff.);[338]

iii. Hebrews' presentation of faithfulness as the *only* necessary condition for continued participation within Christ's people (cf. 3:6, 14) also echoes the description of this people/οἶκος in 1 Samuel 2:35 using the sole adjective πιστός (cf. οἶκον πιστόν, 1 Samuel 2:35).

When read together, these intertextual connections reveal that (LXX) 1 Chronicles 17:14 and 1 Samuel 2:35 play a far more significant role in shaping the vocabulary, form and topic of Hebrews 3:2 and its surrounds than has been generally recognized, making clear the author's understanding:

1. that the οἶκος of Hebrews 3, which includes "us" (3:6), represents the *singular fulfilment* of both houses promised in 1 Chronicles and 1 Samuel 2;

2. that Jesus represents *both* the υἱός and τὸ σπέρμα of David described in 1 Chronicles 17 and the priest and (possibly) King (cf. Χριστοῦ) of 1 Sam 2:35; and

3. that the emphasis of Jesus' description as πιστός in Hebrews 3:2 lies upon his faithful completion of his appointed task as *the builder of God's house*.

In conclusion, this analysis confirms with increased precision previous observations of parallelism within 3:1-8 while also drawing

---

338. Cf. the further promise in 2 Sam 7:16 (which represents a parallel text of 1 Chronicles 17:14): καὶ πιστωθήσεται ὁ οἶκος αὐτοῦ καὶ ἡ βασιλεία αὐτοῦ ("and his house and his kingdom will be made faithful").

attention to a number of further connections within this material. It now remains for us to examine the location of repetition within this cluster for any evidence of a combined structural function.

c. *The location and formal function of repetition in Hebrews 3:1-8*

While several scholars have identified various concentric structures within this text, spanning 3:1-6 (Rhee and Heil),[339] 3:2-6 (Ellingworth),[340] and 3:3-4 (Lane),[341] none of these proposals, though convincing in part, have succeeded in accounting adequately for the relationship between each of the parallels identified in the previous section (4.2.8b).[342]

---

339. Rhee, *Faith*, 91; and Heil, *Chiastic Structures*, 76.
340. Ellingworth, *Hebrews*, 200, 206-7.
341. Lane, *Hebrews 1-8*, n.p.
342. Our analysis most closely resembles Ellingworth's findings, *Hebrews*, 200, of a parallel relationship between vv. 2-3 and vv. 5-6, which together surround the symmetrical v. 4, supplementing these insights with the further evidence of connectedness between 2:18—3:1 and 3:7 (noted above). Rhee, *Faith*, 91-92, for instance, draws attention to plausible links between B / B' and C / C' yet misses the connections between 3:2-3 and 5-6 and ignores strong(er) formal evidence of symmetry within 3:4. Though he claims that "the center sections (D and D' [i.e. vv. 3 and 4]) show parallelism by the words οἶκος (house) and κατασκευάζω (to build)," οἶκος occurs 6 times within this unit, meaning that this connection is not obviously significant. Indeed, a closer relationship seems to exist between the verbal references to κατασκευάζω in v. 3 than between both together and ὁ κατασκευάσας in v. 4. Rhee also fails to provide adequate justification for his perception of a link between κατασκοήσατε (3:1) and κατάσχωμεν (3:6), claiming, without explanation: "sections A and A' show parallelism by the word 'consider' (κατανοήσατε) (3:1) and 'hold firm' (κατάσχωμεν) (3:6). Both terms express similar concepts." Cf. also Lane's suggestion, *Hebrews 1-8*, n.p., of a chiastic relationship within the "argument" of verses 3-4 (see below) which overlooks the more obvious formal symmetry within verse 4.

A   Jesus is worthy of more glory than Moses
    B   as the house-builder receives more honor than the house
    B'   for every house is built by someone
A'   but God is the builder of everything

Heil, *Chiastic Structures*, 76, meanwhile, notes a number of important lexical links within 3:1-6. However, his decision to read verses 3:1 and 3:6 as parallel texts (A and A') on the basis of the lexical link between ἡμῶν (3:1) and ἡμεῖς (3:6) seems arbitrary given that the same group are addressed in the second person in 3:7 onwards and his outline obscures the formal and topical parallelism seen in 3:2-3 and 5-6 and within verse 4.

When viewed together as a whole, the location of repetition suggests that 3:1-8 is best understood as a carefully arranged concentric unit (see below). The majority of significant connections occur on one side or other of a midpoint which lies between verse 4a and b and divide the cluster into two halves which may be further subdivided into three matched pairs of sentences (A, A'; B, B'; C, C'). The unit begins in 3:1 and ends after verse 8 with the introduction of new material concerning God's response to the testing of the wilderness generation. As such, though novel, our proposal is consistent with the widespread perception of the unity of 3:1-6, while avoiding the difficulties noted previously.

A. ³:¹ ὅθεν ἀδελφοὶ ἅγιοι κλήσεως ἐπουρανίου μέτοχοι κατανοήσατε τὸν ἀπόστολον καὶ ἀρχιερέα τῆς ὁμολογίας ἡμῶν Ἰησοῦν

B. ² πιστὸν ὄντα τῷ ποιήσαντι αὐτὸν ὡς καὶ Μωϋσῆς ἐν τῷ οἴκῳ αὐτοῦ πλείονος ³ γὰρ οὗτος δόξης παρὰ Μωϋσῆν ἠξίωται καθ' ὅσον πλείονα τιμὴν ἔχει τοῦ οἴκου ὁ κατασκευάσας αὐτόν

C. ⁴ πᾶς γὰρ οἶκος κατασκευάζεται ὑπό τινος

C'. ὁ δὲ πάντα κατασκευάσας θεός

B'. ⁵ καὶ Μωϋσῆς μὲν πιστὸς ἐν ὅλῳ τῷ οἴκῳ αὐτοῦ ὡς θεράπων εἰς μαρτύριον τῶν λαληθησομένων ⁶ Χριστὸς δὲ ὡς υἱὸς ἐπὶ τὸν οἶκον αὐτοῦ

A'. οὗ οἶκός ἐσμεν ἡμεῖς ἐὰν τὴν παρρησίαν καὶ τὸ καύχημα τῆς ἐλπίδος κατάσχωμεν 7 διὸ καθὼς λέγει τὸ πνεῦμα τὸ ἅγιον σήμερον ἐὰν τῆς φωνῆς αὐτοῦ ἀκούσητε ⁸ μὴ σκληρύνητε τὰς καρδίας ὑμῶν

d. The topical function of repetition in Hebrews 3:1-8

Having determined its form, this section seeks to uncover evidence of coherence between its formally related parts (A / A', B / B', C / C'; and ABC and C'B'A') so as to better understand the combined topical function of this material.

When read together, 3:1 and 3:7-8 (A and A') are best understood as *parallel injunctions* which call on Hebrews' audience to respond appropriately to the word they have heard and continue to hear. Although some have read verses 7-11 as a lengthy citation which introduces the warning proper in 3:12 yet contains no imperatival force of its own,[343] the similarity noted earlier between κατανοήσατε in 3:1 and the phrase μὴ σκληρύνητε τὰς καρδίας ὑμῶν in 3:7 indicates that the quotation from (LXX) Psalm 94 functions as *more than supporting testimony* in this context, serving as *a direct and immediate command* from the Holy Spirit through the words of the Psalmist to those now reading Hebrews.[344] The point is not that the Holy Spirit once spoke these words long ago in the past, but that he *says them to us "today."*[345]

Heb 3:1   "Holy Brothers who share a heavenly call, *pay attention* to the apostle and high priest of our confession, Jesus!"

Heb 3:7   "As the Holy Spirit says today: "If you hear his voice, *do not harden* your hearts!"

Both imperatives are also located within similar contexts in which a link is drawn between the people's ongoing faithfulness and their participation and association with Jesus. In A, the appeal to "pay attention" is presented as an inference (ὅθεν, "therefore") arising from Jesus' present ability to help those being tested (cf. 2:18). The implication is clear: if they do not continue to pay attention to him, he will neither identify with them nor be able to help them. In A′ this need for faithfulness is made explicit: For we are his people *if* (ἐάν [περ]) we "hold fast the

---

343. Johnson, *Hebrews*, 117, claims that the διό in v. 7 properly attaches to βλέπετε in v. 12 rather than μὴ σκληρύνητε in v. 8 so that "if we eliminate the actual citation, the sentence in 3:7–12 would run, 'Just as the Holy Spirit says... watch out... admonish.'" However, as Lane, *Hebrews 1–8*, n.p., observes, this reading "blunts the force of the admonition and obscures the central importance of the quotation to the entire section." Cf. Ellingworth, *Hebrews*, 217; Attridge, *Hebrews*, 114; Guthrie, *Hebrews*, 129; Adam, *The Majestic Son*, 48.

344. Peake's objection, cited in Ellingworth, *Hebrews*, 217, that "the writer would not make the words of the Holy Ghost his own" misses the point for the exhortation of 3:7 (διό... μὴ σκληρύνητε) is indeed presented as coming from the Holy Spirit himself. Johnson, *Hebrews*, 23, comments: "by constantly citing passages from the LXX, and by introducing such passages with verbs of speaking, Hebrews in effect treats *texts* as the voices of the 'prophets' through whom God spoke in the past. And because many of his verbs of introduction are in the present tense, the hearer experiences these voices as God's speech to the present."

345. Read in this way, καθώς functions not to introduce a quotation which functions as a preamble to the exhortation in 3:12 but to identify the speaker of the exhortation (καθὼς λέγει τὸ πνεῦμα τὸ ἅγιον).

confidence and boast of hope [until the end]" (3:6)³⁴⁶ and "therefore" (διό) "do not harden" our hearts (3:7).³⁴⁷

Perhaps most importantly, in each case, Jesus is depicted as the *one to whom we must listen*: he is "the apostle and high priest of our confession" (τὸν ἀπόστολον καὶ ἀρχιερέα τῆς ὁμολογίας ἡμῶν Ἰησοῦν, 3:1) and it is "his voice" (τῆς φωνῆς αὐτοῦ/, 3:7) we are commanded to heed. In its grammatical context, the ambiguous αὐτός in 3:7 clearly links back to Χριστός or υἱός in 3:6, functioning in either case as a reference to Jesus.³⁴⁸

Meanwhile, both B and B' provide further support for the appeal in A/A' to pay attention to Jesus by demonstrating the overwhelming superiority of what he achieved by his faithfulness in comparison to what Moses achieved by his.³⁴⁹ The numerous points of contact between B and B' make clear that verses 2–3 and 5–6 function not as *two separate comparisons* between Moses and Jesus, as some suggest,³⁵⁰ but as parallel statements which together make *the same basic comparison and contrast* between the two men in slightly different forms.

In the light of 1 Chronicles 17:14/1 Samuel 2:35, verses 2–3 represent a statement *about Jesus in comparison to Moses*. The reference to Moses is parenthetical: "He [Jesus] was faithful to him who appointed him in his house (as Moses was too)." While similar to Moses at this point, however, Hebrews 3:2–3 also stresses the great difference between the two men for (γάρ) Jesus has been found worthy of *as much greater*

---

346. Ellingworth, *Hebrews*, 211, notes that "here as in 3:14, ἐάνἶπερÐ introduces a condition which may or may not be fulfilled."

347. The use of διό, which indicates that the appeal in 3:7 flows from what was said in 3:6, makes clear that hardening one's heart represents the opposite of what it means to hold fast. As in 3:1, the author assumes that they already have this "confidence" and "boast" and urges them to continue to hold on to them.

348. Although this reading is not what might have been expected from a plain reading of the Psalm in its original context, Ellingworth's suggestion, *Hebrews*, 219, that "there is nothing in the first part of Psalm 95 which would have been likely to make the author of Hebrews think of a second divine person" overstates the case. For the intriguing title of the Psalm in the LXX reads αἶνος ᾠδῆς τῷ Δαυιδ. While most obviously rendered as "a song of praise by David," an author with an eye for ambiguity such as ours may well have seen the possibilities here of an alternative reading at this point: "a song of praise *to/about the* David (i.e. Jesus)."

349. The point here is not that Jesus was more faithful than Moses for both men are presented as equally faithful. Cf. Lane, *Hebrews 1–8*, n.p., who notes that the author begins his comparison from the likeness between Jesus and Moses, rather than from the difference between them. Cf. Johnson, *Hebrews*, 105; Guthrie, *Hebrews*, 127.

350. Cf. Vanhoye, *La Structure*, 88; and Hanson, "Christ in the Old Testament," 394–96.

glory than Moses *as* the builder of a house has in comparison with the house which he has built (πλείονος ... δόξης ... ἠξίωται καθ' ὅσον πλείονα τιμήν).[351] In this way, Jesus is quite unlike the great OT leader.

Conversely, B' represents a statement *about Moses in comparison to Jesus* in the light of Numbers 12:7, which both affirms, once again, the faithfulness of both men while also providing further evidence for the assertion of verse 3 (above). For the Son's role as Christ (Χριστός) and his position "*over* his house" (ἐπὶ τὸν οἶκον αὐτοῦ, 3:6) both demonstrate Jesus' incomparable greatness relative to Moses, who served *in* the whole of his house" (cf. ἐν ὅλῳ τῷ οἴκῳ αὐτοῦ ὡς θεράπων, 3:5).

The clear parallels between verses 4a and b make similarly clear that, while different words are used, C and C' both affirm the *same* basic truth: that Jesus is the builder of God's house (see below).

Subject/ Agent	Action	Object
Τινος	κατασκευάζεται	πᾶς οἶκος
Θεός	κατασκευάσας	ὁ πάντα

Verse 4a makes explicit what has been plainly implied in B: that Jesus is in fact the house-builder (and therefore worthy of more honor than Moses). For (γάρ), the author clarifies, "every house" (πᾶς ... οἶκος), i.e. *even* God's is built by "someone" (τινος, i.e. Jesus not Moses).[352] Verse 4b, meanwhile, reinforces the content of 4a within a statement which both includes 4a within it[353] and draws attention to the qualitative difference between Jesus'

---

351. Ellingworth, *Hebrews*, 103, suggests that: "no particular degree of superiority is specified; the meaning is simply 'A is greater than B, just as C is greater than D.'" However, the syntax suggests the opposite (as in 1:3–4): Jesus is to be considered worthy of as much greater honor than Moses as a builder has honour in comparison with the house he builds. The reason for this proportional relationship between "the house" and its "builder" on the one hand and Jesus and Moses on the other is not made explicit until verse 4. Yet the implication is clear both from the syntax in verse 3 and from Hebrews' identification of Jesus as the Seed-of-David/Son/house-builder spoken of in 1 Chronicles 17: Jesus must be thought incomparably superior to Moses for by his faithfulness, he has built God's house, a people including not only the present hearers but even Moses himself.

352. The author's use of the present indicative κατασκευάζεται is gnomic at this point, clarifying the logical necessity that *in order* for Moses to serve within a "House," *someone* must first have built it.

353. In context, Θεός (3:4) functions to describe the builder's nature. In the same way that there is more to ὁ πάντα than πᾶς οἶκος, so there is more to Θεός than the Son (τινος). Nonetheless, in his essential nature, he is truly (i.e. 100%) God. Cf. John 1:1.

nature as God the maker/builder of all things and that of "his house" (and indeed all the rest of creation, cf. 1:2, 10).

Some scholars have struggled to account for the coherence within verse 4 due to the understandable reading that θεός in verse 4b refers to God the Father, rather than the Son. Lane, for example, argues against reading τινος ("someone") as Jesus despite the context of 3:3, because in verse 4 "the action of building is assigned to God, and not to Jesus."[354] Johnson, meanwhile, attributes what he sees as a "murky" argument to the author's desire to affirm both God the Father as "source of all things" and the Son as "participant in the creation of all things":

> The impossibility of stating these apparently contradictory propositions in any coherent fashion accounts, I think, for the confused sequence of statements of this section.[355]

In fact, however, the "confusion" stems from the attempt to read θεός as a reference to anyone other than the Son. For the parallelism within verse 4, read in the light of its immediate context (v. 3), the allusion to 1 Chronicles 17:14 in verse 2 and the three previous references to τίς in relation to a person (in 1:5; 1:13 and 2:6) all make perfectly clear that *Jesus is the builder* of God's house who therefore *must be* the "someone" of verse 4.[356] As such, θεός functions in much the same way as it does in 1:8 (and indeed John 1:1), as a reaffirmation of Jesus' divine nature.

Read together, the first half of the unit (A, B, C) appeals to Jesus' sanctified brothers to pay attention to their apostle and high priest, Jesus, because of his relative greatness in comparison to Moses. For as the seed of David/ the builder of God's house (C) who has been "made faithful" in fulfilment of 1 Chronicles 17:14, he is worthy of much greater honor *and therefore much greater attention* than Moses (B). Given the strong likelihood that the first readers of Hebrews would have agreed with the author that Moses was an authority who must be listened to, 3:1–4a functions as a "how much more" argument built upon an implicit assumption as follows:

---

354. Lane, *Hebrews 1-8*, n.p.
355. Johnson, *Hebrews*, 109. Cf. Attridge, *Hebrews*, 110.
356. Cf. Bruce, *Hebrews*, 57; D'Angelo, *Moses*, 166–77. *Contra* Attridge, *Hebrews*, 110.

Stated Premise	Jesus is even greater than Moses
Unstated Premise	We know that we must listen to what Moses has said
Conclusion	How much more must we listen to Jesus then

Meanwhile, C', B' and A' function together to make much the same points in reverse order. The δέ in 3:4b, καί in 3:5 and δέ in 3:6 all relate back to the γάρ of 3:4a and indicate that verses 4b-6 function as further support material for 3:3, explaining once more why Jesus "has been found worthy of so much greater honor than Moses." For as "the builder" of God's house (ὁ κατασκευάσας, 3:3), Jesus is in very nature God who has made all things (C') and the King (cf. Χριστός) who rules as the Son over his house (B'). Because of this and because we who hold fast "the confidence and boast of hope [until the end]" are this house, the author urges "us" again to respond to Jesus, this time using the form of a negative exhortation from Ps 95 (3:7).[357] For he is worthy of much greater honor than Moses and we will not escape if we rebel like the Israelites on the Day of Testing.

Taken together, the author thus presents the "holy brethren" with two arguments in 3:1-8 to pay attention to Jesus, which may be summarized below:

1. Because he is worthy of greater honor than Moses: (a) by as much as the house-builder has in comparison to the house (vv. 2-4a); (b) by as much as is due the house-building Son, who sits over the house, in comparison to the servant, who sits within it (vv. 4b-6);

2. (implied) Because of what happened to "the house of Moses" (3:7ff.).

e. *Further implications for meaning in light of the parallelism in Hebrews 3:1-8*

Once more, the identification of parallelism within 3:1-8 draws attention to a number of further connections between words and phrases in this context, which assist in clarifying meaning as follows.

---

357. The διό in 3:7 does not join together two distinct blocks of text (3:1-6 and 3:7-15/19) as is commonly assumed (cf. Vanhoye, *Structure*, 84; Guthrie, *Structure*, 129, and *Hebrews*, 129; Ellingworth, *Hebrews*, 50; Adam, *The Majestic Son*, 48; Johnson, *Hebrews*, 111; and Westfall, *Discourse Analysis*, 118), but functions rather to link the exhortation of 3:7-8 with the arguments regarding Jesus' superiority to Moses and the identity of the audience as his house (vv. 2-6).

First, although commonly described as a "problem,"³⁵⁸ the clear parallels between B and B' and between these texts and 1 Chronicles 17:14/1 Samuel 2:35 indicate that the repetition of αὐτός, which occurs 3 x in relation to an οἶκος (3:2b, 5 and 6), is best understood as a reference to *Jesus* in each case: he is the owner of the house in which Moses served (3:5). In terms of grammar, αὐτός in 3:2b and 5 can be read as a reference to Moses, Jesus, or God the Father. However, while there is considerable ambiguity with regard to its meaning in verse 2,³⁵⁹ the confirmation of 1 Chronicles as the primary background to 3:2 which makes clear that αὐτός in the verse is *not* a reference to Moses,³⁶⁰ the identification of Jesus as the builder of verse 4, and the fact that each mention of οἶκος seems likely to refer to the *same* house in this context,³⁶¹ suggests that αὐτός is Jesus and that "the house" represents a single group of people, including even Moses (3:5), over which he now rules as Son (3:6). In this way, Hebrews' author once again describes Jesus using words which in the LXX are only ever applied to God. Cf. 1:8–9, 10–12; 2:6–8, 12–13 and the description of Jesus as "the Sanctifier" (2:11; cf. Ex 31:13; Lev 20:8; 21:8, 15, 23; 22:9, 16, 32; Ezek 20:12; 37:28) and "helper" of his people (cf. 2:18; Isa 41:10). A translation of verses 2 and 5 may be seen below:

---

358. Ellingworth, *Hebrews*, 195, for example, claims that this section demonstrates "Hebrews' tendency to use personal pronouns without specifying to whom they refer" and suggests that "the difficulty arises partly because, for both stylistic and reverential reasons, the author makes economical use of explicit references to God and to Jesus, and partly because the activity of Jesus as God's ἀπόστολος is not always clearly distinguished from that of God who sent him."

359. Interestingly, the ambiguity at this point reflects that found in Hebrews' source material. In 1 Samuel 2:35, God promises οἰκοδομήσω αὐτῷ οἶκον πιστόν ("I will make him [Jesus] a house"), suggesting that the house, having been built by God, will belong to Jesus. Cf. 2 Sam 7:16. In 1 Chronicles 17:12, however, God prophecies of his Son αὐτὸς οἰκοδομήσει μοι οἶκον ("he will build a house for me"), suggesting precisely the *opposite* of 1 Samuel 2:35, that the house would be built by Jesus for his Father.

360. Further support for this is seen in the fact that the LXX never speaks of a house "belonging" to Moses and that in Numbers 12:7 (the background material to verse 5), the house belongs to the divine speaker and *not* Moses: ὁ θεράπων μου Μωυςῆς ἐν ὅλῳ τῷ οἴκῳ μου. *Contra* Westfall, *Discourse Analysis*, 299, who entitles 3:1–6 "We are Jesus' house like the Israelites were Moses" house."

361. There is no evidence of a second house or owner in Hebrews: (a) the word οἶκος is always singular, (b) only one builder is mentioned in 3:2–6 (who is identified as θεός); (c) by equating Moses with house and Jesus with builder in a general context, the author seems to connect the two into a single process (one house, one builder); and (d) the very idea of Moses as "owner" of a house would work against the rhetorical point made by the author at this point, which presents him as mere "servant" and "witness" (v. 5).

Heb 3:2 "He [Jesus] was faithful in *his* house to him who appointed him (as Moses was)"

Heb 3:5 "And Moses was faithful in the whole of *Jesus'* house . . . but Christ was faithful as the Son over *his* (own) house"

This parallelism also makes clear, second, that the author sees an extremely close relationship between Jesus' identification as ὁ κατασκευάσας ("the house-builder," 3:3, 4) and his title Χριστός ("Christ," 3:6), reflecting the collocation of these terms within his LXX source material.[362]

The key words and phrases indicated by repetition relate to the need for Jesus' "house" to faithfully pay attention to their "house-builder," Jesus, in view of his all-surpassing greatness in comparison with Moses. Less prominent material includes the as-yet-unexplored conditional clause of verse 6 and the historical description of the wilderness generation in v7.[363]

With regard to topic, though many have understood this material to be *about* Jesus (e.g., Vanhoye who labels 3:1-6 as "The Faithful and Merciful High priest"),[364] when read within its proper formal context, 3:1-7 becomes a meditation on and comparison of three primary LXX texts (1 Chronicles 17:12-34, 1 Samuel 2:35 and Numbers 12:7) which calls on Hebrews' audience to respond with faithfulness to Jesus (not Moses) in light of the completion of his labors (as described in Heb 2:9-18) on their behalf. For because he has suffered, having been tested, Jesus has proved himself worthy of their attention as the faithful messianic builder of God's house,[365] a group of people united through time and space and marked by faithfulness, which includes those of "us" who now hear the voice of Jesus and hold fast.[366] The logic of the

---

362. See 1 Chronicles 17:11-14; 2 Sam 7:12-16; and Isaiah 9.

363. The ambiguity in the phrase ἐὰν τὴν παρρησίαν καὶ τὸ καύχημα τῆς ἐλπίδος κατάσχωμεν (3:6b) raises questions which are not answered within this unit and thus serves to direct attention forwards in the discourse.

364. Vanhoye, *Structure and Message*, 83; Ellingworth, *Hebrews*, 193, 266; Lane, *Hebrews 1-8*, 68. See too Guthrie, *Hebrews*, 125, "A Positive Example: Jesus' Faithfulness as a Son (3:1-6)"; and Westfall, *Discourse Analysis*, 299, "We are Jesus' house like the Israelites were Moses' house."

365. Hebrews makes clear that Jesus "built" his house on the cross when he established salvation (2:10, 12:2).

366. The beneficiaries of Jesus' work of salvation are described as πᾶς (2:9) and the "seed of Abraham" (2:16), both of which terms include even those who lived before Jesus came (i.e. Moses). Against the charge of anachronism, cf. Rom 3; Heb 11; 6:17 etc.

unit (and thus summary of the topic) may be seen below, followed by a translation:

- A. House of God, pay attention/be faithful to Jesus, who speaks to you now!
- B. *For* he is greater than faithful Moses.
- C. *For* he built God's house (further clarification of B).

This may be translated as follows:

- A. ³:¹ Therefore, holy brothers, sharers of a heavenly call, pay attention to the apostle and high priest of our confession, Jesus,
   - B. ² who was faithful to him who appointed him within his house (as Moses also was). ³ For he has been counted worthy of greater glory than Moses by as much more as the builder of the house has compared with the house itself.
      - C. ⁴ For every house is built by someone.
      - C′. And God is the builder of everything.
   - B′. ⁵ And Moses was faithful on the one hand in the whole of his house as a servant, to testify to what would be spoken later, ⁶ but the Christ as Son upon his house, which we are if we hold fast the confidence and boast of hope.
- A′. Therefore as the Holy Spirit says: "Today if you hear his voice, do not harden your hearts."

f.   *Summary of findings in 3:1–8*

This examination of the link cluster at Hebrews 3:1–8:

a. clarifies with increased precision connections noted previously between 3:2–6, and between this text and 1 Chronicles 17:14, 1 Samuel 2:35 and Numbers 12:7, while also drawing attention to a number of further connections of significance, previously unobserved, between 3:1 and 3:7–8;

b. identifies, in response to the structural difficulties associated with the conventional understanding, that 3:1–8 is better understood as a concentric unit consisting of three matched pairs of parallel components (A, A'; B, B'; and C, C'), which displays a high degree of topical coherence between its formally linked material;

c. presents fresh evidence, in light of the parallelism (described above), which makes clear:

- that verses 2-3 and 5-6 function as parallel statements which demonstrate Jesus' incomparable superiority over Moses as ὁ κατασκευάσας ("the house-builder," 3:3, 4) and Χριστός ("Christ");
- that Jesus is the person referred to as τὶς ("someone") and θεός ("God") in v. 4;
- that Jesus is the owner of both the "house" in verses 3-6 and the "voice" of 3:7 (i.e. Jesus is αὐτός in 2:18, 3:2 [x2], 3, 5 and 6).

d. shows with regard to the author's use of the LXX:

- that the frequent repetition of the masculine personal pronoun αὐτός within this unit reflects the patterning of its source material, 1 Chronicles 17:12-14;
- that (LXX) Psalm 94 functions in its new context (i.e. v. 7ff.) not only as supporting testimony but as a parallel injunction with 3:1 spoken by the Holy Spirit calling on Hebrews' audience to respond appropriately to Jesus and his word which they have already heard and continue to hear;
- that the seemingly disparate elements of Hebrews 3:2-6 and 3:7ff., i.e. the description of Jesus and the command not to harden hearts, are both reflective of the promise of a faithful priest who would build a faithful house in 1 Samuel 2:35;
- that the faithfulness described in 3:2 (cf. πιστὸν ὄντα) refers specifically to the completion of Jesus' housebuilding appointment as prophesied in 1 Chronicles 17:14 and 1 Samuel 2:35;

e. concludes that the topic of this material may be summarized as follows: Holy brethren, be faithful to Jesus who speaks to you now! For he is far greater than even faithful Moses as the builder of God's house.

4.3 Conclusions

This chapter has shown:

First, that link clusters represent a commonly occurring and significant feature of the text in Hebrews 1:1–3:8 which reflect authorial *design* rather than an accident of transmission. Evidence for this may be seen by (i) the strength, frequency and range of connections within each cluster, (ii) the careful and concentric internal arrangement of individual links within them, and (iii) Hebrews' distinctive use of language throughout these chapters: Namely, that the author repeatedly uses words and phrases which form lexical and other kinds of connections with other words and phrases in the near vicinity, even when their referents are different (e.g., τοῖς ἀκουσθεῖσιν, 2:1, and τῶν ἀκουσάντων, 2:3) and their inclusion is awkward (e.g., λαβοῦσα, 2:3) and/or not easily explicable on conventional topical grounds (e.g., ποιησάμενος, 1:3, and παντὸς, 2:15).

Second, that intratextual link clusters play a far more significant structural role within Hebrews 1:1–3:8 than has been previously recognized. By means of micro link clusters, the author structures Hebrews 1:1–3:8 into a series of seven overlapping units, each of which is comprised of two or more pairs of balanced parallel phrases which have been concentrically arranged: 1:1–4; 1:3–6; 1:7–14; 1:13—2:5; 2:5–9; 2:8c–18; 3:1–8. Though this understanding of the structure of this part of Hebrews differs from earlier presentations, corresponding only at 1:1–4 and 2:5–9, it confirms previous intuitions of overlap within Hebrews, demonstrating that a relatively large proportion of this text is transitional material which properly belongs to more than one unit simultaneously (i.e. 1:3–4, 13–14; 2:5, 8–9). It also solves many of the structural challenges identified within this part of the text, consistently accounting better for Hebrews' use of conjunctions (especially γάρ, cf. 1:5, 2:5, 10, 16, 18) than previous presentations.

Third, that Hebrews also utilizes intertextual link clusters throughout chapters 1–3 to establish similar kinds of formal connections, again involving multiple points of contact, with a wide range of external texts from the LXX, presented here in approximate order of appearance (Pss 110:1; 2:7; 88:28; 2 Sam 7:14; 1 Chron 17:13; Deut 6:10/11:29; Pss 103:4, 44:7–8 and 101:26–28; Psalm 8:5–7; 21:23; Isa 8:17, 41:8–10; 1 Chron 17:14, 1 Sam 2:35; Num 12:7; and Ps 94:7–11). While the importance of many of these texts for Hebrews has been recognized previously, the identification of intratextual link clusters represents fresh evidence which *clarifies* the precise location of Hebrews' source material in certain places and *confirms* the significance of other largely neglected texts (e.g., Psalm 88:28 and Isaiah 41:8-10).

Fourth, that intra- and intertextual link clusters both serve a similar *topical function* by indicating to Hebrews' readers/hearers the presence of coherent relationships between otherwise unrelated material, *thereby marking out parallel contexts by which the author's intended meaning can be clearly identified*. While this parallelism within Hebrews has been largely overlooked by modern scholarship, leading to considerable distortion in meaning at times (see the widespread misunderstanding of ὁ δι' ἀγγέλων λαληθεὶς λόγος in 2:2 as a reference to the Law), Hebrews' author frequently and consistently uses intratextual link clusters to describe *the same event/person/action/exhortation twice* from slightly different perspectives, thereby (a) indicating the point of his interest with precision and (b) emphasizing the relative importance of this material through repetition.

This analysis has demonstrated that:

- 1:2b, 3d, and 1:6 represent parallel descriptions of the *same* event, the Son's heavenly enthronement in fulfilment of Psalm 88:28 and 110:1;
- τῶν ἀγγέλων in 1:4 describes the *same* group of messengers which is contrasted with the Son in 1:1-2;
- the twin descriptions of the Son in 1:3 affirm the *same* truth (the unity and distinction between him and the Father);
- both ὁ δι' ἀγγέλων λαληθεὶς λόγος (2:2) and τηλικαύτης ἀμελήσαντες ἀμελήσαντες σωτηρίας (2:3) describe the *same* message of salvation;
- 1:7-9 and 13-14 represent the *same* basic contrast between the status and permanency of the Son in comparison to the messengers;
- ἀκουσάντοι (2:3) describes the *same* group as that labelled ἀγγέλων in 2:2;
- 2:9-10 and 14-15 describe the *same* act of rescue from slightly different perspectives;
- 3:2-3 and 5-6 serve to make the *same* basic contrast between Jesus and Moses;
- 3:4a and b refer to the *same* builder (i.e. Jesus); and

- The exhortations of 3:1 and 7 call on readers to respond in the *same* way by paying attention to Jesus who speaks to them today;

Structuring his discourse in this way also allows the author to clarify meaning through (i) subtle yet significant variations, (ii) the juxtaposition of opposite ideas, and (iii) the establishment of instantial equivalents between parallel texts. For example, with regard to (i), by replacing αὐτόν and αὐτόν (2:7) with τόν and Ἰησοῦν (2:9) and changing the tense used within the formally parallel contexts of 2:5-7 and 2:9, the author alerts readers to his distinctive interpretation of Psalm 8 as messianic prophecy which has been fulfilled by Jesus. By juxtaposing the descriptions from (LXX) Psalm 101 of the Son's work at the beginning (1:10) and end (1:12) of time, meanwhile, (ii), he emphasizes Jesus' eternal nature in contrast to that of the creation. Finally, with regard to (iii), the clear parallelism between 2:8c-10 and 14-17 makes clear that the description of Jesus as τὸν ἀρχηγὸν τῆς σωτηρίας αὐτῶν (2:10) is best understood in light of his later identification as ἀρχιερεύς in 2:17 as a descriptor of his role as "pioneer leader/ initiator/first cause" of salvation, who brings forgiveness through his offering of a perfect sacrifice for sins.

Further exegetical insights of significance from this chapter, additional to those noted already, arising from the identification of parallelism between intratextual clusters, include the following.

- The implicit appeal of 2:1 functions in context *not* as a digression based on a tangential reference to the Law as commonly understood, *but* as the direct and urgent application of the topical content of Hebrews 1:13—2:5;
- The reference to τῶν ἀκουσάντων in 2:3 does *not* reveal the author of Hebrews as a "second-generation Christian," as is commonly assumed, but further describes the ἀγγέλων of 2:2;
- ἑνός in 2:11 is best understood as a reference to God (cf. αὐτῷ; and ὁ θεός);
- πάλιν in 2:13 functions as a formal marker which indicates the moment of transition from one component of the chiasm to the next (C' to B' and B' to A' respectively) thereby assisting the reader/hearer to understand the form of the discourse;
- 2:11-13 represents a carefully and chiastically arranged series of assertions and supporting pieces of evidence spoken by Jesus, which

proves that he rejoices in the fraternal relationship he enjoys with the people of God;

- The repetition of πειράζω in 2:18 demonstrates that through testing, Jesus has indeed become "like the brothers in every way" (κατὰ πάντα τοῖς ἀδελφοῖς, 2:17);
- The "help" (cf. βοηθέω) described in 2:18 refers in 2:16–3:2 to Jesus' capacity to *save* people from their sins and lead them into glory, having come as the "pioneer leader" of salvation in fulfilment of Isaiah 41:8–10;
- πειρασθείς (2:18) modifes δύναται rather than πέπονθεν, making clear that Jesus' ability to fulfil his appointed ministry required him to experience human suffering first hand;
- τὸν ἀπόστολον καὶ ἀρχιερέα τῆς ὁμολογίας ἡμῶν (3:1) serves as a title which makes clear that, "having been faithful" (πιστὸν ὄντα, 3:2) to him who *sent* him, Jesus has been immersed in the full range of human experience as the ultimate apostle and offered an acceptable sacrifice for sin as *high priest*;
- Jesus is the owner of both the "house" in 3:3–6 and the "voice" of 3:7 (i.e. Jesus is αὐτός in 3:2 [x2], 3, 5 and 6).

Much the same kind of topical function has also been found with regard to Hebrews' use of intertextual link clusters. At times, Hebrews employs material from the LXX without significant variation to its original form, function and meaning (e.g., the quotation of Psalm 2:7 in Hebrews 1:5) as authoritative testimony in support of assertions in his argument. More commonly, however, by means of intertextual link clusters, the author establishes formal parallels between his text and his source material which allow him *to bring out new meanings from old forms of words* by:

i. introducing subtle yet significant variations to the text of his source material. For example, by replacing πῦρ φλέγον ([LXX] Ps 103:4) with πυρὸς φλόγα in Hebrews 1:7, the author transforms the meaning of this verse from a statement about the winds to one about the messengers;

ii. changing (or at least sharpening) their referent. Thus 1:10–12 applies the words of Psalm 101:3 regarding God the creator specifically to Jesus; and

iii. re-interpreting the meaning of particular words and phrases: e.g., in its new context, ἐπ' αὐτῷ (Isa 8:17) means "about this" rather than "about him."

Further exegetical insights, in addition to those noted already, arising from the observation of parallelism between intertextual clusters in this chapter include the following.

- The ambiguous κλήσεως ἐπουρανίου μέτοχοι (3:1) is best understood in light of Isaiah 41:8–10 as a description of Hebrews' readers as those who in Christ have come to share in the call *from* Heaven;
- The faithfulness described in 3:2 (πιστὸν ὄντα) refers specifically to Jesus' completion of his housebuilding appointment as described in 1 Chronicles 17:14 and 1 Samuel 2:35;
- The enigmatic 1:6 represents a further description of the Son's exaltation (cf. 1:3–4) which speaks "again" (πάλιν) of Jesus' entry into the "heavenly world" (οἰκουμένη) in fulfilment Psalm (LXX) 88:28.

In summary, this chapter has found that intratextual and intertextual link clusters play a crucial role within Hebrews 1–3 by forming parallel contexts, both within and without this text, in light of which meaning might be properly understood. And that this meaning may be discerned by reading texts within their immediate literary context in light of both these additional parallel contexts in combination, noting the points at which they differ from their "partner" texts. Given the consistency and comprehensiveness of this patterning, the meaning of *every* word, phrase and larger textual unit within Hebrews 1:1–3:8 can be clearly identified, since *every* part of Hebrews has been paired with at least one, two, or three such co-texts within Hebrews and/or the LXX.

5

The Combined Function of Micro and Macro Link Clusters in Hebrews Chapters 1–4

5.1 Introduction

IN CHAPTER 4, WE embarked on an analysis of Hebrews 1–3:8 which sought to ascertain the location of link clusters within this material and to understand their function within the text. We found:

1. that the author of Hebrews makes frequent and consistent use of this compositional technique in the first section of his discourse;
2. strong evidence of at least two distinct types of clusters (intra- and inter-textual) within this text;
3. that the author uses this technique primarily to indicate a relationship between his text and one or more additional texts, thereby providing an additional context (or contexts) by which to understand the meaning of individual words, phrases, sentences and paragraphs in his discourse;
4. that link clusters also function to structure this part of the discourse at the micro level into a series of overlapping concentric textual units as follows: Hebrews 1:1–4; 1:3–6; 1:7–14; 2:1–4; 2:5–9; 2:8b–18; 3:1–8.

Following this, chapter 5 investigates the relationships *between* the units identified in chapter 4 according to the final step of our method (see 3.4) and in light of further evidence of macro link clusters and topic markers within the text. It seeks to uncover *why* the author has structured his text in this way and *how* each of these units combines together within Hebrews 1–4. Since Hebrews clearly represents much more than a collection of discrete units, our findings must be deemed unsuccessful if a meaningful relationship cannot be shown to exist between them. On the other hand, the demonstration of such a relationship between these and other larger units of text would represent strong confirmation of our results and provide valuable insight into the structure of this discourse.

The chapter begins (5.2) with an investigation into a further type of textual patterning involving repetition (and typically contrast) at the micro level which has been largely overlooked despite being found consistently throughout Hebrews. It proposes that this patterning serves to draw the attention of its readers/hearers to the start of each new topical point in the discourse. This is followed in 5.3, second, by the identification and examination of four macro link clusters (between 1:1–5 and 1:13—2:4; 2:1–5 and 2:16—3:2; 3:1–3 and 4:14; and 1:1–4 and 4:12–14) which, it argues, function as parallel topic sentences, serving both to group the text into subsections and sections and to summarize its topical content. After this, third (5.4), an attempt is made to understand the relationship between micro and macro clusters and their combined contribution to the flow of thought in 1:1–4:16. Finally, Hebrews' use of overlap is considered in 5.5 in light of all the assembled evidence, at the end of which a number of conclusions will be drawn (5.6).

5.2 Topic Markers

As has been widely recognized, the lexical repetition of λαλέω (1:1 and 2), in association with four relations of opposition regarding the timing, recipients, agents and ways (implied) of God's address, sets up a relationship of antithetical parallelism between the first two clauses and represents a striking beginning to the discourse: Where God once spoke "long ago" (πάλαι), he has now spoken "at the end of these days" (ἐπ' ἐσχάτου τῶν ἡμερῶν τούτων); where he once spoke "to the fathers" (τοῖς πατράσιν), he has now spoken "to us" (ἡμῖν); where he once spoke "by the prophets" (ἐν τοῖς προφήταις), he has now spoken "by the Son" (ἐν υἱῷ); where he once spoke "in many parts and places" (πολθμερῶς καὶ πολυτρόπως), he has now spoken in one way.[1]

---

[1]. Black, "Hebrews 1:1–4," 177, 189. Cf. Ellingworth, *Hebrews*, 91; Adam, *The*

Heb 1:1-2

Πολυμερῶς καὶ πολυτρόπως πάλαι ὁ θεὸς λαλήσας τοῖς πατράσιν ἐν τοῖς προφήταις 2 ἐπ' ἐσχάτου τῶν ἡμερῶν τούτων ἐλάλησεν ἡμῖν ἐν υἱῷ

> "**Having spoken** in many parts and places of old to the fathers by the prophets, in the last of these days God **has spoken** to us by the Son"

Almost as striking, though largely overlooked, is the fact that Hebrews makes use of a similar kind of patterning within the A (and sometimes A and B) components, i.e. the introduction, of *each unit* examined to this point.

This similarity may be seen most clearly within the first part of the four units below, each of which, like 1:1-2, (i) share a common repeated element (marked in **bold**) and (ii) contain a contrast which is grammaticalized in various ways. At times the contrast involves only one element (cf. the contrasting objects of the Son's help in 2:16).[2] At others, two or three elements are contrasted simultaneously. For instance the repetition of ὁ οἶκος αὐτοῦ in 3:5-6 sets up contrasts between (i) Χριστός and Μωϋσῆς, (ii) their respective locations with regard to the house (ἐν / ἐπί), and (iii) roles (ὡς θεράπων / ὡς υἱός).

Heb 1:7-8   καὶ **πρὸς** μὲν τοὺς ἀγγέλους **λέγει** / **πρὸς** δὲ τὸν υἱόν [**λέγει**][3]

"and he says to the messengers on the one hand / but [he says] to the Son on the other"

Heb 2:5-6   οὐ γὰρ ἀγγέλοις ὑπέταξεν ... περὶ ἧς **λαλοῦμεν** / **διεμαρτύρατο** δέ **πού** τις **λέγων** τί ἐστιν ἄνθρωπος

"for he has not subjected to the messengers [about which we speak] but he has testified somewhere, saying "what is man"?"

Majestic Son, 18; Guthrie, *Hebrews*, 46; and O'Brien, *Hebrews*, 47-48. This material is made even more prominent by the use in 1:1 of alliteration based on the "p" sound: πολυμερῶς, πολυτρόπως, πάλαι, πατράσιν, προφήταις.

2. Lane, *Hebrews 1-8*, notes that "by casting the statement in the form of an antithetic parallelism, and then heightening the parallelism by the identity of the last words (i.e., antistrophe), he [the author] could be assured of arresting the attention of his hearers."

3. Cf. the additional repetition of τοὺς ἀγγέλους in 1:7.

Heb 2:8c-9   νῦν δὲ οὔπω **ὁρῶμεν αὐτῷ** τὰ πάντα ὑποτεταγμένα / τὸν δὲ
βραχύ τι παρ' ἀγγέλους ἠλαττωμένον **βλέπομεν Ἰησοῦν**

"and we don't yet see all things subjected to him now / but
we see Jesus who was made lower than messengers for a little
while"

Heb 3:5-6   καὶ Μωϋσῆς μὲν **πιστὸς** ἐν ὅλῳ τῷ **οἴκῳ αὐτοῦ** ὡς θεράπων /
Χριστὸς δὲ [**πιστὸς**] ὡς υἱὸς ἐπὶ **τὸν οἶκον αὐτοῦ**

"and Moses on the one hand was faithful in his house as a
servant / but Christ [was faithful] as Son upon his house"

Similarities of form are also evident in the comparisons which begin 1:3-6 and 3:1-8, and which both represent a two-part clause complex containing repetition. These may be seen below:

Heb 1:4   τοσούτῳ **κρείττων** γενόμενος τῶν ἀγγέλων ὅσῳ **διαφορώτερον**
παρ' αὐτοὺς κεκληρονόμηκεν ὄνομα

"having become greater than the messengers by as much
greater is the name he has inherited than theirs"

Heb 3:2   **πιστὸν ὄντα τῷ ποιήσαντι αὐτὸν** ὡς καὶ Μωϋσῆς ἐν [ὅλῳ] τῷ
οἴκῳ αὐτοῦ

"being faithful to the one who appointed him as also Moses
[was]"

Finally, although grammatically unrelated, 1:13 and 14 are linked by a question/answer construction in which the answer expected by 1:13 ("not one of the messengers") represents *the opposite* of the answer implied by the question of 1:14 ("all of the messengers").[4] In other words, much the same pattern of repetition and contrast emerges once again, as may be seen below.

Heb 1:13-14

πρὸς τίνα δὲ τῶν ἀγγέλων εἴρηκέν ποτε . . . οὐχὶ πάντες εἰσὶν [τῶν ἀγγέλων]

"and to which one of the messengers has he ever said . . . Are not all [the messengers]"

---

4. Verse 14 depends on the previous verse for its referents (i.e. they all = the messengers as a whole).

There is thus clear evidence that Hebrews makes use of *a regularly occurring pattern of repetition (and frequently contrast)* at the micro level of the text, and that this pattern is located in each case *at the beginning of each of the first seven units of the discourse*. Given the consistency of this patterning, this phenomenon is unlikely to represent an accident of the text and almost certainly reflects authorial design. This impression is strengthened even more by the observation of much the same kind of patterning throughout the text of Hebrews, *always* within the introduction (i.e. A and sometimes A and B component) to a unit (see below). Examples which follow those already examined may be seen below:

Heb 4:14—5:2	ἔχοντες οὖν ἀρχιερέα . . . οὐ . . . ἔχομεν ἀρχιερέα
Heb 6:9–20	ἀγαπητοί . . . τῆς ἀγάπης[5]
Heb 6:19—7:3	ἀσφαλῆ τε καὶ βεβαίαν καὶ εἰσερχομένην εἰς τὸ ἐσώτερον . . . εἰσῆλθεν Ἰησοῦς[6]
Heb 7:4–10	δεκάτην Ἀβραὰμ ἔδωκεν . . . ὁ πατριάρχης καὶ οἱ μὲν ἐκ τῶν υἱῶν . . . ἀποδεκατοκατὰ τὴν τάξιν Μελχισέδεκ . . . κατὰ τὴν τάξιν Ἀαρὼν + νενομοθέτηται and νόμου + ἱερωσύνης and ἱερέα
Heb 7:11–17	κατὰ . . . κατὰ[7]
Heb 8:6–13	νυνὶ δὲ διαφορωτέρας τέτυχεν λειτουργίας ὅσῳ καὶ κρείττονός ἐστιν διαθήκης μεσίτης ἥτις ἐπὶ κρείττοσιν ἐπαγγελίαις νενομοθέτηται

The significance of this observation for our understanding of the text of Hebrews is seen in at least two ways. First, it represents important formal evidence which further corroborates our findings concerning unit boundaries. Second, since repetition, contrast, and comparison all represent common tactics by which a skilful writer might mark out particular text as more prominent than its surrounds,[8] *it is likely that Hebrews uses this eye-catching (or, perhaps more accurately, ear-catching) formal device* to alert readers/hearers to the beginning of each new unit/topic in the discourse. As our micro-analysis has already shown, the "A" component of each unit conforms to the methodological criteria

---

5. The adjective ἀγαπητοί ("beloved," 6:9) occurs only here in Hebrews in close proximity to its related noun ἀγάπης ("love," 6:10) which occurs once more in 10:24.

6. Cf. also γενόμενος (6:20) which may be rendered as "having come in."

7. The phoneme κατὰ occurs six times in verses 15–17 (4 x as κατὰ, and within κατάδηλόν and ἀκαταλύτου).

8. Westfall, *Discourse Analysis*, 55, 69, 75.

outlined in chapter 3 for the detection of topic announcements.[9] Meanwhile, in each case, the repeated words or phrases *seem central to the argument*, suggesting their likely function as key words, as would be consistent with such a proposal.[10]

5.3 Macro Link Clusters within Hebrews 1:1—4:16

5.3.1 Overview

In addition to the micro-repetition noted in 5.2 which draws readers/hearers' attention to the beginning of each of the eight micro link clusters identified in chapter 4, 1:1—4:16 also contains four macro link clusters which join together the following texts:

1. 1:1–5 and 1:13—2:4
2. 2:1–5 and 2:16—3:2
3. 3:1–3 and 4:14
4. 1:1–4 and 4:12–14

This section represents an investigation into each of these clusters in turn, seeking to itemize all links within them so as to assess the presence or otherwise of a coherent relationship between partner texts. It argues that each pair of sentences might be plausibly read as topic sentences which both unite the intervening material into subsections and together summarize its content.

5.3.2 Hebrews 1:1–5 and 1:13—2:4

The first macro link cluster in the text occurs between Hebrews 1:1–5 and 1:13-2:4.

> Heb 1:1–5
> ¹ <u>πολυμερῶς καὶ πολυτρόπως πάλαι ὁ θεὸς λαλήσας τοῖς πατράσιν ἐν τοῖς προφήταις</u> ² ἐπ' ἐσχάτου τῶν ἡμερῶν τούτων ἐλάλησεν

---

9. In other words, it represents material which is both discontinuous in some way with the immediately preceding material and continuous with the material it introduces.

10. While this connection with the content is obvious in most cases, it is equally true with regard to 1:13 in which the opposition between τίνα and πάντες stresses the point that out of *all* the messengers who have ever spoken for God, *not one* has ever been addressed in the way that God has spoken to/about his Son.

ἡμῖν ἐν υἱῷ ὃν ἔθηκεν κληρονόμον πάντων δι' οὗ καὶ ἐποίησεν τοὺς αἰῶνας ³ ὃς ὢν ἀπαύγασμα τῆς δόξης καὶ χαρακτὴρ τῆς ὑποστάσεως αὐτοῦ φέρων τε τὰ πάντα τῷ ῥήματι τῆς δυνάμεως καθαρισμὸν τῶν ἁμαρτιῶν ποιησάμενος ἐκάθισεν ἐν δεξιᾷ τῆς μεγαλωσύνης ἐν ὑψηλοῖς ⁴ τοσούτῳ κρείττων γενόμενος τῶν ἀγγέλων ὅσῳ διαφορώτερον παρ' αὐτοὺς κεκληρονόμηκεν ὄνομα ⁵ <u>τίνι γὰρ εἶπέν ποτε τῶν ἀγγέλων</u> υἱός μου εἶ σύ ἐγὼ σήμερον γεγέννηκά σε

Heb 1:13—2:4

¹³ <u>πρὸς τίνα δὲ τῶν ἀγγέλων εἴρηκέν ποτε</u> κάθου ἐκ δεξιῶν μου ἕως ἂν θῶ τοὺς ἐχθρούς σου ὑποπόδιον τῶν ποδῶν σου οὐχὶ πάντες εἰσὶν λειτουργικὰ πνεύματα εἰς διακονίαν ἀποστελλόμενα διὰ τοὺς μέλλοντας κληρονομεῖν σωτηρίαν ²:¹ διὰ τοῦτο δεῖ περισσοτέρως προσέχειν ἡμᾶς τοῖς ἀκουσθεῖσιν μήποτε παραρυῶμεν ² εἰ γὰρ ὁ δι' ἀγγέλων λαληθεὶς λόγος ἐγένετο βέβαιος καὶ πᾶσα παράβασις καὶ παρακοὴ ἔλαβεν ἔνδικον μισθαποδοσίαν ³ πῶς ἡμεῖς ἐκφευξόμεθα τηλικαύτης ἀμελήσαντες σωτηρίας ἥτις ἀρχὴν λαβοῦσα λαλεῖσθαι διὰ τοῦ κυρίου ὑπὸ τῶν ἀκουσάντων εἰς ἡμᾶς ἐβεβαιώθη ⁴ <u>συνεπιμαρτυροῦντος τοῦ θεοῦ σημείοις τε καὶ τέρασιν καὶ ποικίλαις δυνάμεσιν καὶ πνεύματος ἁγίου μερισμοῖς κατὰ τὴν αὐτοῦ θέλησιν</u>

As may be seen both in the diagram above and in the inventory below, correspondences in vocabulary between these texts are both numerous and striking. See in particular:

- the cluster of terms relating to speech: λαλέω which occurs 2x in each text and not at all in the intervening material; λέγω (1:5, 13); συνεπιμαρτθρέω (1:4); and τό ῥῆμα (1:3) / ὁ λόγος (2:2);
- the cluster of terms used to describe the messengers: ἄγγελοι (1:4, 5; 13; 2:2); τοῖς προφήταις (1:1); λειτουργικὰ πνεύματα (1:14); ποικίλαις δυνάμεσιν καὶ πνεύματος ἁγίου μερισμοῖς (2:4);
- the cluster of terms relating to the idea of greatness: ἡ μεγαλωσύνη (1:3); κρείσσων (1:4); διαφορώτερον (1:4); and τηλικοῦτος (2:3);[11]

additional lexical repetition involving:

τίθημι (1:2, 13, and only once more in Hebrews in 10:13);

καθίζω (1:3,13, and twice elsewhere: cf. 10:12; 12:2);

δεξιός (1:3, 13, and also in 8:1; 10:12; 12:2);

---

11. Ellingworth, *Hebrews*, 139, reads τηλικοῦτος as "a (possibly stronger) synonym of τοσοῦτος, used in comparisons in 1:4; 7:22; 10:25."

δύναμις (1:3, 2:4, out of 6 occurences in Hebrews. Cf. 6:5; 7:16; 11:11, 34);

cognates of κληρονομέω (in 1:2, 4 and 14, out of 7 occurrences in Hebrews: cf. 6:12, 17; 11:7; 12:17);

γίνομαι (1:4; 2:2);

πᾶς (1:2, 3, 14; 2:2);

ὁ θεός (1:1; 2:4; cf. τῆς μεγαλωσύνης ἐν ὑψηλοῖς); and

the first person plural and second person singular personal pronouns, ἡμεῖς (1:2; 2:1, 3 x2) and σύ (1:5 x2; 1:13 x2);

- the relationship of similarity between the adverb πολυμερῶς ("many parts / apportionments," 1:1), which represents a *hapax legomenon* in the New Testament and the plural noun μερισμοί ("distributions / apportionments," 2:4) which occurs only twice in the LXX and once more in Hebrews in 4:12, within a context which is also formally related to 1:1–4 (see 5.3.5);
- the similarity between the adjectives διάφορος ("various," 1:4) and ποικίλος ("of various kinds," 2:4);
- the possibility of a connection between the reference to Jesus as κληρονόμος πάντων ("heir of all," 1:2) and his title as κύριος ("lord," 2:3, i.e. one who controls property).

More broadly, both passages contain the same basic field of participants (God, the Son, the messengers and "us").[12] There are also a large number of parallel or otherwise similar phrases as follows.

a. The statement in 1:1 is extremely closely related to that in 2:4 (see below):

Heb 1:1   πολυμερῶς καὶ πολυτρόπως πάλαι ὁ θεὸς λαλήσας τοῖς πατράσιν
"God having spoken in many ways and places to the fathers long ago in the prophets"

---

12. 1:1–5 also contains a reference to τοῖς πατράσιν (1:1) while 1:13–2:4 makes mention of τοὺς ἐχθρούς (1:13). In view of subsequent negative references to "the fathers" in 3:9 and 8:9 and use of this term in both Numbers 14 and Psalm 94, the correlation between these last groups is perhaps not accidental.

Heb 2:4 συνεπιμαρτυροῦντος τοῦ θεοῦ σημείοις τε καὶ τέρασιν καὶ ποικίλαις δυνάμεσιν καὶ πνεύματος ἁγίου μερισμοῖς κατὰ τὴν αὐτοῦ θέλησιν

"God having testified by both signs and wonders and various powers and distributions of the holy spirit according to his will"

b. As many have recognized,[13] the question in 1:13 is both formally and topically related to 1:5, with both introducing quotations from the Psalms:

Heb 1:5 τίνι γὰρ εἶπέν ποτε τῶν ἀγγέλων

"for to which of the messengers has he ever said"

Heb 1:13 πρὸς τίνα δὲ τῶν ἀγγέλων εἴρηκέν ποτε

"but to which of the messengers has he ever said"

c. The prominent participial phrase καθαρισμὸν τῶν ἁμαρτιῶν ποιησάμενος ("having made purification for sins," 1:3), which scholars have claimed seems not to "belong" to its immediate context,[14] corresponds to references to this same event in 1:14 ff.[15]

d. The statement *about the Son* ἐκάθισεν ἐν δεξιᾷ τῆς μεγαλωσύνης ἐν ὑψηλοῖς ("He sat down at the right hand of the Majesty in the heights") in 1:3 is matched by God's statement *to the Son* in 1:13/ Psalm 110:1 κάθου ἐκ δεξιῶν μου ("sit at my right hand").

On the other hand:

a. the similarities of speaker (God, implied in the second case), agent (ἐν υἱῷ / διὰ τοῦ κυρίου)[16] and verbal repetition of λαλέω in 1:2 and 2:3 establish a chronological contrast between the Son's speech at the beginning and end of time:

---

13. Guthrie, *Structure*, 77, reads 1:5 and 1:13 as head and tail members of an inclusion based on the "close approximation of the same question" in both cases plus a quotation from the LXX (Ps 2:7 and 100:1 respectively). Cf. Ellingworth, *Hebrews*, 108.

14. Cf. Ellingworth, *Hebrews*, 95.

15. Cf. σωτηρίαν (1:14); ὁ δι' ἀγγέλων λαληθεὶς λόγος ἐγένετο βέβαιος καὶ πᾶσα παράβασις καὶ παρακοὴ ἔλαβεν ἔνδικον μισθαποδοσίαν (2:2); and τηλικαύτης ἀμελήσαντες σωτηρίας ἥτις ... εἰς ἡμᾶς ἐβεβαιώθη (2:3).

16. The second is best understood as a genitive of agency (Wallace, *Greek Grammar*, 741), describing the Lord as the one through whom God spoke.

Heb 1:2   ἐπ' ἐσχάτου τῶν ἡμερῶν τούτων ἐλάλησεν ἡμῖν ἐν υἱῷ
"In the last of these days he has spoken to us by the Son"

Heb 2:3   ἥτις ἀρχὴν λαβοῦσα λαλεῖσθαι διὰ τοῦ κυρίου
"which was received in the beginning having been spoken through the Lord"

b. although God (ὁ θεός) is depicted as the ultimate speaker in both cases, the author reverses the order of his presentation of speech acts involving the Son and the messengers in 1:1–2 in 2:3–4, perhaps to remove the possibility of mounting an argument for the angels' superiority based on their precedence. This may be seen in the diagram below:

Heb 1:1–2	Heb 2:3
long ago (πάλαι)	in the beginning (se ἀρχὴν)
God spoke by messengers (ὁ θεὸς λαλήσας τοῖς πατράσιν)	God spoke (implied) by the Son (διὰ τοῦ κυρίου)
by the Son (διὰ τοῦ κυρίου)	God adding co-testimony through messengers

Turning to address matters of topic, as was repeatedly found with regard to link clusters at the micro level of the text, there is once again strong evidence of coherence between formally linked material. Both 1:1–5 and 1:13—2:4 make use of similar vocabulary, configured differently, to make essentially the same point regarding the Son's superiority to the messengers. The author begins his discourse by announcing that (i) having spoken in many and various ways in the past, (ii) God has now spoken at the end of these days to us (iii) through the Son who, (iv) having made atonement for sins (v) has sat down at his Father's side, (vi) having become greater than the messengers (vii) by as much as his name is greater than theirs. 1:13–2:4, meanwhile, begins where 1:5 ends, demonstrating once again (vi) the Son's superiority over the messengers (v and vii) in light of the contrast seen between God's invitation to him to sit at his right hand and his labelling of them as "ministering spirits." Therefore, the author concludes, voicing the obvious implication, it is necessary (ii) for us to pay attention to what we have heard (iii) spoken first by *him* lest we neglect the (iv) great Salvation which has been established for us, (iii) spoken first through the Son, (i) God having added his testimony in various ways.

Westfall and others have also drawn attention to the general coherence *within* 1:1—2:4 as a whole.[17] There is thus clear and demonstrable coherence between the formally linked texts of 1:1–5 and 1:13–2:4 and the intervening material, which suggests that these passages function as topic sentences which surround and summarize the first subsection of the text.

5.3.3 Hebrews 2:1–5 and 2:16—3:2

The second macro link cluster occurs between Hebrews 2:1–5 and 2:16—3:2.

Heb 2:1–5

¹ <u>διὰ τοῦτο δεῖ περισσοτέρως προσέχειν ἡμᾶς τοῖς ἀκουσθεῖσιν μήποτε παραρυῶμεν</u> ² εἰ γὰρ ὁ δι' ἀγγέλων λαληθεὶς λόγος ἐγένετο βέβαιος καὶ πᾶσα παράβασις καὶ παρακοὴ ἔλαβεν ἔνδικον μισθαποδοσίαν ³ πῶς ἡμεῖς ἐκφευξόμεθα τηλικαύτης ἀμελήσαντες σωτηρίας ἥτις ἀρχὴν λαβοῦσα λαλεῖσθαι διὰ τοῦ κυρίου ὑπὸ τῶν ἀκουσάντων εἰς ἡμᾶς ἐβεβαιώθη ⁴ συνεπιμαρτυροῦντος τοῦ θεοῦ σημείοις τε καὶ τέρασιν καὶ ποικίλαις δυνάμεσιν καὶ πνεύματος ἁγίου μερισμοῖς κατὰ τὴν αὐτοῦ θέλησιν ⁵ <u>οὐ γὰρ ἀγγέλοις ὑπέταξεν τὴν οἰκουμένην τὴν μέλλουσαν</u> περὶ ἧς λαλοῦμεν

Heb 2:16–3:2

¹⁶ <u>οὐ γὰρ δήπου ἀγγέλων ἐπιλαμβάνεται ἀλλὰ σπέρματος Ἀβραὰμ ἐπιλαμβάνεται</u> ¹⁷ ὅθεν ὤφειλεν κατὰ πάντα τοῖς ἀδελφοῖς ὁμοιωθῆναι ἵνα ἐλεήμων γένηται καὶ πιστὸς ἀρχιερεὺς τὰ πρὸς τὸν θεόν εἰς τὸ ἱλάσκεσθαι τὰς ἁμαρτίας τοῦ λαοῦ ¹⁸ ἐν ᾧ γὰρ πέπονθεν

---

17. Westfall, *Discourse Analysis*, 89–99, reads 1:1–2:4 as the first unit of her analysis and is critical of the common designation of 1:1–4 as a prologue or exordium rather than an introduction because of the "disassociation" this creates between these opening verses, the comparison of Jesus with the angels in 1:5–14 and the encouragement of 2:1–4. She claims (p. 98) that "the first four verses provide an essential point of departure for what follows, which is demonstrated by the complex of anaphoric links as well as the distinct semantic chains that link the unit," suggesting also that the fact that the subject is unexpressed between 1:5–14 indicates that "the interpretation of these four verses is dependent on 1:1" for its referent (θεός, 1:1) and constitutes an elaboration of the contrast of the ways in which God spoke in 1:1–2 (p. 92). Cf. deSilva, *Perseverance*, 94–95; and Rhee, *Faith*, 69, who notes "the general consensus among scholars" that 1:5–14 is the scriptural proof of the Christological statements made in 1:2b–4.

αὐτὸς πειρασθεὶς δύναται τοῖς πειραζομένοις βοηθῆσαι ³:¹ <u>ὅθεν</u> <u>ἀδελφοὶ ἅγιοι κλήσεως ἐπουρανίου μέτοχοι κατανοήσατε τὸν</u> <u>ἀπόστολον καὶ ἀρχιερέα τῆς ὁμολογίας ἡμῶν Ἰησοῦν</u> ² πιστὸν ὄντα τῷ ποιήσαντι αὐτὸν ὡς καὶ Μωϋσῆς ἐν τῷ οἴκῳ αὐτοῦ

Lexical connections include:

- the repetition of ὁ θεός (2:4, 17); ἅγιος (2:4; 3:1); ἄγγελοι (2:2, 16); πᾶς (2:2, 17); and the first person plural personal pronoun, ἡμεῖς (2:1, 3 x2; 3:1);
- the cluster of terms used in both passages to describe the addressees / future recipients of salvation (ἡμεῖς, 2:1, 3 x 2; σπέρματος Ἀβραὰμ, 2:16; ἀδελφοί; 2:17; τοῖς πειραζομένοις, 2:18; ἀδελφοὶ ἅγιοι and κλήσεως ἐπουρανίου μέτοχοι, 3:1);
- the author's use of three terms which convey the notion of "certainty / uncertainty": βέβαιος (2:2, 3) and πιστός (3:2) which both pertain to "being certain/sure" and μήποτε (2:1) which pertains "to not being certain."[18]

There are also relations of similarity between:

- the phrase διὰ τοῦτο (2:1) and the adverb ὅθεν (2:17 and 3:1) which both indicate a deduction from a statement yet to be made or (more commonly, as here) from a previous statement;[19]
- the verbs δεῖ ("it is necessary," 2:1) and ὀφείλω (3:1), which carry a sense of obligation or duty ("compulsion of any kind");[20]
- the verbs προσέχω ("pay attention to," 2:1) and κατανοέω ("look at, consider," 3:1) which both occur within Louw Nida's semantic domain of "to think."

Links also exist between a number of other words and phrases in these texts:

a. though the form is dissimilar, the indicative statement δεῖ περισσοτέρως προσέχειν ("it is necessary to pay much closer attention," 2:1) expresses much the same content as the imperative κατανοήσατε ("pay attention," 3:1);

---

18. Louw and Nida include each of these three words within the same semantic domain, "Mode—certain, uncertain" which contains only seven words in total.

19. Ellingworth, *Hebrews*, 135.

20. Ellingworth, *Hebrews*, 135.

b. the ambiguous περὶ ἧς λαλοῦμεν ("about which we speak," 2:5) is closely related to τῆς ὁμολογίας ἡμῶν ("our confession") in 3:1;

c. our status as "sharers of a heavenly call" (κλήσεως ἐπουρανίου μέτοχοι, 3:1) reflects the fact that "we" have heard/received a Word of Salvation which was first "spoken through the Lord" (λαλεῖσθαι διὰ τοῦ κυρίου, 2:1-3);

d. the reference to πᾶσα παράβασις καὶ παρακοή ("every transgression and disobedience," 2:2) matches the reference to τὰς ἁμαρτίας τοῦ λαοῦ ("the sins of the people," 2:17).[21]

More broadly still:

a. the central exhortation in 2:1 may be read as the functional equivalent to 3:1. Although most commentators read τὸν ἀπόστολον καὶ ἀρχιερέα τῆς ὁμολογίας ἡμῶν as a reference primarily *to a person* (i.e., "Jesus, the apostle and high priest of our confession"), and therefore as unrelated to τοῖς ἀκουσθεῖσιν of 2:1, the parallels between the texts which represent the immediate context of each phrase are striking and suggest a much closer connection between the two. Both 2:1 and 3:1 represent (i) inferences (διὰ τοῦτο / ὅθεν) (ii) containing imperatives which (iii) call on the same group of people to respond in much the same way to (iv) the things they have heard. It is not unlikely then that both τῆς ὁμολογίας ἡμῶν Ἰησοῦν and τοῖς ἀκουσθεῖσιν function in the present context as bookends which refer to *the author's own teaching about Jesus* (i.e. *"what we have been saying about Jesus"*) as elucidated both in the intervening material and the discourse as a whole.

Heb 2:1   διὰ τοῦτο δεῖ περισσοτέρως προσέχειν ἡμᾶς τοῖς ἀκουσθεῖσιν

"therefore, it is necessary for us to pay much more attention to the things heard"

Heb 3:1   ὅθεν ἀδελφοὶ ἅγιοι κλήσεως ἐπουρανίου μέτοχοι κατανοήσατε τὸν ἀπόστολον καὶ ἀρχιερέα τῆς ὁμολογίας ἡμῶν Ἰησοῦν

"Therefore, holy brothers, who share in a call from Heaven, pay attention to the Jesus, the apostle and high priest of our confession."

---

21. Gingrich, BDAG, glosses παρακοή as "unwillingness to hear, disobedience." Cf. Rom 5:19; 2 Cor 10:6.

b. the statements in 2:2 and 2:17 both refer to the same event: Christ's sanctifying work which he achieved through his death (cf. 1:3):

Heb 2:2   πᾶσα παράβασις καὶ παρακοὴ ἔλαβεν ἔνδικον μισθαποδοσίαν
"every transgression and disobedience received due penalty"

Heb 2:17 εἰς τὸ ἱλάσκεσθαι τὰς ἁμαρτίας τοῦ λαοῦ
"in order to atone for the sins of the people"

c. while many have commented on the obvious formal similarities between 2:5 and 2:16 (see below), a topical connection may also be identified between these texts which both provide clarification that the yet-to-be-experienced Salvation is for people and not ἀγγέλοις. In 2:5, the statement functions to clarify the earlier assertion that Salvation has been "established for us" (εἰς ἡμᾶς ἐβεβαιώθη, 2:3). *For* God has not subjected this coming world "about which we are speaking" (περὶ ἧς λαλοῦμεν, since 1:14) to ἀγγέλοις. So too, following the author's elaboration on his theme in 2:6–15, the author emphatically sums up his argument, "for surely" it is not ἀγγέλους that he helps but the Seed of Abraham (later "those being tested," i.e. "us"). The author's use of the emphatic δήπου suggests that we should be aware of what he is saying at this point, clarifying the nature of this help as related to his having provided atonement for his people (see too the causal relationship between Christ's having suffered and his capacity to help in 2:18).

Heb 2:5   οὐ γὰρ ἀγγέλοις
"for not to messengers"

Heb 2:16 οὐ γὰρ δήπου ἀγγέλων
"for surely not of messengers"

d. Finally, 2:2–3 and 3:1–2 represent statements which involve both a comparison and contrast between the Son and other messengers involving speech. In 2:2 both the word spoken through messengers and that spoken through the Lord (which as we have seen represents the same Word at two different stages of transmission) are described as "having been established/made certain," thereby creating a comparison between the reliability of the speakers. At the same time, the identification of the Son as ὁ κύριος together with the εἰ... πῶς construction to form an *a fortiori* argument between the relative greatness of the speakers and the need to listen, makes clear the chasm which exists between him and all of them. Similarly, the characterization of Jesus as πιστὸν ὄντα τῷ ποιήσαντι αὐτὸν ὡς καὶ Μωϋσῆς ("faithful to the One who appointed him as was Moses as well," 3:1) in connection to his role as ὁ ἀπόστολος ("*the* apostle") makes clear once more the certainty of what was said by both men, while also drawing attention to Jesus' towering supremacy as Speaker *par excellence*, to whom readers must pay especial attention.

Having completed our formal inventory, which reveals the connectedness of this material, it is important, once again, to acknowledge the coherent topical relationship which exists between 2:1–5 and 2:16—3:2. As seen previously (see 5.3.2), so here again the author makes use of many of the same words, phrases, and concepts in both texts to make much the same point twice. 2:1-4 represents (i) a warning to pay attention to the things heard (i.e. the τηλικαύτης σωτηρίας of 2:3, cf. 1:2) in view of the complete impossibility of any hope of escape if these are neglected. Three main motivators are given in support of this action, which relate to: (ii) the relative greatness of ὁ κύριος to all other messengers; (iii) the fact that the Word spoken by both messengers and the Son *has now been established* such that every sin has received full recompense; and (iv) the fact that this Salvation has been established *for us*. For (v) the author offers by way of further clarification of points (ii) and (iii), God has not subjected the world-to-come to messengers.

Meanwhile in 2:16—3:2, having first re-iterated (iv and v) that we, "the seed of Abraham" rather than ἄγγελοι, represent the beneficiaries of the Son's help (2:16), the author insists (iii) that Jesus has done what was necessary in order to establish Salvation and atone for our sins. Consequently, those for whom Christ suffered and died (further described as his suffering yet holy brothers and sisters) are exhorted (i) to pay attention to what they have heard about Jesus, *the* apostle and high priest of our confession. Thus, each of the five points made in 2:1–5 with the exception of (ii) is repeated in 2:16–3:2 and the texts may be seen to exhibit an extremely close topical relationship.[22]

---

22. The reason for the omission of (ii) is discussed further in the following section (5.4).

This indicates that Hebrews 2:1–5 and 2:16–3:2 are likely to function as topic sentences which surround and summarize the second subsection of the text.

5.3.4 Hebrews 3:1–3 and 4:14

A third macro-cluster may be detected between Hebrews 3:1–3 and 4:14.

Heb 3:1–3
3:1 ὅθεν ἀδελφοὶ ἅγιοι κλήσεως ἐπουρανίου μέτοχοι, κατανοήσατε τὸν ἀπόστολον καὶ ἀρχιερέα τῆς ὁμολογίας ἡμῶν Ἰησοῦν ² πιστὸν ὄντα τῷ ποιήσαντι αὐτὸν ὡς καὶ Μωϋσῆς ἐν [ὅλῳ] τῷ οἴκῳ αὐτοῦ 3:1 πλείονος γὰρ οὗτος δόξης παρὰ Μωϋσῆν ἠξίωται καθ᾽ ὅσον πλείονα τιμὴν ἔχει τοῦ οἴκου ὁ κατασκευάσας αὐτόν

Heb 4:14
ἔχοντες οὖν ἀρχιερέα μέγαν διεληλυθότα τοὺς οὐρανούς Ἰησοῦν τὸν υἱὸν τοῦ θεοῦ κρατῶμεν τῆς ὁμολογίας

Several scholars argue for a literary unit beginning at 3:1 and ending either at 4:13 (O'Brien) or 4:14 (Vanhoye and Guthrie) based on their identification of four lexical links between 3:1 and 4:14:[23] Ἰησοῦς ("Jesus," 3:1; 4:14); ἀρχιερεύς ("high priest," 3:1; 4:14); ἐπουράνιος ("heavenly," 3:1) and τοὺς οὐρανούς ("the heavens," 4:14); and ἡ ὁμολογία ("the confession," 3:1; 4:14).

To these may be added additional lexical links between:

- ἔχει ("has," 3:3) and ἔχοντες ("having," 4:14);
- πλείνος, πλείονα ("more," 3:3) and μέγαν ("great," 4:14).

There is a further relation of similarity between the imperative καταωοήσατε ("pay attention") in 3:1 and first person subjunctive κρατῶν ("hold fast," 4:14), both of which represent non-literal metaphors of sight and touch respectively, which call on readers to respond in similar fashion to "the confession" (τῆς ὁμολογίας).

Moreover, although superficially dissimilar, 3:2–3 and 4:14a both make the same two points: that Jesus, our high priest, *was faithful* to his priestly appointment and *is uniquely great*.

---

23. Vanhoye, *Structure*, 86; Guthrie, *Structure*, 78; and O'Brien, *Hebrews*, 125, who criticizes Vanhoye for making a sharp division between 4:14 and 15.

Heb 3:2-3

² πιστὸν ὄντα τῷ ποιήσαντι αὐτὸν ὡς καὶ Μωϋσῆς ἐν [ὅλῳ] τῷ οἴκῳ αὐτοῦ ³:¹ πλείονος γὰρ οὗτος δόξης παρὰ Μωϋσῆν ἠξίωται καθ' ὅσον πλείονα τιμὴν ἔχει τοῦ οἴκου ὁ κατασκευάσας αὐτόν

Heb 4:14

ἔχοντες οὖν ἀρχιερέα μέγαν διεληλυθότα τοὺς οὐρανοὺς Ἰησοῦν τὸν υἱὸν τοῦ θεοῦ

In 3:2-3, the author states by means of a comparison and contrast with Moses that Jesus was both *like Moses* in faithfulness (v. 2) and *unlike him* with regard to honor due him as house-builder in comparison with the house (v. 3).[24] Meanwhile, in 4:14, Jesus' high priestly greatness is indicated not only by the apparently "redundant"[25] adjective μέγας but also through the reminder of his ultimate identity as "the Son of God" (τὸν υἱὸν τοῦ θεοῦ, 4:14), while his faithfulness is implied by the phrase διεληλυθότα τοὺς οὐρανούς ("having passed through the Heavens"). Whether read as a description of Jesus' upward journey towards God,[26] or as a reference to his journey *from* Heaven *to* earth, the phrase makes clear that Jesus has done what was necessary to fulfil his high priestly appointment. A further connection between these verses may be seen in their similar function, with each providing the readers with reasons to pay attention/hold fast τὴν ὁμολογίαν.

Once again, the many formal connections between 3:1-3 and 4:14 are matched by similarities of content within the same material. 3:1-3 calls on (i) the brethren (ii) to pay attention to Jesus, (iii) the apostle and (iv) high priest of our (v) confession, who (vi) was faithful to the one who appointed him and (vii) has been found worthy of far greater glory than Moses. Meanwhile, in 4:14, the author states that since Jesus has become a (vii) great (iv) high priest, (iii and vi) having passed through the Heavens, (i) we should (ii) hold fast (v) the confession.

Thus the evidence of both form and content indicates that 3:1-3 and 4:14 function as topic sentences which surround and summarize the second subsection of the text.

---

24. Several scholars have noticed the formal similarities between 1:4 and 3:3.

25. O'Brien, *Hebrews*, 180, claims that "at first glance the adjective *great* seems redundant" in 4:14.

26. Cf. O'Brien, *Hebrews*, 180.

As was the case at the micro level, the evident parallelism between these texts is also instructive in further clarifying meaning. First, the fact that 2:17—3:2 contains a single imperative (κατανοήσατε, 3:1) in contrast to the pair of hortatory subjunctives in 4:14 (κρατῶμεν, 3:14, and προσερχώμεθα, 4:16) indicates the likelihood that the author envisages the exhortation of 3:1 as involving a two-dimensional response, corresponding to the different ways the phrase κατανοήσατε τὸν ἀπόστολον καὶ ἀρχιερέα τῆς ὁμολογίας ἡμῶν Ἰησοῦν can be read. In the first place, to "pay attention" means to commit to persisting with a pattern of teaching *about* Jesus. Yet it also entails drawing near to a person, Jesus, our high priest, presumably through prayer (as depicted metaphorically in 4:16). Second, in its context, the confidence (παρρησία) we can have in approaching Jesus is presumably based both on his having made atonement for sins and his being able to understand and sympathize with our human experience and therefore to welcome us without condemnation.

5.3.5 Hebrews 1:1–4 and 4:12–14

One final link cluster may be identified within this material between Hebrews 1:1–4 and 4:12–14.

> Heb 1:1–4
>
> ¹ πολυμερῶς καὶ πολυτρόπως πάλαι ὁ θεὸς λαλήσας τοῖς πατράσιν ἐν τοῖς προφήταις ² ἐπ' ἐσχάτου τῶν ἡμερῶν τούτων ἐλάλησεν ἡμῖν ἐν υἱῷ ὃν ἔθηκεν κληρονόμον πάντων δι' οὗ καὶ ἐποίησεν τοὺς αἰῶνας ³ ὃς ὢν ἀπαύγασμα τῆς δόξης καὶ χαρακτὴρ τῆς ὑποστάσεως αὐτοῦ φέρων τε τὰ πάντα τῷ ῥήματι τῆς δυνάμεως καθαρισμὸν τῶν ἁμαρτιῶν ποιησάμενος <u>ἐκάθισεν ἐν δεξιᾷ τῆς μεγαλωσύνης ἐν ὑψηλοῖς</u> ⁴ <u>τοσούτῳ κρείττων γενόμενος τῶν ἀγγέλων ὅσῳ διαφορώτερον παρ' αὐτοὺς κεκληρονόμηκεν ὄνομα</u>

> Heb 4:12–14
>
> ¹² Ζῶν γὰρ ὁ λόγος τοῦ θεοῦ καὶ ἐνεργὴς καὶ τομώτερος ὑπὲρ πᾶσαν μάχαιραν δίστομον καὶ διϊκνούμενος ἄχρι μερισμοῦ ψυχῆς καὶ πνεύματος ἁρμῶν τε καὶ μυελῶν καὶ κριτικὸς ἐνθυμήσεων καὶ ἐννοιῶν καρδίας ¹³ καὶ οὐκ ἔστιν κτίσις ἀφανὴς ἐνώπιον αὐτοῦ πάντα δὲ γυμνὰ καὶ τετραχηλισμένα τοῖς ὀφθαλμοῖς αὐτοῦ, πρὸς ὃν ἡμῖν ὁ λόγος ¹⁴ ἔχοντες οὖν ἀρχιερέα <u>μέγαν διεληλυθότα τοὺς οὐρανούς</u> Ἰησοῦν τὸν υἱὸν τοῦ θεοῦ κρατῶμεν τῆς ὁμολογίας

Several scholars have argued for a connection between these texts (or more precisely between parts thereof) for various reasons. Most famously, Nauck proposed that the "hymn" of 4:12-13 complements the "hymn" of 1:2b-3.[27] While the hymn theory has been widely discredited,[28] Attridge observes that these verses "bring to a climax the theme of God's speech which has been a major motif in the opening chapters."[29] Meanwhile Guthrie notes verbal parallels between the following:

- θεός in 1:1 and 4:12;
- τῷ ῥήματι τῆς δυνάμεως ("the powerful word," 1:3) and ὁ λόγος τοῦ θεοῦ as ἐνεργὴς ("the Word of God" as "active," 4:12); and
- the reference to the created order (ἐποίησεν τοὺς αἰῶνας) and κτίσις ("creation," 4:13).[30]

In addition to the links above, there are many other links than previously noted between these verses, with the strongest connections in fact occurring between 1:1-4 and 4:14, a verse left unconsidered by Nauck most likely because of his assumptions regarding a break between 4:13 and 14.[31] Further lexical repetition includes references to:

- ὁ θεός in 4:14 ("God," cf. 1:1; 4:12) and τῆς μεγαλωσύνης ἐν ὑψηλοῖς ("the Majesty in the Heights," 1:3);
- υἱός ("son," 1:1; 4:15);
- πᾶς ("every," 1:2, 3; 4:12, 13);
- μεγαλωσύνη ("greatness," 3) and μέγας ("great," 4:14);
- ἡ ὁμολογία ("the confession," 4:14), which corresponds to both ὁ λόγος (4:12)/ὁ ῥῆμα (1:13) and to λαλήσας and ἐλάλησεν in 1:1 and 2;

---

27. Nauck, "Zum Aufbau des Hebräerbriefes," 200-05; and Guthrie, *Structure*, 81.

28. O'Brien, *Hebrews*, comments: "Although it has been claimed that vv.12-13 are a poem or a hymn, these proposals are unconvincing. Rather, the sentence is a carefully crafted piece of prose for which the author is responsible." Cf. Guthrie, *Structure*, 81; Attridge, *Hebrews*, 133; and Robinson, "Literary Structure," 178-86.

29. Attridge, *Hebrews*, 133. Guthrie, *Structure*, 81, also notes "a conceptual parallel between the notion of God "speaking" (1:1) and the statement concerning the "Word of God" in 4:12-13" but suggests that 4:12-13 is more closely related to 2:1-4 "though it does not form an inclusio with that passage."

30. Guthrie, *Structure*, 81.

31. Guthrie, *Structure*, 81.

- πολυμερῶς ("of many parts," 1:1) and μερισμός ("the point at which parts meet," 4:12); and
- φέρω ("bear," 1:3) and κρατέω ("hold fast," 4:14) which Louw and Nida include within the same semantic domain: "to cause a state to continue."

There are also a number of connections between larger textual units as follows.

a. The description of the multiplicity of ways, means and times in which God has spoken (1:1-2a) corresponds with the description of God's word as "living and active" in 4:12a.
b. The description of the Son's session "at the right hand of the Majesty on High" (ἐν δεξιᾷ τῆς μεγαλωσύνης ἐν ὑψηλοῖς, cf. 1:3) parallels his "having passed through the Heavens" (διεληλυθότα τοὺς οὐρανούς, 4:14), with the latter phrase clearly depicting an upward journey in this context.
c. The reference to Jesus "having made cleansing for sins" (καθαρισμὸν τῶν ἁμαρτιῶν ποιησάμενος, 1:3) is related to his role as "High Priest" (ἀρχιερεύς) in 4:14.
d. 1:2b-4 as a whole gives many reasons for why Jesus might be described as "great" (μέγας) in 4:14.
e. Finally, it is not unlikely that the grammatically and thematically central statement of 1:2 finds its desired reciprocal response in 4:14. Read in this sense, "the confession" of 4:14 represents all that God has ever spoken to his people through messengers and his Son (as summarized in 1:1-2a).

Heb 1:2   ἐλάλησεν ἡμῖν ἐν υἱῷ
"He [God] has spoken to us by the Son"

Heb 4:14 ἔχοντες οὖν ... τὸν υἱὸν τοῦ θεοῦ κρατῶμεν τῆς ὁμολογίας
"therefore, since we have Jesus, the Son of God, let us hold fast the confession"

A further connection of note between these passages may be seen in the fact that both 1:1-4 and 4:12-14 contain evidence of literary dependence on (LXX) Psalm 32, a Psalm which, like Hebrews 1:1-4, displays "considerable regularity of the internal structure and balance," makes "repeated use of the same words, or word forms derived from the same root" throughout, and which can be read as a hymn of praise to "the (personal) word of the Lord" (ὁ λόγος τοῦ κυρίου).[32] The lexical connections are both striking and numerous in both cases. More remarkable still is the fact that virtually all of the Psalm's topics are represented within one or other of these clusters or the text they surround (Hebrews 1-4).

When read together, these formal connections and the clear coherence between 1:1-4 and 4:12-14 strongly suggest that these texts function as topic sentences which surround and summarize the first section of Hebrews. This parallelism also indicates that the reference to ὁ λόγος τοῦ θεοῦ ("the word of God," 4:12) may well function in a Christological sense as an instantial equivalent of υἱός in 1:2 (see John 1:14). Read in this way, the title provides the third of a trio of metaphors which describe the closeness of the relationship between Father and Son (see below) and 4:12-13 serves together with 1:1-2 to make the point that the Son through whom God now speaks is also the active Word of God described in Psalm 32 who will one day judge the thoughts and intentions of all hearts:

ἀπαύγασμα τῆς δόξης (1:3)	"the radiance of his glory"
χαρακτὴρ τῆς ὑποστάσεως αὐτοῦ (1:3)	"the imprint of his substance"
ὁ λόγος τοῦ θεοῦ (4:12)	"the word of God"

5.3.6 Conclusions Regarding Macro Link Clusters in Hebrews Chapters 1-4

This section has shown that the four macro link clusters described above may be understood to serve both a formal and topical function within the discourse. Formally, each pair of clusters has been arranged

---

32. Craigie notes: "In the analysis of the Psalm, it is possible to distinguish vv 4-5 from vv 6-9 . . . Verses 4-5 are thus understood as the introduction to the central hymn of praise (vv 4-19) and at the same time they provide in essence the reason (introduced by כי "for" in v 4) for the preceding call to praise." Read in this way, the Psalm is not so much a hymn to the Lord for his Word *and works* (of creation, vv. 6-7) as a song of praise to "the Word of the Lord" *and all that he has done*. In this sense, "all his works" referred to in vv. 4-5 (πάντα τὰ ἔργα αὐτοῦ) belong not to the Lord directly but to the personal Word himself. See following discussion for the possibility of this reading in Hebrews.

to mark the outer limits of three overlapping subsections (1:1—2:4; 2:1—3:2 and 3:1—4:14 respectively) and one section (1:1—4:14) within the discourse. At the same time, the obvious coherence between these sentences and the material they surround also makes clear that each pair also serves as parallel *topic sentences* which introduce and conclude each (sub)section with a summary of its content. These findings also make clear that, as in the micro discourse, transitional material which properly belongs to more than one subsection represents a distinctive feature of this discourse (cf. 2:1-4 and 3:1-2).

5.4 The Combined Topical Effect of Link Clusters in Hebrews 1:1—4:14

5.4.1 Overview

In section 5.2 and 3 we argued that Hebrews 1:1—4:14 may best be understood as the first section of the discourse which is subdivided into three overlapping subsections (1:1—2:4; 2:1—3:2 and 2:17—4:16) and fourteen overlapping paragraphs, the beginning of each of which is also marked as prominent by repetition. In light of these observations, what can be said with regard to the relationship between micro and macro link clusters within this section? This section (5.4) represents an attempt to understand the synchronic arrangement of this material in light of our findings concerning repetition to this point.

5.4.2 Subsection 1 (Hebrews 1:1—2:4)

The discourse begins with a two-part claim in 1:1-4 which is backed up by supporting evidence in verse 5. Having spoken in many ways of old, God has spoken uniquely to humanity in the Son (unit 1), who, having sat down after making purification for sins, has become *greater* than all other messengers *by as much as* his "name" (ὄνομα) is greater than theirs (unit 2). For (γάρ), the author explains, God has spoken to him alone as "Son" (υἱός).

Having outlined his thesis and its primary evidentiary basis (Psalm 2:7), the author next furnishes his hearers with two additional pieces of evidence from the LXX (each stated twice) designed to further support his starting assertion.[33] In context, the καίς of 1:7 and 10 are best understood as functional equivalents of καὶ γάρ, introducing a list of reasons which begin in verse 5 (γάρ ... καὶ [γὰρ] ... καὶ [γὰρ]).

1. *For* (καὶ [γὰρ]) the Son is God, the eternal King, where the messengers are but transient servants (Pss 44:7-8; 110:1).

2. *For* (καὶ [γὰρ]) he is indeed the Lord, the beginning and end of all creation (Ps 101:26-28), as was claimed in 1:2c.

It is important to recognize that, as with 1:5, each of these arguments for the Son's supremacy over "the messengers" (1:5; 1:7-9; and 1:10-11) rests upon testimony from these messengers themselves. More important still, each of Psalms 2, 44 and 101 describe instances of divine speech in which God directly addresses a particular individual using a "far more excellent" (διαφορώτερον, 1:4) name than has ever been given to a messenger: "Son" (υἱός), "God" (ὁ θεός), and "Lord" (κύριε) respectively.

Ps 2:7/Heb 1:5	υἱός μου εἶ σύ	"You are my Son"
Ps 44:7/Heb 1:8	ὁ θρόνος σου ὁ θεός	"Your throne, O God"
Ps 101:26/Heb 1:10	σὺ κατ' ἀρχάς κύριε	"You, Lord"

When read together, the point is clear: As the one addressed by God in Scripture as "Son," "Lord," and "God," Jesus truly represents "*the* radiance of glory" (ἀπαύγασμα τῆς δόξης) as claimed in 1:2, whose "name" is incomparably greater than all other messengers. And *that* is the degree, the author insists, by which the Son has become greater than "the angels," now that he has sat down at the right hand of the Majesty in the Heavens after making atonement for sins.

Following this, the author indicates that he has reached the end of his argumentation by both repeating the question formula used in v. 5 in v. 13 and summarizing the content of the earlier citation from Psalm 103 within an inferential assertion in v. 14: *For* (καὶ [γὰρ]) which of the messengers has ever been invited to sit at God's right hand? Are not they all "ministering spirits" sent to serve all (on the basis of what has been shown already in Ps 104:4)? Read together, it is likely that 1:13-14 represents the

---

33. The greater prominence of the material in 1:5 relative to 1:7ff is indicated both by its inclusion of 1:5 and 1:13-14 within the unit's introduction and its prominent location at the head of the list of testimony.

chief evidential basis in this section (cf. Psalm 8) for the identification of the Son as κληρονόμος πάντων ("heir of all") in 1:2.

"Because of this" (διὰ τοῦτο, 2:1), he continues, reaching the highpoint and culmination of his argument, it is necessary for "us" (ἡμεῖς, i.e. those to whom God has now spoken in this special way, 1:2) to pay much closer attention to what we have heard, lest we drift. Although διὰ τοῦτο may be understood as a reference to verse 14 or verses 13–14 taken together (as argued previously in its micro-context, cf. 4.2.4d), it can also function as a reference to the assertion of 1:3–4, as supported by all the "angelic testimony" assembled to this point.[34] In this sense, 2:1–3a constitutes the author's *application* of the first part of his discourse, indicating his understanding of what the Son's superiority should mean for the behaviour of his audience. Since the Son is so great, "because of this" (διὰ τοῦτο) we must pay much more attention "to the things heard" (τοῖς ἀκουσθεῖσιν) "spoken through the Lord" than we would to what has been spoken by any other messenger lest we fail to escape.

The key words and phrases of subsection 1 (1:1—2:4), as indicated by repetition, include various verbs of speaking, words related to the concept of greatness and expressions of contrast between the Son and the messengers.

Thus, the first four micro units of the discourse function together topically within the first subsection (1:1—2:4) to communicate a message whose topic can be stated as follows: Since God has spoken to us by his Son, the Creator, Savior, Heir and Image of God, who is so much greater than all other messengers, it is necessary for us to pay much more attention to what we have heard from him (than to that spoken by anyone else).

Subsection 1 may be diagrammatically represented as follows:

Subsection 1 (Hebrews 1:1—2:4)

1. *Introduction* (1:1–4): God has spoken to us through the Son (the Heir and Creator of all things, the Image of his Glory) who, having made purification for sin, has become greater than all other messengers by as much as his name surpasses theirs.

2. *Rationale A* (1:5): *For* God has addressed him alone as Son (i.e. Messiah King, Ps 2:7).

3. *Support Material* (1:7–11)

---

34. Cf. Westfall, *Discourse Analysis*, 98–99.

i. He is also called God (ὁ θεός), the eternal King where they are transient spirits.

   ii. He is also called Lord (κύριε), the Beginning and End of Creation.

   4. *Rationale B* (1:13-14): *For* God has not addressed the messengers as ruler of the world-to-come (Ps 110:1) but as serving spirits (Ps 103:4).

   5. *Conclusion* (2:1-4): *Because of this* it is necessary for us to pay much more attention to what we have heard lest we drift. *For* (γάρ) we will not escape if we neglect that which has been spoken (λαλέω x 2) not only by messengers but ultimately by the Lord.

5.4.3 Subsection 2 (Hebrews 2:1—3:2)

Concurrent to its concluding function, the mention of "new" information within verses 13-14 (namely that the Son will rule the future world and that "we" are about to inherit salvation) signals that διὰ τοῦτο ("because of this," 2:1) also functions as a point of departure for the discourse.[35] We must pay much closer attention to the things we have heard, the author insists, *not only* because of the greatness of the speaker *but also because of what he has said*. For (γάρ, 2:2) since this message (concerning τηλικαύτης ... σωτηρίας, 2:3) spoken through both messengers and the Son "has been established for us" (εἰς ἡμᾶς ἐβεβαιώθη, cf. 2:3), we will not escape if we neglect it.

Having stated in summary his second point (2:1-4), the author next offers a rationale (2:5) supported by a three-step argument designed to demonstrate from Psalm 8 the truth of both his assertions that "we," Jesus' brethren, are indeed the recipients of future Salvation; and that God has already subjected (ὑπέταξεν, 2:5) all things to Jesus, the Man/Son of Man prophesied in Psalm 8, having established this salvation by his human life, death and resurrection.

For (γάρ, 2:5), the author insists, God has not subjected the world-to-come to ἀγγέλοι but to ἄνθρωπος/υἱὸς ἀνθρώπου.[36] The argument which follows may be represented as below:

---

35. See 5.5 for a more detailed analysis of the multifunctionality of this material.

36. In its present context, the γάρ indicates that 2:5ff. (and thus Psalm 8) functions as support material for 2:1-4.

1. Even though we don't see this yet,[37] Psalm 8 testifies that God has indeed subjected the world-to-come (as part of πάντα, v. 7) to Jesus (ἄνθρωπος/υἱὸς ἀνθρώπου), who was made lower than the angels for a while (vv. 8b–11).

2. God did this because he deemed it "fitting" (ἔπρεπεν) for Jesus, the Savior, to come to resemble those he came to save (vv. 10–15).

3. Therefore (οὖν), since Jesus' brothers experience "flesh and blood," he too partook of these things so that through death he might save them (vv. 14–17).

Read together, step one affirms the assertion of 2:5 in face of the contrafactual evidence of experience, step two identifies God's will as the ultimate ground beneath his plan of salvation, while step three clarifies its implications for Jesus' actions.

The presence of the emphatic δήπου ("surely," 2:16), the formal similarity between verses 5 and 16 and the fact that the verse reiterates many of the concepts previously discussed (cf. 2:9–10) indicates that verse 16 functions in parallel with 2:5 as a summary rationale for the intervening material. "For surely" (γὰρ δήπου), the author insists, Jesus came to help the "seed of Abraham" *not* ἀγγέλους.

"Because of this" (ὅθεν, 2:17), the author concludes, he (Jesus) was "obligated" (ὤφειλεν) to become like his brothers in all things to serve as their merciful and faithful high priest, making atonement for their sins. "For" (γάρ) "because he has suffered" (ἐν ᾧ πέπονθεν αὐτός, 2:18), "having been tested" (πειρασθείς), he *is now able to help* those being tested. Although the phrase δύναται τοῖς πειραζομένοις βοηθῆσαι is commonly understood as a reference to Jesus' capacity to offer mercy and sympathy,[38] when read in light of its parallel text (2:1–5) as part of the "conclusion" to 2:1—3:2, it seems better understood in this context as a reference to Jesus' present capacity to *save* his brothers from sin and death and lead them as the Pioneer of their Salvation (τὸν ἀρχηγὸν τῆς σωτηρίας) into the glorious world-to-come (2:5), having atoned for their sins through his own death. In other words, the author declares, returning to the starting point of the subsection (2:2, 3), salvation has indeed been established for us by Jesus!

---

37. The author's use of δὲ in 2:8c acknowledges the seeming disjunction between the claim of 2:5 and his readers" experience: "we do not yet see" (οὔπω ὁρῶμεν) all things subject to Jesus "now" (νῦν).

38. Cf. O'Brien, *Hebrews*, 123.

"Because of this" (ὅθεν, 3:1), he continues by way of application, *"pay attention"* to the confession of Jesus, the apostle and high priest, who was faithful to him who appointed him. The repetition of ὅθεν (2:17) in 3:1 establishes a formal connection between what *was* (but is no longer) *necessary* for Jesus to do and what *is necessary* for the readers to do now. Just as there could be no hope of salvation for humanity had Jesus not become a man, so there can be no hope of salvation for the man or woman who fails to pay attention to the message of that salvation. In this way, the message of Jesus' faithfulness to his appointment serves as a motivation for action in much the same way as in 2:1–4.

Key words and phrases within subsection 2 (2:1—3:2), as indicated by repetition, relate to salvation, death, the accomplishment of Jesus' earthly mission, and the need for "us" to pay closer attention to the things we have heard. On the other hand, the different ways in which God has previously spoken is less prominent here.

In summary, the fourth to seventh micro link clusters in Hebrews function together within the second subsection of the discourse (2:1—3:2) to communicate a message whose topic may be expressed as follows: It is necessary for us to pay much more attention to what we have heard because of the greatness of the message of salvation spoken and established for us by Jesus.

Subsection 2 may be diagrammatically represented as follows:

Subsection 2 (Hebrews 2:1—3:2)

1. Introduction (2:1–4): *Because of this* it is necessary for us to pay much closer attention to the things we have heard lest we drift. For (γάρ) we will not escape if we neglect "such a great Salvation" (τηλικαύτης ... σωτηρίας, 2:3) which has been established for us, having been first spoken by the Lord.

   2. Rationale A (2:5): For (γάρ) God has not subjected the world-to-come (about which we are speaking) to ἀγγέλοις but to ἄνθρωπος/υἱὸς ἀνθρώπου (Psalm 8).

      3. Support Material (2:8b–15)

      Jesus is the ἄνθρωπος/υἱὸς ἀνθρώπου spoken of in Psalm 8, who was made lower than angels for a while so as to fittingly save and lead his brothers into the glory of the world-to-come which he will rule.

4. Rationale B (2:16): *For surely* (γὰρ δήπου) Jesus came to help the "Seed of Abraham" not ἀγγέλους.

5. Proposition (2:17—3:2) *Because of this* (ὅθεν), Jesus was "obligated" to become like his brothers in all things to make atonement for their sins as high priest. "For" (γάρ) because he has suffered, he is able to help. "Therefore" (ὅθεν), holy brothers who share a call from Heaven (3:1), "pay attention" to the apostle and high priest of our confession, Jesus, who was faithful to him who appointed him.

5.4.4 Subsection 3 (Hebrews 3:1—4:14)

As well as forming part of the conclusion to B, the comparison between Jesus and Moses and mention of God's "house" in 3:1-2 also serve together to indicate a new beginning for the discourse.[39] "Because of this" (ὅθεν), namely, the fact that Jesus, our high priest, is able to "help" by making atonement for our sin, the preacher exhorts his hearers to "pay attention to the apostle and high priest of our confession" (3:1), who, *like* Moses, was faithful to God's appointment within his house (3:2). For *unlike* Moses, he explains, Jesus has been counted worthy of as much greater glory than Moses as is due the builder of a house in comparison to the house itself (3:3).

The γάρ of 3:3 makes clear that the primary reason for action in this new context relates to Jesus' all-surpassing greatness as divine house builder (3:3), while the many formal and other echoes between 3:3 and 1:4 (see below) suggest that the verse represents a specific application of the earlier general statement about ἄγγελοι. Since, as has been established, Jesus is greater than *all* God's earlier messengers, he is therefore also necessarily greater than Moses. For, in addition to the earlier argument, he alone is the builder of the house.[40]

---

39. Noting both the transitional nature of material in 3:1 and its unusual prominence, Westfall, *Discourse Analysis*, 297, describes the verse as the "discourse deixis," claiming that it represents a summary of the "topic structure" of Hebrews as a whole.

40. By tying Jesus' superiority over Moses to a different proportional relationship to that offered in 1:4 (involving a house and its builder instead of various names), the author indicates a new direction for the discourse.

Heb 1:4   τοσούτῳ κρείττων γενόμενος τῶν ἀγγέλων ὅσῳ διαφορώτερον παρ' αὐτοὺς κεκληρονόμηκεν ὄνομα

"having become greater than the messengers by as much as the name he has inherited is greater than theirs"

Heb 3:3   πλείονος γὰρ οὗτος δόξης παρὰ Μωϋσῆν ἠξίωται καθ' ὅσον πλείονα τιμὴν ἔχει τοῦ οἴκου ὁ κατασκευάσας αὐτόν

"for he has been found worthy of as much more glory than Moses as the honor due the builder of the house in comparison to the house itself"

Having outlined the chief reason for his readers to take action in this way, the body of subsection C (3:4—4:13), which is approximately double the length of the first two, consists of additional argumentation and, for the first time, additional exhortation which supports, amplifies and elaborates on verses 2 and 3.

In the first place, the author first offers two additional reasons for why Jesus might be thought of as superior to Moses which relate to his title and position relative to the "house") in verses 5 and 6, together with a warning concerning the conditional nature of inclusion within "his house." "Because of this" (διό, 3:7, i.e. both i and ii), the author continues, "if you hear his voice, do not harden your hearts, as in the rebellion on the day of testing in the desert!"

The introduction of the words of (LXX) Psalm 94 at this point (3:7) allows the author both to reinforce the exhortation of 3:1 with a similar command and to introduce a further reason to pay attention based on the example of the wilderness generation which, in contrast to Moses, "tested" God by refusing to listen and thereby experienced his anger. This warning gives way in turn to yet another closely-related exhortation in 3:12–13 which, once more, serves both to apply the previous point to the readers and to introduce yet another reason to do so. For (γάρ, 3:14) our participation within "those who share" (μέτοχοι, 3:14) depends on holding fast the ὑπόστασις until the end, as Psalm 94 makes clear.

Therefore (οὖν, 4:1), let us fear lest by neglecting the Promise to enter, any one of you should be found to miss out. For (γάρ, 4:2), he insists, we have been evangelized (ἐσμεν εὐγγελισμένοι) just like they were, yet the Word they heard did not benefit those not combining the things heard (τοῖς ἀκούσασιν, cf. 2:1) with faith (4:2). For ultimately, he insists, *we who believe* enter into Rest, as may be extrapolated from Genesis 2:2 and Psalm 94:11 (vv. 3b–6). On the basis of his reading of Genesis 2:2

and Psalm 94, the author claims that it remains "therefore" (οὖν) for some to enter into this Rest afterwards *and* that those formerly evangelized did not enter through unbelief. Though this reading of these verses is distinctly different to the conventional understanding, it is based on (i) the detection of a symmetrical arrangement within 4:1–10 similar to that observed within each of the micro-units previously examined and (ii) a translation of ἐπεί as "afterwards" rather than "since."[41]

For (γάρ), the Preacher continues, offering a further reason for us to fear (4:1), the Word of God is living and powerful, sharper than every two-edged sword and piercing to the division of soul and spirit, joints and marrow, and it is able to judge the thoughts and intentions of the heart.

While many scholars have commented on the frequent interchange of expository and hortatory material throughout 3:5—4:13 (the body of this subsection), what stands out from our analysis is the remarkable topical *unity* within this material, as seen most clearly between the various exhortations. Indeed, when the parallels identified in the previous two chapters are taken into consideration, Hebrews' author presents his readers with *essentially the same appeal to hold fast the message of Christ on no less than five occasions* between 3:1 and 4:14 (cf. 3:1, 7–8, 12–13; 4:1 and 14).[42] Each of these may be seen in the diagram below:

---

41. The overwhelming majority read ἐπεί as "since." Cf. Ellingworth, *Hebrews*, 250; Guthrie, *Hebrews*, 153; Westfall, *Discourse Analysis*, 131. However, Friberg, *Analytical Lexicon*, n.p., notes that the conjunction may also be translated inferentially (else, otherwise, in that case); or with a temporal sense (when).

42. While scholars have found difficulty in defining the scope of some of these warnings (e.g., Ellingworth, *Hebrews*, 222), the links between these exhortations may be understood as follows: (i) The parallelism between 2:18—3:1 and 3:7–8 (cf. 4.2.8c and d) makes clear the close relationship between the imperatives of 3:1 and 3:7–8. (ii) Both of these appeals are further related to 3:12–13 which like 3:7ff. warns the same group of people against "hardening" one's heart to the word of God within the same temporal context (σήμερον, "today") in light of the same event (the rebellion at Kadesh Barnea), using the same language (seen in **bold** below) and a similar form:

Heb 3:7   μὴ σκληρύνητε τὰς καρδίας ὑμῶν

           "Do not harden your hearts!"

Heb 3:12   **μήποτε ἔσται ἔν τινι ὑμῶν καρδία** πονηρὰ ἀπιστίας . . . ἀλλ
            ἀπαρακαλεῖτε ἑαυτοὺς . . . **ἵνα μὴ σκληρυνθῇ τις ἐξ ὑμῶν**

            "Let not there be in any one of you an evil heart of unbelief . . . but encourage yourselves . . . so that no-one from you becomes hardened"

(iii) The immediate context makes clear that although superficially dissimilar, much

Hortatory material within 3:1—4:14

Heb 3:1	*Pay attention* to the apostle and high priest of our confession, Jesus (3:1)!
Heb 3:7-8	*Do not harden your hearts* (3:7-8)!
Heb 3:12-13	*Let no-one harden your heart* but *encourage one another* (3:12-13)!
Heb 4:1	*Let us fear* lest we fail to enter rest (4:1)!
Heb 4:14	*Let us hold fast the confession* (4:14)!

Similarly, while slightly more diverse than the hortatory material, each of the five expository points made in support of these injunctions expresses the need to be faithful/have faith in some way or other.[43] In effect then, from the beginning to the end of the subsection, the author repeatedly and urgently calls on his hearers to respond with ongoing faith and obedience to what they have heard. Though the words, phrases and expressions used vary considerably throughout, the message is always the same: "If you hear his voice today, do not harden your hearts!"

Following on from the body of the unit, the inferential conjunction οὖν in 4:14 together the reintroduction of the key word ἀρχιερεύς for the first time since 3:1, in association with the adjective μέγας ("great," cf. 3:3) and indicates that the author has reached the close of his third subsection and has returned to its start to again summarize what he has said. Since we the house have a great high priest, Jesus, the Son of God, let us therefore hold fast the confession. For ours is a high priest who is able to sympathize with our weakness and to offer mercy and grace for the time of help.

---

the same response is also also called for by the hortatory subjunctive of 4:1 (and 4:11). For, as 4:2 makes clear, to "fear" *is* to combine one's hearing of the word with faith (i.e. the opposite of what those who did not benefit did). Finally, (iv), the clear parallelism between 3:1-3 and 4:14 indicates that the imperative of 3:1 is similar to the hortatory subjunctive of 4:14. Cf. Ellingworth, *Hebrews*, 222; and Attridge, *Hebrews*, 117.

43. In 3:5-6, following additional argumentation in support of the claim of greatness made in 3:3, the author raises the need for faithfulness in the final conditional clause: we are God's house if we remain faithful. In 3:8-11, the point is made by way of a negative example: the Israelites were not faithful and experienced God's wrath. In 3:14-15, the author stresses the need for persisting *until the end.* 4:2, meanwhile, makes clear that the word only benefits those who respond with faith, while 4:12 warns that the God who searches the heart is able to discern those who truly trust him and those who do not.

Thus the seventh to the fourteenth micro level link clusters in Hebrews function together within the third subsection of the text (2:17–4:14), a section dominated by exhortation rather than exposition, to repeatedly call on hearers to respond by paying attention to Hebrews' message about Jesus. The logic is clear: Just as it was necessary for Jesus to live and die as one of us to help us by making atonement for our sins (subsection 2), so it is necessary for us to pay attention in order to receive this help.

Subsection 3 may be diagrammatically represented as follows:

Subsection 3 (Hebrews 3:1—4:14)

1. *Introduction* (3:1): "Because of this" (ὅθεν), "pay attention" to the apostle and high priest of our confession, Jesus,

   2. *Rationale A* (3:2–3): who was faithful to his appointment like Moses and has been counted worthy of far greater glory than him as house builder compared to house.

      3. *Support Material* (3:5—4:13)

      i. *And (γάρ)* Jesus is greater than Moses and we are in his house if we hold fast the confidence and boast of hope (3:5-6).

      Therefore do not harden your hearts (3:7-8)!

      ii. *For* Moses' generation tested God and saw his anger (3:9–10).

      Let no-one harden your heart but encourage one another (3:12–13)!

      iii. *For* we have come to share if we hold fast "Today" until the end (3:14–15).

      Therefore let us fear lest we fail to enter Rest (4:1)!

      iv. *For* the Word only benefits those who respond with faith (4:2–6).

      v. *For* the Word of God is able to penetrate and judge the heart (4:11–12).

   4. *Rationale B* (4:14a): Since therefore (οὖν) we have a great high priest who has passed through the Heavens, Jesus, the Son of God,

5. *Conclusion* (4:14b): Let us hold fast the confession.

5.4.5 Summary of Findings regarding the Combined Topical Effect of Link Clusters in Hebrews 1:1—4:14

This analysis demonstrates, in light of the combined evidence of micro and macro link clusters within this text, that Hebrews 1–4 is best understood as *a three-part argument which proceeds in linear fashion from beginning to end* and which develops logically by means of a series of fourteen steps corresponding to the first half of each of the units identified in chapter 4.[44] The concentric design of each unit means that each micro point is effectively stated twice so as to avoid any confusion. A similar concern for clarity may also be seen in the author's use of macro link clusters as topic sentences which introduce the beginning and end of each of his three main sections by summarizing their contents. In this way, he concludes each main point in his discourse in similar fashion to how he began it, indicating the relative prominence of this formally linked material.

Understood in this way, there is a remarkable formal correspondence between each of the first three subsections of Hebrews and "the most complete and perfect" form of argument outlined and exemplified in various ancient rhetorical treatises.[45] According to Cicero's *Rhetorica ad Herennium*:

> The most complete and perfect argument, then, is that which is comprised of five parts: the Proposition, the Reason, the Proof of the Reason, the Embellishment, and the Résumé. Through the Proposition we set forth summarily what we intend to prove. The Reason, by means of a brief explanation subjoined, sets forth the causal basis for the Proposition, establishing the truth of what we are urging. The Proof of the Reason corroborates, by means of additional arguments, the briefly presented Reason. Embellishment we use in order to adorn and enrich the argument, after the Proof has been established. The Résumé is a brief conclusion, drawing together the parts of the argument.[46]

As may be seen in the diagram below, this model may be applied without substantial alteration to our analysis of Hebrews 1:1—2:4 with

---

44. *Contra* the macrochiastic proposals of Vanhoye, *Structure*, 40a and b; and Heil, *Chiastic Structures*, 13–16.

45. Cf. Robbins, *Exploring the Texture of Texts*, 53.

46. Cicero, *Rhetorica ad Herennium*, 2.18.28—19.30, cited in Robbins, *Exploring the Texture of Texts*, 53.

the only difference relating to the fact that Hebrews 1:1—2:4 possesses two rationales (or reasons) in line with its concentric structure.

Subsection 1 (Hebrews 1:1—2:4)

1. Proposition (1:1–4) — God has spoken to us through the Son (the Heir through whom He created the world, the Image of Glory) who has become greater than all other messengers by as much as his name surpasses the greatness of theirs.

2. Rationale A (1:5) — *For* God has addressed him alone as Son (Ps 2:7).

3. Proof (1:7–11) —
i. He is also called God (ὁ θεός), the eternal King where they are transient spirits.

ii. He is also called Lord (κύριε), the Beginning and End of Creation

4. Rationale B (1:13–14) — *For* God has addressed him alone as ruler of the world-to-come (Ps 110:1), the heirs of which they serve.

5. Résumé (2:1–4) — Therefore it is necessary for us to pay much more attention to what we have heard from the Lord than to any other messenger.

Moreover, a summary of Hebrews 1–4 and its three subsections may be attained by reading together each of the introductory topic sentences discussed previously in sequence as follows:

1:1–5

Long ago, at many times and in many ways, God spoke to our fathers by the prophets, ² but in these last days he has spoken to us by his Son, whom he appointed the heir of all things, through whom also he created the world. ³ He is the radiance of the glory of God. And bearing the exact imprint of his nature, and the universe by the word of his power, having made purification for sins, he sat down at the right hand of the Majesty on high, ⁴ having become as much superior to angels as the name he has inherited is more excellent than theirs. For to which of the messengers has God ever said: "You are my Son, today I have given birth to you"?

2:1—3:2

Because of this, it is necessary for us to pay much more attention to the things we have heard, lest we drift. For if the word spoken through messengers has been established and every transgression and sin received due penalty, how will we escape if we neglect such a great salvation, which, having been received in the beginning spoken through the Lord by those who heard, has been established for us, God having added testimony by both signs and wonders and various powers and distributions of the Holy Spirit according to his will? For surely he has not subjected the world to come, about which we speak, to messengers!

3:1—4:14

Therefore, holy brothers, who share in a heavenly call, pay attention to the apostle and high priest of our confession, Jesus, who was faithful to him who appointed him as Moses also was in his house. For he [Jesus] has been found worthy of as much more glory than Moses as the builder of a house has in proportion to the house itself.

5.5 The Function of Transitional Material at Hebrews 2:1-4 and 2:17—3:2

Having considered the combined effect of repetition on the structure and meaning of Hebrews 1-4, this section seeks to better understand one of the key findings of these chapters—Hebrews' frequent use of transitional material—by investigating the function of 2:1-4 and 2:17—3:2 within the text. It asks two questions: *Why* do so many of Hebrews' boundaries overlap? And *how* does this overlap affect our understanding of meaning within the discourse?

As noted above (see 5.4), Hebrews 2:1-4 represents a conglomerate of material which serves two distinct functions simultaneously. It acts as part of the conclusion of subsection 1, and of the introduction of subsection 2. It is therefore unsurprising to find some elements which play a more prominent topical role within the conclusion of section one, some whose function is best explained within section two, and some which seem to serve an equally important role in both. With regard to the first, while the reference to the various ways and means God has testified previously to his will (2:4) echoes the opening two clauses of the discourse (1:1-2) and corresponds more generally with the theme of God's speech throughout 1:1—2:4, it apparently plays no role of any real significance within 2:1—3:2. With regard to the second, although formally linked to the mention of the Son's completed atoning work in 1:3, the description of this Salvation as εἰς ἡμᾶς ἐβεβαιώθη ("established for us," 2:3) and the reference to πᾶσα παράβασις καὶ παρακοὴ ἔλαβεν ἔνδικον μισθαποδοσίαν ("every transgression and disobedience has received just reward") in 2:2 seems of far greater significance within the second section than the first.[47] Meanwhile, 2:1–3a taken as a whole, with the exception of the phrase mentioned above, is clearly topically significant within both contexts.

The difference in function of this material may be seen in the diagram below: material which belongs primarily to the first section is underlined, that which belongs to the second in **bold**, and that which belongs to both in normal text.

> [2:1] διὰ τοῦτο δεῖ περισσοτέρως προσέχειν ἡμᾶς τοῖς ἀκουσθεῖσιν μήποτε παραρυῶμεν ² εἰ γὰρ ὁ δι' ἀγγέλων λαληθεὶς λόγος ἐγένετο βέβαιος **καὶ πᾶσα παράβασις καὶ παρακοὴ ἔλαβεν ἔνδικον μισθαποδοσίαν**³ πῶς ἡμεῖς ἐκφευξόμεθα τηλικαύτης ἀμελήσαντες σωτηρίας ἥτις <u>ἀρχὴν λαβοῦσα λαλεῖσθαι διὰ τοῦ κυρίου ὑπὸ τῶν ἀκουσάντων</u> **εἰς ἡμᾶς ἐβεβαιώθη** ⁴ <u>συνεπιμαρτυροῦντος τοῦ θεοῦ σημείοις τε καὶ τέρασιν καὶ ποικίλαις δυνάμεσιν καὶ πνεύματος ἁγίου μερισμοῖς κατὰ τὴν αὐτοῦ θέλησιν</u>

The different emphases within 2:1–4 which arise from the participation of this material within two distinct subsections is also evident in the author's three labels for the message discussed in both units. First described as "the things heard" (cf. τοῖς ἀκουσθεῖσιν, 2:1), a description which equally suits both contexts, the author next refers to the same entity as "the word spoken through messengers and the Son" (ὁ δι' ἀγγέλων λαληθεὶς λόγος . . . καὶ διὰ τοῦ κυρίου 2:2, 3), which functions topically within section one, and τηλικαύτης . . . σωτηρίας ("so great salvation," 2:3), which functions topically within section two.

Much the same kind of tri-functionality can also be seen within the second main transitional unit, 3:1–2, which stitches together subsections 2 and 3 (2:1—3:2 and 3:1—4:14 respectively). On the one hand, the description of the readers as ἀδελφοὶ ἅγιοι κλήσεως ἐπουρανίου μέτοχοι ("holy brothers, sharers of a heavenly call," 2:18), with its emphasis on

---

47. Indeed, aside from these mentions, the theme is otherwise entirely absent in 1:1–2:4.

the efficacious results of Christ's completed mission of salvation for his church, clearly "belongs" to subsection 2 and serves no apparent ongoing topical function beyond the close of the section. On the other hand, mention of Moses and the house of God in 3:2 lacks any strong connection with the material which precedes it, serving instead to introduce a shift in topic. Meanwhile, references to Jesus' faithfulness to his appointment (3:2) seem significant to the topic of both units. These functional differences may be seen represented in the diagram below.[48]

^{3:1} ὅθεν <u>ἀδελφοὶ ἅγιοι κλήσεως ἐπουρανίου μέτοχοι</u> κατανοήσατε τὸν ἀπόστολον καὶ ἀρχιερέα τῆς ὁμολογίας ἡμῶν Ἰησοῦν ² πιστὸν ὄντα τῷ ποιήσαντι αὐτὸν **ὡς καὶ Μωϋσῆς ἐν τῷ οἴκῳ αὐτοῦ**

When viewed together in its context, the evidence above suggests that Hebrews' use of transitional material serves at least two important roles in the discourse.

First, it allows the author to employ *a minimum number of words to maximum effect*. In the case of 2:1–4, rather than craft a separate conclusion and introduction for subsections 1 and 2 respectively, since the response desired from readers is essentially the same in each case, these verses perfectly fulfil both roles, serving together as a formal and topical pivot, marking the common material as doubly prominent, and effecting a seamless transition from the first to the second section. This may be seen in diagrammatic form below.

> 1. Since God has spoken to us by his Son, who is so much greater than all other messengers,
>
> **it is necessary for us to pay much more attention to what we have heard** (Subsections 1 and 2)
>
> 2. because of the greatness of the message of salvation spoken and established for us by Jesus.

The appeal to "consider" Jesus, the apostle and high priest also functions in much the same way, joining together two separate reasons to do so by the similar inferential response.

> 2. Since Jesus has established salvation for us,
>
> **consider the apostle and high priest of our confession** (2 and 3)

---

48. As above, material which belongs primarily to the first section is underlined, that which belongs primarily to the second in **bold**, and that which belongs to both in normal text.

3. who has been found worthy of greater honour than Moses.

Second, by linking the same passage to more than one partner text in this way, transitional material also allows the author to utilize ambiguity to his advantage, *bringing out two or more different meanings from the same pattern of words* without ever descending into meaningless subjectivism.

Although there is no evidence that the author makes use of such a technique in either of the two transitions examined thus far, a potential example may be found in 4:14 which speaks of Jesus διεληλυθότα τοὺς οὐρανούς ("having passed through the heavens"). What does this phrase refer to? Is it a description of Jesus' upward journey towards God and the heavenly realm, as most commentators believe?[49] Or does it speak rather of Jesus' great journey *from* Heaven *to* earth as the faithful "apostle" (i.e. "sent one") of our confession? Our analysis suggests that the correct answer is *both*, with meaning to be determined by a careful examination of the phrase in its proper context. For as transitional material, διεληλυθότα τοὺς οὐρανούς properly belongs to more than one unit simultaneously. In other words, the phrase has been *purposely crafted to be ambiguous* so as to serve the topical interests of more than one unit. Thus, when 4:14 is read as part of the conclusion to Subsection 3 (3:1—4:14) together with its parallel text in 3:1-3 (see 5.3.4), which refers to Jesus'accomplished faithfulness to his high-priestly mission, διεληλυθότα τοὺς οὐρανούς is best understood as a reference to great Jesus'*downward* journey. However, as part of the introduction to the second major section of the text (4:14—5:1),[50] in light of references to Jesus'newly-won greatness as the perfected messianic Son of God of 7:28—8:3, who has now "sat down at the right hand of the throne of the greatness in Heaven" (ἐκάθισεν ἐν δεξιᾷ τοῦ θρόνου τῆς μεγαλωσύνης ἐν τοῖς οὐρανοῖς, 8:1), the phrase is better understood as a reference to Jesus'*upward* journey within this context

These differences may be seen represented diagrammatically below:

An Ambiguous Phrase (4:14)	διεληλυθότα τοὺς οὐρανούς
Meaning within Subsection 3 (3:1—4:14)	having *come down* through the heavens
Meaning within Section 3 (4:14—8:3)	having *gone up* into the heavens

49. Cf. O'Brien, *Hebrews*, 180.
50. Cf. discussion in the next chapter at 6.3.1.

Thus the formal connections between 4:14 and its macro partner texts reveal the author's intention that his words be understood *in more than one way simultaneously*, corresponding to their participation within more than one section.[51] At the same time, however, they also serve to constrain meaning by ruling out alternative possibilities not intended by the author.

In summary then, while frequently overlooked, Hebrews use of transitional material in 2:1-4 and 2:17—3:2 represents a key feature of this text at both the macro and micro level of the discourse which serves at least two important purposes within this discourse. First, it allows the author to move smoothly from one section to the next without wasting words. Second, it adds a "two-edged" dimension to the "Word of Encouragement" (4:12) by which its author is able to effectively say twice as much through particular words and phrases as would be possible through a more conventional arrangement without allowing his discourse to slide into meaningless subjectivism. For by ensuring that each text has at least one partner text by which to discern its meaning, the author retains rigorous control over which of all the different possibilities represents his intended meanings.

5.6 Conclusions

This chapter has shown:

First, that macro link clusters (between 1:1-5 and 1:13-2:4, 2:1-5 and 2:16-3:2, 3:1-3 and 4:14, and 1:1-4 and 4:12-14) function as matched pairs of topic sentences which mark out the beginning and end of three overlapping subsections (1:1-2:4; 2:1—3:2 and 3:1—4:14) and one section (1:1—4:14) within the text with a summary of its content.

Second, that Hebrews also makes consistent use of a further type of textual patterning involving repetition (and typically contrast) at the micro level of the text to mark the introduction of each of the units identified in chapter 4, thereby drawing the attention of his hearers to each new point in the discourse.

Third, that the topical content of Hebrews 1-4 and its three subsections may be summarized by reading together each of the

---

51. The phrase, διεληλυθότα τοὺς οὐρανούς (4:14), also belongs to a third, additional context to the two discussed above, serving also as part of the introduction to Hebrews' fourth subsection (4:14-5:10).

introductory topic sentences at the subsection level (i.e. 1:1–5, 2:1–5, 3:1–3) in sequence.

Fourth, that overlap, while frequently overlooked, represents a key feature of the text of Hebrews at both the macro and micro level of the discourse; and that it is used by Hebrews' author to move seamlessly from one section to the next without wasting words and to bring out more than one meaning from certain words and phrases (e.g., διεληλυθότα τοὺς οὐρανούς, 4:14) by their common participation within two or more different parallel contexts.

Fifth, that despite its formal complexity, Hebrews 1–4 functions topically to make the following simple point: Since God has spoken through his "greater" Son (subsection 1), who has established salvation for us (subsection 2), let us "pay attention"/hold fast to Jesus, the apostle and high priest of our confession (subsection 3).

6

Macro Link Clusters in Hebrews 4:14—13:22 and the Epilogue of 13:22-25

6.1 Introduction

IN VIEW OF THE previous chapter's identification of the significant structural and topical role played by macro link clusters in Hebrews 1–4, chapter 6 investigates the remaining macro clusters within Hebrews so as to better understand the overall structure and meaning of this discourse. It also briefly examines the final micro link cluster in the text (13:22–25) for important clues regarding Hebrews' authorship. While the absence of a corresponding micro analysis (similar to that in chapter 4) lends some degree of provisionality to these findings, the chapter argues:

First, the location of macro link clusters in the text reveals Hebrews as a discourse consisting of four overlapping sections (1:1—4:14; 4:14—8:3; 7:25—10:22; and 10:19—13:22) and thirteen overlapping subsections (1:1—2:4; 2:1—3:2; 2:17—4:16; 4:14—5:10; 5:11—6:12; 6:9–18; 6:17—8:2; 8:1—9:12; 9:11—10:24; 10:19–38; 10:35—12:2; 12:1-13; 12:12—13:21) plus an epilogue (13:22–25), which are surrounded in each case by parallel topic sentences (i.e. macro link clusters).

Second, by reading these macro link clusters together, it is possible both to attain an accurate summary of each part of the discourse and to gain considerable insight into the structure and meaning of Hebrews as a whole.

Third, Hebrews 13:22–25 is best understood as a discrete textual unit whose concentric arrangement corresponds to that found within each of the micro units addressed in chapter 4, and makes clear that Hebrews was sent to its original readers from an author in Italy through Timothy.

The chapter begins with an investigation of the remaining ten subsectional link clusters in Hebrews (6.2), after which the four sectional link clusters (6.3) and the epilogue (6.4) will be briefly identified and analyzed and a number of conclusions drawn (6.5). Important new insights into the meaning and significance of various words, phrases and even large portions of the text (e.g., chapter 11) arising from this approach will be presented as they are discovered along the way.

6.2 Subsection-level Link Clusters in Hebrews 4:14—13:21

6.2.1 Hebrews 4:14–16 and 5:7–10

The fourth section-level link cluster occurs between Hebrews 4:14–16 and 5:7–10.

> Heb 4:14–16
>
> ¹⁴ ἔχοντες οὖν ἀρχιερέα μέγαν διεληλυθότα τοὺς οὐρανοὺς Ἰησοῦν τὸν υἱὸν τοῦ θεοῦ, κρατῶμεν τῆς ὁμολογίας ¹⁵ οὐ γὰρ ἔχομεν ἀρχιερέα μὴ δυνάμενον συμπαθῆσαι ταῖς ἀσθενείαις ἡμῶν πεπειρασμένον δὲ κατὰ πάντα καθ' ὁμοιότητα χωρὶς ἁμαρτίας ¹⁶ προσερχώμεθα οὖν μετὰ παρρησίας συγκεκερασμένους τῷ θρόνῳ τῆς χάριτος ἵνα λάβωμεν ἔλεος καὶ χάριν εὕρωμεν εἰς εὔκαιρον βοήθειαν

> Heb 5:7–10
>
> ⁵:⁷ ὃς ἐν ταῖς ἡμέραις τῆς σαρκὸς αὐτοῦ δεήσεις τε καὶ ἱκετηρίας πρὸς τὸν δυνάμενον σῴζειν αὐτὸν ἐκ θανάτου μετὰ κραυγῆς ἰσχυρᾶς καὶ δακρύων προσενέγκας καὶ εἰσακουσθεὶς ἀπὸ τῆς εὐλαβείας ⁸ καίπερ ὢν υἱὸς ἔμαθεν ἀφ' ὧν ἔπαθεν τὴν ὑπακοήν ⁹ καὶ τελειωθεὶς ἐγένετο πᾶσιν τοῖς ὑπακούουσιν αὐτῷ αἴτιος σωτηρίας αἰωνίου ¹⁴ προσαγορευθεὶς ὑπὸ τοῦ θεοῦ ἀρχιερεὺς κατὰ τὴν τάξιν Μελχισέδεκ

Instances of lexical repetition include:

- ἀρχιερεύς ("chief priest," 4:14, 15; 5:10);
- υἱός ("son," 4:14; 5:8);
- δύναμαι ("I am able," 4:15; 5:7);
- πᾶς ("every," 4:15; 5:9);

- κατά ("according to," 4:15 x 2; 5:10);
- μετά ("with" + genitive, 4:16; 5:7); and
- ὁ θεός ("God," 4:14; 5:10);

Additional lexical links include:

- a relation of opposition between the noun ἀσθένεια ("weakness," 4:15) and the adjective ἰσχυρός ("strong," 5:7);
- the root connection between λαμβάνω ("I accept," 4:16) and εὐλάβεια ("acceptable," 5:7);
- the root connection between συμπαθέω ("I sympathize/suffer with," 4:15) and πάσχω ("I suffer," 5:8).

More broadly:

a. when read in the light of preceding context (see especially 2:10, 17–18), the description of Jesus as πεπειρασμένον ... κατὰ πάντα καθ' ὁμοιότητα χωρὶς ἁμαρτίας ("having been tested like us in everything without sin, 4:15) makes much the same point as the statement that, having experienced suffering (5:8), Jesus τελειωθεὶς ἐγένετο ("has been perfected," 5:9);

b. the description of ταῖς ἡμέραις τῆς σαρκὸς αὐτοῦ ("the days of his flesh," 5:7) in which Jesus drew near to God with loud cries and tears represents a clear embodiment of εὔκαιρον βοήθειαν ("the time of need," 4:16) when we too are encouraged to draw near to God through him;

c. There is also a strong resemblance between Jesus' response to this situation of weakness described in 5:7 and the way in which we are called to respond in 4:16 (as may be seen below).

Heb 4:16 προσερχώμεθα οὖν μετὰ παρρησίας συγκεκερασμένους τῷ θρόνῳ τῆς χάριτος

"Let us draw near therefore with confidence to the throne of grace"

Heb 5:7 ὃς ... δεήσεις τε καὶ ἱκετηρίας πρὸς τὸν δυνάμενον σῴζειν αὐτὸν ἐκ θανάτου μετὰ κραυγῆς ἰσχυρᾶς καὶ δακρύων προσενέγκας

"He ... offered prayers and supplications towards him who is able to save him from death with loud shouts and cries"

Both statements (i) describe movement *towards* God (ii) in prayer (iii) in similar contexts of need (see c above) (iv) "with" confidence/loud shouts and cries respectively (v) using verbs commonly used in association with worship;

d. the fact that Jesus has been designated by God the αἴτιος σωτηρίας αἰωνίου ("source of eternal salvation," 5:9) explains both why we should go to him in order to find mercy and grace, as urged in 4:16, and why we might do this μετὰ παρρησίας ("with confidence").[1]

Though largely overlooked by modern scholars, who commonly read 5:1-10 as a discrete unit separate from 4:14-16,[2] the range and frequency of these formal connections, when read together, represents strong evidence that 4:14—5:10 functions as a textual unit framed by parallel sentences at 4:14-16 and 5:7-10.

This suggestion is further supported by the topical evidence. When read together, there is demonstrable coherence between 4:14—5:1 and 5:7-10 with both sentences making clear that notwithstanding his greatness, *Jesus is able to sympathize as high priest with our weaknesses*, having come to share our humanity. These truths serve as the foundation in 4:14—5:1 of a twin appeal to hold fast (κρατῶμεν) to the teaching about Jesus and to follow in his footsteps by drawing near (προσερχώμεθα) to God through him in prayer. Similar coherence is also evident between this frame material and the body of the subsection which makes clear, first, the need for all appointed priests to be chosen from among men so as able "to deal gently" (μετριοπαθεῖν, 5:2)[3] with those they represent (5:1-4) and, second, that God's appointed priest, Jesus, has indeed fully

---

1. Cf. 9:13-14; 10:10, 14, 19-23 for further grounds for confidence.

2. Guthrie, *Structure*, 80-82, for instance, reads verses 1 and 10 as head and tail members of an inclusion on the basis of repetition involving ἀρχιερεύς, θεός and καθίστημι/προσαγορεύω, yet fails to mention the similar lexical repetition involving υἱός (4:14; 5:8) and δύναμαι (4:15; 5:7) which also occurs in the immediate vicinity. Cf. Ellingworth, *Hebrews*, 270; Michel, *Der Brief*, 214. Others (e.g., Vanhoye, *La Structure*, 107-13) have argued for a chiasm at 5:1-10. However, Ellingworth, *Hebrews*, 271, cautions that while "the generally chiastic structure of 5:1-10 is widely recognized," it "cannot be pressed in detail." Rare exceptions include Gelardini, "From "Linguistic Turn," 58, and Lane, *Hebrews 1-8*, n.p., who argues for a unit beginning at 4:15 (though not 4:14) on the basis that "a relationship with 4:15-16 is established by the conjunction γάρ ("for") in 5:1.

3. Notice that the same root word is used here once more as in συμπαθέω (4:15) and πάσχω (5:8).

experienced all aspects of human "flesh" (ἡ σάρξ, 5:7) and is thus able to understand us (5:5-10).

Thus the formal and topical evidence strongly suggests that Hebrews 4:14-16 and 5:7-10 serve as topic sentences which summarize and frame a section of the text between 4:14-5:10 whose content may be summarized as follows: Let us draw near to Jesus who is able to sympathize as high priest with our weaknesses.

Hebrews 4:14-16 and 5:7-10 may be translated as follows:

> Therefore, since we have a great high priest who has passed through the heavens, Jesus, the Son of God, let us hold fast the confession! For we do not have a high priest who is unable to sympathize with our weaknesses, but one who has been tested like us in everything without sin. Therefore let us draw near with confidence to the throne of grace so that we might receive mercy and find grace for the time of need (4:14-16).
>
> In the days of his flesh, he offered up prayers and supplications with loud cries and tears to him who was able to save him from death and was heard because of his reverence. Although he was a Son, he learned obedience from what he suffered and has been perfected as the source of eternal salvation for all those who obey him, having been designated by God high priest according to the order of Melchizedek (5:7-10).

6.2.2 Hebrews 5:11 and 6:11-12

The fifth subsection level link cluster occurs between Hebrews 5:11 and 6:9-12.

> Heb 5:11
> περὶ οὗ πολὺς ἡμῖν ὁ λόγος καὶ δυσερμήνευτος λέγειν ἐπεὶ νωθροὶ γεγόνατε ταῖς ἀκοαῖς

> Heb 6:11-12
> ἐπιθυμοῦμεν δὲ ἕκαστον ὑμῶν τὴν αὐτὴν ἐνδείκνυσθαι σπουδὴν πρὸς τὴν πληροφορίαν τῆς ἐλπίδος ἄχρι τέλους ἵνα μὴ νωθροὶ γένησθε

Lexical connections between these sentences include the repetition of:

- νωθροί ("sluggish/lazy," 5:11; 6:12);

- γίνομαι ("to become," 5:11; 6:12); and
- ἡμεῖς ("we," 5:11; 6:11).

There is also a relation of (near) opposition between δυσερμήνευτος ("not easy to make clear," 5:11) and ἐνδείκνυμι ("to show clearly," 6:11).[4]

Connections also exist between a number of other words and phrases in these texts.

a. The purpose/result clause ἵνα μὴ νωθροὶ γένησθε ("that you not be lazy," 6:12), which represents the author's ideal goal for his hearers, contrasts sharply with his perception of their current situation: νωθροὶ γεγόνατε ταῖς ἀκοαῖς ("you have become lazy with regard to your listening!," 5:11).

b. Both 5:11 and 6:11–12 express similar dissatisfaction with regard to the present progress made by Hebrews' original audience by means of comparisons involving Jesus and their own past actions respectively. In 5:11 the repetition of γίνομαι (cf. 5:9) establishes a sharp contrast between what the hearers had *become* (νωθροί, "lazy") and what Jesus *became* through suffering (τελειωθείς, "perfected"). Meanwhile by speaking in 6:11 of his desire for his hearers "to show the same zeal" (τὴν αὐτὴν ἐνδείκνυσθαι σπουδήν) as they had shown previously (as described in 6:10), the author implicitly reminds his audience that their present response is not up to scratch.

c. Though εἰ οὕτως λαλοῦμεν ("even if we speak this way," 6:9) is typically understood as a reference to 6:4–6,[5] it functions equally well as an acknowledgement of the bluntness of the author's accusation in 5:11: νωθροὶ γεγόνατε ταῖς ἀκοαῖς ("you have become dull of hearing).

When read together, the range and frequency of these formal connections strongly suggest that 5:11—6:12 represents a textual unit framed by parallel sentences at 5:11 and 6:11–12. Although the majority of scholars read 5:11—6:20 as a somewhat abrupt parenetic digression which "interrupts" the exposition of Christ the high priest,[6] the follow-

---

4. Friberg, *Analytical Lexicon*, n.p., translates δυσερμένευτος as "not easy to make clear" and ἐνδείκνυμι as "to show, demonstrate."

5. Cf. O'Brien, *Hebrews*, 230; Ellingworth, *Hebrews*, 329.

6. Cf. Michel, *Der Brief an die Hebräer*, 231; 5; Bruce, *Hebrews*, 106; Buchanan, *Hebrews*, 100–101; Vanhoye, *Structure*, 281; Ellingworth, *Hebrews*, 56. Alternatively Lane, *Hebrews 1–8*, n.p., and Gelardini, "Linguistic Turn," 61, argue for a unit between 5:11–6:12.

ing additional points may be made in favor of our proposal. First, there is no general agreement concerning the character or logical scheme of this part of Hebrews, with Westfall criticizing the discourse for "a lack of coherence (or at least disorganization)" at this point.[7] Second, against the conventional understanding, there is a stark difference both in the tone and content of material on either side of 6:9–12. Third, Lane (and Vanhoye before him) sees the repetition of the colorful νωθρός ("sluggish") in 5:11 and 6:12 in and of itself as sufficient proof of a structural connection between these verses:

> The word occurs only here in Hebrews, and nowhere else in the NT. Its literary function corresponds to the use of ἀπιστία in 3:12 and 3:19 to indicate the limits of a paragraph of comment on the biblical citation of Psalm 95:7b–11. . . . The writer's proven dependence upon literary procedures to enable his readers and auditors to follow the conceptual development of the sermon is the crucial consideration in determining the limits of this section.[8]

The suggestion that 5:11—6:12 is best understood as a subsection of this text framed by parallel sentences at 5:11 and 6:11–12 is also supported by the evidence of topic. The clear coherence between both of these texts together and the material they surround indicates that they might reasonably be thought of as topic sentences. Both urge flagging listeners *to press on and not be lazy with regard to their listening in light of the coming salvation*, a message which also rings throughout the subsection as seen in the call to be brought into "completion" (ἡ τελειότης, 6:1), the frequent use of teaching and learning terminology and the "agricultural" warning of 6:7–8.

Thus, far from being a "digression," 5:11—6:12 represents the next subsection of the discourse which logically flows from the section before. The transitional nature of the material in 5:8–11 allows the author *both* to conclude his discussion on completion of the process of suffering undertaken by Jesus so as to become sympathetic with our weakness (section four) *and* to introduce his concerns about the distinct lack of progress made by his hearers in their own journey towards completion, a concern which drives the hortatory material of section five.

---

7. Westfall, *Discourse Analysis*, 141.

8. Lane, *Hebrews 1–8*, n.p. Cf. Vanhoye, *La Structure*, 115; Guthrie, *Structure*, 83–84; and Ellingworth, *Hebrews*, 54, who sees the second reference as the "structural counterpart" to the first.

A translation of both sentences follows:

> We have much to say about this but it is difficult to say because you have become lazy with regard to your listening (5:11).

> But we desire for each one of you that you show the same zeal until the end so that you might have the full assurance of hope and not become lazy (6:11-12).

6.2.3 Hebrews 6:9-18

The sixth subsection level link cluster in Hebrews occurs between 6:9-18. In contrast to the five examined previously, the most distinctive feature of this cluster is that it *functions at two discourse levels simultaneously*. At the micro level, 6:9-18 lies between units at 5:11—6:12 and 6:19—7:3. The same material also serves, however, as a section in its own right between 5:11—6:12 and 6:19—8:1, albeit one without a "body" (i.e. less prominent material not included in the topic sentences). See 10:19-38 and 12:1-13 for further examples of this phenomenon in Hebrews.

Heb 6:9-18

A. ⁹ πεπείσμεθα δὲ περὶ ὑμῶν ἀγαπητοί τὰ κρείσσονα καὶ ἐχόμενα σωτηρίας εἰ καὶ οὕτως λαλοῦμεν ⁹ οὐ γὰρ ἄδικος ὁ θεὸς ἐπιλαθέσθαι τοῦ ἔργου ὑμῶν καὶ τῆς ἀγάπης ἧς ἐνεδείξασθε εἰς τὸ ὄνομα αὐτοῦ διακονήσαντες τοῖς ἁγίοις καὶ διακονοῦντες

B. ¹¹ ἐπιθυμοῦμεν δὲ ἕκαστον ὑμῶν τὴν αὐτὴν ἐνδείκνυσθαι σπουδὴν πρὸς τὴν πληροφορίαν τῆς ἐλπίδος ἄχρι τέλους ¹² ἵνα μὴ νωθροὶ γένησθε μιμηταὶ δὲ τῶν διὰ πίστεως καὶ μακροθυμίας κληρονομούντων τὰς ἐπαγγελίας

C. ¹³ τῷ γὰρ Ἀβραὰμ ἐπαγγειλάμενος ὁ θεός ἐπεὶ κατ' οὐδενὸς εἶχεν μείζονος ὀμόσαι ὤμοσεν καθ' ἑαυτοῦ 14 λέγων Εἰ μὴν εὐλογῶν εὐλογήσω σε καὶ πληθύνων πληθυνῶ σε

D. ¹⁵ καὶ οὕτως μακροθυμήσας ἐπέτυχεν τῆς ἐπαγγελίας

C'. ¹⁶ ἄνθρωποι γὰρ κατὰ τοῦ μείζονος ὀμνύουσιν καὶ πάσης αὐτοῖς ἀντιλογίας πέρας εἰς βεβαίωσιν ὁ ὅρκος

Β'. ¹⁷ ἐν ᾧ περισσότερον βουλόμενος ὁ θεὸς ἐπιδεῖξαι τοῖς κληρονόμοις τῆς ἐπαγγελίας τὸ ἀμετάθετον τῆς βουλῆς αὐτοῦ ἐμεσίτευσεν ὅρκῳ

Α'. ¹⁸ ἵνα διὰ δύο πραγμάτων ἀμεταθέτων ἐν οἷς <u>ἀδύνατον ψεύσασθαι θεόν ἰσχυρὰν παράκλησιν ἔχωμεν οἱ καταφυγόντες κρατῆσαι τῆς προκειμένης ἐλπίδος</u>

Connections between these sentences include the lexical repetition of:

- ἔχω ("I have," 6:9, 13, 18);
- ἐλπίς ("hope," 6:11, 18);
- ἡ ἐπαγγελία (6:12, 15, 17) and its cognate verb ἐπαγγέλλομαι ("I promise," 6:13);
- ἐπιθυμέω ("I desire," 6:11), βούλομαι ("I desire," 6:17) and ἡ βουλή ("the will/desire," 6:17).
- κληρονομέω ("I inherit," 6:12) and ὁ κληρονόμος ("the heir," 6:17);
- ὄμνυμι ("I swear," 6:13 x2, 16) and its near relation ὅρκος ("oath," 6:16, 17); and
- ὁ θεός (6:10, 13, 17, 18).

To these may be added relations of similarity between:

- ἐνδείκνυμι ("I show for proof," 6:10, 11)[9] and its near relation ἐπιδείκνυμι ("I show beyond doubt, prove, demonstrate convincingly,"[10] 6:17), neither of which occur again in Hebrews;
- the adjective ἄδικος ("dishonest," 6:10) and the verb ψεύδομαι ("I lie," 6:18), both of which are used with regard to God;
- a large number of words and phrases which convey the idea of complete confidence and certainty: πεπείσμεθα ("we have been convinced/persuaded," 6:9); τὴν τπληροφορίαν ("full assurance/ complete certainty," 6:11[11]); βεβαίωσις ("confirmation," 6:16); and τὸ ἀμετάθετον τῆς βουλῆς αὐτοῦ ("the unchangeability of his will," 6:17). See too the use of repetition in the quotation of the

---

9. Ellingworth, *Hebrews*, 331, notes that ἐνδείκνυσθαι is used in papyri "of producing legal proof, and in the present passage could mean by extension that the readers' work was evidence of their love."

10. Friberg, *Analytical Lexicon*, n.p.

11. Louw and Nida, *Greek-English Lexicon*, n.p.

oath from Genesis 22:17, the form of which seems designed to emphasize the certainty of God doing what he says he will: εἰ μὴν εὐλογῶν εὐλογήσω σε καὶ πληθύνων πληθυνῶ σε ("I will surely bless you and multiply you," 6:14).

- a further group of words and phrases linked by concepts of running/fast movement: σπουδή ("haste," 6:11); οἱ καταφυγόντες ("those fleeing," 6:18); and its near opposite νωθροί ("sluggish/slow ones," 6:12);
- the verbs ἐπιτυγχάνω ("I obtain," 6:15), κρατέω ("I seize," 6:18); ἐπιθυμοῦμεν ("desire to possess something") which all include the notion of taking hold of something;[12]
- οὐδενός ("not one," 6:13) and πάσης ("all," 6:16).

More broadly:

a. the mention of τὰ κρείσσονα καὶ ἐχόμενα σωτηρίας ("the better things which also have salvation," 6:9)—which most commentators agree are left unexplained in 6:9—clearly relate to the τῆς προκειμένης ἐλπίδος ("the hope which lies ahead," 6:18);

b. there is little difference in meaning between the prepositional phrases περὶ ὑμῶν ("for us," 6:9) and ὑπὲρ ἡμῶν ("on behalf of us," 6:20);

c. τὴν πληροφορίαν τῆς ἐλπίδος ("the full assurance of hope") described in 6:11 is closely related in present context to the ἰσχυρὰν παράκλησιν ("strong encouragement) we might have with regard to hope (ἐλπίς) spoken of in verse 18 (above);

d. in both 6:10 and 6:18 God's righteous character stands as the ultimate grounds for the confidence believers can have in the future. With regard to the first, we can be sure that God will not overlook the past love and service of his people οὐ γὰρ ἄδικος ὁ θεός ("for God is not dishonest," 6:10). With regard to the second, we can be sure that God will do what he says and keep his oath-bound promise because ἀδύνατον ψεύσασθαι θεόν ("it is impossible for God to lie," 6:18);

e. οἱ κληρονόμοι τῆς ἐπαγγελίας ("the heirs of the promise," 6:17) represents a contraction of τῶν διὰ πίστεως καὶ μακροθυμίας κληρονομούντων τὰς ἐπαγγελίας ("those who inherit the promises through faith and patience," 6:12) referring in both cases to the same

---

12. Ellingworth, *Hebrews*, 332.

group of people which includes both Abraham and "us" (6:17).[13] When viewed in light of its wider context (6:12), this parallelism implies that the way to become an heir is to become an "imitator" (μιμητής, 6;12) of the faith and patience demonstrated by the other heirs of the promises.

Although the suggestion that 6:9–18 forms a single, concentrically-arranged section/unit is unusual (once again),[14] the strong formal evidence in its favor (assembled above) is supported by the equally compelling evidence of coherence between both halves (6:9–15 and 6:16–20) and between each component part of the chiasm. A and A′ speak with certainty of great things which lie ahead for believers; B and B′ express the desire of the author and God that hearers might experience this same confident assurance for themselves offering up various reasons for this certainty, while C and C′ reflect on the significance of God's oath-bound promise of Genesis 22:17.[15]

Viewed as a whole, the topic of the subsection/unit relates to God's desire that we might have complete certainty regarding our hope of salvation. And to this end, the author provides no fewer than four distinct reasons for us to be confident as follows:

1. a reminder of our identity as ἀγαπητοί ("loved ones," 6:9);[16]
2. the fact that God is "not unjust" (οὐ ἄδικος) to forget the proof of love and service done in his name (6:12);
3. God's oath-bound promise of blessing and increase to Abraham (6:14; cf. Gen 22:17); and
4. the fact that God cannot lie (6:18).

13. God's desire that the heirs of the promise might know the certainty of his will (6:17) is presented as fulfilled by the statement: ἣν ὡς ἄγκυραν ἔχομεν τῆς ψυχῆς ἀσφαλῆ τε καὶ βεβαίαν ("which [hope] we have as a sure and certain anchor," 6:19) suggesting an overlap in identity between οἱ κληρονόμοι τῆς ἐπαγγελίας ("the heirs of the promises," 6:17), οἱ καταφυγόντες κρατῆσαι τῆς προκειμένης ἐλπίδος ("those who have fled to take hold of the hope lying ahead," 6:18) and "us" (from the repetition of the 1st person plural form of ἔχω in 6:18, 19).

14. As noted previously (cf. 6.2.2), the majority of scholars read 5:11–6:20 as a somewhat abrupt parenetic digression which "interrupts" the exposition of Christ the high priest. Cf. Michel, Der Brief an die Hebräer, 231; 5; Bruce, Hebrews, 106; Buchanan, Hebrews, 100–01; Vanhoye, Structure, 281; Ellingworth, Hebrews, 56.

15. See comments below on the meaning of ἐπέτυχεν τῆς ἐπαγγελίας in 6:15.

16. The adjective ἀγαπητός ("beloved," 6:9) occurs only here in Hebrews in close proximity to its related noun ἀγάπη ("love," 6:10), which occurs once more in 10:24.

Consequently, subsection six, as a whole, represents a wonderful reassurance which follows on immediately from the warnings of the previous section (5:8–6:12).

The clear parallelism within this material is also instructive in clarifying meaning in at least two further ways. First, although 6:11 may be translated as "we desire each of you to show the same zeal until the final and full realization of hope,"[17] God's desire that the heirs might have confidence in his will expressed in B', together with the importance of the theme of certainty, and the lexical root connection between πληροφορία and the oath formula of 6:14 (πληθύνων πληθυνῶ), suggests that the verse is better rendered as: "We desire each of you to show the same zeal until the end *so that you might have full assurance* of hope" (cf. 9:13–14; 10:19–22).[18]

Second, the claim in 6:15 that Abraham "obtained the promise" (ἐπέτυχεν τῆς ἐπαγγελίας) has been a source of difficulty for scholars who note that it is apparently contradicted by statements in 11:13 and 39.[19] When read in parallel with 6:16 (C'), however, the meaning becomes clearer. 6:15 makes no comment on the *reception* of the promise itself, but describes rather the moment its reception became secure. For just as people who receive a promise accept the swearing of an oath as sure and certain confirmation that the thing promised now belongs to them (6:16), so from the moment God swore an oath to Abraham, there was no doubt whatsoever that he would receive the promised blessing of Genesis 22:17. "In this way" (οὕτως) Abraham *obtained* the promise.[20] "Because of

---

17. Cf. Bruce, *Hebrews*, 151; Attridge, *Hebrews*, 175–6; Lane, *Hebrews 1–8*, 1:130.

18. Ellingworth, *Hebrews*, 332.

19. Noting the apparent contradiction between 6:15 and both κατὰ πίστιν ἀπέθανον οὗτοι πάντες μὴ λαβόντες τὰς ἐπαγγελίας (Heb 11:13) and καὶ οὗτοι πάντες μαρτυρηθέντες διὰ τῆς πίστεως οὐκ ἐκομίσαντο τὴν ἐπαγγελίαν (Heb 11:39), Koester, *Hebrews*, 111, claims "Abraham received the fulfillment of the promises in a limited sense through the blessing given to him by Melchizedek (7:1,6), by the birth of Isaac (6:15; 11:11), and by temporary residence in the promised land"; Ellingworth, *Hebrews*, 338–39, proposes that "there is no significant difference between ἐπιτυγχάνω τῆς ἐπαγγελίας here, and κληρονομέω τὰς ἐπαγγελίας in verse 12; the variation is stylistic"; Bruce, *Hebrews*, 153, suggests that "in the restoration to Abraham of the son upon whose survival the promise depended Abraham did, in a very substantial sense, 'obtain the promise.'"

20. Our understanding is closest to Lane at this point, *Hebrews 1–8*, 326, who suggests that the phrase means that Abraham obtained *a confirmation of "the promise,"* but not the fulfilment of the promise itself. This sense is consistent with our understanding of the similarly misunderstood 11:1.

which" (ἐν ᾧ),[21] the author continues, i.e. because an oath seals the deal, when God wished to show the unchangeability of his will "even more" (περισσότερον, i.e. even more than he had already shown to Abraham), he guaranteed it with an(other) oath (Ps 110:4).

A translation of Hebrews 6:9–18, which also demonstrates its structural arrangement, may be seen below:

> A. [6:9] But we have been persuaded of things which are better and have salvation for you, beloved, even if we speak in this way. [10] For God is not unjust to forget your work and the love you have shown in his name by serving the saints and continuing to serve.
>
>> B. [11] But we desire for each of you to show the same zeal until the end [12] so that you might have the full assurance of hope and not become lazy but rather imitators of those who inherit the promises through faith and patience.
>>
>>> C. [13] For when God promised Abraham, because there was no-one greater by whom to swear, he swore by himself [14] saying: "I will bless and multiply you."
>>>
>>>> D. [15] And thus he obtained the promise through patience.
>>>
>>> C'. [16] For people swear according to someone greater, and in all of their disputes the oath is final for confirmation.
>>
>> B'. [17] Because of this when God wished to prove to the heirs of the promises the unshakeability of his will even more he swore an oath,
>
> A'. [18] so that through two unshakeable things in which it is impossible for God to lie, we who have fled to take hold of the hope lying before us might have strong encouragement.

6.2.4 Hebrews 6:19–20 and 7:28—8:1

The seventh subsectional link cluster in Hebrews occurs between 6:19–20 and 7:28—8:1:

---

21. Ellingworth, *Hebrews*, 340–41.

Heb 6:19-20

¹⁹ ἣν ὡς ἄγκυραν ἔχομεν τῆς ψυχῆς ἀσφαλῆ τε καὶ βεβαίαν καὶ εἰσερχομένην εἰς τὸ ἐσώτερον τοῦ καταπετάσματος ²⁰ ὅπου πρόδρομος ὑπὲρ ἡμῶν εἰσῆλθεν Ἰησοῦς κατὰ τὴν τάξιν Μελχισέδεκ ἀρχιερεὺς γενόμενος εἰς τὸν αἰῶνα

Heb 7:28—8:1

²⁸ ὁ νόμος γὰρ ἀνθρώπους καθίστησιν ἀρχιερεῖς ἔχοντας ἀσθένειαν ὁ λόγος δὲ τῆς ὁρκωμοσίας τῆς μετὰ τὸν νόμον υἱόν εἰς τὸν αἰῶνα τετελειωμένον ⁸:¹ κεφάλαιον δὲ ἐπὶ τοῖς λεγομένοις τοιοῦτον ἔχομεν ἀρχιερέα ὃς ἐκάθισεν ἐν δεξιᾷ τοῦ θρόνου τῆς μεγαλωσύνης ἐν τοῖς οὐρανοῖς

Lexical connections between these sentences include the repetition of:

- ἀρχιερεύς ("chief priest," 6:20; 7:28; and 8:1);
- ἔχω ("I have," 6:19; 7:28; and 8:1); and
- the phrase εἰς τὸν αἰῶνα ("forever," 6:20; 7:28), which occurs on 3 further occasions within this section (7:17, 21, 24) and twice more in the rest of the discourse (1:8; 5:6).

Relations of opposition may be detected between ἀσφαλῆ τε καὶ βεβαίαν ("both sure and steadfast," 6:19) and the noun ἀσθένεια ("weakness," 7:28).

There are also ties of reference between Ἰησοῦς ("Jesus," 6:20) and υἱός ("Son," 7:28), which refer to the Son.

More broadly:

a. the author makes use of a number of words and phrases to convey a sense of God's purpose as having been confirmed/established for us: ἄγκυραν ἔχομεν τῆς ψυχῆς ἀσφαλῆ τε καὶ βεβαίαν ("we have a firm and secure anchor," 6:19); τελειόω ("I fully accomplish," 7:28); and πήγνυμι ("I make firm," 8:2);[22]

b. in both 6:19-20 and 7:28-8:1, the grounds for the author's confidence of a welcome into the heavenlies for his readers are directly linked to Jesus having appeared as Melchizedian high priest "forever" (εἰς τὸν αἰῶνα, 6:20; 7:28);

22. Friberg, *Analytical Lexicon*, n.p.

c. Jesus' journey "into the inside of the curtain" (εἰς τὸ ἐσώτερον τοῦ καταπετάσματος, 6:19–20)[23] corresponds with the depiction of him as presently "seated at the right hand of the throne of the Majesty in the heavens" (ἐκάθισεν ἐν δεξιᾷ τοῦ θρόνου τῆς μεγαλωσύνης ἐν τοῖς οὐρανοῖς, 8:1);[24]

d. both 6:20 and 7:28b–8:1 affirm that we now have a great and eternal high priest who has been appointed by God according to the order of Melchizedek (see below):[25]

Heb 6:20   ὑπὲρ ἡμῶν εἰσῆλθεν Ἰησοῦς κατὰ τὴν τάξιν Μελχισέδεκ ἀρχιερεὺς γενόμενος εἰς τὸν αἰῶνα

"Jesus has entered for us, having become high priest forever according to the order of Melchizedek"

Heb 7:28–8:1   ὁ νόμος γὰρ ἀνθρώπους καθίστησιν ἀρχιερεῖς ἔχοντας ἀσθένειαν ὁ λόγος δὲ τῆς ὀρκωμοσίας τῆς μετὰ τὸν νόμον υἱόν εἰς τὸν αἰῶνα τετελειωμένον κεφάλαιον δὲ ἐπὶ τοῖς λεγομένοις τοιοῦτον ἔχομεν ἀρχιερέα

"But the word of the oath which came after the Law [appoints] the Son who has been perfected forever. The point of what we are saying is that we have this kind of High Priest"

e. if, as seems most likely, ἥν in 6:19 refers back to τῆς προκειμένης ἐλπίδος ("the hope which lies before") in 6:18 and signifies not hope itself but the *object* of hope (in context, God's oath-bound promise of forgiveness in Jesus, cf. 3:6, 14), this referent is further described in 7:28 as ὁ λόγος τῆς ὀρκωμοσίας τῆς μετὰ τὸν νόμον ("the word of the oath which is *after* the law," 7:28).[26] Note the potential word-play between "before" and "after";

---

23. Note the emphatic concentration of words which convey the notion of movement "inside" within this part of the text: εἰσερχομένην εἰς τὸ ἐσώτερον . . . εἰσῆλθεν Ἰησοῦς (6:19–20).

24. Scholars have also noted the strong echoes between the reference to Christ's heavenly session in 1:3 and 8:1. Cf. Ellingworth, *Hebrews*, 399.

25. In context, "this kind" of priest (τοιοῦτος, 8:1) refers to God's great Son who has been appointed by "the word of the oath" (i.e. Ps 110:4) and perfected forever.

26. Second, while the phrase ἰσχυρὰν παράκλησιν ἔχωμεν οἱ καταφυγόντες κρατῆσαι τῆς προκειμένης ἐλπίδος in 6:18 may be rendered as "we who flee might have strong encouragement *to take hold of the hope ahead*" (οἱ καταφυγόντες taken in a substantival sense), the author's statement of present certainty about his hearers' future in 6:9 together with the fact that in the wider context, the author writes to people who have already taken hold of (and must not let go of) this hope (cf. 3:6, 14; 10:23) suggests that

f. the phrase κατὰ τὴν τάξιν Μελχισέδεκ ἀρχιερεὺς γενόμενος εἰς τὸν αἰῶνα ("having become high priest forever according to the order of Melchizedek," 6:20) both echoes the form and summarizes the contents of Psalm 110:4, termed ὁ λόγος . . . τῆς ὁρκωμοσίας τῆς μετὰ τὸν νόμον ("the word of the oath which is after the law") in 7:29).

Once more, the suggestion of a subsection spanning 6:19 and 8:1 is unusual, with most scholars arguing for a section between 7:1–28 consisting of two paragraphs (7:1–10 and 7:11–28)[27] on the basis of its overall Melchizedekian content, the dependence of 7:1–10 on Genesis 14:17–20, and perceptions of inclusions between 7:1 and 10 and 7:11 and 28.[28] However, against the conventional understanding, 6:19–20 seems far more intrinsically related to the topic of material in chapter 7 than is generally recognized, summarizing the *significance* for readers of the coming Melchizedekian material in terms of the assurance of their hope and thereby providing them with further reason to pay attention.[29] Furthermore, the almost universal decision to end the unit at 7:28 results in the amputation of this chapter from the κεφάλαιον ("chief summary point") of 8:1, which seems highly unlikely.[30]

The topical evidence is also strongly in favor of our proposal that 6:19–8:1 represents a subsection of Hebrews framed by parallel topic sentences since both these sentences, 6:19–20 and 7:28–8:1, make the same basic point. Namely, that we can be sure of a welcome into the holy places

---

the participle is better understood in connection with the infinitive and translated as: "we who have fled to take hold of the hope might have strong encouragement."

27. Cf. Guthrie, *Structure*, 84; O'Brien, *Hebrews*, 244; Rhee, *Faith*, 131; Ellingworth, *Hebrews*, 350, who finds a further division between 7:11–19 and 7:20–28; Vanhoye, *Structure*, 89–91, who argues for further divisions based on inclusions between 7:1 and 3 (ἱερεύς), 4 and 10 (Ἀβραάμ and δέκατος, both of which may be found in vv. 4 and 9), 7:11, 19 and 28 (τελείωσις / τελειόω), 20 and 28 (ὁρκωμοσία), and 11 and 28 (νόμος). For an alternative, see Westfall, *Discourse Analysis*, 168–9, 300–03, who proposes a significant break between 4:11–7:3 and 7:4–28.

28. Guthrie, *Structure*, 84, argues for an inclusion between 7:1 and 10 based on Μελχισέδεκ and συναντάω, and for another between 7:11–28 on the basis of the author's use of τελείωσις, ἱερωσύνης, and νενομοθέτηται, which he suggests are "roughly paralleled at 7:28."

29. For example, in addition to the many connections noted above between 6:17–20 and 7:28–8:2, the mention of the strong encouragement we might have regarding hope in connection with Melchizedek in 6:17–18 clearly relates to the "better hope" of 6:18. Contra Vanhoye, *Structure*, 27, who analyzes the mention of Melchizedek in 6:20 in purely formal terms as a hook word, linking 5:11–6:20 and 7:1–28.

30. Cf. discussion in Ellingworth, *Hebrews*, 400.

because Jesus has gone before us as a forerunner, having become high priest forever according to the order of Melchizedek in fulfilment of God's oath-bound promise of Psalm 110:4.[31] As such, these sentences follow on logically from the desire expressed in section six that readers might have "the full assurance of hope" (τὴν πληροφορίαν τῆς ἐλπίδος, 6:11) by offering a most convincing basis for that confidence. They also together provide a fitting summary of a section which touches both on Melchizedek's historical significance (as unpacked from Genesis 14:18–20), and the significance of Jesus being named high priest in Psalm 110:4 according to the Melchizedekian rather than the Levitical order.

Hebrews 6:19–20 and 7:28—8:1 may thus reasonably be understood as the introduction and conclusion respectively to the seventh section of this text. A translation of both may be seen below:

> This *we have* as an anchor for the soul, safe and secure and an entry inside the curtain since Jesus has entered for us as a forerunner on our behalf, having become high priest forever according to the order of Melchizedek. (6:19–20)

> For the Law appoints men with weakness as high priests, but the Word of the oath which came after the law appoints the Son who has been perfected forever. And the point of what we are saying is that we have this kind of high priest, who is seated at the right hand of the throne of the Majesty in the Heavens (7:28—8:1).

6.2.5 Hebrews 8:1–3 and 9:9–12

The eighth subsectional link cluster in Hebrews occurs between 8:1–3 and 9:9–12.

---

31. Though in 7:28–8:2 this point is made implicitly, it is no less clearly expressed by the statement κεφάλαιον δὲ ἐπὶ τοῖς λεγομένοις τοιοῦτον ἔχομεν ἀρχιερέα ("and the main point of what we are saying is that we have this kind of priest," 8:1) which in context refers to the perfected Son whose priesthood has been guaranteed by God's oath by himself in contrast to the weak men who serve without an oath as priests of the law (7:28). For since *we have* this kind of priest, we can be far more confident of an entrance into the heavenly places than those who trust in the access provided by the Levitical priesthood.

Heb 8:1-3

Κεφάλαιον δὲ ἐπὶ τοῖς λεγομένοις τοιοῦτον ἔχομεν ἀρχιερέα ὃς ἐκάθισεν ἐν δεξιᾷ τοῦ θρόνου τῆς μεγαλωσύνης <u>ἐν τοῖς οὐρανοῖς</u> τῶν ἁγίων λειτουργὸς καὶ <u>τῆς σκηνῆς τῆς ἀληθινῆς ἣν ἔπηξεν ὁ κύριος οὐκ ἄνθρωπος</u> πᾶς γὰρ ἀρχιερεὺς εἰς τὸ προσφέρειν δῶρά τε καὶ θυσίας καθίσταται ὅθεν ἀναγκαῖον ἔχειν τι καὶ τοῦτον ὃ προσενέγκῃ

Heb 9:9-12

καθ' ἣν δῶρά τε καὶ θυσίας προσφέρονται μὴ δυνάμεναι κατὰ συνείδησιν τελειῶσαι τὸν λατρεύοντα μόνον ἐπὶ βρώμασιν καὶ πόμασιν καὶ διαφόροις βαπτισμοῖς δικαιώματα σαρκὸς μέχρι καιροῦ διορθώσεως ἐπικείμενα Χριστὸς δὲ παραγενόμενος ἀρχιερεὺς τῶν γενομένων ἀγαθῶν διὰ <u>τῆς μείζονος καὶ τελειοτέρας σκηνῆς οὐ χειροποιήτου</u> τοῦτ' ἔστιν οὐ ταύτης τῆς κτίσεως οὐδὲ δι' αἵματος τράγων καὶ μόσχων διὰ δὲ τοῦ ἰδίου αἵματος εἰσῆλθεν ἐφάπαξ εἰς τὰ ἅγια αἰωνίαν λύτρωσιν εὑράμενος

Connections between these sentences include lexical repetition of:

- ἅγιος ("holy," 8:2; 9:12);
- σκηνή ("tent," 8:2; 9:11);
- προσφέρω ("I offer," 8:3; 9:9)
- ἀρχιερεύς ("chief priest," 7:28; 8:1, 3; 9:11). See too the closely related leitourgo,j ("minister," 8:2) and λατρεύω ("I worship," 9:9);
- the phrase δῶρά τε καὶ θυσίας ("both gifts and sacrifices," 8:3; 9:9).

Additional lexical links may also be observed between:

- ἄνθρωπος ("man," 8:2) and χειροποίητος ("man-made," 9:11);
- μεγαλωσύνη ("greatness," 8:1) and μεγάλη ("great," 9:11).

Furthermore, while at the micro level, καθ ἣν ("according to which," 9:9) is best understood together with ἥτις (also 9:9) as a reference to the "first tent" in 9:8,[32] it functions equally well at the macro level as a back reference to the statement of 8:3a. In this sense its meaning may be understood as follows: in accordance with the fact that every high priest

---

32. Pace Lane, *Hebrews 1-8*, n.p., who notes that elsewhere in Hebrews, "the writer consistently uses ἥτις to refer to a specific antecedent, and the gender and number are modified accordingly (2:3; 8:6; 9:2; 10:9, 11, 35; 12:5). *Contra* Windisch, *Der Hebräerbrief*, 77; and Michel, *Der Brief an die Hebräer*, 307.

is appointed to offer gifts and sacrifices (as described in 8:3a), gifts and sacrifices are offered which are not able to perfect the conscience of the worshipper (9:9).
More broadly:

a. the summary expression "gifts and sacrifices" in 8:3 finds its expansion in 9:10 and 12 with regard to the sacrifices offered by the law and Jesus respectively (cf. 5:1);

b. in its wider context (cf. 1:3; 10:11–14), much the same meaning is conveyed by the description of Jesus' heavenly session in 8:1 (ὃς ἐκάθισεν ἐν δεξιᾷ τοῦ θρόνου τῆς μεγαλωσύνης ἐν τοῖς οὐρανοῖς) and the statement that he has entered once-for-all-time into the holies, "having secured an eternal redemption" (9:12, αἰωνίαν λύτρωσιν εὑράμενος)(cf. 1:3; 10:11–14);

c. the description of the location into which Jesus entered in 8:2 strongly resembles that of 9:11, with each stressing its divine construction (the second by implication as may be seen below):

Heb 8:2   τῆς σκηνῆς τῆς ἀληθινῆς ἣν ἔπηξεν ὁ κύριος οὐκ ἄνθρωπος
"the true tent, which the Lord built, not man"

Heb 9:11 τῆς μείζονος καὶ τελειοτέρας σκηνῆς οὐ χειροποιήτου τοῦτ' ἔστιν οὐ ταύτης τῆς κτίσεως
"the greater and more perfect tent which is not man-made, that is not of this creation"

d. 9:12 makes clear that the offering needed by Jesus in order to gain high priestly access into the heavenlies (τι . . . ὃ προσενέγκῃ, "something . . . to offer," 8:3) has now been supplied. For Jesus has now entered once-for-all into the holy place *"through* his own blood" (διὰ . . . τοῦ ἰδίου αἵματος, 9:12).

Though the suggestion of a subsection between 8:1–9:12 is entirely novel, the range and frequency of the connections (above), together with the complete absence of scholarly agreement regarding any alternative position,[33] represents strong evidence in its favour. Further support is

---

33. Scholars have read this material as part of a larger unit spanning 4:14—10:25 (Guthrie, *Structure*, 144), 5:1—10:39 (Lane, *Hebrews 1-8*, n.p.), 5:11—10:39 (Vanhoye [following Vaganay], *Structure*, 79), or 8:1—10:18 (cf. Ellingworth, *Hebrews*, 51; O'Brien, *Hebrews*, 51; Westfall, *Discourse Analysis*, 300). There is similar disagreement

provided by the clear topical coherence which may be detected between these linked sentences and the intervening material as a whole.

When read together, 8:1–3 and 9:9–12 both represent *similar statements* which contrast Christ's vastly superior priesthood with that of the Law in terms of notions of completion/fulfillment versus inefficacy/imperfection and reality versus the shadow. For while, Hebrews insists, Christ *"has sat down"* at God's right hand in the heavens (ἐκάθισεν, 8:1) as "high priest of the good things which *have now come"* (9:11), *"having secured"* an eternal redemption (εὐράμενος, 9:12) and having entered once-for-all-time through *"the greater and more perfect tent which has not been made with human hands"* (9:11), the priests of the Law for their part continue to offer sacrifices which *"are not able to perfect* the conscience of the worshippers" (μὴ δυνάμεναι κατὰ συνείδησιν τελειῶσαι τὸν λατρεύοντα, 9:9) in the [by implication] *less perfect* tent of 9:11, seemingly unaware that the "time of reformation" (καιροῦ διορθώσεως, 9:10) has now come.

Within its wider context, having outlined previously the hope we might have through Jesus' personal superiority as eternal priest in contrast to the weak and mortal priests of the law (6:17—8:2), subsection 8 turns its attention to two other aspects of his ministry which are also markedly superior to the priesthood of the law: namely (i) the covenant he mediates (8:6–13); and (ii) the place in which he ministers (9:1–8). With regard to the first, Jesus' role as λειτουργός (8:2) is further clarified by the reference to the better ministry he now presides over, which in context is best understood as that connected to the new covenant (9:15). With regard to the second, Jesus' entry into "the greater and more perfect tent" (9:11) contrasts sharply with the "earthly holy place (ἅγιον κοσμικόν, 9:1) with its "regulations of worship" (δικαιώματα λατρείας, 9:1) of the law.

The topic of this section may be summarized as follows: In the Son, we have a perfect priest who, unlike the priests of the law, has become minister of a much better covenant and is now seated in a better place.[34]

---

regarding how the text is structured at the micro-level. Alternatives include: 8:1—9:28; 10:1–18 (Vanhoye, *Structure*, 79); 8:1–13; 9:1–28; 10:1–18 (Adam, *The Majestic Son*, 85, 92 and 103); 8:1–7, 8–13; 9:1–5, 6–10, 11–14, 15–22, 23–28; 10:1–4, 5–10, 11–18 (Ellingworth, *Hebrews*, 51); 8:1–13; 9:1–10, 11–28; 10:1–18 (Lane, *Hebrews 1–8*, n.p.); 8:1–2, 3–6, 7–13; 9:1—10:18 (Guthrie, *Structure*, 144, and O'Brien, *Hebrews*, ix); 8:1–13; 9:1–14, 15–28; 10:1–18 (Westfall, *Discourse Analysis*, 300).

34. Although Jesus' sacrifice is mentioned in both, the lack of specific detail in the introduction of 8:3 indicates that it is not yet topically central (until 9:11, which serves as the introduction to the next unit). This suggestion is further confirmed by an examination of the content of the section.

Taken together, then, the formal and topical evidence strongly suggests that Hebrews 7:28—8:3 and 9:9-12 be understood as topic sentences which summarize and frame the eighth section of the text. They may be translated as follows:

> And the point of what we are saying is that we have this kind of high priest, who is seated at the right hand of the throne of the Majesty in the Heavens, a *minister* in the holies and the true tent, which the Lord built, not man. For every high priest is appointed to offer gifts and sacrifices, which is why it was necessary that this high priest also have something to offer. (8:1-3)
>
> According to this arrangement, gifts and sacrifices are being offered that cannot perfect the conscience of the worshiper, being only food and drink and various washings, regulations for the body imposed until the time of the new order. But when Christ became high priest of the good things which have come, he went in through the greater and more perfect tent which is not man-made—that is not of this creation—into the holies, not through the blood of goats and bulls but through his own blood, having secured an eternal redemption. (8:9-12)

6.2.6 Hebrews 9:11-14 and 10:19-24

The ninth subsectional link cluster in Hebrews occurs between 9:11-14 and 10:19-24:

Heb 9:11-14

[11] Χριστὸς δὲ παραγενόμενος ἀρχιερεὺς τῶν γενομένων ἀγαθῶν διὰ τῆς μείζονος καὶ τελειοτέρας σκηνῆς οὐ χειροποιήτου τοῦτ' ἔστιν οὐ ταύτης τῆς κτίσεως [12] οὐδὲ δι' αἵματος τράγων καὶ μόσχων διὰ δὲ τοῦ ἰδίου αἵματος εἰσῆλθεν ἐφάπαξ εἰς τὰ ἅγια αἰωνίαν λύτρωσιν εὑράμενος [13] εἰ γὰρ τὸ αἷμα τράγων καὶ ταύρων καὶ σποδὸς δαμάλεως ῥαντίζουσα τοὺς κεκοινωμένους ἁγιάζει πρὸς τὴν τῆς σαρκὸς καθαρότητα [14] πόσῳ μᾶλλον τὸ αἷμα τοῦ Χριστοῦ ὃς διὰ πνεύματος αἰωνίου ἑαυτὸν προσήνεγκεν ἄμωμον τῷ θεῷ <u>καθαριεῖ τὴν συνείδησιν ἡμῶν ἀπὸ νεκρῶν ἔργων εἰς τὸ λατρεύειν θεῷ ζῶντι</u>

Heb 10:19-24

[19] Ἔχοντες οὖν ἀδελφοὶ παρρησίαν εἰς τὴν εἴσοδον τῶν ἁγίων ἐν τῷ αἵματι Ἰησοῦ [20] ἣν ἐνεκαίνισεν ἡμῖν ὁδὸν πρόσφατον καὶ ζῶσαν διὰ τοῦ καταπετάσματος τοῦτ' ἔστιν τῆς σαρκὸς αὐτοῦ [21] καὶ ἱερέα μέγαν ἐπὶ τὸν οἶκον τοῦ θεοῦ [22] προσερχώμεθα <u>μετὰ ἀληθινῆς</u>

<u>καρδίας ἐν πληροφορίᾳ πίστεως ῥεραντισμένοι τὰς καρδίας ἀπὸ συνειδήσεως πονηρᾶς καὶ λελουσμένοι τὸ σῶμα ὕδατι καθαρῷ</u> ²³ κατέχωμεν τὴν ὁμολογίαν τῆς ἐλπίδος ἀκλινῆ πιστὸς γὰρ ὁ ἐπαγγειλάμενος ²⁴ καὶ κατανοῶμεν ἀλλήλους εἰς παροξυσμὸν ἀγάπης καὶ καλῶν ἔργων

Connections between these sentences include lexical repetition involving:

- αἷμα ("blood," 9:12 x2, 13, 14; 10:19);³⁵
- the verb καθαρίζω ("I cleanse," 9:14) and its cognate noun καθαρότης ("cleansing," 9:13) and adjective (καθαρός, 10:22).³⁶
- ῥαντίζω ("I cleanse," 9:13, 10:22), which occurs on two further occasions in Hebrews (9:19, 21) and nowhere else in the New Testament;
- ἡ σάρξ ("the flesh," 9:13; 10:20) and the closely related τὸ σῶμα ("the body," 10:22);
- συνείδησις ("conscience," 9:14, 10:22), which occurs on three further occasions in Hebrews (9:9; 10:2; 13:8);
- μέγας ("great") in both its regular (10:21) and comparative (9:11) forms;
- ἔργον ("work," 9:14; 10:24), out of nine appearances in Hebrews;
- ἅγιος ("holy," 9:12; 10:19) and its cognate verb ἁγιάζω ("I make holy," 9:13);
- ὁ θεὸς ("God," 9:14; 10:21);
- and the epexegetical τοῦτ' ἔστιν ("this is," 9:11, 10:20).

Additional links may also be found between:

- the verbs used to describe Christ's and our own approach: παραγίνομαι ("I come to," 9:11), ("I go in," 9:12), and προσέρχομαι ("I draw near," 10:23);
- ἀγαθός ("good," 9:11), its near relation καλός ("good," 10:24), and opposite πονηρός ("evil," 10:22);

35. The word αἷμα appears 20 x in chapters 9–13 and only once in the rest of the discourse (2:14). As such it functions as a characteristic term giving a distinctive color to this portion of the text in similar fashion to ἄγγελος (which appears 11x in chapters 1 and 2 and only twice in the rest o the discourse, 12:22, 13:2).

36. The verb καθαρίζω occurs on three further occasions in Hebrews all within this section (9:22, 23; 10:2), while the noun and adjective represent *hapax legomena* (though see καθαρισμός in 1:3).

- the verb ζάω ("I live," 9:14; 10:20) and its opposite adjective νεκρός ("dead," 9:14);
- ἀρχιερεύς ("chief priest," 9:11) and the related ἱερεύς μέγας ("great priest," 10:21);
- the verbs of cleansing above and the similar λούω ("I wash," 10:22) and related adjective ἄμωμος ("without blemish," 9:14);
- λατρεύω ("I serve," 9:14, often with a cultic sense), προσφέρω ("I offer," 9:14), and the similar sounding adjective πρόσφατος ("new/freshly killed," 10:20);[37]
- Χριστός ("Christ," 9:11, 14) and Ἰησοῦς ("Jesus," 10:19) which share the same referent in this context.

In addition to the many lexical connections (above), further connections also exist between a number of other words and phrases in these texts.

a. Though different terminology is used, both passages are saturated with references to Jesus's self-offering: οὐδὲ δι' αἵματος τράγων καὶ μόσχων διὰ δὲ τοῦ ἰδίου αἵματος ("not through the blood of bulls and goats but through his own blood," 9:12); τὸ αἷμα τοῦ Χριστοῦ ("the blood of Christ," 9:14); ἑαυτὸν προσήνεγκεν ("he offered himself," 9:14); ἐν τῷ αἵματι Ἰησοῦ ("by the blood of Jesus," 10:19); τοῦτ' ἔστιν τῆς σαρκὸς αὐτοῦ ("this is his flesh, 10:20);[38] and the metaphorical ὕδατι καθαρῷ ("by pure water," 10:22).[39]

b. The formally similar phrases διὰ τῆς μείζονος καὶ τελειοτέρας σκηνῆς οὐ χειροποιήτου ("through the greater and more perfect tent not man-made," 9:11) and διὰ τοῦ καταπετάσματος ("through the curtain," 10:20) are best understood as parallel references to Jesus' journey "into the holies" (εἰς τὰ ἅγια, "into the holies," 9:12) where, in fulfilment of the Day of atonement ritual, he approached God as high priest, bearing the once-for-all-time offering for sin, his own blood. Although some read διὰ τοῦ καταπετάσματος (10:20) as a reference to Jesus' "flesh" in light of the immediately

---

37. Although commonly translated as "new and living," the immediate context which is rich with words of sacrifice (προσφέρω occurs 8x in this section) suggests the likelihood of this rendering. Cf. Friberg, *Analytical Lexicon*, n.p.

38. See further discussion on the meaning of this phrase.

39. See following for further discussion on the meaning of this phrase.

following phrase τοῦτ' ἔστιν τῆς σαρκὸς αὐτοῦ ("that is, through his own flesh," 10:20),[40] this is doubtful given: (i) that neither the partner text (9:11-14) nor any other part of Hebrews speaks of Jesus leaving his flesh behind to enter into heaven; (ii) the formal similarity between 9:11 and 10:20 (with each making use of a διά + genitive construction; (iii) the apparent connection in 10:19-20 between the confidence we can have to enter "into the holies" (τῶν ἁγίων, 10:19); and Jesus' entry διὰ τοῦ καταπετάσματος.

c. 9:11-4 and 10:22-24 both describe *the same three outcomes* from Jesus' completed sacrifice in slightly different ways: (i) the forgiveness of sin; (ii) the cleansing of the conscience, which leads to (iii) the doing of good (as opposed to evil) works in service of God.

With regard to (i), in 9:11-14 the forgiveness of sin is depicted by the metaphorical description of Christ "having found an eternal redemption" (αἰωνίαν λύτρωσιν εὑράμενος, 9:12), while in 10:23 it is seen in the reference to the λελουσμένοι τὸ σῶμα ὕδατι καθαρῷ ("the body having been washed with pure water," 10:22). Although 10:23 is commonly translated as a plural and the phrase understood as a reference to Christian baptism,[41] the strong formal links between these passages suggest that the "water" (ὕδωρ) is better understood as a metaphor for the blood of Jesus, given the concentration of words for washing in both passages, their use in 9:13-14 where the cleansing agent is clearly blood, the fact that αἷμα represents a key word in this part of the text, and various LXX references, most notably Ezekiel 36:25, in which God promises καὶ ῥανῶ ἐφ' ὕδωρ καθαρόν ("and I will wash you with clean water") in reference to the day on which he will cleanse (καθαρίζω, Ezek 36:33; cf. Heb 9:13, 14; 10:22) his people. Read in this way, 10:23 makes clear that by shedding blood, Jesus has won forgiveness of sins for his people (= τὸ σῶμα, "the body," cf. 13:3, i.e. "we," "the house of God" in context, 10:10-22).[42] It is because of this, that we now have παρρησίαν εἰς τὴν εἴσοδον τῶν ἁγίων ("confidence of an entry into the holies," 10:19).

---

40. Ellingworth, *Hebrews*, 519, notes that such a reading is particularly favored by those who, following Käsemann, find gnostic influence in the text.

41. "Pure water" (Num 5:17) and "washing" were used for purification under the Law (Lev 16:4; 14:9; 15:11, etc. Cf. Peterson, *Hebrews and Perfection*, 155; Attridge, *Hebrews*, 289; and Ellingworth, *Hebrews*, 523-24; and ESV, NAS, KJV.

42. *Pace* Guthrie, *Hebrews*, 344, who notes the lack of overt signals "that he has the Christian rite in mind"; and O'Brien, *Hebrews*, 368.

MACRO LINK CLUSTERS

Both 9:14 and 10:22 also represent a cleansed conscience (ii) as presently available to God's people in light of Christ's sacrifice. In 9:14, the author makes clear by means of a conditional construction (εἰ ... πόσῳ μᾶλλον) that if the blood of bulls and goats was considered sufficient to cleanse according to the flesh, πόσῳ μᾶλλον τὸ αἷμα τοῦ Χριστοῦ ... καθαριεῖ τὴν συνείδησιν ἡμῶν ἀπὸ νεκρῶν ἔργων ("how much more will the blood of Jesus ... cleanse our conscience from dead works!," 9:14). Similarly, by calling on readers to approach God "with true hearts in full assurance of faith, hearts having been washed clean from an evil conscience" (10:22), the author assumes that this is in fact now possible.

Finally (iii), both passages also describe Christ's sacrifice as in some sense causative of a new way by which people might worship and serve God. In 9:13-14, Jesus' blood is described as cleansing our conscience ἀπὸ νεκρῶν ἔργων εἰς τὸ λατρεύειν θεῷ ζῶντι ("from dead works in order to serve the living God"). Meanwhile, immediately after describing the cleansing effects of Jesus' blood, the author calls on readers to consider one another εἰς παροξυσμὸν ἀγάπης καὶ καλῶν ἔργων ("in order to provoke love and good works," 10:24). The similarity between these contexts and grammatical constructions suggests that "love and good deeds" are descriptive of the new "living" worship which we are now called to offer (9:13-14). Cf. 12:28—13:19 where the call to worship in a manner pleasing to God (λατρεύωμεν εὐαρέστως τῷ θεῷ, 12:28) is followed by a list of similar such good deeds in which love is prominent.

Though the suggestion of a section spanning 9:11—10:24 is unusual, there is no scholarly consensus regarding the structure of this part of the text.[43] Moreover, the formal evidence of connectedness is once again strongly supported by the clear coherence which exists between 9:11-14 and 10:19-24. Where the previous section was concerned primarily with the location into which Christ entered as high priest of the good things which have come, the focus here is squarely upon the once-for-all-time (ἐφάπαξ, 9:12) self-offering made by Jesus, our great high priest, and its wondrous efficacy in cleansing both mind and body, thereby opening up the possibility of a new kind of worship for the sanctified community.

Hebrews 9:11-14 and 10:19-24 may be translated as follows:

43. Vanhoye, *Structure*, 40a, b, makes divisions between 8:1—9:28 and 10:1-18 and also reads 9:11 as the center of his macro-chiasm; Guthrie, *Structure*, 144 (and O'Brien, *Hebrews*, 343), argues for a section spanning 9:1-10:18; Rhee, *Faith*, 130-34, proposes a major doctrinal section between 7:1-10:18 (which may be further subdivided into 7:1-28; 8:1-13; 91-28; 10:1-18); while Westfall, *Discourse Analysis*, 300, sees 8:1—10:18 as a single section of text.

But when Christ became high priest of the good things which have come, he went in once for all time through the greater and more perfect tent which is not man-made—that is not of this creation—into the holies, not through the blood of goats and bulls but through his own blood, having secured an eternal redemption. For if the blood of bulls and goats and the sprinkling of the ashes of a heifer cleanses those defiled for the purification of the flesh, *how much more* will the blood of Jesus, who through the eternal Spirit offered himself without blemish to God, cleanse our conscience from dead works in order to serve the living God! (9:11–14)

Therefore, since we have confidence of an entrance into the Holies by the blood of Jesus, a freshly killed and living way which he has opened up for us through the curtain, this is his flesh, and a great high priest over the House of God, let us draw near with a true heart in full assurance of faith, hearts having been sprinkled from an evil conscience and the body washed with pure water. Let us hold fast the confession of hope without swerving, for the promiser is faithful. And let us consider one another with a view to the stimulation of love and good works. (10:19–24)

6.2.7 Hebrews 10:19–38

The tenth subsectional link cluster in Hebrews occurs between 10:19–38.

A. ¹⁹ ἔχοντες οὖν ἀδελφοί παρρησίαν εἰς τὴν εἴσοδον τῶν ἁγίων ἐν τῷ αἵματι Ἰησοῦ ²⁰ ἣν ἐνεκαίνισεν ἡμῖν ὁδὸν πρόσφατον καὶ ζῶσαν διὰ τοῦ καταπετάσματος τοῦτ' ἔστιν τῆς σαρκὸς αὐτοῦ ²¹ καὶ ἱερέα μέγαν ἐπὶ τὸν οἶκον τοῦ θεοῦ ²² <u>προσερχώμεθα μετὰ ἀληθινῆς καρδίας ἐν πληροφορίᾳ πίστεως</u> ῥεραντισμένοι τὰς καρδίας ἀπὸ συνειδήσεως πονηρᾶς καὶ λελουσμένοι τὸ σῶμα ὕδατι καθαρῷ

   B. ²³ κατέχωμεν τὴν ὁμολογίαν τῆς ἐλπίδος ἀκλινῆ <u>πιστὸς γὰρ ὁ ἐπαγγειλάμενος</u>

      C. ²⁴ καὶ κατανοῶμεν ἀλλήλους εἰς παροξυσμὸν ἀγάπης καὶ καλῶν ἔργων ²⁵ μὴ ἐγκαταλείποντες τὴν ἐπισυναγωγὴν ἑαυτῶν καθὼς ἔθος τισίν ἀλλὰ παρακαλοῦντες καὶ τοσούτῳ μᾶλλον ὅσῳ βλέπετε ἐγγίζουσαν τὴν ἡμέραν

D. ²⁶ ἑκουσίως γὰρ ἁμαρτανόντων ἡμῶν μετὰ τὸ λαβεῖν τὴν ἐπίγνωσιν τῆς ἀληθείας οὐκέτι περὶ ἁμαρτιῶν ἀπολείπεται θυσία ²⁷ φοβερὰ δέ τις ἐκδοχὴ κρίσεως καὶ πυρὸς ζῆλος ἐσθίειν μέλλοντος τοὺς ὑπεναντίους

E. ²⁸ ἀθετήσας τις νόμον Μωϋσέως χωρὶς οἰκτιρμῶν <u>ἐπὶ δυσὶν ἢ τρισὶν μάρτυσιν</u> ἀποθνῄσκει

F. ²⁹ πόσῳ δοκεῖτε χείρονος ἀξιωθήσεται τιμωρίας ὁ <u>τὸν υἱὸν τοῦ θεοῦ</u> καταπατήσας

E'. <u>καὶ τὸ αἷμα τῆς διαθήκης κοινὸν</u> ἡγησάμενος ἐν ᾧ ἡγιάσθη <u>καὶ τὸ πνεῦμα τῆς χάριτος</u> ἐνυβρίσας ὑμῶν μετὰ χαρᾶς προσεδέξασθε

D'. ³⁰ οἴδαμεν γὰρ τὸν εἰπόντα ἐμοὶ ἐκδίκησις ἐγὼ ἀνταποδώσω καὶ πάλιν κρινεῖ κύριος τὸν λαὸν αὐτοῦ ³¹ φοβερὸν τὸ ἐμπεσεῖν εἰς χεῖρας θεοῦ ζῶντος

C'. ³² Ἀναμιμνῄσκεσθε δὲ τὰς πρότερον ἡμέρας ἐν αἷς φωτισθέντες πολλὴν ἄθλησιν ὑπεμείνατε παθημάτων ³³ τοῦτο μὲν ὀνειδισμοῖς τε καὶ θλίψεσιν θεατριζόμενοι τοῦτο δὲ κοινωνοὶ τῶν οὕτως ἀναστρεφομένων γενηθέντες ³⁴ καὶ γὰρ τοῖς δεσμίοις συνεπαθήσατε

B'. καὶ τὴν ἁρπαγὴν τῶν ὑπαρχόντων ὑμῶν μετὰ χαρᾶς προσεδέξασθε <u>γινώσκοντες ἔχειν ἑαυτοὺς κρείττονα ὕπαρξιν καὶ μένουσαν</u>

A'. ³⁵ μὴ ἀποβάλητε οὖν τὴν παρρησίαν ὑμῶν ἥτις ἔχει μεγάλην μισθαποδοσίαν ³⁶ ὑπομονῆς γὰρ ἔχετε χρείαν ἵνα τὸ θέλημα τοῦ θεοῦ ποιήσαντες κομίσησθε τὴν ἐπαγγελίαν ³⁷ ἔτι γὰρ μικρὸν ὅσον ὅσον ὁ ἐρχόμενος ἥξει καὶ οὐ χρονίσει ³⁸ <u>ὁ δὲ δίκαιός μου ἐκ πίστεως ζήσεται καὶ ἐὰν ὑποστείληται οὐκ εὐδοκεῖ ἡ ψυχή μου ἐν αὐτῷ</u>

As was the case with the subsection six (6:9–18; cf. also 12:1–13), 10:19–38 seemingly *functions at two discourse levels simultaneously*, serving both as a unit at the micro level (between 10:5–21 and 10:35–11:1), and as the tenth subsection of the discourse, albeit one which lacks any less prominent "body" material.

Lexical connections include the repetition of:

- ἔχω ("I have," 10:19, 34, 35, 36);
- παρρησία ("confidence," 10:19, 35);[44]
- πίστις ("faith," 10:22, 38);
- ζάω ("I live," 10:20, 31, 38);
- μέγας ("great," 10:21, 35) and its opposite μικρός ("small," 10:37);
- ὁ θεός ("God," 10:21, 29, 31, 36);
- φοβερός ("fearful," 10:27, 31);
- κρίσις ("judgement," 10:27) and κρίνω ("I will judge," 10:30);
- ἐπαγγέλλομαι ("I promise," 10:23) and ἐπαγγελία ("promise," 10:36);
- ἡμέρα ("day," 10:25, 32);
- ἑαυτοῦ ("himself," 10:25, 34).

Additional links of similarity and opposition include those between:

- καρδία ("heart/inner self," 10:22 x2); ψυχή ("inner self," 10:38); and συνείδησις ("conscience," 10:22);
- a number of verbs which denote motion towards/away from a place: προσέρχομαι ("I approach," 10:22); ἐγγίζω ("I approach," 10:25); ἔρχομαι ("I come," 10:37); ἥκω ("I come," 10:37); ὑποστέλλω ("I draw back," 38); ἐμπίπτω ("I fall from," 10:31); and
- κατανοέω ("I see/consider," 10:24) and φωτίζω ("I shine light on/make known," 10:23), which both convey notions of understanding and physical sight and are thereby related to a range of other such words in the section: συνείδησις ("conscience," 10:22); ἐπίγνωσις ("knowledge," 26); βλέπω ("I see," 10:25); δοκέω ("I seem," 10:29); ἡγέομαι ("I consider," 10:29); οἶδα ("I know," 10:30); ἀναμιμνῄσκω ("I keep in mind," 10:32); and θεατρίζω ("I set forth as a spectacle," 10:33).

More broadly:

---

44. Both Vanhoye, *Structure*, 98–99, and Ellingworth, *Hebrews*, 516, see structural significance in the repetition of παρρησία (10:19, 35), which they claim marks out the head and tail of an inclusion between 10:19–39.

a. ἡ παρρησία ὑμῶν ("your confidence," 10:35) functions in this context as a contraction of the παρρησίαν εἰς τὴν εἴσοδον τῶν ἁγίων ("confidence of a welcome into the holies," 10:19) which we now "have" by the blood of Jesus;

b. though formally unrelated, much the same meaning is conveyed by the encouragement κατέχωμεν τὴν ὁμολογίαν τῆς ἐλπίδος ἀκλινῆ ("let us hold fast the confession of hope without swerving," 10:23) and the imperatival phrase of 10:35: μὴ ἀποβάλητε οὖν τὴν παρρησίαν ὑμῶν ("therefore do not cast away your confidence"). Although the content of τὴν ὁμολογίαν τῆς ἐλπίδος (10:23) is left unspecified, it is best understood in light of its immediate context (10:19-20) as a reference to the confidence we now possess of a "welcome" (εἴσοδος) into God's eternal presence through the blood of Jesus;[45]

c. a further connection also exists between the reason given for readers to *hold fast* in 10:23b (πιστὸς γὰρ ὁ ἐπαγγειλάμενος, "for the promiser is faithful") and that given to *not cast off* this confidence in 10:35-39. In addition to the lexical links between ἐπαγγέλλομαι and ἐπαγγελία in 10:23 and 36, and πιστός and πίστις in 10:23 and 38, both passages seek to motivate in light of the certainty of future fulfilment.[46] These connections suggest the likelihood that by referring to God as ὁ ἐπαγγειλάμενος ("the promiser"), the author has in mind the promise of Habakkuk 2:3-4 *in particular*. Read in this way, the compressed statement of 10:23 may be expanded as follows:

We must hold fast the confession of hope because God has promised that Jesus will return and that when he does, ὁ δίκαιός μου ἐκ πίστεως ζήσεται ("my righteous one will live from faith," 10:38) while the one who fails to endure by shrinking back will not please him;[47]

d. the imperative to consider τὰς πρότερον ἡμέρας ("the former days," 10:32) directs the attention of hearers in the opposite direction to

---

45. *Pace* Guthrie, *Hebrews*, 344; and Ellingworth, *Hebrews*, 524-25. This suggestion is strengthened by our previous observation that in both previous mentions (3:1 and 4:14) the ὁμολογία is related to the author's own teaching about Jesus as high priest.

46. The fact that the promiser is "faithful" (πιστός) entails that believers will indeed one day receive the "great reward" (μεγάλην μισθαποδοσίαν) he has promised them.

47. According to this understanding, faith is demonstrated *by* holding fast the confession unswervingly (10:23).

the call to consider one another in light of τὴν ἡμέραν ("the Day [still to come]," 10:25);[48]

e. The language used in 10:23 and 34 is suggestive of a degree of opposition between these verses, with the willingness of hearers to accept τὴν ἁρπαγὴν τῶν ὑπαρχόντων ὑμῶν ("the plundering of your possessions," 10:34) seemingly describing the very opposite of what the author calls on readers to do in the encouragement "let us hold fast" (κατέχωμεν, 10:23) to one possession in particular, the confession of hope. In fact, however, verse 34 describes a time when the community to whom Hebrews is addressed did indeed hold fast to what they knew was a κρείττονα ὕπαρξιν καὶ μένουσαν ("better and abiding possession," 10:34), even though it meant losing all other possessions. These connections thus suggest that the κρείττονα ὕπαρξιν καὶ μένουσαν is closely related to τὴν ὁμολογίαν τῆς ἐλπίδος ("the confession of hope," 10:23) in this context,[49] with verse 34 functioning as an encouragement from their past when the original readers did what the author calls on them to continue to do now;

f. the "love and good deeds" (ἀγάπης καὶ καλῶν ἔργων, 10:24) expressed through meeting together to encourage, which are called for in verses 24–25, are also seemingly exemplified by the hearers in the past who "became partners" (κοινωνοὶ ... γενηθέντες, 10:33) with those who were exposed to reproach and affliction and even had compassion on those in chains 10:34);

g. the unusual use of the word παροξυσμός ("provocation," 10:24)[50] establishes a further connection between this verse and verses 32 and 33, which mention a previous "great conflict ... of sufferings" (πολλὴν ἄθλησιν ... παθημάτων) and "troubles and afflictions" (ὀνειδισμοῖς τε καὶ θλίψεσιν);

h. the connection between the twin statements regarding God's coming judgement (see below) is further strengthened by the mention

---

48. In context, the day (ἡ ἡμέρα, 10:25) is best understood as a reference to the day on which Jesus' enemies will be placed under his feet as described in 10:13 (cf. Ps 110:1).

49. The reference to κρείττονα ὕπαρξιν καὶ μένουσαν is commonly understood by commentators in a more general sense as a reference to the inheritance stored up for believers in heaven. Cf. Ellingworth, *Hebrews*, 549–50.

50. Most commentators note that the word παροξυσμός, which occurs here in a positive context, is typically used to convey "intense emotion, almost always of a negative kind." Cf. Ellingworth, *Hebrews*, 527.

of fear in association with both (φοβερός, "fearful," 10:27, 31) and the similarity in sound between ἐκδοχή ("expectation," 10:27) and ἐκδίκησις ("vengeance," 10:30);[51]

Heb 10:27   φοβερὰ δέ τις ἐκδοχὴ κρίσεως καὶ πυρὸς ζῆλος ἐσθίειν μέλλοντος τοὺς ὑπεναντίους

"but a somewhat fearful expectation of judgement and a fire of fury about to consume the adversaries"

Heb 10:30   ἐμοὶ ἐκδίκησις ἐγὼ ἀνταποδώσω καὶ πάλιν κρινεῖ κύριος τὸν λαὸν αὐτοῦ

"'Vengeance is mine, I will repay'. And again, 'The Lord will judge his people.'"

i. finally, though they are grammatically inseparable, it is also possible to detect a number of further connections within verses 28 and 29 which split these verses in similar fashion to the patterning described in 2:1-3)[52] and seem designed to heighten the degree to which it will be worse for those turning their back on the new covenant in comparison to the old.

There is also a link in this context between the references to μέγας ἱερεύς ("great priest," 10:21), Ἰησοῦς ("Jesus," 10:19), and ὁ ἐρχόμενος ("the coming one," 10:37) which all share the same referent (Jesus).

The suggestion of a subsection between 10:19-38 is (almost) consistent with the majority of modern scholars who read 10:19-39 as a coherent section,[53] though the observation of a concentric structure within

---

51. Vanhoye, *Structure*, 98, reads the repetition of φοβερός and κρίσις as an inclusion marking out a unit between 10:26-31.

52. Cf. the relations of similarity between οἰκτιρμός ("mercy," 10:28) / χάρις ("grace," 10:29); various descriptions of the rejection of a covenant; and the "two or three witnesses" of v. 28 and the Son of God, blood of the covenant and Spirit of Grace of v. 29 (cf. Ellingworth, *Hebrews*, 538); and of contrast between Μωϋσέως ("Moses," 10:28) and ὁ υἱός τοῦ θεου ("the Son of God," 10:29). These links suggest the likelihood of a further contrast between νόμον (10:28) and πνεῦμα (10:29) at this point consistent with Pauline theology.

53. Cf. Vanhoye, *Structure*, 40b; Ellingworth, *Hebrews*, 515; Adam, *The Majestic Son*, 111; Attridge, *Hebrews*, 283; and Rhee, *Faith*, 159. Alternatively, Guthrie, *Structure*, 144, Westfall, *Discourse Analysis*, 301, and O'Brien, *Hebrews*, 34, read this text as three separate paragraphs at 10:19-25, 26-31, and 32-39, which (according to Westfall and O'Brien) form part of a wider section spanning 10:19-12:2 on the basis primarily of perceptions of parallelism between 4:14-16 and 10:19-25 (to which we will return in 6.3.1).

this section is new. It is also supported by an examination into its topical content. Read as a whole, subsection ten *functions both as an encouragement and warning* which calls on readers to respond to Jesus' completed self-sacrifice (section nine) by drawing near to God through Christ (A and A′), holding fast the confession in hope (B and B′), and considering one another in love (C and C′) in light both of the wondrous confidence we now have of a heavenly welcome on the one hand (A and A′) and the dreadful future which awaits those who fail to approach, hold fast and love on the other (D, D′, E, E′, and F). The relationship between its component parts and overall flow may be seen in the diagram below:[54]

    A. Since we have confidence, let us draw near to God through the new and living way in faith;

        B. let us hold fast the confession of hope in light of the future reception of the promise;

            C. And let us consider how to love one another in light of the day to come!

                D. For fearful judgement awaits those who knowingly go on sinning.

                    E. If it was bad for those who rejected the Law,

                        F. how much worse will it be for those who reject the Son?

                    E′. And the blood of the covenant, and the Spirit of Grace?

                D′. For we know him who has spoken of fearful judgement ahead.

            C′. Consider also the former days when you loved one another well,

        B′. letting go of other possessions but not the abiding possession.

---

54. Although verses 23 and 24 express quite different responses by means of separate hortatory subjunctives (κατέχωμεν and κατανοῶμεν respectively), the interconnectedness of these ideas in the parallel text (vv. 32–34) and the similarity in sound between κατέχωμεν and κατανοῶμεν suggest that they are better understood together within component B.

A'. Therefore do not throw away your confidence! For the righteous will live by faith and God will not be pleased with the one who shrinks back.

Hebrews 10:19–38 may be translated as follows:

A. [10:19] Therefore, since we have confidence of an entrance into the Holies by the blood of Jesus, [20] a freshly killed and living way which he has opened up for us through the curtain, this is his flesh, [21] and a great high priest over the house of God, [22] let us draw near with a true heart in full assurance of faith, hearts having been sprinkled from an evil conscience and the body washed with pure water.

    B. [23] Let us hold fast the confession of hope without swerving, for the Promiser is faithful.

        C. [24] And let us consider one another with a view to the stimulation of love and good works, [25] not neglecting our gatherings, as is the habit of some, but encouraging, and this by as much more as you see the Day draw near.

            D. [26] For if we go on wilfully sinning after receiving knowledge of the truth, there no longer remains a sacrifice for sins [27] but only a fearful expectation of judgement and a fury of fire which is about to consume the adversaries.

                E. [28] Anyone setting aside the Law of Moses died without mercy on the basis of two or three witnesses.

                    F. [29] How much worse do you suppose will be the punishment deserved by the one who tramples the Son of God?

                E'. And considers the blood of the covenant by which he was sanctified as unholy, and outrages the Spirit of Grace?

            D'. [30] For we know him who has said: "Vengeance is mine, I will repay." And again, "The Lord will judge his people." [31] It is fearful to fall in to the hands of the living God.

C'. ³² But keep in mind the former days, in which having been enlightened you endured a great struggle of sufferings, ³³ sometimes being exposed to insults and tribulations, sometimes becoming partners with those so treated. ³⁴ For you even sympathized with my chains.

B'. And you welcomed the seizure of your possessions knowing yourselves to have a better and abiding possession.

A'. ³⁵ Therefore do not cast off your confidence, which has a great reward. ³⁶ For you need to endure in order that having done God's will you might experience the promise. ³⁷ "For in such a little while, the one who is coming will come and will not delay. ³⁸ And my righteous one will live by faith. And if he shrinks back, my soul will not delight in him."

6.2.8 Hebrews 10:35—11:2 and 11:39—12:2

The eleventh subsection level link cluster in Hebrews occurs between 10:35—11:2 and 11:39—12:2.

Heb 10:35—11:2

³⁵ μὴ ἀποβάλητε οὖν τὴν παρρησίαν ὑμῶν ἥτις ἔχει μεγάλην μισθαποδοσίαν ³⁶ ὑπομονῆς γὰρ ἔχετε χρείαν ἵνα τὸ θέλημα τοῦ θεοῦ ποιήσαντες <u>κομίσησθε τὴν ἐπαγγελίαν</u> ³⁷ ἔτι γὰρ μικρὸν ὅσον ὅσον ὁ ἐρχόμενος ἥξει καὶ οὐ χρονίσει ³⁸ ὁ δὲ δίκαιός μου ἐκ πίστεως ζήσεται καὶ ἐὰν ὑποστείληται οὐκ εὐδοκεῖ ἡ ψυχή μου ἐν αὐτῷ ³⁹ ἡμεῖς δὲ οὐκ ἐσμὲν ὑποστολῆς εἰς ἀπώλειαν ἀλλὰ πίστεως εἰς περιποίησιν ψυχῆς ¹¹:¹ <u>Ἔστιν δὲ πίστις ἐλπιζομένων ὑπόστασις</u> πραγμάτων ἔλεγχος οὐ βλεπομένων ² ἐν ταύτῃ γὰρ ἐμαρτυρήθησαν οἱ πρεσβύτεροι

Heb 11:39—12:2

³⁹ καὶ οὗτοι πάντες μαρτυρηθέντες διὰ τῆς πίστεως <u>οὐκ ἐκομίσαντο τὴν ἐπαγγελίαν</u> ⁴⁰ τοῦ θεοῦ περὶ ἡμῶν κρεῖττόν τι προβλεψαμένου ἵνα μὴ χωρὶς ἡμῶν τελειωθῶσιν ¹²:¹ Τοιγαροῦν καὶ ἡμεῖς τοσοῦτον ἔχοντες περικείμενον ἡμῖν νέφος μαρτύρων ὄγκον ἀποθέμενοι πάντα καὶ τὴν εὐπερίστατον ἁμαρτίαν δι' ὑπομονῆς τρέχωμεν τὸν προκείμενον ἡμῖν ἀγῶνα ² ἀφορῶντες εἰς τὸν τῆς πίστεως ἀρχηγὸν καὶ τελειωτὴν Ἰησοῦν ὃς ἀντὶ τῆς προκειμένης αὐτῷ χαρᾶς

ὑπέμεινεν σταυρὸν αἰσχύνης καταφρονήσας ἐν δεξιᾷ τε τοῦ θρόνου
τοῦ θεοῦ κεκάθικεν

Links within this section include lexical repetition involving:

- κομίζω ("I obtain," 10:37; 11:39) which appears only once more in Hebrews (11:19).

- ὑπομονή ("endurance," 10:36; 12:1) and its cognate verb ὑπομένω ("I endure," 12:2, which also appears in 10:32; 12:3, and 7.

- μαρτυρέω ("I attest," 11:2, 39) and μάρτυς ("attested one," 11:40);[55]

- ἐπαγγελία ("promise," 10:36; 11:39);

- ἔχω ("I have," 10:35, 36; 11:40);

- πίστις ("faith," 10:38, 39, 40; 11:39; 12:2); and

- ὁ θεός ("God," 10:36; 11:40).

Further links of similarity and opposition also exist between:

- ἀποβάλλω ("I cast off," 10:35) and ἀποτίθημι ("I cast off," 12:1), neither of which appears again in the text;

- εὐδοκέω ("I enjoy," 10:38) and χαρά ("joy," 12:2);

- μικρὸν ὅσον ὅσον ("so small," 10:37), τοσοῦτος ("so great," 12:1) and μέγας ("great," 10:35); and

- various verbs of perception βλέπω ("I see," 11:1), προβλέπω ("I foresee," 11:40) and ἀφοράω ("I fix my eyes," 12:2).

Ties of reference may also be detected between various descriptors of a group of Scriptural saints described as "witnesses" in Hebrews 11: οἱ πρεσβύτεροι ("the elders," 11:2), οὗτοι πάντες ("all of these," 11:39), and the νέφος μαρτύρων ("cloud of witnesses") of 12:1; the addressees of Hebrews: ὑμεῖς ("you") or ἡμεῖς ("we" respectively, 10:35, 39l 11:40 x2; 12:1 x3); and between ὁ ἐρχόμενος ("the coming one," 10:37) and ὁ τῆς πίστεως ἀρχηγός καὶ τελειωτής ("the pioneer and perfecter of faith," 12:2) which in context both refer to Jesus.

More broadly:

a. both 10:35–36 and 12:1–2 call on readers to respond with similar endurance for much the same reason: that they might experience

---

55. The word μαρτυρέω appears as a verb on a further six occasions (in 7:8, 17; 10:15; 11:4 x2, and 5) and as a verb in 10:28.

the final fulfilment of God's promises. In 10:35, the author implores his readers μὴ ἀποβάλητε οὖν τὴν παρρησίαν ὑμῶν ("do not cast off your confidence," 10:35)—which 10:36 makes clear would represent the opposite of "endurance" (ὑπομονή)—so that "you may obtain the promise" (κομίσησθε τὴν ἐπαγγελίαν, 10:36). Meanwhile 12:1 calls on readers to δι' ὑπομονῆς τρέχωμεν τὸν προκείμενον ἡμῖν ἀγῶνα ("run through endurance the race lying ahead") in view of the hope of "perfection/completion" (11:40), a hope which in context is closely related once more to obtaining "the promise" [of Habakkuk 2:3-4] (cf. οὐκ ἐκομίσαντο τὴν ἐπαγγελίαν, 11:39);[56]

b. there is little difference in meaning between phrases in 11:2 and 11:39 (see below), with both identifying faith as the *means* by which God commended the saints of old;[57]

> Heb 11:2   ἐν ταύτῃ γὰρ ἐμαρτυρήθησαν οἱ πρεσβύτεροι
> "for by this [πίστις, 11:1] the ancients were commended"
>
> Heb 11:39 καὶ πάντες μαρτυρηθέντες διὰ τῆς πίστεως
> "and all these though commended through faith"

c. although there is no consensus among the scholarly community with regard to the precise meaning of 11:1, if ὑπόστασις and ἔλεγχος are translated according to their common usage as "substance" and "proof" respectively, the author's assertion ἔστιν δὲ πίστις ἐλπιζομένων ὑπόστασις πραγμάτων ἔλεγχος οὐ βλεπομένων ("faith is the substance of the things hoped for, the proof of things not seen") which he claims may be seen by the experience of the commended ancients seems *directly contradicted* by the statement of 11:39.[58] For though "commended through faith," *not one* of the numerous ancients chronicled in chapter received what was promised (which in context clearly relates to the hoped for things of 11:39).

---

56. Though not explicitly identified, the immediate context of 10:35—11:2 strongly suggests that this "promise" is the promise of life through faith of Habakkuk 2:3-4 (10:38).

57. Contra Lane, *Hebrews*, 9-13, who translates ἐν ταύτῃ as "on account of/because of this," 11:2 makes clear that "all the fathers from the beginning of the world, were approved by God in no other way than by being united to him by faith." Cf. Calvin, *Hebrews*, 263; Koester, *Hebrews*, 473; Ellingworth, *Hebrews*, 567.

58. The γάρ of 11:2 marks this verse out as support material on which the author's assertion in 11:1 rests.

Heb 11:1-2   ἔστιν δὲ πίστις ἐλπιζομένων ὑπόστασις πραγμάτων ἔλεγχος οὐ βλεπομένων ἐν ταύτῃ γὰρ ἐμαρτυρήθησαν οἱ πρεσβύτεροι

"And faith is the substance of things hoped for, the proof of what may not be seen for by this the Ancients were commended."

Heb 11:39   καὶ οὗτοι πάντες μαρτυρηθέντες διὰ τῆς πίστεως οὐκ ἐκομίσαντο τὴν ἐπαγγελίαν

"And all of these, though commended through faith, did not receive what was promised"

The contradiction is only apparent, however, as 11:40 makes clear for while "they" might not yet have received what they were waiting for, they (together with us) surely will when Jesus, "the perfecter" returns;

d. both passages depict the fulfilment of hope as yet to come. In 10:35—11:2, the author speaks of our need for endurance (10:36) until the second coming of Jesus (in fulfilment of Habakkuk 2), while 11:39-40 describe the whole of God's people from Abel to the present day waiting for the perfection that still lies ahead;

e. given the many links, it is not unlikely that Jesus himself, who having endured the cross is now seated at God's right hand, serves as the ultimate example demonstrating the need for those who would one day inherit the promises to endure.

Although the suggestion that 10:35—12:2 forms a section of text framed by an introduction (10:35—11:2) and conclusion (11:39—12:2) is (once more) unusual, with modern scholars almost universally reading 11:1-40 as a discrete unit, our proposal better accounts for the connections between the end of chapter 10 and the beginning of chapter 12,[59] and between 11:1-2 and its immediately preceding context. The repetition of the verb εἰμί ("I am") in indicative form in 10:39 and 11:1 suggests that these verses should in fact be read together as twin statements—the first of which builds on the second—which together apply

---

59. Ellingworth, *Hebrews*, 53, notes that while Hebrews 11 is "almost universally agreed to constitute a distinct unit . . . the theme of faith is carefully prepared in 10:35-39, and linked with what follows, not only by the strong logical connective τοιγαροῦν (12:1), but by the verbal echo of μαρτυρηθέντες (11:39) in μαρτύρων (12:1)." Cf. Cosby, *Rhetorical Composition*, 85, who states: "So similar is the language in 12:1-13 to that of 10:19-39 that, if the mention of the great cloud of witnesses in 12:1 were omitted, all of Hebrews 11 could be left out and the sermon would proceed quite smoothly."

the promise of Habakkuk 2:3, 4 to the situation of the readers. Moreover, as Calvin observes:

> Whoever made this the beginning of the eleventh chapter, has unwisely disjointed the context; for the object of the Apostle was to prove what he had already said—that there is need of patience.[60]

There is also demonstrable topical continuity between these sentences with each encouraging hearers to persevere in faith in light of the certain and glorious future ahead for all who trust in God's promises, as shown by the experience of the ancients. When read together with the material these verses surround (11:3–38), our findings suggest that Hebrews 11 functions *not*, as is so often assumed, as a list of heroes whose faithful example we are called to follow, *but* rather as the "proof of the reason" (πίστις) which follows and demonstrates the author's "proposition" that unseen faith surely gives way to a substantial visible reality (10:35—11:1) and "reason" of 11:2.[61]

Hebrews 10:35—11:2 and 11:39—12:2 may be translated as follows:

> Therefore do not cast off your confidence, which has a great reward. For you have need of endurance in order that having done God's will you might experience the promise. For in such a little while, the coming one will come and will not delay and my righteous one will live by faith. And if he shrinks back, my soul will not be pleased with him. But *we are not* of those who shrink back into destruction but of faith for the preservation of the soul. And *faith is* the substance of the things hoped for, the proof of things which may not be seen. For by this the Ancients were commended (10:35—11:2).

> And all of these, though commended through faith, did not receive what was promised, God having foreseen something better, that they might not be perfected apart from us. Therefore since we also have such a great cloud of witnesses surrounding us, let us run the race before us with endurance, throwing off every obstacle and the sin that entangles, fixing our eyes on the pioneer and perfecter of faith, who instead of the joy before

---

60. Calvin, *Hebrews*, 260.

61. The πίστις or "proof of the reason" represents the third of five parts of the perfect argument in ancient Greek thought. Cf. Robbins, *Exploring the Texture of Texts*, 53. Given the author of Hebrews' obvious love of wordplay, it is not hard to imagine his delight in conceiving a πίστις all about πίστις.

him endured the cross, despising the shame and sat down at the right hand of the throne of God (11:39—12:2).

6.2.9 Hebrews 12:1-13

The twelfth subsectional link cluster occurs in Hebrews between 12:1-13.

A. ¹²:¹ τοιγαροῦν καὶ ἡμεῖς τοσοῦτον ἔχοντες περικείμενον ἡμῖν νέφος μαρτύρων ὄγκον ἀποθέμενοι πάντα καὶ τὴν εὐπερίστατον ἁμαρτίαν δι' ὑπομονῆς τρέχωμεν τὸν προκείμενον ἡμῖν ἀγῶνα ² ἀφορῶντες εἰς τὸν τῆς πίστεως ἀρχηγὸν καὶ τελειωτὴν Ἰησοῦν

    B. <u>ὃς ἀντὶ τῆς προκειμένης αὐτῷ χαρᾶς ὑπέμεινεν σταυρὸν</u> αἰσχύνης καταφρονήσας ἐν δεξιᾷ τε τοῦ θρόνου τοῦ θεοῦ κεκάθικεν

        C. ³ ἀναλογίσασθε γὰρ τὸν τοιαύτην ὑπομεμενηκότα ὑπὸ τῶν ἁμαρτωλῶν εἰς ἑαυτοὺς ἀντιλογίαν ἵνα μὴ κάμητε ταῖς ψυχαῖς ὑμῶν ἐκλυόμενοι ⁴ οὔπω μέχρις αἵματος ἀντικατέστητε πρὸς τὴν ἁμαρτίαν ἀνταγωνιζόμενοι

            D. ⁵ καὶ ἐκλέλησθε τῆς παρακλήσεως ἥτις ὑμῖν ὡς υἱοῖς διαλέγεται υἱέ μου <u>μὴ ὀλιγώρει παιδείας κυρίου μηδὲ ἐκλύου ὑπ' αὐτοῦ ἐλεγχόμενος</u> ⁶ <u>ὃν γὰρ ἀγαπᾷ κύριος παιδεύει μαστιγοῖ δὲ πάντα υἱὸν ὃν παραδέχεται</u>

            D'. ⁷ <u>εἰς παιδείαν ὑπομένετε</u> ὡς υἱοῖς ὑμῖν προσφέρεται ὁ θεός τίς γὰρ υἱὸς ὃν οὐ παιδεύει πατήρ; ⁸ <u>εἰ δὲ χωρίς ἐστε παιδείας ἧς μέτοχοι γεγόνασι πάντες ἄρα νόθοι καὶ οὐχ υἱοί ἐστε</u>

        C'. ⁹ εἶτα τοὺς μὲν τῆς σαρκὸς ἡμῶν πατέρας εἴχομεν παιδευτὰς καὶ ἐνετρεπόμεθα οὐ πολὺ μᾶλλον ὑποταγησόμεθα τῷ πατρὶ τῶν πνευμάτων καὶ ζήσομεν; ¹⁰ οἱ μὲν γὰρ πρὸς ὀλίγας ἡμέρας κατὰ τὸ δοκοῦν αὐτοῖς ἐπαίδευον ὁ δὲ ἐπὶ τὸ συμφέρον εἰς τὸ μεταλαβεῖν τῆς ἁγιότητος αὐτοῦ

    B'. ¹¹ <u>πᾶσα δὲ παιδεία πρὸς μὲν τὸ παρὸν οὐ δοκεῖ χαρᾶς εἶναι ἀλλὰ λύπης</u> ὕστερον δὲ καρπὸν εἰρηνικὸν τοῖς δι' αὐτῆς γεγυμνασμένοις ἀποδίδωσιν δικαιοσύνης

A'. ¹² διὸ τὰς παρειμένας χεῖρας καὶ τὰ παραλελυμένα γόνατα ἀνορθώσατε ¹³ καὶ τροχιὰς ὀρθὰς ποιεῖτε τοῖς ποσὶν ὑμῶν ἵνα μὴ τὸ χωλὸν ἐκτραπῇ ἰαθῇ δὲ μᾶλλον

Links within this section include lexical repetition involving:

- the noun ὑπομονή ("endurance," 12:1) and its cognate verb ὑπομένω ("I endure," 12:2, 3 and 7);
- χαρά ("joy," 12:2) and its antonym λύπη ("sorrow," 12:11);
- υἱός ("son," 12:5 x2, 6, 7 x2, 8);
- the noun παιδείας (12:5, 7, 8, 11), its cognate adjective παιδεύω ("I discipline," 12:6, 7), and the related γυμνάζω ("I undergo discipline," 12:12);
- πᾶς ("everyone/all," 12:1, 6, 8, and 11);
- κύριος ("lord," 12:5, 6);
- the verb ὀλιγωρέω ("I make light of," 12:5) and its cognate adjective ὀλίγος ("few," 12:10); and
- ὁ θεός ("God," 12:2, 7).

Links of similarity and opposition also exist between:

- αἰσχύνη ("shame," 12:2) and ἐντρέπω ("I make ashamed," 12:9);
- ψυχή ("soul," 12:3), πνεῦμα ("spirit," 12:9) and σάρξ ("flesh," 12:9);
- αἷμα ("blood," 12:4, as a metaphor for death in this context) and ζάω ("I live," 12:9);
- ἁμαρτωλός ("sinner," 12:3), ἁμαρτία ("sin," 12:4), and ἁγιότης ("holiness," 12:10);
- παραδέχομαι ("I accept," 12:6), μεταλαμβάνω ("I accept," 12:10), and their opposite προσφέρω ("I offer up," 12:7);
- ἡ παράκλησις ("the encouragement," 12:5) and τὰ παραλελυμένα γόνατα ἀνορθώσατε (12:12) which Louw and Nida translate as "I become encouraged."

More broadly:

a. The appeal of 12:1 δι' ὑπομονῆς τρέχωμεν τὸν προκείμενον ἡμῖν ἀγῶνα is similar to the injunction of 12:12–13 with each urging readers by way of the same metaphor to endure in light of much the same goal (expressed as future perfection (τελειόω) in 12:1 and healing in 12:13 (ἰάομαι, "I heal"). Further connections also exist between these verses, the purpose/ result clause of 12:3 (ἵνα μὴ κάμητε ταῖς ψυχαῖς ὑμῶν ἐκλυόμενοι) which is used by Philo to describe a weary runner in the stadium,[62] and the language of physical training listed above (i.e. παιδείας, 12:5, 7, 8, 11, παιδεύω, 12:6, 7, and γυμνάζω, 12:12);

b. The summary statement of Jesus' humiliation and exaltation in 12:2 follows the same broad trajectory as the general statement about discipline in verse 11, each emphasizing both the unpleasantness of the experience by way of a similar contrast involving χαρά ("joy," 12:2, 11) and the magnificence of the outcome that makes such an experience worthwhile. A further connection is also possible between the outcomes themselves in both cases. For while the καρπὸν εἰρηνικὸν . . . δικαιοσύνης ("harvest consisting of peace and righteousness," 12:11)[63] is commonly understood as a reference to the fruit of the Spirit arising within individual believers as a result of discipline, it also neatly captures the much greater harvest of peace and righteousness (i.e. salvation) achieved by Christ for humanity as a whole by his crucifixion and heavenly exaltation. This suggests that the author of Hebrews sees Christ's crucifixion as God the Father's discipline of his son in fulfilment of 2 Samuel 7:14, making Jesus the ultimate examplar of how we should respond to it ourselves;

c. in addition to the lexical links noted previously, verses 3-4 and 9-10 are further connected by notions of opposition and advantage seen in words such as ἀντιλογία ("opposition," 12:3), ἀντικαθίστημι ("I resist," 12:4) and ἀνταγωνίζομαι ("I struggle against," 12:4) on the one hand, and the phrases εἰς ἑαυτοὺς ἀντιλογίαν, ἵνα μὴ κάμητε ταῖς ψυχαῖς ὑμῶν ἐκλυόμενοι ("for your sake that your souls might not grow weary or faint-hearted," 12:3) and ἐπὶ τὸ συμφέρον εἰς τὸ μεταλαβεῖν τῆς ἁγιότητος αὐτοῦ ("for our advantage that we might receive his holiness," 12:10) on the other. Scholars have typically replaced the phrase εἰς ἑαυτοὺς with the "inadequately supported" εἰς ἑαυτόν, translated as "against himself" on the grounds that the former "does

---

62. Ellingworth, *Hebrews*, 644, notes that "the verb is used by Philo, Migr. Abr. 133, of a weary runner in the stadium," but concludes "this image is not present in the Proverbs passage and has probably been left behind in the present verse." However, the consistency of imagery within this unit argues against this.

63. Cf. O'Brien, *Hebrews*, 470.

not make much sense."⁶⁴ However, if εἰς ἑαυτοὺς is read as marking out advantage rather than opposition ("for the sake of yourselves") the difficulty is removed with ἑαυτούς referring not to sinners but to a different group, the readers, called to consider Jesus' sufferings in verse 3. Read in this way, the point made is that Jesus suffered *for our sake* in order that we might not grow weary.

Moreover, both 12:3-4 and 9-10 seemingly function to provide readers with perspective on the degree of suffering they are called to endure so that they don't become overwhelmed at the thought of it. This is achieved in the first by means of a contrast with the greatness of what Jesus suffered (verses 3-4), and in the second through a comparison with their own previous experience of suffering at the hands of their fathers. See too the grammatical link between τὸν τοιαύτην ("how great," 12:3) and πολὺ ... μᾶλλον ("how much ... greater," 12:9);

d. the "encouragement" from Proverbs 3:11-12 in verses 5 and 6 is more or less repeated in similar language differently arranged in verses 7-8.

Though unusual, there is thus strong formal evidence to support our decision to read 12:1-13 as a section of text comprised of a single chiasm. Moreover, there is no agreement amongst alternative proposals.⁶⁵ Read in this way, section 12 functions topically to call on readers to persevere in the light of (i) the glory to come, (ii) the example of Jesus who has gone before us, and (iii) the reminder from Proverbs that as part of discipline, our sufferings are proof of God's love.

> A. ¹²:¹ Therefore since we also have such a great cloud of witnesses surrounding us, let us run the race before us with endurance, throwing off every obstacle and sin which entangles, ² and fixing our eyes on Jesus, the pioneer and perfecter of faith,
>
> > B. who, instead of the joy surrounding him, endured the cross, despising the shame, and is seated at the right hand of the throne of God.

---

64. O'Brien, *Hebrews*, 460-61.

65. The following textual units have been proposed by scholars: 12:1-13 (Vanhoye, *Structure*, 40b; Ellingworth, *Hebrews*, 637; and Lane, *Hebrews 9-13*, 403); 12:1-2, 3-17 (Guthrie, *Structure*, 144); 12:4-13 (Adam, *The Majestic Son*, 133); 12:1-29 (Rhee, *Faith*, 221; and Westfall, *Discourse Analysis*, 301).

MACRO LINK CLUSTERS

C.   ³ For consider him who endured such great hostility from sinners for our sake so that your souls might not grow weary or faint-hearted. ⁴ You have not yet resisted to the point of bloodshed in your struggles with sin.

D.   ⁵ And have you completely forgotten the encouragement which addresses you as sons: "My Son, do not belittle the discipline of the Lord nor give up when reproved by him. ⁶ For the Lord disciplines the one he loves and chastises every son he accepts"?

D'.   ⁷ Endure for the purpose of discipline! God is offering you up as sons. For which son is there whom his father does not discipline? ⁸ And if you are without discipline, in which all have shared, you are indeed bastards not sons.

C'.   ⁹ And besides, we have had fathers of flesh disciplining us and we submitted to them. How much more should we then submit to the Father of spirits and live? ¹⁰ For they disciplined us as seemed best for a few days, but he to our advantage that we might receive his holiness.

B'.   ¹¹ And at the time every discipline seems painful rather than joy, but later it yields a peaceable harvest of righteousness to those who have been trained by it.

A'.   ¹² Therefore straighten up your weakened hands and paralysed knees ¹³ and make straight paths for your feet so that what is lame might not be put out of joint but instead healed!

6.2.10 Hebrews 12:12–16 and 13:20–21

The final subsection-level link cluster in Hebrews occurs between 12:12–16 and 13:20–21.

Heb 12:12–16

¹² διὸ τὰς παρειμένας χεῖρας καὶ τὰ παραλελυμένα γόνατα ἀνορθώσατε ¹³ καὶ τροχιὰς ὀρθὰς ποιεῖτε τοῖς ποσὶν ὑμῶν ἵνα μὴ τὸ χωλὸν ἐκτραπῇ ἰαθῇ δὲ μᾶλλον ¹⁴ εἰρήνην διώκετε μετὰ πάντων καὶ

τὸν ἁγιασμόν οὗ χωρὶς οὐδεὶς ὄψεται τὸν κύριον [15] ἐπισκοποῦντες μή τις ὑστερῶν ἀπὸ τῆς χάριτος τοῦ θεοῦ μή τις ῥίζα πικρίας ἄνω φύουσα ἐνοχλῇ καὶ δι' αὐτῆς μιανθῶσιν πολλοί [16] μή τις πόρνος ἢ βέβηλος ὡς Ἠσαῦ

Heb 13:20-21

[20] Ὁ δὲ θεὸς τῆς εἰρήνης ὁ ἀναγαγὼν ἐκ νεκρῶν τὸν ποιμένα τῶν προβάτων τὸν μέγαν ἐν αἵματι διαθήκης αἰωνίου τὸν κύριον ἡμῶν Ἰησοῦν [21] <u>καταρτίσαι ὑμᾶς ἐν παντὶ ἀγαθῷ εἰς τὸ ποιῆσαι τὸ θέλημα αὐτοῦ</u> ποιῶν ἐν ἡμῖν τὸ εὐάρεστον ἐνώπιον αὐτοῦ διὰ Ἰησοῦ Χριστοῦ ᾧ ἡ δόξα εἰς τοὺς αἰῶνας ἀμήν

Links of lexical repetition within this section include connections:

- εἰρήνη ("peace," 12:14; 13:20) which occurs only twice more in Hebrews (7:22; 11:31);[66]
- κύριος ("lord," 12:14; 13:20);
- ποιέω ("I make," 12:13; 13:21 x2);
- πᾶς ("everyone/all," 12:14; 13:21);
- ὁ θεός ("God," 12:15; 13:20).

Further links of similarity also exist between:

- the verb ἐπισκοπέω ("I oversee, 12:15) with its shepherding connotations (cf. 1 Pet 5:2) and the description of Jesus as τὸν ποιμένα τῶν προβάτων τὸν μέγαν ("the great shepherd of the flock," 13:20);

More broadly:

a. the injunctions of 12:12-14, read together, describe in detail the author's understanding of what it means for his hearers to live the life pleasing to God (mentioned in 13:20-21. Cf. εἰς τὸ ποιῆσαι τὸ θέλημα αὐτοῦ ποιῶν ἐν ἡμῖν τὸ εὐάρεστον ἐνώπιον αὐτοῦ διὰ Ἰησοῦ Χριστοῦ);

---

66. Lane, *Hebrews 9-13*, n.p., claims that "the emphatic position of εἰρήνη in the initial directive of the division and its striking repetition at the end serve to bracket 12:14—13:21 as an integrated unit within the larger structure of the sermon." Cf. Vanhoye, "Discussions," 361-63, 373-74, 379. The fact that εἰρήνη is used also in connection with Rahab, who welcomed the spies in peace (11:31), suggests that Rahab's actions in leaving behind her old life and switching allegiances demonstrate what it means to "pursue peace."

b. the exhortation of 12:12-13, which presses the metaphor of the marathon from the previous unit into fresh service by calling on readers to strengthen themselves so as to live in a way which pleases God, corresponds with and is complemented by the prayer of 13:20-21 that God might equip them to do his will (see below);

Heb 12:12-3   διὸ τὰς παρειμένας χεῖρας καὶ τὰ παραλελυμένα γόνατα ἀνορθώσατε καὶ τροχιὰς ὀρθὰς ποιεῖτε τοῖς ποσὶν ὑμῶν

"therefore strengthen your weak hands and paralysed knees and make straight paths for your feet"

Heb 13:20   ὁ δὲ θεὸς . . . καταρτίσαι ὑμᾶς ἐν παντὶ ἀγαθῷ εἰς τὸ ποιῆσαι τὸ θέλημα αὐτοῦ

"may God . . . strengthen you in everything good that you might do his will"

c. (c) τὸν ἁγιασμόν οὗ χωρὶς οὐδεὶς ὄψεται τὸν κύριον ("the sanctification without which no-one will see the Lord," 12:14) which readers are called upon to pursue is also closely related with the mention of the αἵματι διαθήκης αἰωνίου ("blood of the eternal covenant" (cf. 9:11-14; 10:14, 19-23).[67]

When read together, 12:12-16 and 13:20-21 both encourage Hebrews' audience to commit themselves anew to the life pleasing to the Lord Jesus in view of the grace shown by his blood shed for them. Having exhorted his readers to endure in the previous subsection (12:1-13), the author now calls on them to pursue εἰρήνη ("peace," 12:14) and ὁ ἁγιασμός ("the sanctification," 12:14) in a shift which reflects the movement of thought in his source material. In Proverbs (LXX) 4:26, the command to ὀρθὰς τροχιὰς ποίει σοῖς ποσὶν ("make straight paths for your feet") is supported in the following verse by the certainty that God will act to make the path of his servant straight and will direct him ἐν εἰρήνῃ ("in peace," Proverbs 4:27).[68]

These sentences may be translated as follows:

---

67. ὁ ἁγιασμός only occurs once in Jewish literature to this point (2 Maccabees 2:17). Pace Lane, *Hebrews 9-13*, n.p., ὁ ἁγιασμός "does not possess an ethical significance" in this context but refers to "the objective gift of Christ achieved through his sacrificial death on the cross" (10:29; 13:12). Cf. Michel, *Der Brief*, 451, n. 3.

68. Cf. also the καρπὸν εἰρηνικὸν . . . δικαιοσύνης ("harvest consisting of peace and righteousness") in verse 11 which is presented as the result of discipline.

Therefore strengthen your weakened hands and paralysed knees and make straight paths for your feet so that what is lame might not be put out of joint but instead healed. Pursue peace with all and the sanctification without which no-one will see the Lord, guarding lest anyone fall from the grace of God, lest any bitter root spring up and through this defile many, lest anyone be immoral or worldly like Esau (12:12–16)!

And may the God of peace, who led up from the dead the great shepherd of the sheep by the blood of the eternal covenant, our Lord Jesus, strengthen you in everything good that you might do his will, working among you that which is pleasing before him through Jesus Christ. To him be glory forever. Amen (13:20–21).

6.3 Section-level Link Clusters in Hebrews 4:14—13:22

In addition to the thirteen subsection level link clusters outlined above (cf. 5.3 and 6.2), Hebrews also contains three further section-level link clusters between 4:14—5:1 and 7:28—8:3; 7:25—8:3 and 10:19-22; and 10:19-25 and 13:18–22.

6.3.1 Hebrews 4:14—5:1 and 7:28—8:3

Following Nauck's identification of a number of parallels between 4:14-16 and 10:19-23/31 (which may be seen below in light of modifications by George Guthrie), these texts are commonly thought to function together as a macro inclusion.[69]

---

69. Guthrie, *Structure*, 79–81. Cf. Nauck, "Zum Aufbau," 204–05; Joslin, "Can Hebrews be Structured?," 108; Westfall, *Discourse Analysis*, 13; and O'Brien, *Hebrews*, 360.

Heb 4:14-16	Heb 10:19-23
ἔχοντες οὖν	ἔχοντες οὖν
ἀρχιερέα μέγαν	ἱερέα μέγαν
διεληλυθότα τοὺς οὐρανούς	διὰ τοῦ καταπετάσματος
Ἰησοῦν	Ἰησοῦ
τὸν υἱὸν τοῦ θεοῦ	τὸν οἶκον τοῦ θεοῦ
κρατῶμεν τῆς ὁμολογίας	κατέχωμεν τὴν ὁμολογίαν
προσερχώμεθα ... μετὰ παρρησίας	προσερχώμεθα ... ἐν πληροφορίᾳ πίστεως

However, 4:14-16 and 10:19-23/31 are probably better understood as the introduction and conclusion (or part thereof) of two separate sections (4:14—8:3 and 7:25—10:22) which share an overlapping boundary at 7:25—8:3 for the following reasons. First, the lexical and other kinds of formal connections between 4:14-16 and 7:28—8:3 and 7:25—8:3 and 10:19-22 are stronger and include (in the first case) the repetition of approximately the same phrase in 5:1 and 8:3.[70] Second, though there is clearly some degree of conceptual overlap between these passages, 4:14-16 and 10:19-23 do not appear to be saying the same thing. 10:19-25 makes no mention of Jesus' ability to sympathize with our weaknesses (4:15). Conversely, 4:14-16 has nothing to say about the "new and living way" by which we might enter God's presence which so dominates discussion in 10:19-22. Moreover, the "confidence" described by both texts (παρρησία, cf. 4:16 and 10:19) clearly rests on different grounds in each case (Jesus' greatness and capacity to sympathize in the first and the welcome won by his bloodshed in the second). On the other hand, there is a strongly coherent relationship between 4:14-16 and 7:28-8:3 (cf. 6.3.1 and 2). Third, the use of the extremely prominent κεφάλαιον in 8:1 formally indicates a major conclusion at this point consistent with our proposal.

In light of the above, the second section-level link cluster in Hebrews occurs between 4:14-5:1 and 7:28-8:3.

---

70. According to Guthrie, *Structure*, 85, "the parallel statements found at 5:1 and 8:3 do not form an *inclusio*. The *inclusio* begun in Heb. 5:1-3 has already been shown to close at 7:26-28. Rather, 5:1 and 8:3 form a special type of transition referred to in the present study as "parallel introductions." However, while 8:3 may well function as part of an introduction as Guthrie suggests, this doesn"t entail that it cannot also serve as part of a conclusion to the previous unit.

Heb 4:14-5:1

¹⁴ <u>ἔχοντες οὖν ἀρχιερέα μέγαν διεληλυθότα τοὺς οὐρανούς Ἰησοῦν τὸν υἱὸν τοῦ θεοῦ</u> κρατῶμεν τῆς ὁμολογίας ¹⁵ οὐ γὰρ ἔχομεν ἀρχιερέα μὴ δυνάμενον συμπαθῆσαι ταῖς ἀσθενείαις ἡμῶν πεπειρασμένον δὲ κατὰ πάντα καθ' ὁμοιότητα χωρὶς ἁμαρτίας ¹⁶ προσερχώμεθα οὖν μετὰ παρρησίας συγκεκερασμένους τῷ θρόνῳ τῆς χάριτος ἵνα λάβωμεν ἔλεος καὶ χάριν εὕρωμεν εἰς εὔκαιρον βοήθειαν ⁵:¹ πᾶς γὰρ ἀρχιερεὺς ἐξ ἀνθρώπων λαμβανόμενος ὑπὲρ ἀνθρώπων καθίσταται τὰ πρὸς τὸν θεόν ἵνα προσφέρῃ δῶρά τε καὶ θυσίας ὑπὲρ ἁμαρτιῶν

Heb 7:28-8:3

²⁸ <u>ὁ νόμος γὰρ ἀνθρώπους καθίστησιν ἀρχιερεῖς ἔχοντας ἀσθένειαν ὁ λόγος δὲ τῆς ὁρκωμοσίας τῆς μετὰ τὸν νόμον υἱόν εἰς τὸν αἰῶνα τετελειωμένον</u> ⁸:¹ <u>κεφάλαιον δὲ ἐπὶ τοῖς λεγομένοις τοιοῦτον ἔχομεν ἀρχιερέα ὃς ἐκάθισεν ἐν δεξιᾷ τοῦ θρόνου τῆς μεγαλωσύνης ἐν τοῖς οὐρανοῖς</u> ² τῶν ἁγίων λειτουργὸς καὶ τῆς σκηνῆς τῆς ἀληθινῆς ἣν ἔπηξεν ὁ κύριος οὐκ ἄνθρωπος ³ πᾶς γὰρ ἀρχιερεὺς εἰς τὸ προσφέρειν δῶρά τε καὶ θυσίας καθίσταται

Instances of lexical repetition between 4:14-16 and 7:28—8:3 include:

- ἀρχιερεύς ("High Priest," 4:14, 15; 5:1; 7:28 and 8:1, 3);
- ἔχοντες and ἔχομεν (4:14, 15) / ἔχοντας and ἔχομεν (7:28; 8:1);
- ἄνθρωπος ("person," 5:1 x2; 7:28, 8:2);
- καθίστημι ("I appoint," 5:1, 7:28 and 8:3), which occurs nowhere else in Hebrews;
- ὁ θρόνος ("the throne," 4:16 and 8:1) out of only 4 appearances in Hebrews (cf. 1:8; 12:2);
- ἀσθένεια ("weakness," 4:15 and 7:28, out of only 4 appearances in Hebrews (cf. 5:2; 11:34);
- υἱός ("son," 4:14; 7:28);
- οἱ οὐρανοί ("the heavens," 4:14 and 8:1) out of 7 occurences in plural form within Hebrews; and
- προσφέρω ("I offer," 5:1 and 8:3);

Further relations of similarity may also be identified between:

- μέγας ("great," 4:14) and μεγαλωσύνης ("greatness," 8:1);
- ἡ ὁμολογία ("the confession," 4:14) / τοῖς λεγομένοις ("the things said," 8:1); and
- the lexical string δῶρά τε καὶ θυσίας ("both gifts and sacrifices," 5:1) which is repeated without variation in 8:3;

Most strikingly, much the same phrase is repeated in both 5:1 and 8:3 within minimal alterations.

Heb 5:1	πᾶς γὰρ ἀρχιερεὺς ... καθίσταται ... ἵνα προσφέρῃ δῶρά τε καὶ θυσίας
	"for every high priest ... is appointed ... to offer both gifts and sacrifices"
Heb 8:3	πᾶς γὰρ ἀρχιερεὺς εἰς τὸ προσφέρειν δῶρά τε καὶ θυσίας καθίσταται
	"for every high priest is appointed to offer both gifts and sacrifices"

More broadly:

a. the description of Jesus' upward ascent into the heavens (cf. διεληλυθότα τοὺς οὐρανούς in 4:14) corresponds to the statement that "he sat down at the right hand of the throne of the Majesty in the heavens" in 8:1 (ὃς ἐκάθισεν ἐν δεξιᾷ τοῦ θρόνου τῆς μεγαλωσύνης ἐν τοῖς οὐρανοῖς);

b. the depiction of Jesus as δυνάμενον συμπαθῆσαι ταῖς ἀσθενείαις ἡμῶν πεπειρασμένον δὲ κατὰ πάντα καθ' ὁμοιότητα ("able to sympathize with our weaknesses, having been tested according to everything like us," 4:15) is encapsulated and included within his description as τετελειωμένον ("having been perfected") in 7:28;[71]

c. 7:28—8:1 as a whole represents an expanded version of the statement in 4:14 ἔχοντες οὖν ἀρχιερέα μέγαν ... Ἰησοῦν τὸν υἱὸν τοῦ θεοῦ ("therefore since we have a great high priest ... Jesus the Son of God") which makes much the same point again by way of a contrast between Jesus and the priests of the Law.

---

71. Cf. Peterson, *Hebrews and Perfection*, 118. Cf. comments on the concept of "perfection" in 2:10 in 4.2.6e.

When 4:14—5:1 and 7:28—8:3 are read together, there is also clear topical coherence between these paragraphs with both declaring that in Jesus we have exactly the kind of high priest we need. For he is incomparably great, having sat down at God's right hand in the heavens, yet is able to sympathize with our weaknesses, having been "perfected" forever. A close topical relationship also exists between the frame material and the body of the section with each main part of the introduction corresponding to one of the sub-units within it. Jesus' capacity to sympathize with his brothers is dealt with first (4:14—5:10), before the author exhorts us again to "pay attention" to his message by holding fast the confession (5:8—6:12), after which he returns to the topic of Jesus' greatness as seen by his entry into the Heavens as high priest (6:9—8:3).

Thus combined evidence of repetition suggests that 4:14—5:1 and 7:28—8:3 function as the introduction and conclusion respectively to the second section of the discourse (4:14—8:3), whose topic may be summarized as follows. Since Jesus, our high priest, is both great, having become a priest forever according to the order of Melchizedek, and yet able to sympathize with our weaknesses, having been tested like us, let us draw near to him with confidence for mercy.

A translation of the topic sentences may be seen below.

> Therefore, since we have a great high priest who has passed through the Heavens, Jesus, the Son of God, let us hold fast the confession! For we do not have a high priest who is unable to sympathize with our weaknesses, but one who has been tested in all things like us without sin. Let us therefore draw near with confidence to the throne of Grace, so that we might receive mercy and find grace for the time of need. For every high priest chosen from men is appointed on behalf of men to the things of God, in order that he might offer up gifts and sacrifices for sins. (4:14—5:1)

> For the law appoints men in their weakness as high priests, but the Word of the Oath which came after the Law appoints the Son who has been perfected forever! And the summary of what we are saying is that we have this kind of high priest, who is seated at the right hand of the Throne of the Majesty in the Heavens, a minister of the holies and the true tent, which the Lord built, not man. For every high priest is appointed to offer gifts and sacrifices. (7:28—8:3)

6.3.2 Hebrews 8:1–3 and 10:19–22

The third section-level link cluster in Hebrews occurs between 8:1–3 and 10:19–22.

> Heb 8:1–3
>
> ⁸:¹ κεφάλαιον δὲ ἐπὶ τοῖς λεγομένοις <u>τοιοῦτον ἔχομεν ἀρχιερέα ὃς ἐκάθισεν ἐν δεξιᾷ τοῦ θρόνου τῆς μεγαλωσύνης ἐν τοῖς οὐρανοῖς</u> ² τῶν ἁγίων λειτουργὸς καὶ τῆς σκηνῆς τῆς ἀληθινῆς ἣν ἔπηξεν ὁ κύριος οὐκ ἄνθρωπος ³ πᾶς γὰρ ἀρχιερεὺς εἰς τὸ προσφέρειν δῶρά τε καὶ θυσίας καθίσταται ὅθεν ἀναγκαῖον ἔχειν τι καὶ τοῦτον ὃ προσενέγκῃ

> Heb 10:19–22
>
> ¹⁹ ἔχοντες οὖν ἀδελφοὶ παρρησίαν εἰς τὴν εἴσοδον τῶν ἁγίων ἐν τῷ αἵματι Ἰησοῦ ²⁰ ἣν ἐνεκαίνισεν ἡμῖν ὁδὸν πρόσφατον καὶ ζῶσαν διὰ τοῦ καταπετάσματος τοῦτ' ἔστιν τῆς σαρκὸς αὐτοῦ ²¹ καὶ <u>ἱερέα μέγαν ἐπὶ τὸν οἶκον τοῦ θεοῦ</u> ²² προσερχώμεθα μετὰ ἀληθινῆς καρδίας ἐν πληροφορίᾳ πίστεως ῥεραντισμένοι τὰς καρδίας ἀπὸ συνειδήσεως πονηρᾶς καὶ λελουσμένοι τὸ σῶμα ὕδατι καθαρῷ

Lexical connections between these sentences include the repetition of:

- ἔχω ("I have," 8:1; 8:3; and 10:19);
- μεγαλωσύνη ("greatness," 8:1) and μέγας ("great," 10:21);
- ἡ ἁγία ("the holy places," 8:2; 10:19);
- ἀληθινος ("true" 8:2; 10:22).

Further relations of similarity may be detected between:

- ἀρχιερεύς ("high priest," 8:1), λειτουργός ("[priestly] minister") and ἱερέα ("priest," 10:21);
- ὁ κύριος ("the Lord," 8:2), ἡ μεγαλωσύνης ἐν τοῖς οὐρανοῖς ("the greatness in the heavens," 8:1) and ὁ θεός ("God," 10:21), which all refer to God, the Father, in context;
- ἡ ἁγία ("the holy places," 8:2; 10:19), ἐν τοῖς οὐρανοῖς ("in the heavens," 8:1), τῆς σκηνῆς τῆς ἀληθινῆς ἣν ἔπηξεν ὁ κύριος οὐκ ἄνθρωπος ("the true tent, which the Lord built, not man," 8:2), and διὰ τοῦ καταπετάσματος ("through the curtain," 10:20) which describe the same location, the dwelling-place of God;

- various words and phrases found in both 8:1–3 and 10:19–22 drawn from the background of temple sacrifice: τὸ προσφέρειν δῶρά τε καὶ θυσίας ("to offer both gifts and sacrifices," 8:1); τι ... ὃ προσενέγκῃ ("something ... to offer," 8:1); ἐν τῷ αἵματι Ἰησοῦ ("by the blood of Jesus," 10:19); and ὁδὸν πρόσφατον καὶ ζῶσαν διὰ τοῦ καταπετάσματος τοῦτ' ἔστιν τῆς σαρκὸς αὐτοῦ ("a new and freshly-killed way through the curtain, that is by his flesh, 10:19–20).[72]

More broadly:

a. there is a strong correspondence between κεφάλαιον δὲ ἐπὶ τοῖς λεγομένοις ("the summary of what we are saying," 8:1) and 10:19–22, taken as a whole, which, as some have noted, offers up a further summary (in addition to 8:1) of the message of Hebrews up to that point;

b. the phrase, τοιοῦτον ἔχομεν ἀρχιερέα ("we have this kind of high priest," 8:1, i.e. "the Son, who has been perfected forever," 7:28), communicates virtually the same information about the same person as ἔχοντες οὖν ἀδελφοί ... ἱερέα μέγαν ἐπὶ τὸν οἶκον τοῦ θεοῦ in 10:19–22 ("having therefore, brethren, a great priest over the house of God"), especially when read in light of 3:6;

c. the description of what Jesus has achieved is also closely related in both texts: Within context of the wider discourse, the significance of the statement, ὃς ἐκάθισεν ἐν δεξιᾷ τοῦ θρόνου τῆς μεγαλωσύνης ἐν τοῖς οὐρανοῖς ("he [Jesus] sat down at the right hand of the throne of the Majesty in the heavens), is primarily seen in terms of what Jesus' heavenly session means *for us* (the brethren) and our access into heaven (cf., for example, 1:3; 6:19–20; 9:11–12 etc.). Much the same emphasis may also be found in 10:19ff, which describes the "confidence with regard to a welcome" (παρρησίαν εἰς τὴν εἴσοδον, 10:19) *we* now enjoy since Jesus has opened up a "way" into the heavenlies for us (ὁδός, 10:20).

d. Christ's blood is portrayed in both 8:1–3 and 10:19–22 as the means by which Christ was able to enter heaven. In 8:1–3, the point is made obliquely: As high priest, namely someone specifically appointed

---

72. Although commonly translated as "new and living," the immediate context which is rich with words of sacrifice (προσφέρω occurs 8x in this section) suggests that the two-part description πρόσφατον καὶ ζῶσαν is better rendered as "freshly killed and living," corresponding to the way in which this way to the Father was opened (through Jesus' death and resurrection).

by God "to offer up gifts and sacrifices" (εἰς τὸ προσφέρειν δῶρά τε καὶ θυσίας, 8:3), it was "necessary" (ἀναγκαῖον, 8:3) for Christ, like the priests of the Law, to have *something* to offer in order to enter the holy places. Although this "something" is not identified in the passage, its identity is clarified in 9:12, which insists that Christ entered the true heavenly tent "*not* by means of the blood of goats and calves *but* by his own blood." Meanwhile, in 10:19-22 the point is made explicit: Our confidence of a welcome into heaven is ἐν τῷ αἵματι Ἰησοῦ ("by the blood of Jesus," 10:19). For "by his flesh" (τῆς σαρκὸς αὐτοῦ, 10:20), he has opened up the way.

There is also clear topical continuity between these sentences. Chapter 8:1-3 declares that the "main point/summary" (κεφάλαιον, 8:1) of Hebrews' message is that we now have a great high priest, Jesus, the Son of God himself who has already begun his heavenly ministry, having offered up a suitable sacrifice on our behalf. Much the same content is restated in the second "summary" of 10:19-22. Therefore (οὖν), the preacher concludes, since we have *both* the certainty of a welcome into the holy places by Jesus' own blood *and* a great high priest who even now ministers over us in heaven, let us draw near in the full assurance of faith, knowing in our hearts and minds that we have indeed been washed clean once-for-all by Christ's completed sacrifice of himself.

Similar thematic agreement also exists between 8:1-3 and 10:19-22 and the intervening material with its emphasis on the overwhelming superiority of Jesus' perfect and true priesthood in comparison to the Law's "old" way to God (8:1—9:12; cf. 6.2.5) and the wondrous efficacy of Jesus' once-for-all-time sacrifice for sin (9:11—10:24; cf. 6.2.6).

Thus the formal and topical evidence strongly suggests that Hebrews 8:1-3 and 10:19-22 might reasonably be understood as the introduction and conclusion respectively to the third section of the discourse (7:25-27), marking out 7:25—8:3 as transitional material common to Hebrews' second and third sections. Having established Jesus' suitability as our high priest in section 2, the focus of this section is now squarely upon what Jesus has accomplished by his death and resurrection and its topic may be summarized as follows: Jesus has offered up once-for-all-time an acceptable sacrifice for sin—his own precious blood, which has the power to sanctify all who draw near to God through him—and now serves in the heavenly places as our great, exalted high priest.

A translation of the topic sentences may be seen below.

And the summary of what we are saying is that we have this kind of high priest, who is seated at the right hand of the throne of the Majesty in the Heavens, a minister of the holies and the true tent, which the Lord built, not man. For every high priest is appointed to offer gifts and sacrifices; thus it was necessary for this priest also to have something to offer. (8:1–3)

Therefore, brothers, since we have confidence to enter the holy places by the blood of Jesus, by the new and living way that he opened for us through the curtain, that is, through his flesh, and since we have a great priest over the house of God, let us draw near with a true heart in full assurance of faith, with our hearts sprinkled clean from an evil conscience and our bodies washed with pure water. Let us hold fast the confession of hope without swerving, for the Promiser is faithful. (10:19–22)

6.3.3 Hebrews 10:19–25 and 13:18–22

The fourth section-level link cluster in Hebrews may be seen between 10:19–25 and 13:18–22.

Heb 10:19–25

¹⁹ Ἔχοντες οὖν ἀδελφοί παρρησίαν εἰς τὴν εἴσοδον τῶν ἁγίων <u>ἐν τῷ αἵματι Ἰησοῦ</u> ²⁰ ἣν ἐνεκαίνισεν ἡμῖν ὁδὸν πρόσφατον καὶ ζῶσαν διὰ τοῦ καταπετάσματος τοῦτ' ἔστιν τῆς σαρκὸς αὐτοῦ ²¹ καὶ <u>ἱερέα μέγαν ἐπὶ τὸν οἶκον τοῦ θεοῦ</u> ²² προσερχώμεθα μετὰ ἀληθινῆς καρδίας ἐν πληροφορίᾳ πίστεως ῥεραντισμένοι τὰς καρδίας ἀπὸ συνειδήσεως πονηρᾶς καὶ λελουσμένοι τὸ σῶμα ὕδατι καθαρῷ ²³ <u>κατέχωμεν τὴν ὁμολογίαν τῆς ἐλπίδος ἀκλινῆ</u> πιστὸς γὰρ ὁ ἐπαγγ ειλάμενος ²⁴ καὶ κατανοῶμεν ἀλλήλους εἰς παροξυσμὸν ἀγάπης καὶ καλῶν ἔργων ²⁵ μὴ ἐγκαταλείποντες τὴν ἐπισυναγωγὴν ἑαυτῶν καθὼς ἔθος τισίν ἀλλὰ παρακαλοῦντες καὶ τοσούτῳ μᾶλλον ὅσῳ βλέπετε ἐγγίζουσαν τὴν ἡμέραν

Heb 13:18–22

¹⁸ Προσεύχεσθε περὶ ἡμῶν πειθόμεθα γὰρ ὅτι καλὴν συνείδησιν ἔχομεν ἐν πᾶσιν καλῶς θέλοντες ἀναστρέφεσθαι ¹⁹ περισσοτέρως δὲ παρακαλῶ τοῦτο ποιῆσαι ἵνα τάχιον ἀποκατασταθῶ ὑμῖν ²⁰ ὁ δὲ θεὸς τῆς εἰρήνης, ὁ ἀναγαγὼν ἐκ νεκρῶν <u>τὸν ποιμένα τῶν προβάτων τὸν μέγαν ἐν αἵματι διαθήκης αἰωνίου</u> τὸν κύριον ἡμῶν Ἰησοῦν ²¹ καταρτίσαι ὑμᾶς ἐν παντὶ ἀγαθῷ εἰς τὸ ποιῆσαι τὸ θέλημα αὐτοῦ

ποιῶν ἐν ἡμῖν τὸ εὐάρεστον ἐνώπιον αὐτοῦ διὰ Ἰησοῦ Χριστοῦ ᾧ ἡ δόξα εἰς τοὺς αἰῶνας ἀμήν ²² Παρακαλῶ δὲ ὑμᾶς ἀδελφοί <u>ἀνέχεσθε τοῦ λόγου τῆς παρακλήσεως</u>

Potentially significant lexical connections between these texts include:

- καλός ("good," 10:24 and 13:18) and καλῶς ("well," 13:18) out of a total 5 occurences in Hebrews;
- ἀδελφοί ("brothers," 10:19; 13:22);
- συνείδησις ("conscience," 10:22; 13:18) out of 5 occurrences in Hebrews;
- Ἰησοῦς ("Jesus," 10:19; 13:20, 21);
- παρακαλέω ("I encourage," 10:25; 13:19, 22. Cf. also παράκλησις in 13:22);
- ἔχω ("I have," 10:19; 13:18);
- αἷμα ("blood," 10:19; 13:20);
- μέγας ("great," 10:21; 13:20).

Connections may also be seen between:

- the similar phrases ἐν τῷ αἵματι Ἰησοῦ ("by the blood of Jesus," 10:19) and ἐν αἵματι διαθήκης αἰωνίου ("by the blood of the eternal covenant," 13:20), which both refer to the same blood;
- παρρησία ("confidence," 10:19), πληροφορίᾳ πίστεως ("full assurance of faith," 10:21) and πειθόμεθα ("we are convinced," 13:18), which each convey notions of complete certainty about something.

More broadly:

a. both ὁδὸν πρόσφατον καὶ ζῶσαν ("freshly killed and living way," 10:19) and ὁ ἀναγαγὼν ἐκ νεκρῶν τὸν ποιμένα τῶν προβάτων τὸν μέγαν ("the one who leads up from the dead, the great shepherd of the sheep," 13:20) refer to Jesus' *death and resurrection*;

b. the subjunctival phrase κατέχωμεν τὴν ὁμολογίαν τῆς ἐλπίδος ἀκλινῆ ("let us hold fast the confession of hope without deviation," 10:23) exhorts readers to respond in much *the same way* as the imperatival clause ἀνέχεσθε τοῦ λόγου τῆς παρακλήσεως ("bear with the word of encouragement," 13:22) with the connection further strengthened by the probable link between the objects in each case. In context ὁ λόγος τῆς παρακλήσεως ("the word of encouragement," 13:22) clearly functions as the author's description of his own composition. Similarly, given both the formally related parallel phrases in 3:6 and 14 (cf. κατέχω) and the earlier references to ἡ ὁμολογία in 3:1 and 4:14, it is likely that ἡ ὁμολογία τῆς ἐλπίδος also functions as a reference to this *same* message (i.e. Hebrews), which is here characterized as one of hope;

Heb 3:6   ἐάν[περ] τὴν παρρησίαν καὶ τὸ καύχημα τῆς ἐλπίδος κατάσχωμεν

Heb 3:14   ἐάνπερ τὴν ἀρχὴν τῆς ὑποστάσεως μέχρι τέλους βεβαίαν κατάσχωμεν

c. there is a correspondence of promise / fulfilment between the description of God as the faithful promiser in 10:23 and his identification as ὁ ἀναγαγὼν ἐκ νεκρῶν τὸν ποιμένα τῶν προβάτων τὸν μέγαν ἐν αἵματι διαθήκης αἰωνίου ("the one who leads up from the dead the great shepherd of the sheep by the blood of the eternal covenant," 13:20). Indeed, the language of 13:20 seems calculated to emphasize God's faithfulness to his word as seen by its seeming encapsulation of so many promises in the LXX;

d. the encouragement to love and good deeds (cf. εἰς παροξυσμὸν ἀγάπης καὶ καλῶν ἔργων) in 10:24–25 is also related to the author's prayer in 13:21 that God might strengthen "you" ἐν παντὶ ἀγαθῷ εἰς τὸ ποιῆσαι τὸ θέλημα αὐτοῦ ποιῶν ἐν ἡμῖν τὸ εὐάρεστον ἐνώπιον αὐτοῦ διὰ Ἰησοῦ Χριστοῦ "in everything good that you might do his will, working in you that which is pleasing before him through Jesus Christ") with each describing a similar goal in slightly different dress.

From a topical perspective, both 10:19–25 and 13:19–22 serve (implicitly in the second case) to call Hebrews' audience to hold fast to the word they have heard (described variously throughout the discourse) and to persist with the love and good deeds they had shown previously (cf. 6:9–10) in light of all that God has done for them through the death and resurrection of the Lord Jesus Christ.

A translation of the topic sentences may be seen below.

> Therefore, brothers, since we have confidence with respect to an entry into the holy places by the blood of Jesus, by the new and living way that he opened for us through the curtain, that is, through his flesh, and a great priest over the house of God,

let us draw near with a true heart in full assurance of faith, with our hearts sprinkled clean from an evil conscience and the body washed with pure water. Let us hold fast the confession of hope unswervingly, for he who has promised is faithful, and let us consider how to stir up one another into love and good works, not neglecting our gathering, as is the habit of some, but encouraging. And do this by as much more as you see the Day draw near. (10:19-25)

Pray for us for we are sure that we have a good conscience, wishing to conduct ourselves well in all things. And I encourage you to do this much more that I might be returned to you soon. And may the God of peace, who raised up from the dead the great shepherd of the sheep by the blood of the eternal covenant, our Lord Jesus Christ, strengthen you in everything good in order to do his will, working among you that which is pleasing before him through Jesus Christ, to whom be glory for ever. Amen. And I encourage you, brothers, to bear with the word of encouragement. (13:18-22)

6.4 The Epilogue (Hebrews 13:22-25)

Following Hebrews' fourth section, the author concludes his discourse with one final, stand-alone micro link cluster (13:22-25), the beginning of which (v. 22) overlaps with the end of the section. Commonly described as an "Epilogue," this passage is conventionally read as a final encouragement from the author to his readers to accept his "word of encouragement" (13:22a) which is followed by a statement concerning its brevity (13:22b),[73] "news" of Timothy's release from prison[74] and a future visit (13:23), an instruction to greet the leaders and saints within their community, the passing on of a greeting from οἱ ἀπὸ τῆς Ἰταλίας ("those from Italy," 13:24) and some final words of encouragement: ἡ χάρις μετὰ πάντων ὑμῶν ("may grace be with all of you," 13:25).

Such a reading poses a number of problems, however. In the first place, there is no other historical evidence of (the biblical) Timothy's

---

73. The phrase διὰ βραχέων (13:22) is invariably translated in a temporal sense (i.e. "briefly") in light of its similar use in other ancient (non-Biblical) literature. Cf. Guthrie, *Hebrews*, 443.

74. The statement γινώσκετε τὸν ἀδελφὸν ἡμῶν Τιμόθεον ἀπολελυμένον (13:23) is typically read as "you know our brother Timothy having been released." Cf. Guthrie, *Hebrews*, 443; Westfall, *Discourse Analysis*, 293; ESV.

incarceration.⁷⁵ Second, if the author's purpose in 13:23 is to share information with his hearers about a mutual acquaintance (as Paul does in Romans 16), why does he mention Timothy *alone* (unlike in Romans 16)?

When the evidence of repetition and its location within Hebrews 13:22–25 is considered, there are clear signs of symmetry within this material which raise the possibility of an alternative understanding of these verses.

Lexical repetition includes:

- ἀδελφός ("brother," 13:22, 23); and
- ὑμεῖς ("we," which occurs seven times within this relatively small unit in 13:22 [x2], 23 [x2], 24 [x2] and 25).

Further relations of similarity may also be found between the verbs:

- ἐπιστέλλω ("I send a word to," 13:22) and ἀπολύω ("I send," 13:22); and
- ἀνέχω ("I accept," 13:22) and ἀσπάζομαι ("I embrace/welcome," 13:24 [x2]).

If, as seems likely (cf. Heb 3:1, 6–8), the "word of encouragement" is taken as a means of grace, there is also a correspondence between the author's injunction of 13:22 and the expression of his ultimate desire in verse 25 (see below), since the latter will only be possible if his hearers heed the former.

Heb 13:22	παρακαλῶ δὲ ὑμᾶς ἀδελφοί ἀνέχεσθε τοῦ λόγου τῆς παρακλήσεως
	"I urge you, brothers, to bear with the word of encouragement."
Heb 13:25	ἡ χάρις μετὰ πάντων ὑμῶν
	"let grace be with all of you"

Finally, the prominent repetition in 13:22 involving the verb παρακαλέω ("I encourage," 13:19) and the noun παράκλησις

---

75. Ellingworth, *Hebrews*, 30. This assumes, in agreement with most scholars, that the "Timothy" referred to in 13:23 is Paul's associate.

("encouragement") corresponds to the patterning described in 5.2 and suggests that the verse marks the beginning of a microtextual unit.

Viewed in combination, this repetition and its location suggest that 13:22-25 is better understood as a four-part concentric unit, the formal arrangement of which is entirely consistent with that found within each of the micro link clusters analyzed in chapter 4 (see below).

A. ²² παρακαλῶ δὲ ὑμᾶς ἀδελφοί <u>ἀνέχεσθε τοῦ λόγου τῆς παρακλήσεως</u>

B. καὶ γὰρ διὰ βραχέων ἐπέστειλα ὑμῖν

B'. ²³ γινώσκετε τὸν ἀδελφὸν ἡμῶν Τιμόθεον ἀπολελυμένον μεθ' οὗ ἐὰν τάχιον ἔρχηται ὄψομαι ὑμᾶς

A'. ²⁴ ἀσπάσασθε πάντας τοὺς ἡγουμένους ὑμῶν καὶ πάντας τοὺς ἁγίους ἀσπάζονται ὑμᾶς οἱ ἀπὸ τῆς Ἰταλίας ²⁵ <u>ἡ χάρις μετὰ πάντων ὑμῶν</u>

By this reading, 13:22a (A) functions as a parallel to 13:24-25 (A') which clarifies that Hebrews' author is likely to represent one of those ἀπὸ τῆς Ἰταλίας ("from Italy") mentioned in 13:25. In this sense ἀσπάζονται ὑμᾶς οἱ ἀπὸ τῆς Ἰταλίας does not describe a greeting additional to the author's own final greeting of verse 25 from a separate group of people (as commonly assumed) but represents a second and final reference to himself as the one who now greets his readers.

Meanwhile 13:22b (B) and 13:23 (B') represent parallel descriptions of the agency of Hebrews' transmission. In context, verse 13 does not state that Timothy has been "released" from prison but *functions instead to identify him as one of those through whom Hebrews has been sent* (as described in 13:22). In other words, the parallelism in this text indicates that "our brother" Timothy *is* a "little one" (βραχύς, 13:22), one of those through whom Hebrews has been *sent* (ἀπολελυμένον)[76] In further support of this suggestion, it is interesting to note that Timothy is described in the Apostle Paul's letters as an ἀδελφός ("brother," 1 Thess 3:2; Phil 1:1), a τέκνον ("child," i.e. *little one*, cf. 1 Cor 4:17; 1 Tim 1:2; 2 Tim 1:2), and functionally as one "sent" (cf. ἔπεμψα) to minister to the church of Corinth (1 Cor 4:17).

---

76. Interestingly, ἀπολύω is used similarly in Acts 13:3 to describe the church at Antioch's sending of Saul and Barnabas: τότε νηστεύσαντες καὶ προσευξάμενοι καὶ ἐπιθέντες τὰς χεῖρας αὐτοῖς ἀπέλυσαν.

1 Cor 4:17

διὰ τοῦτο ἔπεμψα ὑμῖν Τιμόθεον ὅς ἐστίν μου τέκνον ἀγαπητὸν καὶ πιστὸν ἐν κυρίῳ ὃς ὑμᾶς ἀναμνήσει τὰς ὁδούς μου τὰς ἐν Χριστῷ Ἰησοῦ

Because of this I sent Timothy to you, who is my beloved child and faithful one in the Lord, who will remind you of my ways in Christ [Jesus].

In summary, the application of our method to the final micro link cluster in Hebrews, 13:22–25, yields potentially significant new evidence regarding Hebrews' authorship. Namely, that *Hebrews was sent to its first readers from an author in Italy through Timothy*. The clear correspondence demonstrated between the form of 13:22–25 and that of each of the micro link clusters examined also serves as further confirmation that the epilogue is indeed part of the original text of Hebrews.[77]

- A. [22] I encourage you, brothers, to accept the word of encouragement
  - B. for I also have sent to you through "little ones."
  - B'. [23] You know our brother Timothy who has been sent, with whom I will see you if he comes soon.
- A'. [24] Greet all your leaders and all the saints. Those from Italy greet you. [25] May grace be with you all!

6.5 Conclusions

This investigation into macro link clusters has found that Hebrews is a discourse comprised of four overlapping sections which may be further subdivided into thirteen sections and an epilogue. Since each subsection and section begins and ends with a topic sentence which unites together the information it summarizes,[78] a summary of the discourse as a whole may be obtained by compiling these sentences in one summary (consisting

---

77. *Contra* Vanhoye, *Structure*, 31–36, who reads 13:22–25 as a later addition to the text. Cf. Ellingworth, *Hebrews*, 692, who notes that "various factors have led some scholars to believe that this chapter, or parts of it, did not originally form part of Hebrews."

78. Cf. discussion in 3.4; Levinsohn, *Discourse Features*, 198; and Westfall, *Discourse Analysis*, 73.

of either thirteen or four parts). A summary of the discourse at the subsection level (beginning at subsection 4) may be seen below.[79]

> **4.** Therefore, since we have a great high priest who has passed through the heavens, Jesus, the Son of God, let us hold fast the confession! For we do not have a high priest who is unable to sympathize with our weaknesses, but one who has been tested in all things like us without sin. Let us therefore draw near with confidence to the throne of grace, so that we might receive mercy and find grace for the time of need. (4:14–16)
>
> **5.** We have much to say about this but it is difficult to say because you have become lazy with regard to your listening. (5:11)
>
> **6.** But we have been persuaded of things which are better and have salvation for you, beloved, even if we speak in this way. For God is not unjust to forget your work and the love you have shown in his name by serving the saints and continuing to serve. But we desire for each of you to show the same zeal until the end so that you might have the full assurance of hope and not become lazy but rather imitators of those who inherit the promises through faith and patience. For when God promised Abraham, because there was no-one greater by whom to swear, he swore by himself saying: "I will bless and multiply you." And thus he obtained the promise through patience. (6:9–15)
>
> **7.** This we have as an anchor for the soul, safe and secure and an entry inside the curtain since Jesus has entered for us as a forerunner on our behalf, having become high priest forever according to the order of Melchizedek. (6:19–20)
>
> **8.** And the point of what we are saying is that we have this kind of high priest, who is seated at the right hand of the throne of the Majesty in the heavens, a *minister* in the holies and the true tent, which the Lord built, not man. For every high priest is appointed to offer gifts and sacrifices, which is why it was necessary that this high priest also have something to offer. (8:1–3)
>
> **9.** But when Christ became high priest of the good things which have come, he went in once for all time through the greater and more perfect tent which is not man-made—that is not of this creation—into the holies, not through the blood of goats and bulls but through his own blood, having secured an eternal

---

79. In cases where the subsection has been arranged concentrically (i.e. subsections 6, 10 and 12), only the first half is here represented.

redemption. For if the blood of bulls and goats and the sprinkling of the ashes of a heifer cleanses those defiled for the purification of the flesh, *how much more* will the blood of Jesus, who through the eternal Spirit offered himself without blemish to God, cleanse our conscience from dead works in order to serve the living God! (9:11–14)

10. Therefore, since we have confidence of an entrance into the holies by the blood of Jesus, a freshly killed and living way which he has opened up for us through the curtain, this is his flesh, and a great high priest over the House of God, let us draw near with a true heart in full assurance of faith, hearts having been sprinkled from an evil conscience and the body washed with pure water. Let us hold fast the confession of hope without swerving, for the promiser is faithful. And let us consider one another with a view to stimultation of love and good works, not neglecting our gatherings, as is the habit of some, but encouraging, and this by as much more as you see the day draw near. For if we go on wilfully sinning after receiving knowledge of the truth, there no longer remains a sacrifice for sins but only a fearful expectation of judgement and a fury of fire which is about to consume the adversaries. Anyone setting aside the Law of Moses died without mercy on basis of two or three witnesses. How much worse do you suppose will be the punishment deserved by the one who tramples the Son of God? (10:19–29)

11. Therefore do not cast off your confidence, which has a great reward. For you have need of endurance in order that having done God's will you might experience the promise. For in such a little while, the coming one will come and will not delay and my righteous one will live by faith. And if he shrinks back, my soul will not be pleased with him. But *we are not* of those who shrink back into destruction but of faith for the preservation of the soul. And *faith is* the substance of the things hoped for, the proof of things which may not be seen. For by this the ancients were commended. (10:35—11:2)

12. Therefore since we also have such a great cloud of witnesses surrounding us, let us run the race before us with endurance, throwing off every obstacle and sin which entangles, and fixing our eyes on Jesus, the pioneer and perfecter of faith, who, instead of the joy surrounding him, endured the cross, despising the shame, and is seated at the right hand of the throne of God. For consider him who endured such great hostility from sinners for our sake so that your souls might not grow weary or faint-hearted. You have not yet resisted to the point of bloodshed in your struggles with sin. And have you completely forgotten the encouragement which addresses you as sons: "My Son, do not despise the discipline of the Lord nor give up when reproved by him. For the Lord disciplines the one he loves and chastises every son he accepts"? (12:1–6)

13. Therefore strengthen your weakened hands and paralysed knees and make straight paths for your feet so that what is lame might not be put out of joint but instead healed. Pursue peace with all and the sanctification without which no-one will see the Lord, guarding lest anyone fall from the grace of God, lest any bitter root spring up and through this defile many, lest anyone be immoral or worldly like Esau, who gave up his birthright for a single meal! (12:12–16)

Epilogue: I encourage you, brothers, to accept the word of encouragement for I also have sent to you through "little ones."

The message of Hebrews may also be sketched in four parts at the section level as follows.

I. 1:1–4

Long ago, at many times and in many ways, God spoke to our fathers by the prophets, but in these last days he has spoken to us by his Son, whom he appointed the heir of all things, through whom also he created the world. He is the radiance of the glory of God. And bearing the exact imprint of his nature, and the universe by the word of his power, having made purification for sins, he sat down at the right hand of the Majesty on high, having become as much superior to angels as the name he has inherited is more excellent than theirs.

II. 4:14—5:1

Therefore, since we have a great high priest who has passed through the Heavens, Jesus, the Son of God, let us hold fast the confession! For we do not have a high priest who is unable to sympathize with our weaknesses, but one who has been tested in all things like us without sin. Let us therefore draw near with confidence to the throne of Grace, so that we might receive mercy and find grace for the time of need. For every high priest chosen from men is appointed on behalf of men to the things of God, in order that he might offer up gifts and sacrifices for sins.

III. 8:1–3

And the summary of what we are saying is that we have this kind of high priest, who is seated at the right hand of the Throne of the Majesty in the Heavens, a minister of the holies and the true tent, which the Lord built, not man. For every high priest is appointed to offer gifts and sacrifices; thus it was necessary for this priest also to have something to offer.

IV. 10:19–25

Therefore, brothers, since we have confidence to enter the holy places by the blood of Jesus, by the new and living way that he opened for us through the curtain, that is, through his flesh, and since we have a great priest over the house of God, let us draw near with a true heart in full assurance of faith, with our hearts sprinkled clean from an evil conscience and our bodies washed with pure water. Let us hold fast the confession of hope without wavering, for he who promised is faithful. And let us consider how to stir up one another to love and good works, not neglecting to meet together, as is the habit of some, but encouraging one another, and all the more as you see the Day drawing near.

Based on observations of parallelism within the epilogue (13:22–25), this chapter also concludes that Hebrews was composed by an author residing in Italy and sent to its original readers through Timothy.

7
Conclusion

THIS STUDY HAS EXAMINED the location and function of link clusters within Hebrews in order to cast light on Hebrews' choice and use of language, literary structure, relationship to the LXX, genre, authorship, and overall meaning. For present purposes, "link clusters" have been defined as two sentences or larger semantic units which demonstrate a higher degree of linkage than would be expected from common lexical repetition and thereby show convincing evidence of textual organization.[1]

Chapter 2 presented an enquiry into the findings of previous scholarship regarding the phenomenon of link clusters within Hebrews. It considered and critiqued the work of six scholars who have made the greatest contributions to the topic to date (Nauck, Vanhoye, Guthrie, Rhee, Westfall, and Heil) and showed that while many have recognized unusual patterns of repetition in Hebrews, and that on occasion these patterns seem to serve a structural purpose within the discourse, the *significance*, *extent* and *combined structural function* of this repetition has not been fully appreciated.

Chapter 3 outlined a method, informed by the wider linguistic discipline of cohesion analysis, by which link clusters might be identified and their function analyzed within the discourse. Clear parameters for the types and forms of repetition to be addressed were established, the terms "link" and "link cluster" carefully defined, and a four-step heuristic device developed by which link clusters might be detected and examined (as follows): (i) identify link clusters within the text; (ii) examine the location of links within each cluster for evidence of any potential structuring

---

1. Cf. 3.3.2 for discussion on the meaning of common lexical repetition and the criteria by which a "higher degree of linkage" might be observed.

function for repetition; (iii) seek to understand the topical function of repetition within individual clusters; (iv) seek to understand the relationship between link clusters within the discourse as a whole.

In chapters 4 to 6, which contain the analysis proper, it was shown that link clusters represent a commonly occurring and significant feature of Hebrews which may be found throughout the discourse at both the micro and macro level of the text and which serve a range of important functions. Chapter 4 embarked on a detailed analysis of the first seven micro link clusters in Hebrews which was supplemented by additional evidence of intertextual link clusters within the same part of the text (1:1–3:8). The chapter demonstrated that the author repeatedly uses link clusters to group his discourse into a series of overlapping concentric units, each of which consists of two or more pairs of balanced parallel phrases which in combination clarify its meaning and emphasis.

Following this, chapter 5 investigated the formal and topical relationships between these micro clusters and other macro link clusters within Hebrews 1–4, seeking to uncover the reasons for the author's decision to structure his text in this way and to understand the combined function of link clusters within the text. It found that micro clusters function as overlapping steps in an argument which proceeds in linear fashion and which is grouped into three subsections (1:1—2:4; 2:1—3:2; 4:1—4:14) and one section (1:1—4:14) by macro link clusters which also serve as matched pairs of topic sentences, summarizing the content of each. It also detected a further kind of textual patterning involving repetition which occurs throughout Hebrews and seemingly functions as topic markers which draw the attention to readers/hearers to each new point in the discourse.

Lastly, chapter 6 identified and examined each of the remaining macro link clusters in Hebrews, showing that they function consistently as parallel topic sentences which both summarize the content of each section and subsection within the text and reveal the structure of Hebrews as a whole. The chapter also offered a brief analysis of the final micro link cluster in Hebrews (13:22–25), demonstrating the parallelism within it (consistent with the form of each of the units identified in chapter 4), and offering a new reading of these verses which yields two important clues regarding the authorship of Hebrews (see following discussion on authorship).

CONCLUSION

Based on these investigations, a number of conclusions of a more general nature may be drawn together with several suggestions for further research.

First, this study has demonstrated that link clusters in Hebrews reflect authorial *design* rather than an accident of transmission. This has been seen not only in the strength, frequency, and range of connections and their careful concentric arrangement within each cluster addressed, but also in the author's tendency to use similar groups of words and phrases within adjacent texts, even when their referents are obviously different (e.g., τοῖς ἀκουσθεῖσιν, 2:1, and τῶν ἀκουσάντων, 2:3) and their inclusion is awkward (e.g., λαβοῦσα, 2:3) and/or not easily explained on conventional topical grounds (e.g., ποιησάμενος, 1:3, and παντός, 2:15).

Second, this study has shown that, though previously overlooked, intratextual link clusters at both the micro and macro level of the text serve in combination to reveal the literary structure of Hebrews. By means of micro link clusters, the discourse is grouped into a series of thirty nine overlapping units, each of which is comprised of two or more pairs of balanced parallel phrases which have been concentrically arranged: Hebrews 1:1-4; 1:3-6; 1:7-14; 2:1-4; 2:5-9; 2:8c-18; 3:1-8; 3:5-19; 4:1-12; 4:12-13; 4:14—5:10; 5:11—6:12; 6:9-18; 6:19—7:3; 7:4-10; 7:11-17; 7:15-26; 7:26—8:1; 8:1-5; 8:6-13; 9:1-8; 9:6-12; 9:11-28; 10:1-4; 10:5-22; 10:19-38; 10:39—11:4; 11:3-7; 11:8-16; 11:17-22; 11:23-28; 11:29-40; 12:1-13; 12:14-25; 12:25-29; 12:28—13:10; 13:10-14; 13:15-21; and 13:22-25.

Macro link clusters, meanwhile, mark out the beginning and end of each of four overlapping sections (1:1—4:14; 4:14—8:3; 8:1—10:22; and 10:19—13:22) and thirteen overlapping subsections (1:1—2:4; 2:1—3:2; 2:17—4:16; 4:14—5:10; 5:11—6:12; 6:9-18; 6:17—8:2; 8:1—9:12; 9:11—10:24; 10:19-38; 10:35—12:2; 12:1-13; 12:12—13:21) within the discourse. The interaction between these units, subsections and sections and the overall structure which results may be seen in the diagram below, which also summarizes the topical content of each section (fig. 21).[2]

I. Hebrews 1:1—4:14

Pay attention to Jesus, the Son, apostle and high priest of our confession, through whom God has spoken salvation to us!

---

2. Sections and exhortatory material are marked in **bold**, subsections in italics, and units in unmarked text.

1. 1:1—2:4   1:1-4
                1:3-6
                1:7-14
2. 2:1—3:2   2:1-4
                2:5-9
                2:8c-18
3. 3:1—4:14   3:1-8
                3:5-19
                4:1-12
                4:12-13

II. Hebrews 4:14—8:3

Since Jesus, our high priest, is both great, having become priest forever according to the order of Melchizedek, and yet able to sympathize with our weaknesses, having been tested like us, **let us draw near** to him with confidence for mercy.

4. 4:14—5:10   4:14-5:10
5. 5:11—6:12   5:11-6:12
6. 6:9-18   6:9-18
7. 6:19—8:1   6:19-7:3
                7:4-10
                7:11-17
                7:15-26
                7:26-8:1

III. Hebrews 8:1—10:22

Jesus has offered up once-for-all-time an acceptable sacrifice for sin—his own precious blood, which has the power to sanctify all who draw near to God through him—and now serves in the heavenly places as our great, exalted high priest.

8. 8:1—9:12   8:1-5
                8:6-13
                9:1-8
                9:6-12
9. 9:11—10:24 9:11-28
                10:1-4
                10:5-22

IV. Hebrews 10:19—13:22

*Therefore, being confident of an entry into the holy places by Jesus' blood, **let us draw near** by faith, **let us hold fast** to what we hope for even in suffering, and **let us persist with love and good deeds** while we await his return.*

10.	10:19–38	10:19–38
11.	10:35—12:2	10:39—11:4
		11:3–7
		11:8–16
		11:17–22
		11:23–28
		11:29–40
12.	12:1–13	12:1–13
13.	12:12—13:21	12:14–25
		12:25–29
		12:28—13:10
		13:10–14
		13:15–21
	Epilogue	13:22–25

Viewed in light of these assembled findings, Hebrews emerges as a multi-connected, intricately assembled discourse in which repetition serves a number of important functions simultaneously at three distinct levels of discourse (micro, subsectional and sectional). Although this presentation differs from previous structural offerings, it better accounts for Hebrews' use of conjunctions (and especially γάρ, e.g., 1:5, 2:5, 10, 16, 18) than previous attempts. It also confirms and develops earlier intimations regarding Hebrews' use of transitional material, demonstrating that overlap represents a key feature of this text which allows its author *both* to move seamlessly from one unit/subsection/section to the next without wasting words *and* to bring out more than one meaning from certain words and phrases by their shared participation within two or more different contexts (e.g., διεληλυρότα τοὺς οὐρανούς, 4:14, which belongs to both 3:1—4:14 and 4:14—5:10).

While further research is clearly needed to confirm and/or correct our analysis and to examine each of the remaining micro link clusters in Hebrews (a provisional sketch of which may be found in the Appendix), this study thus represents a potential solution to the "unsolved problem"[3] of the structure of Hebrews.

Third, this dissertation has shown that Hebrews also utilizes intertextual link clusters throughout chapters 1–3 to establish similar kinds of formal connections (to those noted above), again involving multiple points of contact, with a wide range of external texts from the LXX (Num 12:7; Deut 6:10/11:29; 1 Chron 17:14; 1 Sam 2:35; 2 Sam 7:14; 1 Chron 17:13; Pss 2:7; 8:5–7; 21:23; 44:7–8; 88:28; 94:7–11; 101:26; 103:4; and 110:1; Isa 8:17; 41:8–10). In this way, the author clarifies his source material with precision. The significance of this observation lies in the fact that it identifies a means by which the importance of a particular LXX text to Hebrews' author, and thereby its likely influence in the discourse, might be objectively determined. For where multiple connections may be found between the vocabulary used in Hebrews and an external text (e.g., Isa 41:8–10), this represents a firm basis for its interpretation in light of the earlier context.

The identification of intertextual link clusters in Hebrews also opens up three further avenues for research into Hebrews' relationships with other literature, as follows. Further work is needed, first, to uncover and analyze intertextual link clusters involving the LXX within chapters 3–13 (i.e. the part of the text not addressed by this study), and particularly those marked as most significant by the extent of repetition (e.g., Ps 94:7–11 and Jer 31:31–34). Second, given Hebrews' tendency to derive meaning from more than one formally related text in combination, more attention should be paid to the relationship between these background texts themselves, and how this combined interaction shapes Hebrews' interpretation. By way of example, the extraordinary correlation between the language of Ps 94:7–11/Heb 3:7–4:1 and Numbers 14 and 32:6–15 strongly suggests a far more significant topical role for these Numbers texts in Hebrews 1–4 than has been generally recognized. Third, given that Hebrews' form and language is also almost certainly influenced by a number of non-LXX texts (e.g., Sirach in Hebrews 11), more needs to be done to understand the extent and significance of these connections for Hebrews according to the method used in this study.

Fourth, this study has demonstrated that both intra- and intertextual link clusters serve a similar and crucial *topical* function within Hebrews by the creation of parallelism between otherwise unrelated texts,

---

3. Aune, *New Testament*, 213.

which helps to clarify their meaning. As was shown in chapter 4, by carefully arranging his discourse into a series of balanced parallel phrases or sentences so that any given text has at least one partner text, the author is able both to indicate the point of his interest with precision and to emphasize its relative importance by describing the same event/person/action/exhortation twice from slightly different perspectives. This kind of textual patterning also allows him to further illuminate the meaning of his material by (i) introducing subtle yet significant variations, (ii) juxtaposing opposite ideas, and (iii) establishing instantial equivalents between partner texts. For example (i), by replacing αὐτόν and αὐτόν (2:7) with τόν and Ἰησοῦν (2:9) and changing the tense, the author alerts readers to his distinctive interpretation of Psalm 8 as messianic prophecy which has now been fulfilled by Jesus. Alternatively (ii), by juxtaposing the descriptions from (LXX) Psalm 101 of the Son's work at the beginning (1:10) and end (1:12) of time, he emphatically contrasts Jesus' eternal nature with the temporality of all creation. Finally, with regard to (iii), the clear parallelism between 2:8c–10 and 14–17 makes clear that the description of Jesus as τὸν ἀρχηγὸν τῆς σωτηρίας αὐτῶν (2:10) is best understood in the light of ἀρχιερεύς in 2:17 as denoting his role as the "pioneer leader/ initiator/first cause" of salvation, who brings forgiveness through his offering of a perfect sacrifice for sins.[4]

Given that this parallelism has been largely overlooked by modern scholarship, the identification of a topical function for link clusters represents one of the most important findings of this study and has yielded a raft of new exegetical insights into Hebrews 1:1–3:8 (cf. the list at 4.3). Since there is good evidence to suggest that the remainder of the text (3:9–13) has been similarly patterned by repetition, it also opens up an avenue for further study which promises to be equally fruitful.

Fifth, this study has found that macro clusters also serve an additional topical role in Hebrews, functioning as topic sentences which introduce each section and subsection of the text (noted above) with a summary of its content. On the basis of this observation, a summary of the discourse as a whole may be attained by reading together each of

---

4. As noted previously (see 4.2.9), much the same kind of topical function has also been found with regard to Hebrews' use of link clusters, with the author commonly bringing out new meanings from old forms of words by introducing subtle yet significant variation to his source material, changing (or at least sharpening) its referents, and re-interpreting its meaning in its new context.

the introductory topic sentences in sequence at either the subsection or section level (cf. 6.5).

Sixth, Hebrews' distinctive use of repetition and various other rhetorical devices aimed to catch the ear of its hearers represents fresh evidence in support of the growing consensus of opinion that, whatever else it might be, Hebrews is most clearly not a "true" epistle.[5] This is not to suggest, as some have argued, that "the written text was *not* crafted for the eye but for the ear"[6] as though literary analysis were no longer necessary. Quite the contrary, this study has substantially added to the view that Hebrews bears all the hallmarks of having been written by a skillful author using the most sophisticated techniques.[7] Nevertheless, the study demonstrates and strongly affirms the need to analyze Hebrews *both* as written document *and* preached word.[8] The importance of this insight cannot be overstated for, as has been seen, blindness to the dual nature of Hebrews can lead modern readers to miss not only "the persuasive element"[9] of the discourse but also many of the most important determinants of its meaning. Put simply, it is no longer appropriate to read Hebrews as one might read Romans or 1 Corinthians without regard to the significant body of evidence which attests to its orality. Clearly, further research is needed in this area and especially into the existence or otherwise of other genetically related texts within antiquity.[10]

---

5. Trotter, *Interpreting the Epistle to the Hebrews*, 64. See Guthrie, "New Testament Exegesis," 597, who notes that "the book is replete with qualities pointing to the orality of this text; for example, alliteration, rhyme, short sentence structuree, and forms of direct address"; deSilva, *Despising the Shame*, 31–33; Eisenbaum, *Heroes*, 137; and Cosby, *Rhetorical Composition*, 4.

6. Lane, *Hebrews 1–8*, lxxvi. Cf. Eisenbaum, *Heroes*, 137, who differentiates between the work "originally intended for oral presentation, and the text in its timeless written form," claiming that "oral presentation provides the primary context for rhetorical writing"; and Cosby, *Rhetorical Composition*, 4.

7. Cf. Ellingworth, *Hebrews*, 54; and Trotter, *Interpreting the Epistle to the Hebrews*, 64, who claims that "since the final form of Hebrews is a written document, it is perhaps correct to say that oral elements are embedded in its writing, so that even some elements that . . . were intended primarily for oral persuasion, now serve the ultimate purpose of written persuasion."

8. Noting the "dual nature" of this composition, Trotter, *Interpreting*, 62, observes that "near the end of the epistle, the author asks his readers to "bear with my word of exhortation, for I have written to you briefly" (Heb 13:22). The two parts of the sentence are equally important for our understanding of Hebrews' genre: it is a document to be understood from both an oral and a written perspective."

9. Trotter, *Interpreting*, 71.

10. See, for example, Vanhoye's suggestion, *Structure*, 22, of a number of similarities between Hebrews and Wisdom.

Seventh and finally, while a full-scale investigation into the subject lies beyond the scope of this present enquiry, this study has uncovered some important new evidence concerning the vexed issue of Hebrews' authorship. Although no suitable replacement has been found,[11] modern scholars have almost universally abandoned the traditional claim of Pauline authorship, commonly citing the same two arguments, which both appear in Calvin's statement below:

> The manner of teaching and style sufficiently show that Paul was not the author, and the writer himself confesses in the second chapter that he was one of the disciples of the apostles, which is totally different from the way in which Paul spoke of himself.[12]

In response to the argument of "style," this study has demonstrated that the obvious differences between Hebrews' choice and use of language and that found in Paul may easily be explained by Hebrews' consistent and characteristic use of repetition and symmetrical parallelism for reasons of communication and *do not necessarily* point to its having been composed by a different author. Just as the same Luther who produced "The Freedom of the Christian" also penned the (formally distinct) hymn "A Mighty Fortress is our God," so it is entirely possible that the author of Romans might have chosen to express himself in Hebrews through a completely unrelated genre. With regard to the second argument, the identification of parallelism within 2:1–4 makes clear that the commonly held belief that Hebrews 2:3 reveals the author as a "second-generation Christian" is in fact the result of misexegesis. Furthermore, the detection of similar parallelism within the epilogue suggests that, whoever he was, the author wrote from Italy to his readers through Timothy (cf. 6.4). While this evidence is not sufficient, in and of itself, to reinstate Paul as the author of Hebrews, it casts serious doubt on the counter arguments and perhaps warrants a fresh appraisal.

---

11. See Ellingworth, *Hebrews*, 3–21, for discussion of each of the thirteen candidates who have been put forward in the past: namely Paul, Clement of Rome, Luke, Barnabas, Peter, Jude, Stephen, Philip the deacon, Aristion, Priscilla (and Aquila), Mary, Epaphras and Apollos; and Eisenbaum, "Locating Hebrews," 217, who speaks of the "futility" of seeking to identify the author with "a specific person known from the pages of history."

12. Calvin, *Hebrews*, 1; Cf. Eisenbaum, "Locating Hebrews," 220, who speaks of "many dissimilarities [between the letters of Paul and Hebrews], most glaringly of style."

Appendix

Micro Link Clusters in Hebrews

1:1–4

A. ¹:¹ Πολυμερῶς καὶ πολυτρόπως πάλαι ὁ θεὸς λαλήσας τοῖς πατράσιν ἐν τοῖς προφήταις ² ἐπ' ἐσχάτου τῶν ἡμερῶν τούτων ἐλάλησεν ἡμῖν ἐν υἱῷ

    B. ²ᵇ <u>ὃν ἔθηκεν κληρονόμον πάντων</u>

        C. ²ᶜ δι' οὗ καὶ ἐποίησεν τοὺς αἰῶνας

            D. ³ᵃ ὃς ὢν ἀπαύγασμα τῆς δόξης

            D' ³ᵇ καὶ χαρακτὴρ τῆς ὑποστάσεως αὐτοῦ

        C'. ³ᶜ φέρων τε τὰ πάντα τῷ ῥήματι τῆς δυνάμεως αὐτοῦ

    B'. ³ᵈ καθαρισμὸν τῶν ἁμαρτιῶν ποιησάμενος <u>ἐκάθισεν ἐν δεξιᾷ τῆς μεγαλωσύνης ἐν ὑψηλοῖς</u>

A'. ⁴ τοσούτῳ κρείττων γενόμενος τῶν ἀγγέλων ὅσῳ διαφορώτερον παρ' αὐτοὺς κεκληρονόμηκεν ὄνομα

    A. ¹:¹ While God spoke long ago in many ways and places to the Fathers by the Prophets, ² in the last of these days, he has spoken to us by the Son,

        B. whom he appointed as the heir of all,

            C. through whom he also made the universe.

                D. ³ He being the image of the Glory.

APPENDIX: MICRO LINK CLUSTERS IN HEBREWS

    D′. And the exact imprint of his substance.

    C′. And bearing all things by the word of his power,

    B′. having made atonement for sins, he sat down at the right hand of the Majesty in the Heavens,

A′. ⁴ having become greater than the messengers by as much as the name he has inherited stands out from theirs.

1:3–6

A. ¹:³ᶜ καθαρισμὸν τῶν ἁμαρτιῶν ποιησάμενος <u>ἐκάθισεν ἐν δεξιᾷ τῆς μεγαλωσύνης ἐν ὑψηλοῖς</u> ⁴ <u>τοσούτῳ κρείττων γενόμενος τῶν ἀγγέλων</u> ὅσῳ διαφορώτερον παρ' αὐτοὺς κεκληρονόμηκεν ὄνομα

    B. ⁵ τίνι γὰρ εἶπέν ποτε τῶν ἀγγέλων <u>υἱός μου εἶ σύ ἐγὼ σήμερον γεγέννηκά σε</u>

    B′. καὶ πάλιν <u>ἐγὼ ἔσομαι αὐτῷ εἰς πατέρα, καὶ αὐτὸς ἔσται μοι εἰς υἱόν</u>

A′. ⁶ ὅταν δὲ πάλιν εἰσαγάγῃ τὸν πρωτότοκον εἰς τὴν οἰκουμένην λέγει καὶ <u>προσκυνησάτωσαν αὐτῷ πάντες ἄγγελοι θεοῦ</u>

A. ¹:³ᶜ Having made atonement for sins, he is seated at the right hand of the Majesty in the Heights, ⁴ having become as much greater than the messengers as the name he has inherited stands out from theirs.

    B. ⁵ For to which of the messengers did he ever say "you are my Son, today I have begotten you"?

    B′. And again: "I will be to him as a father, and he will be to me as Son."

A′. ⁶ And again, when he leads up the Firstborn into the Heavenly world, he says: "Let even all the messengers of God worship him" (1:5–6).

1:7–14

A. ¹:⁷ καὶ πρὸς μὲν τοὺς ἀγγέλους λέγει <u>ὁ ποιῶν τοὺς ἀγγέλους αὐτοῦ πνεύματα καὶ τοὺς λειτουργοὺς αὐτοῦ πυρὸς φλόγα</u>

APPENDIX: MICRO LINK CLUSTERS IN HEBREWS

    B. ⁸ πρὸς δὲ τὸν υἱόν <u>ὁ θρόνος σου ὁ θεὸς εἰς τὸν αἰῶνα τοῦ αἰῶνος</u> καὶ ἡ ῥάβδος τῆς εὐθύτητος ῥάβδος τῆς βασιλείας σου ⁹ ἠγάπησας δικαιοσύνην καὶ ἐμίσησας ἀνομίαν διὰ τοῦτο ἔχρισέν σε ὁ θεός ὁ θεός σου ἔλαιον ἀγαλλιάσεως παρὰ τοὺς μετόχους σου

        C. ¹⁰ καί σὺ κατ' ἀρχάς κύριε τὴν γῆν ἐθεμελίωσας καὶ ἔργα τῶν χειρῶν σού εἰσιν οἱ οὐρανοί αὐτοὶ ¹¹ <u>ἀπολοῦνται σὺ δὲ διαμένεις</u>

        C'. καὶ πάντες ὡς ἱμάτιον παλαιωθήσονται ¹² καὶ ὡσεὶ περιβόλαιον ἑλίξεις αὐτούς ὡς ἱμάτιον καὶ <u>ἀλλαγήσονται σὺ δὲ ὁ αὐτὸς εἶ καὶ τὰ ἔτη σου οὐκ ἐκλείψουσιν</u>

    B'. ¹³ πρὸς τίνα δὲ τῶν ἀγγέλων εἴρηκέν ποτε <u>κάθου ἐκ δεξιῶν μου</u> ἕως ἂν θῶ τοὺς ἐχθρούς σου ὑποπόδιον τῶν ποδῶν σου

A'. ¹⁴ <u>οὐχὶ πάντες εἰσὶν λειτουργικὰ πνεύματα εἰς διακονίαν ἀποστελλόμενα</u> διὰ τοὺς μέλλοντας κληρονομεῖν σωτηρίαν

A. ¹:⁷ And about the messengers on the one hand, he says: "He makes his messengers winds and servants of him, flames of fire."

    B. ⁸ But to the Son he says, "your throne, O God, is forever. And the scepter of uprightness is the scepter of your Kingdom. ⁹ You love righteousness and hate lawlessness. Therefore God, your God, has anointed you with the oil of joy beyond your companions."

        C. ¹⁰ And "you, Lord, founded the earth in the beginning, and the Heavens are the works of your hands. ¹¹ They will perish but you remain.

        C'. "And all things will wear out like clothing ¹² and like a coat you will roll them up and they will be exchanged like a garment. But you are the same and your years will not end."

    B'. ¹³ And to which one of the messengers has he ever said: "Sit at my right hand until I make your enemies a footstool for your feet"?

APPENDIX: MICRO LINK CLUSTERS IN HEBREWS

A'. ¹⁴ Are not they all ministering spirits sent out to serve those about to inherit salvation? (1:13–14)

2:1–4

A. ²:¹ Διὰ τοῦτο δεῖ περισσοτέρως προσέχειν ἡμᾶς τοῖς ἀκουσθεῖσιν μήποτε παραρυῶμεν ² εἰ γὰρ ὁ δι' ἀγγέλων λαληθεὶς λόγος ἐγένετο βέβαιος καὶ πᾶσα παράβασις καὶ παρακοὴ ἔλαβεν ἔνδικον μισθαποδοσίαν

B. ³ **πῶς ἡμεῖς ἐκφευξόμεθα τηλικαύτης ἀμελήσαντες σωτηρίας**

A'. ἥτις ἀρχὴν λαβοῦσα λαλεῖσθαι διὰ τοῦ κυρίου ὑπὸ τῶν ἀκουσάντων εἰς ἡμᾶς ἐβεβαιώθη 4 συνεπιμαρτυροῦντος τοῦ θεοῦ σημείοις τε καὶ τέρασιν καὶ ποικίλαις δυνάμεσιν καὶ πνεύματος ἁγίου μερισμοῖς κατὰ τὴν αὐτοῦ θέλησιν;

A. 2:1 Because of this, it is necessary for us to pay much closer attention to what we have heard lest we drift. ² For if the word spoken through messengers has been established and every transgression and sin received due penalty

B. ³ **How will we escape if we neglect such a great salvation?**

A'. . . . which, having been first received spoken through the Lord by those who heard, has been established for us, 4 God adding his testimony with signs and wonders and various kinds of powers and distributions of the Holy Spirit according to his will.

2:5–9

A. ²:⁵ οὐ γὰρ ἀγγέλοις ὑπέταξεν τὴν οἰκουμένην τὴν μέλλουσαν περὶ ἧς λαλοῦμεν ⁶ διεμαρτύρατο δέ πού τις λέγων· Τί ἐστιν ἄνθρωπος ὅτι μιμνῄσκῃ αὐτοῦ ἢ υἱὸς ἀνθρώπου ὅτι ἐπισκέπτῃ αὐτόν; ⁷ ἠλάττωσας αὐτὸν βραχύ τι παρ' ἀγγέλους δόξῃ καὶ τιμῇ ἐστεφάνωσας αὐτόν

B. ⁸ <u>πάντα ὑπέταξας ὑποκάτω τῶν ποδῶν αὐτοῦ</u>

B'. <u>ἐν τῷ γὰρ ὑποτάξαι οὐδὲν ἀφῆκεν αὐτῷ ἀνυπότακτον</u>

APPENDIX: MICRO LINK CLUSTERS IN HEBREWS

A'. νῦν δὲ οὔπω ὁρῶμεν αὐτῷ τὰ πάντα ὑποτεταγμένα ⁹ τὸν δὲ βραχύ τι παρ' ἀγγέλους ἠλαττωμένον βλέπομεν Ἰησοῦν διὰ τὸ πάθημα τοῦ θανάτου δόξῃ καὶ τιμῇ ἐστεφανωμένον ὅπως χωρὶς θεοῦ ὑπὲρ παντὸς γεύσηται θανάτου

A. ²:⁵ For he has not subjected the world to come, about which we speak, to angels. ⁶ But someone has testified somewhere, saying: "What is man that you remember him? Or the Son of Man that you shepherd him? ⁷ You have made him lower than the messengers for a while. And you have crowned him with glory and honor."

B. ⁸ You have placed all things under his feet.

B'. For when he subjected all things, he left nothing unsubject to him.

A'. But now we don't yet see everything subject to him. ⁹ But we see him who was made lower than angels for a while, Jesus, crowned with glory and honor because of the suffering of death, so that by the grace of God he might taste death for all.

2:8c–18

A. ²:⁸ᶜ νῦν δὲ οὔπω ὁρῶμεν αὐτῷ τὰ πάντα ὑποτεταγμένα τὸν δὲ βραχύ τι παρ' ἀγγέλους ἠλαττωμένον ⁹ βλέπομεν Ἰησοῦν διὰ τὸ πάθημα τοῦ θανάτου δόξῃ καὶ τιμῇ ἐστεφανωμένον <u>ὅπως χωρὶς θεοῦ ὑπὲρ παντὸς γεύσηται θανάτου</u>

B. ¹⁰ ἔπρεπεν γὰρ αὐτῷ, δι' ὃν τὰ πάντα καὶ δι' οὗ τὰ πάντα <u>πολλοὺς υἱοὺς εἰς δόξαν ἀγαγόντα τὸν ἀρχηγὸν</u> τῆς σωτηρίας αὐτῶν διὰ παθημάτων τελειῶσαι

C. ¹¹ ὅ τε γὰρ ἁγιάζων καὶ οἱ ἁγιαζόμενοι ἐξ ἑνὸς πάντες

D. δι' ἣν αἰτίαν οὐκ ἐπαισχύνεται ἀδελφοὺς αὐτοὺς καλεῖν

E. ¹² λέγων ἀπαγγελῶ τὸ ὄνομά σου τοῖς ἀδελφοῖς μου

E'. ἐν μέσῳ ἐκκλησίας ὑμνήσω σε

D'. ¹³ καὶ πάλιν ἐγὼ ἔσομαι πεποιθὼς ἐπ' αὐτῷ

APPENDIX: MICRO LINK CLUSTERS IN HEBREWS

    C'. καὶ πάλιν ἰδοὺ ἐγὼ καὶ τὰ παιδία ἅ μοι ἔδωκεν ὁ θεός

  B'. ¹⁴ ἐπεὶ οὖν τὰ παιδία κεκοινώνηκεν αἵματος καὶ σαρκός καὶ αὐτὸς παραπλησίως μετέσχεν τῶν αὐτῶν ἵνα διὰ τοῦ θανάτου καταργήσῃ τὸν τὸ κράτος ἔχοντα τοῦ θανάτου τοῦτ' ἔστιν τὸν διάβολον ¹⁵ <u>καὶ ἀπαλλάξῃ τούτους ὅσοι φόβῳ θανάτου διὰ παντὸς τοῦ ζῆν ἔνοχοι ἦσαν δουλείας</u>

A'. ¹⁶ οὐ γὰρ δήπου ἀγγέλων ἐπιλαμβάνεται ἀλλὰ σπέρματος Ἀβραὰμ ἐπιλαμβάνεται ¹⁷ ὅθεν ὤφειλεν κατὰ πάντα τοῖς ἀδελφοῖς ὁμοιωθῆναι ἵνα ἐλεήμων γένηται καὶ πιστὸς ἀρχιερεὺς τὰ πρὸς τὸν θεόν <u>εἰς τὸ ἱλάσκεσθαι τὰς ἁμαρτίας τοῦ λαοῦ</u> ⁹ ἐν ᾧ γὰρ πέπονθεν αὐτὸς πειρασθείς <u>δύναται τοῖς πειραζομένοις βοηθῆσαι</u>

A. ²:⁸ᶜ But now, we don't yet see all things subject to him. ⁹ But we see him who was made lower than the messengers for a little while, Jesus, crowned with glory and honor through the suffering of death so that by the grace of God he might taste death for everyone.

  B. ¹⁰ For it was fitting for him for whom and through whom are everyone to perfect the pioneer of their salvation through suffering, so as to lead many sons into glory.

    C. ¹¹ For he who sanctifies and those being sanctified are both from the same one.

      D. Because of which, he is not ashamed to call them brothers,

        E. ¹² saying: "I will proclaim your name among my brothers."

        E'. "In the midst of the gathering I will praise you."

      D'. ¹³ And again, "I will be certain about this!"

    C'. And look again! I and the children God has given to me.

  B'. ¹⁴ Therefore, because the children have experienced blood and flesh, he also partook of these in this way

APPENDIX: MICRO LINK CLUSTERS IN HEBREWS

in order that through death he might nullify the one with authority ¹⁵ and deliver those who through fear of death were slaves throughout all of life.

A'. ¹⁶ For surely it is not angels that he helps, but the seed of Abraham! ¹⁷ Therefore he had to become like his brothers in every way, in order that he might become a merciful and faithful high priest so as to make atonement for the sins of the people. For because he himself has suffered, having been tested, he is able to help those who are being tested.

3:1-8

A. ³:¹ ὅθεν ἀδελφοὶ ἅγιοι κλήσεως ἐπουρανίου μέτοχοι <u>κατανοήσατε τὸν ἀπόστολον καὶ ἀρχιερέα τῆς ὁμολογίας ἡμῶν Ἰησοῦν</u>

B. ² πιστὸν ὄντα τῷ ποιήσαντι αὐτὸν ὡς καὶ Μωϋσῆς ἐν τῷ οἴκῳ αὐτοῦ πλείονος ³ γὰρ οὗτος δόξης παρὰ Μωϋσῆν ἠξίωται καθ' ὅσον πλείονα τιμὴν ἔχει τοῦ οἴκου ὁ κατασκευάσας αὐτόν

C. ⁴ πᾶς γὰρ οἶκος κατασκευάζεται ὑπό τινος

C'. ὁ δὲ πάντα κατασκευάσας θεός

B'. ⁵ καὶ Μωϋσῆς μὲν πιστὸς ἐν ὅλῳ τῷ οἴκῳ αὐτοῦ ὡς θεράπων εἰς μαρτύριον τῶν λαληθησομένων ⁶ Χριστὸς δὲ ὡς υἱὸς ἐπὶ τὸν οἶκον αὐτοῦ

A'. οὗ οἶκός ἐσμεν ἡμεῖς ἐὰν τὴν παρρησίαν καὶ τὸ καύχημα τῆς ἐλπίδος κατάσχωμεν ⁷ διὸ καθὼς λέγει τὸ πνεῦμα τὸ ἅγιον <u>σήμερον ἐὰν τῆς φωνῆς αὐτοῦ ἀκούσητε ⁸ μὴ σκληρύνητε τὰς καρδίας ὑμῶν</u>

A. ³:¹ Therefore, holy brothers, sharers of a heavenly call, pay attention to the apostle and high priest of our confession, Jesus,

B. ² who was faithful to him who appointed him within his house (as Moses also was). ³ For he has been counted worthy of greater glory than Moses by as much more as the builder of the house has compared with the house itself.

- C. ⁴ For every house is built by someone.
- C'. And God is the builder of everything.
- B'. ⁵ And Moses was faithful on the one hand in the whole of his house as a servant, to testify to what would be spoken later, ⁶ but the Christ as Son upon his house, which we are if we hold fast the confidence and boast of hope.
- A'. Therefore as the Holy Spirit says: "Today if you hear his voice, do not harden your hearts."

3:5–19

- A. ⁵ καὶ Μωϋσῆς μὲν πιστὸς ἐν ὅλῳ τῷ οἴκῳ αὐτοῦ ὡς θεράπων εἰς μαρτύριον τῶν λαληθησομένων
  - B. ⁶ Χριστὸς δὲ ὡς υἱὸς ἐπὶ τὸν οἶκον αὐτοῦ <u>ὅς οἶκός ἐσμεν ἡμεῖς ἐὰν τὴν παρρησίαν καὶ τὸ καύχημα τῆς ἐλπίδος κατάσχωμεν</u>
    - C. ⁷ διὸ καθὼς λέγει τὸ πνεῦμα τὸ ἅγιον <u>σήμερον ἐὰν τῆς φωνῆς αὐτοῦ ἀκούσητε</u> ⁸ **μὴ σκληρύνητε τὰς καρδίας ὑμῶν ὡς ἐν τῷ παραπικρασμῷ** κατὰ τὴν ἡμέραν τοῦ πειρασμοῦ ἐν τῇ ἐρήμῳ ⁹ οὗ ἐπείρασαν οἱ πατέρες ὑμῶν ἐν δοκιμασίᾳ καὶ εἶδον τὰ ἔργα μου ¹⁰ τεσσεράκοντα ἔτη
      - D. διὸ προσώχθισα τῇ γενεᾷ ταύτῃ καὶ εἶπον ἀεὶ πλανῶνται τῇ καρδίᾳ αὐτοὶ
      - D'. δὲ οὐκ ἔγνωσαν τὰς ὁδούς μου ¹² ὡς ὤμοσα ἐν τῇ ὀργῇ μου εἰ εἰσελεύσονται εἰς τὴν κατάπαυσίν μου
    - C'. ¹² βλέπετε ἀδελφοί **μήποτε ἔσται** ἔν τινι ὑμῶν <u>καρδία πονηρὰ ἀπιστίας</u> ἐν τῷ ἀποστῆναι ἀπὸ θεοῦ ζῶντος ¹³ ἀλλ ἀπαρακαλεῖτε ἑαυτοὺς καθ' ἑκάστην ἡμέραν ἄχρις οὗ τὸ Σήμερον καλεῖται <u>ἵνα **μὴ σκληρυνθῇ**</u> τις ἐξ ὑμῶν ἀπάτῃ τῆς ἁμαρτίας
  - B'. ¹⁴ <u>μέτοχοι γὰρ τοῦ Χριστοῦ γεγόναμεν ἐάνπερ τὴν ἀρχὴν τῆς ὑποστάσεως μέχρι τέλους βεβαίαν κατάσχωμεν</u> ¹⁵ ἐν τῷ λέγεσθαι Σήμερον ἐὰν τῆς φωνῆς αὐτοῦ ἀκούσητε μὴ σκληρύνητε τὰς καρδίας ὑμῶν ὡς ἐν τῷ παραπικρασμῷ

APPENDIX: MICRO LINK CLUSTERS IN HEBREWS

A'.   ¹⁶ τίνες γὰρ ἀκούσαντες παρεπίκραναν ἀλλ' οὐ πάντες οἱ ἐξελθόντες ἐξ Αἰγύπτου διὰ Μωϋσέως ¹⁷ τίσιν δὲ προσώχθισεν τεσσεράκοντα ἔτη οὐχὶ τοῖς ἁμαρτήσασιν ὧν τὰ κῶλα ἔπεσεν ἐν τῇ ἐρήμῳ ¹⁸ τίσιν δὲ ὤμοσεν μὴ εἰσελεύσεσθαι εἰς τὴν κατάπαυσιν αὐτοῦ εἰ μὴ τοῖς ἀπειθήσασιν ¹⁹ καὶ βλέπομεν ὅτι οὐκ ἠδυνήθησαν εἰσελθεῖν δι' ἀπιστίαν

A.   ⁵ And Moses was faithful in the whole of his house as servant, as evidence for what would be spoken in the future,

    B.   ⁶ But Christ [was faithful] as the Son over his house, which we are if we hold fast the confidence and boast of hope.

        C.   ⁷ Therefore, as the Holy Spirit says today: "If you hear his voice, ⁸ **do not harden your hearts** as in the wilderness on the day of testing in the desert, ⁹ where your fathers tested by testing and saw my works ¹⁰ for forty years".

            D.   Because of this I was angry with *this generation* and said: "*They* always go astray in their heart"

            D'.   And *they* did not know my ways ¹¹ as I swore in my anger. Will they enter into my rest?

        C'.   ¹² Brothers, **let there not** be in anyone of you an evil heart of unbelief by which you fall from the living God. ¹³ But encourage each other every day, while-ever it is still called "today" so that not one of you might be hardened by the deceitfulness of sin.

    B'.   ¹⁴ For we have become sharers of Christ, if we hold fast the beginning of the substance until the end ¹⁵ while it says: "Today, If you hear his voice, do not harden your hearts as in the rebellion".

A'.   ¹⁶ For who were those who heard and yet rebelled? Were they not all those who went out from Egypt through Moses? ¹⁷ And with whom was he angry for forty years? Was it not those who sinned whose bodies fell in the desert? ¹⁸ And to whom did he swear that they would not enter his rest if not those who disobeyed? ¹⁹ And we see that they were not able to enter because of unbelief.

4:1-12

A. ⁴:¹ **Φοβηθῶμεν οὖν μήποτε** καταλειπομένης ἐπαγγελίας εἰσελθεῖν εἰς τὴν κατάπαυσιν αὐτοῦ δοκῇ τις ἐξ ὑμῶν ὑστερηκέναι ² καὶ γάρ ἐσμεν εὐηγγελισμένοι καθάπερ κἀκεῖνοι ἀλλ' οὐκ ὠφέλησεν ὁ λόγος τῆς ἀκοῆς ἐκείνους μὴ συγκεκερασμένους τῇ πίστει τοῖς ἀκούσασιν

    B. ³ εἰσερχόμεθα γὰρ εἰς κατάπαυσιν οἱ πιστεύσαντες καθὼς εἴρηκεν ὡς ὤμοσα ἐν τῇ ὀργῇ μου εἰ εἰσελεύσονται εἰς τὴν κατάπαυσίν μου καίτοι τῶν ἔργων ἀπὸ καταβολῆς κόσμου γενηθέντων

        C. ⁴ εἴρηκεν γάρ που περὶ τῆς ἑβδόμης οὕτως καὶ κατέπαυσεν ὁ θεὸς ἐν τῇ ἡμέρᾳ τῇ ἑβδόμῃ ἀπὸ πάντων τῶν ἔργων αὐτοῦ ⁵ καὶ ἐν τούτῳ πάλιν εἰ εἰσελεύσονται εἰς τὴν κατάπαυσίν μου ⁶ ἐπεὶ οὖν ἀπολείπεται τινὰς εἰσελθεῖν εἰς αὐτήν καὶ οἱ πρότερον εὐαγγελισθέντες οὐκ εἰσῆλθον δι' ἀπείθειαν

        C'. ⁷ πάλιν τινὰ ὁρίζει ἡμέραν Σήμερον ἐν Δαυὶδ λέγων μετὰ τοσοῦτον χρόνον καθὼς προείρηται Σήμερον ἐὰν τῆς φωνῆς αὐτοῦ ἀκούσητε μὴ σκληρύνητε τὰς καρδίας ὑμῶν ⁸ εἰ γὰρ αὐτοὺς Ἰησοῦς κατέπαυσεν οὐκ ἂν περὶ ἄλλης ἐλάλει μετὰ ταῦτα ἡμέρας ⁹ ἄρα ἀπολείπεται σαββατισμὸς τῷ λαῷ τοῦ θεοῦ

    B'. ¹⁰ ὁ γὰρ εἰσελθὼν εἰς τὴν κατάπαυσιν αὐτοῦ καὶ αὐτὸς κατέπαυσεν ἀπὸ τῶν ἔργων αὐτοῦ ὥσπερ ἀπὸ τῶν ἰδίων ὁ θεός

A'. ¹¹ **σπουδάσωμεν οὖν εἰσελθεῖν** εἰς ἐκείνην τὴν κατάπαυσιν **ἵνα μὴ** ἐν τῷ αὐτῷ τις ὑποδείγματι **πέσῃ** τῆς ἀπειθείας ¹² Ζῶν γὰρ ὁ λόγος τοῦ θεοῦ καὶ ἐνεργὴς καὶ τομώτερος ὑπὲρ πᾶσαν μάχαιραν δίστομον καὶ διϊκνούμενος ἄχρι μερισμοῦ ψυχῆς καὶ πνεύματος

A. ⁴:¹ Therefore, let us fear lest while the promise to enter into his rest remains, anyone of you should seem to be found wanting. ² For we too have been evangelized just as they

APPENDIX: MICRO LINK CLUSTERS IN HEBREWS

were but the word which they heard did not help those who were not united together to what was heard by faith.

B. ³ For *we who believe* enter into rest, just as surely as he has said: "As I swore in my wrath, *they will not* enter into my rest", even though works were finished from the creation of the world.

C. ⁴ For he has spoken about the Sabbath somewhere as follows: "And God rested on the seventh day from all of his works", ⁵ and again in this: "They will not enter into my rest". ⁶ It remains therefore for some to enter into this *afterwards*, while those who were evangelized formerly did not enter because of disobedience.

C'. ⁷ Again He appoints a particular day, "today", in David, saying so long afterwards as he had said before: "Today, if you hear his voice, do not harden your hearts". ⁸ For if Jesus had given rest to them, He would not have spoken of another day after this. ⁹ Therefore there remains a Sabbath for the people of God.

B'. ¹⁰ For the one entering into his rest has rested himself also from his works, just as God has from his own.

A'. ¹¹ Therefore let us hasten to enter into that rest in order that no-one among you might fall by the same example of disobedience. ¹² For the word of God is living and effective and sharper than every two-edged sword, piercing even until the division of soul and spirit.

4:12–13

A. ¹² Ζῶν γὰρ ὁ λόγος τοῦ θεοῦ καὶ ἐνεργὴς καὶ <u>τομώτερος ὑπὲρ πᾶσαν μάχαιραν δίστομον</u>

B. καὶ διϊκνούμενος ἄχρι μερισμοῦ ψυχῆς καὶ πνεύματος ἁρμῶν τε καὶ μυελῶν

B'. ¹³ καὶ κριτικὸς ἐνθυμήσεων καὶ ἐννοιῶν καρδίας

A'. καὶ οὐκ ἔστιν κτίσις ἀφανὴς ἐνώπιον αὐτοῦ <u>πάντα δὲ γυμνὰ καὶ τετραχηλισμένα τοῖς ὀφθαλμοῖς αὐτοῦ</u> πρὸς ὃν ἡμῖν ὁ λόγος

A. ¹² For the Word of God is alive and powerful and sharper than every two-edged sword,

    B. and piercing even until the division of soul and spirit, joints and marrow.

    B′. ¹³ And it is able to judge the thoughts and intentions of the heart,

A′. And no living being is hidden before it, but all are naked and exposed before the eyes of Him *with whom* is the Word for us.

4:14–5:10

A. ¹⁴ Ἔχοντες οὖν ἀρχιερέα μέγαν διεληλυθότα τοὺς οὐρανοὺς Ἰησοῦν τὸν υἱὸν τοῦ θεοῦ κρατῶμεν τῆς ὁμολογίας ¹⁵ <u>οὐ γὰρ ἔχομεν ἀρχιερέα μὴ δυνάμενον συμπαθῆσαι ταῖς ἀσθενείαις ἡμῶν πεπειρασμένον δὲ κατὰ πάντα καθ' ὁμοιότητα χωρὶς ἁμαρτίας</u> ¹⁶ προσερχώμεθα οὖν μετὰ παρρησίας συγκεκερασμένους τῷ θρόνῳ τῆς χάριτος ἵνα λάβωμεν ἔλεος καὶ χάριν εὕρωμεν εἰς εὔκαιρον βοήθειαν

    B. ⁵:¹ πᾶς γὰρ ἀρχιερεὺς ἐξ ἀνθρώπων λαμβανόμενος ὑπὲρ ἀνθρώπων καθίσταται τὰ πρὸς τὸν θεόν ἵνα προσφέρῃ δῶρά τε καὶ θυσίας ὑπὲρ ἁμαρτιῶν ² μετριοπαθεῖν δυνάμενος τοῖς ἀγνοοῦσι καὶ πλανωμένοις ἐπεὶ καὶ αὐτὸς περίκειται ἀσθένειαν ³ καὶ δι' αὐτὴν ὀφείλει καθὼς περὶ τοῦ λαοῦ οὕτως καὶ περὶ αὐτοῦ προσφέρειν περὶ ἁμαρτιῶν

        C. ⁴ καὶ <u>οὐχ ἑαυτῷ τις λαμβάνει τὴν τιμὴν ἀλλὰ καλούμενος ὑπὸ τοῦ θεοῦ καθώσπερ καὶ Ἀαρών</u>

        C′. ⁵ <u>οὕτως καὶ ὁ Χριστὸς οὐχ ἑαυτὸν ἐδόξασεν γενηθῆναι ἀρχιερέα ἀλλ' ὁ λαλήσας πρὸς αὐτόν υἱός μου εἶ σύ ἐγὼ σήμερον γεγέννηκά σε ⁶ καθὼς καὶ ἐν ἑτέρῳ λέγει Σὺ ἱερεὺς εἰς τὸν αἰῶνα κατὰ τὴν τάξιν Μελχισέδεκ</u>

    B′. ⁷ ὃς ἐν ταῖς ἡμέραις τῆς σαρκὸς αὐτοῦ δεήσεις τε καὶ ἱκετηρίας πρὸς τὸν δυνάμενον σῴζειν αὐτὸν ἐκ θανάτου μετὰ κραυγῆς ἰσχυρᾶς καὶ δακρύων προσενέγκας καὶ εἰσακουσθεὶς ἀπὸ τῆς εὐλαβείας

A'. ⁸ <u>καίπερ ὢν υἱός ἔμαθεν ἀφ' ὧν ἔπαθεν τὴν ὑπακοήν</u> ⁹ καὶ τελειωθεὶς ἐγένετο πᾶσιν τοῖς ὑπακούουσιν αὐτῷ αἴτιος σωτηρίας αἰωνίου ¹⁰ προσαγορευθεὶς ὑπὸ τοῦ θεοῦ ἀρχιερεὺς κατὰ τὴν τάξιν Μελχισέδεκ

A. ⁴:¹⁴ Since then we have a great high priest who has passed through the heavens, Jesus, the Son of God, let us hold fast our confession. ¹⁵ For we do not have a high priest who is unable to sympathize with our weaknesses, but one who in every respect has been tempted as we are, yet without sin. ¹⁶ Let us then with confidence draw near to the throne of grace, that we may receive mercy and find grace to help in time of need.

    B. ⁵:¹ For every high priest, having been chosen from men, is appointed on behalf of men to the things of God in order that he might offer gifts and sacrifices for sins, ² being able to deal gently with the ignorant and wayward, because he too is surrounded by weakness. ³ And because of this he is obligated to offer sacrifices for his own sins just as he does for those of the people.

        C. ⁴ And no-one takes the honor for himself but only when called by God.

        C'. ⁵ Thus even the Christ did not glorify himself to become high priest but he said to him: "You are my Son, Today I have begotten you" ⁶ just as he says in another place: "You are a Priest forever according to the order of Melchizedek".

    B'. ⁷ He, in the days of his flesh, offered up prayers and supplications with loud cries and tears and was heard because of his reverent obedience.

A'. ⁸ Although he was the Son, he learned obedience from what he suffered. ⁹ And having been perfected has become for all those who obey him the source of eternal Salvation, ¹⁰ being designated by God high priest according to the order of Melchizedek.

APPENDIX: MICRO LINK CLUSTERS IN HEBREWS

5:11—6:12 (cf. 6.2.2)

A. ⁵:¹¹ περὶ οὗ πολὺς ἡμῖν ὁ λόγος καὶ δυσερμήνευτος λέγειν ἐπεὶ νωθροὶ γεγόνατε ταῖς ἀκοαῖς

B. ¹² καὶ γὰρ ὀφείλοντες εἶναι διδάσκαλοι διὰ τὸν χρόνον πάλιν χρείαν ἔχετε τοῦ διδάσκειν ὑμᾶς τινὰ τὰ στοιχεῖα τῆς ἀρχῆς τῶν λογίων τοῦ θεοῦ καὶ γεγόνατε χρείαν ἔχοντες γάλακτος οὐ στερεᾶς τροφῆς

C. ¹³ πᾶς γὰρ ὁ μετέχων γάλακτος ἄπειρος λόγου δικαιοσύνης νήπιος γάρ ἐστιν ¹⁴ τελείων δέ ἐστιν ἡ στερεὰ τροφή τῶν διὰ τὴν ἕξιν <u>τὰ αἰσθητήρια γεγυμνασμένα ἐχόντων πρὸς διάκρισιν καλοῦ τε καὶ κακοῦ</u>

D. ⁶:¹ διὸ ἀφέντες τὸν τῆς ἀρχῆς τοῦ Χριστοῦ λόγον ἐπὶ τὴν τελειότητα φερώμεθα μὴ πάλιν θεμέλιον καταβαλλόμενοι μετανοίας ἀπὸ νεκρῶν ἔργων καὶ πίστεως ἐπὶ θεόν βαπτισμῶν διδαχὴν ἐπιθέσεώς τε χειρῶν ἀναστάσεώς τε νεκρῶν καὶ κρίματος αἰωνίου

D'. ³ καὶ τοῦτο ποιήσομεν ἐάνπερ ἐπιτρέπῃ ὁ θεός ⁴ ἀδύνατον γὰρ τοὺς ἅπαξ φωτισθέντας γευσαμένους τε τῆς δωρεᾶς τῆς ἐπουρανίου καὶ μετόχους γενηθέντας πνεύματος ἁγίου ⁵ καὶ καλὸν γευσαμένους θεοῦ ῥῆμα δυνάμεις τε μέλλοντος αἰῶνος ⁶ καὶ παραπεσόντας πάλιν ἀνακαινίζειν εἰς μετάνοιαν ἀνασταυροῦντας ἑαυτοῖς τὸν υἱὸν τοῦ θεοῦ καὶ παραδειγματίζοντας

C'. ⁷ γῆ γὰρ ἡ πιοῦσα τὸν ἐπ' αὐτῆς ἐρχόμενον πολλάκις ὑετόν καὶ <u>τίκτουσα βοτάνην εὔθετον ἐκείνοις δι' οὓς καὶ γεωργεῖται</u> μεταλαμβάνει εὐλογίας ἀπὸ τοῦ θεοῦ ⁸ ἐκφέρουσα δὲ ἀκάνθας καὶ τριβόλους ἀδόκιμος καὶ κατάρας ἐγγύς ἧς τὸ τέλος εἰς καῦσιν

B'. ⁹ Πεπείσμεθα δὲ περὶ ὑμῶν ἀγαπητοί τὰ κρείσσονα καὶ ἐχόμενα σωτηρίας εἰ καὶ οὕτως λαλοῦμεν ¹⁰ οὐ γὰρ ἄδικος ὁ θεὸς ἐπιλαθέσθαι τοῦ ἔργου ὑμῶν καὶ τῆς ἀγάπης ἧς ἐνεδείξασθε εἰς τὸ ὄνομα αὐτοῦ διακονήσαντες τοῖς ἁγίοις καὶ διακονοῦντες

APPENDIX: MICRO LINK CLUSTERS IN HEBREWS

A′. ¹¹ ἐπιθυμοῦμεν δὲ ἕκαστον ὑμῶν τὴν αὐτὴν ἐνδείκνυσθαι σπουδὴν πρὸς τὴν πληροφορίαν τῆς ἐλπίδος ἄχρι τέλους ¹² ἵνα μὴ νωθροὶ γένησθε

A. ⁵:¹¹ We have much to say about this and it is not easy to say it because you have become slack with regard to your listening.

    B. ¹² For although you ought to be teachers by now, you need someone to again teach you the basics of the beginning of the words of God. And you have come to need milk, not solid food.

        C. ¹³ For everyone who partakes of milk is unpracticed with the word of righteousness for he is a baby. ¹⁴ And solid food is for the mature, for those who through constant practice have exercised their faculties to distinguish good from evil.

            D. ⁶:¹ Therefore, leaving the beginning word of Christ, press on to maturity, not again laying a foundation of repentance from dead works and faith in God, ² teaching of baptisms and the laying on of hands, the Resurrection and eternal judgement.

                D′. ³ And we will do this if God permits. ⁴ For it is impossible for those once enlightened, who have tasted the heavenly gift and become sharers of the Holy Spirit ⁵ and tasted the good word of God and the powers of the age to come ⁶ and fallen to again renew into repentance, since they are re-crucifying the son of God to themselves and disgracing him.

        C′. ⁷ For land which often drinks of the rain which falls on it and bears a crop pleasing to those for whom it has been farmed receives blessing from God. ⁸ But if it bears thorns and thistles, it is worthless and near the curse, the end of which is burning.

    B′. ⁹ But we have been persuaded of things which are better and have salvation for you, beloved, even if we speak in this way. ¹⁰ For God is not unjust to forget your work and the love you have shown in his name by serving the saints and continuing to serve.

A'. ¹¹ But we desire for each of you to show the same zeal until the end ¹² so that you might have the full assurance of hope and not become lazy but rather imitators of those who inherit the promises through faith and patience.

6:9–18 (cf. 6.2.3)

A. ⁹ <u>πεπείσμεθα δὲ περὶ ὑμῶν ἀγαπητοί τὰ κρείσσονα καὶ ἐχόμενα</u> σωτηρίας εἰ καὶ οὕτως λαλοῦμεν ⁹ <u>οὐ γὰρ ἄδικος ὁ θεὸς</u> ἐπιλαθέσθαι τοῦ ἔργου ὑμῶν καὶ τῆς ἀγάπης ἧς ἐνεδείξασθε εἰς τὸ ὄνομα αὐτοῦ διακονήσαντες τοῖς ἁγίοις καὶ διακονοῦντες

B. ¹¹ ἐπιθυμοῦμεν δὲ ἕκαστον ὑμῶν τὴν αὐτὴν ἐνδείκνυσθαι σπουδὴν πρὸς τὴν πληροφορίαν τῆς ἐλπίδος ἄχρι τέλους ¹² ἵνα μὴ νωθροὶ γένησθε μιμηταὶ δὲ τῶν διὰ πίστεως καὶ μακροθυμίας κληρονομούντων τὰς ἐπαγγελίας

C. ¹³ τῷ γὰρ Ἀβραὰμ ἐπαγγειλάμενος ὁ θεὸς ἐπεὶ κατ' οὐδενὸς εἶχεν μείζονος ὀμόσαι ὤμοσεν καθ' ἑαυτοῦ ¹⁴ λέγων Εἰ μὴν εὐλογῶν εὐλογήσω σε καὶ πληθύνων πληθυνῶ σε

D. ¹⁵ καὶ οὕτως μακροθυμήσας ἐπέτυχεν τῆς ἐπαγγελίας

C'. ¹⁶ ἄνθρωποι γὰρ κατὰ τοῦ μείζονος ὀμνύουσιν καὶ πάσης αὐτοῖς ἀντιλογίας πέρας εἰς βεβαίωσιν ὁ ὅρκος

B'. ¹⁷ ἐν ᾧ περισσότερον βουλόμενος ὁ θεὸς ἐπιδεῖξαι τοῖς κληρονόμοις τῆς ἐπαγγελίας τὸ ἀμετάθετον τῆς βουλῆς αὐτοῦ ἐμεσίτευσεν ὅρκῳ

A'. ¹⁸ ἵνα διὰ δύο πραγμάτων ἀμεταθέτων ἐν οἷς <u>ἀδύνατον ψεύσασθαι θεὸν ἰσχυρὰν παράκλησιν ἔχωμεν οἱ καταφυγόντες κρατῆσαι τῆς προκειμένης ἐλπίδος</u>

A. ⁶:⁹ But we have been persuaded of things which are better and have salvation for you, beloved, even if we speak in this way. ¹⁰ For God is not unjust to forget your work and the love you have shown in his name by serving the saints and continuing to serve.

B. ¹¹ But we desire for each of you to show the same zeal until the end ¹² so that you might have the full assurance of hope and not become lazy but rather imitators of those who inherit the promises through faith and patience.

C. ¹³ For when God promised Abraham, because there was no-one greater by whom to swear, he swore by himself ¹⁴ saying: "I will bless and multiply you."

D. ¹⁵ And thus he obtained the promise through patience.

C'. ¹⁶ For people swear according to someone greater, and in all of their disputes the oath is final for confirmation.

B'. ¹⁷ Because of this when God wished to prove to the heirs of the promises the unshakeability of his will even more he swore an oath,

A'. ¹⁸ so that through two unshakeable things in which it is impossible for God to lie, we who have fled to take hold of the hope lying before us might have strong encouragement.

6:19—7:3

A. ⁶:¹⁹ ἣν ὡς ἄγκυραν ἔχομεν τῆς ψυχῆς ἀσφαλῆ τε καὶ βεβαίαν καὶ εἰσερχομένην εἰς τὸ ἐσώτερον τοῦ καταπετάσματος ²⁰ ὅπου <u>πρόδρομος ὑπὲρ ἡμῶν εἰσῆλθεν Ἰησοῦς κατὰ τὴν τάξιν Μελχισέδεκ ἀρχιερεὺς γενόμενος εἰς τὸν αἰῶνα</u>

B. ⁷:¹ οὗτος γὰρ ὁ Μελχισέδεκ βασιλεὺς Σαλήμ ἱερεὺς τοῦ θεοῦ τοῦ ὑψίστου

C. ὁ συναντήσας Ἀβραὰμ ὑποστρέφοντι ἀπὸ τῆς κοπῆς τῶν βασιλέων καὶ εὐλογήσας αὐτόν

C'. ² ᾧ καὶ δεκάτην ἀπὸ πάντων ἐμέρισεν Ἀβραάμ

B'. πρῶτον μὲν ἑρμηνευόμενος βασιλεὺς δικαιοσύνης ἔπειτα δὲ καὶ βασιλεὺς Σαλήμ ὅ ἐστιν βασιλεὺς εἰρήνης

A'. ³ ἀπάτωρ ἀμήτωρ ἀγενεαλόγητος μήτε ἀρχὴν ἡμερῶν μήτε ζωῆς τέλος ἔχων <u>ἀφωμοιωμένος δὲ τῷ υἱῷ τοῦ θεοῦ μένει ἱερεὺς εἰς τὸ διηνεκές</u>

A. 6:19 We have this as a safe and secure anchor for the soul and an entry inside the curtain ²⁰ since Jesus has entered for us as a fore-runner on our behalf, having become high priest forever according to the order of Melchizedek

    B. 7:1 For this Melchizedek was the King of Salem, Priest of God Most High

        C. who met Abraham when returning from the slaughter of the kings and blessed him.

        C'. ² And Abraham gave a tenth of everything to him,

    B'. who may be translated first as King of Righteousness and then as King of Salem, which is King of Peace,

A'. ³ who is without father or mother or genealogy, not having beginning of days nor end of life, but resembling the Son of God, remains a priest forever.

7:4–10

A. ⁷:⁴ Θεωρεῖτε δὲ πηλίκος οὗτος ᾧ δεκάτην Ἀβραὰμ ἔδωκεν ἐκ τῶν ἀκροθινίων ὁ πατριάρχης

    B. ⁵ καὶ οἱ μὲν ἐκ τῶν υἱῶν Λευὶ τὴν ἱερατείαν λαμβάνοντες ἐντολὴν ἔχουσιν ἀποδεκατοῦν τὸν λαὸν κατὰ τὸν νόμον τοῦτ' ἔστιν τοὺς ἀδελφοὺς αὐτῶν καίπερ ἐξεληλυθότας ἐκ τῆς ὀσφύος Ἀβραάμ

        C. ⁶ ὁ δὲ μὴ γενεαλογούμενος ἐξ αὐτῶν δεδεκάτωκεν Ἀβραὰμ καὶ τὸν ἔχοντα τὰς ἐπαγγελίας εὐλόγηκεν

        C'. ⁷ χωρὶς δὲ πάσης ἀντιλογίας τὸ ἔλαττον ὑπὸ τοῦ κρείττονος εὐλογεῖται

    B'. ⁸ καὶ ὧδε μὲν δεκάτας ἀποθνῄσκοντες ἄνθρωποι λαμβάνουσιν ἐκεῖ δὲ μαρτυρούμενος ὅτι ζῇ

A'. ⁹ καὶ ὡς ἔπος εἰπεῖν δι' Ἀβραὰμ καὶ Λευὶ ὁ δεκάτας λαμβάνων δεδεκάτωται ¹⁰ ἔτι γὰρ ἐν τῇ ὀσφύϊ τοῦ πατρὸς ἦν ὅτε συνήντησεν αὐτῷ Μελχισέδεκ

APPENDIX: MICRO LINK CLUSTERS IN HEBREWS

A. ⁷:⁴ Behold how great is he to whom [*even*] Abraham, the Patriarch, gave a tenth of the plunder!

B. ⁵ The sons of Levi who receive the priesthood also have a command to take a tenth from the people according to the Law, that is from their brothers, although they themselves have come out from the loins of Abraham.

C. ⁶ But he who is not descended from them tithed Abraham and blessed the one who had the promises.

C'. ⁷ And beyond all dispute the greater is blessed by the lesser.

B'. ⁸ And here dying men receive the tithes, but there one about whom it is testified that he lives.

A'. ⁹ And one might even say that through Abraham, *even* Levi who receives tithes has paid the tithe. ¹⁰ For he was still in the loins of his father when Melchizedek met him.

7:11–17

A. ⁷:¹¹ εἰ μὲν οὖν τελείωσις διὰ τῆς Λευιτικῆς ἱερωσύνης ἦν ὁ λαὸς γὰρ ἐπ' αὐτῆς νενομοθέτηται τίς ἔτι χρεία κατὰ τὴν τάξιν Μελχισέδεκ ἕτερον ἀνίστασθαι ἱερέα καὶ οὐ κατὰ τὴν τάξιν Ἀαρὼν λέγεσθαι; ¹² <u>μετατιθεμένης γὰρ τῆς ἱερωσύνης ἐξ ἀνάγκης καὶ νόμου μετάθεσις γίνεται</u>

B. ¹³ <u>ἐφ' ὃν γὰρ λέγεται ταῦτα φυλῆς ἑτέρας μετέσχηκεν ἀφ' ἧς οὐδεὶς προσέσχηκεν τῷ θυσιαστηρίῳ</u>

B'. ¹⁴ <u>πρόδηλον γὰρ ὅτι ἐξ Ἰούδα ἀνατέταλκεν ὁ κύριος ἡμῶν εἰς ἣν φυλὴν περὶ ἱερέων οὐδὲν Μωϋσῆς ἐλάλησεν</u>

A'. ¹⁵ καὶ περισσότερον ἔτι κατάδηλόν ἐστιν εἰ κατὰ τὴν ὁμοιότητα Μελχισέδεκ ἀνίσταται ἱερεὺς ἕτερος ¹⁶ <u>ὃς οὐ κατὰ νόμον ἐντολῆς σαρκίνης γέγονεν ἀλλὰ κατὰ δύναμιν ζωῆς ἀκαταλύτου</u> ¹⁷ μαρτυρεῖται γὰρ ὅτι Σὺ ἱερεὺς εἰς τὸν αἰῶνα κατὰ τὴν τάξιν Μελχισέδεκ

A.   **7:11** Therefore, if perfection was possible through the Levitical priesthood (for the people receive the Law through this), what need would there still be for another priest to arise according to the order of Melchizedek and not called according to the order of Aaron? ¹² For a change of priesthood also necessitates a change of law.

B.   ¹³ For the one, about whom these things is spoken, belonged to another tribe from which no-one has ever offered at the altar.

B′.   ¹⁴ For it is clear that our Lord was descended from Judah, about which tribe Moses said nothing about priests.

A′.   ¹⁵ And <u>this</u> is made even clearer if another priest rises up ¹⁶ who has not come according to the law of flesh but according to the power of an indestructible life. ¹⁷ For it is testified: "You are a priest forever according to the order of Melchizedek".

7:15-26

A.   **7:15** καὶ περισσότερον ἔτι κατάδηλόν ἐστιν εἰ κατὰ τὴν ὁμοιότητα Μελχισέδεκ ἀνίσταται ἱερεὺς ἕτερος ¹⁶ ὃς οὐ κατὰ νόμον ἐντολῆς σαρκίνης γέγονεν ἀλλὰ <u>κατὰ δύναμιν ζωῆς ἀκαταλύτου</u> ¹⁷ μαρτυρεῖται γὰρ ὅτι Σὺ ἱερεὺς εἰς τὸν αἰῶνα κατὰ τὴν τάξιν Μελχισέδεκ

B.   ¹⁸ ἀθέτησις μὲν γὰρ γίνεται προαγούσης ἐντολῆς διὰ τὸ αὐτῆς ἀσθενὲς καὶ ἀνωφελές ¹⁹ οὐδὲν γὰρ ἐτελείωσεν ὁ νόμος ἐπεισαγωγὴ δὲ κρείττονος ἐλπίδος <u>δι' ἧς ἐγγίζομεν τῷ θεῷ</u>

C.   ²⁰ καὶ **<u>καθ' ὅσον οὐ χωρὶς ὀρκωμοσίας</u>** οἱ μὲν γὰρ χωρὶς ὀρκωμοσίας εἰσὶν ἱερεῖς γεγονότες ²¹ ὁ δὲ μετὰ ὀρκωμοσίας διὰ τοῦ λέγοντος πρὸς αὐτόν Ὤμοσεν κύριος καὶ οὐ μεταμεληθήσεται Σὺ ἱερεὺς εἰς τὸν αἰῶνα

C′.   ²² **<u>κατὰ τοσοῦτο</u>** κρείττονος διαθήκης γέγονεν ἔγγυος Ἰησοῦς

B′.   ²³ Καὶ οἱ μὲν πλείονές εἰσιν γεγονότες ἱερεῖς διὰ τὸ θανάτῳ κωλύεσθαι παραμένειν ²⁴ ὁ δὲ διὰ τὸ μένειν αὐτὸν εἰς τὸν αἰῶνα ἀπαράβατον ἔχει τὴν ἱερωσύνην ²⁵ ὅθεν καὶ σῴζειν εἰς τὸ παντελὲς δύναται <u>τοὺς προσερχομένους δι' αὐτοῦ</u> <u>τῷ θεῷ</u> πάντοτε ζῶν εἰς τὸ ἐντυγχάνειν ὑπὲρ αὐτῶν

A'. ²⁶ τοιοῦτος γὰρ ἡμῖν καὶ ἔπρεπεν ἀρχιερεύς <u>ὅσιος ἄκακος</u> <u>ἀμίαντος κεχωρισμένος ἀπὸ τῶν ἁμαρτωλῶν καὶ ὑψηλότερος</u> <u>τῶν οὐρανῶν γενόμενος</u>

A. ⁷:¹⁵ And this is made even clearer if another priest rises up according to the likeness of Melchizedek, ¹⁶ who has not come according to the law of fleshly descent but according to the power of an indestructible life. ¹⁷ For it is testified: "You are a priest forever according to the order of Melchizedek".

B. ¹⁸ For on the one hand the former command is annulled because of its weakness and uselessness— ¹⁹ for the Law perfected nothing—on the other, a better hope is brought in through which we draw near to God.

C. ²⁰ And it is better to the degree that it is not without the swearing of an oath. For there are those who are priests without the making of an oath, ²¹ but he became priest with an oath through who said to him: "The Lord has sworn and will not change his mind: You are a priest forever".

C'. ²² To the same degree Jesus has become guarantor of a better covenant.

B'. ²³ And those who have become priests are many, having been prevented through death from remaining. ²⁴ But because he remains forever, he has the priesthood without change. ²⁵ Therefore he is able to save completely those drawing near to God through him, since he always lives to intercede for them.

A'. ²⁶ For a high priest like this is clearly suitable for us—holy, innocent, unstained, having been separated from sinners and lifted up above the Heavens.

7:26–8:1

A. ⁷:²⁶ <u>τοιοῦτος γὰρ ἡμῖν καὶ ἔπρεπεν ἀρχιερεύς</u> ὅσιος ἄκακος ἀμίαντος κεχωρισμένος ἀπὸ τῶν ἁμαρτωλῶν καὶ ὑψηλότερος τῶν οὐρανῶν γενόμενος

B. ²⁷ ὃς οὐκ ἔχει καθ' ἡμέραν ἀνάγκην ὥσπερ οἱ ἀρχιερεῖς πρότερον ὑπὲρ τῶν ἰδίων ἁμαρτιῶν θυσίας ἀναφέρειν ἔπειτα τῶν τοῦ λαοῦ τοῦτο γὰρ ἐποίησεν ἐφάπαξ ἑαυτὸν ἀνενέγκας

B'. ²⁸ ὁ νόμος γὰρ ἀνθρώπους καθίστησιν ἀρχιερεῖς ἔχοντας ἀσθένειαν ὁ λόγος δὲ τῆς ὁρκωμοσίας τῆς μετὰ τὸν νόμον υἱόν εἰς τὸν αἰῶνα τετελειωμένον

A'. ⁸:¹ κεφάλαιον δὲ ἐπὶ τοῖς λεγομένοις <u>τοιοῦτον ἔχομεν ἀρχιερέα</u> ὃς ἐκάθισεν ἐν δεξιᾷ τοῦ θρόνου τῆς μεγαλωσύνης ἐν τοῖς οὐρανοῖς

A. ⁷:²⁶ For this is exactly the kind of Priest who is suitable for us: holy, innocent, unstained, separated from sinners, and having been exalted above the Heavens.

B. ²⁷ He does not have need, as these high priests, to offer sacrifices daily first for his own sins and later for those of the people for he did this once-for-all when he offered himself.

B'. ²⁸ For the Law appoints men who have weaknesses as high priests, but the Word of the Oath (which came after the Law), the Son who has been perfected forever.

A'. ⁸:¹ And the point of what we have been saying is that we have a Priest like this, who is seated at the right-hand of the Throne of the Greatness in the Heavens.

8:1–5

A. ⁸:¹ κεφάλαιον δὲ ἐπὶ τοῖς λεγομένοις τοιοῦτον <u>ἔχομεν ἀρχιερέα ὃς ἐκάθισεν ἐν δεξιᾷ τοῦ θρόνου τῆς μεγαλωσύνης ἐν τοῖς οὐρανοῖς</u> ² τῶν ἁγίων λειτουργὸς καὶ τῆς σκηνῆς τῆς ἀληθινῆς ἣν ἔπηξεν ὁ κύριος οὐκ ἄνθρωπος

APPENDIX: MICRO LINK CLUSTERS IN HEBREWS

- B. ³ πᾶς γὰρ ἀρχιερεὺς εἰς τὸ προσφέρειν δῶρά τε καὶ θυσίας καθίσταται ὅθεν ἀναγκαῖον ἔχειν τι καὶ τοῦτον ὃ προσενέγκῃ

- B'. ⁴ εἰ μὲν οὖν ἦν ἐπὶ γῆς οὐδ' ἂν ἦν ἱερεύς ὄντων τῶν προσφερόντων κατὰ νόμον τὰ δῶρα

- A'. ⁵ <u>οἵτινες ὑποδείγματι καὶ σκιᾷ λατρεύουσιν τῶν ἐπουρανίων</u> καθὼς κεχρημάτισται Μωϋσῆς μέλλων ἐπιτελεῖν τὴν σκηνήν ὅρα γάρ φησίν ποιήσεις πάντα κατὰ τὸν τύπον τὸν δειχθέντα σοι ἐν τῷ ὄρει

- A. ⁸:¹ And the point of what we are saying is that we have this kind of high priest, who is seated at the right hand of the throne of the Majesty in the Heavens, ² a *minister* in the holies and the true tent, which the Lord built, not man.

- B. ³ For every high priest is appointed to offer gifts and sacrifices. Because of which even he needed something to offer.

- B'. ⁴ If therefore he was on earth, he would not be a priest, since there are those who offer gifts according to the law

- A'. ⁵ who serve in a copy and shadow of the heavenlies, as Moses was warned when about to erect the tent. For he was told: 'make everything according to the type which you saw on the mountain.

8:6-13

- A. ⁸:⁶ νυνὶ δὲ διαφορωτέρας τέτυχεν λειτουργίας ὅσῳ καὶ κρείττονός ἐστιν διαθήκης μεσίτης ἥτις ἐπὶ κρείττοσιν ἐπαγγελίαις νενομοθέτηται ⁷ Εἰ γὰρ ἡ πρώτη ἐκείνη ἦν ἄμεμπτος οὐκ ἂν δευτέρας ἐζητεῖτο τόπος ⁸ μεμφόμενος γὰρ αὐτοὺς λέγει

- B. Ἰδοὺ ἡμέραι ἔρχονται λέγει κύριος καὶ συντελέσω ἐπὶ τὸν οἶκον Ἰσραὴλ καὶ ἐπὶ τὸν οἶκον Ἰούδα διαθήκην καινήν ⁹ οὐ κατὰ τὴν διαθήκην ἣν ἐποίησα τοῖς πατράσιν αὐτῶν ἐν ἡμέρᾳ ἐπιλαβομένου μου τῆς χειρὸς αὐτῶν ἐξαγαγεῖν αὐτοὺς ἐκ γῆς Αἰγύπτου ὅτι αὐτοὶ οὐκ ἐνέμειναν ἐν τῇ διαθήκῃ μου κἀγὼ ἠμέλησα αὐτῶν λέγει κύριος ¹⁰ ὅτι

> αὕτη ἡ διαθήκη ἣν διαθήσομαι τῷ οἴκῳ Ἰσραὴλ μετὰ τὰς ἡμέρας ἐκείνας λέγει κύριος διδοὺς νόμους μου εἰς τὴν διάνοιαν αὐτῶν καὶ ἐπὶ καρδίας αὐτῶν ἐπιγράψω αὐτούς, καὶ ἔσομαι αὐτοῖς εἰς θεόν καὶ αὐτοὶ ἔσονταί μοι εἰς λαόν ¹¹ καὶ οὐ μὴ διδάξωσιν ἕκαστος τὸν πολίτην αὐτοῦ καὶ ἕκαστος τὸν ἀδελφὸν αὐτοῦ λέγων γνῶθι τὸν κύριον ὅτι πάντες εἰδήσουσίν με ἀπὸ μικροῦ ἕως μεγάλου αὐτῶν ¹² ὅτι ἵλεως ἔσομαι ταῖς ἀδικίαις αὐτῶν καὶ τῶν ἁμαρτιῶν αὐτῶν οὐ μὴ μνησθῶ ἔτι

A'. ¹³ ἐν τῷ λέγειν καινὴν πεπαλαίωκεν τὴν πρώτην τὸ δὲ παλαιούμενον καὶ γηράσκον ἐγγὺς ἀφανισμοῦ

A. ⁸:⁶ But now he has obtained a ministry which is as much greater as the covenant of which he is mediator, being legislated on better promises. ⁷ For if the first (covenant) was without fault, what place would be sought for a second? ⁸ For finding fault he says:

> B. "Behold, days are coming! Says the Lord, and I will establish a new covenant with the House of Israel and the House of Judah, ⁹ not like the Covenant which I made with their fathers in the day when I took them by the hand to bring them out of the land of Egypt, because they did not remain in my covenant, and so I neglected them, says the Lord. ¹⁰ This is the covenant which I will make with the House of Israel after those days, says the Lord. I will give my laws into their mind and I will write them upon their heart, and I will be God to them, and they will be as people to me. ¹¹ And each will not teach his neighbor and each his brother, saying 'know the Lord', because they will all know me from small to great, ¹² because I will be merciful to their acts of unrighteousness and will no longer remember their sins".

A'. ¹³ By speaking of a new one, he has declared the former one obsolete. And what has become obsolete and old is near to vanishing.

9:1-8

A. ⁹:¹ εἶχε μὲν οὖν ἡ πρώτη δικαιώματα λατρείας τό τε ἅγιον κοσμικόν

B. ² σκηνὴ γὰρ κατεσκευάσθη ἡ πρώτη ἐν ᾗ ἥ τε λυχνία καὶ ἡ τράπεζα καὶ ἡ πρόθεσις τῶν ἄρτων ἥτις λέγεται Ἅγια ³ μετὰ δὲ τὸ δεύτερον καταπέτασμα σκηνὴ ἡ λεγομένη Ἅγια Ἁγίων ⁴ χρυσοῦν ἔχουσα θυμιατήριον καὶ τὴν κιβωτὸν τῆς διαθήκης περικεκαλυμμένην πάντοθεν χρυσίῳ ἐν ᾗ στάμνος χρυσῆ ἔχουσα τὸ μάννα καὶ ἡ ῥάβδος Ἀαρὼν ἡ βλαστήσασα καὶ αἱ πλάκες τῆς διαθήκης ⁵ ὑπεράνω δὲ αὐτῆς Χερουβὶν δόξης κατασκιάζοντα τὸ ἱλαστήριον περὶ ὧν οὐκ ἔστιν νῦν λέγειν κατὰ μέρος

B'. ⁶ τούτων δὲ οὕτως κατεσκευασμένων εἰς μὲν τὴν πρώτην σκηνὴν διὰ παντὸς εἰσίασιν οἱ ἱερεῖς τὰς λατρείας ἐπιτελοῦντες ⁷ εἰς δὲ τὴν δευτέραν ἅπαξ τοῦ ἐνιαυτοῦ μόνος ὁ ἀρχιερεύς οὐ χωρὶς αἵματος ὃ προσφέρει ὑπὲρ ἑαυτοῦ καὶ τῶν τοῦ λαοῦ ἀγνοημάτων

A'. ⁸ τοῦτο δηλοῦντος τοῦ πνεύματος τοῦ ἁγίου μήπω πεφανερῶσθαι τὴν τῶν ἁγίων ὁδὸν ἔτι τῆς πρώτης σκηνῆς ἐχούσης στάσιν

A. ⁹:¹ Therefore the first covenant has had regulations of worship and an *earthly* sanctuary.

B. ² For a tent is erected with regard to the first in which are the lamp stand and the table and the bread of the presence, which is said to be holy. ³ And after a second curtain, a tent which is called 'Holy of Holies', ⁴ having the golden altar of incense and the ark of the covenant covered on all sides with gold, in which was a golden urn holding the manna and Aaron's staff that budded and the tablets of the covenant ⁵ and above which were the cherubim of glory over-shadowing the mercy seat. It is not possible to speak in detail now about these.

B'. ⁶ And these things having been set up in this way, the priests always enter into the first tent, performing their worship. ⁷ But only the high priest enters the second once a year, and not without blood which he offers for himself and for the of the people,

A'. ⁸ the Holy Spirit indicating by this that the way into the Holies has still not been made manifest whilever the first tent has standing.

9:6-12

A. ⁹:⁶ τούτων δὲ οὕτως κατεσκευασμένων <u>εἰς μὲν τὴν πρώτην σκηνὴν διὰ παντὸς εἰσίασιν οἱ ἱερεῖς</u> τὰς λατρείας ἐπιτελοῦντες ⁷ <u>εἰς δὲ τὴν δευτέραν</u> ἅπαξ τοῦ ἐνιαυτοῦ <u>μόνος ὁ ἀρχιερεύς</u> οὐ χωρὶς αἵματος ὃ προσφέρει ὑπὲρ ἑαυτοῦ καὶ τῶν τοῦ λαοῦ ἀγνοημάτων

  B. ⁸ τοῦτο δηλοῦντος τοῦ πνεύματος τοῦ ἁγίου μήπω πεφανερῶσθαι τὴν τῶν ἁγίων ὁδὸν ἔτι <u>τῆς πρώτης σκηνῆς ἐχούσης στάσιν</u> ⁹ ἥτις παραβολὴ <u>εἰς τὸν καιρὸν τὸν ἐνεστηκότα</u>

  B'. καθ' ἣν δῶρά τε καὶ θυσίαι προσφέρονται μὴ δυνάμεναι κατὰ συνείδησιν τελειῶσαι τὸν λατρεύοντα ¹⁰ μόνον ἐπὶ βρώμασιν καὶ πόμασιν καὶ διαφόροις βαπτισμοῖς δικαιώματα σαρκὸς <u>μέχρι καιροῦ διορθώσεως ἐπικείμενα</u>

A'. ¹¹ <u>Χριστὸς δὲ παραγενόμενος ἀρχιερεὺς τῶν γενομένων ἀγαθῶν διὰ τῆς μείζονος καὶ τελειοτέρας σκηνῆς</u> οὐ χειροποιήτου τοῦτ' ἔστιν οὐ ταύτης τῆς κτίσεως ¹² οὐδὲ δι' αἵματος τράγων καὶ μόσχων διὰ δὲ τοῦ ἰδίου αἵματος <u>εἰσῆλθεν ἐφάπαξ</u> εἰς τὰ ἅγια αἰωνίαν λύτρωσιν εὑράμενος

A. ⁹:⁶ And these things having been set up in this way, the priests continually enter into the first tent performing their worship, ⁷ but only the high priest enters the second once a year, and not without blood which he offers for himself and for the of the people,

  B. ⁸ the Holy Spirit signifying by this that the way into the Holies has not yet been disclosed whilever the first tent has standing, ⁹ which is symbolic of the present time.

  B'. According to which, gifts and sacrifices are offered which are not able to perfect the conscience of the worshippers, ¹⁰ being only about food and drink and various washings, regulations of flesh in force until the time of correction.

APPENDIX: MICRO LINK CLUSTERS IN HEBREWS

A'. ¹¹ But when Christ became high priest of the good things which have come, he went in through the greater and more perfect tent which is not man-made—that is not of this creation—into the holies, ¹² not through the blood of goats and bulls but through his own blood, having secured an eternal redemption.

9:11-28

A. ⁹:¹¹ Χριστὸς δὲ παραγενόμενος ἀρχιερεὺς τῶν γενομένων ἀγαθῶν διὰ τῆς μείζονος καὶ τελειοτέρας σκηνῆς οὐ χειροποιήτου τοῦτ' ἔστιν οὐ ταύτης τῆς κτίσεως ¹² οὐδὲ δι' αἵματος τράγων καὶ μόσχων διὰ δὲ τοῦ ἰδίου αἵματος <u>εἰσῆλθεν</u> ἐφάπαξ εἰς τὰ ἅγια <u>αἰωνίαν λύτρωσιν εὑράμενος</u>

B. ¹³ εἰ γὰρ τὸ αἷμα τράγων καὶ ταύρων καὶ σποδὸς δαμάλεως ῥαντίζουσα τοὺς κεκοινωμένους ἁγιάζει πρὸς τὴν τῆς σαρκὸς καθαρότητα ¹⁴ πόσῳ μᾶλλον τὸ αἷμα τοῦ Χριστοῦ ὃς διὰ πνεύματος αἰωνίου ἑαυτὸν προσήνεγκεν ἄμωμον τῷ θεῷ καθαριεῖ τὴν συνείδησιν ἡμῶν ἀπὸ νεκρῶν ἔργων εἰς τὸ λατρεύειν θεῷ ζῶντι

C. ¹⁵ καὶ διὰ τοῦτο διαθήκης καινῆς μεσίτης ἐστίν ὅπως θανάτου γενομένου εἰς ἀπολύτρωσιν τῶν ἐπὶ τῇ πρώτῃ διαθήκῃ παραβάσεων τὴν ἐπαγγελίαν λάβωσιν οἱ κεκλημένοι τῆς αἰωνίου κληρονομίας

D. ¹⁶ <u>ὅπου γὰρ διαθήκη θάνατον ἀνάγκη φέρεσθαι τοῦ διαθεμένου</u>

D'. ¹⁷ <u>διαθήκη γὰρ ἐπὶ νεκροῖς βεβαία ἐπεὶ μήποτε ἰσχύει ὅτε ζῇ ὁ διαθέμενος</u>

C'. ¹⁸ ὅθεν οὐδὲ ἡ πρώτη χωρὶς αἵματος ἐγκεκαίνισται ¹⁹ λαληθείσης γὰρ πάσης ἐντολῆς κατὰ τὸν νόμον ὑπὸ Μωϋσέως παντὶ τῷ λαῷ λαβὼν τὸ αἷμα τῶν μόσχων μετὰ ὕδατος καὶ ἐρίου κοκκίνου καὶ ὑσσώπου αὐτό τε τὸ βιβλίον καὶ πάντα τὸν λαὸν ἐράντισεν ²⁰ λέγων τοῦτο τὸ αἷμα τῆς διαθήκης ἧς ἐνετείλατο πρὸς ὑμᾶς ὁ θεός

B'. ²¹ καὶ τὴν σκηνὴν δὲ καὶ πάντα τὰ σκεύη τῆς λειτουργίας τῷ αἵματι ὁμοίως ἐράντισεν ²² καὶ σχεδὸν ἐν αἵματι πάντα καθαρίζεται κατὰ τὸν νόμον καὶ χωρὶς αἱματεκχυσίας οὐ γίνεται ἄφεσις ²³ Ἀνάγκη οὖν τὰ μὲν ὑποδείγματα τῶν ἐν τοῖς οὐρανοῖς τούτοις καθαρίζεσθαι αὐτὰ δὲ τὰ ἐπουράνια κρείττοσι θυσίαις παρὰ ταύτας [24] οὐ γὰρ εἰς χειροποίητα εἰσῆλθεν ἅγια Χριστός ἀντίτυπα τῶν ἀληθινῶν ἀλλ' εἰς αὐτὸν τὸν οὐρανόν νῦν ἐμφανισθῆναι τῷ προσώπῳ τοῦ θεοῦ ὑπὲρ ἡμῶν [25] οὐδ' ἵνα πολλάκις προσφέρῃ ἑαυτόν ὥσπερ ὁ ἀρχιερεὺς εἰσέρχεται εἰς τὰ ἅγια κατ' ἐνιαυτὸν ἐν αἵματι ἀλλοτρίῳ [26] ἐπεὶ ἔδει αὐτὸν πολλάκις παθεῖν ἀπὸ καταβολῆς κόσμου

A'. <u>νυνὶ δὲ ἅπαξ ἐπὶ συντελείᾳ τῶν αἰώνων εἰς ἀθέτησιν ἁμαρτίας διὰ τῆς θυσίας αὐτοῦ πεφανέρωται</u> [27] καὶ καθ' ὅσον ἀπόκειται τοῖς ἀνθρώποις ἅπαξ ἀποθανεῖν μετὰ δὲ τοῦτο κρίσις [28] οὕτως καὶ <u>ὁ Χριστὸς ἅπαξ προσενεχθεὶς εἰς τὸ πολλῶν ἀνενεγκεῖν ἁμαρτίας</u> ἐκ δευτέρου χωρὶς ἁμαρτίας ὀφθήσεται τοῖς αὐτὸν ἀπεκδεχομένοις εἰς σωτηρίαν

A. [11] But when Christ became high priest of the good things which have come, he went in through the greater and more perfect tent which is not man-made—that is not of this creation—into the holies, [12] not through the blood of goats and bulls but through his own blood, having secured an eternal redemption.

B. [13] For if the blood of bulls and goats and the sprinkling of the ashes of a heifer cleanses those defiled for the purification of the flesh, [14] *how much more* will the blood of Jesus, who through the eternal Spirit offered himself without blemish to God, cleanse our conscience from dead works in order to serve the living God!

C. [15] And because of this, he is the mediator of the new covenant, so that a death having occurred for the redemption of those sins of the first covenant, those called might receive the promise of the eternal inheritance.

D. [16] For where there is a covenant, it is necessary for the death of the covenant maker to be established.

D'. [17] For a covenant is established by deaths, because it is not yet in force while the covenant maker lives.

APPENDIX: MICRO LINK CLUSTERS IN HEBREWS

C'. ¹⁸ Therefore not even the first [covenant] was inaugurated without blood. ¹⁹ For when every covenant according to the law of Moses was spoken by Moses to all the people, taking the blood of goats [and bulls] with water and scarlet wool and hyssop, he sprinkled both the book itself and all the people ²⁰ saying: 'This is the blood of the covenant which God commanded for you'.

B'. ²¹ And he sprinkled even the tent and all the vessels of worship with blood in the same way. ²² Indeed, almost everything is cleansed in blood according to the law and apart from the flow of blood there is no forgiveness. ²³ Therefore it was necessary for the copies of the heavenly things to be cleansed, but the heavenly things themselves through better sacrifices than these. ²⁴ For Christ did not enter into a holy place made by hands, an antitype of the true holies, but into Heaven itself, now to appear before the face of God for us, ²⁵ nor in order to offer himself repeatedly as the high priest enters into the Holies each year by the blood of another, ²⁶ because it would be necessary for him to suffer many times from the creation of the world.

A'. But now he has appeared once at the culmination of the ages in order to put away sin through the sacrifice of himself. ²⁷ And as it is appointed for people to die once and afterwards face judgement, ²⁸ so Christ having been offered up once to bear the sins of many, will appear for a second time without sin for the salvation of those waiting for him.

10:1-4

A. ¹⁰:¹ <u>σκιὰν γὰρ ἔχων ὁ νόμος τῶν μελλόντων ἀγαθῶν οὐκ αὐτὴν τὴν εἰκόνα τῶν πραγμάτων κατ'</u> ἐνιαυτὸν <u>ταῖς αὐταῖς θυσίαις ἃς προσφέρουσιν εἰς τὸ διηνεκὲς οὐδέποτε δύναται τοὺς προσερχομένους τελειῶσαι</u>

B. ² ἐπεὶ οὐκ ἂν ἐπαύσαντο προσφερόμεναι διὰ τὸ μηδεμίαν ἔχειν ἔτι συνείδησιν ἁμαρτιῶν τοὺς λατρεύοντας ἅπαξ κεκαθαρισμένους;

B'. ³ ἀλλ' ἐν αὐταῖς ἀνάμνησις ἁμαρτιῶν κατ' ἐνιαυτόν

A'. ⁴ <u>ἀδύνατον γὰρ αἷμα ταύρων καὶ τράγων ἀφαιρεῖν ἁμαρτίας</u>

APPENDIX: MICRO LINK CLUSTERS IN HEBREWS

- A. ^{10:1} For the law, having only a shadow of the good things to come, not itself being the image of the realities, is never able by these sacrifices which they offer continually to perfect those drawing near.
  - B. ² Else would not they have ceased to be offered since having been cleansed once the worshippers would have no more consciousness of sin?
  - B'. ³ But in these there is an annual reminder of sins.
- A'. ⁴ For it is impossible for the blood of bulls and goats to take away sins.

10:5-22

- A. ^{10:5} διὸ <u>εἰσερχόμενος εἰς τὸν κόσμον λέγει θυσίαν καὶ προσφορὰν οὐκ ἠθέλησας σῶμα δὲ κατηρτίσω μοι</u> ⁶ ὁλοκαυτώματα καὶ περὶ ἁμαρτίας οὐκ εὐδόκησας ⁷ τότε εἶπον <u>ἰδοὺ ἥκω</u> ἐν κεφαλίδι βιβλίου γέγραπται περὶ ἐμοῦ <u>τοῦ ποιῆσαι ὁ θεός τὸ θέλημά σου</u>
  - B. ⁸ ἀνώτερον λέγων ὅτι θυσίας καὶ προσφορὰς καὶ ὁλοκαυτώματα καὶ περὶ ἁμαρτίας οὐκ ἠθέλησας οὐδὲ εὐδόκησας αἵτινες κατὰ νόμον προσφέρονται ⁹ τότε εἴρηκεν ἰδοὺ ἥκω τοῦ ποιῆσαι τὸ θέλημά σου <u>ἀναιρεῖ τὸ πρῶτον ἵνα τὸ δεύτερον στήσῃ</u>
    - C. ¹⁰ ἐν ᾧ θελήματι <u>ἡγιασμένοι ἐσμὲν διὰ τῆς προσφορᾶς τοῦ σώματος Ἰησοῦ Χριστοῦ ἐφάπαξ</u>
      - D. ¹¹ καὶ πᾶς μὲν ἱερεὺς ἕστηκεν καθ' ἡμέραν λειτουργῶν καὶ τὰς αὐτὰς πολλάκις προσφέρων θυσίας αἵτινες οὐδέποτε δύνανται περιελεῖν ἁμαρτίας
      - D'. ¹² οὗτος δὲ μίαν ὑπὲρ ἁμαρτιῶν προσενέγκας θυσίαν εἰς τὸ διηνεκὲς ἐκάθισεν ἐν δεξιᾷ τοῦ θεοῦ ¹³ τὸ λοιπὸν ἐκδεχόμενος ἕως τεθῶσιν οἱ ἐχθροὶ αὐτοῦ ὑποπόδιον τῶν ποδῶν αὐτοῦ
    - C'. ¹⁴ <u>μιᾷ γὰρ προσφορᾷ τετελείωκεν εἰς τὸ διηνεκὲς τοὺς ἁγιαζομένους</u>
  - B'. ¹⁵ μαρτυρεῖ δὲ ἡμῖν καὶ τὸ πνεῦμα τὸ ἅγιον μετὰ γὰρ τὸ εἰρηκέναι ¹⁶ αὕτη ἡ διαθήκη ἣν διαθήσομαι πρὸς αὐτοὺς μετὰ τὰς ἡμέρας ἐκείνας λέγει κύριος διδοὺς νόμους μου

APPENDIX: MICRO LINK CLUSTERS IN HEBREWS

ἐπὶ καρδίας αὐτῶν καὶ ἐπὶ τὴν διάνοιαν αὐτῶν ἐπιγράψω αὐτούς ¹⁷ καὶ τῶν ἁμαρτιῶν αὐτῶν καὶ τῶν ἀνομιῶν αὐτῶν οὐ μὴ μνησθήσομαι ἔτι ¹⁸ <u>ὅπου δὲ ἄφεσις τούτων οὐκέτι προσφορὰ περὶ ἁμαρτίας</u>

A'. ¹⁹ <u>ἔχοντες οὖν ἀδελφοί παρρησίαν εἰς τὴν εἴσοδον τῶν ἁγίων ἐν τῷ αἵματι Ἰησοῦ</u> ²⁰ ἣν ἐνεκαίνισεν ἡμῖν ὁδὸν πρόσφατον καὶ ζῶσαν διὰ τοῦ καταπετάσματος τοῦτ᾽ ἔστιν τῆς σαρκὸς αὐτοῦ ²¹ καὶ ἱερέα μέγαν ἐπὶ τὸν οἶκον τοῦ θεοῦ ²² προσερχώμεθα μετὰ ἀληθινῆς καρδίας ἐν πληροφορίᾳ πίστεως

A. ¹⁰:⁵ Therefore, coming into the world he says: "Sacrifices and offerings you do not desire, but a body you have established for me. ⁶ You do not desire burnt offerings and those for sin". ⁷ Then I said: "Behold I have come, it is written in the book about me, to do your will, God".

    B. ⁸ Having said earlier, "You do not want nor desire sacrifices and offerings and burnt offerings and those for sin", then he *has said*: "Behold I have come to do your will". He abolishes the first in order to establish the second,

        C. by which will we have been sanctified through the once-for-all-time offering of the body of Jesus Christ.

            D. ¹¹ And every priest stands ministering every day and offering the same sacrifices all the time which are not able to take away sins.

            D'. ¹² But He, having offered a single sacrifice for sins has sat down forever at the right hand of God, ¹³ waiting until the enemies will be placed as a footstool beneath his feet.

        C'. ¹⁴ For by a single sacrifice, he has perfected those being sanctified forever.

    B'. ¹⁵ And the Holy Spirit also testifies to us. For after saying: ¹⁶ "This is the covenant which I will make with them after those days", the Lord says: "I will give my laws upon their hearts and I will write them on their conscience, ¹⁷ and their sins and lawlessness I will remember no more". And where there is forgiveness of these, there is no longer offering for sins.

A'. [19] Therefore, since we have confidence of an entrance into the Holies by the blood of Jesus, [20] a freshly killed and living way which he has opened up for us through the curtain, this is his flesh, [21] and a great High Priest over the House of God, [22] let us draw near with a true heart in full assurance of faith.

10:19–38 (cf. 6.2.7)

A. [19] ἔχοντες οὖν ἀδελφοί παρρησίαν εἰς τὴν εἴσοδον τῶν ἁγίων ἐν τῷ αἵματι Ἰησοῦ [20] ἣν ἐνεκαίνισεν ἡμῖν ὁδὸν πρόσφατον καὶ ζῶσαν διὰ τοῦ καταπετάσματος τοῦτ' ἔστιν τῆς σαρκὸς αὐτοῦ [21] καὶ ἱερέα μέγαν ἐπὶ τὸν οἶκον τοῦ θεοῦ [22] <u>προσερχώμεθα μετὰ ἀληθινῆς καρδίας ἐν πληροφορίᾳ πίστεως</u> ῥεραντισμένοι τὰς καρδίας ἀπὸ συνειδήσεως πονηρᾶς καὶ λελουσμένοι τὸ σῶμα ὕδατι καθαρῷ

    B. [23] κατέχωμεν τὴν ὁμολογίαν τῆς ἐλπίδος ἀκλινῆ <u>πιστὸς γὰρ ὁ ἐπαγγειλάμενος</u>

        C. [24] καὶ κατανοῶμεν ἀλλήλους εἰς παροξυσμὸν ἀγάπης καὶ καλῶν ἔργων [25] μὴ ἐγκαταλείποντες τὴν ἐπισυναγωγὴν ἑαυτῶν καθὼς ἔθος τισίν ἀλλὰ παρακαλοῦντες καὶ τοσούτῳ μᾶλλον ὅσῳ βλέπετε ἐγγίζουσαν τὴν ἡμέραν

           D. [26] ἑκουσίως γὰρ ἁμαρτανόντων ἡμῶν μετὰ τὸ λαβεῖν τὴν ἐπίγνωσιν τῆς ἀληθείας οὐκέτι περὶ ἁμαρτιῶν ἀπολείπεται θυσία [27] φοβερὰ δέ τις ἐκδοχὴ κρίσεως καὶ πυρὸς ζῆλος ἐσθίειν μέλλοντος τοὺς ὑπεναντίους

               E. [28] ἀθετήσας τις νόμον Μωϋσέως χωρὶς οἰκτιρμῶν <u>ἐπὶ δυσὶν ἢ τρισὶν μάρτυσιν</u> ἀποθνῄσκει

                    F. [29] πόσῳ δοκεῖτε χείρονος ἀξιωθήσεται τιμωρίας ὁ <u>τὸν υἱὸν τοῦ θεοῦ</u> καταπατήσας

               E'. <u>καὶ τὸ αἷμα τῆς διαθήκης κοινὸν</u> ἡγησάμενος ἐν ᾧ ἡγιάσθη <u>καὶ τὸ πνεῦμα</u>

    <u>τῆς χάριτος</u> ἐνυβρίσας ὑμῶν μετὰ χαρᾶς προσεδέξασθε

D'. ³⁰ οἴδαμεν γὰρ τὸν εἰπόντα ἐμοὶ ἐκδίκησις ἐγὼ ἀνταποδώσω καὶ πάλιν κρινεῖ κύριος τὸν λαὸν αὐτοῦ ³¹ φοβερὸν τὸ ἐμπεσεῖν εἰς χεῖρας θεοῦ ζῶντος

C'. ³² Ἀναμιμνήσκεσθε δὲ τὰς πρότερον ἡμέρας ἐν αἷς φωτισθέντες πολλὴν ἄθλησιν ὑπεμείνατε παθημάτων ³³ τοῦτο μὲν ὀνειδισμοῖς τε καὶ θλίψεσιν θεατριζόμενοι τοῦτο δὲ κοινωνοὶ τῶν οὕτως ἀναστρεφομένων γενηθέντες ³⁴ καὶ γὰρ τοῖς δεσμίοις συνεπαθήσατε

B'. καὶ τὴν ἁρπαγὴν τῶν ὑπαρχόντων ὑμῶν μετὰ χαρᾶς προσεδέξασθε <u>γινώσκοντες ἔχειν ἑαυτοὺς κρείττονα ὕπαρξιν καὶ μένουσαν</u>

A'. ³⁵ μὴ ἀποβάλητε οὖν τὴν παρρησίαν ὑμῶν ἥτις ἔχει μεγάλην μισθαποδοσίαν ³⁶ ὑπομονῆς γὰρ ἔχετε χρείαν ἵνα τὸ θέλημα τοῦ θεοῦ ποιήσαντες κομίσησθε τὴν ἐπαγγελίαν ³⁷ ἔτι γὰρ μικρὸν ὅσον ὅσον ὁ ἐρχόμενος ἥξει καὶ οὐ χρονίσει ³⁸ <u>ὁ δὲ δίκαιός μου ἐκ πίστεως ζήσεται καὶ ἐὰν ὑποστείληται οὐκ εὐδοκεῖ ἡ ψυχή μου ἐν αὐτῷ</u>

A. ¹⁰:¹⁹ Therefore, since we have confidence of an entrance into the Holies by the blood of Jesus, ²⁰ a freshly killed and living way which he has opened up for us through the curtain, this is his flesh, ²¹ and a great high priest over the house of God, ²² let us draw near with a true heart in full assurance of faith, hearts having been sprinkled from an evil conscience and the body washed with pure water.

B. ²³ Let us hold fast the confession of hope without swerving, for the Promiser is faithful.

C. ²⁴ And let us consider one another with a view to the stimulation of love and good works, ²⁵ not neglecting our gatherings, as is the habit of some, but encouraging, and this by as much more as you see the Day draw near.

D. ²⁶ For if we go on wilfully sinning after receiving knowledge of the truth, there no longer remains a sacrifice for sins ²⁷ but only a fearful expectation of judgement and a fury of fire which is about to consume the adversaries.

E. ²⁸ Anyone setting aside the Law of Moses died without mercy on the basis of two or three witnesses.

F. ²⁹ How much worse do you suppose will be the punishment deserved by the one who tramples the Son of God?

E'. And treats the blood of the covenant by which he was sanctified as unholy, and outrages the Spirit of Grace?

D'. ³⁰ For we know him who has said: "Vengeance is mine, I will repay." And again, "The Lord will judge his people." ³¹ It is fearful to fall in to the hands of the living God.

C'. ³² But keep in mind the former days, in which having been enlightened you endured a great struggle of sufferings, ³³ sometimes being exposed to insults and tribulations, sometimes becoming partners with those so treated. ³⁴ For you even sympathized with my chains.

B'. And you welcomed the seizure of your possessions knowing yourselves to have a better and abiding possession.

A'. ³⁵ Therefore do not cast off your confidence, which has a great reward. ³⁶ For you need to endure in order that having done God's will you might experience the promise. ³⁷ "For in such a little while, the one who is coming will come and will not delay. ³⁸ And my righteous one will live by faith. And if he shrinks back, my soul will not delight in him."

10:39—11:4

A. ¹⁰:³⁹ ἡμεῖς δὲ οὐκ ἐσμὲν ὑποστολῆς εἰς ἀπώλειαν ἀλλὰ πίστεως εἰς περιποίησιν ψυχῆς

B. ¹¹:¹ ἔστιν δὲ πίστις ἐλπιζομένων ὑπόστασις πραγμάτων ἔλεγχος οὐ βλεπομένων ² <u>ἐν ταύτῃ γὰρ ἐμαρτυρήθησαν οἱ πρεσβύτεροι</u>

B'. ³ <u>πίστει νοοῦμεν κατηρτίσθαι τοὺς αἰῶνας ῥήματι θεοῦ εἰς τὸ μὴ ἐκ φαινομένων τὸ βλεπόμενον γεγονέναι</u>

A'. ⁴ πίστει πλείονα θυσίαν Ἄβελ παρὰ Κάϊν προσήνεγκεν τῷ θεῷ δι' ἧς ἐμαρτυρήθη εἶναι δίκαιος μαρτυροῦντος ἐπὶ τοῖς δώροις αὐτοῦ τοῦ θεοῦ καὶ δι' αὐτῆς ἀποθανὼν ἔτι λαλεῖ

A. ¹⁰:³⁹ And *we are not* of those who shrink back into destruction *but* of faith which leads to the preservation of the soul.

B. ¹¹:¹ And *faith is* the substance of things hoped for, the proof of things which cannot be seen. ² For by *it* the Ancients were commended.

B'. ³ *By faith* we understand the ordering of the ages in the Word of God that what may be seen comes from what is not visible.

A'. ⁴ By faith Abel offered to God a better sacrifice than Cain, through which he was testified to be righteous, being commended by God's acceptance of his gifts. And because of this, though he died he still speaks.

11:3-7

A. ¹¹:³ πίστει νοοῦμεν κατηρτίσθαι τοὺς αἰῶνας ῥήματι θεοῦ εἰς τὸ μὴ ἐκ φαινομένων τὸ βλεπόμενον γεγονέναι

B. ⁴ πίστει πλείονα θυσίαν Ἄβελ παρὰ Κάϊν προσήνεγκεν τῷ θεῷ δι' ἧς ἐμαρτυρήθη εἶναι δίκαιος μαρτυροῦντος ἐπὶ τοῖς δώροις αὐτοῦ τοῦ θεοῦ

C. καὶ δι' αὐτῆς ἀποθανὼν ἔτι λαλεῖ

C'. ⁵ πίστει Ἑνὼχ μετετέθη τοῦ μὴ ἰδεῖν θάνατον καὶ οὐχ ηὑρίσκετο διότι μετέθηκεν αὐτὸν ὁ θεός

B'. πρὸ γὰρ τῆς μεταθέσεως μεμαρτύρηται εὐαρεστηκέναι τῷ θεῷ ⁶ χωρὶς δὲ πίστεως ἀδύνατον εὐαρεστῆσαι πιστεῦσαι γὰρ δεῖ τὸν προσερχόμενον τῷ θεῷ ὅτι ἔστιν καὶ τοῖς ἐκζητοῦσιν αὐτὸν μισθαποδότης γίνεται

A'. ⁷ πίστει χρηματισθεὶς Νῶε περὶ τῶν μηδέπω βλεπομένων εὐλαβηθεὶς κατεσκεύασεν κιβωτὸν εἰς σωτηρίαν τοῦ οἴκου αὐτοῦ δι' ἧς κατέκρινεν τὸν κόσμον καὶ τῆς κατὰ πίστιν δικαιοσύνης ἐγένετο κληρονόμος

A. ¹¹:³ By faith we understand with regard to the ordering of the ages in the Word of God that what may be seen comes from what is not visible.

  B. ⁴ By faith, Abel offered to God a better sacrifice than Cain, through which he was commended as righteous, testimony having been given by God about his gifts

   C. And through this, though he died he still speaks.

   C'. ⁵ By faith Enoch was taken so that he should not see death and was not found because God took him.

  B'. For before he was taken it is testified that he pleased God, ⁶ And apart from faith it is impossible to please him. For it is necessary for the one approaching God to believe that he is and that he rewards those who seek him.

A'. ⁷ By faith Noah, being warned about things not yet able to see, built a boat in reverent fear for the salvation of his house, through which he condemned the world, and became an heir of the righteousness according to faith.

11:8-16

A. ⁸ πίστει καλούμενος Ἀβραὰμ ὑπήκουσεν ἐξελθεῖν <u>εἰς τόπον ὃν ἤμελλεν λαμβάνειν εἰς κληρονομίαν</u> καὶ ἐξῆλθεν <u>μὴ ἐπιστάμενος ποῦ ἔρχεται</u>

  B. ⁹ πίστει παρῴκησεν εἰς γῆν τῆς ἐπαγγελίας ὡς ἀλλοτρίαν ἐν σκηναῖς κατοικήσας μετὰ Ἰσαὰκ καὶ Ἰακὼβ τῶν συγκληρονόμων τῆς ἐπαγγελίας τῆς αὐτῆς ¹⁰ <u>ἐξεδέχετο γὰρ τὴν τοὺς θεμελίους ἔχουσαν πόλιν ἧς τεχνίτης καὶ δημιουργὸς ὁ θεός</u>

   C. ¹¹ <u>πίστει καὶ αὐτῇ Σάρρᾳ δύναμιν εἰς καταβολὴν σπέρματος ἔλαβεν</u> καὶ παρὰ καιρὸν ἡλικίας ἐπεὶ πιστὸν ἡγήσατο τὸν ἐπαγγειλάμενον

APPENDIX: MICRO LINK CLUSTERS IN HEBREWS

    D. ¹² διὸ καὶ ἀφ' ἑνὸς ἐγεννήθησαν καὶ ταῦτα νενεκρωμένου καθὼς τὰ ἄστρα τοῦ οὐρανοῦ τῷ πλήθει

    D'. καὶ ὡς ἡ ἄμμος ἡ παρὰ τὸ χεῖλος τῆς θαλάσσης ἡ ἀναρίθμητος ¹³ Κατὰ πίστιν ἀπέθανον οὗτοι πάντες

  C'. <u>μὴ λαβόντες τὰς ἐπαγγελίας</u> ἀλλὰ πόρρωθεν αὐτὰς ἰδόντες καὶ ἀσπασάμενοι

 B'. καὶ ὁμολογήσαντες ὅτι ξένοι καὶ παρεπίδημοί εἰσιν ἐπὶ τῆς γῆς ¹⁴ <u>οἱ γὰρ τοιαῦτα λέγοντες ἐμφανίζουσιν ὅτι πατρίδα ἐπιζητοῦσιν</u> ¹⁵ καὶ εἰ μὲν ἐκείνης μνημονεύουσιν ἀφ' ἧς ἐξέβησαν εἶχον ἂν καιρὸν ἀνακάμψαι

A'. ¹⁶ νῦν δὲ <u>κρείττονος</u> ὀρέγονται τοῦτ' ἔστιν <u>ἐπουρανίου</u> διὸ οὐκ ἐπαισχύνεται αὐτοὺς ὁ θεὸς θεὸς ἐπικαλεῖσθαι <u>αὐτῶν ἡτοίμασεν γὰρ αὐτοῖς πόλιν</u>

A. ⁸ By faith Abraham obeyed when he was called to go out to a place that he was to receive as an inheritance. And he went out, not knowing where he was going.

  B. ⁹ By faith he lived in the land of promise, as in a foreign land, living in tents with Isaac and Jacob, heirs with him of the same promise. ¹⁰ For he was looking forward to the city that has foundations, whose designer and builder is God (cf. v.6).

    C. ¹¹ By faith Sarah herself also received power to conceive, even when she was past the age, since she considered him faithful who had promised.

      D. ¹² Therefore from one man, and him as good as dead, were born descendants as many as the stars of heaven.

      D'. And as many as the innumerable grains of sand by the seashore, ¹³ these all died in faith,

    C'. not having received the things promised, but having seen them and greeted them from afar,

  B'. and acknowledging that they were aliens and strangers on earth. ¹⁴ For this kind of speaking reveals that they were seeking a Fatherland. ¹⁵ And if they had been thinking of that land from which they had gone out, they would have had time to return.

A'. ¹⁶ But as it is, they desire a better country, that is, a heavenly one. Therefore God is not ashamed to be called their God, for he has prepared for them a city.

11:17–22

A. ¹¹:¹⁷ πίστει προσενήνοχεν Ἀβραὰμ τὸν Ἰσαὰκ πειραζόμενος καὶ τὸν μονογενῆ προσέφερεν ὁ τὰς ἐπαγγελίας ἀναδεξάμενος ¹⁸ πρὸς ὃν ἐλαλήθη ὅτι Ἐν Ἰσαὰκ κληθήσεταί σοι σπέρμα ¹⁹ λογισάμενος ὅτι καὶ ἐκ νεκρῶν ἐγείρειν δυνατὸς ὁ θεός ὅθεν αὐτὸν καὶ ἐν παραβολῇ ἐκομίσατο

B. ²⁰ πίστει καὶ περὶ μελλόντων εὐλόγησεν Ἰσαὰκ τὸν Ἰακὼβ καὶ τὸν Ἠσαῦ

B'. ²¹ πίστει Ἰακὼβ ἀποθνῄσκων ἕκαστον τῶν υἱῶν Ἰωσὴφ εὐλόγησεν καὶ προσεκύνησεν ἐπὶ τὸ ἄκρον τῆς ῥάβδου αὐτοῦ

A'. ²² πίστει Ἰωσὴφ τελευτῶν περὶ τῆς ἐξόδου τῶν υἱῶν Ἰσραὴλ ἐμνημόνευσεν καὶ περὶ τῶν ὀστέων αὐτοῦ ἐνετείλατο

A. ¹¹:¹⁷ By faith Abraham offered up Isaac when tested and he who received the promises was about to offer up his only begotten son, ¹⁸ of whom it was said: "in Isaac will seed be called to you", ¹⁹ because he reckoned that God was even able to raise from the dead. Because of which he received him back in symbolic fashion.

B. ²⁰ By faith also Isaac blessed Jacob and Esau regarding things that were about to come.

B'. ²¹ By faith Jacob, when dying, blessed the sons of Joseph and worshipped on the top of his staff.

A'. ²² By faith Joseph, dying, was mindful of the Exodus of the sons of Israel and gave directions regarding his bones.

APPENDIX: MICRO LINK CLUSTERS IN HEBREWS

11:23-28

A. ¹¹:²³ πίστει Μωϋσῆς γεννηθεὶς ἐκρύβη τρίμηνον ὑπὸ τῶν πατέρων αὐτοῦ διότι εἶδον ἀστεῖον τὸ παιδίον καὶ οὐκ ἐφοβήθησαν τὸ διάταγμα τοῦ βασιλέως

B. ²⁴ πίστει Μωϋσῆς μέγας γενόμενος ἠρνήσατο λέγεσθαι υἱὸς θυγατρὸς Φαραώ ²⁵ μᾶλλον ἑλόμενος συγκακουχεῖσθαι τῷ λαῷ τοῦ θεοῦ ἢ πρόσκαιρον ἔχειν ἁμαρτίας ἀπόλαυσιν

B'. ²⁶ μείζονα πλοῦτον ἡγησάμενος τῶν Αἰγύπτου θησαυρῶν τὸν ὀνειδισμὸν τοῦ Χριστοῦ ἀπέβλεπεν γὰρ εἰς τὴν μισθαποδοσίαν

A'. ²⁷ πίστει κατέλιπεν Αἴγυπτον μὴ φοβηθεὶς τὸν θυμὸν τοῦ βασιλέως τὸν γὰρ ἀόρατον ὡς ὁρῶν ἐκαρτέρησεν ²⁸ πίστει πεποίηκεν τὸ πάσχα καὶ τὴν πρόσχυσιν τοῦ αἵματος ἵνα μὴ ὁ ὀλοθρεύων τὰ πρωτότοκα θίγῃ αὐτῶν

A. ¹¹:²³ By faith Moses was hidden by his parents for three months when he was born, because they saw the child as pleasing and did not fear the command of the King.

B. ²⁴ By faith Moses, when he became great, refused to be called the Son of the daughter of Pharoah, ²⁵ choosing instead to be mistreated with the people of God than to have the fleeting pleasure of sin.

B'. ²⁶ he considered the reproach of Christ a greater wealth than the treasures of Egypt for he looked to the reward.

A'. ²⁷ By faith he left Egypt not fearing the wrath of the king. For he endured as if seeing what was invisible. ²⁸ By faith he performed the Passover and the sprinkling of blood so that the destroyer of the firstborn might not touch them.

11:29-40

A. ¹¹:²⁹ πίστει <u>διέβησαν τὴν Ἐρυθρὰν Θάλασσαν</u> ὡς διὰ ξηρᾶς γῆς ἧς πεῖραν λαβόντες οἱ Αἰγύπτιοι κατεπόθησαν ³⁰ πίστει <u>τὰ τείχη Ἰεριχὼ ἔπεσαν κυκλωθέντα ἐπὶ ἑπτὰ ἡμέρας</u> ³¹ πίστει

Ῥαὰβ ἡ πόρνη οὐ συναπώλετο τοῖς ἀπειθήσασιν δεξαμένη τοὺς κατασκόπους μετ' εἰρήνης

B. ³² καὶ τί ἔτι λέγω; ἐπιλείψει με γὰρ διηγούμενον ὁ χρόνος περὶ Γεδεών Βαράκ Σαμψών Ἰεφθάε Δαυίδ τε καὶ Σαμουὴλ καὶ τῶν προφητῶν ³³ οἳ διὰ πίστεως κατηγωνίσαντο βασιλείας εἰργάσαντο δικαιοσύνην ἐπέτυχον ἐπαγγελιῶν ἔφραξαν στόματα λεόντων ³⁴ ἔσβεσαν δύναμιν πυρός <u>ἔφυγον στόματα μαχαίρης</u>

    C. <u>ἐδυναμώθησαν ἀπὸ ἀσθενείας ἐγενήθησαν ἰσχυροὶ ἐν πολέμῳ παρεμβολὰς ἔκλιναν ἀλλοτρίων</u>

        D. ³⁵ <u>ἔλαβον γυναῖκες ἐξ ἀναστάσεως τοὺς νεκροὺς αὐτῶν</u>

        D′. ἄλλοι δὲ ἐτυμπανίσθησαν οὐ προσδεξάμενοι τὴν ἀπολύτρωσιν ἵνα κρείττονος ἀναστάσεως τύχωσιν

    C′. ³⁶ <u>ἕτεροι δὲ ἐμπαιγμῶν καὶ μαστίγων πεῖραν ἔλαβον ἔτι δὲ δεσμῶν καὶ φυλακῆς</u>

B′. ³⁷ ἐλιθάσθησαν ἐπρίσθησαν <u>ἐν φόνῳ μαχαίρης</u> ἀπέθανον περιῆλθον ἐν μηλωταῖς ἐν αἰγείοις δέρμασιν ὑστερούμενοι θλιβόμενοι κακουχούμενοι

A′. ³⁸ ὧν οὐκ ἦν ἄξιος ὁ κόσμος ἐπὶ ἐρημίαις πλανώμενοι καὶ ὄρεσι καὶ σπηλαίοις καὶ ταῖς ὀπαῖς τῆς γῆς ³⁹ καὶ πάντες μαρτυρηθέντες διὰ τῆς πίστεως <u>οὐκ ἐκομίσαντο τὴν ἐπαγγελίαν</u> ⁴⁰ τοῦ θεοῦ περὶ ἡμῶν κρεῖττόν τι προβλεψαμένου ἵνα μὴ χωρὶς ἡμῶν τελειωθῶσιν

A. By faith the people passed through death and saw fulfilment

    B. The people do amazing things (active voice)

        C. Amazing things are done for them (passive voice)

            D. Dead received back from the resurrection

            D′. Others refuse to get them back for a better resurrection

        C′. Others receive terrible things (passive voice)

    B′. they died and wandered destitute and afflicted (active voice)

A'. They wandered on the world, commended through faith yet not receiving the Promise

12:1-13 (cf. 6.2.9)

A. ¹²:¹ τοιγαροῦν καὶ ἡμεῖς τοσοῦτον ἔχοντες περικείμενον ἡμῖν νέφος μαρτύρων ὄγκον ἀποθέμενοι πάντα καὶ τὴν εὐπερίστατον ἁμαρτίαν δι' ὑπομονῆς τρέχωμεν τὸν προκείμενον ἡμῖν ἀγῶνα ² ἀφορῶντες εἰς τὸν τῆς πίστεως ἀρχηγὸν καὶ τελειωτὴν Ἰησοῦν

   B. <u>ὃς ἀντὶ τῆς προκειμένης αὐτῷ χαρᾶς ὑπέμεινεν σταυρὸν</u> αἰσχύνης καταφρονήσας ἐν δεξιᾷ τε τοῦ θρόνου τοῦ θεοῦ κεκάθικεν

      C. ³ ἀναλογίσασθε γὰρ **τὸν τοιαύτην** ὑπομεμενηκότα ὑπὸ τῶν ἁμαρτωλῶν εἰς ἑαυτοὺς ἀντιλογίαν ἵνα μὴ κάμητε ταῖς ψυχαῖς ὑμῶν ἐκλυόμενοι ⁴ οὔπω μέχρις αἵματος ἀντικατέστητε πρὸς τὴν ἁμαρτίαν ἀνταγωνιζόμενοι

         D. ⁵ καὶ ἐκλέλησθε τῆς παρακλήσεως ἥτις ὑμῖν ὡς υἱοῖς διαλέγεται υἱέ μου <u>μὴ ὀλιγώρει παιδείας κυρίου μηδὲ ἐκλύου ὑπ' αὐτοῦ ἐλεγχόμενος ⁶ ὃν γὰρ ἀγαπᾷ κύριος παιδεύει μαστιγοῖ δὲ πάντα υἱὸν ὃν παραδέχεται</u>

         D'. ⁷ <u>εἰς παιδείαν ὑπομένετε</u> ὡς υἱοῖς ὑμῖν προσφέρεται ὁ θεός τίς γὰρ υἱὸς ὃν οὐ παιδεύει πατήρ; ⁸ <u>εἰ δὲ χωρίς ἐστε παιδείας ἧς μέτοχοι γεγόνασι πάντες ἄρα νόθοι καὶ οὐχ υἱοί ἐστε</u>

      C'. ⁹ εἶτα τοὺς μὲν τῆς σαρκὸς ἡμῶν πατέρας εἴχομεν παιδευτὰς καὶ ἐνετρεπόμεθα οὐ **πολὺ μᾶλλον** ὑποταγησόμεθα τῷ πατρὶ τῶν πνευμάτων καὶ ζήσομεν; ¹⁰ οἱ μὲν γὰρ πρὸς ὀλίγας ἡμέρας κατὰ τὸ δοκοῦν αὐτοῖς ἐπαίδευον ὁ δὲ ἐπὶ τὸ συμφέρον εἰς τὸ μεταλαβεῖν τῆς ἁγιότητος αὐτοῦ

   B'. ¹¹ <u>πᾶσα δὲ παιδεία πρὸς μὲν τὸ παρὸν οὐ δοκεῖ χαρᾶς εἶναι ἀλλὰ λύπης</u> ὕστερον δὲ καρπὸν εἰρηνικὸν τοῖς δι' αὐτῆς γεγυμνασμένοις ἀποδίδωσιν δικαιοσύνης

A'. ¹² διὸ τὰς παρειμένας χεῖρας καὶ τὰ παραλελυμένα γόνατα ἀνορθώσατε ¹³ καὶ τροχιὰς ὀρθὰς ποιεῖτε τοῖς ποσὶν ὑμῶν ἵνα μὴ τὸ χωλὸν ἐκτραπῇ ἰαθῇ δὲ μᾶλλον

A. ¹²:¹ Therefore since we also have such a great cloud of witnesses surrounding us, let us run the race before us with endurance, throwing off every obstacle and sin which entangles, ² and fixing our eyes on Jesus, the pioneer and perfecter of faith,

    B. who, instead of the joy surrounding him, endured the cross, despising the shame, and is seated at the right hand of the throne of God.

        C. ³ For consider him who endured such great hostility from sinners for our sake so that your souls might not grow weary or faint-hearted. ⁴ You have not yet resisted to the point of bloodshed in your struggles with sin.

            D. ⁵ And have you completely forgotten the encouragement which addresses you as sons: "My Son, do not belittle the discipline of the Lord nor give up when reproved by him. ⁶ For the Lord disciplines the one he loves and chastises every son he accepts"?

            D'. ⁷ Endure for the purpose of discipline! God is offering you up as sons. For which son is there whom his father does not discipline? ⁸ And if you are without discipline, in which all have shared, you are indeed bastards not sons.

        C'. ⁹ And besides, we have had fathers of flesh disciplining us and we submitted to them. How much more should we then submit to the Father of spirits and live? ¹⁰ For they disciplined us as seemed best for a few days, but he to our advantage that we might receive his holiness.

    B'. ¹¹ And at the time every discipline seems painful rather than joy, but later it yields a peaceable harvest of righteousness to those who have been trained by it.

A'. ¹² Therefore straighten up your weakened hands and paralysed knees ¹³ and make straight paths for your feet so that what is lame might not be put out of joint but instead healed!

12:14-25

A. ¹⁴ Εἰρήνην διώκετε μετὰ πάντων καὶ τὸν ἁγιασμόν οὗ χωρὶς οὐδεὶς ὄψεται τὸν κύριον ¹⁵ ἐπισκοποῦντες μή τις ὑστερῶν ἀπὸ τῆς χάριτος τοῦ θεοῦ μή τις ῥίζα πικρίας ἄνω φύουσα ἐνοχλῇ καὶ δι' αὐτῆς μιανθῶσιν πολλοί ¹⁶ μή τις πόρνος ἢ βέβηλος ὡς Ἠσαῦ ὃς ἀντὶ βρώσεως μιᾶς ἀπέδετο τὰ πρωτοτόκια ἑαυτοῦ ¹⁷ ἴστε γὰρ ὅτι καὶ μετέπειτα θέλων κληρονομῆσαι τὴν εὐλογίαν ἀπεδοκιμάσθη

    B. μετανοίας γὰρ τόπον οὐχ εὗρεν καίπερ μετὰ δακρύων ἐκζητήσας αὐτήν

        C. οὐ γὰρ προσεληλύθατε ψηλαφωμένῳ καὶ κεκαυμένῳ πυρὶ καὶ γνόφῳ καὶ ζόφῳ καὶ θυέλλῃ ¹⁹ καὶ σάλπιγγος ἤχῳ καὶ φωνῇ ῥημάτων ἧς οἱ ἀκούσαντες παρῃτήσαντο μὴ προστεθῆναι αὐτοῖς λόγον ²⁰ οὐκ ἔφερον γὰρ διαστελλόμενον Κἂν θηρίον θίγῃ τοῦ ὄρους λιθοβοληθήσεται ²¹ καὶ οὕτω φοβερὸν ἦν τὸ φανταζόμενον Μωϋσῆς εἶπεν Ἔκφοβός εἰμι καὶ ἔντρομος

        C'. ²² ἀλλὰ προσεληλύθατε Σιὼν ὄρει καὶ πόλει θεοῦ ζῶντος Ἰερουσαλὴμ ἐπουρανίῳ καὶ μυριάσιν ἀγγέλων πανηγύρει ²³ καὶ ἐκκλησίᾳ πρωτοτόκων ἀπογεγραμμένων ἐν οὐρανοῖς καὶ κριτῇ θεῷ πάντων καὶ πνεύμασι δικαίων τετελειωμένων ²⁴ καὶ διαθήκης νέας μεσίτῃ Ἰησοῦ

    B'. καὶ αἵματι ῥαντισμοῦ κρεῖττον λαλοῦντι παρὰ τὸν Ἄβελ

A'. ²⁵ Βλέπετε μὴ παραιτήσησθε τὸν λαλοῦντα εἰ γὰρ ἐκεῖνοι οὐκ ἐξέφυγον ἐπὶ γῆς παραιτησάμενοι τὸν χρηματίζοντα πολὺ μᾶλλον ἡμεῖς οἱ τὸν ἀπ' οὐρανῶν ἀποστρεφόμενοι

A. ¹⁴ Pursue peace with all and the holiness without which noone will see the Lord, watching lest anyone fall from the grace of God, ¹⁵ lest any bitter root spring up and through this defile many, lest anyone be immoral or worldly like Esau, who gave up his birthright for a single meal. ¹⁷ For you see also that afterward, when he wanted to inherit the blessing, he was rejected.

    B. For he found no place of repentance, though he sought it with tears.

APPENDIX: MICRO LINK CLUSTERS IN HEBREWS

    C. For *you have not come* to what may be touched, a blazing fire and darkness and gloom and a tempest [19] and the sound of a trumpet and a voice of words which made the hearers beg that no further word be added to them. [20] For they could not bear what was commanded, "If even a beast touches the mountain, it shall be stoned" [21] and so terrifying was the sight that even Moses said, "I tremble with fear."

    C'. But *you have come* to Mount Zion and to the city of the living God, the heavenly Jerusalem, and to innumerable angels in festal gathering, [23] and to the assembly of the firstborn who are enrolled in heaven, and to God, the judge of all, and the spirits of the righteous made perfect, [24] and to Jesus, the mediator of a new covenant.

  B'. And to the sprinkled blood that speaks a better word than the blood of Abel.

A'. [25] See that you do not refuse him the one who speaks! For if they did not escape, who refused him who warned them on earth, how much less will we if we reject him who warns from heaven!

12:25–29

  A. [25] Βλέπετε μὴ παραιτήσησθε τὸν λαλοῦντα εἰ γὰρ ἐκεῖνοι οὐκ ἐξέφυγον ἐπὶ γῆς παραιτησάμενοι τὸν χρηματίζοντα πολὺ μᾶλλον ἡμεῖς οἱ τὸν ἀπ' οὐρανῶν ἀποστρεφόμενοι

    B. [26] οὗ ἡ φωνὴ τὴν γῆν ἐσάλευσεν τότε νῦν δὲ ἐπήγγελται λέγων Ἔτι ἅπαξ ἐγὼ σείσω οὐ μόνον τὴν γῆν ἀλλὰ καὶ τὸν οὐρανόν

    B'. [27] τὸ δὲ Ἔτι ἅπαξ δηλοῖ τῶν σαλευομένων μετάθεσιν ὡς πεποιημένων ἵνα μείνῃ τὰ μὴ σαλευόμενα

  A'. [28] διὸ βασιλείαν ἀσάλευτον παραλαμβάνοντες ἔχωμεν χάριν δι' ἧς λατρεύωμεν εὐαρέστως τῷ θεῷ μετὰ εὐλαβείας καὶ δέους [29] καὶ γὰρ ὁ θεὸς ἡμῶν πῦρ καταναλίσκον

APPENDIX: MICRO LINK CLUSTERS IN HEBREWS

A. ²⁵ Watch out that you do not refuse him who is speaking. For if they did not escape when they refused him who warned them on earth, much less will we if we turn from him who warns from heaven.

B. ²⁶ Then his voice shook the earth, but now he has promised, 'Yet once more I will shake not only the earth but also the heavens'.

B′. ²⁷ This phrase, 'Yet once more', indicates the removal of things that are shaken—that is, things that have been made—in order that the things that cannot be shaken may remain.

A′. ²⁸ Therefore since we are receiving a kingdom that cannot be shaken, let us have grace, through which let us offer to God acceptable worship, with reverence and awe ²⁹ for our God is a consuming fire.

12:28—13:10

A. ¹²:²⁸ διὸ βασιλείαν ἀσάλευτον παραλαμβάνοντες ἔχωμεν χάριν δι' ἧς λατρεύωμεν εὐαρέστως τῷ θεῷ μετὰ εὐλαβείας καὶ δέους ²⁹ καὶ γὰρ ὁ θεὸς ἡμῶν πῦρ καταναλίσκον

B. ¹³:¹ <u>Ἡ φιλαδελφία μενέτω</u> ² τῆς φιλοξενίας μὴ ἐπιλανθάνεσθε διὰ ταύτης γὰρ ἔλαθόν τινες ξενίσαντες ἀγγέλους

C. ³ μιμνῄσκεσθε τῶν δεσμίων ὡς συνδεδεμένοι τῶν κακουχουμένων ὡς καὶ αὐτοὶ ὄντες ἐν σώματι

D. ⁴ τίμιος ὁ γάμος ἐν πᾶσιν καὶ ἡ κοίτη ἀμίαντος <u>πόρνους γὰρ καὶ μοιχοὺς κρινεῖ ὁ θεός</u> ⁵ ἀφιλάργυρος ὁ τρόπος ἀρκούμενοι τοῖς παροῦσιν αὐτὸς γὰρ εἴρηκεν

E. <u>Οὐ μή σε ἀνῶ οὐδ' οὐ μή σε ἐγκαταλίπω</u>

D′. ⁶ ὥστε θαρροῦντας ἡμᾶς λέγειν <u>Κύριος ἐμοὶ βοηθός</u> οὐ φοβηθήσομαι τί ποιήσει μοι ἄνθρωπος;

C′. ⁷ Μνημονεύετε τῶν ἡγουμένων ὑμῶν οἵτινες ἐλάλησαν ὑμῖν τὸν λόγον τοῦ θεοῦ ὧν ἀναθεωροῦντες τὴν ἔκβασιν τῆς ἀναστροφῆς μιμεῖσθε τὴν πίστιν

APPENDIX: MICRO LINK CLUSTERS IN HEBREWS

B'. ⁸ <u>Ἰησοῦς Χριστὸς ἐχθὲς καὶ σήμερον ὁ αὐτὸς καὶ εἰς τοὺς αἰῶνας</u> ⁹ διδαχαῖς ποικίλαις καὶ ξέναις μὴ παραφέρεσθε

A'. καλὸν γὰρ χάριτι βεβαιοῦσθαι τὴν καρδίαν οὐ βρώμασιν ἐν οἷς οὐκ ὠφελήθησαν οἱ περιπατοῦντες ¹⁰ ἔχομεν θυσιαστήριον ἐξ οὗ φαγεῖν οὐκ ἔχουσιν ἐξουσίαν οἱ τῇ σκηνῇ λατρεύοντες

A. ^{12:28} Therefore, since we are receiving an unshakeable kingdom, let us have grace, through which let us worship God acceptably with reverence and awe. ²⁹ For our God is also a consuming fire.

    B. ^{13:1} Let brotherly love remain: ² Do not neglect hospitality to strangers, for through this some have entertained angels without realizing.

        C. ³ Keep in mind those in chains as if in chains with them, those treated badly as these are also in the body.

            D. ⁴ Let marriage be honored by all and the bed kept unstained. For God will judge the immoral and adulterous. ⁵ Keep your life free from the love of money, being content with what you have!

                E. For He has said "I will never ever leave you nor will I ever forsake you"

            D'. ⁶ Therefore we may be confident to say "The Lord is my help, I will not fear. What can man do for me?"

        C'. ⁷ Remember your leaders, who spoke the word of God to you. Considering the outcome of their walk, imitate their faith.

    B'. ⁸ Jesus Christ is the same yesterday, today and forever. ⁹ Do not be carried away by strange teachings.

A'. For it is good for the heart to be strengthened by grace, not by foods by which those devoted have not been helped. We have an altar from which those serving in the tent do not have authority to eat.

APPENDIX: MICRO LINK CLUSTERS IN HEBREWS

13:10-14

- A. ¹⁰ ἔχομεν θυσιαστήριον **ἐξ** οὗ φαγεῖν οὐκ ἔχουσιν **ἐξουσίαν** οἱ τῇ σκηνῇ λατρεύοντες ¹¹ <u>ὧν γὰρ εἰσφέρεται ζῴων τὸ αἷμα περὶ ἁμαρτίας **εἰς** τὰ ἅγια διὰ τοῦ ἀρχιερέως τούτων τὰ σώματα κατακαίεται</u> **ἔξω** τῆς παρεμβολῆς

  - B. ¹² διὸ καὶ <u>Ἰησοῦς</u> ἵνα ἁγιάσῃ διὰ τοῦ ἰδίου αἵματος τὸν λαόν **ἔξω** τῆς πύλης ἔπαθεν

  - B'. ¹³ τοίνυν <u>ἐξερχώμεθα πρὸς αὐτὸν</u> **ἔξω** τῆς παρεμβολῆς τὸν ὀνειδισμὸν αὐτοῦ φέροντες

- A'. ¹⁴ οὐ γὰρ ἔχομεν ὧδε μένουσαν πόλιν ἀλλὰ τὴν μέλλουσαν ἐπιζητοῦμεν δι' αὐτοῦ οὖν <u>ἀναφέρωμεν θυσίαν αἰνέσεως διὰ παντὸς τῷ θεῷ</u>

- A. ¹⁰ We have an altar from which those serving *within* the tent have no right to eat. ¹¹ For the bodies of those animals whose blood is offered for sins by the High Priest inside the sanctuary are burned *outside* the camp.

  - B. ¹² Therefore Jesus also suffered *outside* the gate in order that he might sanctify the people through his own blood

  - B'. ¹³ Therefore let us go *out* to him *outside* the camp, bearing his shame.

- A'. ¹⁴ For we do not have here an abiding city but seek that which is to come. ¹⁵ Through him [therefore] let us offer up a continual sacrifice of praise to God.

13:15-21

- A. ¹⁵ δι' αὐτοῦ οὖν <u>ἀναφέρωμεν θυσίαν αἰνέσεως διὰ παντὸς τῷ θεῷ</u> τοῦτ' ἔστιν καρπὸν χειλέων ὁμολογούντων τῷ ὀνόματι αὐτοῦ ¹⁶ τῆς δὲ εὐποιΐας καὶ κοινωνίας μὴ ἐπιλανθάνεσθε τοιαύταις γὰρ θυσίαις εὐαρεστεῖται ὁ θεός

  - B. ¹⁷ Πείθεσθε τοῖς ἡγουμένοις ὑμῶν καὶ ὑπείκετε αὐτοὶ γὰρ ἀγρυπνοῦσιν ὑπὲρ τῶν ψυχῶν ὑμῶν ὡς λόγον ἀποδώσοντες ἵνα μετὰ χαρᾶς τοῦτο ποιῶσιν καὶ μὴ στενάζοντες ἀλυσιτελὲς γὰρ ὑμῖν τοῦτο

B'. ¹⁸ Προσεύχεσθε περὶ ἡμῶν πειθόμεθα γὰρ ὅτι καλὴν συνείδησιν ἔχομεν ἐν πᾶσιν καλῶς θέλοντες ἀναστρέφεσθαι ¹⁹ περισσοτέρως δὲ παρακαλῶ τοῦτο ποιῆσαι ἵνα τάχιον ἀποκατασταθῶ ὑμῖν

A'. ²⁰ Ὁ δὲ θεὸς τῆς εἰρήνης ὁ ἀναγαγὼν ἐκ νεκρῶν τὸν ποιμένα τῶν προβάτων τὸν μέγαν ἐν αἵματι διαθήκης αἰωνίου τὸν κύριον ἡμῶν Ἰησοῦν ¹⁵ καταρτίσαι ὑμᾶς ἐν παντὶ ἀγαθῷ <u>εἰς τὸ ποιῆσαι τὸ θέλημα αὐτοῦ ποιῶν ἐν ἡμῖν τὸ εὐάρεστον ἐνώπιον</u> αὐτοῦ διὰ Ἰησοῦ Χριστοῦ ᾧ ἡ δόξα εἰς τοὺς αἰῶνας ἀμήν

A. ¹³:¹⁵ Through him [therefore] let us offer up a continual sacrifice of praise to God. This is the fruit of lips which confess his name. ¹⁶ Do not neglect the doing of good and fellowship! For God delights in sacrifices such as these.

    B. ¹⁷ Be convinced about your leaders and submit for they keep watch over your souls as those who must give an account—so that they may do this with joy and not grumbling. For this would not be advantageous to you.

    B'. ¹⁸ Pray for us. For we are convinced that we have a good conscience, wanting to act honorably in everything. ¹⁹ And I urge you to do this more and more that I might be returned to you sooner.

A'. ²⁰ And may the God of peace, who raised up from the dead the great shepherd of the sheep by the blood of the eternal covenant, our Lord Jesus Christ, ²¹ strengthen you in everything good that you might do his will, working among us what is pleasing before him through Jesus Christ, to whom be glory forever. Amen.

13:22–25

A. ²² <u>παρακαλῶ</u> δὲ ὑμᾶς ἀδελφοί <u>ἀνέχεσθε τοῦ λόγου τῆς παρακλήσεως</u>

    B. καὶ γὰρ διὰ βραχέων ἐπέστειλα ὑμῖν

    B'. ²³ γινώσκετε τὸν ἀδελφὸν ἡμῶν Τιμόθεον ἀπολελυμένον μεθ' οὗ ἐὰν τάχιον ἔρχηται ὄψομαι ὑμᾶς

APPENDIX: MICRO LINK CLUSTERS IN HEBREWS

A'. ²⁴ ἀσπάσασθε πάντας τοὺς ἡγουμένους ὑμῶν καὶ πάντας τοὺς ἁγίους ἀσπάζονται ὑμᾶς οἱ ἀπὸ τῆς Ἰταλίας ²⁵ <u>ἡ χάρις μετὰ πάντων ὑμῶν</u>

A. ²² I encourage you, brothers, to accept the word of encouragement

    B. for I also have sent to you through "little ones."

    B'. ²³ You know our brother Timothy, who has been sent, with whom I will see you if he comes soon.

A'. ²⁴ Greet all your leaders and all the saints. Those from Italy greet you. ²⁵ May grace be with you all!

Bibliography

Andriessen, P. "La teneur judéo-chrétienne de Hébr. I,6 et II,14b–III,2." *Novum Testamentum* 18 (1976) 293–313.
Andriessen, P., and A. Lenglet. "Quelques passages difficiles de l'Épître aux Hébreux (5:7–11; 10:20; 12:2)." *Biblica* 51 (1970) 207–20.
Attridge, Harold W. "Paraenesis in a Homily (λόγος παρακλήσεως): The Possible Location of, and Socialization in, the Epistle to the Hebrews." *Semeia* 50 (1990) 211–27.
———. *The Epistle to the Hebrews: A Commentary on the Epistle to the Hebrews*. Hermeneia. Philadelphia: Fortress, 1989.
Auffret, P. "Essai sur la structure littéraire et l'interprétation d'Hébreux 3, 1–6." *New Testament Studies* 26 (1980) 380–96.
———. "Note sur la Structure Littérraire d'Hb II. 1–4." *New Testament Studies* 25 (1979) 166–79.
Aune, David E. *The New Testament in Its Literary Environment*. Library of Early Christianity 8. Philadelphia: Westminster, 1987.
Bateman, Herbert W., IV. *Early Jewish Hermeneutics and Hebrews 1:5–13: The Impact of Early Jewish Exegesis on the Interpretation of a Significant New Testament Passage*. New York: Lang, 1997.
Baugh, S. M. "The Cloud of Witnesses in Hebrews 11." *Westminster Theological Journal* 68 (2006) 113–32.
Beekman, John, and John Callow. *Translating the Word of God*. Grand Rapids: Zondervan, 1974.
Berger, Klaus. "Rhetorical Criticism, New Form Criticism, and New Testament Hermeneutics." In *Rhetoric and the New Testament: Essays from the 1992 Heidelberg Conference*, edited by Stanley E. Porter and Thomas H. Olbricht, 390–96. Journal for the Study of the New Testament Supplementary Series 90. Sheffield: Sheffield Academic, 1993.
Berlin, Adele. *The Dynamics of Biblical Parallelism*. Rev. ed. Grand Rapids: Eerdmans, 2008.
Black, David Alan. "Hebrews 1:1–4: A Study in Discourse Analysis." *Westminster Theological Journal* 49 (1987) 175–94.

———. "The Problem of the Literary Structure of Hebrews: An Evaluation and a Proposal." *Grace Theological Journal* 7 (1986) 163–77.
Bligh, J. *Chiastic Analysis of the Epistle to the Hebrews*. Oxford: Athenaeum, 1966.
Brown, Gillian, and George Yule. *Discourse Analysis*. Cambridge: Cambridge University Press, 1983.
Bruce, F. F. *Commentary on the Epistles to the Hebrews*. Grand Rapids: Eerdmans, 1990.
Buchanan, George Wesley. *To the Hebrews*. Anchor Bible 36. Garden City, NY: Doubleday, 1972.
Caneday, Ardel B. "The Eschatological World Already Subjected to the Son: The οἰκουμένη of Hebrews 1:6 and the Son's Enthronement." In *A Cloud of Witnesses: The Theology of Hebrews in Its Ancient Contexts*, edited by Richard Bauckham et al., 28–39. London: T. & T. Clark, 2008.
Calvin, John. *The Epistle of Paul the Apostle to the Hebrews and the First and Second Epistles of St Peter*. Edited by David W. Torrance and Thomas F. Torrance. Translated by William B. Johnston. Calvin's Commentaries 12. Grand Rapids: Eerdmans, 1989.
Campbell, J. Y. "κοινωνία and Its Cognates in the New Testament." *Journal of Biblical Literature* 51 (1932) 352–80.
Carson, D. A. *Exegetical Fallacies*. 2nd ed. Grand Rapids: Paternoster, 1996.
Cockerill, Gareth Lee. "The Better Resurrection (Heb 11:35): A Key to the Structure and Rhetorical Purpose of Hebrews 11." *Tyndale Bulletin* 51 (2000) 215–35.
Cosby, Michael R. "The Rhetorical Composition of Hebrews 11." *Journal of Biblical Literature* 107 (1988) 257–73.
———. *The Rhetorical Composition and Function of Hebrews 11: In Light of Example Lists in Antiquity*. Macon, GA: Mercer University Press, 1988.
Coste, J. "Notion grecque et notion biblique de la "souffrance éducatrice" (A propos d'Hébreux, v. 8)." *Recherches de Science Religieuse* 43 (1955) 481–523.
Cotterell, Peter, and Max Turner. *Linguistics and Biblical Interpretation*. London: SPCK, 1989.
Cruse, D. A. *Meaning in Language: An Introduction to Semantics and Pragmatics*. Oxford: Oxford University Press, 2000.
Culpepper, R. Alan. "A Superior Faith: Hebrews 10:19—12:2." *Review and Expositor* 82 (1985) 375–90.
D'Angelo, Mary Rose. *Moses in the Letter to the Hebrews*. Society of Biblical Literature Dissertation Series 42. Missoula, MT: Scholars, 1979.
Davies, G. Henton. "Psalm 95." *Zeitschrift für die alttestamentliche Wissenschaft* 88 (1973) 183–95.
Deibler, Ellis W., Jr. *A Semantic and Structural Analysis of Hebrews*. Dallas: SIL International, 2017.
Descamps, A. "La Structure de l'Épître aux Hébreux." *Rassegna di Teologia* 9 (1954) 251–58; 333–38.
deSilva, David Arthur. *Despising Shame: Honour Discourse and Community Maintenance in the Epistle to the Hebrews*. Society of Biblical Literature Dissertation Series 152. Atlanta: Scholars, 1995.
———. *Perseverance in Gratitude: A Socio-Rhetorical Commentary on the Epistle "to the Hebrews."* Grand Rapids: Eerdmans, 2000.
Downing, F. Gerald. "Ambiguity, Ancient Semantics, and Faith." *New Testament Studies* 56 (2009) 139–62.

Dunning, Benjamin. "The Intersection of Alien Status and Cultic Discourse in the Epistle to the Hebrews." In *Hebrews: Contemporary Methods—New Insights*, edited by Gabriella Gelardini, 177–98. Biblical Interpretation Series 75. Leiden: Brill, 2005.

Durnbaugh, Donald F. "Go Forth in Faith." *Brethren Life and Thought* 15 (1990) 160–67.

Dussaut, Louis. *Synopse structurelle de l'Épître aux Hébreux*. Paris: Cerf, 1982.

Ebert, Daniel J. IV. "The Chiastic Structure of the Prologue to Hebrews." *Trinity Journal* 13 (1992) 163–79.

Eggins, Suzanne. *An Introduction to Systemic Functional Linguistics*. London: Pinter, 1994.

Eisenbaum, Pamela M. "Heroes and History in Hebrews 11." In *Early Christian Interpretation of the Scriptures of Israel: Investigations and Proposals*, edited by Craig A. Evans and James A. Sanders, 380–96. Studies in Scripture in Early Judaism and Christianity 5. Sheffield: Sheffield Academic, 1997.

———. *The Jewish Heroes of Christian History: Hebrews 11 in Literary Context*. Society of Biblical Literature Dissertation Series 156. Atlanta: Scholars, 1997.

———. "Locating Hebrews within the Literary Landscape of Christian Origins." In *Hebrews: Contemporary Methods—New Insights*, edited by Gabriella Gelardini, 213–37. Biblical Interpretation Series 75. Leiden: Brill, 2005.

Ellingworth, Paul. "Jesus and the Universe in Hebrews." *Evangelical Quarterly* 58 (1986) 337–50.

———. *The Epistle to the Hebrews: A Commentary on the Greek Text*. New International Greek Testament Commentary. Grand Rapids: Eerdmans, 1993.

Enns, Peter E. "Creation and Re-creation: Psalm 95 and its Interpretation in Hebrews 3:1–4:13." *Westminster Theological Journal* 55 (1993) 255–80.

Fredrickson, David E. "Παρρησία in the Pauline Epistles." In *Friendship, Flattery, and Frankness of Speech: Studies on Friendship in the New Testament World*, edited by John T. Fitzgerald, 203–26. Novum Testamentum Supplements 82. Leiden: Brill, 1996.

Friberg, Timothy, and Barbara Friberg. *Analytical Lexicon to the Greek New Testament on CD-ROM*. BibleWorks Version 7.0. 1994, 2006. Print ed.: Grand Rapids: Baker, 2000.

Gelardini, Gabriella. "From "Linguistic Turn" and Hebrews Scholarship to *Anapidlosis Iterata*." In *Deciphering the Worlds of Hebrews: Collected Essays*, edited by Gabriella Gelardini, 38–66. Novum Testamentum Supplements 184. Leiden: Brill, 2021.

———. "Hebrews, Homiletics, and Liturgical Scripture Interpretation." In *Deciphering the Worlds of Hebrews: Collected Essays*, edited by Gabriella Gelardini, 67–91. Novum Testamentum Supplements 184. Leiden: Brill, 2021.

———. "Rhetorical Criticism in Hebrews Scholarship: Avenues and Aporias." In *Deciphering the Worlds of Hebrews: Collected Essays*, edited by Gabriella Gelardini, 113–41. Novum Testamentum Supplements 184. Leiden: Brill, 2021.

Gheorghita, Radu. *The Role of the Septuagint in Hebrews: An Investigation of Its Influence with Special Consideration to the Use of Hab 2:3–4 in Heb 10:37–38*. Wissenschaftliche Untersuchungen zum Neuen Testament 2/160. Tübingen: Mohr Siebeck, 2003.

Guthrie, George H. *Hebrews*. The NIV Application Commentary. Grand Rapids: Zondervan, 1998.

———. "Hebrews' Use of the Old Testament: Recent Trends in Research." *Currents in Biblical Research* 1/2 (2003) 271–94.

———. "Hebrews." In *Commentary on the New Testament Use of the Old Testament*, edited by G. K. Beale and D. A. Carson, 919–96. Grand Rapids: Baker Academic, 2007.

———. "New Testament Exegesis of Hebrews and the Catholic Epistles.' In *Handbook to Exegesis of the New Testament*, edited by Stanley E. Porter, 591–606. New Testament Tools and Studies 25. Leiden: Brill, 1997.

———. *The Structure of Hebrews: A Text-Linguistic Analysis*. Grand Rapids: Baker, 1994.

Halliday, M. A. K., and Ruquaiya Hasan. *Cohesion in English*. London: Longman, 1976.

———. *Language, Context and Text: Aspects of Language in a Social-Semiotic*. Waurn Ponds, Victoria: Deakin University, 1985.

Hamm, Dennis. "Faith in the Epistle to the Hebrews: The Jesus Factor." *Catholic Biblical Quarterly* 52 (1990) 270–91.

Harris, Dana M. "The Use of the Old Testament in the Epistle to the Hebrews." *Southwestern Journal of Theology* 64 (2021) 91–106.

Hasan, Ruquaiya. "Coherence and Cohesive Harmony." In *Understanding Reading Comprehension*, edited by J. Flood, 181–219. Delaware: International Reading Association, 1984.

Hanson, A. T. "Christ in the Old Testament according to Hebrews." *Studia Evangelica* 2 (1964) 394–96.

Hays, Richard B. *Echoes of Scripture in the Letters of Paul*. New Haven: Yale University Press, 1989.

Heen, Erik M. *Hebrews*. Edited by Erik M. Heen and Philip D.W. Krey. . Ancient Christian Commentary on Scripture. New Testament. Downers Grove, IL: InterVarsity Press, 2005.

Heil, John Paul. *Hebrews: Chiastic Structures and Audience Response*. Catholic Biblical Quarterly Monograph Series 46. Washington, DC: Catholic Biblical Association of America, 2010.

Hofius, O. *Katapausis: Die Vorstellung vom endzeitlichen Ruheort im Hebräerbrief*. Wissenschaftliche Untersuchungen zum Neuen Testament 11. Tübingen: Mohr Siebeck, 1972.

Horning, E. B. "Chiasmus, Creedal Structure, and Christology in Hebrews 12:1–2." *Biblical Research* 23 (1978) 37–48.

Hoey, Michael. *Patterns of Lexis in Text*. Describing English Language. Oxford: Oxford University Press, 1991.

Hughes, Graham. *Hebrews and Hermeneutics: The Epistle to the Hebrews as a New Testament Example of Biblical Interpretation*. Society for New Testament Studies Monograph Series 36. Cambridge: Cambridge University Press, 1979.

Hughes, Philip Edgcumbe. *A Commentary on the Epistle to the Hebrews*. Grand Rapids: Eerdmans, 1977.

Johnson, Luke Timothy. *Hebrews: A Commentary*. New Testament Library. Louisville: Westminster John Knox, 2006.

Joslin, Barry C. "Can Hebrews Be Structured? An Assessment of Eight Approaches." *Currents in Biblical Research* 6.2 (2007) 99–129.

Käsemann, Ernst. *The Wandering People of God: An Investigation of the Letter to the Hebrews.* Translated by Roy A. Harrisville and Irving L. Sandberg. Minneapolis: Augsburg, 1984.

Kennedy, George A. *New Testament through Rhetorical Criticism.* Chapel Hill: University of North Carolina Press, 1984.

Kistemaker, Simon J. *Exposition of the Epistle to the Hebrews.* Grand Rapids: Baker, 1984.

———. "The Psalm Citations in the Epistle to the Hebrews." PhD diss., Amsterdam: van Soest, 1961.

Koester, Craig R. *Hebrews: A New Translation with Introduction and Commentary.* Anchor Bible. New York: Doubleday, 2001.

Kuss, Otto. *Der Brief an die Hebräer.* Regensburger Neues Testament 8. Regegensburg: Pustet, 1966.

Lane, William L. *Hebrews 1–8, 9–13 on CD-ROM.* Libronix Digital Library System Version 2.1b, 2000–2004. Print ed.: Bruce M. Metzger et al., eds. 2 vols. Dallas: Word, 1991.

Lee, John A. L. *A History of New Testament Lexicography.* Studies in Biblical Greek 8. New York: Lang, 2003.

Lee, Thomas R. *Studies in the Form of Sirach 44–50.* Society of Biblical Litrature Dissertation Series 75. Atlanta: Scholars, 1986.

Levinsohn, Stephen H. *Discourse Features of New Testament Greek: A Coursebook on the Informational Structure of New Testament Greek.* 2nd ed. Dallas: SIL International, 2000.

———. Review of George H. Guthrie, *The Structure of Hebrews: A Text-Linguistic Analysis. Novum Testamentum* 43 (2001) 182–88.

Lincoln, Andrew T. "Sabbath, Rest and Eschatology in the New Testament." In *From Sabbath to Lord's Day: Biblical, Historical and Theological Investigation,* edited by D. A. Carson, 197–220. Grand Rapids: Zondervan, 1982.

Lindars, Barnabas. "The Rhetorical Structure of Hebrews." *New Testament Studies* 35 (1989) 382–406.

Löhr, Hermut. "Reflections of Rhetorical Terminology in Hebrews." In *Hebrews: Contemporary Methods—New Insights,* edited by Gabriella Gelardini, 199–210. Biblical Interpretation 75. Leiden: Brill, 2005.

Louw, J. P. *Semantics of New Testament Greek.* Semeia Studies. Philadelphia: Fortress, 1982.

Louw, J. P., and E. A. Nida. *Greek-English Lexicon of the New Testament Based on Semantic Domains on CD-ROM.* BibleWorks Version 7.0. 2006. Print ed.: 2nd ed. New York: United Bible Societies, 1988.

Mackie, Scott D. "Confession of the Son of God in Hebrews." *New Testament Studies* 53 (2007) 114–29.

———. *Eschatology and Exhortation in the Epistle to the Hebrews.* Wissenschaftliche Untersuchungen zum Neuen Testament 2/223. Tübingen: Mohr Siebeck, 2007.

Man, Ronald E. "The Value of Chiasm for New Testament Interpretation." *Bibliotheca Sacra* 141 (1984) 148–54.

Macleod, David J. "The Literary Structure of the Book of Hebrews." *Bibliotheca Sacra* 146 (1989) 185–97.

Martin, Michael Wade, and Jason A. Whitlark. *Inventing Hebrews: Design and Purpose in Ancient Rhetoric*. Society for New Testament Studies Monograph Series 171. Cambridge: Cambridge University Press, 2018.

Meier, John P. "Structure and Theology in Heb 1,1–14." *Biblica* 66 (1985) 168–89.

———. "Symmetry and Theology in the Old Testament Citations of Heb. 1, 5–14." *Biblica* 66 (1985) 504–33.

Metzger, Bruce M. *A Textual Commentary on the Greek New Testament*. 2nd ed. Stuttgart: Deutsche Bibelgesellschaft, 1994.

Michel, Otto. *Der Brief an die Hebräer*. Kritisch-exegetischer Kommentar über das Neue Testament 13. Göttingen: Vandenhoeck & Ruprecht, 1949.

Miller, Merland Ray. "What Is the Literary Form of Hebrews 11?' *Journal of the Evangelical Theological Society* 29 (1986) 411–17.

Moffatt, James. *A Critical Commentary on the Epistle to the Hebrews*. Edinburgh: T. & T. Clark, 1924.

Nauck, Wolfgang. "Zum Aufbau des Hebräerbriefes." In *Jüdentum Urchristentum Kirche: Festschrift für Joachim Jeremias*, edited by Walther Eltester, 199–206. Berlin: Töpelmann, 1960.

O'Brien, Peter T., *The Letter to the Hebrews*. Pillar New Testament Commentary. Grand Rapids: Eerdmans, 2010.

Ó Fearghail, Fearghus. "Apropos the Literary Structure of Hebrews." *Proceedings of the Irish Biblical Association* 39 (2016) 45–64.

Peterson, David. *Hebrews and Perfection: An Examination of the Concept of Perfection in "The Epistle to the Hebrews"*. Society for the Study of the New Testament Monograph Series 47. Cambridge: Cambridge University Press, 1982.

Phillips, Martin. *Aspects of Text Structure: An Investigation of the Organisation of Text*. Amsterdam: North-Holland, 1985.

Pierce, Madison N. *Divine Discourse in the Epistle to the Hebrews: The Recontextualization of Spoken Quotations of Scripture*. Society for New Testament Studies Monograph Series 178. Cambridge: Cambridge University Press, 2020.

Porter, Stanley E. "Discourse Analysis and New Testament Studies: An Introductory Survey." In *Discourse Analysis and Other Topics in Biblical Greek*, edited by Stanley E. Porter and D. A. Carson, 14–35. Journal for the Study of the New Testament Supplementary Series 113. Sheffield: Sheffield Academic, 1995.

———. "How Can Biblical Discourse Be Analyzed?: A Response to Several Attempts." In *Discourse Analysis and Other Topics in Biblical Greek*, edited by Stanley E. Porter and D. A. Carson, 107–17. Journal for the Study of the New Testament Supplementary Series 113. Sheffield: Sheffield Academic d, 1995.

———. "The Basic Tools of Exegesis of the New Testament: A Bibliographical Essay." In *Handbook to Exegesis of the New Testament*, edited by Stanley E. Porter, 23–44. New Testament Tools and Studies 25. Leiden: Brill, 1997.

———. *Verbal Aspect in the Greek of the New Testament with Reference to Tense and Mood*. Studies in Biblical Greek. New York: Lang, 1989.

Radday, Y. T. "Chiasmus in Hebrew Biblical Narrative." In *Chiasmus in Antiquity*, edited by John W. Welch, 50–117. Provo, UT: Research Press, 1999.

Reed, Jeffrey T. "The Cohesiveness of Discourse: Towards a Model of Linguistic Criteria for Analyzing New Testament Discourse." In *Discourse Analysis and the New Testament: Approaches and Results*, edited by Stanley E. Porter and Jeffrey T. Reed, 28–46. Journal for the Study of the New Testament Supplementary Series 170. Studies in New Testament Greek 4. Sheffield: Sheffield Academic, 1999.

Rhee, Victor (Sung-Yul). *Faith in Hebrews: Analysis within the Context of Christology, Eschatology, and Ethics.* Studies in Biblical Literature 19. New York: Lang, 2001.

———. "Chiasm and the Concept of Faith in Hebrews 11." *Bibliotheca Sacra* 155 (1998) 327–45.

Robbins, Vernon K. "A Socio-Rhetorical Response: Contexts of Interaction and Forms of Exhortation." *Semeia* 50 (1990) 229–42.

———. *Exploring the Texture of Texts: A Guide to Socio-Rhetorical Interpretation.* Valley Forge, PA: Trinity, 1996.

———. *The Tapestry of Early Christian Discourse: Rhetoric, Society and Ideology.* London: Routledge, 1996.

Robinson, D. W. B. "The Literary Structure of Hebrews 1:1–4." *Australian Journal of Biblical Archaeology* 2 (1972) 178–86.

Ryken, Leland. *The Literature of the Bible.* Grand Rapids: Zondervan, 1974.

Sanford, A. J., and S. C. Garrod. *Understanding Written Language: Explorations of Comprehension beyond the Sentence.* Chichester, UK: Wiley, 1981.

Silva, Moisés. *Biblical Words and their Meaning: An Introduction to Lexical Semantics.* 2nd ed. Grand Rapids: Zondervan, 1994.

Smith, Claire. *Pauline Communities as "Scholastic Communities": A Study of the Vocabulary of "Teaching' in 1 Corinthians, 1 and 2 Timothy, and Titus.* Wissenschaftliche Untersuchungen zum Neuen Testament 2/335. Tübingen: Mohr Siebeck, 2012.

Stamps, Dennis L. "Rhetorical and Narratological Criticism." In *Handbook to Exegesis of the New Testament*, edited by Stanley E. Porter, 219–40. New Testament Tools and Studies 25. Leiden: Brill, 1997.

Steyn, Gert Jacobus. "Quotations from Scripture and the Compilation of Hebrews in an Oral World." *Journal of Early Christian History* 4 (2014) 68–87.

Swetnam, James. "Form and Content in Hebrews 1–6." *Biblica* 53 (1972) 368–85.

———. *Jesus and Isaac: A Study of the Epistle to the Hebrews in Light of the Aqedah.* Analecta Biblica 94. Rome: Pontifical Biblical Institute Gregorian and Biblical Press, 1981.

———. *Hebrews: An Interpretation.* Subsidia Biblica 47. Rome: Pontifical Biblical Insitute Gregorian and Biblical Press, 2016.

Thiselton, Anthony C. "Semantics and New Testament Interpretation." In *New Testament Interpretation*, edited by I. Howard Marshall, 75–104. 4th ed Carlisle, UK: Paternoster, 1997.

Tönges, Elke. "The Epistle to the Hebrews as a 'Jesus-Midrash.'" In *Hebrews: Contemporary Methods—New Insights*, edited by Gabriella Gelardini, 89–105. Biblical Interpretation 75. Leiden: Brill, 2005.

Trotter, Andrew H. *Interpreting the Epistle to the Hebrews.* Grand Rapids; Baker, 1997.

Vaganay, L. "Le Plan de l'Épître aux Hébreux." In *Mémorial Lagrange*, edited by L. H. Vincent, 269–77. Paris: Gabalda, 1940.

Vanhoye, Albert. "Discussions sur la structure de l'Épître aux Hébreux." *Biblica* 55 (1974) 349–80.

———. "La Question Littéraire de l'Épître aux Hébreux XIII. I–6." *New Testament Studies* 23 (1976–77) 121–39.

———. *La Structure Littéraire de l'Épître aux Hébreux.* Paris: Desclée de Brouwer, 1976.

———. "L'épître aux Éphésiens et l'épître aux Hébreux." *Biblica* 59 (1975) 198–230.

———. *Situation du Christ: Hébreux 1–2*. Paris: Cerf, 1969.

———. *Structure and Message of the Epistle to the Hebrews*. Subsidia Biblica 12. Rome: Editrice Pontificio Istituto Biblico, 1989.

Wallace, Daniel B. *Greek Grammar beyond the Basics: An Exegetical Syntax of the New Testament with Scripture, Subject, and Greek Word Indexes*. Grand Rapids: Zondervan, 1996.

Welch, John W. "Chiasm in the New Testament." In *Chiasmus in Antiquity: Structures, Analyses, Exegesis*, edited by John W. Welch, 211–49. Provo, UT: Research Press, 1999.

Westcott, B. F. *The Epistle to the Hebrews: The Greek Text with Notes and Essays*. Biblical Criticism in the United States and Great Britain 98. Grand Rapids: Eerdmans, 1892.

Westfall, Cynthia Long. *A Discourse Analysis of the Letter to the Hebrews: The Relationship between Form and Meaning*. Library of New Testament Studies 297. London: T. & T. Clark, 2005.

———. "Moses and Hebrews 3:1–6: Approach or Avoidance?' In *Christian-Jewish Relations through the Centuries*, edited by Stanley E. Porter and Brook W. R. Pearson, 175–201. Journal for the Study of the New Testament Supplementary Series 192. Sheffield: Sheffield Academic, 2000.

Windisch, Hans. *Der Hebräerbrief*. 2nd ed. Handbuch zum Neuen Testament 14. Tübingen: Mohr Siebeck, 1931.

Winter, Eugene O. "Replacement as a Fundamental Function of the Sentence in Context." *Forum Linguisticum* 4/2 (1979) 95–133.

www.ingramcontent.com/pod-product-compliance
Lightning Source LLC
Chambersburg PA
CBHW071144300426
44113CB00009B/1076